The

WILEY
advantage

W9-BSN-719

Dear Valued Customer,

We realize you're a busy professional with deadlines to hit. Whether your goal is to learn a new technology or solve a critical problem, we want to be there to lend you a hand. Our primary objective is to provide you with the insight and knowledge you need to stay atop the highly competitive and ever-changing technology industry.

Wiley Publishing, Inc., offers books on a wide variety of technical categories, including security, data warehousing, software development tools, and networking — everything you need to reach your peak. Regardless of your level of expertise, the Wiley family of books has you covered.

- For Dummies – The *fun* and *easy* way to learn
- The Weekend Crash Course –The *fastest* way to learn a new tool or technology
- Visual – For those who prefer to learn a new topic *visually*
- The Bible – The *100% comprehensive* tutorial and reference
- The Wiley Professional list – *Practical* and *reliable* resources for IT professionals

The book you hold now, *Mastering Unix Shell Scripting*, is the first book to provide end-to-end scripting solutions that will solve real-world system administration problems for those who have to automate these often complex and repetitive tasks. Starting with a sample task and targeting the most common Unix systems: Solaris, Linux, AIX, and HP-UX with specific command structures, this book will save precious time with hands-on detail. The companion Web site contains all the timesaving scripts from the book.

Our commitment to you does not end at the last page of this book. We'd want to open a dialog with you to see what other solutions we can provide. Please be sure to visit us at www.wiley.com/compbooks to review our complete title list and explore the other resources we offer. If you have a comment, suggestion, or any other inquiry, please locate the "contact us" link at www.wiley.com.

Thank you for your support and we look forward to hearing from you and serving your needs again in the future.

Sincerely,

Richard K. Swadley

Richard K. Swadley
Vice President & Executive Group Publisher
Wiley Technology Publishing

Bible

Wiley Publishing, Inc.

Mastering Unix
Shell Scripting

Mastering Unix
Shell Scripting

Randal K. Michael

WILEY

Wiley Publishing, Inc.

Publisher: Robert Ipsen
Executive Editor: Carol Long
Developmental Editor: Scott Amerman
Managing Editor: Angela Smith
Text Design & Composition: Wiley Composition Services

This book is printed on acid-free paper. ∞

Published by Wiley Publishing, Inc., Indianapolis, Indiana

Published simultaneously in Canada

For general information on our other products and services please contact our Customer Care Department within the United States at (800) 762-2974, outside the United States at (317) 572-3993 or fax (317) 572-4002.

Wiley also publishes its books in a variety of electronic formats. Some content that appears in print may not be available in electronic books.

Library of Congress Cataloging-in-Publication Data:

ISBN: 0-471-21821-9

Printed in the United States of America

10 9 8 7 6 5 4 3 2 1

This book is dedicated to

My Wife Robin,

and the girls, Andrea and Ana

Acknowledgments

The information that I gathered together in this book is the result of working with some of the most talented UNIX professionals on the topic. I have enjoyed every minute of my association with these UNIX gurus and it has been my pleasure to have the opportunity to gain so much knowledge from the pros. I want to thank every one of these experts for asking and answering questions over the last fifteen years. If my brother, Jim, had not kept telling me, "you should write a book," after querying me for UNIX details on almost a weekly basis, I doubt this book would have ever been written. So, thanks Jim!

I especially want to thank Jack Renfro at Daimler/Chrysler Corporation for giving me my first shell scripting project so long ago. I had to start with the **man** pages, but that is how I learned to dig deep to get an answer. Since then I have been on a mission to automate, through shell scripting, everything on every system that I come in contact with. I certainly value the years that I was able to work with Jack.

I must also thank the talented people at Wiley Publishing. Margaret Eldridge started me on this project by letting me do my own thing, and Carol Long kept me going. Scott Amerman kept me on schedule, and Angela Smith did the edits that make my writing flow with ease. It has been a valuable experience for me to work with such a fine group of professionals at Wiley. I also want to thank Carole McClendon at Waterside Productions for all of the support on this project. Carole is the best Agent that anyone could ever ask for. She is a true professional with the highest ethics.

Of course my family had a lot to do with my success on this and every project. I want to thank Mom, Gene, Jim, Marcia, Rusty, Mallory, and Anica. I want to thank my Wife Robin for her understanding and support. The girls, Andrea and Ana, always keep a smile on my face, and Steve is always on my mind.

I could not have written this book without the support of all of these people and the many others that remain unnamed. It has been an honor!

Contents

Acknowledgments   **vii**

Introduction   **xix**

Chapter 1   **Scripting Quick Start and Review**   **1**

Case Sensitivity   1

Unix Special Characters   2

Shells   2

Shell Scripts   2

Functions   2

    A Function Has the Form   3

Running a Shell Script   3

    Declare the Shell in the Shell Script   3

Comments and Style in Shell Scripts   4

Control Structures   6

Using break, continue, exit, and return   9

Here Document   9

    Syntax for a Here Document   9

Shell Script Commands   10

Symbol Commands   13

Variables   13

Command-Line Arguments   13

Shift Command   14

Special Parameters $* and $@   15

    Special Parameter Definitions   15

Double Quotes ", Forward Tics ', and Back Tics `   16

Math in a Shell Script   17

    Operators   17

Built-in Mathematical Functions   18

File Permissions, suid and sgid Programs   18
   chmod Command Syntax for Each Purpose   19
Running Commands on a Remote Host   20
Setting Traps   21
User Information Commands   22
   who Command   22
   w Command   22
   last Command   22
ps Command   23
Communicating with Users   23
Uppercase or Lowercase Text for Easy Testing   24
Check the Return Code   25
Time-Based Script Execution   27
   cron tables   27
      Cron Table Entry Syntax   27
      Wildcards   28
   at Command   28
Output Control   28
   Silent Running   28
   Using getopts to Parse Command-Line Arguments   29
   Making a Co-Process with Background Function   30
Catching a Delayed Command Output   32
Fastest Ways to Process a File Line -by Line   33
Mail Notification Techniques   34
   Using the mail and mailx Commands   34
   Using the sendmail Command to Send Outbound Mail 34
Creating a Progress Indicator   35
   A Series of Dots   35
   A Rotating Line   35
Creating a Psuedo-Random Number   36
Checking for Stale Disk Partitions in AIX   37
Automated Host Pinging   37
Highlighting Specific Text in a File   38
Keeping the Printers Printing   38
   AIX "Classic" Printer Subsystem   38
   System V Printing   39
Automated FTP File Transfer   39
Capturing a List of Files Larger than $MEG   39
Capturing a User's Keystrokes   40
Using the bc Utility for Floating-Point Math   40
Number Base Conversions   41
   Using the typeset Command   41
   Using the printf Command   41
Create a Menu with the select Command   42
Sending Pop-Up Messages to Windows   43
Removing Repeated Lines in a File   43
Removing Blank Lines from a File   44

Testing for a Null Variable   44
Directly Access the Value of the Last Positional Parameter, $#   45
Remove the Columns Heading in a Command Output   45
Arrays   46
   Loading an Array   46
Testing a String   47
Summary   51

Chapter 2   Twelve Ways to Process a File Line by Line   53
Command Syntax   53
   Using File Descriptors   54
   Creating a Large File to Use in the Timing Test   54
Twelve Methods to Parse a File Line by Line   56
   Method 1: cat $FILENAME | while read LINE   57
   Method 2: while read $FILENAME from Bottom   58
   Method 3: while_line_LINE_Bottom   58
   Method 4: cat $FILENAME | while LINE=`line`   59
   Method 5: cat $FILENAME | while line LINE   60
   Method 6: while LINE=`line` from the Bottom   61
   Method 7: cat $FILENAME | while LINE=$(line)   61
   Method 8: while LINE=$(line) from the Bottom   62
   Method 9: while read LINE Using File Descriptors   63
   Method 10: while LINE='line' Using File Descriptors   64
   Method 11: while LINE=$(line) Using File Descriptors   65
   Method 12: while line LINE Using File Descriptors   66
Timing Each Method   66
   Timing Script   67
      Timing Data for Each Method   73
   Timing Command Substitution Methods   77
Summary   78

Chapter 3   Automated Event Notification   79
Basics of Automating Event Notification   79
   Using the mail and mailx Commands   80
Problems with Outbound Mail   82
   Create a "Bounce" Account with a .forward File   82
   Using the sendmail Command to Send Outbound Mail   83
Dial-Out Modem Software   84
SNMP Traps   85
Summary   86

Chapter 4   Progress Indicator Using a Series of Dots,
a Rotating Line, or a Countdown to Zero   87
Indicating Progress with a Series of Dots   87
Indicating Progress with a Rotating Line   89
Creating a Countdown Indicator   91
Other Options to Consider   95
Summary   96

Chapter 5	**File System Monitoring**	**97**
	Syntax	98
	Adding Exceptions Capability to Monitoring	103
	The Exceptions File	103
	Using the MB of Free Space Method	110
	Using MB of Free Space with Exceptions	113
	Percentage Used—MB Free and Large Filesystems	118
	Running on AIX, Linux, HP-UX, and Solaris	128
	Command Syntax and Output Varies between	
	Operating Systems	130
	Other Options to Consider	143
	Event Notification	143
	Automated Execution	143
	Modify the egrep Statement	144
	Summary	144
Chapter 6	**Monitoring Paging and Swap Space**	**145**
	Syntax	146
	AIX lsps Command	146
	HP-UX swapinfo Command	147
	Linux free Command	148
	Solaris swap Command	148
	Creating the Shell Scripts	149
	AIX Paging Monitor	149
	HP-UX Swap Space Monitor	155
	Linux Swap Space Monitor	160
	Solaris Swap Space Monitor	164
	All-in-One Paging and Swap Space Monitor	169
	Other Options to Consider	176
	Event Notification	177
	Log File	177
	Scheduled Monitoring	177
	Summary	177
Chapter 7	**Monitoring System Load**	**179**
	Syntax	180
	Syntax for uptime	180
	AIX	180
	HP-UX	181
	Linux	182
	Solaris	183
	What Is the Common Denominator?	183
	Scripting an uptime Field Test Solution	184
	Syntax for iostat	186
	AIX	186
	HP-UX	186

Linux	187
Solaris	187
What Is the Common Denominator?	187
Syntax for sar	188
AIX	188
HP-UX	189
Linux	189
Solaris	190
What Is the Common Denominator?	190
Syntax for vmstat	191
AIX	191
HP-UX	191
Linux	192
Solaris	192
What Is the Common Denominator?	192
Scripting the Solutions	193
Using uptime to Measure the System Load	194
Scripting with the uptime Command	194
Using sar to Measure the System Load	197
Scripting with the sar Command	198
Using iostat to Measure the System Load	203
Scripting with the iostat Command	203
Using vmstat to Measure the System Load	208
Scripting with the vmstat Command	208
Other Options to Consider	212
Stop Chasing the Floating uptime Field	212
Try to Detect Any Possible Problems for the User	213
Show the User the Top CPU Hogs	213
Gathering a Large Amount of Data for Plotting	214
Summary	214
Chapter 8 Process Monitoring and Enabling Preprocess, Startup, and Postprocess Events	**215**
Syntax	216
Monitoring for a Process to Start	216
Monitoring for a Process to End	218
Monitor and Log as a Process Starts and Stops	223
Timed Execution for Process Monitoring, Showing each PID, and Time Stamp with Event and Timing Capability	228
Other Options to Consider	248
Common Uses	248
Modifications to Consider	248
Summary	249
Chapter 9 Monitoring Processes and Applications	**251**
Monitoring Local Processes	252
Remote Monitoring with Secure Shell	254
Checking for Active Oracle Databases	256
Checking If the HTTP Server/Application Is Working	259

Other Things to Consider   260
  Application APIs and SNMP Traps   261
Summary   261

Chapter 10   Creating Pseudo-Random Passwords   263
Randomness   263
Creating Pseudo-Random Passwords   264
Syntax   264
  Arrays   265
    Loading an Array   265
Building the Password Creation Script   266
  Order of Appearance   266
    Define Variables   266
    Define Functions   267
    Testing and Parsing Command-Line Arguments   275
  Beginning of Main   279
    Setting a Trap   280
    Checking for the Keyboard File   280
    Loading the "KEYS" Array   280
    Using the LENGTH Variable to Build a Loop List   281
    Building a New Pseudo-Random Password   282
    Printing the Manager's Password Report for Safe Keeping   283
Other Options to Consider   294
  Password Reports?   294
  Which Password?   295
  Other Uses?   295
Summary   295

Chapter 11   Monitor for Stale Disk Partitions   297
AIX Logical Volume Manager (LVM)   298
The Commands and Methods   298
  Disk Subsystem Commands   298
  Method 1: Monitoring for Stale PPs at the LV Level   299
  Method 2: Monitoring for Stale PPs at the PV Level   304
  Method 3: VG, LV, and PV Monitoring with a resync   308
Other Options to Consider   315
  SSA Disks   315
  Log Files   316
  Automated Execution   316
  Event Notification   316
Summary   317

Chapter 12   Automated Hosts Pinging with Notification   319
Syntax   320
Creating the Shell Script   321
  Define the Variables   321
  Creating a Trap   323
  The Whole Shell Script   324

Other Options to Consider   332
    $PINGLIST Variable Length Limit Problem   332
    Ping the /etc/hosts File Instead of a List File   333
    Logging   333
    Notification of "Unknown host"   334
    Notification Method   334
    Automated Execution Using a Cron Table Entry   335
Summary   335

Chapter 13   Taking a System Snapshot   337
Syntax   338
Creating the Shell Script   340
Other Options to Consider   367
Summary   367

Chapter 14   Compiling, Installing, Configuring, and Using sudo   369
The Need for sudo   369
Downloading and Compiling sudo   370
Compiling sudo   371
Configuring sudo   378
Using sudo   384
Using sudo in a Shell Script   385
The sudo Log File   389
Summary   390

Chapter 15   hgrep: Highlighted grep Script   391
Reverse Video Control   392
Building the hgrep.ksh Shell Script   393
Other Options to Consider   400
    Other Options for the tput Command   400
Summary   401

Chapter 16   Print Queue Hell: Keeping the Printers Printing   403
System V versus BSD Printer Subsystems   404
    AIX Print Control Commands   404
        Classic AIX Printer Subsystem   404
        System V Printing on AIX   408
        More System V Printer Commands   412
    HP-UX Print Control Commands   414
    Linux Print Control Commands   417
        Controlling Queuing and Printing Individually   422
    Solaris Print Control Commands   425
        More System V Printer Commands   429
Putting It All Together   431
Other Options to Consider   438
    Logging   439
    Exceptions Capability   439
    Maintenance   439
    Scheduling   439
Summary   439

Chapter 17 **Automated FTP Stuff** 441
Syntax 441
Automating File Transfers and Remote Directory Listings 444
Using FTP for Directory Listings on a Remote Machine 444
Getting One or More Files from a Remote System 446
Pre and Post Events 449
Script in Action 449
Putting One or More Files to a Remote System 450
Replacing Hard-Coded Passwords with Variables 452
Example of Detecting Variables in a Script's Environment 453
Modifying Our FTP Scripts to Use Password Variables 456
Other Options to Consider 463
Use Command-Line Switches to Control Execution 463
Keep a Log of Activity 463
Add a Debug Mode to the Scripts 463
Summary 464

Chapter 18 **Finding "Large" Files** 465
Syntax 466
Creating the Script 466
Other Options to Consider 472
Summary 473

Chapter 19 **Monitoring and Auditing User Key Strokes** 475
Syntax 476
Scripting the Solution 477
Logging User Activity 478
Starting the Monitoring Session 479
Where Is the Repository? 479
The Scripts 480
Logging root Activity 483
Some sudo Stuff 486
Monitoring Other Administration Users 489
Other Options to Consider 492
Emailing the Audit Logs 493
Compression 493
Need Better Security? 493
Inform the Users 493
Sudoers File 494
Summary 494

Chapter 20 **Turning On/Off SSA Identification Lights** 495
Syntax 496
Translating an hdisk to a pdisk 496
Identifying an SSA Disk 496
The Scripting Process 497
Usage and User Feedback Functions 497
Control Functions 501
The Full Shell Script 507

Other Things to Consider   520
   Error Log   520
   Cross-Reference   520
   Root Access and sudo   520
Summary   521

Chapter 21   Pseudo-Random Number Generation   **523**
What Makes a Random Number?   523
The Methods   524
   Method 1: Creating Numbers between 0 and 32,767   525
   Method 2: Creating Numbers between 1 and a
     User-Defined Maximum   526
   Method 3: Fixed-Length Numbers between 1 and a
     User-Defined Maximum   527
     Why Pad the Number with Zeros the Hard Way?   529
Shell Script to Create Pseudo-Random Numbers   530
Creating Unique Filenames   535
Summary   543

Chapter 22   Floating-Point Math and the bc Utility   **545**
Syntax   545
Creating Some Shell Scripts Using bc   546
   Creating the float_add.ksh Shell Script   546
   Testing for Integers and Floating-Point Numbers   552
   Building a Math Statement for the bc Command   554
   Using a Here Document   555
   Creating the float_subtract.ksh Shell Script   556
   Using getopts to Parse the Command Line   561
   Building a Math Statement String for bc   563
   Here Document and Presenting the Result   564
   Creating the float_multiply.ksh Shell Script   565
   Parsing the Command Line for Valid Numbers   570
   Creating the float_divide.ksh Shell Script   573
   Creating the float_average.ksh Shell Script   580
Other Options to Consider   582
   Remove the Scale from Some of the Shell Scripts   582
   Create More Functions   582
Summary   583

Chapter 23   Scripts for Number Base Conversions   **585**
Syntax   585
   Example 23.1: Converting from Base 10 to Base 16   586
   Example 23.2: Converting from Base 8 to Base 16   586
   Example 23.3 Converting Base 10 to Octal   587
   Example 23.4 Converting Base 10 to Hexadecimal   587
Scripting the Solution   587
   Base 2 (binary) to Base 16 (hexadecimal) Shell Script   587
   Base 10 (Decimal) to Base 16 (Hexadecimal) Shell Script   590

Script to Create a Software Key Based on the Hexadecimal
Representation of an IP Address   594
Script to Translate between *Any* Number Base   597
Using getopts to Parse the Command Line   602
Example 23.5 Correct Usage of the Equate_any_base.ksh
Shell Script   603
Example 23.6 Incorrect Usage of the Equate_any_base.ksh
Shell Script   603
Continuing with the Script   604
Beginning of Main   606
Other Options to Consider   608
Software Key Shell Script   608
Summary   608

Chapter 24   Menu Program Suitable for Operations Staff   609
Reverse Video Syntax   610
Creating the Menu   610
Creating a Message Bar for Feedback   611
From the Top   616
Other Options to Consider   617
Shelling Out to the Command Line   618
Good Candidate for Using sudo   618
Summary   618

Chapter 25   Sending Pop-Up Messages from Unix to Windows   619
About Samba and the smbclient Command   619
Syntax   620
Building the broadcast.ksh Shell Script   621
Sending a Message to All Users   621
Adding Groups to the Basic Code   623
Adding the Ability to Specify Destinations Individually   623
Using getopts to Parse the Command Line   624
Testing User Input   627
Testing and Prompting for WINLIST Data   627
Testing and Prompting for Message Data   628
Sending the Message   629
Putting It All Together   630
Watching the broadcast.ksh Script in Action   640
Downloading and Installing Samba   642
Testing the smbclient Program the First Time   643
Other Options to Consider   644
Producing Error Notifications   645
Add Logging of Unreachable Machines   645
Create Two-Way Messanging   645
Summary   645

Appendix A   What's on the Web Site   647

Index   663

Introduction

In Unix there are many ways to accomplish a given task. Given a problem to solve, we may be able to get to a solution in any number of ways. Of course, some will be more efficient, be more readable, use less disk space or memory, may or may not give the user feedback on what is going on or give more accurate details and more precision to the result. In this book we are going to step through every detail of writing a shell script to solve real-world Unix problems and tasks. The shell scripts range from using a pseudo-random number generator to create pseudo-random passwords to checking for full filesystems on Unix machines and to sending pop-up messages to Windows desktops. The details required to write these shell scripts include using good style and providing good comments throughout the shell script by describing each step. Other details include combining many commands into just one command statement when desirable, separating commands on several lines when readability and understanding of the concept may be diminished, and making a script readable and easy to maintain. We will see the benefit of using variables and files to store data, show methods to strip out unwanted or unneeded data from a command output, and format the data for a particular use. Additionally, we are going to show how to write and include functions in our shell scripts and demonstrate the benefits of functions over a shell script written without functions.

This book is intended for any flavor of Unix, but its emphasis includes AIX, Linux, HP-UX, and Solaris operating systems. Most every script in the book is also included on the book's companion Web site (www.wiley.com/compbooks/michael). Many of the shell scripts are rewritten for each different operating system, when it is necessary. Other shell scripts are not platform dependent. These script rewrites are sometimes needed because command syntax and output vary, sometimes in a major way, between Unix flavors. The variations are sometimes as small as pulling the data out of a different column or using a different command switch, or they can be as major as putting several commands together to accomplish the same task to get similar output or result on different flavors of Unix.

In each chapter we start with the very basic concepts and work our way up to some very complex and difficult concepts. The primary purpose of a shell script is automating repetitive and complex functions. This alleviates keystroke errors and allows for time-scheduled execution of the shell script. It is always better to have the system tell us that it has a problem than to find out too late to be proactive. This book will help us to be more proactive in our dealings with the system. At every level we will gain more knowledge to allow us to move on to ever increasingly complex ideas with ease. We are going to show different ways to solve our real-world *example tasks*. There is not just one correct way to solve a challenge, and we are going to look at the pros and cons of attacking a problem in various ways. Our goal is to be confident and flexible problem solvers. Given a task, we can solve it in any number of ways, and the solution will be intuitively obvious when you complete this book.

Overview of the Book and Technology

This book is intended as a learning tool and study guide to learn how to write shell scripts to solve a multitude of problems by starting with a clear goal. While studying with this book we will cover most shell scripting techniques about seven times, each time from a different angle, solving a different problem. I have found this learning technique to work extremely well for retention of the material to memory.

I urge everyone to read this book from cover to cover to get the maximum benefit. Every script is written using Korn shell, which is the industry standard for scripting solutions in Unix, although some may argue this point. There are several versions of the Korn shell shipped with Unix, depending on the Unix operating system (OS) and the version of the OS release. I have found that the shell scripts in this book will run on any of the Korn shell versions without any modification.

This book goes from some trivial task solutions to some rather advanced concepts that Systems Administrators will benefit from, and a lot of stuff in between. There are several chapters for each level of complexity scattered throughout this book. The shell scripts presented in this book are complete shell scripts, which is one of the things that sets this book apart from other shell scripting books on the market. The solutions are explained thoroughly, with each part of the shell script explained in minute detail down to the philosophy and mindset of the author.

How This Book Is Organized

Each chapter starts with a typical Unix challenge that occurs every day in the computing world. With each challenge we define a specific goal and start the shell script by defining the correct command syntax to solve the problem. When we have a goal and the command syntax, we start building the shell script around the commands. The next step is to filter the command(s) output to strip out the unneeded data, or we may decide to just extract the data we need from the output. If the syntax varies between Unix flavors we show the correct syntax to get the same, or a similar, result. When we get to this point we go further to build options into the shell script to give the end user more flexibility on the command line.

When a shell script has to be rewritten for each operating system, a combined shell script is shown at the end of the chapter that joins the Unix flavor differences together into one shell script that will run on all of the OS flavors. To do this last step we query the system for the Unix flavor using the **uname** command. By knowing the flavor of the operating system we are able to execute the proper commands for each Unix flavor by using a simple **case** statement. If this is new to you, do not worry; everything is explained throughout the book in detail.

Each chapter targets a different real-world problem. Some challenges are very complex, while others are just interesting to play around with. Some chapters hit the problem from several different angles in a single chapter, and others leave you the challenge to solve on your own—of course, with a few hints to get you started. Each chapter solves the challenge presented and can be read as a single unit without referencing other chapters in the book. Some of the material, though, is explained in great detail in one chapter and lightly covered in other chapters. Because of this variation we recommend that you start at the beginning of the book and read and study every chapter to the end of the book because this is a learning experience!

Who Should Read This Book

This book is intended for anyone who works with Unix on a daily basis from the command line. The topics studied in the book are mainly for Unix professionals—Programmers, Programmer-Analysts, System Operators, Systems Administrators, and anyone who is interested in getting ahead in the support arena. Beginners will get a lot out of this book, too, but some of the material may be a little high level, so a basic Unix book may be needed to answer some questions. Everyone should have a good working knowledge of common Unix commands before starting this book, because we do not explain common Unix commands at all.

I started my career in Unix by learning on the job how to be a Systems Operator. I wish I had a book like this when I started. Having this history I wanted others to get a jump start on their careers. I wrote this book with the knowledge that I was in your shoes at one time, and I remember that I had to learn everything from the **man** pages, one command at a time. Use this book as a study guide, and you will have a jump start to get ahead quickly in the Unix world, which is getting bigger all of the time.

Tools You Will Need

To get the most benefit from this book you need access to a Unix machine, preferably with AIX, HP-UX, Linux, or Solaris installed. You can run Linux and Solaris on standard PC hardware, and it is relatively inexpensive. It is a good idea to make your default shell environment the Korn shell (ksh); the standard shell on Linux is the Bourne Again shell (bash) shell, and some others use Bourne shell (sh) as the default. You can find your default shell by entering **echo $SHELL** from the command line. None of the shell scripts in this book requires a graphical terminal, but it sure does not hurt to have GNOME, CDE, KDE2, or X-Windows running. This way you can work in multiple windows at the same time and cut and paste code between windows.

You also need a text editor that you are comfortable using. Most Unix operating systems come with the **vi** editor, and a lot also include **emacs.** Remember that the editor must be a text editor that stores files in a standard ANSII format. The CDE and other X-editors work just fine, too. You will also need some time, patience, and an open, creative mind that is ready to learn.

Another thing to note is that all of the variables used in the shell scripts and functions in this book are in uppercase. I did this because it is much easier to follow along with a shell script if you know quickly where the variables are located in the code. When you write your own shell scripts, please use lowercase for all shell script and function variables. The reason this is important is that the operating system, and applications, use *environment variables* that are in uppercase. If you are not careful, you can overwrite a critical system or application variable with your own value and hose up the system; however this is dependent on the scope of where the variable is visible in the code. Just a word of warning, be careful with uppercase variables!

What's on the Web Site

On the book's companion Web site, www.wiley.com/compbooks/michael, all of the shell scripts and most of the functions that are studied in the book can be found. The functions are easy to cut and paste directly into your own shell scripts to make the scripting process a little easier. Additionally, there is a shell script *stub* that you can copy to another filename. This script stub has everything to get you started writing quickly. The only thing you need to do is fill in the fields for the following: Script Name, Author, Date, Version, Platform, Purpose, and Rev List, when revisions are made. There is a place to define variables and functions, and then you have a "BEGINNNG OF MAIN" section to start the main body of the shell script.

Summary

This book is for learning how to be creative, proactive, and a professional problem solver. Given a task, the solution will be *intuitively obvious* to you on completion of this book. This book will help you attack problems logically and present you with a technique of building on what you know. With each challenge presented you will see how to take the basic syntax and turn it into the basis for a shell scripting solution. We always start with the basics and build more and more logic into the solution before we add other options the end user can use for more flexibility.

Speaking of end users, we must always keep our users informed about how processing is progressing. Giving a user a blank screen to look at is the worst thing that you can do, so for this we can create progress indicators. You will learn how to be proactive by building tools that monitor for specific situations that indicate the beginning stages of an upcoming problem. This is where knowing how to query the system puts you ahead of the rest of your staff.

With the techniques presented in this book, you will learn. You will learn about problem resolution. You will learn about starting with what you know about a situation and building a solution effectively. You will learn how to make a single shell script work on other platforms without further modification. You will learn how to be proactive. You will learn how to write a shell script that is easily maintained. You will learn how to use plenty of comments in a shell script. You will learn how to write a shell script that is easy to read and follow through the logic. Basically, you will learn to be an effective problem solver where the solution to any challenge is *intuitively obvious!*

CHAPTER 1

Scripting Quick Start and Review

We are going to start out by giving a very targeted refresher course. The topics that follow are short explanations of techniques that we always have to search the book to find; here they are all together in one place. The explanations range from showing the fastest way to process a file line by line to the simple matter of case sensitivity of Unix and shell scripts. This should not be considered a full and complete list of scripting topics, but it is a very good starting point and it does point out a sample of the topics covered in the book. For each topic listed in this chapter there is a very detailed explanation later in the book.

I urge everyone to study this entire book. Every chapter hits a different topic using a different approach. The book is written this way to emphasize that there is never only one technique to solve a challenge in Unix. All of the shell scripts in this book are real-world examples of how to solve a problem. Thumb through the chapters, and you can see that I tried to hit most of the common (and some uncommon!) tasks in Unix. All of the shell scripts have a good explanation of the thinking process, and we always start out with the correct command syntax for the shell script targeting a specific goal. I hope you enjoy this book as much as I enjoyed writing it. Let's get started!

Case Sensitivity

Unix is case sensitive. Because Unix is case sensitive our shell scripts are also case sensitive.

1

Unix Special Characters

All of the following characters have a special meaning or function. If they are used in a way that their special meaning is not needed then they must be *escaped*. To escape, or remove its special function, the character must be immediately preceded with a back-slash, \, or enclosed within ' ' forward tic marks (single quotes).

```
\ ( ; # $ ? & * ( ) [ ] ` ' " +
```

Shells

A shell is an environment in which we can run our commands, programs, and shell scripts. There are different flavors of shells, just as there are different flavors of operating systems. Each flavor of shell has its own set of recognized commands and functions. This book works entirely with the Korn shell.

```
Korn Shell      /bin/ksh   OR   /usr/bin/ksh
```

Shell Scripts

The basic concept of a shell script is a list of commands, which are listed in the order of execution. A good shell script will have comments, preceded by a pound sign, #, describing the steps. There are conditional tests, such as value A is greater than value B, loops allowing us to go through massive amounts of data, files to read and store data, and variables to read and store data, and the script may include *functions*.

We are going to write a lot of scripts in the next several hundred pages, and we should always start with a *clear goal* in mind. By clear goal, we have a specific purpose for this script, and we have a set of expected results. We will also hit on some tips, tricks, and, of course, the gotchas in solving a challenge one way as opposed to another to get the same result. All techniques are not created equal.

Shell scripts and functions are both *interpreted*. This means they are not compiled. Both shell scripts and functions are ASCII text that is read by the Korn shell command interpreter. When we execute a shell script, or function, a command interpreter goes through the ASCII text line by line, loop by loop, test by test and executes each statement, as each line is reached from the top to the bottom.

Functions

A function is written in much the same way as a shell script but is different in that it is defined, or written, within a shell script, most of the time, and is called within the script. This way we can write a piece of code, which is used over and over, just once and use it without having to rewrite the code every time. We just call the function instead.

We can also define functions at the system level that is always available in our environment, but this is a later topic for discussion.

A Function Has the Form

```
function function_name
{

     commands to execute

}


or


function_name ()
{

     commands to execute

}
```

When we write functions into our scripts we must remember to declare, or write, the function *before* we use it: The function must appear above the command statement calling the function. We can't use something that does not yet exist.

Running a Shell Script

A shell script can be executed in the following ways:

```
ksh  shell_script_name
```

will create a Korn shell and execute the shell_script_name in the newly created Korn shell environment.

```
shell_script_name
```

will execute shell_script_name *if the execution bit is set on the file* (see the **man** page on the **chmod** command). The script will execute in the shell that is *declared* on the first line of the shell script. If no shell is declared on the first line of the shell script, it will execute in the default shell, which is the user's system-defined shell. Executing in an unintended shell may result in a failure and give unpredictable results.

Declare the Shell in the Shell Script

Declare the shell! If we want to have complete control over how a shell script is going to run and in which shell it is to execute, we MUST *declare* the shell in *the very first line of the script.* If no shell is declared, the script will execute in the default shell, defined by the system for the user executing the shell script. If the script was written, for example, to execute in Korn shell ksh, and the default shell for the user executing the shell script is the C shell csh, then the script will most likely have a failure during execution. To declare a shell, one of the declaration statements in Table 1.1 must appear on the *very first line* of the shell script:

NOTE This book uses only the Korn shell, `#!/usr/bin/ksh` **OR** `#!/bin/ksh`.

Comments and Style in Shell Scripts

Making good comments in our scripts is stressed throughout this book. What is intuitively obvious to us may be total Greek to others who follow in our footsteps. We have to write code that is readable and has an easy flow. This involves writing a script that is easy to read and easily maintained, which means that it must have plenty of comments describing the steps. For the most part, the person who writes the shell script is not the one who has to maintain it. There is nothing worse than having to hack through someone else's code that has no comments to find out what each step is supposed to do. It can be tough enough to modify the script in the first place, but having to figure out the mind set of the author of the script will sometimes make us think about rewriting the entire shell script from scratch. We can avoid this by writing a clearly readable script and inserting plenty of comments describing what our philosophy is and how we are using the input, output, variables, and files.

For good style in our command statements, we need it to be readable. For this reason it is sometimes better, for instance, to separate a command statement onto three separate lines instead of stringing, or *piping*, everything together on the same line of code; in some cases, it is more desirable to create a long pipe. In some cases, it may be just too difficult to follow the pipe and understand what the expected result should be for a new script writer. And, again, it should have comments describing our thinking step by step. This way someone later will look at our code and say, "Hey, now that's a groovy way to do that."

Table 1.1   Different Types of Shells to Declare

#!/usr/bin/sh	OR	#!/bin/sh	Declares a Bourne shell
#!/usr/bin/ksh	OR	#!/bin/ksh	Declares a Korn shell
#!/usr/bin/csh	OR	#!/bin/csh	Declares a C shell
#!/usr/bin/bash	OR	#!/bin/bash	Declares a Bourne-Again shell

Command readability and step-by-step comments are just the very basics of a well-written script. Using a lot of comments will make our life much easier when we have to come back to the code after not looking at it for six months, and believe me, we will look at the code again. Comment everything! This includes, but is not limited to, describing what our variables and files are used for, describing what loops are doing, describing each test, maybe including expected results and how we are manipulating the data and the many data fields.

A hash mark, #, precedes each line of a comment.

The *script stub* that follows is on this book's companion Web site at www.wiley.com/compbooks/michael. The name is `script.stub`. It has all of the comments ready to get started writing a shell script. The `script.stub` file can be copied to a new filename. Edit the new filename, and start writing code. The `script.stub` file is shown in Listing 1.1.

```
#!/usr/bin/ksh
#
# SCRIPT: NAME_of_SCRIPT
# AUTHOR: AUTHORS_NAME
# DATE:   DATE_of_CREATION
# REV:    1.1.A (Valid are A, B, D, T and P)
#               (For Alpha, Beta, Dev, Test and Production)
#
# PLATFORM: (SPECIFY: AIX, HP-UX, Linux, Solaris
#                     or Not platform dependent)
#
# PURPOSE: Give a clear, and if necessary, long, description of the
#          purpose of the shell script. This will also help you stay
#          focused on the task at hand.
#
# REV LIST:
#         DATE: DATE_of_REVISION
#         BY:   AUTHOR_of_MODIFICATION
#         MODIFICATION: Describe what was modified, new features, etc--
#
#
# set -n   # Uncomment to check your syntax, without execution.
#          # NOTE: Do not forget to put the comment back in or
#          #       the shell script will not execute!
# set -x   # Uncomment to debug this shell script (Korn shell only)
#
############################################################
########### DEFINE FILES AND VARIABLES HERE ##############
############################################################


############################################################
```

Listing 1.1   script.stub shell script starter listing. *(continues)*

```
############## DEFINE FUNCTIONS HERE ###################
#########################################################




#########################################################
############### BEGINNING OF MAIN #######################
#########################################################



# End of script
```

Listing 1.1   script.stub shell script starter listing. *(continued)*

The shell script starter shown in Listing 1.1 gives you the framework to start writing the shell script with sections to declare variables and files, create functions, and write the final section, BEGINNING OF MAIN, where the main body of the shell script is written.

Control Structures

The following control structures will be used extensively.

if ... then Statement

```
if [ test_command ]
then

        commands

fi
```

if ... then ... else Statement

```
if [ test_command ]
then

     commands

else

     commands

fi
```

if ... then ... elif ... (else) Statement

```
if  [ test_command ]

then

    commands
elif [ test_command ]
then

    commands

elif [ test_command ]
then

    commands
.
.
.
else    (Optional)

    commands

fi
```

for ... in Statement

```
for loop_variable in argument_list
do

    commands

done
```

while Statement

```
while test_command_is_true
do

    commands

done
```

until Statement

```
until  test_command_is_true
do
```

```
        commands

done
```

case Statement

```
case $variable  in

match_1)

        commands_to_execute_for_1

        ;;

match_2)

        commands_to_execute_for_2

        ;;

match_3)

        commands_to_execute_for_3

        ;;
    .
    .
    .


*)      (Optional - any other value)

        commands_to_execute_for_no_match

        ;;

esac
```

NOTE **The last part of the case statement:**

```
    *)

            commands_to_execute_for_no_match

  ;;
```

is optional.

Using break, continue, exit, and return

It is sometimes necessary to *break* out of a **for** or **while** loop, *continue* in the next block of code, *exit* completely out of the script, or *return* a function's result back to the script that called the function.

break is used to terminate the execution of the entire loop, after completing the execution of all of the lines of code up to the **break** statement. It then steps down to the code following the end of the loop.

continue is used to transfer control to the next set of code, but it continues execution of the loop.

exit will do just what one would expect: It exits the entire script. An integer may be added to an **exit** command (for example, `exit 0`), which will be sent as the return code.

return is used in a function to send data back, or *return a result*, to the calling script.

Here Document

A *here document* is used to redirect input *into* an interactive shell script or program. We can run an interactive program within a shell script without user action by supplying the required input for the interactive program, or interactive shell script. This is why it is called a here document: The required input is here, as opposed to somewhere else.

Syntax for a Here Document

```
program_name <<LABEL

Program_Input_1
Program_Input_2
Program_Input_3

Program_Input_#


LABEL
```

EXAMPLE:

```
/usr/local/bin/My_program << EOF
Randy
Robin
Rusty
Jim
EOF
```

Notice in the here documents that there are *no spaces* in the program input lines, between the two EOF labels. If a space is added to the input, then the here document may fail. The input that is supplied must be the *exact* data that the program is expecting, and many programs will fail if spaces are added to the input.

Shell Script Commands

The basis for the shell script is the automation of a series of commands. We can execute most any command in a shell script that we can execute from the command line. (One exception is trying to set an execution *suid* or *sgid, sticky bit*, within a shell script is not supported for security reasons.) For commands that are executed often, we reduce errors by putting the commands in a shell script. We will eliminate typos and missed device definitions, and we can do conditional tests that can ensure there are not any failures due to unexpected input or output. Commands and command structure will be covered extensively throughout this book.

Most of the commands shown in Table 1.2 are used at some point in this book, depending on the task we are working on in each chapter.

Table 1.2   Unix Commands Review

COMMAND	DESCRIPTION
passwd	Change user password
pwd	Print current directory
cd	Change directory
ls	List of files in a directory
wildcards	* matches any number of characters, ? matches a single character
file	Print the type of file
cat	Display the contents of a file
pr	Display the contents of a file
pg or page	Display the contents of a file one page at a time
more	Display the contents of a file one page at a time
clear	Clear the screen
cp or copy	Copy a file
chown	Change the owner of a file
chgrp	Change the group of a file
chmod	Change file modes, permissions

Table 1.2 *(Continued)*

COMMAND	DESCRIPTION
rm	Remove a file from the system
mv	Rename a file
mkdir	Create a directory
rmdir	Remove a directory
grep	Pattern matching
egrep	grep command for extended regular expressions
find	Used to locate files and directories
>>	Append to the end of a file
>	Redirect, create, or overwrite a file
|	Pipe, used to string commands together
||	Logical OR—command1 || command2—execute command2 if command1 fails
&	Execute in background
&&	Logical AND—command1 && command2—execute command2 if command1 succeeds
date	Display the system date and time
echo	Write strings to standard output
sleep	Execution halts for the specified number of seconds
wc	Count the number of words, lines, and characters in a file
head	View the top of a file
tail	View the end of a file
diff	Compare two files
sdiff	Compare two files side by side (requires 132-character display)
spell	Spell checker
lp, lpr, enq, qprt	Print a file
lpstat	Status of system print queues
enable	Enable, or start, a print queue
disable	Disable, or stop, a print queue

(continues)

Table 1.2 Unix Commands Review *(Continued)*

COMMAND	DESCRIPTION
cal	Display a calendar
who	Display information about users on the system
w	Extended **who** command
whoami	Display $LOGNAME or $USER environment parameter
who am I	Display login name, terminal, login date/time, and where logged in
f, finger	Information about logged-in users including the users .plan and .project
talk	Two users have a split screen conversation
write	Display a message on a user's screen
wall	Display a message on all logged-in users' screens
rwall	Display a message to all users on a remote host
rsh or remsh	Execute a command, or log in, on a remote host
df	Filesystems statistics
ps	Information on currently running processes
netstat	Show network status
vmstat	Show virtual memory status
iostat	Show input/output status
uname	Name of the current operating system, as well as machine information
sar	System activity report
basename	Base filename of a string parameter
man	Display the on-line reference manual
su	Switch to another user, also known as super-user
cut	Write out selected characters
awk	Programming language to parse characters
sed	Programming language for character substitution
vi	Start the vi editor
emacs	Start the emacs editor

Most of the commands shown in Table 1.2 are used at some point in this book, depending on the task we are working on in each chapter.

Symbol Commands

The symbols shown in Table 1.3 are actually commands.

All of the symbol commands shown in Table 1.3 are used extensively in this book.

Variables

A variable is a character string to which we assign a value. The value assigned could be a number, text, filename, device, or any other type of data. A variable is nothing more than a pointer to the actual data. We are going to use variables so much in our scripts that it will be unusual for us not to use them. In this book we are always going to specify a variable in uppercase—for example, UPPERCASE. Using uppercase variable names is not recommended in the real world of shell programming, though, because these uppercase variables may step on system environment variables, which are also in uppercase. Uppercase variables are used in this book to emphasize the variables and to make them stand out in the code. When you write your own shell scripts or modify the scripts in this book, make the variables lowercase text. To assign a variable to point to data, we use UPPERCASE="value_to_assign" as the assignment syntax. To access the data that the variable, UPPERCASE, is pointing to, we must add a dollar sign, **$**, as a prefix—for example, $UPPERCASE. To view the data assigned to the variable, we use echo $UPPERCASE, print $UPPERCASE for variables, or cat $UPPERCASE, if the variable is pointing to a file, as a command structure.

Command-Line Arguments

The command-line arguments $1, $2, $3, ...$9 are positional parameters, with **$0** pointing to the actual command, program, shell script, or function and $1, $2, $3, ...$9 as the arguments to the command.

Table 1.3 Symbol Commands

( )	Run the enclosed command in a sub-shell
(( ))	Evaluate and assign value to variable and do math in a shell
$(( ))	Evaluate the enclosed expression
[ ]	Same as the test command
[[ ]]	Used for string comparison
$( )	Command substitution
`command`	Command substitution

The positional parameters, $0, $2, etc., in a *function*, are for the function's use and may not be in the environment of the shell script that is calling the function. Where a variable is known in a function or shell script is called the *scope* of the variable.

Shift Command

The **shift** command is used to move positional parameters to the left; for example, **shift** causes $2 to become $1. We can also add a number to the **shift** command to move the positions more than one position; for example, **shift 3** causes $4 to move to the $1 position.

Sometimes we encounter situations where we have an unknown or varying number of arguments passed to a shell script or function, $1, $2, $3... (also known as positional parameters). Using the **shift** command is a good way of processing each positional parameter in the order they are listed.

To further explain the **shift** command, we will show how to process an unknown number of arguments passed to the shell script shown in Listing 1.2. Try to follow through this example shell script structure. This script is using the **shift** command to process an unknown number of command-line arguments, or positional parameters. In this script we will refer to these as *tokens*.

```
#!/usr/bin/sh
#
# SCRIPT: shifting.sh
#
# AUTHOR: Randy Michael
#
# DATE:   01-22-1999
#
# REV:    1.1.A
#
# PLATFORM: Not platform dependent
#
# PURPOSE: This script is used to process all of the tokens which
# Are pointed to by the command-line arguments, $1, $2, $3,etc...
#
# REV. LIST:
#
#
# Initialize all variables
COUNT=0          # Initialize the counter to zero
NUMBER=$#        # Total number of command-line arguments to process

#  Start a while loop

while [ $COUNT -lt $NUMBER ]
```

Listing 1.2 Example of using the shift command.

```
do
        COUNT=`expr $COUNT + 1`   # A little math in the shell script

        TOKEN='$'$COUNT                  # Loops through each token starting with $1

                                 process each $TOKEN

        shift                            # Grab the next token, i.e. $2 becomes $1

done
```

Listing 1.2   Example of using the shift command. *(continued)*

We will go through similar examples of the **shift** command in great detail later in the book.

Special Parameters $* and $@

There are special parameters that allow accessing *all* of the command-line arguments at once. **$*** and **$@** both will act the same unless they are enclosed in double quotes, " ".

Special Parameter Definitions

The $* special parameter specifies *all* command-line arguments.

The $@ special parameter also specifies *all* command-line arguments.

The "$*" special parameter takes the entire list as one argument with spaces between.

The "$@" special parameter takes the entire list and separates it into separate arguments.

We can rewrite the shell script shown in Listing 1.2 to process an unknown number of command-line arguments with either the **$*** or **$@** special parameters:

```
#!/usr/bin/sh
#
# SCRIPT: shifting.sh
# AUTHOR: Randy Michael
# DATE:    01-22-1999
# REV:     1.1.A
# PLATFORM: Not platform dependent
#
# PURPOSE: This script is used to process all of the tokens which
```

```
# Are pointed to by the command-line arguments, $1, $2, $3, etc... -
#
# REV LIST:
#
#

#  Start a for loop

for TOKEN in $*
do

        process each $TOKEN

done
```

We could have also used the $@ special parameter just as easily. As we see in the previous code segment, the use of the $@ or $* is an alternative solution to the same problem, and it was less code to write. Either technique accomplishes the same task.

Double Quotes ", Forward Tics ', and Back Tics `

How do we know which one of these to use in our scripts, functions, and command statements? This decision causes the most confusion in writing scripts. We are going to set this straight now.

Depending on what the task is and the output desired, it is very important to use the correct enclosure. Failure to use these correctly will give unpredictable results.

We use ", double quotes, in a statement where we want to allow character or command substitution. The "-key is located next to the Enter key on a standard USA QWERT keyboard. Use the SHIFT "-key sequence.

We use ', forward tics, in a statement where we do *not* want character or command substitution. Enclosing in ', forward tics, is intended to use the *literal text* in the variable or command statement, without any substitution. All special meanings and functions are removed. It is also used when you want a variable reread each time it is used; for example, '$PWD' is used a lot in processing the PS1 command-line prompt. The '-key is located next to the Enter key on a standard USA QWERT keyboard. Additionally, preceding the same string with a backslash, \, also removes the special meaning of a character, or string.

We use `, back tics, in a statement where we want to execute a command, or script, and have its output substituted instead; this is *command substitution*. The `-key is located below the Escape key, Esc, in the top-left corner of a standard USA QWERT keyboard. Command substitution is also accomplished by using the $(command) command syntax. We are going to see many different examples of these throughout this book.

Math in a Shell Script

We can do arithmetic in a shell script easily. The Korn shell `let` command and the `((expr))` command expressions are the most commonly used methods to evaluate an integer expression. Later we will also cover the **bc** function to do floating-point arithmetic.

Operators

The Korn shell uses arithmetic operators from the C programming language (see Table 1.4), in decreasing order of precedence.

A lot of these math operators are used in the book, but not all. In this book we try to keep things very straightforward and not confuse the reader with obscure expressions.

Table 1.4   Math Operators

OPERATOR	DESCRIPTION
++ −	Auto-increment and auto-decrement, both prefix and postfix
+	Unary plus
-	Unary minus
! ~	Logical negation; binary inversion (one's complement)
* / %	Multiplication; division; modulus (remainder)
+ -	Addition; subtraction
<< >>	Bitwise left shift; bitwise right shift
<= >=	Less than or equal to; greater than or equal to
< >	Less than; greater than
== !=	Equality; inequality (both evaluated left to right)
&	Bitwise AND
^	Bitwise exclusive OR
|	Bitwise OR
&&	Logical AND
||	Logical OR

Built-In Mathematical Functions

The Korn shell provides access to the standard set of mathematical functions. They are called using C function call syntax. Table 1.5 shows a list of shell functions.

We do not have any shell scripts in this book that use any of these built-in Korn shell functions except for the `int` function to extract the integer portion of a floating-point number.

File Permissions, suid and sgid Programs

After writing a shell script we must remember to set the file permissions to make it *executable*. We use the **chmod** command to change the file's mode of operation. In addition to making the script executable, it is also possible to change the mode of the file to always execute as a particular user (`suid`) or to always execute as a member of a particular system group (`sgid`). This is called setting the *sticky bit*. If you try to `suid` or `sgid` a shell script, it is ignored for security reasons.

Table 1.5   Built-In Shell Functions

NAME	FUNCTION
abs	Absolute value
log	Natural logarithm
acos	Arc cosine
sin	Sine
asin	Arc sine
sinh	Hyperbolic sine
cos	Cosine
sqrt	Square root
cosh	Hyperbolic cosine
tan	Tangent
exp	Exponential function
tanh	Hyperbolic tangent
int	Integer part of floating-point number

Setting a program to always execute as a particular user, or member of a certain group, is often used to allow all users, or a set of users, to run a program in the proper environment. As an example, most system check programs need to run as an administrative user, sometimes `root`. We do not want to pass out passwords so we can just make the program always execute as `root` and it makes everyone's life easier. We can use the options shown in Table 1.6 in setting file permissions. Also, please review the `chmod` **man** page.

By using combinations from the **chmod** command options, you can set the permissions on a file or directory to anything that you want. Remember that setting a shell script to `suid` or `sgid` is ignored by the system.

chmod Command Syntax for Each Purpose

To Make a Script Executable

```
chmod 754 my_script.sh
```

or

```
chmod u+rwx,g+rx,o+r my_script.ksh
```

Table 1.6   `chmod` Permission Options

4000	Sets user ID on execution.
2000	Sets group ID on execution.
1000	Sets the link permission to directories or sets the save-text attribute for files.
0400	Permits read by owner.
0200	Permits write by owner.
0100	Permits execute or search by owner.
0040	Permits read by group.
0020	Permits write by group.
0010	Permits execute or search by group.
0004	Permits read by others.
0002	Permits write by others.
0001	Permits execute or search by others.

The owner can read, write, and execute. The group can read and execute. The world can read.

To Set a Program to Always Execute as the Owner

```
chmod 4755 my_program
```

The program will always execute as the owner of the file, if it is not a shell script. The owner can read, write, and execute. The group can read and execute. The world can read and execute. So no matter who executes this file it will always execute as if the owner actually executed the program.

To Set a Program to Always Execute as a Member of the File Owner's Group

```
chmod 2755 my_program
```

The program will always execute as a member of the file's group, as long as the file is not a shell script. The owner of the file can read, write, and execute. The group can read and execute. The world can read and execute. So no matter who executes this program it will always execute as a member of the file's group.

To Set a Program to Always Execute as Both the File Owner and the File Owner's Group

```
chmod 6755 my_program
```

The program will always execute as the file's owner and as a member of the file owner's group, as long as the program is not a shell script. The owner of the file can read, write, and execute. The group can read and execute. The world can read and execute. No matter who executes this program it will always execute as the file owner and as a member of the file owner's group.

Running Commands on a Remote Host

We sometimes want to execute a command on a remote host and have the result displayed locally. An example would be getting filesystem statistics from a group of machines. We can do this with the **rsh** command. The syntax is rsh *hostname command_to_execute*. This is a handy little tool but two system files will need to be set up on all of the hosts before the **rsh** command will work. The files are .rhosts, which would be created in the user's home directory and have the file permissions of 600, and the /etc/hosts.equiv file.

For security reasons the .rhosts and hosts.equiv files, by default, are not set up to allow the execution of a remote shell. *Be careful!* The systems' security could be threatened. Refer to each operating system's documentation for details on setting up these files.

Speaking of security, a better solution is to use Open Secure Shell (OpenSSH) instead of **rsh**. OpenSSH is a freeware encrypted replacement for **rsh**, **telnet**, and **ftp**, for the most part. To execute a command on another machine using OpenSSH use the following syntax.

```
ssh user@hostname command_to_execute
```

This command prompts you for a password if the encryption key pairs have not been set up on both machines. Setting up the key pair relationships usually takes less than one hour. The details of the procedure are shown in the **ssh** man page (**man ssh**). The OpenSSH code can be downloaded from the following URL: www.openssh.org.

Setting Traps

When a program is terminated before it would normally end, we can catch an exit signal. This is called a *trap*. Table 1.7 lists some of the exit signals.

To see the entire list of supported signals for your operating system, enter the following command:

```
# kill -l      [That's kill -(ell)]
```

This is a really nice tool to use in our shell scripts. On catching a trapped signal we can execute some cleanup commands before we actually exit the shell script. Commands can be executed when a signal is trapped. If the following command statement is added in a shell script, it will print to the screen "EXITING on a TRAPPED SIGNAL" and then make a clean exit on the signals 1, 2, 3, and 15. We cannot trap a `kill -9`.

```
trap 'echo "\nEXITING on a TRAPPED SIGNAL";exit' 1 2 3 15
```

We can add all sorts of commands that may be needed to clean up before exiting. As an example we may need to delete a set of files that the shell script created before we exit.

Table 1.7   Exit Signals

0	—	Normal termination, end of script
1	**SIGHUP**	Hang up, line disconnected
2	**SIGINT**	Terminal interrupt, usually CONTROL-C
3	**SIGQUIT**	Quit key, child processes to die before terminating
9	**SIGKILL**	**kill -9** command, **cannot trap this type of exit status**
15	**SIGTERM**	kill command's default action
24	**SIGSTOP**	Stop, usually CONTROL-z

User Information Commands

Sometimes we need to query the system for some information about users on the system.

who Command

The **who** command gives this output for each logged-in user: *username, tty, login time,* and *where* the user *logged in from*:

```
rmichael      pts/0        Mar 13 10:24        10.10.10.6
root          pts/1        Mar 15 10:43        (yogi)
```

w Command

The **w** command is really an extended **who**. The output looks like the following:

```
12:29PM     up 27 days,    21:53,2 users, load average  1.03,  1.17, 1.09
User        tty       login@        idle      JCPU  PCPU    what
rmichael    pts/0     Mon10AM 0     3:00      1             w
root        pts/1     10:42AM 37    5:12      5:12          tar
```

Notice that the top line of the preceding output is the same as the output of the **uptime** command. The **w** command gives a more detailed output than the **who** command by listing job process time, total user process time, but it does not reveal *where* the users have logged in *from*. We often are interested in this for security purposes. One nice thing about the **w** command's output is that it also lists *what* the users are doing at the instant the command is entered. This can be very useful.

last Command

The **last** command shows the history of who has logged into the system since the wtmp file was created. This is a good tool when you need to do a little investigation of who logged into the system and when. The following is example output:

```
root        ftp       booboo         Aug 06 19:22 - 19:23   (00:01)
root        pts/3     mrranger       Aug 06 18:45    still logged in.
root        pts/2     mrranger       Aug 06 18:45    still logged in.
root        pts/1     mrranger       Aug 06 18:44    still logged in.
root        pts/0     mrranger       Aug 06 18:44    still logged in.
root        pts/0     mrranger       Aug 06 18:43 - 18:44   (00:01)
root        ftp       booboo         Aug 06 18:19 - 18:20   (00:00)
root        ftp       booboo         Aug 06 18:18 - 18:18   (00:00)
root        tty0                     Aug 06 18:06    still logged in.
```

```
root        tty0                        Aug 02 12:24 - 17:59 (4+05:34)
reboot      ~                           Aug 02 12:00
shutdown    tty0                        Jul 31 23:23
root        ftp     booboo              Jul 31 21:19 - 21:19  (00:00)
root        ftp     bambam              Jul 31 21:19 - 21:19  (00:00)
root        ftp     booboo              Jul 31 20:42 - 20:42  (00:00)
root        ftp     bambam              Jul 31 20:41 - 20:42  (00:00)
```

The output of the **last** command shows the username, the login port, where the user logged in from, the time of the login/logout, and the duration of the login session.

ps Command

The **ps** command will show information about current system processes. The **ps** command has many switches that will change what we look at. Some common command options are listed in Table 1.8.

Communicating with Users

Communicate with the system's users and let them know what is going on! All Systems Administrators have the *maintenance window* where we can finally get control and handle some offline tasks. This is just one example of a need to communicate with the systems' users, if any are still logged in.

The most common way to get information to the system users is to use the /etc/motd file. This file is displayed each time the user logs in. If users stay logged in for days at a time they will not see any new messages of the day. This is one reason why real-time communication is needed. The commands shown in Table 1.9 allow communication to, or between, users who are currently logged in the system.

Table 1.8 Some **ps** Command Options

ps	The user's currently running processes
ps -f	Full listing of the user's currently running processes
ps -ef	Full listing of all processes, except kernel processes
ps -A	All processes including kernel processes
ps -Kf	Full listing of kernel processes
ps auxw	Wide listing sorted by percentage of CPU usage, %CPU

Table 1.9 Commands for Real-Time User Communication

wall	Writes a message on the screen of all logged-in users on the *local* host.
rwall	Writes a message on the screen of all logged-in users on a *remote* host.
write	Writes a message to an individual user. The user must currently be logged-in.
talk	Starts an interactive program that allows two users to have a conversation. The screen is split in two, and both users can see what each person is typing.

NOTE When using these commands be aware that if a user is using a program—for example, an accounting software package—and has that program's screen on the terminal, then the user may not get the message or the user's screen may become scrambled.

In addition to the preceding commands, there is a script on the Web site that accompanies this book named broadcast.ksh that can be used to send pop-up messages in a Windows (95, 98, and NT) environment. The script uses Samba, and it must be installed, and enabled, for broadcast.ksh to work. The details are in Chapter 25.

Uppercase or Lowercase Text for Easy Testing

We often need to test text strings like filenames, variables, file text, and so on, for comparison. It can vary so widely that it is easier to uppercase or lowercase the text for ease of comparison. The **tr** and **typeset** commands can be used to uppercase and lowercase text. This makes testing for things like variable input a breeze. Here is an example using the **tr** command:

VARIABLE VALUES

Expected input: TRUE

Real input: TRUE

Possible input: true TRUE True True, etc...

UPCASING

```
UPCASEVAR=$(echo $VARIABLE | tr '[a-z]' '[A-Z]')
```

DOWNCASING

```
DOWNCASEVAR=$(echo $VARIABLE | tr '[A-Z]' '[a-z]')
```

In the preceding example of the **tr** command, we **echo** the string and use a pipe (|) to send the output of the **echo** statement to the **tr** command. As the preceding examples show, uppercasing uses `'[a-z]' '[A-Z]'` .

NOTE The single quotes are required around the square brackets.

```
'[a-z]' '[A-Z]'      Used for lower to uppercase
'[A-Z]' '[a-z]'      Used for upper to lowercase
```

No matter what the user input is, we will always have the *stable* input of TRUE, if uppercased, and `true`, if lowercased. This reduces our code testing and also helps the readability of the script.

We can also use **typeset** to control the attributes of a variable in the Korn shell. In the previous example we are using the variable, VARIABLE. We can set the attribute to always translate all of the characters to uppercase or lowercase. To set the case attribute of VARIABLE to always translate characters to uppercase we use:

```
typeset -u VARIABLE
```

The **-u** switch to the **typeset** command is used for uppercase. After we set the attribute of the variable VARIABLE, using the **typeset** command, any time we assign text characters to VARIABLE they are automatically translated to uppercase characters.

EXAMPLE:

```
typeset -u VARIABLE
VARIABLE="True"
echo $VARIABLE
```

```
TRUE
```

To set the case attribute of the variable VARIABLE to always translate characters to lowercase we use:

```
typeset -l VARIABLE
```

EXAMPLE:

```
typeset -l VARIABLE
VARIABLE="True"
echo $VARIABLE
true
```

Check the Return Code

Whenever we run a command there is a response back from the system about the last command that was executed, known as the **return code**. If the command was successful the return code will be 0, zero. If it was *not* successful the return will be something other than 0, zero. To check the return code we look at the value of the $? shell variable.

As an example, we want to check if the /usr/local/bin directory exists. Each of these blocks of code accomplishes the exact same thing:

```
test   -d   /usr/local/bin
if  [ "$?" -eq 0 ]  # Check the return code
then          # The return code is zero

     echo '/usr/local/bin does exist'

else         # The return code is NOT zero


     echo '/usr/local/bin  does NOT exist'

fi
```

or

```
if  test  -d  /usr/local/bin
then          # The return code is zero

     echo '/usr/local/bin  does exist'

else         # The return code is NOT zero

     echo '/usr/local/bin does NOT exist'
fi
```

or

```
If [ -d  /usr/local/bin ]
then          # The return code is zero

     echo '/usr/local/bin does exist'

else          # The return code is NOT zero

     echo '/usr/local/bin does NOT exist'
fi
```

Notice that we checked the return code using $? once. The other examples use the control structure's built-in test. The built-in tests do the same thing of processing the return code, but the built-in tests hide this step in the process. All three of the previous examples give the exact same result. This is just a matter of personal choice and readability.

Time-Based Script Execution

We write a lot of shell scripts that we want to execute on a timed interval or run once at a specific time. This section addresses these needs with several examples.

Cron Tables

A *cron table* is a system file that is read every minute by the system and will execute any entry that is scheduled to execute in that minute. By default, any user can create a cron table with the **crontab -e** command, but the Systems Administrator can control which users are allowed to create and edit cron tables with the `cron.allow` and `cron.deny` files. When a user creates his or her own cron table the commands, programs, or scripts will execute in that user's environment. It is the same thing as running the user's `$HOME/.profile` before executing the command.

The **crontab -e** command starts the default text editor, **vi** or **emacs**, on the user's cron table.

> **NOTE** When using the crontab command, the current user ID is the cron table that is acted on. To list the contents of the current user's cron table, issue the crontab -l command.

Cron Table Entry Syntax

It is important to know what each field in a cron table entry is used for. Figure 1.1 shows the usage for creating a cron table entry.

This cron table entry in Figure 1.1 executes the script, `/usr/local/bin/somescript.ksh`, at 3:15AM, January 8, on any day of the week that January 8 falls on. Notice that we used a *wildcards* for the weekday field. The following **cron table** entry is another example:

```
1 0 1 1 *  /usr/bin/banner "Happy New Year" > /dev/console
```

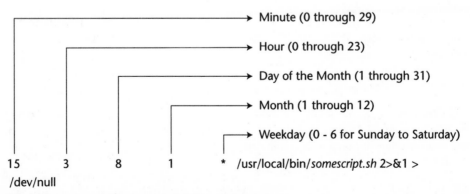

Figure 1.1 Cron table entry definitions and syntax.

At 1 minute after midnight on January 1, on any weekday, this cron table entry writes to the system's console (**/dev/console**) **Happy New Year** in large *banner* letters.

Wildcards

*   Match any number of characters
?   Match a single character

at Command

Like a cron table, the **at** command executes commands based on time. Using the **at** command we can schedule a job to run *once*, at a specific time. When the job is executed the **at** command will send an e-mail, of the standard output and standard error, to the user who scheduled the job to run, unless the output is redirected. As a Systems Administrator we can control which users are allowed to schedule jobs with the at.allow and at.deny files. Refer to each operating system's man pages before modifying these files and the many ways to use the **at** command for timed controlled command execution.

Output Control

How is the script going to run? Where will the output go? These questions come under job control.

Silent Running

To execute a script in *silent mode* we can use the following syntax:

```
/PATH/script_name 2>&1 > /dev/null
```

In this command statement the script_name shell script will execute without any output to the screen. The reason for this is that the command is terminated with the following:

```
2>&1 > /dev/null
```

By terminating a command like this it redirects standard error (stderr), specified by file descriptor 2, to standard output (stdout), specified by file descriptor 1. Then we have another redirection to /dev/null, which sends all of the output to the bit bucket.

We can call this *silent running*. This means that there is absolutely no output from the script going to our screen. Inside the script there may be some output directed to files or devices, a particular terminal, or even the system's console, /dev/console, but none to the user screen. This is especially useful when executing a script from one of the system's cron tables.

In the following example cron table entry, we want to execute a script named /usr/local/bin/systemcheck.ksh, which needs to run as the **root** user, every 15 minutes, 24 hours a day, 7 days a week and not have any output to the screen. There will not be any screen output because we are going to end the cron table entry with:

```
2>&1 > /dev/null
```

Inside the script it may do some kind of notification such as paging staff or sending output to the system's console, writing to a file or a tape device, but output such as echo "Hello world" would go to the *bit bucket*. But echo "Hello world" > /dev/console *would* go to the system's defined console if this command statement was within the shell script.

This cron table entry would need to be placed in the **root** cron table (must be logged in as the **root** user) with the following syntax.

```
5,20,35,50 * * * *  /usr/local/bin/systemcheck.ksh  2>&1 >/dev/null
```

NOTE Most system check type scripts need to be in the root cron table. Of course, a user must be logged in as root to edit root's cron table.

The previous cron table entry would execute the /usr/local/bin/system check.ksh every 15 minutes, at 5, 20, 35, and 50 minutes, each hour, 24 hours a day, 7 days a week. It would not produce any output to the screen due to the final 2>&1 > /dev/null. Of course, the minutes selected to execute can be any. We sometimes want to spread out execution times in the cron tables so that we don't have a lot of CPU-intensive scripts and programs starting execution at the same time.

Using getopts to Parse Command-Line Arguments

The **getopts** command is built in to the Korn shell. It retrieves valid command-line options specified by a single character preceded by a - (minus sign) or + (plus sign). To specify that a command switch requires an argument to the switch, it is followed by a : (colon). If the switch does not require any argument then the : should be omitted. All of the options put together are called the OptionString, and this is followed by some variable name. The argument for each switch is stored in a variable called $OPTARG. If the entire OptionString is preceded by a : (colon), then any unmatched switch option causes a ? to be loaded into the VARIABLE. The form of the command follows:

```
getopts OptionString VARIABLE [ Argument ... ]
```

The easiest way to explain this is with an example. For our script we need seconds, minutes, hours, days, and a process to monitor. For each one of these we want to supply an argument—that is, -s 5 -m10 -p my_backup. In this we are specifying 5 seconds,

10 minutes, and the process is my_backup. Notice that there does not have to be a space between the switch and the argument. This is what makes **getopts** so great! The command line to set up our example looks like this:

```
SECS=0          # Initialize all to zero
MINUTES=0
HOURS=0
DAYS=0
PROCESS=          # Initialize to null

while getopts :s:m:h:d:p: TIMED 2>/dev/null
do
    case $TIMED in
      s) SECS=$OPTARG
         ;;
      m) (( MINUTES = $OPTARG * 60 ))
         ;;
      h) (( HOURS = $OPTARG * 3600 ))
         ;;
      d) (( DAYS = $OPTARG * 86400 ))
         ;;
      p) PROCESS=$OPTARG
         ;;
     \?) usage
         exit 1
         ;;
    esac
done

(( TOTAL_SECONDS = SECONDS + MINUTES + HOURS + DAYS ))
```

There are a few things to note in the **getopts** command. The **getopts** command needs to be part of a **while** loop with a **case** statement within the loop for this example. On each option we specified, s, m, h, d, and p, we added a : (colon) after each switch. This tells **getopts** that an argument is required. The : (colon) *before* the OptionString list tells getopts that if an unspecified option is given, to set the $TIMED variable to the ? character. This allows us to call the usage function and exit with a return code of 1. The first thing to be careful of is that **getopts** does not care what arguments it receives so we have to take action if we want to exit. The last thing to note is that the first line of the **while** loop has redirection of standard error (file descriptor 2) to the bit bucket. Any time an unexpected argument is encountered, **getopts** sends a message to standard error. Because we expect this to happen, we can just ignore the messages and discard them to /dev/null. We will study **getopts** a lot in this book.

Making a Co-Process with Background Function

We also need to cover setting up a co-process. A co-process is a communications link between a foreground and a background process. The most common question is *why* is this needed? In one of the scripts we are going to call a function that will handle all of the process monitoring for us while we do the timing control in the main script. A problem arises because *we need to run this function in the background and it has an infinite loop.* Within this background process-monitoring function there is an infinite loop. Without the ability to tell the loop to break out, it will continue to execute on its own after the main script, and function, is interrupted. We know what this causes—*one or more defunct processes!* From the main script we need a way to communicate with this loop, thus background function, to tell it to break out of the loop and exit the function cleanly when the countdown is complete and if the script is interrupted, CTRL-C. To solve this little problem we kick off our `proc_watch` function as a **co-process**, in the background. How do we do this, you ask? *"Pipe it to the background"* is the simplest way to put it, and that is also what it looks like, too. Look at the next example code block:

```
###########################
function trap_exit
{
     # Tell the co-process to break out of the loop
     BREAK_OUT='Y'
     print -p $BREAK_OUT    # Use "print -p" to talk to the co-process
}
###########################
function proc_watch
{
# This function is started as a co-process!!!

     while :      # Loop forever
     do
          Some Code Here

          read $BREAK_OUT  # Do NOT need a "-p" to read!
          if [[ $BREAK_OUT = 'Y' ]]
          then
               return 0
          fi
     done
}


###########################
##### Start of Main ########
###########################

### Set a Trap ###

trap 'trap_exit; exit 2' 1 2 3 15

TOTAL_SECONDS=300
BREAK_OUT='N'

proc_watch |&         # Start proc_watch as a co-process!!!!

PW_PID=$1             # Process ID of the last background job
```

```
until (( TOTAL_SECONDS == 0 ))
do
      (( TOTAL_SECONDs = TOTAL_SECONDS - 1 ))
      sleep 1
done

BREAK_OUT='Y'

# Use "print -p" to communicate with the co-process variable

print -p $BREAK_OUT

kill $PW_PID      # Kill the background co-process

exit 0
```

In this code segment we defined two functions. The `trap_exit` function will execute on exit signals 1, 2, 3, and 15. The other function is the `proc_watch` function, which is the function that we want to start as a background process. As you can see in `proc_watch`, it has an infinite loop. If the main script is interrupted then without a means to exit the loop, within the function, the loop *alone* will continue to execute! To solve this we start the `proc_watch` as a co-process by "piping it to the background" using *pipe ampersand* , `|&`, as a suffix. Then when we want to communicate to this co-process background function we use `print -p $VARIABLE_NAME`. Inside the co-process function we just use the standard `read $VARIABLE_NAME`. This is the mechanism that we are going to use to break out of the loop if the main script is interrupted on a trapped signal; of course, we cannot catch a **kill -9** with a trap.

Try setting up the scenario described previously with a background function that has an infinite loop. Then press the CTRL-C key sequence to kill the main script, and do a **ps -ef | more**. You will see that the background *loop* is still executing! Get the PID, and do a **kill -9** on that PID to kill it. Of course, if the loop's exit criteria is ever met, the loop will exit on its own.

Catching a Delayed Command Output

Have you ever had a hard time trying to catch the output of a command that has a delayed output? This can cause a lot of frustration when you *just miss it*! There is a little technique that allows you to catch these delayed responses. The trick is to use an **until** loop. Look at the code shown here.

```
OUTFILE="/tmp/outfile.out"   # Define the output file
cat /dev/null > $OUTFILE      # Create a zero size output file

# Start an until loop to catch the delayed response

until [ -s $OUTFILE ]
do
```

```
          delayed_output_command >> $OUTFILE
done

# Show the resulting output

more $OUTFILE
```

This code segment first defines an output file to store the delayed output data. We start with a zero-sized file and then enter an **until** loop that will continue until the $OUTFILE is no longer a zero-sized file, and the **until** loop exits. The last step is to show the user the data that was captured from the delayed output.

Fastest Ways to Process a File Line by Line

Most shell scripts work with files, and some use a file for data input. The two fastest techniques for processing a file line by line are shown in this section. The first technique feeds a **while** loop from the bottom. The second technique uses file descriptors.

```
function while_read_LINE_bottom
{
while read LINE
do
        echo "$LINE"
        :

done < $FILENAME
}
```

The function shown in the previous code feeds the **while** loop from the bottom, after the **done**.

```
function while_read_LINE_FD
{
exec 3<&0
exec 0< $FILENAME

while read LINE
do
        echo "$LINE"
        :
done

exec 0<&3
}
```

The function shown in the previous code uses file descriptors to process the file line by line.

Mail Notification Techniques

In a lot of the shell scripts in this book it is a good idea to send notifications to users when errors occur, when a task is finished, and for many other reasons. Some of the email techniques are shown in this section.

Using the mail and mailx Commands

The most common notification method uses the **mail** and **mailx** commands. The basic syntax of both these commands is shown here.

```
mail -s "This is the subject" $MAILOUT_LIST < $MAIL_FILE
OR
cat $MAIL_FILE | mail -s "This is the subject" $MAILOUT_LIST

mailx -s "This is the subject" $MAILOUT_LIST < $MAIL_FILE
OR
cat $MAIL_FILE | mailx -s "This is the subject" $MAILOUT_LIST
```

Not all systems support the **mailx** command, but the systems that do have support use the same syntax as the **mail** command. To be safe when dealing with multiple Unix platforms always use the **mail** command.

Using the sendmail Command to Send Outbound Mail

In one shop I worked at I could not send outbound mail from the any user named **root**. The *from* field had to be a valid email address that is recognized by the mail server, and **root** is not valid. To get around this little problem I changed the command that I used from **mail** to **sendmail**. The **sendmail** command allows us to add the **-f** switch to indicate a valid internal email address for the *from* field. The **sendmail** command is in /usr/sbin/sendmail on AIX, HP-UX, and Linux, but on SunOS the location changed to /usr/lib/sendmail. Look at the function in Listing 3.3.

```
function send_notification
{
if [ -s $MAIL_FILE -a  "$MAILOUT" = "TRUE" ];
then
        case $(uname) in
        AIX|HP-UX|Linux) SENDMAIL="/usr/sbin/sendmail"
                         ;;
        SunOS)           SENDMAIL="/usr/lib/sendmail"
                         ;;
        esac
```

```
            echo "\nSending e-mail notification"
            $SENDMAIL -f randy@$THISHOST $MAIL_LIST < $MAIL_FILE
fi
}
```

Both techniques should allow you to get the message out quickly.

Creating a Progress Indicator

Any time that a user is forced to wait as a long process runs, it is an excellent idea to give the user some feedback. This section deals with progress indicators.

A Series of Dots

The **echo** command prints a single dot on the screen, and the backslash c, \c, specifies a continuation on the same line without a new line or carriage return. To make a series of dots we will put this single command in a loop with some sleep time between each dot. We will use a **while** loop that loops forever with a 10-second sleep between printing each dot on the screen.

```
while true
do
     echo ".\c"
     sleep 10
done
```

A Rotating Line

The function shown here shows what appears to be a rotating line as the process runs.

```
function rotate_line
{
INTERVAL=1      # Sleep time between "twirls"
TCOUNT="0"       # For each TCOUNT the line twirls one increment

while :         # Loop forever...until this function is killed
do
     TCOUNT=`expr $TCOUNT + 1`   # Increment the TCOUNT

     case $TCOUNT in
         "1")    echo '-'"\b\c"
                 sleep $INTERVAL
```

```
               ;;
        "2")      echo '\\'"\b\c"
                  sleep $INTERVAL
                  ;;
        "3")      echo "|\b\c"
                  sleep $INTERVAL
                  ;;
        "4")      echo "/\b\c"
                  sleep $INTERVAL
                  ;;
        *)       TCOUNT="0" ;;  # Reset the TCOUNT to "0", zero.
     esac
done
}
```

To use this in a shell script, use this technique to start and stop the rotation.

```
#####################################
########## Begin of Main ############
#####################################

rotate_line &   # Run the function in the background

ROTATE_PID=$!   # Capture the PID of the last background process

/usr/local/bin/my_time_consuming_task.ksh

# Stop the rotating line function

kill -9 $ROTATE_PID

# Cleanup...this removes the left over line.

echo "\b\b  "
```

Creating a Psuedo-Random Number

There is a built-in Korn shell variable that will create a pseudo-random number called RANDOM. The following code segment creates a pseudo-random number between 1 and a upper limit defined by the user.

```
RANDOM=$$   # Set the seed to the PID of the script
UPPER_LIMIT=$1

RANDOM_NUMBER=$(($RANDOM % $UPPER_LIMIT + 1))

echo "$RANDOM_NUMBER"
```

If the user specified the UPPER_LIMIT to be 100 then the result would be a pseudo-random number between 1 and 100.

Checking for Stale Disk Partitions in AIX

Ideally we want the stale disk partition value to be zero, 0. If the value is greater than zero we have a problem. Specifically, the mirrored disks in this Logical Volume are not in sync, which translates to a worthless mirror. Take a look at the following command statement.

```
LV=hd6

NUM_STALE_PP=$(lslv -L $LV | grep "STALE PP" | awk '{print $3}'
```

The previous statement saves the number of stale PPs into the NUM_STALE_PP variable. We accomplish this feat by command substitution, specified by the VARIABLE=$(*commands*) notation.

Automated Host Pinging

Depending on the operating system that you are running, the **ping** command varies if you want to send three pings to each host to see if the machines are up. The function shown here can **ping** from AIX, HP-UX, Linux, and SunOS machines.

```
function ping_host
{
HOST=$1 # Grab the host to ping from ARG1.
PING_COUNT=3
PACKET_SIZE=54

# This next case statement executes the correct ping
# command based on the Unix flavor

case $(uname) in

AIX|Linux)
        ping -c${PING_COUNT} $HOST 2>/dev/null
        ;;
HP-UX)
        ping $HOST $PACKET_SIZE $PING_COUNT 2>/dev/null
        ;;
SunOS)
        ping -s $HOST $PACKET_SIZE $PING_COUNT 2>/dev/null
        ;;
*)
        echo "\nERROR: Unsupported Operating System - $(uname)"
        echo "\n\t...EXITING...\n"
        exit 1
esac
}
```

The main body of the shell script must supply the hostname to ping. This is usually done with a **while** loop.

Highlighting Specific Text in a File

The technique shown here highlights specific text in a file with reverse video while displaying the entire file. To add in the reverse video piece, we have to do some command substitution within the **sed** statement using the **tput** commands. Where we specify the *new_string*, we will add in the control for reverse video using command substitution, one to turn highlighting on and one to turn it back off. When the command substitution is added, our **sed** statement will look like the following:

```
sed s/current_string/$(tput smso)new_string$(tput rmso)/g
```

In our case the *current_string* and *new_string* will be the same because we only want to highlight existing text without changing it. We also want the string to be assigned to a variable as in the next command:

```
sed s/"$STRING"/$(tput smso)"$STRING"$(tput rmso)/g
```

Notice the double quotes around the string variable, "$STRING". Do not forget to add the double quotes around variables!

As an experiment using command substitution, try this next command statement to highlight the machine's host name in the /etc/hosts file on any Unix machine:

```
cat /etc/hosts | sed s/`hostname`/$(tput smso)`hostname`$(tput rmso)/g
```

Keeping the Printers Printing

Keeping the printers enabled in a large shop can sometimes be overwhelming. There are two techniques to keep the printers printing. One technique is for the AIX "classic" printer subsystem, and the other is for System V printing.

AIX "Classic" Printer Subsystem

To keep AIX "classic" printer subsystem print queues running use either of the following commands.

```
enable $(enq -AW | tail +3 | grep DOWN | awk '{print $1}') 2>/dev/null
```

or

```
enable $(lpstat -W | tail +3 | grep DOWN | awk '{print $1}') 2>/dev/null
```

System V Printing

To keep System V printers printing use either of the following commands.

```
lpc enable $(lpstat -a | grep 'not accepting' | awk '{print $1}')

lpc start $( lpstat -p | grep disabled | awk '{print $2}')

lpc up all        # Enable all printing and queuing
```

It is a good idea to use the **root** cron table to execute the appropriate command every 15 minutes or so.

Automated FTP File Transfer

You can use a here document to script an FTP file transfer. The basic idea is shown here.

```
ftp -i -v -n wilma <<END_FTP

user randy mypassword
binary
lcd /scripts/download
cd /scripts
get auto_ftp_xfer.ksh
bye

END_FTP
```

Capturing a List of Files Larger than $MEG

Who filled up that filesystem? If you want to look quickly for large files use the following syntax.

```
# Search for files > $MEG_BYTES starting at the $SEARCH_PATH
#
HOLD_FILE=/tmp/largefiles.list
MEG_BYTES=$1
SEARCH_PATH=$(pwd)  # Use the current directory

find $SEARCH_PATH -type f -size +${MEG_BYTES}000000c -print > $HOLDFILE
```

Note that in the **find** command after the **-size** parameter there is a plus sign (+) preceding the file size, and there is a **c** added as a suffix. This combination specifies files larger than **$MEG_BYTES** measured in bytes, as opposed to blocks.

Capturing a User's Keystrokes

In most large shops there is a need, at least occasionally, to monitor a user's actions. You may even want to audit the keystrokes of anyone with root access to the system or other administration type accounts such as oracle. Contractors on site can pose a particular security risk. Typically when a new application comes into the environment, one or two contractors are on site for a period of time for installation, troubleshooting, and training personnel on the product.

The code shown next uses the **script** command to capture all of the keystrokes.

```
TS=$(date +%m%d%y%H%M%S)        # File time stamp
THISHOST=$(hostname|cut -f1-2 -d.) # Host name of this machine
LOGDIR=/usr/local/logs/script   # Directory to hold the logs
LOGFILE=${THISHOST}.${LOGNAME}.$TS # Creates the name of the log file
touch $LOGDIR/$LOGFILE           # Creates the actual file


# Set the command prompt
export PS1="[$LOGNAME:$THISHOST]@"'$PWD> '

################### RUN IT HERE #########################

chown  $LOGNAME ${LOGDIR}/${LOGFILE} # Let the user own the file during
the script
chmod 600 ${LOGDIR}/${LOGFILE}      # Change permission to RW for the
owner

script ${LOGDIR}/${LOGFILE}         # Start the script monitoring session

chown root ${LOGDIR}/${LOGFILE}  # Change the ownership to root
chmod 400 ${LOGDIR}/${LOGFILE}   # Set permission to read-only by root
```

Using the bc Utility for Floating-Point Math

On Unix machines there is a utility called **bc** that is an interpreter for arbitrary-precision arithmetic language. The **bc** command is an interactive program that provides arbitrary-precision arithmetic. You can start an interactive **bc** session by typing **bc** on the command line. Once in the session you can enter most complex arithmetic expressions as you would in a calculator.

The code segment shown next creates the mathematical expression for the **bc** utility and then uses a here document to load the expression into **bc**.

```
# Loop through each number and build a math statement that
# will add all of the numbers together.

for X in $NUM_LIST
do
     ADD="$ADD $PLUS $X"
```

```
        PLUS="+"
done


##########################################################

# Do the math here by using a here document to supply
# input to the bc command. The sum of the numbers is
# assigned to the SUM variable.

SUM=$(bc <<EOF
scale=$SCALE
(${ADD})
EOF)
```

This is about as simple as **bc** gets. This is just a taste. Look for more later in the book.

Number Base Conversions

There are a lot of occasions when we need to convert numbers between bases. The code that follows shows some examples of how to change the base.

Using the typeset Command

```
Convert a base 10 number to base 16

# typeset -i16 BASE_16_NUM
# BASE_16_NUM=47295
# echo $BASE_16_NUM

16#b8bf

Convert a base 8 number to base 16

[root@yogi:/scripts]> typeset -i16 BASE_16_NUM
[root@yogi:/scripts]> BASE_16_NUM=8#472521
[root@yogi:/scripts]> echo $BASE_16_NUM

16#735c9
```

Using the printf Command

```
Convert a base 10 number to base 8

# printf %o 20398

47656
```

```
Convert a base 10 number to base 16

# printf %x 20398

4fae
```

Create a Menu with the select Command

There are many times when you just need to provide a menu for the end user to select from, and this is where a **select** statement comes in. The menu prompt is assigned to the **PS3** system variable, and the **select** statement is used a lot like a **for** loop. A **case** statement is used to specify the action to take on each selection.

```
PS3="Is today your birthday? "

echo "\n"

select menu_selections in Yes No Quit
do
      case $menu_selections in
      Yes) echo "\nHappy Birthday!\n"
           ;;
      No)  print "\nIt is someone's birthday today...\
Sorry it is not yours\n"
           ;;
      Quit) print "\nLater tater!\n"
            break
            ;;
      *)   print "\nInvalid Answer...Please try again\n"
           ;;
      esac
done
```

Notice in this code segment the use of the **select** statement. This looks just like a **for** loop with a list of possible values. Next is an embedded **case** statement that allows us to specify the action to take when each selection is made. The output of this simple menu is shown here with a selection of each possible answer.

```
./select_menu.ksh

1) Yes
2) No
3) Quit
Is today your birthday? 4

Invalid Answer...Please try again
```

```
Is today your birthday? 1

Happy Birthday!

Is today your birthday? 2

It is someone's birthday today...Sorry it is not yours

Is today your birthday? 3

Later tater!
```

Sending Pop-Up Messages to Windows

When we need to get the word out quickly to the clients using Windows desktops, we can use Samba on the Unix machine to send a pop-up message. A list of the Windows machines is used in a **while** loop, and one by one the message is sent to each desktop that is reachable and powered on. If a message is not sent to the target Windows machine, no error is produced. We cannot guarantee that all of the messages were received. The code segment to send the message is shown here.

```
# Loop through each host in the $WINLIST and send the pop-up message

for NODE in $WINLIST
do
     echo "Sending to ==> $NODE"
     echo $MESSAGE | $SMBCLIENT -M $NODE # 1>/dev/null
     if (($? == 0))
     then
          echo "Sent OK    ==> $NODE"
     else
          echo "FAILED to  ==> $NODE Failed"
     fi
done
```

The WINLIST variable contains a list of Windows machines. The MESSAGE contains the message to send, and the SMBCLIENT variable contains the fully qualified pathname to the **smbclient** command.

Removing Repeated Lines in a File

The **uniq** command is used to report and remove repeated lines in a file. This is a valuable tool for a lot of scripting and testing. The syntax is shown here.

If you have a file that has repeated lines named `my_list` and you want to save the list without the repeated lines in a file called `my_list_no_repeats`, use the following command:

```
# uniq my_list my_list_no_repeats
```

If you want to see a file's output without repeated lines use the following command:

```
# cat repeat_file | uniq
```

Removing Blank Lines from a File

The easiest way to remove blank lines from a file is to use a **sed** statement. The following syntax removes the blank lines.

```
# cat my_file | sed /^$/d
```

Testing for a Null Variable

Variables that have nothing assigned to them are sometimes hard to deal with. The following test will ensure that a variable is either Null or has a value assigned to it. The double quotes are very important and must be used!

```
VAL=    # Creates a NULL variable

if [[ -z "$VAL" && "$VAL" = '' ]]
then
     echo "The VAL variable is NULL"
fi
```

or

```
VAL=25

if [[ ! -z "$VAL" && "$VAL" != '' ]]
then
     echo "The VAL variable is NOT NULL"
fi
```

Directly Access the Value of the Last Positional Parameter, $#

To access the value of the $# positional parameter directly, use the following command:

```
eval '$'$#
```

or

```
eval \$$#
```

There are a lot of uses for this technique, as you will see later in this book.

Remove the Columns Heading in a Command Output

There are many instances when we want to get rid of the columns heading in a command's output. A lot of people try to use **grep -v** to pattern match on something unique in the heading. A much easier and more reliable method is to use the **tail** command. An example is shown with the **df** command output.

```
[root:yogi]@/scripts# df -k
Filesystem     1024-blocks      Free %Used    Iused %Iused Mounted on
/dev/hd4           32768       15796   52%     1927    12% /
/dev/hd2          1466368      62568   96%    44801    13% /usr
/dev/hd9var         53248       8112   85%     1027     8% /var
/dev/hd3           106496      68996   36%      245     1% /tmp
/dev/hd1             4096       3892    5%       55     6% /home
/proc                  -          -     -        -      - /proc
/dev/hd10opt       655360      16420   98%    16261    10% /opt
/dev/scripts_lv    102400      24012   77%     1137     5% /scripts
/dev/lv_temp       409600     147452   65%       29     1% /tmpfs
```

Now look at the same output with the column headings removed.

```
[root:yogi]@/scripts# df -k | tail +2
/dev/hd4           32768       15796   52%     1927    12% /
/dev/hd2          1466368      62568   96%    44801    13% /usr
/dev/hd9var         53248       8112   85%     1027     8% /var
/dev/hd3           106496      68996   36%      245     1% /tmp
```

```
/dev/hd1            4096      3892     5%        55      6% /home
/proc                  -         -      -         -       - /proc
/dev/hd10opt      655360     16420    98%     16261     10% /opt
/dev/scripts_lv   102400     24012    77%      1137      5% /scripts
/dev/lv_temp      409600    147452    65%        29      1% /tmpfs
```

Just remember to add one to the total number of lines that you want to remove.

Arrays

The Korn shell supports one-dimensional arrays. The maximum number of array elements is 1024. When an array is defined, it is automatically dimensioned to 1024 elements. A one-dimensional array contains a sequence of *array elements*, which are like the boxcars connected together on a train track. An array element can be just about anything, except for another array. I know, you're thinking that you can use an array to access an array to create two- and three-dimensional arrays. If this can be done, it is beyond the scope of this book.

Loading an Array

An array can be loaded in two ways. You can define and load the array in one step with the **set -A** command, or you can load the array one element at a time. Both techniques are shown here.

```
set -A MY_ARRAY alpha beta gamma
```

or

```
X=0  # Initialize counter to zero.
# Load the array with the strings alpha, beta, and gamma
for ELEMENT in alpha gamma beta
do
        MY_ARRAY[$X]=$ELEMENT
        ((X = X + 1))
done
```

The first array element is referenced by 0, not 1. To access array elements use the following syntax:

```
echo ${MY_ARRAY[2]   # Show the third array element
gamma

echo ${MY_ARRAY[*]   # Show all array elements
alpha beta gamma

echo ${MY_ARRAY[@]   # Show all array elements
alpha beta gamma
```

```
echo ${#MY_ARRAY[*]}  # Show the total number of array elements
3

echo ${#MY_ARRAY[@]}  # Show the total number of array elements
3

echo ${MY_ARRAY}      # Show array element 0 (the first element)
alpha
```

We will use arrays in shell scripts in two chapters in this book.

Testing a String

One of the hardest things to do in a shell script is to test the user's input from the command-line. This shell script will do the trick by using regular expressions to define the string composition.

```
#!/bin/ksh
#
#   SCRIPT: test_string.ksh
#   AUTHOR: Randy Michael
#   REV: 1.0.D  - Used for developement
#   DATE: 10/15/2002
#   PLATFORM: Not Platform Dependent
#
#   PURPOSE: This script is used to test a character
#            string, or variable, for its composition.
#            Examples include numeric, lowercase or uppercase
#            characters, alpha-numeric characters and IP address.
#
#   REV LIST:
#
#
# set -x # Uncomment to debug this script
# set -n # Uncomment to verify syntax without any execution.
#        # REMEMBER: Put the comment back or the script will
#        # NOT EXECUTE!
#
####################################################
############## DEFINE FUNCTIONS HERE ###############
####################################################

test_string ()
{
# This function tests a character string

# Must have one argument ($1)

if (( $# != 1 ))
```

```
then
      # This error would be a programming error

      print "ERROR: $(basename $0) requires one argument"
      return 1
fi
# Assign arg1 to the variable --> STRING

STRING=$1

# This is where the string test begins

case $STRING in

+([0-9]).+([0-9]).+([0-9]).+([0-9]))
         # Testing for an IP address - valid and invalid
         INVALID=FALSE

         # Separate the integer portions of the "IP" address
         # and test to ensure that nothing is greater than 255
         # or it is an invalid IP address.

         for i in $(echo $STRING | awk -F . '{print $1, $2, $3, $4}')
         do
             if (( i > 255 ))
             then
                   INVALID=TRUE
             fi
         done

         case $INVALID in
         TRUE) print 'INVALID_IP_ADDRESS'
               ;;
        FALSE) print 'VALID_IP_ADDRESS'
               ;;
         esac
         ;;
+([0-1])) # Testing for 0-1 only
         print 'BINARY_OR_POSITIVE_INTEGER'
         ;;
+([0-7])) # Testing for 0-7  only
         print 'OCTAL_OR_POSITIVE_INTEGER'
         ;;
+([0-9])) # Check for an integer
         print 'INTEGER'
         ;;
+([-0-9])) # Check for a negative whole number
          print 'NEGATIVE_WHOLE_NUMBER'
          ;;
+([0-9]|[.][0-9]))
```

```
                  # Check for a positive floating point number
                  print 'POSITIVE_FLOATING_POINT'
                  ;;
+(+[0-9][.][0-9]))
                  # Check for a positive floating point number
                  # with a + prefix
                  print 'POSITIVE_FLOATING_POINT'
                  ;;
+(-[0-9][.][0-9]))
                  # Check for a negative floating point number
                  print 'NEGATIVE_FLOATING_POINT'
                  ;;
+([-.0-9]))
                  # Check for a negative floating point number
                  print 'NEGATIVE_FLOATING_POINT'
                  ;;
+([+.0-9]))
                  # Check for a positive floating point number
                  print 'POSITIVE_FLOATING_POINT'
                  ;;
+([a-f])) # Test for hexidecimal or all lowercase characters
          print 'HEXIDECIMAL_OR_ALL_LOWERCASE'
          ;;
+([a-f]|[0-9])) # Test for hexidecimal or all lowercase characters
          print 'HEXIDECIMAL_OR_ALL_LOWERCASE_ALPHANUMERIC'
          ;;
+([A-F])) # Test for hexidecimal or all uppercase characters
          print 'HEXIDECIMAL_OR_ALL_UPPERCASE'
          ;;
+([A-F]|[0-9])) # Test for hexidecimal or all uppercase characters
          print 'HEXIDECIMAL_OR_ALL_UPPERCASE_ALPHANUMERIC'
          ;;
+([a-f]|[A-F]))
                  # Testing for hexidecimal or mixed-case characters
                  print 'HEXIDECIMAL_OR_MIXED_CASE'
                  ;;
+([a-f]|[A-F]|[0-9]))
                  # Testing for hexidecimal/alpha-numeric strings only
                  print 'HEXIDECIMAL_OR_MIXED_CASE_ALPHANUMERIC'
                  ;;
+([a-z]|[A-Z]|[0-9]))
                  # Testing for any alpha-numeric string only
                  print 'ALPHA-NUMERIC'
                  ;;
+([a-z])) # Testing for all lowercase characters only
          print 'ALL_LOWERCASE'
          ;;
+([A-Z])) # Testing for all uppercase numbers only
          print 'ALL_UPPERCASE'
          ;;
```

```
+([a-z]|[A-Z]))
           # Testing for mixed case alpha strings only
           print 'MIXED_CASE'
           ;;
        *) # None of the tests matched the string coposition
           print 'INVALID_STRING_COMPOSITION'
           ;;
esac
}


##################################################

usage ()
{
echo "\nERROR: Please supply one character string or variable\n"
echo "USAGE: $THIS_SCRIPT {character string or variable}\n"
}

##################################################
############ BEGINNING OF MAIN ##################
##################################################

# Query the system for the name of this shell script.
# This is used for the "usage" function.

THIS_SCRIPT=$(basename $0)

# Check for exactly one command-line argument

if (( $# != 1 ))
then
     usage
     exit 1
fi

# Everything looks okay if we got here. Assign the
# single command-line argument to the variable "STRING"

STRING=$1

# Call the "test_string" function to test the composition
# of the character string stored in the $STRING variable.

test_string $STRING

# End of script
```

This is a good start but this shell script does not cover everything. Play around with it and see if you can make some improvements.

Summary

This chapter is just a primer to get you started with a quick review and some little tricks and tips. In the next 24 chapters we are going to write a lot of shell scripts to solve some real-world problems. Sit back and get ready to take on the Unix world!

The first thing that we are going to study is the 12 ways to process a file line by line. I have seen a lot of good and bad techniques for processing a file line by line over the last 10 years, and some have been rather inventive. The next chapter presents the 12 techniques that I have seen the most; at the end of the chapter there is a shell script that times each technique to find the fastest. Read on, and find out which one wins the race. See you in the next chapter!

CHAPTER 2

Twelve Ways to Process a File Line by Line

Have you ever created a really slick shell script to process file data and found that you have to wait until after lunch to get the results? The script may be running so slowly because of how you are processing the file. I have come up with 12 ways to process a file line by line. Some techniques are very fast, and some make you wait for half a day. The techniques used in this chapter are measurable, and I created a shell script that will time each method so that you can see which technique suits your needs.

When processing an ASCII text/data file, we are normally inside a loop of some kind. Then, as we go through the file from the top to the bottom, we process each line of text. A Korn shell script is really not meant to work on text character by character, but you can do it using various techniques. The task for this chapter is to show the line-by-line parsing techniques. We are also going to look at using *file descriptors* as a processing technique.

Command Syntax

First, as always, we need to go over the command syntax that we are going to use. The commands that we want to concentrate on in this chapter have to deal with **while** loops. When parsing a file in a **while** loop, we need a method to read in the entire line to a variable. The most prevalent command is **read**. The **read** command is flexible in that you can extract individual strings as well as the entire line. Speaking of line, the

line command is another alternative to grab a full line of text. Some operating systems do not support the **line** command. I did not find the **line** command on Linux or Solaris; however, the **line** may have been added in subsequent OS releases.

In addition to the **read** and **line,** we need to look at the different ways you can use the **while** loop, which is the major cause of fast or slow execution times. A **while** loop can be used as a standalone loop in a predefined configuration; it can be used in a command pipe or with file descriptors. Each method has its own set of rules. The use of the **while** loop is critical to get the quickest execution times. I have seen many renditions of the proper use of a **while** loop, and some techniques I have seen are unique.

Using File Descriptors

Under the covers of the Unix operating system, files are referenced, copied, and moved by unique numbers known as file descriptors. You already know about three of these file descriptors:

```
0 - stdin
1 - stdout
2 - stderr
```

We have redirected output using the `stdout` (standard output) and `stderr` (standard error) in other scripts in this book. This is the first time we are going to use the `stdin` (standard input) file descriptor. For a short definition of each of these we can talk about the devices on the computer. Standard input usually comes into the computer from the keyboard or mouse. Standard output usually has output to the screen or to a file. Standard error is where error messages are routed by commands, programs, and scripts. We have used `stderr` before to send the error messages to the bit bucket, or `/dev/null`, and also more commonly to combine the `stdout` and `stderr` outputs together. You should remember a command like the following one:

```
some_command 2>&1
```

The previous command sends all of the error messages to the same output device that standard output goes to, which is normally the terminal. We can also use other file descriptors. Valid descriptor values range from 0 to 19 on most operating systems. You have to do a lot of testing when you use the upper values to ensure that they are not reserved by the system for some reason. We will see more on using file descriptors in some of the following code listings.

Creating a Large File to Use in the Timing Test

Before I get into each method of parsing the file, I want to show you a little script you can use to create a file that has the exact number of lines that you want to process. The number of characters to create on each line can be changed by modifying the `LINE_LENGTH` variable in the shell script, but the default value is 80. This script also uses a **while** loop but this time to build a file. To create a file that has 7,500 lines, you add the number of lines as a parameter to the shell script name. Using the shell script in Listing 2.1, you create a 7,500-line file with the following syntax:

```
# mk_large_file.ksh 7500
```

The full shell script is shown in Listing 2.1.

```ksh
#!/bin/ksh
#
# SCRIPT: mk_large_file.ksh
# AUTHOR: Randy Michael
# DATE: 03/15/2002
# REV: 1.2.P
#
# PURPOSE: This script is used to create a text file that
#          has a specified number of lines that is specified
#          on the command line.
#
# set -n # Uncomment to check syntax without any execution
# set -x # Uncomment to debug this shell script
#
##################################################
# Define functions here
##################################################

function usage {

echo "\n...USAGE ERROR...\n"
echo "\nUSAGE: $SCRIPT_NAME  <number_of_lines_to_create>\n"
}
##################################################
# Check for the correct number of parameters
##################################################

if (( $# != 1 )) # Looking for exactly one parameter
then
     usage    # Usage error was made
     exit 1   # Exit on a usage error
fi


##################################################
# Define files and variables here
##################################################

LINE_LENGTH=80             # Number of characters per line

OUT_FILE=/scripts/bigfile  # New file to create
```

Listing 2.1   mk_large_file.ksh shell script listing. *(continues)*

```
>$OUT_FILE                      # Initialize to a zero-sized file
SCRIPT_NAME=$(basename $0)      # Extract the name of the script
TOTAL_LINES=$1                  # Total number of lines to create
LINE_COUNT=0                    # Character counter
CHAR=X                          # Character to write to the file


################################################
#    BEGINNING of MAIN
################################################

while ((LINE_COUNT < TOTAL_LINES)) # Specified by $1
do
    CHAR_COUNT=0   # Initialize the CHAR_COUNT to zero on every new line

    while ((CHAR_COUNT < LINE_LENGTH)) # Each line is fixed length
    do
        echo "${CHAR}\c" >> $OUT_FILE   # Echo a single character
        ((CHAR_COUNT = CHAR_COUNT + 1)) # Increment the character
counter
    done
    ((LINE_COUNT = LINE_COUNT + 1))      # Increment the line counter
    echo>>$OUT_FILE                      # Give a newline character
done
```

Listing 2.1   mk_large_file.ksh shell script listing. *(continued)*

Each line produced by the mk_large_file.ksh script is the same length. The user specifies the total number of lines to create as a parameter to the shell script.

Twelve Methods to Parse a File Line by Line

The following paragraphs describe 12 of the parsing techniques I have commonly seen over the years. I have put them all together in one shell script separated as functions. After the functions are defined, I execute each method, or function, while timing the execution using the **time** command. To get accurate timing results I use a file that has 7,500 lines, where each line is the same length (we built this file using the mk_large_file.ksh shell script). A 7,500-line file is an extremely large file to be parsing line by line in a shell script, about 600 MB, but my Linux machine is so fast that I needed a large file to get the timing data greater than zero!

Now it is time to look at the 12 methods to parse a file line by line. Each method uses a **while** statement to create a loop. The only two commands within the loop are **cat $LINE,** to output each line as it is read, and a *no-op*, specified by the : (colon) character. The thing that makes each method different is how the **while** loop is used.

Method 1: cat $FILENAME | while read LINE

Let's start with the most common method that I see, which is catting a file and piping the file output to a **while read** loop. On each loop iteration a single line of text is read into a variable named LINE. This continuous loop will run until all of the lines in the file have been processed one at a time.

The pipe is the key to the popularity of this method. It is intuitively obvious that the output from the previous command in the pipe is used as input to the next command in the pipe. As an example, if I execute the **df** command to list filesystem statistics and it scrolls across the screen out of view, I can use a pipe to send the output to the **more** command, as in the following command:

```
df | more
```

When the **df** command is executed, the pipe stores the output in a temporary system file. Then this temporary system file is used as input to the **more** command, allowing me to view the **df** command output one page/line at a time. Our use of piping output to a **while** loop works the same way; the output of the **cat** command is used as input to the **while** loop and is read into the LINE variable on each loop iteration. Look at the complete function in Listing 2.2.

```
function while_read_LINE
{
cat $FILENAME | while read LINE
do
        echo "$LINE"
        :
done
}
```

Listing 2.2   while_read_LINE function listing.

Each of these test loops is created as a function so that we can time each method using the shell script. You could also use () C-type function definition if you wanted, as shown in Listing 2.3.

```
while_read_LINE ()
{
cat $FILENAME | while read LINE
do
        echo "$LINE"
        :
done
}
```

Listing 2.3   Using the () declaration method function listing.

Whether you use the function or () technique, you get the same result. I tend to use the function method more often so that when someone edits the script they will know the block of code is a function. For beginners, the word "function" helps understanding the whole shell script a lot. The $FILENAME variable is set in the main body of the shell script. Within the **while** loop notice that I added the no-op (:) after the **echo** statement. A no-op (:) does nothing, but it always has a 0, zero, return code. I use the no-op only as a placeholder so that you can cut the function code out and paste it in one of your scripts. If you should remove the **echo** statement and leave the no-op, the **while** loop will not fail; however, the loop will not do anything either.

Method 2: while read $FILENAME from Bottom

You are now entering one of my favorite methods of parsing through a file. We still use the **while read LINE** syntax, but this time we feed the loop from the bottom instead of using a pipe. You will find that this is one of the fastest ways to process each line of a file. The first time you see this it looks a little unusual, but it works very well.

Look at the code in Listing 2.4, and we will go over the function at the end.

```
function while_read_LINE_bottom
{
while read LINE
do
        echo "$LINE"
        :

done < $FILENAME
}
```

Listing 2.4   while_read_LINE_bottom function listing.

We made a few modifications to the function from Listing 2.3. The **cat $FILENAME** to the pipe was removed. Then we use *input redirection* to let us read the file from the bottom of the loop. By using the **< $FILENAME** notation after the done loop terminator we feed the **while** loop from the bottom, which greatly increases the input throughput to the loop. When we time each technique, this method will stand out at the top of the list.

Method 3: while_line_LINE_Bottom

As with the **read** command you can use the **line** command directly in a **while** loop using the same loop technique. In this function we use the following syntax:

```
while line LINE
```

Whether you use this syntax in a pipe or, as in this function, feed the loop from the bottom, you can see that the **line** command can be used in the same manner as a **read** statement. Study the function in Listing 2.5 and we will go over the method at the end.

```
function while_line_LINE_bottom
{
while line LINE
do
        echo $LINE
        :
done < $FILENAME
}
```

Listing 2.5   while_line_LINE_bottom function listing.

This method is like Method 2 except that we replace **read** with **line**. You will see in our timing tests that both of these techniques may look the same, but you will be surprised at the timing difference. You will have to wait for the timing script to see the results.

The function in Listing 2.5 uses the **line** command to assign a new line of text to the LINE variable on each loop iteration. The **while** loop is fed from the bottom using input redirection after the **done** loop terminator, **done < $FILENAME**. Using this input redirection technique keeps the file open for reading and is one of the fastest methods of supplying input to the loop.

Method 4: cat $FILENAME | while LINE=`line`

Now we are getting into some of the "creative" methods that I have seen in some shell scripts. Not all Unix operating systems support the **line** command, though. I have not found the **line** command in my Red Hat Linux releases, but that does not mean that it is not out there somewhere in the open-source world.

Using this loop strategy replaces the **read** command from Listings 2.2 and 2.4 with the **line** command in a slightly different command structure. Look at the function in Listing 2.6, and we will see how it works at the end.

```
function cat_while_LINE_line
{
cat $FILENAME | while LINE=`line`
do
        echo "$LINE"
        :
done
}
```

Listing 2.6   while_read_LINE_line function listing.

The function in Listing 2.6 is interesting. Because we are not using the **read** command to assign the line of text to a variable, we need some other technique. If your machine supports the **line** command, then this is an option. To see if your Unix box has the **line** command enter the following command:

```
which line
```

The response should be something like /usr/bin/line. Otherwise, you will see the **$PATH** list that was searched, followed by "line" not found.

The **line** command is used to grab one whole line of text at a time. The **read** command does the same thing if you use only one variable with the **read** statement; otherwise the line of text will be broken up between the different variables used in the **read** statement.

On each loop iteration the LINE variable is assigned a whole line of text using *command substitution*. This is done using the **LINE=`line`** command syntax. The **line** command is executed, and the result is assigned to the LINE variable. Of course, I could have used any variable name, for example:

```
MY_LINE=`line`
TEXT=`line`
```

Please notice that the single tic marks are really *back tics* (`command`), which are located in the top left corner of most keyboards below the ESC-key. Executing a command and assigning the output to a variable is called command substitution. Look for the timing data for this technique when you run the timing script. This extra variable assignment may have quite an effect on the timing result.

Method 5: cat $FILENAME | while line LINE

Why do the extra variable assignments when using the **line** command? You really do not have to. Just as the **read** command directly assigns a line of text to the LINE variable, the **line** command can do the same thing. This technique is like Method 1, but we replace the **read** command with the **line** command. Check out Listing 2.7, and we will describe the method at the end.

```
function while_line_LINE
{
cat $FILENAME | while line LINE
do
        echo "$LINE"
        :
done
}
```

Listing 2.7   while_line_LINE function listing.

In Listing 2.7 we **cat** the $FILENAME file and use a pipe (|) to use the **cat $FILE-NAME** output as input to the **while** loop. On each loop iteration the **line** command grabs one line from the $FILENAME file and assigns it to the LINE variable. Using a pipe in this manner does not produce very fast file processing, but it is one of the most popular methods because of its ease of use. When I see a pipe used like this, the **while** loop is normally used with the **read** command instead of the **line** command.

Method 6: while LINE=`line` from the Bottom

Again, this is one of the more obscure techniques that I have seen in any shell script. This time we are going to feed our **while** loop from the bottom, but this time use the **line** command instead of the **read** statement to assign the text to the LINE variable. This method is similar to the last technique, but we removed the **cat $FILENAME** to the pipe and instead redirect input into the loop from the bottom, after the **done** loop terminator.

Look at the function in Listing 2.8, and we will see how it works at the end.

```
function while_LINE_line_bottom
{
while LINE=`line`
do
        echo "$LINE"
        :

done < $FILENAME
}
```

Listing 2.8 while_LINE_line_bottom function listing.

We use command substitution to assign the line of file text to the LINE variable as we did in the previous method. The only difference is that we are feeding the **while** loop from the bottom using input redirection of the $FILENAME file. You should be getting the hang of what we are doing by now. As you can see there are many ways to parse through a file, but you are going to see that not all of these techniques are very good choices. This method is one of the poorer choices.

Next we are going to look at the other method of command substitution. The last two methods used the **line** command using the syntax **LINE=`line`**. We can also use the **LINE=$(line)** technique. Is there a speed difference?

Method 7: cat $FILENAME | while LINE=$(line)

Looks familiar? This is the same method as Method 3 except for the way we use command substitution. As I stated in the beginning, we need a rather large file to parse through to get accurate timing results. When we do our timing tests we may see a difference between the two command substitution techniques.

Study the function in Listing 2.9, and we will cover the function at the end.

```
function while_LINE_line_cmdsub2
{
cat $FILENAME | while LINE=$(line)
do
        echo "$LINE"
        :
done
}
```

Listing 2.9   while_LINE_line_cmdsub2 function listing.

The only thing we are looking for in the function in Listing 2.9 is a timing difference between the two command substitution techniques. As each line of file text enters the loop, the **line** command assigns the text to the LINE variable. Let's see how Methods 4 and 7 show up in the loop timing tests because the only difference is the assignment method.

Method 8: while LINE=$(line) from the Bottom

This method is the same technique used in Listing 2.8 except for the command substitution. In this function we are going to use the **LINE=$(line)** technique. We are again feeding the **while** loop input from the bottom, after the **done** loop terminator. Please review the function in Listing 2.10.

```
function while_LINE_line_bottom_cmdsub2
{
while LINE=$(line)
do
        echo "$LINE"
        :

done < $FILENAME
}
```

Listing 2.10   while_LINE_line_bottom_cmdsub2 function listing.

By the look of the loop structure you might assume that this **while** loop is very fast executing, but you will be surprised at how slow it is. The main reason is the variable assignment, but the **line** command has a large effect, too.

Method 9: while read LINE Using File Descriptors

So far we have been doing some very straightforward kind of loops. Have you ever used *file descriptors* to parse through a file? I saved the next four functions for last. The use of file descriptors is sometimes a little hard to understand. I'm going to do my best to make this easy! Under the covers of the Unix operating system, files are referenced by file descriptors. You should already know three file descriptors right off the bat. The three that I am talking about are stdin, stdout, and stderr. Standard input, or stdin, is specified as file descriptor 0. This is usually the keyboard or mouse. Standard output, or stdout, is specified as file descriptor 1. Standard output can be your terminal screen or some kind of a file. Standard error, or stderr, is specified as file descriptor 2. Standard error is how the system and programs and scripts are able to send out or suppress error messages.

You can use these file descriptors in combination with one another. I'm sure that you have seen a shell script send all output to the bit bucket, or /dev/null. Look at the following command.

```
my_shell_script.ksh >/dev/null  2>&1
```

The result of the previous command is to run completely silent. In other words, there is not any external output produced. Internally the script may be reading and writing to and from files and may be sending output to a specific terminal, such as /dev/console. You may want to use this technique when you run a shell script as a cron table entry or when you just are not interested in seeing any output.

In the previous example we used two file descriptors. We can also use other file descriptors to handle file input and storage. In our next four timing functions we are going to use file descriptor 0 (zero), which is standard input, and file descriptor 3. On most Unix systems valid file descriptors range from 0 to 19. In our case we are going to use file descriptor 3, but we could have just as easily used file descriptor 5.

There are two steps in the method we are going to use. The first step is to close file descriptor 0 by redirecting everything to our new file descriptor 3. We use the following syntax for this step:

```
exec 3<&0
```

Now all of the keyboard and mouse input is going to our new file descriptor 3. The second step is to send our input file, specified by the variable $FILENAME, into file descriptor 0 (zero), which is standard input. This second step is done using the following syntax:

```
exec 0<$FILENAME
```

At this point any command requiring input will receive the input from the $FILENAME file. Now is a good time for an example. Look at the function in Listing 2.11.

```
function while_read_LINE_FD
{
exec 3<&0
exec 0< $FILENAME

while read LINE
do
        echo "$LINE"
        :
done

exec 0<&3
}
```

Listing 2.11 while_read_LINE_FD function listing.

Within the function in Listing 2.11 we have our familiar **while** loop to read one line of text at a time. But the beginning of this function does a little file descriptor redirection. The first **exec** command redirects `stdin` to file descriptor 3. The second **exec** command redirects the `$FILENAME` file into `stdin`, which is file descriptor 0. Now the **while** loop can just execute without our having to worry about how we assign a line of text to the `LINE` variable. When the **while** loop exits we redirect the previously reassigned `stdin`, which was sent to file descriptor 3, back to its original file descriptor 0.

```
exec 0<&3
```

In other words we set it back to the system's default value.

Pay close attention to this method in the timing tests later in this chapter. We have three more examples using file descriptors that utilize some of our previous **while** loops. The next two functions are absolutely the most unusual techniques of parsing a file that I have run across. When you first look at Methods 10 and 11 it seems that the author had some tricks up his or her sleeve. Please make sure you compare all of the timing results at the end of the chapter to see how these methods fare.

Method 10: while LINE='line' Using File Descriptors

Here we go again with the **line** command. In this function the **line** command replaces the **read** command; however, we are still going to use file descriptors to gain access to the `$FILENAME` file as input to our **while** loop. We use the same technique described in Method 9. Study the function in Listing 2.12.

```
function while_LINE_line_FD
{
exec 3<&0
```

Listing 2.12 while_LINE_line_FD function listing.

```
exec 0< $FILENAME

while LINE=`line`
do
        echo "$LINE"
        :
done

exec 0<&3
}
```

Listing 2.12   while_LINE_line_FD function listing. *(continued)*

The nice thing about using file descriptors is that standard input is implied. Standard input is there; we do not have to **cat** the file or use a pipe for data input. We just send the file's data directly into file descriptor 0, stdin. Just don't forget to reset the file descriptor when you are finished using it.

The first **exec** command redirects input of file descriptor 0 into file descriptor 3. The second **exec** command redirects our $FILENAME file into stdin, file descriptor 0. We process the file using a **while** loop and then reset the file descriptor 0 back to its default. File descriptors are really not too hard to use after scripting with them a few times. Even though we are using file descriptors to try to speed up the processing, the **line** command variable assignment will produce slower results than anticipated.

Method 11: while LINE=$(line) Using File Descriptors

This method is just like Method 10 except for the command substitution technique. We are going to use a large file for our timing tests and hope that we can detect a difference between the `command` and $(command) command substitution techniques in overall run time. Please study the function in Listing 2.13.

```
function while_LINE_line_cmdsub2_FD
{
exec 3<&0
exec 0< $FILENAME

while LINE=$(line)
do
        print "$LINE"
        :
done

exec 0<&3
}
```

Listing 2.13   while_LINE_line_cmdsub2_FD function listing.

The function in Listing 2.13 first redirects stdin to file descriptor 3; however, I could have used any valid file descriptor, such as file descriptor 5. The second step is redirecting the $FILENAME file into stdin, which is file descriptor 0. After the file descriptor redirection we execute the **while** loop, and on completion file descriptor 3 is redirected back to stdin. The end result is file descriptor 0, which again references stdin. The variable assignment produced by the command substitution has a negative impact on the timing results.

Method 12: while line LINE Using File Descriptors

Just as in Method 9 when we used a simple **while read LINE** syntax with file descriptors, we can use the **line** command in place of **read**. In our timing tests you will find that these two methods may look the same, but in the speed list you may be surprised with the results. Let's look at the function in Listing 2.14, and we will cover the technique at the end.

```
function while_line_LINE_FD
{
exec 3<&0
exec 0< $FILENAME

while line LINE
do
        echo "$LINE"
        :
done

exec 0<&3
}
```

Listing 2.14   while_line_LINE_FD function listing.

As with all of our functions using file descriptors we first set up our redirection so that the $FILENAME file remains open for reading. The difference in this function is the use of the **while line LINE** loop syntax. When using file descriptors do not forget to reset stdin, file descriptor 0 by default, to use file descriptor 0. The last statement in Listing 2.13 we reset the file descriptor 3 back to 0, zero, using the syntax: **exec 0<&3**.

Timing Each Method

We have created each of the functions for the 12 different methods to parse a file line by line. Now we can set up a shell script to time the execution of each function to see which one is the fastest to process a file. Earlier we wrote the mk_large_file.ksh script that creates a file that has the specified number of 80 character lines of text. This file is called `bigfile`, which is defined by the `OUT_FILE` variable. The default path for this new file is `/scripts/bigfile`. If you do not have a `/scripts` directory or filesystem, then you need to edit the `mk_large_file.ksh` shell script to define your preferred path and filename.

The file used for our timing test is a 7,500-line file. We needed this large a file to get accurate timing results for each of the 12 methods. Before we start the timing let's look at the timing shell script.

Timing Script

The shell script to time each file is not too difficult to understand when you realize where the output will go by default. The timing mechanism is the **time** command. The **time** command is followed by the name of the shell script or program that you want the execution to time. The timing data is broken down to the following fields:

```
real    1m30.34s
user    0m35.50s
sys     0m52.13s
```

In the previous output we have three measurements: `real`, `user`, and `sys`. The `real` time is the total time of execution. The `user` time is the time spent processing at the user/application process level. The `sys` time is the time spent by the system at the system/kernel level. Different Unix flavors produce slightly different output fields, but the concepts are identical.

The one thing that users get confused about using the **time** command is where the timing data output goes. All of the timing data goes to `stderr`, or standard error, which is file descriptor 2. So the shell script or program will execute with the normal `stdin` and `stdout`, and the timing data will go the `stderr`. Study the shell script in Listing 2.15, and we will go through the script at the end. Then we are going show some timing data for each method.

```ksh
#!/usr/bin/ksh
#
# SCRIPT: 12_ways_to_parse.ksh.ksh
#
# AUTHOR: Randy Michael
#
# DATE: 03/15/2001
#
# REV: 1.2.A
#
# PURPOSE:  This script shows the different ways of reading
#         a file line by line.  Again there is not just one way
#         to read a file line by line and some are faster than
#         others and some are more intuitive than others.
```

Listing 2.15 12_ways_to_parse.ksh shell script listing. *(continues)*

```
#
# REV LIST:
#
#       02/19/2002 - Randy Michael
#       Set each of the while loops up as functions and the timing
#       of each function to see which one is the fastest.
#
##########################################################################
#
#       NOTE: To output the timing to a file use the following syntax:
#
#   12_ways_to_parse.ksh file_to_process  > output_file_name 2>&1
#
#       The actaul timing data is sent to standard error, file
#       descriptor (2), and the function name header is sent
#       to standard output, file descriptor (1).
#
##########################################################################
#
# set -n  # Uncomment to check command syntax without any execution
# set -x  # Uncomment to debug this script
#

FILENAME="$1"
TIMEFILE="/tmp/loopfile.out"
>$TIMEFILE
THIS_SCRIPT=$(basename $0)

#####################################
function usage
{
echo "\nUSAGE: $THIS_SCRIPT  file_to_process\n"
echo "OR - To send the output to a file use: "
echo "\n$THIS_SCRIPT  file_to_process  > output_file_name 2>&1 \n"
exit 1
}
#####################################
function while_read_LINE
{
cat $FILENAME | while read LINE
do
        echo "$LINE"
        :
done
}
#####################################
function while_read_LINE_bottom
{
while read LINE
```

Listing 2.15   12_ways_to_parse.ksh shell script listing. *(continued)*

```
do
        echo "$LINE"
        :

done < $FILENAME
}
########################################
function while_line_LINE_bottom
{
while line LINE
do
        echo $LINE
        :
done < $FILENAME
}
########################################
function cat_while_LINE_line
{
cat $FILENAME | while LINE=`line`
do
        echo "$LINE"
        :
done
}
########################################
function while_line_LINE
{
cat $FILENAME | while line LINE
do
        echo "$LINE"
        :
done
}
########################################
function while_LINE_line_bottom
{
while LINE=`line`
do
        echo "$LINE"
        :

done < $FILENAME
}
########################################
function while_LINE_line_cmdsub2
{
cat $FILENAME | while LINE=$(line)
do
        echo "$LINE"
```

Listing 2.15   12_ways_to_parse.ksh shell script listing. *(continues)*

```
        :
done
}
######################################
function while_LINE_line_bottom_cmdsub2
{
while LINE=$(line)
do
        echo "$LINE"
        :

done < $FILENAME
}
######################################
function while_read_LINE_FD
{
exec 3<&0
exec 0< $FILENAME
while read LINE
do
        echo "$LINE"
        :
done
exec 0<&3
}
######################################
function while_LINE_line_FD
{
exec 3<&0
exec 0< $FILENAME
while LINE=`line`
do
        echo "$LINE"
        :
done
exec 0<&3
}
######################################
function while_LINE_line_cmdsub2_FD
{
exec 3<&0
exec 0< $FILENAME
while LINE=$(line)
do
        print "$LINE"
        :
done
exec 0<&3
```

Listing 2.15 12_ways_to_parse.ksh shell script listing. *(continued)*

```
}
######################################
function while_line_LINE_FD
{
exec 3<&0
exec 0< $FILENAME

while line LINE
do
        echo "$LINE"
        :
done

exec 0<&3
}
######################################
########## START OF MAIN ###########
######################################

# Test the Input

# Looking for exactly one parameter
(( $# == 1 )) || usage

# Does the file exist as a regular file?
[[ -f $1 ]] || usage

echo "\nStarting File Processing of each Method\n"

echo "Method 1:"
echo "\nfunction while_read_LINE\n" >> $TIMEFILE
echo "function while_read_LINE"
time while_read_LINE >> $TIMEFILE
echo "\nMethod 2:"
echo "\nfunction while_read_LINE_bottom\n" >> $TIMEFILE
echo "function while_read_LINE_bottom"
time while_read_LINE_bottom >> $TIMEFILE
echo "\nMethod 3:"
echo "\nfunction while_line_LINE_bottom\n" >> $TIMEFILE
echo "function while_line_LINE_bottom"
time while_line_LINE_bottom >> $TIMEFILE
echo "\nMethod 4:"
echo "\nfunction while_read_LINE_line\n" >> $TIMEFILE
echo "function while_read_LINE_line"
time while_read_LINE_line >> $TIMEFILE
echo "\nMethod 5:"
echo "\nfunction while_line_LINE\n" >> $TIMEFILE
echo "function while_line_LINE"
```

Listing 2.15   12_ways_to_parse.ksh shell script listing. *(continues)*

```
time while_line_LINE >> $TIMEFILE
echo "\nMethod 6:"
echo "\nfunction while_LINE_line_bottom\n" >> $TIMEFILE
echo "function while_LINE_line_bottom"
time while_LINE_line_bottom >> $TIMEFILE
echo "\nMethod 7:"
echo "\nfunction while_LINE_line_cmdsub2\n" >> $TIMEFILE
echo "function while_LINE_line_cmdsub2"
time while_LINE_line_cmdsub2 >> $TIMEFILE
echo "\nMethod 8:"
echo "\nfunction while_LINE_line_bottom_cmdsub2\n" >> $TIMEFILE
echo "function while_LINE_line_bottom_cmdsub2"
time while_LINE_line_bottom_cmdsub2 >> $TIMEFILE
echo "\nMethod 9:"
echo "\nfunction while_read_LINE_FD\n" >> $TIMEFILE
echo "function while_read_LINE_FD"
time while_read_LINE_FD >> $TIMEFILE
echo "\nMethod 10:"
echo "\nfunction while_LINE_line_FD\n" >> $TIMEFILE
echo "function while_LINE_line_FD"
time while_LINE_line_FD >> $TIMEFILE
echo "\nMethod 11:"
echo "\nfunction while_LINE_line_cmdsub2_FD\n" >> $TIMEFILE
echo "function while_LINE_line_cmdsub2_FD"
time while_LINE_line_cmdsub2_FD >> $TIMEFILE
echo "\nMethod 12:"
echo "\nfunction while_line_LINE_FD\n" >> $TIMEFILE
echo "function while_line_LINE_FD"
time while_line_LINE_FD >> $TIMEFILE
```

Listing 2.15   12_ways_to_parse.ksh shell script listing. *(continued)*

The shell script in Listing 2.15 first defines all of the functions that we previously covered in the Methods sections. After the functions are defined, we do a little testing of the input. We are expecting exactly one command parameter, and it should be a regular file. Look at the following code block in Listing 2.16 to see the file testing.

```
# Test the Input

# Looking for exactly one parameter
(( $# == 1 )) || usage

# Does the file exist as a regular file?
[[ -f $1 ]] || usage
```

Listing 2.16   Code to test command input.

The first test checks to ensure that the number of command parameters, specified by the $# operator, is exactly one. Notice that we used the *double parentheses* mathematical test, specified as ((`math test`)). Additionally, we used a logical OR, specified by ||, to execute the `usage` function if the number of parameters is not equal to one.

We use the same type of test for the file to ensure that the file exists and the file is a regular file, as opposed to a character or block special file. When we do the test, notice that we used the *double bracket* test for character data, specified by [[`character test`]]. This is an important distinction to note. We again use the logical OR to execute the `usage` function if the return code from the test is nonzero.

Now we start the actual timing tests. In doing these tests we execute the Method functions one at a time. The function's internal **while** loop does the file processing, but we redirect each function's output to a file so that we have some measurable system activity. As I stated before, the timing measurements produced by the **time** commands go to `stderr`, or file descriptor 2, which will just go to the screen by default. When this shell script executes, there are three things that go to the screen, as you will see in Listing 2.17. You can also send all of this output to a file by using the following command syntax:

```
12_ways_to_parse.ksh /scripts/bigfile > /tmp/timing_data.out 2>&1
```

The previous command starts with the script name, followed by the file to parse through. The output is redirected to the file /tmp/timing_data.out with `stderr` (file descriptor 2) redirected to `stdout` (file descriptor 1), specified by 2>&1. Do not forget the ampersand, &, before the 1. If the & is omitted, a file with the name 1 will be created. This is a common mistake when working with file descriptors. The placement of the `stderr` to `stdout` is important in this case. If the 2>&1 is at the end of the command, you will not get the desired result, which is all of the timing data going to a data file. In some cases the placement of the 2>&1 redirection does not matter, but it does matter here.

Timing Data for Each Method

Now all of the hard stuff has been done. We have a 7,500-line file, /scripts/bigfile, and we have our shell script written, so let's look at which function is the fastest in Listing 2.17.

```
Starting File Processing of each Method

Method 1:
function while_read_LINE

real    1m30.34s
user    0m35.50s
sys     0m52.13s
```

Listing 2.17 Timing data for each loop method. *(continues)*

```
Method 2:
function while_read_LINE_bottom

real   0m5.89s
user   0m5.62s
sys    0m0.16s

Method 3:
function while_line_LINE_bottom

real   6m53.71s
user   0m36.62s
sys    6m2.03s

Method 4:
function cat_while_LINE_line

real   7m16.87s
user   0m51.87s
sys    6m8.54s

Method 5:
function while_line_LINE

real   6m50.79s
user   0m36.65s
sys    5m59.66s

Method 6:
function while_LINE_line_bottom

real   7m20.48s
user   0m51.01s
sys    6m14.57s

Method 7:
function while_LINE_line_cmdsub2

real   7m18.04s
user   0m52.01s
sys    6m10.94s

Method 8:
function while_LINE_line_bottom_cmdsub2

real   7m20.34s
```

Listing 2.17   Timing data for each loop method. *(continued)*

```
user   0m50.82s
sys    6m14.26s

Method 9:
function while_read_LINE_FD

real   0m5.89s
user   0m5.53s
sys    0m0.28s

Method 10:
function while_LINE_line_FD

real   8m25.35s
user   0m50.68s
sys    7m15.33s

Method 11:
function while_LINE_line_cmdsub2_FD

real   8m24.58s
user   0m50.04s
sys    7m16.07s

Method 12:
function while_line_LINE_FD

real   7m54.57s
user   0m35.88s
sys    7m2.26s
```

Listing 2.17   Timing data for each loop method. *(continued)*

As you can see, all file processing loops are not created equal. Two of the methods are tied for first place. Methods 2 and 9 produce the exact same `real` execution time at 5.89 seconds to process a 7,500-line file. Method 1 came in second at 1 minute and 30.34 seconds. The remaining methods fall far behind, ranging from almost 7 minutes to over 8 minutes and 25.35 seconds. The sorted timing output for the real time is shown in Listing 2.18.

```
real   0m5.89s    Method 2
real   0m5.89s    Method 9
real   1m30.34s   Method 1
```

Listing 2.18   Sorted timing data by method. *(continues)*

```
real    6m50.79s    Method 5
real    6m53.71s    Method 3
real    7m16.87s    Method 4
real    7m18.04s    Method 7
real    7m20.34s    Method 8
real    7m20.48s    Method 6
real    7m54.57s    Method 12
real    8m24.58s    Method 11
real    8m25.35s    Method 10
```

Listing 2.18   Sorted timing data by method. *(continued)*

Let's take a look at the code for the top three techniques. The order of appearance is Method 2, 9, and 1.

```
function while_read_LINE_bottom
{
while read LINE
do
        echo "$LINE"
        :

done < $FILENAME
}
```

Listing 2.19   Method 2: Tied for first place.

The method in Listing 2.19 is my favorite because it is quick and intuitive to write and understand once the input redirection is explained to the beginner.

```
function while_read_LINE_FD
{
exec 3<&0
exec 0< $FILENAME

while read LINE
do
        echo "$LINE"
        :
done

exec 0<&3
}
```

Listing 2.20   Method 9: Tied for first place.

I tend not to use this method when I write shell scripts because it can be difficult to maintain through the code life cycle. If a user is not familiar with using file descriptors, then a script using this method is extremely hard to understand. The method in Listing 2.19 produces the same timing results, and it is much easier to understand. Listing 2.21 shows the second-place loop method.

```
function while_read_LINE
{
cat $FILENAME | while read LINE
do
        echo "$LINE"
        :
done
}
```

Listing 2.21   Method 1: Made second place in timing tests.

The method in Listing 2.21 is the most popular way to process a file line by line. I see this technique in almost every shell script that does file parsing. Method 1 is 1,433 percent slower than either Method 2 or 9 in execution time. The delta percentage between first and last place is 8,479 percent. These timing tests also point out another factor: Do not use the **line** command when parsing a file in a loop.

Timing Command Substitution Methods

We also want to take a look at the difference in timing when we used the two different methods of command substitution using `` `command` `` versus `$(command)`.

```
Method 4:
function cat_while_LINE_line

real   7m16.87s
user   0m51.87s
sys    6m8.54s

Method 7:
function while_LINE_line_cmdsub2

real   7m18.04s
user   0m52.01s
sys    6m10.94s
```

Listing 2.22   Command substitution timing difference.

In Method 4 the command substitution technique uses *backtic*, `` `command` ``, which are located in the top left corner of a standard keyboard. The command substitution technique used in Method 7 is the dollar parentheses technique, $(command). Both command substitution methods give the same end result, but one method is slightly faster than the other. From the timing of each method in Listing 2.22, the backtic method won the race by only 1.17 seconds when parsing a 7,500-line file. This difference is so small that it is really not an issue.

Summary

Through this chapter we have covered the various techniques for parsing a file line by line that I have seen over the years. You may have seen even more oddball ways to process a file. The two points that I wanted to make in this chapter are these: First, there are many ways to handle any task on a Unix platform, and second, some techniques that are used to process a file waste a lot of CPU time. Most of the wasted time is spent in unnecessary variable assignments and continuously opening and closing the same file over and over. Using a pipe also has a negative impact on the loop timing.

I hope you noticed the second place method in Listing 2.21 is 1,433 percent slower than the tie for first place. On a small file this is not a big deal, but for large parsing jobs this delta in timing can have a huge impact both on the machine resources and on the time involved.

Automated Event Notification

To solve problems proactively, an early warning is essential. In this chapter we are going to look at some techniques of getting the word out by automating the notification when a system event occurs. When we write monitoring shell scripts and there is a failure, success, or request, we need a method of getting a message to the right people. There are really three main strategies of notification in shell scripts. The first is to send an email directly to the user. We can also send an alphanumeric page by email to the user for immediate notification to a pager. The third is to send a text page by dialing a modem to the service provider. We are mainly going to look at the first two methods, but we will also list some good software products that will send text pages by dialing the modem and transferring the message to the pager provider.

In some shops email is so restricted that you have to use a little trick or two to get around some of the restrictions. We will cover some of these situations, too.

Basics of Automating Event Notification

In a shell script there are times when you want to send an automated notification. As an example, if you are monitoring filesystems and your script finds that one of the filesystems has exceeded the maximum threshold, then most likely you want to be informed of this situation. I always like an email notification when the backups complete every night—not just when there is a backup error, but when the backup is successful, too. This way I always know the status of last night's backup every morning just by checking my email. I also know that a major backup problem occurred if no email was sent at all. There are a few ways to do the notification, but the most common is through email to either a text pager or through an email account. In the next few sections we are going to look at the techniques to get the message out, even if only one server has mail access.

Using the mail and mailx Commands

The most common notification method uses the **mail** and **mailx** commands. The basic syntax of both of these commands is shown in the following code:

```
mail -s "This is the subject" $MAILOUT_LIST < $MAIL_FILE
OR
cat $MAIL_FILE | mail -s "This is the subject" $MAILOUT_LIST

mailx -s "This is the subject" $MAILOUT_LIST < $MAIL_FILE
OR
cat $MAIL_FILE | mailx -s "This is the subject" $MAILOUT_LIST
```

Not all systems support the **mailx** command, but the systems that do have support use the same syntax as the **mail** command. To be safe when dealing with multiple Unix platforms, always use the **mail** command.

Notice in the **mail**, and **mailx**, commands the use of the MAILOUT_LIST and MAIL_FILE variables. The MAILOUT_LIST variable contains a list of email addresses, or email aliases, to send the message to. The MAIL_FILE variable points to a filename that holds the message to be sent. Let's look at both of these individually.

Suppose we are monitoring the filesystems on a machine and the /var filesystem has reached 98 percent utilization, which is over the 85-percent threshold, for a filesystem to be considered full. The Systems Administrator needs to get a page about this situation quickly, or we may have a machine crash when /var fills up. In the monitoring shell script there is a MAIL_FILE variable defined to point to the filename /tmp/mailfile.out, MAIL_FILE=/tmp/mailfile. Then we create a zero-sized mail-out file using cat /dev/null > $MAIL_FILE. When an error is found, which in our case is when /var has reached 98 percent, a message is appended to the $MAIL_FILE for later mailing. If more errors are found, they are also appended to the file as the shell script processes each task. At the end of the shell script we can test the size of the $MAIL_FILE. If the $MAIL_FILE has any data in it, then the file will have a size greater than 0 bytes. If the file has data, then we mail the file. If the file is empty with a 0 byte file size, then we do nothing.

To illustrate this idea, let's study the code segment in Listing 3.1.

```
MAIL_FILE=/tmp/mailfile.out
cat /dev/null > $MAIL_FILE
MAIL_LIST="randy@my.domain.com 1234567890@mypage_somebody.net"

check_filesystems    # This function checks the filesystems percentage

if [ -s $MAIL_FILE ]
then
     mail -s "Filesystem Full" $MAIL_LIST < $MAIL_FILE
fi
```

Listing 3.1   Typical mail code segment listing.

In Listing 3.1 we see a code segment that defines the MAIL_FILE and MAIL_LIST variables that we use in the **mail** command. After the definitions this code segment executes the function that looks for filesystems that are over the threshold. If the threshold is exceeded, then a message is appended to the $MAIL_FILE file as shown in the following code segment:

```
FS=/var
PERCENT=98
THISHOST=$(uname -n)

echo "$THISHOST: $FS is $PERCENT" | tee -a $MAIL_FILE
```

This code segment is from the check_filesystems function. For my machine, this **echo** command statement would both display the following message to the screen and append it to the $MAIL_FILE file:

```
yogi: /var is 98%
```

The hostname is **yogi**, the filesystem is /var, and the percentage of used space is 98 percent. Notice the **tee** command after the pipe (|) from the **echo** statement. In this case we want to display the results on the screen and send an email with the same data. The **tee -a** command does this double duty when you pipe the output to | **tee -a** $FILENAME.

After the check_filesystems function finishes, we test the size of the $MAIL_FILE. If it is greater than 0 bytes in size, then we send a mail message using the **mail** command. The following message is sent to the randy@my.domain.com and 1234567890@mypage_somebody.net email addresses:

```
yogi: /var is 98%
```

Problems with Outbound Mail

Before we hard-code the **mail** command into your shell script we need to do a little test to see if we can get the email to the destination without error. To test the functionality, add the **-v** switch to the **mail** or **mailx** command, as shown in Listing 3.2.

```
# echo "Testing: /var is 98%" > /tmp/mailfile.out

# mail -v -s "Filesystem Full" randy@my.domain.com < /tmp/mailfile.out

AND

# mail -v -s "Filesystem Full" 1234567890@mypage_somebody.net \
  < /tmp/mailfile.out
```

Listing 3.2   Testing the mail service using mail -v.

With the **-v** switch added to the **mail** command, all of the details of the delivery are displayed on the user's terminal. From the delivery details we can see any errors that happen until the file is considered "sent" by the local host. If the message is not delivered to the target email address, then further investigation is needed. The next two sections look at some alternative techniques.

Create a "Bounce" Account with a .forward File

I worked at one shop where only one Unix machine in the network, other than the mail server, was allowed to send email outside of the LAN. This presented a problem for all of the other machines to get the message out when a script detected an error. The solution we used was to create a user account on the Unix machine that could send email outbound. Then we locked down this user account so no one could log in remotely. Let's say we create a user account called **bounce**. In the /home/bounce directory we create a file called /home/bounce/.forward. Then in the .forward file we add the email address to which we want to forward all mail. You can add as many email addresses to this file as you want, but be aware that every single email will be forwarded to *each* address listed in the .forward file.

On this single machine that has outside LAN mailing capability we added the user **bounce** to the system. Then in the /home/bounce directory we created a file called .forward that has the following entries:

```
randy@my.domain.com
1234567890@mypage_somebody.net
```

This `.forward` file will forward all mail received by the **bounce** user to the `randy@` `my.domain.com` and `1234567890@mypage_somebody.net` email addresses. This way I have an email to my desktop, and I am also notified by my text pager. On all of the other machines we have two options. The first option is to edit all of the shell scripts that send email notification and change the `$MAIL_LIST` variable to:

```
MAIL_LIST="bounce@dino."
```

This entry assumes that the **dino** host is in the same domain, specified by the period that follows the hostname **dino**. (`dino.`).

An easier way is to create some entries in the `aliases` file for sendmail. The `aliases` file is usually located in `/etc/aliases`, but you may find it in `/etc/mail/aliases` on some operating systems. The format of defining an alias is a name, username, or tag, followed by one or more email addresses. The following is an example of an `aliases` file:

```
admin:      bounce@dino.,randy,brad,cindy,jon,pepe
```

This `aliases` file entry creates a new alias called **admin** that automatically sends email to the **bounce** account on **dino** and also to **randy**, **brad**, **cindy**, **jon**, and **pepe**.

Before these changes will take effect, we need to run the **newaliases** command. The **sendmail -bi** command works, too.

Using the sendmail Command to Send Outbound Mail

In another shop where I worked, I could not send outbound mail from any user named **root**. The *from* field had to be a valid email address that is recognized by the mail server, and **root** is not valid. To get around this little problem I changed the command that I used from **mail** to **sendmail**. The **sendmail** command allows us to add the **-f** switch to indicate a valid internal email address for the *from* field. The **sendmail** command is in `/usr/sbin/sendmail` on AIX, HP-UX, and Linux, but on SunOS the location changed to `/usr/lib/sendmail`. Look at the function in Listing 3.3, and we will cover the details at the end.

```
function send_notification
{
if [ -s $MAIL_FILE -a  "$MAILOUT" = "TRUE" ];
then

        case $(uname) in
        AIX|HP-UX|Linux) SENDMAIL="/usr/sbin/sendmail"
                         ;;
        SunOS)           SENDMAIL="/usr/lib/sendmail"
                         ;;
```

Listing 3.3   send_notification function listing. *(continues)*

```
        esac

        echo "\nSending email notification"
        $SENDMAIL -f randy@$THISHOST $MAIL_LIST < $MAIL_FILE
 fi
 }
```

Listing 3.3   send_notification function listing. *(continued)*

Notice in Listing 3.3 that we added another variable, MAILOUT. This variable is used to turn on/off the email notifications. If the $MAILOUT variable points to TRUE, and the $MAIL_FILE file is nonempty, then the email is sent. If the $MAILOUT variable does not equal the string TRUE, then the email is disabled. This is just another way to control the email notifications.

In the **case** statement we use the output of the **uname** command to set the correct command path for **sendmail** command on the Unix platform. For AIX, HP-UX, and Linux the **sendmail** command path is /usr/sbin. On SunOS the **sendmail** path is /usr/lib. We assign the correct path to the SENDMAIL variable, and we use this variable as the command to send the mail. Once the command is defined we issue the command, as shown here:

```
$SENDMAIL -f randy@$THISHOST $MAIL_LIST < $MAIL_FILE
```

We issue the **sendmail** command using the **-f** switch and follow the switch by a valid email account name, which is randy@$THISHOST. Remember that we defined the THISHOST variable to the local machine's hostname. The *from* address is followed by the list of email addresses, and the message file is used by redirecting input into the **sendmail** command. We can also use the following syntax:

```
cat $MAIL_FILE | $SENDMAIL -f randy@$THISHOST $MAIL_LIST
```

Either **sendmail** statement will send the mail, if the mail server and firewall allow outgoing mail.

Dial-Out Modem Software

Many good products are on the market, both freeware and commercial, that handle large amounts of paging better than any shell script could ever do. They also have the ability to dial the modem and send the message to the provider. A list of such products is shown in Table 3.1.

Table 3.1 Products That Handle High-Volume Paging and Modem Dialing

PRODUCT	DESCRIPTION
FREEWARE AND SHAREWARE PRODUCTS	
QuickPage	Client/server software used to send messages to alphanumeric pagers.
SMS Client	Command-line utility for Unix that allows you to send SMS messages to cell phones and pagers.
HylaFAX	Faxing product for Unix that allows dial-in, dial-out, fax-in, fax-out, and pager notifications.
COMMERCIAL PRODUCTS	
EtherPage	Enterprise-wide alphanumeric pager software product made by MobileSys.
TelAlert	Pager notification and interactive voice response software made by Telamon.
FirstPAGE	Supports all national paging networks using IXO/TAP, made by Netcon Technologies.

Table 3.1 shows only a sample of the products available for paging. The nice thing about these products is the ability to dial-out on a modem. At some level in every shop there is a need to use a phone line for communications instead of the network. This gives you the ability to get the message out even if the network is having a problem.

SNMP Traps

Most large shops use an enterprise monitoring tool to monitor all of the systems from a central management console. The server software is installed on a single machine called the management station. All of the managed/monitored machines have the client software installed. This client software is an SNMP agent and uses a local MIB to define the *managed objects*, or *management variables*. These managed objects define things such as the filesystems to monitor and the trigger threshold for detecting a full filesystem. When the managed object, which in this case is a full filesystem, exceeds the set threshold, a local SNMP *trap* is generated and the management station captures the trap and performs the predefined action, which may be to send a text page to the System Administrator. To understand what an SNMP trap is, let's review a short explanation of each of the pieces:

SNMP (Simple Network Management Protocol). SNMP is a protocol used for agent communications. The most common use for the SNMP protocol is client/server system management software.

MIB (Management Information Base). Each managed machine, or *agent*, in an SNMP-managed network maintains a local database of information (MIB) defined to the network managed machine. An SNMP-compliant MIB contains information about the property definitions of each of the managed resources.

SNMP trap. Event notification to the management server from an agent-generated event, called a trap. The server management station receives and sets objects in the MIB, and the local machine, or agent, notifies the management station of client-generated events, or traps. All of the communication between the network management server and its agents, or management clients, takes place using the Simple Network Management Protocol (SNMP).

The nice thing about using an enterprise management tool is that it utilizes SNMP. With most products you can write your own shell scripts using SNMP traps. The details vary for the specific syntax for each product, but with the software installed you can have your shell scripts perform that same notifications that the enterprise management software produces. Using Tivoli Netview, EcoTools, or BMC Patrol (just to name a few) you have the ability to incorporate SNMP traps into your own shell scripts for event notifications. Please refer to the product documentation for details on creating and using SNMP traps.

Summary

This chapter is intended to give a brief overview of some techniques of getting critical information out to the system management community. This chapter mainly focused on email and some different techniques for using the mail commands.

The topics discussed here form the basics for notification of system problems. You should be able to extend the list of notification techniques without much effort. If you have an enterprise management solution installed at your shop, then study the vendor documentation on using and creating SNMP traps. There are books based entirely on SNMP, and the information is just too long to cover in this book, but it is an important notification method that you need to be familiar with. If you have trouble getting the email solution to work, talk with the Network Manager to find a solution.

In the next chapter we move on to look at creating progress indicators to give our users feedback on long running processes. The topics include a series of dots as the processing continues, a line that appears to rotate as processing continues, and a counter that counts down to zero.

CHAPTER

4

Progress Indicator Using a Series of Dots, a Rotating Line, or a Countdown to Zero

Giving your end users feedback that a script or program is not hung is vital on long processing jobs. We sometimes write shell scripts that take a long time to completely execute—for example, system backup scripts. A good way to keep everyone content is to have some kind of progress indicator. Just about anything can be a progress indicator as long as the end user gets the idea that job processing is continuing. In this chapter we are going to examine the following three progress indicators, which are fairly common:

- A series of dots
- A rotating line
- A counter counting down to zero

The dots and rotating line are more common, but the countdown method does have its place where we want to specify a timeout period. Each of these methods can be started as a separate script, as a function, or we can put the code loop directly in the background. We will cover using each of these methods.

Indicating Progress with a Series of Dots

The simplest form of progress indicator is to print a period to the screen every 5 to 20 seconds. It is simple, clean, and very easy to do. As with every script we start out with the command syntax. All we want to do is **echo** a dot to the screen while continuing on the same line.

```
echo ".\c"
```

The **echo** command prints a single dot on the screen, and the backslash c, \c, specifies a continuation on the same line without a new line or carriage return. To make a series of dots we will put this single command in a loop with some sleep time between each dot. We will use a **while** loop that loops forever with a 10-second sleep between printing each dot on the screen.

```
while true
do
     echo ".\c"
     sleep 10
done
```

If, for instance, we are running a backup script and we want to use this method to indicate progress, we would put this **while** loop in the background and save the process ID, PID, so that we could kill the background process when the backup script is complete. First, we will just put this **while** loop in the background, or we can create a function with this loop and run the function in the background. Both methods are shown in Listings 4.1 and 4.2.

```
while true
do
     echo ".\c"
done &

BG_PID=$!

/usr/local/bin/my_backup.ksh

kill $BG_PID
```

Listing 4.1   Looping in the background.

To accomplish the background loop, notice that we just put an ampersand, &, after the end of the **while** loop, after **done**. The next line uses the $! operator, which saves the PID of the last background process, BG_PID=$!. The background loop starts the dots ticking, and then we kick off the backup script, /usr/local/bin/ my_backup.ksh in the foreground. When the backup script is complete, we use the **kill** command to stop the dots by killing the background job, specified by kill $BG_PID. We can accomplish the same task with a function, as shown in Listing 4.2.

```
function dots
{
     while true
     do
          echo ".\c"
     done
}


####################################
######## Begin of Main ##########
####################################

dots &

BG_PID=$!

/usr/local/bin/my_backup.ksh

kill $BG_PID
```

Listing 4.2   Using a background function.

The script and function in Listing 4.2 accomplish the same task but use a background function instead of just putting the **while** loop in the background. We still capture the PID of the dots function, specified by $!, so we can **kill** the function when the backup script has completed, as we did in the previous example. We could also put the loop in a separate shell script and run the external script in the background, but this would be overkill for three lines of code.

Indicating Progress with a Rotating Line

If a series of dots is too boring, then we could use a rotating line as a progress indicator. To rotate the line we will again use the **echo** command, but this time we need a little more cursor control. This method requires that we display, in a series, the forward slash, /, then a hyphen, -, followed by a backslash, \, and then a pipe, |, and then repeat the process. For this character series to appear seamless we need to backspace over the last character and erase it, or overwrite it with the new character that makes the line appear to rotate. We will use a **case** statement inside a **while** loop, as shown in Listing 4.3.

```
function rotate
{
# PURPOSE: This function is used to give the end user some feedback that
#     "something" is running.  It gives a line twirling in a circle.
#     This function is started as a background process. Assign its PID
#     to a variable using:
#
#             rotate &      # To start
#             ROTATE_PID=$! # Get the PID of the last background job
#
#       At the end of execution just break out by killing the $ROTATE_PID
#       process. We also need to do a quick "cleanup" of the leftover
#       line of rotate output.
#
#         FROM THE SCRIPT:
#             kill -9 $ROTATE_PID
#             echo "\b\b   "

INTERVAL=1     # Sleep time between "twirls"
TCOUNT="0"     # For each TCOUNT the line twirls one increment

while :        # Loop forever...until this function is killed
do
     TCOUNT=`expr $TCOUNT + 1`   # Increment the TCOUNT

     case $TCOUNT in
         "1") echo '-'"\b\c"
              sleep $INTERVAL
              ;;
         "2") echo '\\'"\b\c"
              sleep $INTERVAL
              ;;
         "3") echo "|\b\c"
              sleep $INTERVAL
              ;;
         "4") echo "/\b\c"
              sleep $INTERVAL
              ;;
         *)   TCOUNT="0" ;;  # Reset the TCOUNT to "0", zero.
     esac
done
} # End of Function - rotate
```

Listing 4.3   Rotate function.

In the function in Listing 4.3 we first define an interval to sleep between updates. If we do not have some sleep time, then the load on the system will be noticeable. We just want to give the end user some feedback, not load the system down. At least one second is needed between screen updates. Next we start an infinite **while** loop and use the TCOUNT variable to control which part of the rotating line is displayed during the interval. Notice that each time that we **echo** a piece of the rotating line, we also back up the cursor with \b and continue on the same line with \c; both are needed. This way the next loop iteration will overwrite the previous character with a new character, and then we again back up the cursor and continue on the same line. This series of characters gives the appearance of a rotating line.

We use this function just like the previous example using the dots function in Listing 4.2. We start the function in the background, save the PID of the background function using the $! operator, start our time-consuming task, and **kill** the background rotate function when the task is complete. We could also just put the **while** loop in the background without using a function. In either case, when the rotating line is killed, we need to clean up the last characters on the screen. To do the cleanup we just back up the cursor and overwrite the last character with a blank space. (See Listing 4.4.)

```
#######################################
########## Begin of Main #############
#######################################

rotate &

ROTATE_PID=$!

/usr/local/bin/my_time_consuming_task.ksh

kill -9 $ROTATE_PID

# Cleanup...

echo "\b\b  "

# End of Example
```

Listing 4.4 Example of rotate function in a shell script.

These scripts work well and execute cleanly, but do not forget to give some sleep time on each loop iteration. Now we have shown the series of dots and the rotating line methods. Another method that may sometimes be beneficial is a countdown indicator.

Creating a Countdown Indicator

There may be times when you want something to time out. If we know an approximate amount of time that we want to allow for a task to finish, we can display a countdown indicator; then, when the time is up, we can take some action. Use your imagination with this one. The process we are going to use will depend on how many digits are in the current countdown, for example 0 to 9, 10 to 99, 100 to 999, and 1000 to 9999. The number of digits must be taken into account because we want a smooth transition between 1000 to 999 and 100 to 99 in the countdown, as well as other digit count changes. We also want to update the screen with a new value each second as we count down to zero. This method will again require us to control the cursor as we back up over the previous output and overwrite the characters with a new countdown number. Other than the cursor control this script is not very difficult. Let's look at the script and explain the process afterward (see Listing 4.5).

```ksh
#!/bin/ksh
#
# SCRIPT: countdown.ksh
#
# AUTHOR: Randy Michael - Systems Administrator
# DATE: 02-29-2000
# PLATFORM: Not Platform Dependent
#
# PURPOSE:  This script will do the same thing as a sleep command
#     while giving the user feedback as to the number of seconds
#     remaining.  It takes input between 1 and 9999 seconds only.
#
SCRIPT_NAME=$(basename $0)

#########################################
######## DEFINE FUNCTIONS HERE ##########
#########################################

usage ()
{
    echo "\nUSAGE: $SCRIPT_NAME seconds\n"
}

#########################################

trap_exit ()
{
    echo "\n\n...EXITING on a trapped signal...\n"
}

#########################################

test_string ()
{
    # This function tests for a positive integer!

    if (( $# != 1 ))
    then
```

Listing 4.5 countdown.ksh shell script.

```
        print 'ERROR'
        break
    fi
    STRING=$1

    case $STRING in
    +([0-9])) print 'POS_INT'
            ;;
        *) print 'NOT'
            ;;
    esac
}

#########################################
######### START OF MAIN ################
#########################################

trap 'trap_exit;exit 2' 1 2 3 15

if (( $# != 1 ))
then
    usage
    exit 1
fi

# Test for a positive integer

INT_STRING=$(test_string $1)

if [[ $INT_STRING != 'POS_INT' ]]
then
    echo "\nINVALID INPUT ==> $1 ...EXITING...\n"
    usage
    exit 1
fi

# Check for a valid range 1 - 9999
if (( $1 > 0 && $1 < 10000 ))
then

   S=$1  # Total second to start the countdown from

   echo "Seconds Remaining:  $S\c"


   while (( S > 0 ))  # Start the loop
   do
       # In this loop we back over the previous countdown value
```

Listing 4.5   countdown.ksh shell script. *(continues)*

```
            # and update the screen with a new countdown value. It
            # depends on how many digits the number has to determine
            # how many spaces to back up.

            sleep 1

            if (( S < 10 ))   # For numbers 0-9
            then
                  echo "\b\b  \b\c"

            elif (( S >= 10 && S < 100 )) # For numbers 10-99
            then
                  echo "\b\b\b   \b\b\c"

            elif (( S >= 100 && S < 1000 ))  # For numbers 100-999
            then
                     echo "\b\b\b\b    \b\b\b\c"

            elif (( S >= 1000 && S < 10000 )) # For numbers 1000-9999
            then
                     echo "\b\b\b\b\b     \b\b\b\b\c"
            fi

             ((S = S - 1)) # Decrement the counter by 1

            echo "$S\c"    # Update the screen with the new value
       done

      echo "\n" # Done - give a new line...

else
            echo "Invalid input ==> $1"
            echo "Range 1 - 9999 seconds"
            usage
            exit 1
fi
```

Listing 4.5 countdown.ksh shell script. *(continued)*

Let's review the countdown.ksh shell script in Listing 4.5 from the top. We start the script by defining the shell script's filename. We use the **basename $0** command, which will remove the leading directory path and leave only the filename. We need the script's filename for the usage function, and we never want to hard-code a filename because we may rename the script at some point. Next, we define all of our functions. As always, we have our usage function for incorrect command-line usage. The usage function is where we need the shell script filename that we captured with the preceding **basename $0** command. If the **basename** command were executed in the usage function the result would be usage instead of countdown.ksh. This subtle difference in using the **basename** command is a common mistake.

Next we have the trap_exit function that will execute on trapped exit signals 1, 2, 3, and 15 (of course, we cannot trap **kill -9**). This trap_exit function will display ...EXITING on a trapped signal... as an informational message to the user.

The test_string function is used to test for an integer value greater than or equal to 0, zero. To test for an integer we just use the regular expression +([0-9]) in a **case** statement. This regular expression will be true if the value is an integer value greater than or equal to 0, zero. In Chapter 1 there is a very extensive test_string.ksh shellscript that includes lowercase and uppercase characters, mixed-case strings, and numeric and alphanumeric characters. Regular expressions are great for string tests and are flexible to use.

We start the main part of the script by setting a *trap* to catch exit signals 1, 2, 3, and 15. On these exit signals we execute our trap_exit function that we previously covered. After setting the trap we check to confirm that we have exactly one command-line argument. If we have more or less than one argument, then we run our usage function and exit with a return code of 1.

The integer test for the command-line argument is next. To make this test we use our test_string function and assign the output to the variable INT_STRING. The test_string should return POS_INT, or we inform the user of the invalid value, run the usage function, and exit the script with a return code of 1. If we have got this far we know that we have a positive integer, so we need to make sure that the integer is within the valid range for this shell script. The valid range is 1 to 9999 seconds, which is 2.78 hours. If the value is out of range, then we inform the user that the value is out of range, run the usage function, and exit the script with a return code of 1. All usage errors exit with a return code of 1 in this shell script. Now we are ready to start the countdown. The countdown takes place in a **while** loop. Within this **while** loop notice the **if..then..elif..elif..** control structure and the cursor control. This cursor control is dependent on the number of digits in the current countdown value. We need to control the cursor using this method so that we get a smooth transition between 1000 and 999, 100 to 99, and 10 to 9. If you do not handle the transition by cursor control the digit set will move across the screen during the transitions. For the cursor control we use the **echo** command with a backslash **b**, \b, to back the cursor one space. For three spaces we use \b\b\b\c with the final \c keeping the cursor on the same line without a new line and carriage return. So, in each loop iteration the cursor is controlled depending on the current number of digits in the current countdown value.

When the countdown reaches 0, the script will output one new line and carriage return and exit with a return code of 0.

Other Options to Consider

As with any script, we may be able to improve on the techniques. The series-of-dots method is so simple that I cannot think of any real improvements. The rotating line is a fun little script to play with, and I have accomplished the same result in several different ways. Each method I used produced a noticeable load on the system if the sleep statement was removed, so that the line twirled as fast as possible. Try to see if you can find a technique that will not produce a noticeable load and does not require a sleep of at least one second, using a shell script!

In the countdown indicator the actual countdown time may not be exactly accurate. The inaccuracy is due to the variation in response time due to the load on the system. If your system is not under any load, the countdown time will be fairly stable and accurate. If you have a normally very active system, your countdown time can vary widely depending on the load and the duration of the countdown—the longer the countdown time, the less accurate the timing. A more accurate way to handle an exact timing is to use an **at** command to kick off the job at a specific time in the future. The following **at** command example will execute a script called time_out.ksh in 500 seconds:

```
echo time_out.ksh | at now + 500 seconds
```

The **at** command is very flexible and very accurate for timing purposes.

Another option is to use the shell variable SECONDS. This variable is extremely accurate and easy to use. The first step is to initialize the SECONDS variable to 0, zero. Once the variable is initialized you need only test the variable, which keeps track of the number of seconds since the SECONDS variable was initialized. Type the following lines in on the command line.

```
# SECONDS=0

(Wait 5 seconds...)

# echo $SECONDS
5
```

Play around with each of these techniques, and always strive to keep your end users informed. A blank or "frozen" screen makes people uncomfortable.

Summary

In this chapter we presented three techniques to help keep our script users content. Each technique has its place, and they are all easy to implement within any shell script or function. We covered how to save the PID of the last background job and how to put an entire loop in the background. The background looping can make a script a little easier to follow if you are not yet proficient at creating and using functions.

Remember, informed users are happy users!

In the next chapter we will cover monitoring a system for full filesystems. Methods covered include a typical percentage method to the number of megabytes free, for very large filesystems. Chapter 5 ends with a shell script that does auto detection using the filesystem size to set the monitoring method.

CHAPTER 5

File System Monitoring

The most common monitoring task is monitoring for full filesystems. On different flavors of Unix the monitoring techniques are the same, but the commands and fields in the output vary slightly. This difference is due to the fact that command syntax and the output columns vary depending on the Unix system.

We are going to step through the entire process of building a script to monitor filesystem usage and show the philosophy behind the techniques used. In scripting this solution we will cover five monitoring techniques, starting with the most basic monitoring—percentage of space used in each filesystem.

The next part will build on this original base code and add *exceptions* capability allowing an override of the script's set threshold for a filesystem to be considered full. The third part will deal with *large filesystems*, which is typically considered to be a filesystem larger than 2 gigabytes, 2GB. This script modification will use the megabytes, MB, of free space technique.

The fourth part will add exception capability to the MB of free space method. The fifth part in this series combines both the percentage of used space and MB of free space techniques with an added *auto-detect* feature to decide how to monitor each filesystem. Regular filesystems will be monitored with percent used and large filesystems as MB of free space, and, of course, with the exception capability. The sixth and final script will allow the filesystem monitor script to run on AIX, Linux, HP-UX, or Solaris without any further modification.

In This Chapter

In this chapter, we will cover the following six shell scripts related to filesystem monitoring:

- Percentage of used space method
- Percentage of used space with exceptions capability
- Megabytes of free space method
- Megabytes of free space with exceptions capability
- Combining percentage used and megabytes of free space with exceptions capability
- Enabling the combined script to execute on AIX, HP-UX, Linux, and Solaris

Syntax

Our first task, as usual, is to get the required command syntax. For this initial example we are going to monitor an AIX system (HP-UX, Linux, and Solaris will be covered later). The command syntax to look at the filesystems in kilobytes, KB, or 1024-byte blocks, is **df -k** in AIX.

Let's take a look at the output of the **df -k** command on an AIX 5L machine:

```
Filesystem      1024-blocks     Free %Used    Iused %Iused Mounted on
/dev/hd4              32768    16376   51%     1663    11% /
/dev/hd2            1212416    57592   96%    36386    13% /usr
/dev/hd9var           53248    30824   43%      540     5% /var
/dev/hd3             106496    99932    7%      135     1% /tmp
/dev/hd1               4096     3916    5%       25     3% /home
/proc                     -        -    -        -      - /proc
/dev/hd10opt         638976    24456   97%    15457    10% /opt
/dev/scripts_lv      102400    95264    7%      435     2% /scripts
/dev/cd0             656756        0  100%   328378   100% /cdrom
```

The fields in the command output that we are concerned about are column 1, the **Filesystem** device, column 4, the **%Used**, and **Mounted on** in column 7. There are at least two reasons that we want both the filesystem device and the mount point. The first reason is to know if it is an NFS mounted filesystem. This first column will show the NFS server name as part of the device definition if it is NFS mounted. The second reason is that we will not want to monitor a mounted CD-ROM. A CD-ROM will always show that it is 100 percent used because it is mounted as read-only and you cannot write to it (I know, CD-RW drives, but these are still not the norm in business environments).

As you can see in the bottom row of the preceding output, the /cdrom mount point does indeed show that it is 100 percent utilized. We want to omit this from the output along with the column heading at the top line. The first step is to show everything except for the column headings. We can use the following syntax:

```
df -k | tail +2
```

This delivers the following output without the column headings:

```
/dev/hd4          32768     16376    51%      1663    11% /
/dev/hd2        1212416     57592    96%     36386    13% /usr
/dev/hd9var       53248     30824    43%       540     5% /var
/dev/hd3         106496     99932     7%       135     1% /tmp
/dev/hd1           4096      3916     5%        25     3% /home
/proc                 -         -     -         -      -  /proc
/dev/hd10opt     638976     24456    97%     15457    10% /opt
/dev/scripts_lv  102400     95264     7%       435     2% /scripts
/dev/cd0         656756         0   100%    328378   100% /cdrom
```

This output looks a bit better, but we still have a couple of things we are not interested in. The /cdrom is at 100 percent all of the time, and the /proc mount point has no values, just hyphens. The /proc filesystem is new to AIX 5L, and because it has no values, we want to eliminate it from our output. Notice the device, in column 1, for the CD-ROM is /dev/cd0. This is what we want to use as a tag to pattern match on instead of the mount point because it may at some point be mounted somewhere else, for example /mnt. We may also have devices /dev/cd1 and /dev/cd2, too, if not now perhaps in the future. This, too, is easy to take care of, though. We can expand on our command statement to exclude both lines from the output with one **egrep** statement, as in the following:

```
df -k | tail +2 | egrep -v '/dev/cd[0-9]|/proc'
```

In this statement we used the **egrep** command with a **-v** switch. The **-v** switch means to show everything *except* what it patterned matched on. The **egrep** is used for extended regular expressions; in this case, we want to exclude two rows of output. To save an extra **grep** statement we use **egrep** and enclose what we are pattern matching on within single tic marks, ' ', and separate each item in the list with a pipe symbol, |. The following two commands are equivalent:

```
df -k | tail +2 | grep -v '/dev/cd[0-9]' | grep -v '/proc'
```

```
df -k | tail +2 | egrep -v '/dev/cd[0-9]|/proc'
```

Also notice in both statements the pattern match on the CD-ROM devices. The **grep** and **egrep** statements will match devices /dev/cd0 up through the last device, for example /dev/cd24, using /dev/cd[0-9] as the pattern match. Do not forget the tic marks around '/dev/cd[0-9]' or the **grep/egrep** statement may fail.

Using **egrep** saves a little bit of code, but both commands produce the same output, shown here:

```
/dev/hd4          32768    16376   51%     1663    11% /
/dev/hd2        1212416    57592   96%    36386    13% /usr
/dev/hd9var       53248    30864   43%      539     5% /var
/dev/hd3         106496    99932    7%      134     1% /tmp
/dev/hd1           4096     3916    5%       25     3% /home
/dev/hd10opt     638976    24456   97%    15457    10% /opt
/dev/scripts_lv  102400    95264    7%      435     2% /scripts
```

In this output we have all of the rows of data we are looking for; however, we have some extra columns that we are not interested in. Now let's extract out the columns of interest, 1, 4, and 7. Extracting the columns is easy to do with an **awk** statement. Using an **awk** statement is the cleanest method, and the columns are selected using the positional parameters, or columns, $1, $2, $3, ..., $n. As we keep building this command statement we add in the **awk** part of the command.

```
df -k | tail +2 | egrep -v '/dev/cd[0-9]|/proc' \
 | awk '{print $1, $4, $7}'
```

First, notice that we extended our command onto the next line with the backslash character, \. This convention helps with the readability of the script. In the **awk** part of the statement we placed a comma and a space after each field, or positional parameter. The comma and space are needed to ensure that the fields remain separated by at least one space. This command statement leaves the following output:

```
/dev/hd4 51% /
/dev/hd2 96% /usr
/dev/hd9var 43% /var
/dev/hd3 7% /tmp
/dev/hd1 5% /home
/dev/hd10opt 97% /opt
/dev/scripts_lv 7% /scripts
```

For ease of working with our command output we can write it to a file and work with the file. In our script we can define a file and point to the file with a variable. The following code will work:

```
WORKFILE="/tmp/df.work"    # df output work file
>$WORKFILE                  # Initialize the file to zero size
```

Before we go any further we also need to decide on a trigger threshold for when a filesystem is considered full, and we want to define a variable for this, too. For our example we will say that anything over 85 percent is considered a full filesystem, and we will assign this value to the variable FSMAX:

```
FSMAX="85"
```

From these definitions we are saying that any monitored filesystem that has used *more than* 85 percent of its capacity is considered *full*. Our next step is to loop through each row of data in our output file. Our working data file is /tmp/df.work, which is pointed to by the $WORKFILE variable, and we want to compare the second column, the percentage used for each filesystem, to the $FSMAX variable, which we initialized to 85. But we still have a problem; the $WORKFILE entry still has a %, percent sign, and we need an integer value to compare to the $FSMAX value. We will take care of this conversion with a **sed** statement. We use **sed** for character substitution and, in this case, character removal. The **sed** statement is just before the numerical comparison in a loop that follows. Please study Listing 5.1, and pay close attention to the bold text.

```ksh
#!/usr/bin/ksh
#
# SCRIPT: fs_mon_AIX.ksh
# AUTHOR: Randy Michael
# DATE: 08-22-2001
# REV: 1.1.P
# PURPOSE: This script is used to monitor for full filesystems,
#     which is defined as "exceeding" the FSMAX value.
#     A message is displayed for all "full" filesystems.
#
# REV LIST:
#
# set -n # Uncomment to check syntax without any execution
# set -x # Uncomment to debug this script
#
##### DEFINE FILES AND VARIABLES HERE ####

FSMAX="85"                    # Max. FS percentage value

WORKFILE="/tmp/df.work" # Holds filesystem data
>$WORKFILE                # Initialize to empty
OUTFILE="/tmp/df.outfile" # Output display file
>$OUTFILE                # Initialize to empty
THISHOST=`hostname`  # Hostname of this machine

######## START OF MAIN ############

# Get the data of interest by stripping out /dev/cd#,
# /proc rows and keeping columns 1, 4 and 7

df -k | tail +2 | egrep -v '/dev/cd[0-9] | /proc' \
     | awk '{print $1, $4, $7}' > $WORKFILE

# Loop through each line of the file and compare column 2

while read FSDEVICE FSVALUE FSMOUNT
```

Listing 5.1 fs_mon_AIX.ksh shell script. *(continues)*

```
do
        FSVALUE=$(echo $FSVALUE | sed s/\%//g) # Remove the % sign
        typeset -i FSVALUE
        if [ $FSVALUE -gt $FSMAX ]
        then
            echo "$FSDEVICE mounted on $FSMOUNT is ${FSVALUE}%" \
                >> $OUTFILE
        fi
done < $WORKFILE # Feed the while loop from the bottom!!

if [[ -s $OUTFILE ]]
then
        echo "\nFull Filesystem(s) on $THISHOST\n"
        cat $OUTFILE
        print
fi
```

Listing 5.1   fs_mon_AIX.ksh shell script. *(continued)*

The items highlighted in the script are all important to note. We start with getting the hostname of the machine. We want to know which machine the report is relating to. Next we load the $WORKFILE with the filesystem data. Just before the numerical test is made we remove the **%** sign and then typeset the variable, FSVALUE, to be an integer. Then we make the over-limit test, and if the filesystem in the current loop iteration has exceeded the threshold of 85 percent, we append a message to the $OUTFILE. Notice that the **while** loop is getting its data from the bottom of the loop, after **done**. This is the fastest technique to process a file line by line. After processing the entire file we test to see if the $OUTFILE exists and is greater than zero bytes in size. If it has data, then we print an output header, with a newline before and after, and display the $OUTFILE file followed by another blank line. In Listing 5.1 we used an assortment of commands to accomplish the same task in a different way—for example, using VARIABLE=$(command) and VARIABLE=`command`, to execute a command and assign the command's output to a variable, and the use of the **echo** and **print** commands. In both instances the result is the same. We again see there is not just one way to accomplish the same task.

We also want to explain how we use **sed** for character substitution. The basic syntax of the **sed** statement that we are going to use is as follows:

```
command | sed s/current_string/new_string/g
```

When we extend our command and pipe the last pipe's output to the **sed** statement we get the following:

```
df -k | tail +2 | egrep -v '/dev/cd[0-9]|/proc' \
    | awk '{print $1, $4, $7}' | sed s/\%//g
```

The point to notice about the preceding **sed** part of the command statement is that we had to *escape* the %, percent sign, with a \, backslash. This is because % is a special character in Unix. To remove the special meaning from, or to escape, the function we use a backslash before the % sign, \%. This lets us literally use % as a text character as opposed to its system-defined value or function. See Listing 5.2.

```
Full Filesystem(s) on yogi

/dev/hd2 mounted on /usr is 96%
/dev/hd10opt mounted on /opt is 97%
```

Listing 5.2 Full filesystem script in action.

This script is okay, but we really are not very concerned about these filesystems being at these current values. The reason is that /usr and /opt, on AIX, should remain static in size. The reason is that /usr is where the OS and application code for the system resides, and /opt, new to AIX 5L as a mount point, is where Linux code resides. So how can we give an exception to these two filesystems?

Adding Exceptions Capability to Monitoring

The fs_mon.ksh script is great for what it is written for, but in the real world we always have to make exceptions and we always strive to cover all of the gotchas when writing shell scripts. Now we are going to add the capability to override the default FSMAX threshold. Because we are going to be able to override the default, it would be really nice to be able to either raise or lower the threshold for individual filesystems.

To accomplish this script tailoring, we need a data file to hold our exceptions. We want to use a data file so that people are not editing the shell script every time a filesystem threshold is to be changed. To make it simple, let's use the file /usr/local/bin/exceptions and point to the file with the EXCEPTIONS variable. Now that we know the name of the file, we need a format for the data in the $EXCEPTIONS file. A good format for this data file is the /mount_point and a NEW_MAX%. We will also want to ignore any entry that is commented out with a pound sign, #. This may sound like a lot, but it is really not too difficult to modify the script code and add a function to read the exceptions file. Now we can set it up.

The Exceptions File

To set up our exceptions file we can always use /usr/local/bin, or your favorite place, as a *bin directory*. To keep things nice we can define a bin directory for the script to use. This is a good thing to do in case the files need to be moved for some reason. The declarations are shown here:

```
BINDIR="/usr/local/bin"
EXCEPTIONS="${BINDIR}/exceptions"
```

Notice the curly braces around the BINDIR variable when it is used to define the EXCEPTIONS file. This is always a good thing to do if the variable name will have a character, which is not associated with the variable's name, next to the variable name without a space. Otherwise, an error may occur that could be very hard to find!

```
EXCEPTIONS="$BINDIR/exceptions"
```

versus

```
EXCEPTIONS="${BINDIR}/exceptions"
```

In all of the ways there are to set up exceptions capability, **grep** seems to come up the most. Please *avoid the grep mistake!* The two fields in the $EXCEPTIONS file are the /mount_point and the NEW_MAX% value. The first instinct is to **grep** on the /mount_point, but what if /mount_point is root, /? If you **grep** on /, and the / entry is not the first entry in the exceptions file, then you will get a pattern match on the wrong entry, and thus use the wrong $NEW_MAX% in deciding if the / mount point is full. In fact, if you grep on / in the exceptions file, you will get a match on the first entry in the file every time. Listing 5.3 shows some *wrong code* that made this very grep mistake:

```
while read FSDEVICE FSVALUE FSMOUNT
do
      # Strip out the % sign if it exists
      FSVALUE=$(echo $FSVALUE | sed s/\%//g) # Remove the % sign
      if [[ -s $EXCEPTIONS ]] # Do we have a non-empty file?
      then # Found it!
          # Look for the current $FSMOUNT value in the file
                #WRONG CODE, DON'T MAKE THIS MISTAKE USING grep!!
          cat $EXCEPTIONS | grep -v "^#" | grep $FSMOUNT \
                          | read FSNAME NEW_MAX
          if [ $? -eq 0 ] # Found it!
          then
              if [[ $FSNAME = $FSMOUNT ]] # Sanity check
              then
                      NEW_MAX=$(echo $NEW_MAX | sed s/\%//g)
                      if [ $FSVALUE -gt $NEW_MAX ] # Use the new $NEW_MAX
                      then
                            echo "$FSDEVICE mount on $FSMOUNT is ${FSVALUE}%" \
                                    >> $OUTFILE
                      fi
              elif [ $FSVALUE -gt $FSMAX ] # Not in $EXCEPTIONS file
              then
```

Listing 5.3   The wrong way to use grep.

```
                       echo "$FSDEVICE mount on $FSMOUNT is ${FSVALUE}%" \
                            >> $OUTFILE
            fi
        fi
    else # No exceptions file...use script default
        if [ $FSVALUE -gt $FSMAX ]
        then
                echo "$FSDEVICE mount on $FSMOUNT is ${FSVALUE}%" \
                     >> $OUTFILE
        fi
    fi
done < $WORKFILE
```

Listing 5.3   The wrong way to use grep. *(continued)*

The code in Listing 5.3 really looks as if it should work, and it does *some of the time*! To get around the error that **grep** introduces, we need to just set up a function that will look for an exact match for each entry in the exceptions file.

Now let's look at this new technique. We want to write two functions, one to load the $EXCEPTIONS file data without the comment lines, the lines beginning with a #, while omitting all blank lines into a data file, and one to search through the exceptions file data and perform the tests.

This is a simple one-line function to load the $EXCEPTIONS file data into the $DATA_EXCEPTIONS file:

```
function load_EXCEPTIONS_file
{
# Ignore any line that begins with a pound sign, #
# and also remove all blank lines

cat $EXCEPTIONS | grep -v "^#" | sed /^$/d > $DATA_EXCEPTIONS
}
```

In the preceding function we use the ^, caret character, along with the **grep -v** to ignore any line beginning with a #, pound sign. We also use the ^$ with the **sed** statement to remove any blank lines and then redirect output to a data file, which is pointed to by the $DATA_EXCEPTIONS variable. After we have the exceptions file data loaded, we have the following check_exceptions function that will look in the $DATA_EXCEPTIONS file for the current mount point and, if found, will check the $NEW_MAX value to the system's reported percent used value. The function will present back to the script a return code relating to the result of the test.

```
function check_exceptions
{
# set -x # Uncomment to debug this function
```

```
while read FSNAME NEW_MAX # Feeding data from Bottom of Loop!!!
do
        if [[ $FSNAME = $FSMOUNT ]] # Correct /mount_point?
        then    # Get rid of the % sign, if it exists!
                NEW_MAX=$(echo $NEW_MAX | sed s/\%//g)

                if [ $FSVALUE -gt $NEW_MAX ]
                then #  Over Limit...Return a "0", zero
                        return 0 # FOUND OVER LIMIT - Return 0
                else #  Found in the file but is within limits
                        return 2 # Found OK
                fi
        fi

done < $DATA_EXCEPTIONS # Feed from the bottom of the loop!!

return 1 # Not found in File
}
```

This check_exceptions function is called during each loop iteration in the main script and returns a 0, zero, if the /mount_point is found to exceed the NEW_MAX%. It will return a 2 if the mount point was found to be OK in the exceptions data file and return a 1, one, if the mount point was not found in the $DATA_EXCEPTIONS file. There are plenty of comments throughout this new script, so feel free to follow through and pick up a few pointers—pay particular attention to the bold text in Listing 5.4.

```
#!/usr/bin/ksh
#
# SCRIPT: fs_mon_AIX_excep.ksh
# AUTHOR: Randy Michael
# DATE: 08-22-2001
# REV: 2.1.P
#
# PURPOSE: This script is used to monitor for full filesystems,
#       which is defined as "exceeding" the FSMAX value.
#       A message is displayed for all "full" filesystems.
#
# PLATFORM: AIX
#
# REV LIST:
#       08-23-2001 - Randy Michael
#       Added code to override the default FSMAX script threshold
#       using an "exceptions" file, defined by the $EXCEPTIONS
#       variable, that list /mount_point and NEW_MAX%
#
# set -n # Uncomment to check syntax without any execution
# set -x # Uncomment to debug this script
```

Listing 5.4   fs_mon_AIX_except.ksh shell script.

```
#
##### DEFINE FILES AND VARIABLES HERE ####

FSMAX="85"                    # Max. FS percentage value

WORKFILE="/tmp/df.work" # Holds filesystem data
>$WORKFILE                    # Initialize to empty
OUTFILE="/tmp/df.outfile" # Output display file
>$OUTFILE             # Initialize to empty
BINDIR="/usr/local/bin" # Local bin directory
THISHOST=`hostname`  # Hostname of this machine

EXCEPTIONS="${BINDIR}/exceptions" # Overrides $FSMAX
DATA_EXCEPTIONS="/tmp/dfdata.out" # Exceptions file w/o #, comments


####### DEFINE FUNCTIONS HERE #####

function load_EXCEPTIONS_file
{
# Ignore any line that begins with a pound sign, #
# and omit all blank lines

cat $EXCEPTIONS |  grep -v "^#" | sed /^$/d > $DATA_EXCEPTIONS
}


####################################

function check_exceptions
{
# set -x # Uncomment to debug this function

while read FSNAME NEW_MAX # Feeding data from Bottom of Loop!!!
do
        if [[ $FSNAME = $FSMOUNT ]] # Correct /mount_point?
        then    # Get rid of the % sign, if it exists!
                NEW_MAX=$(echo $NEW_MAX | sed s/\%//g)

                if [ $FSVALUE -gt $NEW_MAX ]
                then #  Over Limit...Return a "0", zero
                        return 0 # FOUND OUT OF LIMITS - Return 0
                fi
        fi

done < $DATA_EXCEPTIONS # Feed from the bottom of the loop!!

return 1 # Not found in File
}
```

Listing 5.4   fs_mon_AIX_except.ksh shell script. *(continues)*

```
################################################
######## START OF MAIN #############
####################################

# If there is an exceptions file...load it...

[[ -s $EXCEPTIONS ]] && load_EXCEPTIONS_file

# Get the data of interest by stripping out /dev/cd#,
# /proc rows and keeping columns 1, 4, and 7

df -k | tail +2 | egrep -v '/dev/cd[0-9]|/proc' \
   | awk '{print $1, $4, $7}' > $WORKFILE

# Loop through each line of the file and compare column 2

while read FSDEVICE FSVALUE FSMOUNT
do   # Feeding the while loop from the BOTTOM!!

     # Strip out the % sign if it exists
     FSVALUE=$(echo $FSVALUE | sed s/\%//g) # Remove the % sign
     if [[ -s $EXCEPTIONS ]] # Do we have a non-empty file?
     then # Found it!

          # Look for the current $FSMOUNT value in the file
          # using the check_exceptions function defined above.

          check_exceptions
          RC=$? # Get the return code from the function
          if [ $RC -eq 0 ] # Found Exceeded in Exceptions File!!
          then
               echo "$FSDEVICE mount on $FSMOUNT is ${FSVALUE}%" \
                    >> $OUTFILE
          elif [ $RC -eq 1 ] # Not found in exceptions, use defaults
          then
               if [ $FSVALUE -gt $FSMAX ] # Use Script Default
               then
                    echo "$FSDEVICE mount on $FSMOUNT is ${FSVALUE}%" \
                         >> $OUTFILE
               fi
          fi
     else # No exceptions file use the script default
               if [ $FSVALUE -gt $FSMAX ] # Use Script Default
               then
                    echo "$FSDEVICE mount on $FSMOUNT is ${FSVALUE}%" \
                         >> $OUTFILE
```

Listing 5.4   fs_mon_AIX_except.ksh shell script. *(continued)*

```
            fi
    fi
done < $WORKFILE # Feed the while loop from the bottom...

# Display output if anything is exceeded...

if [[ -s $OUTFILE ]]
then
      echo "\nFull Filesystem(s) on ${THISHOST}\n"
      cat $OUTFILE
      print
fi
```

Listing 5.4 fs_mon_AIX_except.ksh shell script. *(continued)*

Notice in the script that we never acted on the return code 2. Because the mount point is found to be OK, there is nothing to do except to check the next mount point. The /usr/local/bin/exceptions file will look something like the script shown in Listing 5.5.

```
# FILE: "exceptions"
# This file is used to override the $FSMAX
# value in the filesystem monitoring script
# fs_mon_excep.ksh.  The syntax to override
# is a /mount-point and a NEW_MAX%:
# EXAMPLE:
# /opt 97
# OR
# /usr 96%
# All lines beginning with a # are ignored as well as
# the % sign, if you want to use one...

/opt 96%
/usr 97
/ 50%
```

Listing 5.5 Example exceptions file.

When we execute the fs_mon_AIX_excep.ksh script, with the exception file entries from Listing 5.5, the output looks like the following on yogi (see Listing 5.6).

```
Full Filesystem(s) on yogi

/dev/hd4 mount on / is 51%
/dev/hd10opt mount on /opt is 97%
```

Listing 5.6 Full filesystem on yogi script in action.

Notice that we added a limit for the root filesystem, /, and set it to 50 percent, and also that this root entry is not at the top of the list in the exceptions file so we have solved the **grep** problem. You should be able to follow the logic through the preceding code to see that we met all of the goals we set out to accomplish in this section. There are plenty of comments to help you understand each step.

Are we finished? Not by a long shot! What about monitoring large filesystems? Using the percentage of filesystem space used is excellent for regular filesystems, but if you have a 10GB filesystem and it is at 90 percent you still have 1GB of free space. Even at 99 percent you have 100MB of space left. For large filesystems we need another monitoring method.

Using the MB of Free Space Method

Sometimes a percentage is just not accurate enough to get the detailed notification that is desired. For these instances, and in the case of large filesystems, we can use **awk** on the **df -k** command output to extract the KB of free space field and compare this to a threshold trigger value, specified in either KB or MB. We are going to modify both of the scripts we have already written to use the KB of free space field.

Remember our previous **df -k** command output:

```
Filesystem       1024-blocks     Free %Used     Iused %Iused Mounted on
/dev/hd4              32768     16376   51%      1663    11% /
/dev/hd2            1212416     57592   96%     36386    13% /usr
/dev/hd9var           53248     30824   43%       540     5% /var
/dev/hd3             106496     99932    7%       135     1% /tmp
/dev/hd1               4096      3916    5%        25     3% /home
/proc                     -         -    -          -     -  /proc
/dev/hd10opt         638976     24456   97%     15457    10% /opt
/dev/scripts_lv      102400     95264    7%       435     2% /scripts
/dev/cd0             656756         0  100%    328378   100% /cdrom
```

Instead of the fourth field of the percentage used, we now want to extract the third field with the 1024-blocks, or KB of *free* space. When someone is working with the script it is best that an easy and familiar measurement is used; the most common is MB of free space. To accomplish this we will need to do a little math, but this is just to have a more familiar measurement to work with. As before, we are going to load the command output into the $WORKFILE, but this time we extract columns $1, $3, and $7.

```
df -k | tail +2 | egrep -v '/dev/cd[0-9]|/proc' \
    | awk '{print $1, $3, $7}' > $WORKFILE
```

We also need a new threshold variable to use for this method. The MIN_MB_FREE variable sounds good. But what is an appropriate value to set the threshold? In this example we are going to use 50MB. It could be any value, though.

```
MIN_MB_FREE="50MB"
```

Notice that we added **MB** to the value. We will remove this later, but it is a good idea to add the measurement type just so that the ones who follow will know that the threshold is in MB. Remember that the system is reporting in KB, so we have to multiply our 50MB times 1024 to get the actual value that is equivalent to the system-reported measurement. We also want to strip out the **MB** letters and typeset the MIN_MB_FREE variable to be an integer. In the compound statement that follows, we take care of everything except typesetting the variable:

```
(( MIN_MB_FREE = $(echo $MIN_MB_FREE | sed s/MB//g) * 1024 ))
```

The order of execution for this compound command is as follows: First, the inner-most $() command substitution is executed, which replaces the letters **MB**, if they exist, with null characters. Next is the evaluation of the math equation and assignment of the result to the MIN_MB_FREE variable. Equating MIN_MB_FREE may seem a little confusing, but remember that the system is reporting in KB so we need to get to the same power of 2 to also report in 1024-byte blocks. Other than these small changes, the script is the same as the original, as shown in Listing 5.7.

```
#!/usr/bin/ksh
#
# SCRIPT: fs_mon_AIX_MBFREE.ksh
# AUTHOR: Randy Michael
# DATE: 08-22-2001
# REV: 1.5.P
# PURPOSE: This script is used to monitor for full filesystems,
#     which is defined as "exceeding" the FSMAX value.
#     A message is displayed for all "full" filesystems.
#
# REV LIST:
#         Randy Michael - 08-27-2001
```

Listing 5.7   fs_mon_AIX_MBFREE.ksh shell script. *(continues)*

```
#           Changed the code to use MB of free space instead of
#           the %Used method.
#
# set -n # Uncomment to check syntax without any execution
# set -x # Uncomment to debug this script
#
##### DEFINE FILES AND VARIABLES HERE ####

MIN_MB_FREE="50MB"       # Min. MB of Free FS Space

WORKFILE="/tmp/df.work" # Holds filesystem data
>$WORKFILE                # Initialize to empty
OUTFILE="/tmp/df.outfile" # Output display file
>$OUTFILE          # Initialize to empty
THISHOST=`hostname`    # Hostname of this machine


######## START OF MAIN #############

# Get the data of interest by stripping out /dev/cd#,
# /proc rows and keeping columns 1, 4 and 7

df -k | tail +2 | egrep -v '/dev/cd[0-9] | /proc' \
   | awk '{print $1, $3, $7}' > $WORKFILE


# Format Variables
(( MIN_MB_FREE = $(echo $MIN_MB_FREE | sed s/MB//g) * 1024 ))

# Loop through each line of the file and compare column 2

while read FSDEVICE FSMB_FREE FSMOUNT
do
     FSMB_FREE=$(echo $FSMB_FREE | sed s/MB//g) # Remove the "MB"
     if (( FSMB_FREE < MIN_MB_FREE ))
     then
         (( FS_FREE_OUT = FSMB_FREE / 1000 ))
         echo "$FSDEVICE mounted on $FSMOUNT only has
     ${FS_FREE_OUT}MB Free" >> $OUTFILE
     fi

done < $WORKFILE  # Feed the while loop from the bottom!!

if [[ -s $OUTFILE ]]
then
     echo "\nFull Filesystem(s) on $THISHOST\n"
     cat $OUTFILE
     print
fi
```

Listing 5.7   fs_mon_AIX_MBFREE.ksh shell script. *(continued)*

```
Full Filesystem(s) on yogi

/dev/hd4 mounted on / only has 16MB Free
/dev/hd9var mounted on /var only has 30MB Free
/dev/hd1 mounted on /home only has 3MB Free
/dev/hd10opt mounted on /opt only has 24MB Free
```

Listing 5.8   Shell script in action.

This output in Listing 5.8 is padded by less than 1 MB due to the fact that we divided the KB free column by 1000 for the output, measured in MB. If the exact KB is needed, then the division by 1000 can be omitted. What about giving this script exception capability to raise or lower the threshold, as we did for the percentage technique? We already have the percentage script with the `check_exception` function so that we can modify this script and function to use the same technique of parsing through the `$EXCEPTIONS` file.

Using MB of Free Space with Exceptions

To add exception capability to the `fs_mon_MBFREE.ksh` shell script, we will again need a function to perform the search of the `$EXCEPTIONS` file, if it exists. This time we will add some extras. We may have the characters **MB** in our data, so we need to allow for this. We also need to test for null characters, or no data, and remove all blank lines in the exception file. The easiest way to use the function is to supply an appropriate return code back to the calling script. We will set the function up to return 1, one, if the mount point is found to be out of limits in the `$DATA_EXCEPTIONS` file. It will return 2 if the `/mount_point` is in the exceptions data file but is *not* out of limits. The function will return 3 if the mount point is not found in the exceptions data file. This will allow us to call the function to check the exception file, and based on the return code, we make a decision in the main body of the script.

We already have experience modifying the script to add exception capability, so this should be a breeze, right? When we finish, the exception modification will be intuitively obvious.

Because we are going to parse through the exceptions file, we need to run a sanity check to see if someone made an incorrect entry and placed a colon, **:**, in the file intending to override the limit on an NFS mounted filesystem. This error should never occur, but because a tester I know did so, I now check and correct the error, if possible. We just **cut** out the second field using the colon, **:**, as a delimiter. Listing 5.9 shows the modified `check_exceptions` function. Check out the highlighted parts in particular.

```
function check_exceptions
{
# set -x # Uncomment to debug this function

while read FSNAME FSLIMIT
do
    # Do an NFS sanity check
    echo $FSNAME | grep ":" >/dev/null \
        && FSNAME=$(echo $FSNAME | cut -d ":" -f2)

    # Make sure we do not have a null value
    if [[ ! -z "$FSLIMIT" && "$FSLIMIT" != '' ]]
    then
        (( FSLIMIT = $(echo $FSLIMIT | sed s/MB//g) * 1024 ))
        if [[ $FSNAME = $FSMOUNT ]]
        then
            # Get rid of the "MB" if it exists
            FSLIMIT=$(echo $FSLIMIT | sed s/MB//g)
            if (( FSMB_FREE < FSLIMIT ))
            then
                return 1 # Found out of limit
            else
                return 2 # Found OK
            fi
        fi
    fi
done < $DATA_EXCEPTIONS # Feed the loop from the bottom!!!

return 3 # Not found in $EXCEPTIONS file
}
```

Listing 5.9 New check_exceptions function.

A few things to notice in this function are the NFS and null value sanity checks as well as the way that we feed the **while** loop from the bottom, after the **done** statement. First, the sanity checks are very important to guard against incorrect NFS entries and blank lines, or null data, in the exceptions file. For the NFS colon check we use the double ampersands, &&, as opposed to **if...then...** statement. It works the same but is cleaner in this type of test. The other point is the null value check. We check for both a zero-length variable and null data. The double ampersands, &&, are called a logical AND function, and the double pipes, ||, are a logical OR function. In a logical AND, &&, all of the command statements must be true for the return code of the entire statement to be 0, zero. In a logical OR, ||, at least one statement must be true for the return code to be 0, zero. When a logical OR receives the first true statement in the test list it will immediately exit the test, or command statement, with a return code of 0, zero.

Both are good to use, but some people find it hard to follow. Next we test for an empty/null variable.

```
if [[ ! -z "$FSLIMIT" && "$FSLIMIT" != '' ]]
```

Note that in the null sanity check there are double quotes around both of the $FSLIMIT variables, "$FSLIMIT". These are required! If you omit the double quotes and the variable is actually null, then the test will fail and a system error message is generated and displayed on the terminal. It never hurts to add double quotes around a variable, and sometimes it is required.

For the **while** loop we go back to our favorite loop structure. Feeding the **while** loop from the bottom, after **done**, is the fastest way to loop through a file line by line. With the sanity checks complete, we just compare some numbers and give back a return code to the calling shell script. Please pay attention to the boldface code in Listing 5.10.

```
#!/usr/bin/ksh
#
# SCRIPT: fs_mon_AIX_MB_FREE_excep.ksh
# AUTHOR: Randy Michael
# DATE: 08-22-2001
# REV: 2.1.P
# PURPOSE: This script is used to monitor for full filesystems,
#      which is defined as "exceeding" the FSMAX value.
#      A message is displayed for all "full" filesystems.
#
# PLATFORM: AIX
#
# REV LIST:
#         Randy Michael - 08-27-2001
#         Changed the code to use MB of free space instead of
#         the %Used method.
#
#         Randy Michael - 08-27-2001
#         Added code to allow you to override the set script default
#         for MIN_MB_FREE of FS Space
#
# set -n # Uncomment to check syntax without any execution
# set -x # Uncomment to debug this script
#
##### DEFINE FILES AND VARIABLES HERE ####

MIN_MB_FREE="50MB"      # Min. MB of Free FS Space

WORKFILE="/tmp/df.work" # Holds filesystem data
>$WORKFILE              # Initialize to empty
OUTFILE="/tmp/df.outfile" # Output display file
```

Listing 5.10 fs_mon_AIX_MB_FREE_excep.ksh shell script. *(continues)*

```
>$OUTFILE         # Initialize to empty
EXCEPTIONS="/usr/local/bin/exceptions" # Override data file
DATA_EXCEPTIONS="/tmp/dfdata.out" # Exceptions file w/o # rows
THISHOST=`hostname`    # Hostname of this machine

####### DEFINE FUNCTIONS HERE ########

function check_exceptions
{
# set -x # Uncomment to debug this function

while read FSNAME FSLIMIT
do
    # Do an NFS sanity check
    echo $FSNAME | grep ":" >/dev/null \
        && FSNAME=$(echo $FSNAME | cut -d ":" -f2)
    if [[ ! -z "$FSLIMIT" && "$FSLIMIT" != '' ]] # Check for empty/null
    then
        (( FSLIMIT = $(echo $FSLIMIT | sed s/MB//g) * 1024 ))
        if [[ $FSNAME = $FSMOUNT ]]
        then
            # Get rid of the "MB" if it exists
            FSLIMIT=$(echo $FSLIMIT | sed s/MB//g)
            if (( FSMB_FREE < FSLIMIT )) # Numerical Test
            then
                return 1 # Found out of limit
            else
                return 2 # Found OK
            fi
        fi
    fi
done < $DATA_EXCEPTIONS # Feed the loop from the bottom!!!

return 3 # Not found in $EXCEPTIONS file
}

######## START OF MAIN #############

# Load the $EXCEPTIONS file if it exists

if [[ -s $EXCEPTIONS ]]
then
    # Ignore all lines beginning with a pound sign, #
    # and omit all blank lines

    cat $EXCEPTIONS | grep -v "^#" | sed /^$/d > $DATA_EXCEPTIONS
fi

# Get the data of interest by stripping out /dev/cd#,
```

Listing 5.10   fs_mon_AIX_MB_FREE_excep.ksh shell script. *(continued)*

```
# /proc rows and keeping columns 1, 4 and 7

df -k | tail +2 | egrep -v '/dev/cd[0-9] | /proc' \
   | awk '{print $1, $3, $7}' > $WORKFILE


# Format Variables for the proper MB value
(( MIN_MB_FREE = $(echo $MIN_MB_FREE | sed s/MB//g) * 1024 ))


# Loop through each line of the file and compare column 2

while read FSDEVICE FSMB_FREE FSMOUNT
do
    if [[ -s $EXCEPTIONS ]]
    then
      check_exceptions
      RC="$?"  # Check the Return Code!
      if (( RC == 1 )) # Found out of exceptions limit
      then
          (( FS_FREE_OUT = $FSMB_FREE / 1000 ))
          echo "$FSDEVICE mounted on $FSMOUNT only has\
 ${FS_FREE_OUT}MB Free" \
                >> $OUTFILE
      elif (( RC == 2 )) # Found in exceptions to be OK
      then # Just a sanity check - We really do nothing here...
          # The colon, :, is a NO-OP operator in KSH


          : # No-Op - Do Nothing!

      elif (( RC == 3 )) # Not found in the exceptions file
      then
          FSMB_FREE=$(echo $FSMB_FREE | sed s/MB//g) # Remove the "MB"
          if (( FSMB_FREE < MIN_MB_FREE ))
          then
              (( FS_FREE_OUT = FSMB_FREE / 1000 ))
              echo "$FSDEVICE mounted on $FSMOUNT only has\
 ${FS_FREE_OUT}MB Free" >> $OUTFILE
          fi
      fi
    else # No Exceptions file use the script default
      FSMB_FREE=$(echo $FSMB_FREE | sed s/MB//g) # Remove the "MB"
      if (( FSMB_FREE < MIN_MB_FREE ))
      then
          (( FS_FREE_OUT = FSMB_FREE / 1000 ))
          echo "$FSDEVICE mounted on $FSMOUNT only has\
 ${FS_FREE_OUT}MB Free" >> $OUTFILE
      fi
    fi
done < $WORKFILE
```

Listing 5.10 fs_mon_AIX_MB_FREE_excep.ksh shell script. *(continues)*

```
if [[ -s $OUTFILE ]]
then
        echo "\nFull Filesystem(s) on $THISHOST\n"
        cat $OUTFILE
        print
fi
```

Listing 5.10   fs_mon_AIX_MB_FREE_excep.ksh shell script. *(continued)*

The script in Listing 5.10 is good, and we have covered all of the bases, right? If you want to stop here, you will be left with an incomplete picture of what we can accomplish. There are several more things to consider, and, of course, there are many more ways to do any of these tasks, and no one is *correct*. Let's consider mixing the filesystem percentage used and the MB of free filesystem space techniques. With a mechanism to auto-detect the way we select the usage, the filesystem monitoring script could be a much more robust tool—and a *must-have* tool where you have a mix of regular and large filesystems to monitor.

Percentage Used—MB Free and Large Filesystems

Now we're talking! Even if most of your filesystems are large file enabled or are just huge in size, the small ones will still kill you in the end. For a combination of small and large filesystems, we need a mix of both the percent used and MB of free space techniques. For this combination to work, we need a way to auto-detect the *correct usage*, which we still need to define. There are different combinations of these auto-detect techniques that can make the monitoring work differently. For the large filesystems we want to use the MB of free space, and for regular filesystems we use the percentage method.

We need to define a *trigger* that allows for this free space versus percentage monitoring transformation. The trigger value will vary by environment, but this example uses 1GB as the transition point from percentage used to MB of free space. Of course, the value should be more like 4–6GB, but we need an example. We also need to consider how the $EXCEPTIONS file is going to look. Options for the exceptions file are a combined file or two separate files, one for percentage used and one for MB free. The obvious choice is one combined file. What are combined entries to look like? How are we going to handle the wrong entry *type*? The entries need to conform to the specific test type the script is looking for. The best way to handle this is to require that either a **%** or **MB** be added as a suffix to each new entry in the exceptions file. With the **MB** or

% suffix we could override not only the triggering level, but also the testing method! If an entry has only a number without the suffix, then this exceptions file entry will be ignored and the shell script's default values will be used. This suffix method is the most flexible, but it, too, is prone to mistakes in the exceptions file. For the mistakes, we need to test the entries in the exceptions to see that they conform to the standard that we have decided on.

The easiest way to create this new, more robust script is to take large portions of the previous scripts and convert them into functions. We can simply insert the word *function* followed by a function name and enclose the code within curly braces—for example, `function test_function { `*function_code*` }`. Or if you prefer the C-type function method, we can use this example, `test_function () { `*function_code*` }`. The only difference between the two function methods is one uses the word *function* to define the function while the other just adds a set of parentheses after the function's name. When we use functions, it is easy to set up a logical framework from which to call the functions. It is always easiest to set up the framework first and then fill in the middle. The *logic code* for this script will look like Listing 5.11.

```
load_File_System_data > $WORKFILE
if EXCEPTIONS_FILE exists and is > 0 size
then
    load_EXCEPTIONS_FILE_data
fi
while read $WORKFILE, which has the filesystem data
do
    if EXCEPTIONS data was loaded
    then
        check_exceptions_file
        RC=Get Return code back from function
        case $RC in
            1) Found exceeded by % method
            2) Found out-of-limit by MB Free method
            3) Found OK in exceptions file by a testing method
            4) Not found in exceptions file
        esac
    else # No exceptions file
        Use script defaults to compare
    fi
done

if we have anything out of limits
then
    display_output
fi
```

Listing 5.11   Logic code for a large and small filesystem freespace script.

This is very straightforward and easy to do with functions. From this logical description we already have the main body of the script written. Now we just need to modify the check_exceptions function to handle both types of data and create the load_FS_data, load_EXCEPTIONS_data, and display_output functions. For this script we are also going to do things a little differently because this *is* a learning process. As we all know, there are many ways to accomplish the same task in Unix; shell scripting is a prime example. To make our scripts a little easier to read at a glance, we are going to change how we do numeric test comparisons. We currently use the standard bracketed test functions with the numeric operators, -lt, -le, -eq, -ne, -ge, and -gt:

```
if [ $VAR1 -gt $VAR2 ]
```

We are now going to use the bracketed tests for character strings only and do all of our numerical comparisons with the double parentheses method:

```
if (( VAR1 > VAR2 ))
```

The operators for this method are <, <=, ==, !=, >=, >. When we make this small change, it makes the script much easier to follow because we know immediately that we are dealing with either numeric data or a character string without knowing much at all about the data being tested. Notice that we did *not* reference the variables with a $ (dollar sign) for the numeric tests. The $ omission is not the only difference, but it is the most obvious. The $ is omitted because it is implied that anything that is not numeric is a variable. Other things to look for in this script are compound tests, math and math within tests, the use of curly braces with variables, ${VAR1}MB, a no-op using a : (colon), data validation, error checking, and error notification. These variables are a lot to look for, but you can learn much from studying the script shown in Listing 5.12.

Just remember that all functions must be defined before they can be used! Failure to define functions is the most common mistake when working with them. The second most common mistake has to do with *scope*. Scope deals with *where* a variable and its value are known to other scripts and functions. *Top level down* is the best way to describe where scope lies. The basic rules say that *all* of a shell script's variables are known to the *internal*, lower-level, functions, but *none* of the function's variables are known to any *higher-calling* script or function, thus the top level down definition. We will cover a method called a co-process of dealing with scope in a later chapter.

So, in this script the check_exceptions function will use the *global* script's variables, which are known to all of the functions, and the function will, in turn, reply with a return code, as we defined in the logic flow of Listing 5.11. Scope is a very important concept, as is the placement of the function in the script. The comments in this script are extensive, so please study the code and pay particular attention to the boldface text.

NOTE Remember: You have to define a function before you can use it.

```
#!/usr/bin/ksh
#
# SCRIPT: fs_mon_AIX_PC_MBFREE_excep.ksh
# AUTHOR: Randy Michael
# DATE: 08-22-2001
# REV: 4.3.P
# PURPOSE: This script is used to monitor for full filesystems,
#     which is defined as "exceeding" the MAX_PERCENT value.
#     A message is displayed for all "full" filesystems.
#
# PLATFORM: AIX
#
# REV LIST:
#          Randy Michael - 08-27-2001
#          Changed the code to use MB of free space instead of
#          the %Used method.
#
#          Randy Michael - 08-27-2001
#          Added code to allow you to override the set script default
#          for MIN_MB_FREE of FS Space
#
#          Randy Michael - 08-28-2001
#          Changed the code to handle both %Used and MB of Free Space.
#          It does an "auto-detection" but has override capability
#          of both the trigger level and the monitoring method using
#          the exceptions file pointed to by the $EXCEPTIONS variable
#
# set -n # Uncomment to check syntax without any execution
# set -x # Uncomment to debug this script
#
##### DEFINE FILES AND VARIABLES HERE ####

MIN_MB_FREE="100MB"     # Min. MB of Free FS Space
MAX_PERCENT="85%"       # Max. FS percentage value
FSTRIGGER="1000MB"      # Trigger to switch from % Used to MB Free

WORKFILE="/tmp/df.work" # Holds filesystem data
>$WORKFILE              # Initialize to empty
OUTFILE="/tmp/df.outfile" # Output display file
>$OUTFILE              # Initialize to empty
EXCEPTIONS="/usr/local/bin/exceptions" # Override data file
DATA_EXCEPTIONS="/tmp/dfdata.out" # Exceptions file w/o # rows
EXCEPT_FILE="N"        # Assume no $EXCEPTIONS FILE
```

Listing 5.12 fs_mon_AIX_PC_MBFREE_excep.ksh shell script. *(continues)*

```
THISHOST=`hostname`      # Hostname of this machine

###### FORMAT VARIABLES HERE ######

# Both of these variables need to be multiplied by 1024 blocks
(( MIN_MB_FREE = $(echo $MIN_MB_FREE | sed s/MB//g) * 1024 ))
(( FSTRIGGER = $(echo $FSTRIGGER | sed s/MB//g)  * 1024 ))

####### DEFINE FUNCTIONS HERE ########

function check_exceptions
{
# set -x # Uncomment to debug this function

while read FSNAME FSLIMIT
do
    IN_FILE="N"  # If found in file, which test type to use?

    # Do an NFS sanity check and get rid of any ":".
    # If this is found it is actually an error entry
    # but we will try to resolve it.  It will
    # work only if it is an NFS cross mount to the same
    # mount point on both machines.
    echo $FSNAME | grep ':' >/dev/null \
        && FSNAME=$(echo $FSNAME | cut -d ':' -f2)

    # Check for empty and null variable
    if [[ ! -z "$FSLIMIT" && "$FSLIMIT" != '' ]]
    then
        if [[ $FSNAME = $FSMOUNT ]] # Found it!
        then
            # Check for "MB" Characters...Set IN_FILE=MB
            echo $FSLIMIT | grep MB >/dev/null && IN_FILE="MB" \
                && (( FSLIMIT = $(echo $FSLIMIT \
                    | sed s/MB//g) * 1024 ))
            # check for "%" Character...Set IN_FILE=PC, for %
            echo $FSLIMIT | grep "%" >/dev/null && IN_FILE="PC" \
                && FSLIMIT=$(echo $FSLIMIT | sed s/\%//g)

            case $IN_FILE in
            MB) # Use Megabytes of free space to test
                # Up-case the characters, if they exist
                FSLIMIT=$(echo $FSLIMIT | tr '[a-z]' '[A-Z]')
                # Get rid of the "MB" if it exists
                FSLIMIT=$(echo $FSLIMIT | sed s/MB//g)
                # Test for blank and null values
                if [[ ! -z $FSLIMIT && $FSLIMIT != '' ]]
```

Listing 5.12   fs_mon_AIX_PC_MBFREE_excep.ksh shell script. *(continued)*

```
                    then
                        # Test for a valid filesystem "MB" limit
                        if (( FSLIMIT >= 0 && FSLIMIT < FSSIZE ))
                        then # Check the limit
                           if (( FSMB_FREE < FSLIMIT ))
                           then
                               return 1 # Found out of limit
                                        # using MB Free method
                           else
                               return 3 # Found OK
                           fi
                        else
                           echo "\nERROR: Invalid filesystem MAX for\
$FSMOUNT - $FSLIMIT"
                           echo "         Exceptions file value must be\
less than or"
                           echo "         equal to the size of the filesystem\
measured"
                           echo "         in 1024 bytes\n"
                        fi
                    else
                        echo "\nERROR: Null value specified in exceptions\
file"
                        echo "         for the $FSMOUNT mount point.\n"
                    fi
                    ;;
              PC) # Use the Percent used method to test
                    # Strip out the % sign if it exists
                    PC_USED=$(echo $PC_USED | sed s/\%//g)
                    # Test for blank and null values
                    if [[ ! -z $FSLIMIT && $FSLIMIT != '' ]]
                    then
                        # Test for a valid percentage, i.e. 0-100
                        if (( FSLIMIT >= 0 && FSLIMIT <= 100 ))
                        then
                           if (( PC_USED > FSLIMIT ))
                           then
                               return 2 # Found exceeded by % Used method
                           else
                               return 3 # Found OK
                           fi
                        else
                           echo "\nERROR: Invalid percentage for\
$FSMOUNT - $FSLIMIT"
                           echo "         Exceptions file values must be"
                           echo "         between 0 and 100%\n"
                        fi
```

Listing 5.12   fs_mon_AIX_PC_MBFREE_excep.ksh shell script. *(continues)*

```
                        else
                            echo "\nERROR: Null value specified in exceptions"
                            echo "          file for the $FSMOUNT mount point.\n"
                        fi
                        ;;
                N)  # Test type not specified in exception file, use default

                    # Inform the user of the exceptions file error...
                    echo "\nERROR: Missing testing type in exceptions file"
                    echo "          for the $FSMOUNT mount point.  A \"%\" or"
                    echo "          \"MB\" must be a suffix to the numerical"
                    echo "          entry.  Using script default values...\n"

                    # Method Not Specified - Use Script Defaults
                    if (( FSSIZE >= FSTRIGGER ))
                    then # This is a "large" filesystem
                        if (( FSMB_FREE < MIN_MB_FREE ))
                        then
                            return 1 # Found out of limit using MB Free
                        else
                            return 3 # Found OK
                        fi
                    else # This is a standard filesystem
                        PC_USED=$(echo $PC_USED | sed s/\%//g) #Remove the %
                        FSLIMIT=$(echo $FSLIMIT | sed s/\%//g) #Remove the %
                        if (( PC_USED > FSLIMIT ))
                        then
                            return 2 # Found exceeded by % Used method
                        else
                            return 3 # Found OK
                        fi
                    fi
                    ;;
                esac
            fi
        fi
done < $DATA_EXCEPTIONS # Feed the loop from the bottom!!!

return 4 # Not found in $EXCEPTIONS file
}

#######################################

function display_output
{
if [[ -s $OUTFILE ]]
then
```

Listing 5.12   fs_mon_AIX_PC_MBFREE_excep.ksh shell script. *(continued)*

```
            echo "\nFull Filesystem(s) on $THISHOST\n"
            cat $OUTFILE
            print
fi
}

######################################

function load_EXCEPTIONS_data
{
# Ignore any line that begins with a pound sign, #
# and omit all blank lines

cat $EXCEPTIONS |  grep -v "^#" | sed /^$/d > $DATA_EXCEPTIONS
}

######################################

function load_FS_data
{
   df -k | tail +2 | egrep -v '/dev/cd[0-9]|/proc' \
         | awk '{print $1, $2, $3, $4, $7}' > $WORKFILE
}

######################################
######### START OF MAIN ###########
######################################

load_FS_data

# Do we have a nonzero size $EXCEPTIONS file?

if [[ -s $EXCEPTIONS ]]
then # Found a nonempty $EXCEPTIONS file

    load_EXCEPTIONS_data
    EXCEP_FILE="Y"
fi

while read FSDEVICE FSSIZE FSMB_FREE PC_USED FSMOUNT
do
    if [[ $EXCEP_FILE = "Y" ]]
    then
        check_exceptions
        CE_RC="$?" # Check Exceptions Return Code (CE_RC)

        case $CE_RC in
```

Listing 5.12   fs_mon_AIX_PC_MBFREE_excep.ksh shell script. *(continues)*

```
         1) # Found exceeded in exceptions file by MB Method
            (( FS_FREE_OUT = FSMB_FREE / 1000 ))
            echo "$FSDEVICE mounted on $FSMOUNT has ${FS_FREE_OUT}MB\
Free" \
                >> $OUTFILE
         ;;
         2) # Found exceeded in exceptions file by %Used method
            echo "$FSDEVICE mount on $FSMOUNT is ${PC_USED}%" \
                >> $OUTFILE
         ;;
         3) # Found OK in exceptions file
            : # NO-OP Do Nothing
         ;;

         4) # Not found in exceptions file - Use Script Default Triggers
            if (( FSSIZE >= FSTRIGGER ))
            then # This is a "large" filesystem
              # Remove the "MB", if it exists
              FSMB_FREE=$(echo $FSMB_FREE | sed s/MB//g)
              typeset -i FSMB_FREE
              if (( FSMB_FREE < MIN_MB_FREE ))
              then
                (( FS_FREE_OUT = FSMB_FREE / 1000 ))
                echo "$FSDEVICE mounted on $FSMOUNT has\
${FS_FREE_OUT}MB Free" >> $OUTFILE
              fi
            else # This is a standard filesystem
                PC_USED=$(echo $PC_USED | sed s/\%//g)
                MAX_PERCENT=$(echo $MAX_PERCENT | sed s/\%//g)
                if (( PC_USED > MAX_PERCENT ))
                then
                    echo "$FSDEVICE mount on $FSMOUNT is ${PC_USED}%" \
                        >> $OUTFILE
                fi
            fi
         ;;
        esac

    else # NO $EXECPTIONS FILE USE DEFAULT TRIGGER VALUES

        if (( FSSIZE >= FSTRIGGER  ))
        then # This is a "large" filesystem - Use MB Free Method
          FSMB_FREE=$(echo $FSMB_FREE | sed s/MB//g) # Remove the "MB"
          if (( FSMB_FREE < MIN_MB_FREE ))
          then
            (( FS_FREE_OUT = FSMB_FREE / 1000 ))
            echo "$FSDEVICE mounted on $FSMOUNT has\
```

Listing 5.12   fs_mon_AIX_PC_MBFREE_excep.ksh shell script. *(continued)*

```
      ${FS_FREE_OUT}MB Free" >> $OUTFILE
               fi
          else # This is a standard filesystem - Use % Used Method
               PC_USED=$(echo $PC_USED | sed s/\%//g)
               MAX_PERCENT=$(echo $MAX_PERCENT | sed s/\%//g)
               if (( PC_USED > MAX_PERCENT ))
               then
                    echo "$FSDEVICE mount on $FSMOUNT is ${PC_USED}%" \
                         >> $OUTFILE
               fi
          fi
     fi
done < $WORKFILE # Feed the while loop from the bottom!!!

display_output

# End of Script
```

Listing 5.12   fs_mon_AIX_PC_MBFREE_excep.ksh shell script. *(continued)*

In the script shown in Listing 5.12, we made tests to confirm the data's integrity and for mistakes in the exceptions file (of course, we can go only so far with mistakes!). The reason is that we made the exceptions file more complicated to use. Two of my testers consistently had reverse logic on the MB free override option of the script by thinking *greater than* instead of *less than*. From this confusion, a new exceptions file was created that explained what the script is looking for and gave example entries. Of course, all of these lines begin with a pound sign, #, so they are ignored when data is loaded into the $DATA_EXCEPTIONS file. Listing 5.13 shows the exceptions file that worked best with the testers.

```
# FILE: "exceptions"
#
# This file is used to override both the default
# trigger value in the filesystem monitoring script
# fs_mon_excep.ksh, but also allows overriding the
# monitoring technique used, i.e. Max %Used and
# minimum MB of filesystem space.  The syntax to
# override is a /mount-point and a trigger value.
#
# EXAMPLES:
#
# /usr 96%  # Flag anything ABOVE 96%
# OR
```

Listing 5.13   Example exceptions file. *(continues)*

```
# /usr 50MB # Flag anything BELOW 50 Megabytes
#
# All lines beginning with a # are ignored.
#
# NOTE: All Entries MUST have either "MB" or
#        "%" as a suffix!!!  Or else the script
#        defaults are used.  NO SPACES PLEASE!
#
/opt 95%
/ 50%
/usr 70MB
```

Listing 5.13   Example exceptions file. *(continued)*

The requirement for either **%** or **MB** does help keep the entry mistakes down. In case mistakes are made, the error notifications seemed to get these cleared up very quickly—usually after an initial run. You can find customized shell scripts for each of the operating systems (AIX, HP-UX, Linux, and SunOS) on this book's Web site.

Are we finished with filesystem monitoring? No way! What about the other three operating systems that we want to monitor? We need to be able to execute this script on AIX, Linux, HP-UX, and Solaris without the need to change the script on each platform.

Running on AIX, Linux, HP-UX, and Solaris

Can we run the filesystem scripts on various Unix flavors? You bet! Running our filesystem monitoring script is very easy because we used functions for most of the script. We are going to use the same script, but instead of hard-coding the loading of the filesystem data, we need to use variables to point to the correct OS syntax and columns of interest. Now we need a new function that will determine which flavor of Unix we are running. Based on the OS, we set up the command syntax and command output columns of interest that we want to extract and load the filesystem data for this particular OS. For OS determination we just use the **uname** command. **uname**, and the get_OS_info function, will return the resident operating system, as shown in Table 5.1.

Table 5.1   uname Command and Function Results

OPERATING SYSTEM	COMMAND RESULT	FUNCTION RESULT
Linux	Linux	LINUX
AIX	AIX	AIX
HP-UX	HP-UX	HP-UX
Solaris	SunOS	SUNOS

For the function's output we want to use all UPPERCASE characters, which makes testing much easier. In the following function please notice we use the **typeset** function to ensure that the result is in all uppercase characters.

```
function get_OS_info
{
# For a few commands it is necessary to know the OS to
# execute the proper command syntax.  This will always
# return the Operating System in UPPERCASE characters

typeset -u OS  # Use the UPPERCASE values for the OS variable
OS=`uname`     # Grab the Operating system, i.e. AIX, HP-UX
print $OS      # Send back the UPPERCASE value
}
```

To use the `get_OS_info` function we can assign it to a variable using command substitution, use the function directly in a command statement, or redirect the output to a file. For this script modification we are going to use the `get_OS_info` function directly in a **case** statement. Now we need four different `load_FS_data` functions, one for each of the four operating systems, and that is all of the modification that is needed. Each of the `load_FS_data` functions will be unique in command syntax and the column fields to extract from the **df** statement output, as well as the devices to exclude from testing. Because we wrote this script using functions, we will replace the original `load_FS_data` script, at the `Beginning of Main`, with a **case** statement that utilizes the `get_OS_info` function. The **case** statement will execute the appropriate `load_FS_data` function.

```
case $(get_OS_info) in
    AIX)   # Load filesystem data for AIX
           load_AIX_FS_data
       ;;
    HP-UX) # Load filesystem data for HP-UX
           load_HP_UX_FS_data
       ;;
    LINUX) # Load filesystem data for Linux
           load_LINUX_FS_data
       ;;
    SUNOS) # Load filesystem data for Solaris
           load_Solaris_FS_data
       ;;
    *)     # Unsupported in script
           echo "\nUnsupported Operating System...EXITING\n"
           exit 1
esac
```

Listing 5.14   Operating system test.

Listing 5.14 shows simple enough replacement code. In this **case** statement we either execute one of the functions or exit if the OS is not in the list with a return code of 1, one. In these functions we will want to pay attention to the command syntax for each operating system, the columns to extract for the desired data, and the filesystems that we want to ignore, if any. There is an **egrep**, or extended **grep**, in each statement that will allow for exclusions to the filesystems that are monitored. A typical example of this is a CD-ROM. Remember that a CD-ROM will always show that it is 100% utilized because it is mounted as read-only and you cannot write to it. Also, some operating systems list *mount points* that are really not meant to be monitored, such as /proc in AIX 5L.

Command Syntax and Output Varies between Operating Systems

The command syntax and command output varies between Unix operating systems. To get a similar output of the AIX **df -k** command on other operating systems we sometimes have to change the command syntax. We also extract data from different columns in the output. The command syntax and resulting output for AIX, Linux, HP-UX, and SUN/Solaris are listed in the text that follows as well as the columns of interest for each operating system output. Please review Tables 5.2 through 5.9.

Table 5.2 AIX df -k Command Output

FILESYSTEM	1024-BLOCKS	FREE	%USED	IUSED	%IUSED	MOUNTED ON
/dev/hd4	32768	16376	51%	1663	11%	/
/dev/hd2	1212416	57592	96%	36386	13%	/usr
/dev/hd9var	53248	30824	43%	540	5%	/var
/dev/hd3	106496	99932	7%	135	1%	/tmp
/dev/hd1	4096	3916	5%	25	%	/home
/proc						/proc
/dev/hd10opt	638976	24456	97%	15457	10%	/opt
/dev/scripts_lv	102400	95264	7%	435	2%	/scripts
/dev/cd0	656756	0	100%	328378	100%	/cdrom

Table 5.3 AIX df Output Columns of Interest

DF OUTPUT COLUMNS	COLUMN CONTENTS
Column 1	The filesystem device name, Filesystem
Column 2	The size of the filesystem in 1024 blocks, 1024-blocks
Column 3	The kilobytes of free filesystem space, Free
Column 4	The percentage of used capacity, %Used
Column 7	The mount point of the filesystem, Mounted on

Table 5.4 Linux df -k Command Output

FILESYSTEM	1K-BLOCKS	USED	AVAILABLE	USE%	MOUNTED ON
/dev/hda16	101089	32949	62921	34%	/
/dev/hda5	1011928	104	960420	0%	/backup
/dev/hda1	54416	2647	48960	5%	/boot
/dev/hda8	202220	13	191767	0%	/download
/dev/hda9	202220	1619	190161	1%	/home
/dev/hda12	124427	19	117984	0%	/tmp
/dev/hda6	1011928	907580	52944	94% /usr	—
/dev/hda10	155545	36	147479	0%	/usr/local
/dev/hda11	124427	29670	88333	25%/var	

Table 5.5 Linux df Output Columns of Interest

DF OUTPUT COLUMNS	COLUMN CONTENTS
Column 1	The filesystem device name, Filesystem
Column 2	The size of the filesystem in 1k-blocks, 1k-blocks
Column 4	The kilobytes of free filesystem space, Available
Column 5	The percentage of used capacity, Use%
Column 6	The mount point of the filesystem, Mounted on

Table 5.6 SUN/Solaris df -k Command Output

FILESYSTEM	KBYTES	USED	AVAIL	CAPACITY	MOUNTED ON
/dev/dsk/c0d0s0	192423	18206	154975	11%	
/dev/dsk/c0d0s6	1015542	488678	465932	52%	/usr
/proc	0	0	0	0%	/proc
fd	0	0	0	0%	/dev/fd
mnttab	0	0	0	0%	/etc/mnttab
/dev/dsk/c0d0s3	96455	5931	80879	7%	/var
swap	554132	0	55413	0%	/var/run
/dev/dsk/c0d0s5	47975	1221	41957	3%	/opt
swap	554428	296	554132	1%	/tmp
/dev/dsk/c0d0s7	1015542	1	954598	1%	/export/home
/dev/dsk/c0d0s1	375255	214843	122887	64%	/usr/openwin

Table 5.7 SUN/Solaris df òk Output Columns of Interest

DF OUTPUT COLUMNS	COLUMN CONTENTS
Column 1	The filesystem device name, Filesystem
Column 2	The size of the filesystem in 1k-blocks, kbytes
Column 4	The kilobytes of free filesystem space, avail
Column 5	The percentage of used capacity, capacity
Column 6	The mount point of the filesystem, Mounted on

Table 5.8 HP-UX bdf Command Output

FILESYSTEM	KBYTES	USED	AVAIL	%USED	MOUNTED ON
/dev/vg00/lvol3	151552	89500	58669	60%	/
/dev/vg00/lvol1	47829	24109	18937	56%	/stand
/dev/vg00/lvol9	1310720	860829	422636	67%	/var
/dev/vg00/lvol8	972800	554392	392358	59%	/usr

Table 5.8   *(Continued)*

FILESYSTEM	KBYTES	USED	AVAIL	%USED	MOUNTED ON
/dev/vg13/lvol1	4190208	1155095	2850597	29%	/u2
/dev/vg00/lvol7	102400	4284	92256	4%	/tmp
/dev/vg00/lvol13	2039808	1664073	352294	83%	/test2
/dev/vg00/lvol6	720896	531295	177953	75%	/opt
/dev/vg00/lvol5	409600	225464	176663	56%	/home

Table 5.9   HP-UX `bdf` Output Columns of Interest

DF OUTPUT COLUMNS	COLUMN CONTENTS
Column 1	The filesystem device name, `Filesystem`
Column 2	The size of the filesystem in 1k-blocks, `kbytes`
Column 4	The kilobytes of free filesystem space, `avail`
Column 5	The percentage of used capacity, `%used`
Column 6	The mount point of the filesystem, `Mounted on`

Now that we know how the commands and output vary between operating systems, we can take this into account when creating the shell functions to load the correct filesystem data for each system. Note in each of the following functions that one or more filesystems or devices are set to be ignored, which is specified by the **egrep** part of the statement.

```
####################################

function load_AIX_FS_data
{
   df -k | tail +2 | egrep -v '/dev/cd[0-9]|/proc' \
        | awk '{print $1, $2, $3, $4, $7}' > $WORKFILE
}

####################################

function load_HP_UX_FS_data
{
   bdf | tail +2 | egrep -v '/mnt/cdrom' \
        | awk '{print $1, $2, $4, $5, $6}' > $WORKFILE
```

```
}

######################################

function load_LINUX_FS_data
{
   df -k | tail +2 | egrep -v '/mnt/cdrom'\
        | awk '{print $1, $2, $4, $5, $6}' > $WORKFILE
}


######################################

function load_Solaris_FS_data
{
   df -k | tail +2 | egrep -v '/dev/fd|/etc/mnttab|/proc'\
        | awk '{print $1, $2, $4, $5, $6}' > $WORKFILE
}
```

Each Unix system is different, and these functions may need to be modified for your particular environment. The script modification to execute on all of the four operating systems includes entering the functions into the top part of the script, where functions are defined, and to replace the current `load_FS_data` function with a **case** statement that utilizes the `get_OS_info` function. This is an excellent example of how using functions can make life doing modifications much easier. The *final* script (it is never a final script!) will look like the following code, shown in Listing 5.15. Please scan through the boldface text in detail.

```
#!/usr/bin/ksh
#
# SCRIPT: fs_mon_ALL_OS.ksh
# AUTHOR: Randy Michael
# DATE: 08-22-2001
# REV: 5.1.D
#
# PURPOSE: This script is used to monitor for full filesystems,
#     which are defined as "exceeding" the MAX_PERCENT value.
#     A message is displayed for all "full" filesystems.
#
# PLATFORM: AIX, Linux, HP-UX and Solaris
#
# REV LIST:
#         Randy Michael - 08-27-2001
#         Changed the code to use MB of free space instead of
#         the %Used method.
#
#         Randy Michael - 08-27-2001
#         Added code to allow you to override the set script default
```

Listing 5.15   fs_mon_ALL_OS.ksh shell script.

```
#              for MIN_MB_FREE of FS Space
#
#              Randy Michael - 08-28-2001
#              Changed the code to handle both %Used and MB of Free Space.
#              It does an "auto-detection" but has override capability
#              of both the trigger level and the monitoring method using
#              the exceptions file pointed to by the $EXCEPTIONS variable
#
#              Randy Michael - 08-28-2001
#              Added code to allow this script to be executed on
#              AIX, Linux, HP-UX, and Solaris
#
# set -n # Uncomment to check syntax without any execution
# set -x # Uncomment to debug this script
#
##### DEFINE FILES AND VARIABLES HERE ####


MIN_MB_FREE="100MB"      # Min. MB of Free FS Space
MAX_PERCENT="85%"        # Max. FS percentage value
FSTRIGGER="1000MB"       # Trigger to switch from % Used to MB Free


WORKFILE="/tmp/df.work" # Holds filesystem data
>$WORKFILE               # Initialize to empty
OUTFILE="/tmp/df.outfile" # Output display file
>$OUTFILE                # Initialize to empty
EXCEPTIONS="/usr/local/bin/exceptions" # Override data file
DATA_EXCEPTIONS="/tmp/dfdata.out" # Exceptions file w/o # rows
EXCEPT_FILE="N"          # Assume no $EXCEPTIONS FILE
THISHOST=`hostname`      # Hostname of this machine


###### FORMAT VARIABLES HERE ######


# Both of these variables need to be multiplied by 1024 blocks
(( MIN_MB_FREE = $(echo $MIN_MB_FREE | sed s/MB//g) * 1024 ))
(( FSTRIGGER = $(echo $FSTRIGGER | sed s/MB//g)  * 1024 ))


#######################################
####### DEFINE FUNCTIONS HERE ########
#######################################


function get_OS_info
{
# For a few commands it is necessary to know the OS and its level
# to execute the proper command syntax.  This will always return
# the OS in UPPERCASE

typeset -u OS    # Use the UPPERCASE values for the OS variable
OS=`uname`       # Grab the Operating system, i.e. AIX, HP-UX
```

Listing 5.15 fs_mon_ALL_OS.ksh shell script. *(continues)*

```
print $OS     # Send back the UPPERCASE value
}


######################################

function check_exceptions
{
# set -x # Uncomment to debug this function

while read FSNAME FSLIMIT
do
    IN_FILE="N"

    # Do an NFS sanity check and get rid of any ":".
    # If this is found it is actually an error entry
    # but we will try to resolve it.  It will only
    # work if it is an NFS cross mount to the same
    # mount point on both machines.
    echo $FSNAME | grep ':' >/dev/null \
        && FSNAME=$(echo $FSNAME | cut -d ':' -f2)

    # Check for empty and null variable
    if [[ ! -z $FSLIMIT && $FSLIMIT != '' ]]
    then
        if [[ $FSNAME = $FSMOUNT ]] # Found it!
        then
            # Check for "MB" Characters...Set IN_FILE=MB
          echo $FSLIMIT | grep MB >/dev/null && IN_FILE="MB" \
                && (( FSLIMIT = $(echo $FSLIMIT \
                    | sed s/MB//g) * 1024 ))
            # check for "%" Character...Set IN_FILE=PC, for %
          echo $FSLIMIT | grep "%" >/dev/null && IN_FILE="PC" \
                && FSLIMIT=$(echo $FSLIMIT | sed s/\%//g)

            case $IN_FILE in
            MB) # Use MB of Free Space Method
                # Up-case the characters, if they exist
                FSLIMIT=$(echo $FSLIMIT | tr '[a-z]' '[A-Z]')
                # Get rid of the "MB" if it exists
                FSLIMIT=$(echo $FSLIMIT | sed s/MB//g)
                # Test for blank and null values
                if [[ ! -z $FSLIMIT && $FSLIMIT != '' ]]
                then
                    # Test for a valid filesystem "MB" limit
                    if (( FSLIMIT >= 0 && FSLIMIT < FSSIZE ))
                    then
                        if (( FSMB_FREE < FSLIMIT ))
                        then
```

Listing 5.15 fs_mon_ALL_OS.ksh shell script. *(continued)*

```
                              return 1 # Found out of limit
                                       # using MB Free method
                         else
                              return 3 # Found OK
                         fi
                    else
                         echo "\nERROR: Invalid filesystem MAX for\
$FSMOUNT - $FSLIMIT"
                         echo "           Exceptions file value must be less\
than or"
                         echo "           equal to the size of the filesystem\
measured"
                         echo "           in 1024 bytes\n"
                    fi
               else
                    echo "\nERROR: Null value specified in exceptions\
file"
                    echo "           for the $FSMOUNT mount point.\n"
               fi
               ;;
          PC) # Use Filesystem %Used Method
               # Strip out the % sign if it exists
               PC_USED=$(echo $PC_USED | sed s/\%//g)
               # Test for blank and null values
               if [[ ! -z $FSLIMIT && $FSLIMIT != '' ]]
               then
                    # Test for a valid percentage, i.e. 0-100
                    if (( FSLIMIT >= 0 && FSLIMIT <= 100 ))
                    then
                         if (( $PC_USED > $FSLIMIT ))
                         then
                              return 2 # Found exceeded by % Used method
                         else
                              return 3 # Found OK
                         fi
                    else
                         echo "\nERROR: Invalid percentage for $FSMOUNT -\
$FSLIMIT"
                         echo "           Exceptions file values must be"
                         echo "           between 0 and 100%\n"
                    fi
               else
                    echo "\nERROR: Null value specified in exceptions\
file"
                    echo "           for the $FSMOUNT mount point.\n"
               fi
               ;;
          N)  # Method Not Specified - Use Script Defaults
```

Listing 5.15 fs_mon_ALL_OS.ksh shell script. *(continues)*

```
                    if (( FSSIZE >= FSTRIGGER ))
                    then # This is a "large" filesystem
                        if (( FSMB_FREE < MIN_MB_FREE ))
                        then
                                return 1 # Found out of limit
                                         # using MB Free method
                        else
                                return 3 # Found OK
                        fi
                    else # This is a standard filesystem
                        PC_USED=$(echo $PC_USED | sed s/\%//g) # Remove %
                        FSLIMIT=$(echo $FSLIMIT | sed s/\%//g) # Remove %
                        if (( PC_USED > FSLIMIT ))
                        then
                                return 2 # Found exceeded by % Used method
                        else
                                return 3 # Found OK
                        fi
                    fi
                    ;;
            esac
        fi
    fi
done < $DATA_EXCEPTIONS # Feed the loop from the bottom!!!

return 4 # Not found in $EXCEPTIONS file
}

######################################

function display_output
{
if [[ -s $OUTFILE ]]
then
      echo "\nFull Filesystem(s) on $THISHOST\n"
      cat $OUTFILE
      print
fi
}

######################################

function load_EXCEPTIONS_data
{
# Ignore any line that begins with a pound sign, #
# and omit all blank lines

cat $EXCEPTIONS |  grep -v "^#" | sed /^$/d > $DATA_EXCEPTIONS
```

Listing 5.15 fs_mon_ALL_OS.ksh shell script. *(continued)*

```
}

######################################

function load_AIX_FS_data
{

   df -k | tail +2 | egrep -v '/dev/cd[0-9]|/proc' \
         | awk '{print $1, $2, $3, $4, $7}' > $WORKFILE
}

######################################

function load_HP_UX_FS_data
{

   bdf | tail +2 | egrep -v '/cdrom' \
         | awk '{print $1, $2, $4, $5, $6}' > $WORKFILE
}

######################################

function load_LINUX_FS_data
{

   df -k | tail +2 | egrep -v '/cdrom'\
         | awk '{print $1, $2, $4, $5, $6}' > $WORKFILE
}

######################################

function load_Solaris_FS_data
{

   df -k | tail +2 | egrep -v '/dev/fd|/etc/mnttab|/proc'\
         | awk '{print $1, $2, $4, $5, $6}' > $WORKFILE
}

######################################
######### START OF MAIN ############
######################################

# Query the operating system to find the Unix flavor, then
# load the correct filesystem data for the resident OS

case $(get_OS_info) in
   AIX)    # Load filesystem data for AIX
           load_AIX_FS_data
```

Listing 5.15 fs_mon_ALL_OS.ksh shell script. *(continues)*

```
      ;;
   HP-UX) # Load filesystem data for HP-UX
          load_HP_UX_FS_data
      ;;
   LINUX) # Load filesystem data for Linux
          load_LINUX_FS_data
      ;;
   SUNOS) # Load filesystem data for Solaris
          load_Solaris_FS_data
      ;;
   *)     # Unsupported in script
          echo "\nUnsupported Operating System for this\
 Script...EXITING\n"
          exit 1
esac

# Do we have a nonzero size $EXCEPTIONS file?

if [[ -s $EXCEPTIONS ]]
then # Found a nonempty $EXCEPTIONS file

    load_EXCEPTIONS_data
    EXCEP_FILE="Y"
fi

while read FSDEVICE FSSIZE FSMB_FREE PC_USED FSMOUNT
do
    if [[ $EXCEP_FILE = "Y" ]]
    then
        check_exceptions
        CE_RC="$?" # Check Exceptions Return Code (CE_RC)

        case $CE_RC in
        1) # Found exceeded in exceptions file by MB Method
           (( FS_FREE_OUT = FSMB_FREE / 1000 ))
           echo "$FSDEVICE mounted on $FSMOUNT has ${FS_FREE_OUT}MB\
Free" >> $OUTFILE
          ;;
        2) # Found exceeded in exceptions file by %Used method
           echo "$FSDEVICE mount on $FSMOUNT is ${PC_USED}%" \
                >> $OUTFILE
          ;;
        3) # Found OK in exceptions file
           : # NO-OP Do Nothing.  A ":" is a no-op!
          ;;

        4) # Not found in exceptions file - Use Default Triggers
           if (( FSSIZE >= FSTRIGGER ))
```

Listing 5.15   fs_mon_ALL_OS.ksh shell script. *(continued)*

```
               then # This is a "large" filesystem
                   FSMB_FREE=$(echo $FSMB_FREE | sed s/MB//g) # Remove the\
    "MB"

                   if (( FSMB_FREE < MIN_MB_FREE ))
                   then
                       (( FS_FREE_OUT = FSMB_FREE / 1000 ))
                       echo "$FSDEVICE mounted on $FSMOUNT has {FS_FREE_OUT}MB\
    Free" >> $OUTFILE
                   fi
               else # This is a standard filesystem
                   PC_USED=$(echo $PC_USED | sed s/\%//g)
                   MAX_PERCENT=$(echo $MAX_PERCENT | sed s/\%//g)
                   if (( PC_USED > MAX_PERCENT ))
                   then
                       echo "$FSDEVICE mount on $FSMOUNT is ${PC_USED}%" \
                            >> $OUTFILE
                   fi
               fi
           ;;
         esac

       else # NO $EXCEPTIONS FILE USE DEFAULT TRIGGER VALUES

           if (( FSSIZE >= FSTRIGGER ))
           then # This is a "large" filesystem - Use MB Free Method
               FSMB_FREE=$(echo $FSMB_FREE | sed s/MB//g) # Remove the "MB"
               if (( FSMB_FREE < MIN_MB_FREE ))
               then
                   (( FS_FREE_OUT = FSMB_FREE / 1000 ))
                   echo "$FSDEVICE mounted on $FSMOUNT has ${FS_FREE_OUT}MB
    Free" \
                            >> $OUTFILE
               fi
           else # This is a standard filesystem - Use % Used Method
               PC_USED=$(echo $PC_USED | sed s/\%//g)
               MAX_PERCENT=$(echo $MAX_PERCENT | sed s/\%//g)
               if (( PC_USED > MAX_PERCENT ))
               then
                   echo "$FSDEVICE mount on $FSMOUNT is ${PC_USED}%" \
                        >> $OUTFILE
               fi
           fi
       fi
   fi
done < $WORKFILE # Feed the while loop from the bottom!!!!!

display_output

# End of Script
```

Listing 5.15 fs_mon_ALL_OS.ksh shell script. *(continued)*

A good study of the script in Listing 5.15 will reveal some nice ways to handle the different situations we encounter while writing shell scripts. As always, it *is* intuitively obvious!

The `/usr/local/bin/exceptions` file in Listing 5.16 is used on yogi.

```
# FILE: "exceptions"
#
# This file is used to override the default
# trigger value in the filesystem monitoring script
# fs_mon_ALL_OS_excep.ksh, but also allows overriding the
# monitoring technique used, i.e. Max %Used and
# MINIMUM MB FREE of filesystem space.  The syntax to
# override is a /mount-point and a "trigger value" with
# either "%" or "MB" as a suffix.
#
# EXAMPLES:
#
# /usr 96%
# OR
# /usr 50MB
#
# All lines beginning with a # are ignored.
#
# NOTE: All Entries MUST have either "MB" or
#       "%" as a suffix!!!  Or else the script
#       defaults are used. NO SPACES PLEASE!
#
/opt 95%
/ 50%
/usr 70MB
/home 50MB
```

Listing 5.16 Sample exceptions file.

Listing 5.16 should work, but it gives an error. If the monitoring script is executed using these exception file entries, it will result in the following output:

```
ERROR: Invalid filesystem MINIMUM_MB_FREE specified
       for /home - 50MB -- Current size is 4MB.
       Exceptions file value must be less than or equal
       to the size of the filesystem measured Megabytes


Full Filesystem(s) on yogi

/dev/hd4 mount on / is 51%
/dev/hd2 mounted on /usr has 57MB Free
/dev/hd10opt mount on /opt is 97%
```

The problem is with the /home filesystem entry in the $EXCEPTIONS file. The value specified is 50 Megabytes, and the /home filesystem is only 4MB in size. In a case like this the check_exceptions function will display an error message and then use the shell script default values to measure the filesystem and return an appropriate return code to the calling script. So, if a modification is made to the exceptions file, the script needs to be run to check for any errors.

The important thing to note is that error checking and data validation should take place before the data is used for measurement. This sequence will also prevent any messages from standard error (stderr) that the system may produce.

Other Options to Consider

We can always improve on a script, and the full filesystems script is no exception.

Event Notification

Because monitoring for full filesystems should involve event notification, it is wise to modify the display_output function to send some kind of message, whether by page or email, or otherwise this information needs to be made known so that we can call ourselves proactive. Sending an email to your pager and desktop would be a good start. An entry like the statement that follows might work, but its success depends on the mail server and firewall configurations.

```
echo "Full Filesystem(s) on $THISHOST\n" > $MAILFILE
cat $OUTFILE >> $MAILFILE

mailx -s "Full Filesystem(s) on $THISHOST" $MAIL_LIST < $MAILFILE
```

For pager notification, the text message must be *very short*, but descriptive enough to get the point across.

Automated Execution

If we are to monitor the system, we want the system to tell us when *it* has a problem. We want event notification, but we also want the event notification to be automated. For filesystem monitoring, a cron table entry is the best way to do this. An interval of about 10–15 minutes 24 × 7 is most common. We have the exceptions capability built in so that if pages become a problem, the exceptions file can be modified to stop the filesystem from being *in error*, and thus stop the paging. The cron entry that follows will execute the script every 10 minutes, on the 5s, 24 hours a day, 7 days a week.

```
5,15,25,35,45,55 * * * * /usr/local/bin/fs_mon_ALL_OS.ksh 2>&1
```

To make this cron entry you can either edit a cron table with **crontab -e** or use the following command sequence to append an entry to the end of the cron table.

```
crontab -l > /tmp/cron_hold.out

echo '5,15,25,35,45,55 * * * * /usr/local/bin/fs_mon_ALL_OS.ksh 2>&1' \
      >> /tmp/cron_hold.out

crontab /tmp/cron_hold.out

rm /tmp/cron_hold.out
```

For this to work, the `fs_mon_ALL_OS.ksh` script must be modified to send notification by some method. Paging, email, SNMP traps, and modem dialing are the preferred methods. You could send this output to the systems console, but who would ever see it?

Modify the egrep Statement

It may be wise to remove the **egrep** part of the **df** statement, used for filesystem exclusion, and use another method. As pointed out previously, grepping can be a mistake. Grepping was done here because most of the time we can get a unique character string for a filesystem device to make **grep** and **egrep** work without error, but not always. If this is a problem, then creating a list either in a variable assignment in the script or in a file is the best bet. Then the new $IGNORE_LIST list can be searched and an exact match can be made.

Summary

Through this chapter we have changed our thinking about monitoring for full filesystems. The script that we use can be very simple for the average small shop or more complex as we move to larger and larger storage solutions. All filesystems are not created equal in size, and when you get a mix of large and small filesystems on mixed operating systems, we have shown how to handle the mix with ease.

In the next chapter we will move into monitoring the paging and/or swap space. If we run out of paging or swap space, the system will start thrashing, and if the problem is chronic, the system may crash. We will look at the different monitoring methods for each operating system.

CHAPTER 6

Monitoring Paging and Swap Space

Every Systems Administrator loves paging and swap space because they are the magic bullets to fix a system that does not have enough memory. *Wrong!* This misconception is thought to be true by many people, at various levels, in a lot of organizations. The fact is that if your system does not have enough real memory to run your applications, adding more paging and swap space is not going to help. Depending on the application(s) running on your system, swap space should start at least 1.5 times physical memory. Many high-performance applications require 4 to 6 times real memory so the actual amount of paging and swap space is variable, but 1.5 times is a good place to start. Use the application's recommended requirement, if one is suggested, as a starting point.

Some of you may be asking "What is the difference between *paging* space and *swap* space?" It depends on the Unix flavor whether your system does swapping or paging, but both swap space and paging space are disk storage that makes up virtual memory along with real, or physical, memory. A *page fault* happens when a memory segment, or *page*, is needed in memory but is not currently resident in memory. When a page fault occurs, the system attempts to load the needed data into memory; this is called paging or swapping, depending on the Unix system you are running. When the system is doing a lot of paging in and out of memory we need to be able to monitor this activity. If your system runs out of paging space or is in a state of continuous swapping, such that as soon as a segment is paged out of memory it is immediately needed again, the system is *thrashing*. If this thrashing condition continues for very long, you have a risk of the system crashing. In this chapter we are going to use the terms "paging" and "swapping" interchangeably.

Each of our four Unix flavors, AIX, HP-UX, Linux, and Solaris, use different commands to list the swap space usage; the output for each command and OS varies also. The goal of this chapter is to create five shell scripts: one script of each of the four operating systems and an all-in-one shell script that will run on any of our four Unix flavors. Each of the shell scripts must produce the exact same output, which is shown in Listing 6.1.

```
Paging Space Report for yogi

Wed Jun  5 21:48:16 EDT 2002

Total MB of Paging Space:        336MB
Total MB of Paging Space Used:   33MB
Total MB of Paging Space Free:   303MB

Percent of Paging Space Used:    10%

Percent of Paging Space Free:    90%
```

Listing 6.1   Required paging and swap space report.

Before we get started creating the shell scripts, we need the command syntax for each operating system. Each of the commands produces a different result, so this should be an interesting chapter in which we can try some varied techniques.

Syntax

As usual, we need the correct command syntax before we can write a shell script. As we go through each of the operating systems, the first thing I want you to notice is the command syntax used and the output received back. Because we want each Unix flavor to produce the same output, as shown in Listing 6.1, we are going to have to do some math. This is not going to be hard math, but each of the paging and swap space command outputs is lacking some of the desired information so we must calculate the missing pieces. Now we are going to see the syntax for each operating system.

AIX lsps Command

AIX does paging instead of swapping. This technique uses 4096-byte blocks pages. When a page fault occurs, AIX has a complex algorithm that frees memory of the least used noncritical memory page to disk paging space. When the memory has space available, the page of data is paged in to memory. To monitor paging space usage in AIX, you use the **lsps** command, which stands for *list paging space*. The **lsps** command has two command options, **-a**, to list each paging space separately, and −s, to show a summary of all paging spaces. Both **lsps** options are shown here:

```
# lsps -a

Page Space  Physical Volume  Volume Group   Size   %Used Active Auto  Type
paging00    hdisk2           rootvg        1024MB    11   yes    yes   lv
hd6         hdisk0           rootvg        1024MB     9   yes    yes   lv


# lsps -s

Total Paging Space   Percent Used
      2048MB              10%
```

From the first command output, **lsps -a**, on this system notice that there are two paging spaces defined, paging00 and hd6, both are the same size at 1GB each, and each paging space is on a separate disk. This is an important point. In AIX, paging space is used in a round-robin fashion, starting with the paging space that has the largest area of free space. If one paging space is significantly larger, the round-robin technique is defeated, and the system will almost always use the larger paging space. This has a negative effect on performance because one disk will take all of the paging activity.

In the second output, **lsps -s**, we get a summary of all of the paging space usage. Notice that the only data that we get is the total size of the paging space and the percentage used. From these two pieces of data we must calculate the remaining parts of our required output, which is total paging space in MB, free space in MB, used space in MB, percent used, and percent free. We will cover these points in the scripting section for AIX later in this chapter.

HP-UX swapinfo Command

The HP-UX operating system uses swapping, which is evident by the command **swapinfo**. HP-UX does the best job of giving us the best detailed command output so we need to calculate only one piece of data for our required output, percent of total swap space free. Everything else is provided with the **swapinfo -tm** command. The **-m** switch specifies to produce output in MB, and the **-t** switch specifies to produce a total line for a summary of all virtual memory. This command output is shown here.

```
[root@dino]/> swapinfo -tm
            Mb     Mb     Mb    PCT   START/      Mb
TYPE     AVAIL   USED   FREE   USED  LIMIT  RESERVE  PRI  NAME
dev         96     21     73   22%   928768       -    1  /dev/dsk/c0t6d0
reserve      -     46    -46
memory      15      5     10   33%
total      111     72     37   65%        -       0    -
```

Notice in this output that HP-UX splits up virtual memory into three categories: `dev`, `reserve`, and `memory`. For our needs we could use the summary information that is shown in the `total` line at the bottom. As you can see on the `total` line, the total virtual memory is 111MB, the system is consuming 72MB of this total, which leaves 37MB of free virtual memory. The fifth column shows that the system is consuming 65 percent of the available virtual memory. This `total` row is misleading, though, when we are interested only in the swap space usage. The actual swap space usage is located on the `dev` row of data at the top of the command output. As you can see, we need to calculate only the percent free, which is a simple calculation.

Linux free Command

Linux uses swapping and uses the **free** command to view memory and swap space usage. The **free** command has several command switches, but the only one we are concerned with is the **-m** command switch to list output in MB. The swap information given by the **free -m** command is listed only in MB, and there are no percentages presented in the output. Therefore, from the total MB, used MB, and free MB, we must calculate the percentages for percentage used and percentage free. The following shows the **free -m** command output:

```
# free -m
              total      used      free    shared   buffers    cached
Mem:             52        51         1         0         1        20
-/+ buffers/cache:         30        22
Swap:           211         9       202
```

The last line in this output has the swap information listed in MB, specified by the **-m** switch. This command output shows that the system has 211MB of total swap space, of which 9MB has been used and 202MB of swap space is free.

Solaris swap Command

The Solaris operating system does swapping, as indicated by the command **swap**. Of the **swap** command switches we are concerned with only the **-s** switch, which produces a summary of swap space usage. All output from this command is produced in KB so we have to do a little division by 1,000 to get our standard MB output. Like Linux, the Solaris **swap** output does not show the swap status using percentages, so we must calculate these values. The **swap -s** output is shown here.

```
# swap -s
total: 26788k bytes allocated + 7256k reserved = 34044k used, 557044k
available
```

This is an unusual output to decipher because the data is all on the same line, but because Solaris attempts to create a mathematical statement we will have to use our own mathematical statements to fill in the blanks to get our required script output. The **swap -s** command output shows that the system has used a total of 34MB and it has 557MB of free swap space. We must calculate the total MB, the percentage used, and the percentage of free swap space. These calculations are not too hard to handle as we will see in the shell scripting section for Solaris later in this chapter.

Creating the Shell Scripts

Now that we have the basic syntax of the commands to get paging and swap space statistics, we can start our scripting of the solutions. In each case you should notice which pieces of data are missing from our required output, as shown in Listing 6.1. All of these shell scripts are different. Some pipe command outputs to a **while** loop to assign the values to variables, and some use other techniques to extract the desired data from the output. Please study each shell script in detail, and you will learn how to handle the different situations you are challenged with when working in a heterogeneous environment.

AIX Paging Monitor

As we previously discussed, the AIX **lsps -s** command output shows only the total amount of paging space measured in MB and the percentage of paging space that is currently in use. To get our standard set of data to display we need to do a little math. This is not too difficult when you take one step at a time. In this shell script let's use a file to store the command output data. To refresh your memory the **lsps -s** command output is shown again here (this output is using a different AIX system):

```
# lsps -s
Total Paging Space   Percent Used
       336MB               2%
```

The first thing we need to do is to remove the columns heading. I like to use the **tail** command in a pipe for this purpose. The command syntax is shown in the next statement:

```
# lsps -s | tail +2
       336MB               2%
```

This resulting output contains only the data, without the columns heading. The next step is to store these values in variables so that we can work with them for some calculations. We are going to use a file for initial storage and then use a **while read** loop, which we feed from the bottom using input redirection with the filename. Of course, we could have piped the command output to the **while read** loop, but I want to vary the techniques in each shell script in this chapter. Let's look at the first part of the data gathering and the use of the **while read** loop, as shown in Listing 6.2.

```
PAGING_STAT=/tmp/paging_stat.out # Paging Stat hold file

# Load the $PAGING_STAT file with data

lsps -s | tail +2 > $PAGING_STAT

# Use a while loop to assign the values to variables

while read TOTAL PERCENT
do
      DO CALCULATIONS HERE

done < $PAGING_STAT
```

Listing 6.2   Logical view of AIX lsps -s data gathering.

Notice in Listing 6.2 that we first define a file to hold the data, which is pointed to by the $PAGING_STAT variable. In the next step we redirect output of our paging space status command to the defined file. Next comes a **while** loop where we **read** the file data and assign the first data field to the variable TOTAL and the second data field to the variable PERCENT.

Notice how the $PAGING_STAT file is used to feed the **while** loop from the bottom. As you saw in Chapter 2, "Twelve Ways to Process a File Line by Line," this technique is one of the two fastest methods of reading data from a file. The middle of the **while** loop is where we do our calculations to fill in the blanks of our required output.

Speaking of calculations, we need to do three calculations for this script, but before we can perform the calculations on the data we currently have, we need to get rid of the suffixes attached to the variable data. The first step is to extract the MB from the $TOTAL variable and then extract the percent sign, %, from the $PERCENT variable. We do both of these operations using a **cut** command in a pipe, as shown here:

```
PAGING_MB=$(echo $TOTAL | cut -d 'MB' -f1)
PAGING_PC=$(echo $PERCENT | cut -d% -f1)
```

In both of these statements we use command substitution, specified by the $(command_statement) notation, to execute a command statement and assign the result to the variable specified. In the first statement we **echo** the $TOTAL variable and pipe the output to the **cut** command. For the **cut** command we specify the delimiter to be **MB**, and we enclose it with single tic marks, **'MB'**. Then we specify that we want the first field, specified by **-f1**. In the second statement we do the exact same thing except that this time we specify that the percent sign, %, is the delimiter. The result of these two statements is that we have the PAGING_MB and PAGING_PC variables pointing to integer values without any other characters. Now we can do our calculations!

Let's do the most intuitive calculation first. We have the value of the percent of paging space used stored in the $PAGING_PC variable as an integer value. To get the percent of free paging space, we need to subtract the percent used value from 100, as shown in the next command statement.

```
(( PAGING_PC_FREE = 100 - PAGING_PC ))
```

Notice that we used the double parentheses mathematical method, specified by the `(( Math Statement ))`. I like this method because it is so intuitive to use. Also notice that you do NOT use the dollar sign, $, with variables when using this method. Because the double parentheses method expects a mathematical statement, any character string that is not numeric is assumed to be a variable, so the dollar sign should be omitted. If you add a dollar sign to the variable name, then the statement may fail depending on the OS you are running! I always remove the dollar sign, just in case. This is a common cause of frustration when using math in shell scripts, and it is extremely hard to troubleshoot.

The next calculation is not so intuitive to some. We want to calculate the MB of paging space that is currently in use. Now let's think about this. We have the percentage of paging space used, the percentage of paging space free, and the total amount of paging space measured in MB. To calculate the MB of used paging space, we can use the value of the total MB of paging space and the percentage of paging space used divided by 100, which converts the value of paging space used into a decimal value internally. See how this is done in the next statement.

```
(( MB_USED = PAGING_MB * PAGING_PC / 100 ))
```

One thing to note in the last math statement: This will produce only an integer output. If you want to see the output in floating-point notation, then you need to use the **bc** utility, which you will see in some of the following sections.

The last calculation is another intuitive calculation, to find the MB of free paging space. Because we already have the values for the total paging space in MB, and the MB of paging space in use, then we need only to subtract the used value from the total. This is shown in the next statement.

```
(( MB_FREE = PAGING_MB - MB_USED ))
```

We have completed all of the calculations so now we are ready to produce the required output for the AIX shell script. Take a look at the entire shell script shown in Listing 6.3, and pay particular attention to the boldface type.

```
#!/usr/bin/ksh
#
# SCRIPT: AIX_paging_mon.ksh
#
# AUTHOR: Randy Michael
# DATE: 5/31/2002
# REV: 1.1.P
#
```

Listing 6.3 AIX_paging_mon.ksh shell script listing. *(continues)*

```
# PLATFORM: AIX Only
#
# PURPOSE: This shell script is used to produce a report of
#          the system's paging space statistics including:
#
#          Total paging space in MB, MB of free paging space,
#          MB of used paging space, % of paging space used, and
#          % of paging space free
#
# REV LIST:
#
#
# set -x # Uncomment to debug this shell script
# set -n # Uncomment to check command syntax without any execution
#
##############################################################
################ DEFINE VARIABLES HERE ###################

PC_LIMIT=65                    # Percentage Upper limit of paging space
                               # before notification

THISHOST=$(hostname)     # Host name of this machine
PAGING_STAT=/tmp/paging_stat.out # Paging Stat hold file

##############################################################
################ INITIALIZE THE REPORT ###################

echo "\nPaging Space Report for $THISHOST\n"
date

##############################################################
############# CAPTURE AND PROCESS THE DATA ###############

# Load the data in a file without the column headings

lsps -s | tail +2 > $PAGING_STAT

# Start a while loop and feed the loop from the bottom using
# the $PAGING_STAT file as redirected input, after "done"

while read TOTAL PERCENT
do
     # Clean up the data by removing the suffixes
     PAGING_MB=$(echo $TOTAL | cut -d 'MB' -f1)
     PAGING_PC=$(echo $PERCENT | cut -d% -f1)

     # Calculate the missing data: %Free, MB used and MB free
     (( PAGING_PC_FREE = 100 - PAGING_PC ))
```

Listing 6.3 AIX_paging_mon.ksh shell script listing. *(continued)*

```
(( MB_USED = PAGING_MB * PAGING_PC / 100 ))
(( MB_FREE = PAGING_MB - MB_USED ))


# Produce the rest of the paging space report:
echo "\nTotal MB of Paging Space:\t$TOTAL"
echo "Total MB of Paging Space Used:\t${MB_USED}MB"
echo "Total MB of Paging Space Free:\t${MB_FREE}MB"
echo "\nPercent of Paging Space Used:\t${PERCENT}"
echo "\nPercent of Paging Space Free:\t${PAGING_PC_FREE}%"


# Check for paging space exceeded the predefined limit
if ((PC_LIMIT <= PAGING_PC))
then

      # Paging space is over the limit, send notification

      tput smso  # Turn on reverse video!

      echo "\n\nWARNING: Paging Space has Exceeded the ${PC_LIMIT}% \
Upper Limit!\n"

      tput rmso  # Turn off reverse video
    fi

done < $PAGING_STAT

rm -f $PAGING_STAT

# Add an extra new line to the output

echo "\n"
```

Listing 6.3   AIX_paging_mon.ksh shell script listing. *(continued)*

There is one part of our shell script in Listing 6.3 that we have not covered yet. At the top of the script where we define variables, I added the PC_LIMIT variable. I normally set this threshold to 65 percent so that I will know when I have exceeded a safe system paging space limit. When your system starts running at a high paging space level, you need to find the cause of this added activity. Sometimes developers do not write applications properly when it comes to deallocating memory. If a program runs for a long time and it is not written to clean up and release allocated memory, then the program is said to have a *memory leak*. The result of running this memory leak program for a long time without a system reboot is that your system will run out of memory. When your system runs out of memory, it starts paging in and out to disk, and then your paging space starts edging up. The only way to correct this problem and regain your memory is to reboot the system, most of the time.

Notice at the end of the script that there is a test to see if the percentage of paging space used is greater than or equal to the limit that is set by the PC_LIMIT variable. If the value is exceeded, then reverse video is turned on so the WARNING message stands out on the screen. After the message is displayed, reverse video is turned back off. To turn on reverse video use the **tput smso** command. When reverse video is on, anything that you print to the screen appears in reverse video; however, do not forget to turn it off because this mode will continue *after* the shell script ends execution if you do not turn it off. To turn off the reverse video mode use the **tput rmso** command. Listings 6.4 and 6.5 show the shell script in action. Listing 6.4 shows a report of the system within the set 65 percent limit, while Listing 6.5 shows the report when the system has exceeded the 65 percent paging limit.

```
Paging Space Report for yogi

Fri Jun  7 15:47:08 EDT 2002

Total MB of Paging Space:        336MB
Total MB of Paging Space Used:   6MB
Total MB of Paging Space Free:   330MB


Percent of Paging Space Used:    2%


Percent of Paging Space Free:    98%
```

Listing 6.4 AIX_paging_mon.ksh in action.

As you can see in Listing 6.4, **yogi** is not doing too much right now. Let's produce a little load on the system and set the trigger threshold in the AIX_paging_mon.ksh shell script to 5 percent so that we can see the threshold exceeded, as shown in Listing 6.5.

```
Paging Space Report for yogi

Fri Jun  7 15:54:30 EDT 2002

Total MB of Paging Space:        336MB
Total MB of Paging Space Used:   23MB
Total MB of Paging Space Free:   313MB


Percent of Paging Space Used:    7%


Percent of Paging Space Free:    93%



WARNING: Paging Space has Exceeded the 5% Upper Limit!
```

Listing 6.5 AIX_paging_mon.ksh exceeding a 5 percent paging limit.

This is still not much of a load, but it does make the point of the ability to set a trigger threshold for notification purposes. Of course, the reverse video of the warning message did not come to the page; believe me, it does show up in reverse video on the screen. Let's move on to the HP-UX system.

HP-UX Swap Space Monitor

The HP-UX operating system does swapping, as shown by the **swapinfo** command. To check the statistics of swap space you use the **swapinfo -tm** command. The **-t** command switch adds a summary `total` line to the output, and the **-m** option specifies that the output space measurements are in MB, as opposed to the default of KB. As I said previously, HP-UX does the best job of producing the various virtual memory statistics, so we need to calculate only one piece of our required output, the percent of free swap space. Before we go any further, let's look at the command output we are dealing with, as shown in Listing 6.6.

```
swapinfo -tm
              Mb        Mb      Mb    PCT   START/     Mb
TYPE         AVAIL     USED    FREE   USED  LIMIT  RESERVE  PRI  NAME
dev             96       23      71   24%   928768      -    1
/dev/dsk/c0t6d0
reserve          -       45     -45
memory          15        6       9   40%
total          111       74      35   67%            -     0    -
```

Listing 6.6   HP-UX swapinfo -tm command output.

As you can see, HP-UX shows paging space for devices, reserved memory, and real memory usage. I like to use `total` row of output to get a good summary of what all of the virtual memory is doing. It really does not matter if you use the `dev` row or the `total` row to do your monitoring, but for this exercise I am going to use the `dev` row to monitor only the swap space and not worry about what real memory is doing.

The easiest way to extract the data we want on the `dev` row in the output is to use **grep** to pattern match on the string `dev` because `dev` appears on only one row of data. Piping the **swapinfo** command output to a **grep** statement produces the following output:

```
# swapinfo -tm | grep dev

dev             96       23      71   24%   928768      -    1
/dev/dsk/c0t6d0
```

The output that we want to extract, Total MB, Used MB, Free MB, and Percent Used, is located in fields $2, $3, $4, and $5, respectively. From looking at this we have at least two options to assign the field values to variables. We can use five **awk** statements, or we can pipe the preceding command output to a **while read** loop. Of course, the **while read** loop runs for only one loop iteration. The easiest technique is to pipe to the **while** loop. The following command will get us started:

```
swapinfo -tm | grep dev | while read junk SW_TOTAL SW_USED \
                             SW_FREE PERCENT_USED junk2
```

Notice in the **while read** portion of the previous statement how we assign unneeded fields to variables named junk and junk2. The first field, specified by the junk variable, targets dev; we are not interested in saving this field so it gets a junk assignment. The last variable, junk2, is a catch-all for anything remaining on the line of output; specifically, "928768   -   1 /dev/dsk/c0t6d0", gets assigned to the variable junk2 as one field. This is an extremely important part of the **while read** statement because you must account for everything when reading in a line of data. Had I left out the junk2 variable, the PERCENT_USED variable would point to the data "24% 928768   -   1 /dev/dsk/c0t6d0" when the only thing we want is 24%. The junk2 variable catches all of the remaining data on the line and assigns it to the junk2 variable. This brings up another point. If you want to capture the entire line of data and assign it to a single variable, you can do this too by using the following syntax:

```
while read DATA_LINE
do
     PARSE THE $DATA_LINE DATA HERE

done < $DATA_FILE
```

Using this syntax, all of the data is captured with a single variable, DATA_LINE, and the data is separated into fields just as it appears in the command output.

Back to our previous **swapinfo** statement, we have the data of interest stored in the following variables:

SW_TOTAL.   Total swap space available on the system measured in MB.

SW_USED.   MB of swap space that is currently in use.

SW_FREE.   MB of swap space that is currently free.

PERCENT_USED.   Percentage of total swap space that is in use.

The only part of our required output missing is the percentage of total swap space that is currently free. This is an easy calculation because we already have the $PERCENT_USED. For the calculation we need to remove the percent sign, %, in the $PERCENT_USED variable. The following statement does the removal of the percent sign and makes the calculation in one step.

```
((PERCENT_FREE = 100 - $(echo $PERCENT_USED | cut -d% -f1) ))
```

In the preceding mathematical statement we assign 100 percent minus 24 percent to the variable PERCENT_FREE using command substitution to remove the percent sign from the $PERCENT_USED variable using the **cut** command. In the **cut** part of the statement we define % to be the delimiter, or field separator, specified by **-d%**, then we extract the first field, 24 in this case, using the **-f1** notation. Once the command substitution is complete, we are left with the following math statement:

```
((PERCENT_FREE = 100 - 24))
```

Now let's examine the entire shell script that is shown in Listing 6.7.

```ksh
#!/usr/bin/ksh
#
# SCRIPT: HP-UX_swap_mon.ksh
#
# AUTHOR: Randy Michael
# DATE: 5/31/2002
# REV: 1.1.P
#
# PLATFORM: HP-UX Only
#
# PURPOSE: This shell script is used to produce a report of
#          the system's swap space statistics including:
#
#     Total paging space in MB, MB of free paging space,
#     MB of used paging space, % of paging space used, and
#     % of paging space free
#
# REV LIST:
#
#
# set -x # Uncomment to debug this shell script
# set -n # Uncomment to check command syntax without any execution
#
############### DEFINE VARIABLES HERE ###################

PC_LIMIT=65                 # Percentage Upper limit of paging space
                            # before notification

THISHOST=$(hostname)    # Host name of this machine


##########################################################
############### INITIALIZE THE REPORT ###################

echo "\nSwap Space Report for $THISHOST\n"
date


##########################################################
```

Listing 6.7   HP-UX_swap_mon.ksh shell script listing. *(continues)*

```
############# CAPTURE AND PROCESS THE DATA ###############

# Start a while read loop by using the piped-in input from
# the swapinfo -tm command output.


swapinfo -tm | grep dev | while read junk SW_TOTAL SW_USED \
                          SW_FREE PERCENT_USED junk2
do
    # Calculate the percentage of free swap space

    ((PERCENT_FREE = 100 - $(echo $PERCENT_USED | cut -d% -f1) ))

    echo "\nTotal Amount of Swap Space:\t${SW_TOTAL}MB"
    echo "Total MB of Swap Space Used:\t${SW_USED}MB"
    echo "Total MB of Swap Space Free:\t${SW_FREE}MB"
    echo "\nPercent of Swap Space Used:\t${PERCENT_USED}"
    echo "\nPercent of Swap Space Free:\t${PERCENT_FREE}%"

    # Check if paging space exceeded the predefined limit

    if (( PC_LIMIT <= $(echo $PERCENT_USED | cut -d% -f1) ))
    then
          # Swap space is over the predefined limit, send notification

          tput smso # Turn on reverse video!
          echo "\n\nWARNING: Swap Space has Exceeded the\
 ${PC_LIMIT}% Upper Limit!\n"
          tput rmso # Turn reverse video off!
    fi

done

echo "\n"
```

Listing 6.7   HP-UX_swap_mon.ksh shell script listing. *(continued)*

There are a few things that I want to point out in Listing 6.7. The first point is that any time we use the $PERCENT_USED value we always use command substitution to remove the percent sign, %, as shown in the following command substitution statement:

```
$(echo $PERCENT_USED | cut -d% -f1)
```

The next part I want to go over is our required report output. At the top of the shell script we initialize the report by stating a report header including the hostname of the machine and the date stamp of the time the report was executed. Then we do any calculation that is needed to gather any missing data for our required output. Once all of our required data is gathered, we have a series of **echo** statements that add to the report. In these **echo** statements we spell out the data in an easily readable list. I want you to look at each **echo** statement and then look at the report output in Listing 6.8.

```
Swap Space Report for dino

Sun Oct 21 17:27:20 EDT 2001

Total Amount of Swap Space:      96MB
Total MB of Swap Space Used:     24MB
Total MB of Swap Space Free:     70MB

Percent of Swap Space Used:      25%

Percent of Swap Space Free:      75%
```

Listing 6.8   HP-UX swap space report.

There are three thing I want you to notice in the **echo** statements. First is the use of the **\n** when we want to add another new line to the output, which is a blank line in this case. Second is the use of the **\t** to add a TAB to align the data output. And finally, note the use of the curly braces, {VAR}, around the variable names. The curly braces are needed because we are adding characters to the output, and these characters are adjacent to the variable data and there is not a space, which include MB and % suffixes. To separate the extra characters from the variable name we need to use curly braces to ensure the separation.

At the end of the script in Listing 6.7 we compare the percent used variable to the trigger threshold that is defined in the DEFINE VARIABLES section at the top of the shell script. If the threshold is exceeded, then we turn on reverse video, print a warning message, and then turn reverse video back off. The over threshold warning message is shown in Listing 6.9.

```
Swap Space Report for dino

Sun Oct 21 17:40:35 EDT 2001

Total Amount of Swap Space:      96MB
Total MB of Swap Space Used:     24MB
```

Listing 6.9   HP-UX swap space report with over limit warning. *(continues)*

```
Total MB of Swap Space Free:     70MB

Percent of Swap Space Used:      25%

Percent of Swap Space Free:      75%



WARNING: Swap Space has Exceeded the 20% Upper Limit!
```

Listing 6.9   HP-UX swap space report with over limit warning. *(continued)*

I edited the shell script and changed the PC_LIMIT variable assignment to 20 percent for this example. The reverse video does not show up on paper, but on the screen it stands out so that the user will always notice the warning message. I usually set this threshold to 65 percent. When you exceed this level of swap space usage, you really need to find the cause of the increased swapping.

Linux Swap Space Monitor

The Linux operating system does swapping, and the command to gather swap space statistics is the **free** command. The **free** command output by default lists swap space usage in KB, but the **-m** switch is available for listing the statistics in MB. Additionally, the **free -m** output does not include any statistics measured in percentages, so we must calculate the percentage of free swap space and the percentage of used swap space.

These percentage calculations are relatively easy, but we really want to measure the percentage using floating-point notation this time. We need to use the **bc** utility for the mathematical calculations. Chapter 22 goes into great detail on floating-point math and the use of the **bc** utility. First, let's look at the following **free -m** output so that we know what we are dealing with:

```
# free -m
              total       used       free     shared    buffers     cached
Mem:             52         51          0          0          0         18
-/+ buffers/cache:          32         19
Swap:           211         14        197
```

The row of output that we are interested in is the last line of output, beginning with Swap:. This output shows that we have a total of 211MB of swap space where 14MB is currently being used. This leaves 197MB of free swap space. We have three out of five pieces of our required output, so we need to calculate only the percentage of free swap space and the percentage of used space. For these calculations we need to look at the use of the **bc** utility.

The **bc** utility is a precision calculator language that is a Unix level built-in program. For our purposes we have two techniques for using the **bc** utility. We can place our mathematical statement in an **echo** statement and pipe the output to **bc**. The second option is to use a *here* document with command substitution. For this exercise we are going to use the second option to look at the use of a here document.

To calculate the percentage of used swap space we divide the total amount of swap space into MB of used swap space and multiply this total by 100, as shown in the following statement:

```
($SW_USED / $SW_TOTAL) * 100
```

This looks simple enough, but how do we get a floating-point output in a shell script? This is where the **bc** utility comes in. There is an option in **bc** called **scale**. The scale indicates how many decimal places to the right of the decimal point that we want to use in the calculation. In our case we need to set **scale=4**. Now you are asking, Why four places? Because we are multiplying the result of the division by 100 we will have only two active decimal places with data, and the last two will have zeros in the end. Let's look at the following example to clear up any confusion:

```
PERCENT_USED=$(bc <<EOF
scale=4
($SW_USED / $SW_TOTAL) * 100
EOF
)
```

From the previous values, the result of this calculation is 7.1000 percent of used space because $SW_USED is 15MB and $SW_TOTAL is 211MB. Now let's look more closely at the use of the **bc** utility. We are using command substitution with an enclosed here document. A here document has the following form:

```
command <<LABEL

...
Input to the command
...


LABEL
```

This is a neat way of providing input to a command that usually requires user input, and this is why it is referred to as a **here** document, because the input is *here*, as opposed to being entered by the user at the command line.

In our case we use the here document inside command substitution, which is specified by the $(commands) notation. The result is assigned to the PERCENT_USED variable. The calculation of the percent free is done in the same manner except that this time we divide the MB of free space into the MB of total swap space, as shown here.

```
PERCENT_FREE=$(bc <<EOF
scale=4
($SW_FREE / $SW_TOTAL) * 100
EOF
)
```

In our case, using the previously acquired data we get a result of 92.4100 percent. With these two calculations we have all of the data required for our standard output. We will cover the **bc** command, and we will use it again in the next section that deals with the Solaris swap space monitor. Take a look at the entire shell script in Listing 6.10, and pay particular attention to the boldface type.

```ksh
#!/usr/bin/ksh
#
# SCRIPT: linux_swap_mon.ksh
#
# AUTHOR: Randy Michael
# DATE: 5/31/2002
# REV: 1.1.P
#
# PLATFORM: Linux Only
#
#
# PURPOSE: This shell script is used to produce a report of
#          the system's swap space statistics including:
#
#       Total paging space in MB, MB of free paging space,
#       MB of used paging space, % of paging space used, and
#       % of paging space free
#
# REV LIST:
#
#
# set -x # Uncomment to debug this shell script
# set -n # Uncomment to check command syntax without any execution
#
############################################################
################ DEFINE VARIABLES HERE ##################

THISHOST=$(hostname)    # Host name of this machine
PC_LIMIT=65             # Upper limit of Swap space percentage
                        # before notification


############################################################
################ INITIALIZE THE REPORT ##################

echo "\nSwap Space Report for $THISHOST\n"
date


############################################################
############# CAPTURE AND PROCESS THE DATA ##############

free -m | grep -i swap | while read junk SW_TOTAL SW_USED SW_FREE
```

Listing 6.10 Linux_swap_mon.ksh shell script listing.

```
do

# Use the bc utility in a here document to calculate
# the percentage of free and used swap space.

PERCENT_USED=$(bc <<EOF
scale=4
($SW_USED / $SW_TOTAL) * 100
EOF
)

PERCENT_FREE=$(bc <<EOF
scale=4
($SW_FREE / $SW_TOTAL) * 100
EOF
)

    # Produce the rest of the paging space report:
    echo "\nTotal Amount of Swap Space:\t${SW_TOTAL}MB"
    echo "Total KB of Swap Space Used:\t${SW_USED}MB"
    echo "Total KB of Swap Space Free:\t${SW_FREE}MB"
    echo "\nPercent of Swap Space Used:\t${PERCENT_USED}%"
    echo "\nPercent of Swap Space Free:\t${PERCENT_FREE}%"

    # Grab the integer portion of the percent used to
    # test for the over limit threshold

    INT_PERCENT_USED=$(echo $PERCENT_USED | cut -d. -f1)

    if (( PC_LIMIT <= INT_PERCENT_USED ))
    then
        # Swap space limit has exceeded the threshold, send
notification

        tput smso # Turn on reverse video!
        echo "\n\nWARNING: Paging Space has Exceeded the ${PC_LIMIT}%
Upper Limit!\n"
        tput rmso # Turn off reverse video!
    fi

done

echo "\n"
```

Listing 6.10   Linux_swap_mon.ksh shell script listing. *(continued)*

Notice the **while read** portion of the **free -m** command. We use the variable junk as a place to store the first field, which contains Swap:. This is the same technique that we used in the HP-UX section of this chapter. If we had additional data fields after the MB of free swap space, we could use a junk2 variable to hold this extra unneeded data, too.

Also notice that our **bc** calculations are done inside our **while read** loop. Even though I have indented everything else inside the loop for readability, you *cannot* use indention with these documents! If you do indent anything, the calculation will fail, and this is extremely difficult to troubleshoot because it *looks* as if it should work.

Let's take a look at the shell script in Listing 6.10 in action in Listing 6.11.

```
#  ./linux_swap_mon.ksh

Swap Space Report for bambam

Sun Jun  9 13:01:06 EDT 2002

Total Amount of Swap Space:     211MB
Total KB of Swap Space Used:    16MB
Total KB of Swap Space Free:    195MB


Percent of Swap Space Used:     7.5800%


Percent of Swap Space Free:     92.4100%
```

Listing 6.11   Linux_swap_mon.ksh in action.

Notice that the last two numbers in the percentage of used and free swap space are zeros. I am leaving the task of removing these two numbers as an exercise for you to complete. Now let's move on to the Solaris swap space monitor.

Solaris Swap Space Monitor

The Solaris operating system does swapping, and the command to gather swap space statistics is **swap -s**. The output of the **swap -s** command is all on a single line, which is different from any of the previously studied operating systems. Additionally, all of the swap space statistics are measured in KB as opposed to MB, which is our required measurement. Before we go any further, let's look at the Solaris **swap -s** output.

```
# swap -s
total: 56236k bytes allocated + 9972k reserved = 66208k used, 523884k
available
```

As you can see, the output is a little difficult to understand. We are interested in two fields for our purposes, the ninth field, 66208k, and the eleventh field, 523884k. The ninth field represents the total amount of used swap space, and the eleventh field represents the free swap space, where both are measured in KB. We are not interested in the amount of reserved and allocated swap space individually, but in the total, which is located in the ninth field.

When I say the ninth and eleventh fields I am specifying that each field in the output is separated by at least one blank space, also called white space. From this definition it is intuitively obvious that `total:`, `+`, `=`, and `used` are all individual fields in the command output. This is important to know because we are going to use two **awk** statements to extract the $9 and $11 fields.

As in the Linux section, we do not have any percentages given in the output so we must calculate the percentage of free swap space and the percentage of used swap space. If you looked at the Linux section, then you already know how to use the **bc** utility. If you jumped to the Solaris section, we will cover this again here.

The **bc** utility is a precision calculator language that is a Unix level built-in program. For our purposes, we have two techniques for using the **bc** utility. We can place our mathematical statement in an **echo** statement and pipe the output to **bc**. The second option is to use a *here* document with command substitution. For this exercise we are going to use the second option and look at the use of a here document.

To calculate the percentage of used swap space we divide the total amount of swap space into MB of used swap space and multiply this total by 100, as shown in the following statement:

```
($SW_USED / $SW_TOTAL) * 100
```

This looks simple enough, but how do we get a floating-point output in a shell script? This is where the **bc** utility comes in. There is an option in **bc** called **scale**. The scale indicates how many decimal places to the right of the decimal point that we want to use in the calculation. In our case we need to set **scale=4**. Now you are asking, Why 4 places? Because we are multiplying the result of the division by 100, we will have only two active decimal places with data after this multiplication, and the last two will have zeros. Let's look at this next example to clear up any confusion.

```
PERCENT_USED=$(bc <<EOF
scale=4
($SW_USED / $SW_TOTAL) * 100
EOF
)
```

From the previous values the result of this calculation is 11.2200 percent of used space because `$SW_USED` is 66MB and `$SW_TOTAL` is 590MB. Now let's look more closely at the use of the **bc** utility. We are using command substitution with an enclosed here document. A here document has the following form:

```
command <<LABEL

...

Input to the command

...

LABEL
```

This is a neat way of providing input to a command that usually requires user input, and this is why it is referred to as a **here** document—the input is *here*, as opposed to being entered by the user at the command line.

In our case, we use the here document inside command substitution, which is specified by the $(commands) notation. The result is assigned to the PERCENT_USED variable. The calculation of the percent free is done in the same manner except that this time we divide the MB of free space into the MB of total swap space, as shown in the code that follows.

```
PERCENT_FREE=$(bc <<EOF
scale=4
($SW_FREE / $SW_TOTAL) * 100
EOF
)
```

In our case, the percentage of used swap space is 11.220 percent, and the percentage of free swap space is 88.7800 percent. Of course, to get the total swap space we added the $9 and $11 fields together. The entire shell script is shown in Listing 6.12.

```ksh
#!/usr/bin/ksh
#
# SCRIPT: SUN_swap_mon.ksh
#
# AUTHOR: Randy Michael
# DATE: 5/31/2002
# REV: 1.1.P
#
# PLATFORM: Solaris Only
#
# PURPOSE: This shell script is used to produce a report of
#          the system's swap space statistics including:
#
#       Total paging space in MB, MB of free paging space,
#       MB of used paging space, % of paging space used, and
#       % of paging space free
#
# REV LIST:
#
#
# set -x # Uncomment to debug this shell script
# set -n # Uncomment to check command syntax without any execution
#
##########################################################
############### DEFINE VARIABLES HERE ####################

PC_LIMIT=65              # Upper limit of Swap space percentage
```

Listing 6.12 SUN_swap_mon.ksh shell script listing.

```
                         # before notification
THISHOST=$(hostname)   # Host name of this machine

############################################################
################ INITIALIZE THE REPORT ####################

echo "\nSwap Space Report for $THISHOST\n"
date

############################################################
############# CAPTURE AND PROCESS THE DATA ###############

# Use two awk statements to extract the $9 and $11 fields
# from the swap -s command output

SW_USED=$(swap -s | awk '{print $9}' | cut -dk -f1)
SW_FREE=$(swap -s | awk '{print $11}' | cut -dk -f1)

# Add SW_USED to SW_FREE to get the total swap space

((SW_TOTAL = SW_USED + SW_FREE))

# Calculate the percent used and percent free using the
# bc utility in a here documentation with command substitution

PERCENT_USED=$(bc <<EOF
scale=4
($SW_USED / $SW_TOTAL) * 100
EOF
)

PERCENT_FREE=$(bc <<EOF
scale=4
($SW_FREE / $SW_TOTAL) * 100
EOF
)

# Convert the KB measurements to MB measurements

((SW_TOTAL_MB = SW_TOTAL / 1000))
((SW_USED_MB  = SW_USED / 1000))
((SW_FREE_MB  = SW_FREE / 1000))

# Produce the remaining part of the report

echo "\nTotal Amount of Swap Space:\t${SW_TOTAL_MB}MB"
echo "Total KB of Swap Space Used:\t${SW_USED_MB}MB"
```

Listing 6.12 SUN_swap_mon.ksh shell script listing. *(continues)*

```
echo "Total KB of Swap Space Free:\t${SW_FREE_MB}MB"
echo "\nPercent of Swap Space Used:\t${PERCENT_USED}%"
echo "\nPercent of Swap Space Free:\t${PERCENT_FREE}%"

# Grab the integer portion of the percent used

INT_PERCENT_USED=$(echo $PERCENT_USED | cut -d. -f1)

# Check to see if the percentage used maximum threshold
# has been exceeded

if (( PC_LIMIT <= INT_PERCENT_USED ))
then
    # Percent used has exceeded the threshold, send notification

    tput smso # Turn on reverse video!
    echo "\n\nWARNING: Swap Space has Exceeded the ${PC_LIMIT}% Upper
Limit!\n"
    tput rmso # Turn off reverse video!
fi

echo "\n"
```

Listing 6.12   SUN_swap_mon.ksh shell script listing. *(continued)*

Notice how we used two **awk** statements using two separate reads of the **swap -s** command output. These two measurements occur in such a short amount of time that it should not matter; however, you may want to change the method to a single read and store the output in a variable or file; I'm leaving this modification task for you to do as an exercise. In the next step we add the KB of free swap space to the KB of used swap space to find the total swap space on the system.

With these three KB measurements we calculate the percentage of used and free swap space using the **bc** utility inside a command substitution statement while using a here document to provide input to the **bc** command. There is still one more step before we are ready to print the report—convert the KB measurements to MB. We only need to divide our KB measurements by 1,000, and we are ready to go. Next the remaining portions of the report are printed, and then the test is made to see if the percent used has exceeded the threshold limit, specified by the PC_LIMIT variable. If the percentage used limit is exceeded, then reverse video is turned on, the warning message is displayed, and reverse video is turned back off. The SUN_swap_mon.ksh shell script is in action in Listing 6.13.

```
#  ./SUN_swap_mon.ksh

Swap Space Report for wilma

Mon Jun 10 03:50:29 EDT 2002

Total Amount of Swap Space:      590MB
Total KB of Swap Space Used:     66MB
Total KB of Swap Space Free:     524MB

Percent of Swap Space Used:      11.2200%

Percent of Swap Space Free:      88.7800%
```

Listing 6.13   SUN_swap_mon.ksh script in action.

Notice that the percentages are given as floating-pointing numbers, but there are two extra zeros. These two extra zeros are the result of specifying in the **bc** here document that the **scale=4** and then multiplying the result by 100. As an exercise, add a command to remove the two extra zeros. Are we finished? Not yet; we still need a single shell script that will run on all four operating systems. Let's move on to the all-in-one section.

All-in-One Paging and Swap Space Monitor

Let's put everything together by making the four previous scripts into functions and use the **uname** command in a **case** statement to determine the Unix flavor, and thus which function to run.

Let's look at this combined shell script, and we will go over the details at the end. The combined shell script is called `all-in-one_swapmon.ksh` and is shown in Listing 6.14.

```
#!/usr/bin/ksh
#
# SCRIPT: all-in-one_swapmon.ksh
#
# AUTHOR: Randy Michael
# DATE: 6/6/2002
```

Listing 6.14   all-in-one_swapmon.ksh shell script listing. *(continues)*

```
# REV: 2.0.P
#
# PLATFORM: AIX, Solaris, HP-UX and Linux Only
#
# PURPOSE: This shell script is used to produce a report of
#          the system's paging or swap space statistics including:
#
#       Total paging space in MB, MB of Free paging space,
#       MB of Used paging space, % of paging space Used, and
#       % of paging space Free
#
# REV LIST:
#
#
# set -x # Uncomment to debug this shell script
# set -n # Uncomment to check command syntax without any execution
#
############################################################
############### DEFINE VARIABLES HERE ###################

PC_LIMIT=65             # Upper limit of Swap space percentage
                        # before notification

THISHOST=$(hostname)    # Host name of this machine
############################################################
############### INITIALIZE THE REPORT ###################

echo "\nSwap Space Report for $THISHOST\n"
date


############################################################
############### DEFINE FUNCTIONS HERE ###################

function SUN_swap_mon
{
############# CAPTURE AND PROCESS THE DATA ##############

# Use two awk statements to extract the $9 and $11 fields
# from the swap -s command output

SW_USED=$(swap -s | awk '{print $9}' | cut -dk -f1)
SW_FREE=$(swap -s | awk '{print $11}' | cut -dk -f1)

# Add SW_USED to SW_FREE to get the total swap space

((SW_TOTAL = SW_USED + SW_FREE))
```

Listing 6.14   all-in-one_swapmon.ksh shell script listing. *(continued)*

```
# Calculate the percent used and percent free using the
# bc utility in a here documentation with command substitution

PERCENT_USED=$(bc <<EOF
scale=4
($SW_USED / $SW_TOTAL) * 100
EOF
)

PERCENT_FREE=$(bc <<EOF
scale=4
($SW_FREE / $SW_TOTAL) * 100
EOF
)

# Convert the KB measurements to MB measurements

((SW_TOTAL_MB = SW_TOTAL / 1000))
((SW_USED_MB  = SW_USED / 1000))
((SW_FREE_MB  = SW_FREE / 1000))

# Produce the remaining part of the report

echo "\nTotal Amount of Swap Space:\t${SW_TOTAL_MB}MB"
echo "Total KB of Swap Space Used:\t${SW_USED_MB}MB"
echo "Total KB of Swap Space Free:\t${SW_FREE_MB}MB"
echo "\nPercent of Swap Space Used:\t${PERCENT_USED}%"
echo "\nPercent of Swap Space Free:\t${PERCENT_FREE}%"

# Grab the integer portion of the percent used

INT_PERCENT_USED=$(echo $PERCENT_USED | cut -d. -f1)

# Check to see if the percentage used maximum threshold
# has been exceeded

if (( PC_LIMIT <= INT_PERCENT_USED ))
then
    # Percent used has exceeded the threshold, send notification

    tput smso # Turn on reverse video!
    echo "\n\nWARNING: Swap Space has Exceeded the ${PC_LIMIT}% Upper
Limit!\n"
    tput rmso # Turn off reverse video!
fi
```

Listing 6.14   all-in-one_swapmon.ksh shell script listing. *(continues)*

```
echo "\n"
}

##############################################################

function Linux_swap_mon
{

free -m | grep -i swap | while read junk SW_TOTAL SW_USED SW_FREE
do

# Use the bc utility in a here document to calculate
# the percentage of free and used swap space.

PERCENT_USED=$(bc <<EOF
scale=4
($SW_USED / $SW_TOTAL) * 100
EOF
)

PERCENT_FREE=$(bc <<EOF
scale=4
($SW_FREE / $SW_TOTAL) * 100
EOF
)

    # Produce the rest of the paging space report:
    echo "\nTotal Amount of Swap Space:\t${SW_TOTAL}MB"
    echo "Total KB of Swap Space Used:\t${SW_USED}MB"
    echo "Total KB of Swap Space Free:\t${SW_FREE}MB"
    echo "\nPercent of Swap Space Used:\t${PERCENT_USED}%"
    echo "\nPercent of Swap Space Free:\t${PERCENT_FREE}%"

    # Grab the integer portion of the percent used to
    # test for the over limit threshold

    INT_PERCENT_USED=$(echo $PERCENT_USED | cut -d. -f1)

    if (( PC_LIMIT <= INT_PERCENT_USED ))
    then
        tput smso
        echo "\n\nWARNING: Paging Space has Exceeded the \
${PC_LIMIT}% Upper Limit!\n"
        tput rmso
```

Listing 6.14   all-in-one_swapmon.ksh shell script listing. *(continued)*

```
     fi

done

echo "\n"
}

##########################################################

function HP_UX_swap_mon
{

# Start a while read loop by using the piped in input from
# the swapinfo -tm command output.


swapinfo -tm | grep dev | while read junk SW_TOTAL SW_USED \
                          SW_FREE PERCENT_USED junk2
do
    # Calculate the percentage of free swap space

    ((PERCENT_FREE = 100 - $(echo $PERCENT_USED | cut -d% -f1) ))

    echo "\nTotal Amount of Swap Space:\t${SW_TOTAL}MB"
    echo "Total MB of Swap Space Used:\t${SW_USED}MB"
    echo "Total MB of Swap Space Free:\t${SW_FREE}MB"
    echo "\nPercent of Swap Space Used:\t${PERCENT_USED}"
    echo "\nPercent of Swap Space Free:\t${PERCENT_FREE}%"

    # Check for paging space exceeded the predefined limit

    if (( PC_LIMIT <= $(echo $PERCENT_USED | cut -d% -f1) ))
    then
        # Swap space is over the predefined limit, send notification

      tput smso # Turn on reverse video!
        echo "\n\nWARNING: Swap Space has Exceeded the\
${PC_LIMIT}% Upper Limit!\n"
        tput rmso # Turn reverse video off!
    fi

done

echo "\n"
}
```

Listing 6.14   all-in-one_swapmon.ksh shell script listing. *(continues)*

```
###########################################################

function AIX_paging_mon
{
################ DEFINE VARIABLES HERE ###################

PAGING_STAT=/tmp/paging_stat.out # Paging Stat hold file

############# CAPTURE AND PROCESS THE DATA ###############

# Load the data in a file without the column headings

lsps -s | tail +2 > $PAGING_STAT

# Start a while loop and feed the loop from the bottom using
# the $PAGING_STAT file as redirected input

while read TOTAL PERCENT
do
     # Clean up the data by removing the suffixes
     PAGING_MB=$(echo $TOTAL | cut -d 'MB' -f1)
     PAGING_PC=$(echo $PERCENT | cut -d% -f1)

     # Calculate the missing data: %Free, MB used and MB free
     (( PAGING_PC_FREE = 100 - PAGING_PC ))
     (( MB_USED = PAGING_MB * PAGING_PC / 100 ))
     (( MB_FREE = PAGING_MB - MB_USED ))


     # Produce the rest of the paging space report:
     echo "\nTotal MB of Paging Space:\t$TOTAL"
     echo "Total MB of Paging Space Used:\t${MB_USED}MB"
     echo "Total MB of Paging Space Free:\t${MB_FREE}MB"
     echo "\nPercent of Paging Space Used:\t${PERCENT}"
     echo "\nPercent of Paging Space Free:\t${PAGING_PC_FREE}%"

     # Check for paging space exceeded the predefined limit
     if ((PC_LIMIT <= PAGING_PC))
     then
          # Paging space is over the limit, send notification

          tput smso  # Turn on reverse video!

          echo "\n\nWARNING: Paging Space has Exceeded the ${PC_LIMIT}% \
Upper Limit!\n"

          tput rmso  # Turn off reverse video
```

Listing 6.14 all-in-one_swapmon.ksh shell script listing. *(continued)*

```
     fi

done < $PAGING_STAT

rm -f $PAGING_STAT

# Add an extra new line to the output

echo "\n"
}


############################################################
################# BEGINNING OF MAIN #####################
############################################################


# Find the Operating System and execute the correct function

case $(uname) in

    AIX) AIX_paging_mon
    ;;
    HP-UX) HP_UX_swap_mon
    ;;
    Linux) Linux_swap_mon
    ;;
    SunOS) SUN_swap_mon
    ;;
    *) echo "\nERROR: Unsupported Operating System...EXITING...\n"
       exit 1
       ;;
esac

# End of all-in-one_swapmon.ksh
```

Listing 6.14   all-in-one_swapmon.ksh shell script listing. *(continued)*

As you can see, there is not much to converting a shell script into a function. The only thing required is that you extract out of each shell script the core code that makes up the shell script. The common code should remain in the main body of the new shell script. In our example, the common parts are the PC_LIMIT, which defines the over limit percentage threshold, and the hostname of the machine. Everything else is unique to each of the four shell scripts and functions here.

To turn a shell script into a function, all you need to do is a cut and paste in your favorite editor and copy the main body of the shell script into a new shell script. This new function can be enclosed into a function in two ways, as follows:

```
function was_a_shell_script
{
shell_script_code_here
}

OR

was_a_shell_script ()
{
shell_script_code_here
}
```

I tend to use the **function** definition instead of the C language type definition. This is a personal choice, but both types of function definitions produce the same result. If you are a C programmer you will most likely prefer the C type notation. I like to use the **function** definition so that a person coming behind me trying to edit the shell script will know intuitively that this is a function because it is spelled out in the definition.

Once we have each of the four functions defined inside a single shell script, we need to know only on which operating system that we are running and to execute the appropriate function. To determine the Unix flavor, we use the **uname** command. The following **case** statement runs the correct swap/paging function as defined by the Unix flavor.

```
case $(uname) in

    AIX)    AIX_paging_mon
    ;;
    HP-UX)  HP_UX_swap_mon
    ;;
    Linux)  Linux_swap_mon
    ;;
    SunOS)  SUN_swap_mon
    ;;
    *) echo "\nERROR: Unsupported Operating System...EXITING...\n"
esac
```

Notice that if the Unix flavor is not AIX, HP-UX, Linux, or SunOS, the shell script gives an error message and exits with a return code of 1.

Other Options to Consider

As usual, we can always improve on a shell script, and this chapter is no exception. Each of these shell scripts could stand a little improvement one way or another because there is not just one way to do anything! I have noted a few suggestions here.

Event Notification

The only event notification I have included in these shell scripts and functions is a warning message presented to the user in reverse video. I usually add email notification to my alphanumeric pager also. Just use your preferred method of remote notification, and you will have the upper hand on keeping your systems running smoothly.

Log File

A log file is a great idea for this type of monitoring. I suggest that any time the threshold is crossed that a log file receives an appended message. This is simple to do by using the **tee -a** command in a pipe. See the **man** page on **tee** for more information.

Scheduled Monitoring

If you are going to do paging/swap monitoring, it is an extremely good idea to do this monitoring on a scheduled basis. Different shops have different requirements. I like to monitor every 15 minutes from 6:00 A.M. until 10:00 P.M. This way I have covered everyone from the East Coast to the West Coast. If you have locations in other time zones around the world then you may want to extend your coverage to include these times as well. The monitoring is up to you, but it is best to take a proactive approach and find the problem before someone tells *you* about it. You may also discover some trends of heavy system loads to help in troubleshooting.

Summary

In this chapter we started out with a predetermined output that we had to adhere to for any Unix flavor, and we held to it. Each operating system presented us with a new challenge because in each instance we lacked part of the required data and we had to do a little math to get into the correct format. Each of these shell scripts is a unique piece of work, but in the end we combined everything into a single multi-OS functioning shell script that determines what the Unix flavor is and executes the proper function to get the desired result. If the Unix flavor is not AIX, HP-UX, Linux, or Solaris, then the shell script gives an error message and exits cleanly.

In this chapter we covered various techniques to extract and calculate data to produce an identical output no matter the Unix flavor. I hope you gained some valuable experience with dealing with the challenge of handling different types of data to produce a standard report. This type of experience is extremely important for heterogeneous environments. In the next chapter, we will look at some techniques to monitor the load on a system.

Monitoring System Load

Have you ever seen a system start slowing down as the wait state and uptime stats rise, and finally the system crashes? I have, and it is not a pretty sight when all of the heads start popping up over the cubes. In this chapter, we are going to look at some techniques to monitor the load on a Unix system. When the system is unhappy running under a heavy load, there are many possible causes. The system may have a runaway process that is producing a ton of zombie processes every second, or it may have been up for more than a year due to the competition between System Administrators to see who can run his or her system the longest without a reboot. In any case, we want to be proactive in catching a symptom in the early stages of loading down the system.

There are really only three basic things to look at when monitoring the load on the system. First is to look at the load statistics produced as part of the **uptime** command. This output indicates the average number of jobs in the run queue over the last 5, 10, and 15 minutes in AIX and 1, 5, and 15 minutes for HP-UX, Linux, and Solaris. The second measurement to look at is the percentages of CPU usage for system/kernel, user/application, I/O wait state, and idle time. These four measurements can be obtained from the **iostat**, **vmstat**, and **sar** outputs. We will look at each of these commands individually. The final step in monitoring the CPU load is to find the CPU hogs. Most systems have a **top** like monitoring tool that shows the CPU process users in descending order of CPU usage.

We can also use the **ps auxw** command that displays CPU % usage for each process in descending order from the top. We will look at each of these in this chapter. First, let's look at the command syntax for the commands we use.

Syntax

As usual with Unix, there is not just one way to monitor a system for load. We can use any of the following commands to get system load statictics: **uptime**, **iostat**, **sar**, and **vmstat**. To illustrate the ability of each of these commands, we are going to take a look at each one of the commands individually.

Syntax for uptime

Using the **uptime** command is the most direct method of getting a measurement of the system load. Part of the output of the **uptime** command is a direct measure of the average length of the run queue over the last 5 minutes, last 10 minutes, and the last measurement is averaged over 15 minutes on AIX. For HP-UX, Linux, and Solaris the **uptime** command is a direct measure of the average length of the run queue over the last 1 minute, 5 minutes, and the last measurement is averaged over 15 minutes. The length of the run queue is a direct measurement of how busy the CPU is by the number of runnable processes waiting for CPU time, as an average, over a period of time.

We do need to put a bit of logic into the use of the **uptime** command because the output field positions vary depending on how long it has been since the last system reboot and, possibly, which Unix flavor we are running. We are going to test each of these options and produce a table of the field to extract as it relates to the Unix flavor and the time since the last system reboot. We have five possible variations to look at in this **uptime** output as you will see later. The first is 1–59 minutes, the second is 1–23 hours, and the third measurement is when the system has been up for more than 24 hours. After the system has been up for at least one day, then we have to consider hours and minutes again! Believe it or not, the load fields continue to float during each day. When the system reaches an *exact* hour, to the minute, of the reboot day, then an **hrs** field is added; this is true for the *anniversary* first hour, too. In this case, the **min** field is added along with the **day** field. Follow along through the next few sections to see how the fields vary during these five stages.

AIX

This **uptime** output is shown when the AIX system has been up for 26 minutes. The field we want is in the **$9** position.

```
# uptime
  01:46PM   up 26 mins,   7 users,   load average: 3.11, 1.38, 0.58
```

This **uptime** output is shown when the AIX system has been up for 1 hour and 22 minutes. The field we want is in the **$8** position.

```
# uptime
  01:08PM   up   1:22,   6 users,   load average: 2.74, 1.38, 0.59
```

This **uptime** output is shown when the AIX system has been up for 2 days, 22 hours, and 3 minutes. The field we want is in the **$10** position.

```
# uptime
  04:59PM   up 2 days,  22:03,   4 users,   load average: 1.51, 1.67, 1.70
```

This **uptime** output is shown when the AIX system has been up for 21 days and exactly 17 minutes. The field we want is in the **$11** position.

```
# uptime
  09:16PM   up 21 days, 17 mins,   9 users,   load average: 1.31, 1.82, 1.61
```

This **uptime** output is shown when the AIX system has been up for 21 days and exactly 6 hours. The field we want is in the **$11** position.

```
# uptime
  09:16PM   up 21 days, 6 hrs,   2 users,   load average: 1.01, 1.62, 1.94
```

From these **uptime** command outputs on my AIX machine, notice the last three columns. The load average is the average number of runnable processes over the preceding 5-, 10-, and 15-minute intervals. AIX is different in this respect because our other Unix flavors show the load average over the last 1-, 5-, and 15-minute intervals.

HP-UX

This **uptime** output is shown when the HP-UX system has been up for 17 minutes. The field we want is in the **$9** position.

```
# uptime
  4:33am  up 17 mins,   3 users,   load average: 1.69, 1.36, 0.86
```

This **uptime** output is shown when the HP-UX system has been up for 1 hour and 38 minutes. The field we want is in the **$8** position.

```
# uptime
  5:54am  up  1:38,   3 users,   load average: 1.67, 0.60, 0.38
```

This **uptime** output is shown when the HP-UX system has been up for 1 day, 5 hours, and 32 minutes. The field we want is in the **$10** position.

```
# uptime
  5:49pm  up 1 day,  5:32,   3 users,   load average: 4.25, 1.85, 0.76
```

This **uptime** output is shown when the HP-UX system has been up for 4 days and exactly 22 minutes. The field we want is in the **$11** position.

```
# uptime
  9:16pm  up 4 days, 22 mins,   9 users,   load average: 2.33, 1.99, 1.30
```

This **uptime** output is shown when the HP-UX system has been up for 4 days and exactly 5 hours. The field we want is in the **$11** position.

```
# uptime
   9:16pm  up 4 days, 5 hrs,   2 users,   load average: 1.01, 1.62, 1.94
```

From the **uptime** commands output on my HP-UX machine, notice the last three columns. The load average on an HP-UX machine shows the average number of runnable processes over the preceding 1-, 5-, and 15-minute intervals.

Linux

This **uptime** output is shown when the Linux system has been up 20 minutes. The field we want is in the **$9** position.

```
# uptime
   12:17pm  up 20 min,   4 users,   load average: 2.29, 2.17, 1.51
```

This **uptime** output is shown when the Linux system has been up for 1 hour and 7 minutes. The field we want is in the **$8** position.

```
# uptime
   1:04pm  up  1:07,   4 users,   load average: 1.74, 2.10, 2.09
```

This **uptime** output is shown when the Linux system has been up for 12 days, 19 hours, and 3 minutes. The field we want is in the **$10** position.

```
# uptime
   4:40pm  up 12 days, 19:03,   4 users,   load average: 1.52, 0.47, 0.16
```

This **uptime** output is shown when the Linux system has been up for 14 days and exactly 17 minutes. The field we want is in the **$11** position.

```
# uptime
   9:16pm  up 14 days, 17 mins,   9 users,   load average: 1.31, 1.82, 1.61
```

This **uptime** output is shown when the Linux system has been up for 14 days and exactly 5 hours. The field we want is in the **$11** position.

```
# uptime
   9:16pm  up 14 days, 5 hr,   2 users,   load average: 1.01, 1.69, 1.84
```

From the **uptime** command output on my Linux machine, notice the last three columns. The load average on a Linux machine shows the average number of runnable processes over the preceding 1-, 5-, and 15-minute intervals. For Linux we need to extract the **$11** field from the **uptime** output to look at the CPU load over the last 1-minute interval.

Solaris

This **uptime** output is shown when the Solaris system has been up 11 minutes. The field we want is in the **$9** position.

```
# uptime
  12:31pm  up 11 min(s),  1 user,  load average: 1.01, 0.75, 0.38
```

This **uptime** output is shown when the Solaris system has been up 1 hour and 30 minutes. The field we want is in the **$8** position.

```
# uptime
  1:50pm  up  1:30,  1 user,  load average: 1.35, 1.87, 1.95
```

This **uptime** output is shown when the Solaris system has been up for 1 day, 5 hours, and 41 minutes. The field we want is in the **$10** position.

```
# uptime
  6:01pm  up 1 day(s),  5:41,  1 user,  load average: 2.70, 1.27, 0.53
```

This **uptime** output is shown when the Solaris system has been up for 2 days and exactly 25 minutes. The field we want is in the **$11** position.

```
# uptime
  9:16pm  up 2 day(s), 25 mins, 9 users,  load average: 3.31, 2.83, 2.40
```

This **uptime** output is shown when the Solaris system has been up for 2 days and exactly 7 hours. The field we want is in the **$11** position.

```
# uptime
  9:16pm  up 2 days, 7 hrs,  2 users,  load average: 2.02, 1.92, 0.97
```

From the **uptime** command output on my Solaris machine, notice the last three columns. The load average on a Solaris machine shows the average number of runnable processes over the preceding 1-, 5-, and 15-minute intervals.

What Is the Common Denominator?

In each case, we are interested in the newest available data, which is the last 5 minutes on an AIX machine and the last minute on HP-UX, Linux, and Solaris machines. The easiest way to look at this *floating* field is to make a table of the positional parameter's placement as related to the Unix flavor and the amount of time since the last system reboot. Once we can see how the parameter is moving, we can build some logic into the script to extract the latest load statistics. The field data is shown in Table 7.1.

Table 7.1   Field Movement Based on Uptime and Unix Flavor

TIME SINCE LAST REBOOT:	UNIX FLAVOR			
	AIX	**HP-UX**	**LINUX**	**SOLARIS**
Minutes	$9	$9	$9	$9
Hours	$8	$8	$8	$8
Day(s)	$10	$10	$10	$10
Day(s) on the exact reboot hour anniversary	$11	$11	$11	$11
Day(s) on the first 59 minutes of the reboot hour anniversary	$11	$11	$11	$11

As you can see in Table 7.1, the most current load field varies all the time. It looks as if we are in luck, though, for the operating system! We do not have to worry about the Unix flavor, but we do have to test the time since the last system reboot. From the previous **uptime** command outputs, did you notice anything that will help us determine which field we need to extract? It turns out that we have an indicator for each of the five possible field values in the **uptime** output. If the system has been up for less than one hour, then we **grep** on **min**, which will pattern match on each Unix flavor output. If the system has been up for more than 24 hours, then we **grep** first for **day** *and* **min** in the **uptime** output, then **day** *and* **hr**, and finally just **day**. At the end of the chapter, I will show you a cleaner way to do this data extraction.

Scripting an Uptime Field Test Solution

With the five defined tests we can use **grep** to extract the correct field from the **uptime** command output. Let's look at the code in Listing 7.1 to see how this works.

```
#!/bin/ksh
#
# SCRIPT: uptime_fieldtest.ksh
# AUTHOR: Randy Michael
# DATE: 07/28/2002
# PLATFORM: Any Unix
# PURPOSE: This shell script is used to demonstrate how the
#          average load statistics field shifts depending on
#          how long it has been since the last system reboot.
```

Listing 7.1   uptime_fieldtest.ksh shell script listing.

```
#            The options are "min", "day", "hr" and combinations.
#            If all other tests fail then the system has been running
#            for 1-23 hours.

echo "\n" # Write one blank new line to the screen

# Show a current uptime output

uptime

# Find the correct field based on how long the system has been up.

if $(uptime | grep day | grep min >/dev/null)
then
     FIELD=11
elif $(uptime | grep day | grep hr >/dev/null)
then
     FIELD=11
elif $(uptime | grep day >/dev/null)
then
     FIELD=10
elif $(uptime | grep min >/dev/null)
then
     FIELD=9

else # The machine has been up for 1 to 23 hours.

     FIELD=8
fi

# Display the correct field.

echo "\nField is $FIELD \n"
```

Listing 7.1   uptime_fieldtest.ksh shell script listing. *(continued)*

The shell script in Listing 7.1 shows a method of grepping out the four known options and defaulting to the fifth option field if the system has been up for 1–23 hours because there is nothing to **grep** on. This is the method that is used in the shell script to monitor the system load using the **uptime** command. The remaining load monitoring techniques do not require any special treatment of positional parameters in the command output.

Note: In finding the floating fields in the **uptime** command output, I hope you realize that you need to pay careful attention to each command's output. What looks like a simple, normal, always-the-same output can trick you into programming errors into a shell script without really knowing. The exact error that is produced will likely depend on when the system was last rebooted as related to when the shell script was written and tested.

Syntax for iostat

To get the CPU load statistics from the **iostat** command, we have to be a little flexible between Unix flavors. For AIX and HP-UX machines, we need to use the **-t** command switch, and for Linux and Solaris we use the **-c** switch. Due to the Unix flavor dependency, we need to first check the operating system using the **uname** command. Then, based on the OS, we can assign the proper switch to the **iostat** command.

Let's look at the output of the **iostat** command for each of our Unix flavors, AIX, HP-UX, Linux, and Solaris.

AIX

```
# iostat -t 10 2

tty:    tin      tout    avg-cpu:  % user    % sys    % idle    % iowait
        0.2      33.6                2.4       8.2      84.0       5.4
        0.1    1188.4               16.8      83.2       0.0       0.0
```

In this AIX output, notice the last four fields, %user, %sys, %idle, and %iowait. These four fields are the ones that we want to extract. The field positions are $3, $4, $5, and $6, and we want just the last line of the output because the first line of data is an average since the last system reboot. Also, notice that the rows of actual data consist entirely of numeric characters. This will become important as we look at each operating system.

HP-UX

```
# iostat -t 10 2

                        tty            cpu
                    tin tout     us  ni  sy  id
                      0    2      1   0   1  97

        device   bps    sps    msps

        c0t6d0     0    0.0    1.0


                    tty            cpu
                 tin tout      us  ni  sy  id
                   0    0      41   0  59   0

        device   bps    sps    msps

        c0t6d0     1    0.1    1.0
```

Notice that the HP-UX output differs greatly from the AIX **iostat** output. The only thing that distinguishes the CPU data from the rest of the data is the fact that the entire row of data is numeric. This is an important characteristic of the HP-UX data, and it will help us extract the data that we are looking for. Notice again that the first set of statistics is an average since the last system reboot.

Linux

```
iostat -c 10 2

Linux 2.4.2-2 (bambam)      07/29/2002

avg-cpu:   %user    %nice     %sys     %idle
            0.69     0.00     0.48    98.83
avg-cpu:   %user    %nice     %sys     %idle
           62.80     0.00    37.20     0.00
```

Notice that the Linux **iostat** command switch for CPU statistics is **-c**, instead of the **-t** that we used for AIX and HP-UX. In this output we have the average of the CPU load since the last reboot, and then the current data is shown in the second command output. Also notice that the actual data presented is entirely numeric. It looks as if we have a trend.

Solaris

```
iostat -c 10 2

      cpu
 us sy wt id
  3 14  0 83
 17 81  0  2
```

The Solaris **iostat -c** output shows the load average statistics since the last system reboot on the first line of data and the most current data on the last line. Notice again that the actual data is a row of numeric characters. Knowing that the data is always on a row that is numeric characters allows us to greatly simplify writing this shell script.

What Is the Common Denominator?

The real common denominator for the **iostat** command data between each Unix flavor is that we have a row of numeric data only. The only thing remaining is the fields for each OS, which vary by field and content. We want just the last line of data, which is the most current data. From this set of criteria, let's write a little code to see how we can specify the correct switch and set the proper fields to extract. We can do both of these tasks with a single **case** statement, as shown in Listing 7.2.

```
OS=$(uname)

case $OS in
AIX|HP-UX)   SWITCH='-t'
             F1=3
             F2=4
             F3=5
             F4=6
             echo "\nThe Operating System is $OS\n"
             ;;
Linux|SunOS) SWITCH='-c'
             F1=1
             F2=2
             F3=3
             F4=4
             echo "\nThe Operating System is $OS\n"
             ;;

*) echo "\nERROR: $OS is not a supported operating system\n"
   echo "\n\t...EXITING...\n"
   exit 1
   ;;
esac
```

Listing 7.2   Case statement for the iostat fields of data.

Notice in Listing 7.2 that we use a single **case** statement to set up the environment for the shell script to run the correct **iostat** command for each of the four Unix flavors. If the Unix flavor is not in the list, then the user receives an error message before the script exits with a return code of 1, one. Later we will cover the entire shell script.

Syntax for sar

The **sar** command stands for *system activity report*. Using the **sar** command we can take direct sample intervals for a specific time period. For example, we can take 4 samples that are 10 seconds each, and the **sar** command automatically averages the results for us.

Let's look at the output of the **sar** command for each of our Unix flavors, AIX, HP-UX, Linux, and Solaris.

AIX

```
# sar 10 4

AIX yogi 1 5 000125604800     07/26/02

17:44:54    %usr    %sys    %wio    %idle
17:45:04      25      75       0       0
```

```
17:45:14      25      75        0        0
17:45:24      26      74        0        0
17:45:34      25      75        0        0

Average       25      75        0        0
```

Now let's look at the average of the samples directly.

```
# sar 10 4 | grep Average

Average       26      74        0        0
```

HP-UX

```
# sar 10 4

HP-UX dino B.10.20 A 9000/715    07/29/102

22:48:10     %usr    %sys     %wio     %idle
22:48:20      40      60        0        0
22:48:30      40      60        0        0
22:48:40      12      19        0       68
22:48:50       0       0        0      100

Average       23      35        0       42
```

Now let's only look at the average of the samples directly.

```
# sar 10 4 | grep Average

Average       25      37        0       38
```

Linux

```
# sar 10 4
Linux 2.4.2-2 (bambam)     07/29/2002

10:01:59 PM       CPU     %user    %nice    %system    %idle
10:02:09 PM       all      0.10     0.00       0.00     99.90
10:02:19 PM       all      0.00     0.00       0.10     99.90
10:02:29 PM       all     11.40     0.00       5.00     83.60
10:02:39 PM       all     60.80     0.00      36.30      2.90
Average:          all     18.07     0.00      10.35     71.58
```

Now let's look at the average of the samples directly.

```
# sar 10 4 | grep Average

Average:          all     18.07     0.00      10.35     71.58
```

Solaris

```
# sar 10 4

SunOS wilma 5.8 Generic i86pc    07/29/02

23:01:55    %usr    %sys    %wio    %idle
23:02:05      1       1       0       98
23:02:15     12      53       0       35
23:02:25     15      67       0       18
23:02:35     21      59       0       21


Average      12      45       0       43
```

Now let's look at the average of the samples directly.

```
# sar 10 4 | grep Average
Average      12      45       0       43
```

What Is the Common Denominator?

With the **sar** command the only common denominator is that we can always **grep** on the word "Average." Like the **iostat** command, the fields vary between some Unix flavors. We can use a similar **case** statement to extract the correct fields for each Unix flavor, as shown in Listing 7.3.

```
OS=$(uname)

case $OS in
AIX|HP-UX|SunOS)
        F1=2
        F2=3
        F3=4
        F4=5
        echo "\nThe Operating System is $OS\n"
        ;;
Linux)
        F1=3
        F2=4
        F3=5
        F4=6
        echo "\nThe Operating System is $OS\n"
        ;;
*) echo "\nERROR: $OS is not a supported operating system\n"
   echo "\n\t...EXITING...\n"
   exit 1
   ;;
esac
```

Listing 7.3 Case statement for the sar fields of data.

Notice in Listing 7.3 that a single **case** statement sets up the environment for the shell script to select the correct fields from the **sar** command for each of the four Unix flavors. If the Unix flavor is not in the list, then the user receives an error message before the script exits with a return code of 1, one. Later we will cover the entire shell script.

Syntax for vmstat

The **vmstat** command stands for *virtual memory statistics*. Using the **vmstat** command, we can get a lot of data about the system including memory, paging space, page faults, and CPU statistics. We are concentrating on the CPU statistics in this chapter, so let's stay on track. The **vmstat** commands also allow us to take direct samples over intervals for a specific time period. The **vmstat** command does not do any averaging for us, however, we are going to stick with two intervals. The first interval is the average of the system load since the last system reboot, like the **iostat** command. The last line contains the most current sample.

Let's look at the output of the **vmstat** command for each of our Unix flavors, AIX, HP-UX, Linux, and Solaris.

AIX

```
[root:yogi]@/scripts# vmstat 30 2
kthr     memory            page              faults        cpu
----- ----------- ------------------------ ------------ -----------
 r  b   avm   fre  re  pi  po  fr   sr  cy  in   sy   cs us sy id wa
 0  0 23936   580   0   0   0   0    2   0 103 2715  713  8 25 67  0
 1  0 23938   578   0   0   0   0    0   0 115 9942 2730 24 76  0  0
```

The last line of output is what we are looking for. This is the average of the CPU load over the length of the interval. We want just the last four columns in the output. The fields that we want to extract for AIX are in positions **$14**, **$15**, **$16**, and **$17**.

HP-UX

```
# vmstat 30 2
      procs        memory        page             faults     cpu
 r  b  w  avm  free  re  at  pi  po  fr  de  sr   in    sy   cs us sy id
 0 39  0 8382  290 122  26   2   0   0   0   3  128 2014  146 14 21 65
 1 40  0 7532  148 345  71   0   0   0   0   0  108 5550  379 29 43 27
```

The HP-UX **vmstat** output is a long string of data. Notice for the CPU data that HP-UX supplies only three values: user part, system part, and the CPU idle time. The fields that we want to extract are in positions **$16**, **$17**, and **$18**.

Linux

```
# vmstat 30 2
```

procs			memory				swap		io		system		cpu		
r	b	w	swpd	free	buff	cache	si	so	bi	bo	in	cs	us	sy	id
2	0	0	244	1088	1676	21008	0	0	1	0	127	72	1	1	99
3	0	0	244	1132	1676	21008	0	0	0	1	212	530	37	23	40

Like HP-UX, the Linux **vmstat** output for CPU activity has three fields: user part, system part, and the CPU idle time. The fields that we want to extract are in positions **$14**, **$15**, and **$16**.

Solaris

```
# vmstat 30 2
```

procs		memory		page							disk				faults			cpu		
r	b	w	swap	free	re	mf	pi	po	fr	de	sr	cd	f0	s0	--	in	sy	cs	us	sy	id
0	0	0	558316	33036	57	433	2	0	0	0	0	0	0	0		111	500	77	2	8	90
0	0	0	556192	29992	387	2928	0	0	0	0	0	1	0	0		155	2711	273	14	60	26

As with HP-UX and Linux, the Solaris **vmstat** output for CPU activity consists of the last three fields: user part, system part, and the CPU idle time.

What Is the Common Denominator?

There are at least two common denominators for the **vmstat** command output between the Unix flavors. The first is that the CPU data is in the last fields. On AIX the data is in the last four fields with the added I/O wait state. HP-UX, Linux, and Solaris do not list the wait state. The second common factor is that the data is always on a row that is entirely numeric. Again, we need a **case** statement to parse the correct fields for the command output. Take a look at Listing 7.4.

```
OS=$(uname)

case $OS in
AIX)
        F1=14
        F2=15
        F3=16
        F4=17
        echo "\nThe Operating System is $OS\n"
        ;;
```

Listing 7.4   Case statement for the vmstat fields of data.

```
HP-UX)
        F1=16
        F2=17
        F3=18
        F4=1 # This "F4=1" is bogus and not used for HP-UX

        echo "\nThe Operating System is $OS\n"
        ;;
Linux)
        F1=14
        F2=15
        F3=16
        F4=1 # This "F4=1" is bogus and not used for Linux

        echo "\nThe Operating System is $OS\n"
        ;;
SunOS)
        F1=20
        F2=21
        F3=22
        F4=1 # This "F4=1" is bogus and not used for SunOS

        echo "\nThe Operating System is $OS\n"
        ;;
*) echo "\nERROR: $OS is not a supported operating system\n"
   echo "\n\t...EXITING...\n"
   exit 1
   ;;
esac
```

Listing 7.4   Case statement for the vmstat fields of data. *(continued)*

Notice in Listing 7.4 that the F4 variable gets a valid assignment only on the AIX match. For HP-UX, Linux, and Solaris, the F4 variable is assigned the value of the **$1** field, specified by the F4=1 variable assignment. This bogus assignment is made so that we do not need a special **vmstat** command statement for each operating system. You will see how this works in detail in the scripting section.

Scripting the Solutions

Each of the techniques presented is slightly different in execution and output. Some options need to be timed over an interval for a user-defined amount of time, measured in seconds. We can get an immediate load measurement using the **uptime** command, but the **sar, iostat**, and **vmstat** commands require the user to specify a period of time to measure over and the number of intervals to sample the load. If you enter the **sar, iostat**, or **vmstat** commands without any arguments, then the statistics presented are an average since the last system reboot. Because we want current statistics, the scripts must supply a period of time to sample. We are always going to initialize the INTERVAL variable to equal 2. The first line of output is measured since the last system reboot, and the second line is the current data that we are looking for.

Let's look at each of these commands in separate shell scripts in the following sections.

Using uptime to Measure the System Load

Using **uptime** is one of the best indicators of the system load. The last columns of the output represent the average of the *run queue* over the last 5, 10, and 15 minutes for an AIX machine and over the last 1, 5, and 10 minutes for HP-UX, Linux, and Solaris. A run queue is where jobs wanting CPU time line up for their turn for some processing time in the CPU. The priority of the process, or on some systems a *thread*, has a direct influence on how long a job has to wait in line before getting more CPU time. The lower the priority, the more CPU time. The higher the priority, the less CPU time.

The **uptime** command always has an average of the length of the run queue. The threshold trigger value that you set will depend on the normal load of your system. My little C-10 AIX box starts getting very slow when the run queue hits 2, but the S-80 at work typically runs with a run queue value over 8 because it is a multiprocessor machine running a terabyte database. With these differences in acceptable run queue levels, you will need to tailor the threshold level for notification on a machine-by-machine basis.

Scripting with the uptime Command

Scripting the **uptime** solution is a short shell script, and the response is immediate. As you remember in the "Syntax" section, we had to follow the floating load statistics as the time since the last reboot moved from minutes, to hours, and even days after the machine was rebooted. The good thing is that the floating fields are consistent across the Unix flavors studied in this book. Let's look at the uptime_loadmon.ksh shell shown in Listing 7.5.

```
#!/bin/ksh
#
# SCRIPT: uptime_loadmon.ksh
# AUTHOR: Randy Michael
# DATE: 07/26/2002
# REV: 1.0.P
# PLATFORM: AIX, HP-UX, Linux, and Solaris
#
```

Listing 7.5 uptime_loadmon.ksh shell script listing.

```
# PURPOSE: This shell script uses the "uptime" command to
#          extract the most current load average data. There
#          is a special need in this script to determine
#          how long the system has been running since the
#          last reboot. The load average field "floats"
#          during the first 24 hours after a system restart.
#
# set -x # Uncomment to debug this shell script
# set -n # Uncomment to check script syntax without any execution
#
####################################################
############# DEFINE VARIABLES HERE ##############
####################################################



MAXLOAD=2.00
typeset -i INT_MAXLOAD=$MAXLOAD

# Find the correct field to extract based on how long
# the system has been up, or since the last reboot.

if $(uptime | grep day | grep min >/dev/null)
then
     FIELD=11
elif $(uptime | grep day | grep hrs >/dev/null)
then
     FIELD=11
elif $(uptime | grep day >/dev/null)
then
     FIELD=10
elif $(uptime | grep min >/dev/null)
then
     FIELD=9
else
     FIELD=8
fi


####################################################
######## BEGIN GATHERING STATISTICS HERE ##########
####################################################

echo "\nGathering System Load Average using the \"uptime\" command\n"

# This next command statement extracts the latest
# load statistics no matter what the Unix flavor is.

LOAD=$(uptime | sed s/,//g | awk '{print $'$FIELD'}')
```

Listing 7.5   uptime_loadmon.ksh shell script listing. *(continues)*

```
# We need an integer representation of the $LOAD
# variable to do the test for the load going over
# the set threshold defined by the $INT_MAXLOAD
# variable

typeset -i INT_LOAD=$LOAD

# If the current load has exceeded the threshold then
# issue a warning message. The next step always shows
# the user what the current load and threshold values
# are set to.

((INT_LOAD >= INT_MAXLOAD)) && echo "\nWARNING: System load has \
reached ${LOAD}\n"

echo "\nSystem load value is currently at ${LOAD}"
echo "The load threshold is set to ${MAXLOAD}\n"
```

Listing 7.5 uptime_loadmon.ksh shell script listing. *(continued)*

There are two statements that I want to point out in Listing 7.5 that are highlighted in boldface text. First, notice the LOAD= statement. To make the variable assignment we use command substitution, defined by the VAR=$(command statement) notation. In the command statement we execute the **uptime** command and pipe the output to a **sed** statement. This **sed** statement removes all of the commas (,) from the **uptime** output. We need to take this step because the load statistics are comma separated. Once the commas are removed, the remaining output is piped to the **awk** statement that extracts the correct field that is defined at the top of the shell script by the FIELD variable and based on how long the system has been running.

In this **awk** statement notice how we find the positional parameter that the $FIELD variable is pointing to. If you try to use the syntax $$FIELD, the result is the current process ID ($$) and the *word* FIELD. To get around this little problem of directly accessing what a variable is pointing to, we use the following syntax:

```
# The $8 variable points to the value 34.

FIELD=8

# Wrong usage

echo $$FIELD
3243FIELD

# Correct usage

echo $'$FIELD'
34
```

Notice that the latter usage is correct, and the actual result is the *value* of the $8 field, which is currently 34. This is really telling us the value of what a pointer is pointing to. You will see other uses of this technique as we go through this chapter.

The second command statement that I want to point out is the test of the INT_LOAD value to the INT_MAXLOAD value, which are integer values of the LOAD and MAXLOAD variables. If the INT_LOAD is equal to, or has exceeded, the INT_MAXLOAD, then we use a logical AND (&&) to **echo** a warning to the user's screen. Using the logical AND saves a little code and is faster than an **if..then..else** statement.

You can see the uptime_loadmon.ksh shell script in action in Listings 7.6 and 7.7.

```
#  ./uptime_loadmon.ksh

Gathering System Load Average using the "uptime" command


System load value is currently at 1.86
The load threshold is set to 2.00
```

Listing 7.6 Script in action under "normal" load.

Listing 7.6 shows the uptime_loadmon.ksh shell script in action on a machine that is under a normal load. Listing 7.7 shows the same machine under an excessive load—at least, it is excessive for this little machine.

```
#  ./uptime_loadmon.ksh

Gathering System Load Average using the "uptime" command


WARNING: System load has reached 2.97


System load value is currently at 2.97
The load threshold is set to 2.00
```

Listing 7.7 Script in action under "excessive" load.

This is about all there is to using the **uptime** command. Let's move on to the **sar** command.

Using sar to Measure the System Load

Most Unix flavors have **sar** data collection set up by default. This **sar** data is presented when the **sar** command is executed without any switches. The data that is displayed is automatically collected at scheduled intervals throughout the day and compiled into a report at day's end. By default, the system keeps a month's worth of data available for online viewing. This is great for seeing the basic trends of the machine as it is loaded through the day. If we want to collect data at a specific time of day for a specific period of time, then we need to add the number of seconds for each interval and the total number of intervals to the **sar** command. The final line in the output is an average of all of the previous sample intervals.

This is where our shell script comes into play. By using a shell script with the times and intervals defined, we can take samples of the system load over small or large increments of time without interfering with the system's collection of **sar** data. This can be a valuable tool for things like taking hundreds of small incremental samples as a development application is being tested. Of course, this technique can also help in troubleshooting just about any application. Let's look at how we script the solution.

Scripting with the sar Command

For each of our Unix flavors the **sar** command produces four CPU load statistics. The outputs vary somewhat, but the basic idea remains the same. In each case, we define an INTERVAL variable specifying the total number of samples to take and a SECS variable to define the total number of seconds for each sample interval. Notice that we used the variable SECS as opposed to SECONDS. We do not want to use the variable SECONDS because it is a Korn shell built-in variable used for timing in a shell. As I stated in the introduction, this book uses variable names in uppercase so the reader will quickly know that the code is referencing a variable; however, in the real world you may want to use the lowercase version of the variable name. It really would not matter here because we are defining the variable value and then using it within the same second, hopefully.

The next step in this shell script is to define which positional fields we need to extract to get the **sar** data for each of the Unix operating systems. For this step we use a **case** statement using the **uname** command output to define the fields of data. It turns out that AIX, HP-UX, and SunOS operating systems all have the **sar** data located in the $2, $3, $4, and $5 positions. Linux differs in this respect with the **sar** data residing in the $3, $4, $5, and $6 positions. In each case, these field numbers are assigned to the F1, F2, F3, and F4 variables inside the **case** statement.

Let's look at the `sar_loadmon.ksh` shell script in Listing 7.8 and cover the remaining details at the end.

```
#!/bin/ksh
#
# SCRIPT: sar_loadmon.ksh
# AUTHOR: Randy Michael
# DATE: 07/26/2002
# REV: 1.0.P
# PLATFORM: AIX, HP-UX, Linux, and Solaris
#
```

Listing 7.8 sar_loadmon.ksh shell script listing.

```
# PURPOSE: This shell script takes multiple samples of the CPU
#          usage using the "sar" command. The average of
#          sample periods is shown to the user based on the
#          Unix operating system that this shell script is
#          executing on. Different Unix flavors have differing
#          outputs and the fields vary too.
#
# REV LIST:
#
#
# set -n # Uncomment to check the script syntax without any execution
# set -x # Uncomment to debug this shell script
#
####################################################
############# DEFINE VARIABLES HERE ##############
####################################################

SECS=30   # Defines the number of seconds for each sample
INTERVAL=10 # Defines the total number of sampling intervals
OS=$(uname) # Defines the Unix flavor

####################################################
##### SETUP THE ENVIRONMENT FOR EACH OS HERE ######
####################################################

# These "F-numbers" point to the correct field in the
# command output for each Unix flavor.

case $OS in
AIX|HP-UX|SunOS)
        F1=2
        F2=3
        F3=4
        F4=5
        echo "\nThe Operating System is $OS\n"
        ;;
Linux)
        F1=3
        F2=4
        F3=5
        F4=6
        echo "\nThe Operating System is $OS\n"
        ;;
*) echo "\nERROR: $OS is not a supported operating system\n"
   echo "\n\t...EXITING...\n"
   exit 1
   ;;
```

Listing 7.8   sar_loadmon.ksh shell script listing. *(continues)*

```
esac

######################################################
######## BEGIN GATHERING STATISTICS HERE ##########
######################################################

echo "Gathering CPU Statistics using sar...\n"
echo "There are $INTERVAL sampling periods with"
echo "each interval lasting $SECS seconds"
echo "\n...Please wait while gathering statistics...\n"

# This "sar" command takes $INTERVAL samples, each lasting
# $SECS seconds. The average of this output is captured.

sar $SECS $INTERVAL | grep Average \
        | awk '{print $'$F1', $'$F2', $'$F3', $'$F4'}' \
        | while read FIRST SECOND THIRD FOURTH
do
        # Based on the Unix Flavor, tell the user the
        # result of the statistics gathered.

        case $OS in
        AIX|HP-UX|SunOS)
                echo "\nUser part is ${FIRST}%"
                echo "System part is ${SECOND}%"
                echo "I/O Wait is ${THIRD}%"
                echo "Idle time is ${FOURTH}%\n"
                ;;

        Linux)
                echo "\nUser part is ${FIRST}%"
                echo "Nice part is ${SECOND}%"
                echo "System part is ${THIRD}%"
                echo "Idle time is ${FOURTH}%\n"
                ;;
        esac
done
```

Listing 7.8 sar_loadmon.ksh shell script listing. *(continued)*

In the shell script in Listing 7.8 we start by defining the data time intervals. In these definitions we are taking 10 interval samples of 30 seconds each, for a total of 300 seconds, or 5 minutes. Then we grab the Unix flavor using the **uname** command and assigning the operating system value to the OS variable. Following these definitions we define the data fields that contain the **sar** data for each operating system. In this case Linux is the oddball with an offset of one position.

Now we get to the interesting part where we actually take the data sample. Look at the following **sar** command statement, and we will decipher how it works.

```
sar $SECS $INTERVAL | grep Average \
           | awk '{print $'$F1', $'$F2', $'$F3', $'$F4'}' \
           | while read FIRST SECOND THIRD FOURTH
```

We really need to look at the statement one pipe at a time. In the very first part of the statement we take the sample(s) over the defined number of intervals. Consider the following statement and output:

```
SECS=30
INTERVAL=10

# sar $SECS $INTERVAL

AIX yogi 1 5 000125604800    07/31/02

19:24:00     %usr     %sys     %wio     %idle
19:24:30        0        1        1       98
19:25:00        4       15       13       68
19:25:30       26       28       40        6
19:26:00       13       12       11       64
19:26:30       16       44        0       39
19:27:00       27       73        0        0
19:27:30       20       48        2       30
19:28:00        5        6        9       80
19:28:30       11        9        5       75
19:29:00        9       18        0       73

Average        13       26        8       53
```

The previous output is produced by the first part of the **sar** command statement. Then, all of this output is piped to the next part of the statement, as shown here:

```
sar $SECS $INTERVAL | grep Average

Average        13       26        8       53
```

Now we have the row of data that we want to work with, which we grepped out using the word `Average` as a pattern match. The next step is to extract the positional fields that contain the data for user, system, I/O wait, and idle time for AIX. Remember in the previous script section that we defined the field numbers and assigned them to the F1, F2, F3, and F4 variables, which in our case results in F1=2, F2=3, F3=4, and F4=5. Using the following extension to our previous command we get the following statement:

```
sar $SECS $INTERVAL | grep Average \
    | awk '{print $'$F1', $'$F2', $'$F3', $'$F4'}'
```

Notice that we continued the command statement on the next line by placing a backslash (\) at the end of the first line of the statement. In the **awk** part of the statement you can see a confusing list of dollar signs and "F" variables. The purpose of this set of characters is to *directly* access what the "F" variables are pointing to. Let's run through this in detail by example.

The F1 variable has the value 2 assigned to it. This value is the positional location of the first data field that we want to extract. So we want to access the value at the $2 position. Makes sense? When we extract the $2 data we get the value 13, as defined in the previous step. Instead of going in this roundabout method, we want to *directly* access the *field* that the F1 variable points to. Just remember that a variable is only a pointer to a value, nothing more! We want to point directly to what another variable is pointing to. The solution is to use the following syntax:

```
$'$F1'
```

OR

```
$\$F1
```

In any case, the innermost pointer ($) must be *escaped*, which removes the special meaning. For this shell script we use the $'$F1' notation. The result of this notation, in this example, is 13, which is the value that we want. This is not smoke and mirrors when you understand how it works.

The final part of the **sar** command statement is to pipe the four data fields to a **while** loop so that we can do something with the data, which is where we end the **sar** statement and enter the **while** loop.

The only thing that we do in the **while** loop is to display the results based on the Unix flavor. The sar_loadmon.ksh shell script is in action in Listing 7.9.

```
# ./sar_loadmon.ksh

The Operating System is AIX

Gathering CPU Statistics using sar...

There are 10 sampling periods with
each interval lasting 30 seconds

...Please wait while gathering statistics...


User part is 13%
System part is 26%
I/O wait state is 8%
Idle time is 53%
```

Listing 7.9   sar_loadmon.ksh shell script in action.

From the output presented in Listing 7.9 you can see that the shell script queries the system for its operating system, which is AIX here. Then the user is notified of the sampling periods and the length of each sample period. The output is displayed to the user by field. That is it for using the **sar** command. Now let's move on to the **iostat** command.

Using iostat to Measure the System Load

The **iostat** command is mostly used to collect disk storage statistics, but by using the **-t**, or **-c** command switch, depending on the operating system, we can see the CPU statistics as we saw them in the *syntax* section for the **iostat** command. We are going to create a shell script using the **iostat** command and use almost the same technique as we did in the last section.

Scripting with the iostat Command

In this shell script we are going to use a very similar technique to the **sar** shell script in the previous section. The difference is that we are going to take only two intervals with a long sampling period. As an example, the INTERVAL variable is set to 2, and the SECS variable is set to 300 seconds, which is 5 minutes. Also, because we have two possible switch values, **-t** and **-c**, we need to add a new variable called SWITCH. Let's look at the iostat_loadmon.ksh shell script in Listing 7.10, and we will cover the differences at the end in more detail.

```
#!/bin/ksh
#
# SCRIPT: iostat_loadmon.ksh
# AUTHOR: Randy Michael
# DATE: 07/26/2002
# REV: 1.0.P
# PLATFORM: AIX, HP-UX, Linux, and Solaris
#
# PURPOSE: This shell script take two samples of the CPU
#          usage using the "iostat" command. The first set of
#          data is an average since the last system reboot. The
#          second set of data is an average over the sampling
#          period, or $INTERVAL. The result of the data acquired
#          during the sampling period is shown to the user based
#          on the Unix operating system that this shell script is
#          executing on. Different Unix flavors have differing
#          outputs and the fields vary too.
#
# REV LIST:
#
#
```

Listing 7.10 iostat_loadmon.ksh shell script listing. *(continues)*

```
# set -n # Uncomment to check the script syntax without any execution
# set -x # Uncomment to debug this shell script
#
######################################################
############# DEFINE VARIABLES HERE ##############
######################################################

SECS=300      # Defines the number of seconds for each sample
INTERVAL=2    # Defines the total number of sampling intervals
STATCOUNT=0   # Initializes a loop counter to 0, zero
OS=$(uname)   # Defines the Unix flavor


######################################################
##### SETUP THE ENVIRONMENT FOR EACH OS HERE ######
######################################################

# These "F-numbers" point to the correct field in the
# command output for each Unix flavor.

case $OS in
AIX|HP-UX)    SWITCH='-t'
              F1=3
              F2=4
              F3=5
              F4=6
              echo "\nThe Operating System is $OS\n"
              ;;
Linux|SunOS)  SWITCH='-c'
              F1=1
              F2=2
              F3=3
              F4=4
              echo "\nThe Operating System is $OS\n"
              ;;

*) echo "\nERROR: $OS is not a supported operating system\n"
   echo "\n\t...EXITING...\n"
   exit 1
   ;;
esac


######################################################
######## BEGIN GATHERING STATISTICS HERE ##########
######################################################

echo "Gathering CPU Statistics using vmstat...\n"
```

Listing 7.10   iostat_loadmon.ksh shell script listing. *(continued)*

```
echo "There are $INTERVAL sampling periods with"
echo "each interval lasting $SECS seconds"
echo "\n...Please wait while gathering statistics...\n"

# Use "iostat" to monitor the CPU utilization and
# remove all lines that contain alphabetic characters
# and blank spaces. Then use the previously defined
# field numbers, for example, F1=4,to point directly
# to the 4th position, for this example. The syntax
# for this techniques is ==>  $'$F1'.

iostat $SWITCH $SECS $INTERVAL | egrep -v '[a-zA-Z]|^$' \
        | awk '{print $'$F1', $'$F2', $'$F3', $'$F4'}' \
        | while read FIRST SECOND THIRD FOURTH
do
  if ((STATCOUNT == 1)) # Loop counter to get the second set
  then                  # of data produced by "iostat"

      case $OS in # Show the results based on the Unix flavor
      AIX)
            echo "\nUser part is ${FIRST}%"
            echo "System part is ${SECOND}%"
            echo "Idle part is ${THIRD}%"
            echo "I/O wait state is ${FOURTH}%\n"
            ;;
      HP-UX|Linux)
            echo "\nUser part is ${FIRST}%"
            echo "Nice part is ${SECOND}%"
            echo "System part is ${THIRD}%"
            echo "Idle time is ${FOURTH}%\n"
            ;;
      SunOS)
            echo "\nUser part is ${FIRST}%"
            echo "System part is ${SECOND}%"
            echo "I/O Wait is ${THIRD}%"
            echo "Idle time is ${FOURTH}%\n"
            ;;
      esac

  fi
  ((STATCOUNT = STATCOUNT + 1)) # Increment the loop counter
done
```

Listing 7.10   iostat_loadmon.ksh shell script listing. *(continued)*

The similarities are striking between the **sar** implementation and the **iostat** script shown in Listing 7.10. At the top of the shell script we define an extra variable,

STATCOUNT. This variable is used as a loop counter, and it is initialized to 0, zero. We need this counter because we have only two intervals, and the first line of the output is the load average since the last system reboot. The second, and final, set of data is the CPU load statistics collected during our sampling period, so it is the most current data. Using a counter variable, STATCOUNT, we collect the data and assign it to variables on the second loop iteration, or when the STATCOUNT is equal to 1, one.

In the next section we use the Unix flavor given by the **uname** command in a **case** statement to assign the correct switch to use in the **iostat** command. This is also where the F1, F2, F3, and F4 variables are defined with the positional placement of the data we want to extract from the command output.

Now comes the fun part. Let's look at the **iostat** command statement we use to extract the CPU statistics here.

```
iostat $SWITCH $SECS $INTERVAL | egrep -v '[a-zA-Z]|^$' \
           | awk '{print $'$F1', $'$F2', $'$F3', $'$F4'}' \
           | while read FIRST SECOND THIRD FOURTH
```

The beginning of the **iostat** command statement uses the correct command switch, as defined by the operating system, and the sampling time and the number of intervals, which is two this time. From this first part of the **iostat** statement we get the following output on a Linux system.

```
SWITCH='-c'
SECS=300
INTERVAL=2

iostat $SWITCH $SECS $INTERVAL

Linux 2.4.2-2 (bambam)      07/31/2002

avg-cpu:   %user     %nice      %sys     %idle
           23.15      0.00     26.09     50.76
avg-cpu:   %user     %nice      %sys     %idle
           31.77      0.00     21.79     46.44
```

Remember that the first row of data is an average of the CPU load since the last system reboot, so we are interested in the last row of output. If you remember from the *syntax* section for the **iostat** command, the common denominator for this output is that the data rows are entirely numeric characters. Using this as a criteria to extract data, we add to our **iostat** command statement as shown here.

```
iostat $SWITCH $SECS $INTERVAL | egrep -v '[a-zA-Z]|^$'
```

The **egrep** addition to the previous command statement does two things for us. First, it excludes all lines of the output that have alphabetic characters, leaving only the rows with numbers. The second thing we get is the removal of all blank lines from the output. Let's look at each of these.

To omit the alpha characters we use the **egrep** command with the **-v** option, which says to display everything in the output *except* the rows that the pattern matched. To specify all alpha characters we use the following expression:

```
[a-zA-Z]
```

Then to remove all blank lines we use the expression:

```
^$
```

The caret character means *begins with*, and to specify blank lines we use the dollar sign ($). If you wanted to remove all of the lines in a file that are commented out with a hash mark (#), then use ^#.

When we join these two expressions in a single extended **grep** (**egrep**), we get the following extended regular expression:

```
egrep -v '[a-zA-Z]|^$'
```

At this point we are left with the following output:

```
23.15    0.00    26.09    50.76
31.77    0.00    21.79    46.44
```

This brings us to the next addition to the **iostat** command statement in the shell script. This is where we add the **awk** part of the statement using the F1, F2, F3, and F4 variables, as shown here.

```
iostat $SWITCH $SECS $INTERVAL | egrep -v '[a-zA-Z]|^$' \
        | awk '{print $'$F1', $'$F2', $'$F3', $'$F4'}'
```

This is the same code that we covered in the last section, where we point *directly* to what another pointer is pointing to. For Linux F1=1, F2=2, F3=3, and F4=4. With this information we know that $'$F1' on the first line of output is equal to 23.15, and on the second row this same expression is equal to 31.77. Now that we have the values we have a final pipe to a **while** loop. Remember that in the **while** loop we have added a loop counter, STATCOUNT. On the first loop iteration, the **while** loop does nothing. On the second loop iteration, the values 31.77, 0.00, 21.79, and 46.44 are assigned to the variables FIRST, SECOND, THIRD, and FOURTH, respectively.

Using another **case** statement with the $OS value the output is presented to the user based on the operating system fields, as shown in Listing 7.11.

```
The Operating System is Linux

Gathering CPU Statistics using vmstat...

There are 2 sampling periods with
```

Listing 7.11   iostat_loadmon.ksh shell script in action. *(continues)*

```
each interval lasting 300 seconds

...Please wait while gathering statistics...


User part is 39.35%
Nice part is 0.00%
System part is 31.59%
Idle time is 29.06%
```

Listing 7.11 iostat_loadmon.ksh shell script in action. *(continued)*

Notice that the output is in the same format as the **sar** script output. This is all there is to the **iostat** shell script. Let's now move on to the **vmstat** solution.

Using vmstat to Measure the System Load

The **vmstat** shell script uses the exact same technique as the **iostat** shell script in the previous section. Only AIX produces four fields of output; the remaining Unix flavors have only three data points to measure for the CPU load statistics. The rest of the **vmstat** output is for virtual memory statistics, which is the main purpose of this command anyway. Let's look at the **vmstat** script.

Scripting with the vmstat Command

When you look at this shell script for **vmstat** you will think that you just saw this shell script in the last section. Most of these two shell scripts are the same, with only minor exceptions. Let's look at the vmstat_loadmon.ksh shell script in Listing 7.12 and cover the differences in detail at the end.

```
#!/bin/ksh
#
# SCRIPT: vmstat_loadmon.ksh
# AUTHOR: Randy Michael
# DATE: 07/26/2002
# REV: 1.0.P
# PLATFORM: AIX, HP-UX, Linux, and Solaris
#
# PURPOSE: This shell script takes two samples of the CPU
#          usage using the "vmstat" command. The first set of
#          data is an average since the last system reboot. The
#          second set of data is an average over the sampling
```

Listing 7.12 vmstat_loadmon.ksh shell script listing.

```
#              period, or $INTERVAL. The result of the data acquired
#              during the sampling perion is shown to the user based
#              on the Unix operating system that this shell script is
#              executing on. Different Unix flavors have differing
#              outputs and the fields vary too.
#
# REV LIST:
#
#
# set -n # Uncomment to check the script syntax without any execution
# set -x # Uncomment to debug this shell script
#
####################################################
############# DEFINE VARIABLES HERE ###############
####################################################

SECS=300   # Defines the number of seconds for each sample
INTERVAL=2    # Defines the total number of sampling intervals
STATCOUNT=0   # Initializes a loop counter to 0, zero
OS=$(uname)   # Defines the Unix flavor

####################################################
##### SETUP THE ENVIRONMENT FOR EACH OS HERE ######
####################################################

# These "F-numbers" point to the correct field in the
# command output for each Unix flavor.

case $OS in
AIX)    # AIX has four relative columns in the output
        F1=14
        F2=15
        F3=16
        F4=17

        echo "\nThe Operating System is $OS\n"
        ;;
HP-UX) # HP-UX has only three relative columns in the output
        F1=16
        F2=17
        F3=18
        F4=1    # This "F4=1" is bogus and not used for HP-UX

        echo "\nThe Operating System is $OS\n"
        ;;
Linux) # Linux has only three relative columns in the output
        F1=14
        F2=15
```

Listing 7.12   vmstat_loadmon.ksh shell script listing. *(continues)*

```
        F3=16
        F4=1    # This "F4=1" is bogus and not used for Linux

        echo "\nThe Operating System is $OS\n"
        ;;
SunOS) # SunOS has only three relative columns in the output
        F1=20
        F2=21
        F3=22
        F4=1    # This "F4=1" is bogus and not used for SunOS

        echo "\nThe Operating System is $OS\n"
        ;;
*) echo "\nERROR: $OS is not a supported operating system\n"
   echo "\n\t...EXITING...\n"
   exit 1
   ;;
esac


####################################################
######## BEGIN GATHERING STATISTICS HERE ##########
####################################################

echo "Gathering CPU Statistics using vmstat...\n"
echo "There are $INTERVAL sampling periods with"
echo "each interval lasting $SECS seconds"
echo "\n...Please wait while gathering statistics...\n"

# Use "vmstat" to monitor the CPU utilization and
# remove all lines that contain alphabetic characters
# and blank spaces. Then use the previously defined
# field numbers, for example F1=20,to point directly
# to the 20th position, for this example. The syntax
# for this technique is ==>  $'$F1' and points directly
# to the $20 positional parameter.

vmstat $SECS $INTERVAL | egrep -v '[a-zA-Z]|^$' \
        | awk '{print $'$F1', $'$F2', $'$F3', $'$F4'}' \
        | while read FIRST SECOND THIRD FOURTH
do
   if ((STATCOUNT == 1)) # Loop counter to get the second set
   then                  # of data produced by "vmstat"

        case $OS in  # Show the results based on the Unix flavor
        AIX)
            echo "\nUser part is ${FIRST}%"
```

Listing 7.12 vmstat_loadmon.ksh shell script listing. *(continued)*

```
            echo "System part is ${SECOND}%"
            echo "Idle part is ${THIRD}%"
            echo "I/O wait state is ${FOURTH}%\n"
            ;;
    HP-UX|Linux|SunOS)
            echo "\nUser part is ${FIRST}%"
            echo "System part is ${SECOND}%"
            echo "Idle time is ${THIRD}%\n"
            ;;
    esac


  fi
  ((STATCOUNT = STATCOUNT + 1)) # Increment the loop counter
done
```

Listing 7.12   vmstat_loadmon.ksh shell script listing. *(continued)*

We use the same variables in Listing 7.12 as we did in Listing 7.10 with the **iostat** script. The differences come when we define the "F" variables to indicate the fields to extract from the output and the presentation of the data to the user. As I stated before, only AIX produces a fourth field output.

In the first **case** statement, where we assign the F1, F2, F3, and F4 variables to the field positions that we want to extract for each operating system, notice that only AIX assigns F4 variable to a valid field. HP-UX, Linux, and SunOS all have the F4 variable assigned the field #1, F4=1. I did it this way so that I would not have to rewrite the **vmstat** command statement for a second time to extract just three fields. This method helps to make the code shorter and less confusing—at least I hope it is less confusing! There is a comment next to each F4 variable assignment that states that this field assignment is bogus and not used in the shell script.

Other than these minor changes the shell script for the **vmstat** solution is the same as the solution for the **iostat** command. The vmstat_loadmon.ksh shell script is in action in Listing 7.13 on a Solaris machine.

```
# ./vmstat_loadmon.ksh

The Operating System is SunOS

Gathering CPU Statistics using vmstat...

There are 2 sampling periods with
```

Listing 7.13   vmstat_loadmon.ksh shell script in action. *(continues)*

```
each interval lasting 300 seconds

...Please wait while gathering statistics...


User part is 14%
System part is 54%
Idle time is 31%
```

Listing 7.13   vmstat_loadmon.ksh shell script in action. *(continued)*

Notice that the Solaris output shown in Listing 7.13 does not show the I/O wait state. This information is available only on AIX for the **vmstat** shell script. The output format is the same as the last few shell scripts. It is up to you how you want to use this information. Let's look at some other options that you may be interested in next.

Other Options to Consider

As with any shell script there is always room for improvement, and this set of shell scripts is no exception. I have a few suggestions, but I'm sure that you can think of a few more.

Stop Chasing the Floating uptime Field

In the **uptime** CPU load monitoring shell script we did not really have to trace down the location of the latest CPU statistics. Another approach is to use what we know always to be true. Specifically, we know that the field of interest is always in the third position field from the *end* of the **uptime** command output. Using this knowledge we can use this little function, get_max, to find the total number of fields in the output. If we subtract 2 from the total number of positions, then we always have the correct field. The next code segment is an example of using this technique.

```
function get_max
{
(($# == 0)) && return -1
echo $#
}


########## MAIN #############

MAX=$(get_max $(uptime)) # Get the total number of fields in uptime
```

```
output
((MAX == -1)) && echo "ERROR: Function Error...EXITING..." && exit 2
TARGET_FIELD=$(((MAX - 2)))   # Subtract 2 from the total
CPU_LOAD=$(uptime | sed s/,//g | awk '{print $'$TARGET_FIELD'}')
echo $CPU_LOAD
```

In the previous code segment the get_max function receives the output of the **uptime** command. Using this input the function returns the total number of positional parameters that the **uptime** command output contains. In the MAIN part we assign the result received back from the get_max function to the MAX variable. If the returned value is -1, then a scripting error has occurred and the script will show the user an error and exit with a return code of 2. Otherwise, the MAX variable has 2 subtracted from its value, and it is assigned to the TARGET_FIELD variable. The last step assigns the most recent CPU run queue statistics to the variable CPU_LOAD.

Using a technique like this eliminates the need to track the position of the CPU statistics and reduces the code a bit. I wanted to use the method of tracking the position in this chapter just to make a point: Glancing at a command's output to find a field is not always a good idea. I did not want to leave you hanging around, though, thinking that you always have to track data. As you know, there is more than one way to get the same result in Unix, and this is a perfect example.

Try to Detect Any Possible Problems for the User

One thing that would be valuable when looking at the CPU load statistics is to try to detect any problems. For example, if the system percentage plus the user percentage is consistently greater than 90 percent, then the system may be CPU bound. This is easy to code into any of these shell scripts using the following statement:

```
((SYSTEM + USER > 90)) && echo "\nWarning: This system is CPU-bound\n"
```

Another possible problem happens when the I/O wait percentage is consistently over 80 percent; then the system may be I/O bound. This, too, is easy to code into the shell scripts. System problem thresholds vary widely depending on whom you are talking to, so I will leave the details up to you. I'm sure you can come up with some other problem detection techniques.

Show the User the Top CPU Hogs

Whenever the system is stressed under load, the cause of the problem may be a runaway process or a developer trying out the **fork()** system call during the middle of the day (same problem, different cause!). To show the user the top CPU hogs, you can use the **ps auxw** command. Notice that there is *not* a hyphen before **auxw**! Something like the following command syntax will work.

```
ps auxw | head -n 15
```

The output is sorted by CPU usage in descending order from the top. Also, most Unix operating systems have a **top** like command. In AIX it is **topas**, in HP-UX and Linux it is **top**, and in Solaris it is **prstat**. Any of these commands will show you real-time process statistics.

Gathering a Large Amount of Data for Plotting

Another method is to get a lot of short intervals over a longer period of time. The **sar** command is perfect for this type of data gathering. Using this method of short intervals over a long period, maybe eight hours, gives you a detailed picture of how the load fluctuates through the day. This is the perfect kind of detailed data for graphing on a line chart. It is very easy to take the **sar** data and use a standard spreadsheet program to create graphs of the system load versus time.

Summary

I enjoyed this chapter, but it turned out to be a lot longer than I first intended. With the CPU load data floating based on the time since the system was last rebooted, and just by the time of every day, it made the **uptime** shell script a challenge, but I love a good challenge. This chapter did present some different concepts that are not in any other chapter, and it is always intended that way throughout this book. Play around with these shell scripts, and see how you can improve the usefulness of each script. It is always fun to find a new use for a shell script by playing with the code.

In the next chapter, we are going to study some techniques to monitor a process and wait for it to start up, stop execution, or both. We also allow for pre and post events to be defined for the process. I hope you gained some knowledge in this chapter, and every chapter! See you next time.

CHAPTER

8

Process Monitoring and Enabling Preprocess, Startup, and Postprocess Events

All too often a program or script will die during execution or fail to start up. This type of problem can be hard to nail down due to the unpredictable behavior and the timing required to catch the event as it happens. We also sometimes want to execute some commands before a process starts, as the process starts (or as the monitoring starts), or as a post event when the process dies. Timing is everything! Instead of reentering the same command over and over to monitor a process, we can write scripts to wait for a process to start or end and record the time stamps, or we can perform some other function as a pre, startup, or post event. To monitor the process we are going to use **grep** to grab one or more matched patterns from the process list output. Because we are going to use **grep,** there is a need for the process to be unique in some way—for example, by process name, user name, PID, PPID, or even a date/time.

In this chapter we cover four scripts:

- Monitor for a process (one or more!) to start execution.

- Monitor for a process (one or more!) to stop execution.

- Monitor as the process(es) stops and starts and log the events as they happen with a timestamp.

- Monitor as the process(es) starts and stops while keeping track of the current number of active processes, giving user notification with time stamp and listing of all of the active PIDs. We also add pre, startup, and post event capabilities.

Two examples for using of one of these functions are waiting for a backup to finish before rebooting the system and sending an email as a process starts up.

Syntax

As with all of our scripts, we start out by getting the correct command syntax. To look at the system processes, we want to look at *all* of the processes, not a limited view for a particular user. To list all of the processes, we use the **ps** command with the **-ef** switch. Using **grep** with the **ps -ef** command requires us to filter the output. The **grep** command will produce two additional lines of output. One line will result from the **grep** command, and the other will result from the script name, which is doing the grepping. To remove both of these we can use either **grep -v** or **egrep -v** to exclude this output. From this specification, and using variables, we came up with the following command syntax:

```
ps -ef | grep $PROCESS | grep -v "grep $PROCESS" | grep -v $SCRIPT_NAME
```

The previous command will give a full process listing while excluding the shell script's name and the grepping for the target process. This will leave only the actual processes that we are interested in monitoring. The return code for this command is 0, zero, if at least one process is running, and it will return a nonzero value if no process, specified by the $PROCESS variable, is currently executing. To monitor a process to start or stop we need to remain in a tight loop until there is a transition from running to end of execution, and vice versa.

Monitoring for a Process to Start

Now that we have the command syntax we can write the script to wait for a process to start. This shell script is pretty simple because all it does is run in a loop until the process starts. The first step is to check for the correct number of arguments, one—the process to monitor. If the process is currently running, then we will just notify the user and exit. Otherwise, we will loop until the target process starts and then display the process name that started and exit. The loop is listed in Lisiting 8.1.

```
RC=1

until (( RC == 0 )) # Loop until the return code is zero
do
        # Check for the $PROCESS on each loop iteration

        ps -ef | grep $PROCESS | egrep -v "grep $PROCESS" \
```

Listing 8.1 Process startup loop.

```
                    | grep -v $SCRIPT_NAME >/dev/null 2>&1

        # Check the Return Code!!!
        if (( $? == 0 )) # Has it Started????
        then
                echo "$PROCESS has Started Execution...`date`\n\n"

                # Show the user what started!!

                ps -ef | grep $PROCESS | egrep -v "grep $PROCESS" \
                        | grep -v $SCRIPT_NAME

                echo "\n\n" # A Couple of Blank Lines Before Exit

                exit 0 # Exit time...
        fi
        sleep $SLEEP_TIME # Needed to reduce CPU load!! 1 Second or more
done
```

Listing 8.1 Process startup loop. *(continued)*

There are a few things to point out in Listing 8.1. First, notice that we are using the numeric tests, which are specified by the double parentheses ((numeric_ expression)). The numeric tests can be seen in the **if** and **until** control structures. When using the double parentheses numeric testing method, we *do not* reference any *user-defined numeric variables* with a dollar sign—that is, $RC. If you use a $, the test may fail! This testing method knows the value is a numeric variable and does need to go through the process of converting the character string to a numeric string before the test. This convention saves time by saving CPU cycles. Just leave out the "$". We still must use the $ reference for system variables—for example, $? and $#. Also notice that we use double equal signs when making an equality test—for example, until ((RC == 0)). If you use only one equal sign it is assumed to be an assignment, not an equality test! Failure to use double equal signs is one of the most common mistakes, and it is very hard to find during troubleshooting. Also notice in Listing 8.1 that we **sleep** on each loop iteration. If we do not have a sleep interval, then the load on the CPU can be tremendous. Try programming a loop with and without the sleep interval and monitor the CPU load with either the **uptime** or **vmstat** commands. You can definitely see a big difference in the load on the system. What does this mean for our monitoring? The process must remain running for at least the length of time that the **sleep** is executing on each loop iteration. If you need an interval of less than one second, then you can try setting the sleep interval to 0, zero, but watch out for the heavy CPU load. Even with a 1-second interval the load can get to around 25 percent. An interval of about 3 to 10 seconds is not bad, if you can stand the wait.

Now let's study the loop. We initialize the return code variable, RC, to 1, one. Then we start an **until** loop that tests for the target process on each loop iteration. If the process is not running, then the **sleep** is executed and then the loop is executed again. If the target process is found to be running, then we give user notification that the process has started, with the time stamp, and display to the user the process that actually started. We need to give the user this process information just in case the **grep** command got a pattern match on an unintended pattern. The entire script is on the Web site with the name `proc_wait.ksh`. This is crude, but it works well. (See Listing 8.2.)

```
[root:yogi]@/scripts/WILEY/PROC_MON# ./proc_wait.ksh xcalc


WAITING for xcalc to start...Thu Sep 27 21:11:47 EDT 2001

xcalc has Started Execution...Thu Sep 27 21:11:55 EDT 2001


    root 26772 17866  13 21:11:54  pts/6  0:00 xcalc
```

Listing 8.2   proc_wait.ksh script in action.

Monitoring for a Process to End

Monitoring for a process to end is also a simple procedure because it is really the opposite of the previous shell script. In this new shell script we want to add some extra options. First, we set a **trap** and inform the user if an interrupt occurred—for example, **CTRL-C** is pressed. It would be nice to give the user the option of *verbose* mode. The verbose mode enables the listing of the active process(es). We can use a **-v** switch as a command-line argument to the shell script to turn on the verbose mode. To parse through the command-line arguments we could use the **getopts** command; but for only one or two arguments, we can easily use a nested **case** statement. We will show how to use **getopts** later in the chapter. Again, we will use the double parentheses for numeric tests wherever possible. For the `proc_mon.ksh` script we are going to list out the entire script and review the process at the end. (See Listing 8.3.)

```
#!/usr/bin/ksh
#
# SCRIPT: proc_mon.ksh
# AUTHOR: Randy Michael
# DATE: 02/14/2001
# REV: 1.1.P
# PLATFORM: Not Platform Dependent
#
# PURPOSE: This script is used to monitor a process to end
```

Listing 8.3   proc_mon.ksh shell script listing.

```
#     specified by ARG1 if a single command-line argument is
#     used. There is also a "verbose" mode where the monitored
#     process is displayed and ARG2 is monitored.
#
# USAGE: proc_mon.ksh [-v] process-to-monitor
#
# EXIT STATUS:
#     0 ==> Monitored process has terminated
#     1 ==> Script usage error
#     2 ==> Target process to monitor is not active
#     3 ==> This script exits on a trapped signal
#
# REV. LIST:
#
#     02/22/2001 - Added code for a "verbose" mode to output the
#                  results of the 'ps -ef' command.  The verbose
#                  mode is set using a "-v" switch.
#
# set -x # Uncomment to debug this script
# set -n # Uncomment to debug without any command execution

SCRIPT_NAME=`basename $0`

#########################################################
############ DEFINE FUNCTIONS HERE ###################
#########################################################

function usage
{
    echo "\n\n"
    echo "USAGE: $SCRIPT_NAME [-v] {Process_to_monitor}"
    echo "\nEXAMPLE: $SCRIPT_NAME  my_backup\n"
    echo "OR"
    echo "\nEXAMPLE: $SCRIPT_NAME -v  my_backup\n"
    echo "Try again...EXITING...\n"
}


#########################################################

function exit_trap
{
    echo "\n...EXITING on trapped signal...\n"
}


#########################################################
############### START OF MAIN#########################
#########################################################

###############
```

Listing 8.3   proc_mon.ksh shell script listing. *(continues)*

```
# Set a trap...#
################

trap 'exit_trap; exit 3' 1 2 3 15

# First Check for the Correct Number of Arguments
# One or Two is acceptable

if (( $# != 1 && $# != 2 ))
then
     usage
     exit 1
fi

# Parse through the command-line arguments and see if verbose
# mode has been specified. NOTICE that we assign the target
# process to the PROCESS variable!!!
# Embedded case statement...

case $# in
     1)      case $1 in
              '-v') usage
                    exit 1
                    ;;
                 *) PROCESS=$1
          esac
          ;;

     2) case $1 in
              '-v') continue
                    ;;
          esac

          case $2 in
              '-v') usage
                    exit 1
                    ;;

                 *) PROCESS=$2
                    ;;
          esac
          ;;

     *) usage
        exit 1
        ;;
```

Listing 8.3   proc_mon.ksh shell script listing. *(continued)*

```
esac

# Check if the process is running or exit!

ps -ef | grep "$PROCESS" | grep -v "grep $PROCESS" \
        | grep -v $SCRIPT_NAME >/dev/null

if (( $? != 0 ))
then
     echo "\n\n$PROCESS is NOT an active process...EXITING...\n"
     exit 2
fi

# Show verbose mode if specified...

if (( $# == 2 )) && [[ $1 = "-v" ]]
then
     # Verbose mode has been specified!
     echo "\n"

     # Extract the columns heading from the ps -ef output
     ps -ef | head -n 1

     ps -ef | grep "$PROCESS" | grep -v "grep $PROCESS" \
              | grep -v $SCRIPT_NAME
fi

##### O.K. The process is running, start monitoring...

SLEEP_TIME="1"   # Seconds between monitoring
RC="0"               # RC is the Return Code
echo "\n\n"    # Give a couple of blank lines

echo "$PROCESS is currently RUNNING...`date`\n"

####################################
# Loop UNTIL the $PROCESS stops...

while (( RC == 0 )) # Loop until the return code is not zero
do
     ps -ef | grep $PROCESS | grep -v "grep $PROCESS" \
            | grep -v $SCRIPT_NAME >/dev/null 2>&1

     if (( $? != 0 )) # Check the Return Code!!!!!
     then
          echo "\n...$PROCESS has COMPLETED...`date`\n"
```

Listing 8.3 proc_mon.ksh shell script listing. *(continues)*

```
        exit 0
    fi
    sleep $SLEEP_TIME # Needed to reduce CPU Load!!!
done

# End of Script
```

Listing 8.3   proc_mon.ksh shell script listing. *(continued)*

Did you catch all of the extra hoops we had to jump through? Adding command switches can be problematic. We will see a much easier way to do this later using the **getopts** command.

In Listing 8.3 we first defined two functions, which are both used for abnormal operation. We always need a `usage` function, and in this shell script we added a `trap_exit` function that is to be executed only when a trapped signal is captured. The **trap** definition specifies exit signals 1, 2, 3, and 15. Of course, you cannot trap exit signal 9. This `trap_exit` function will display "`...EXITING on a trapped signal...`". Then the **trap** will execute the second command, `exit 3`. In the next step we check for the correct number of command-line arguments, one or two, and use an embedded **case** statement to assign the target process to a variable, `PROCESS`. If a -**v** is specified in the *first* argument, $1, of two command-line arguments, then verbose mode is used. Verbose mode will display the **ps -ef** output that the **grep** command did the pattern match on. Otherwise, this information is not displayed. This is the first time that we look to see if the target process is active. If the target process is not executing, then we just notify the user and exit with a return code of 2. Next comes the use of verbose mode if the **-v** switch is specified on the command line. Notice how we pull out the **ps** command output columns header information before we display the process using **ps -ef | head -n 1**. This helps the user confirm that this is the correct match with the column header. Now we know the process is currently running so we start a loop. This loop will continue until either the process ends or the program is interrupted—for example, **CTRL-C** is pressed.

The `proc_mon.ksh` script did the job, but we have no logging and the monitoring stops when the process stops. It would be really nice to track the process as it starts and stops. If we can monitor the transition, we can keep a log file to review and see if we can find a trend.

```
[root:yogi]@/scripts/WILEY/PROC_MON# ./proc_mon.ksh xcalc


xcalc is NOT an active process...EXITING...

[root:yogi]@/scripts/WILEY/PROC_MON# ./proc_mon.ksh xcalc


xcalc is currently RUNNING...Thu Sep 27 21:14:08 EDT 2001


...xcalc has COMPLETED...Thu Sep 27 21:14:26 EDT 2001
```

Listing 8.4   proc_mon.ksh shell script in action.

Monitor and Log as a Process Starts and Stops

Catching process activity as it cycles on and off can be a useful tool in problem determination. In this section, we are going to expand on both of our previous scripts and monitor for both startup and end time for a target process. We are also going to log everything and time stamp the start and stop event. Because we are logging everything we also want to see the same data as it happens on the screen. The log file can be reviewed at any time; we want to see it in "real time" (at least close to real time). We are going to make the startup and end time monitoring into functions this time, and as a result we are going to need to capture the current tty device, which may be a pseudo-terminal (pty), to use within these functions. The **tty** command will show the current terminal, and we can save this in a variable. For concurrent display and logging within the script we pipe our output to **tee -a $LOGFILE**. This **tee** command sends the output to both standard output and to the file that $LOGFILE points to. But inside the functions we will use the specific tty device to send our output to, which we assign to a variable called TTY. Enough with the fluff; here is the script (in Listing 8.5), followed by a short explanation.

```
#!/bin/ksh
#
# SCRIPT: proc_watch.ksh
# AUTHOR: Randy Michael
# DATE: 09-12-2001
# REV: 1.0.P
# PLATFORM: Not Platform Dependent
#
# PURPOSE" This script is used to monitor and log
#          the status of a process as it starts and stops.
#
# REV LIST:
#
# set -x # Uncomment to debug this script
# set -n # Uncomment to check syntax without ANY execution
#
####################################################
########## DEFINE FILES AND VARIABLES HERE #########
####################################################

LOGFILE="/tmp/proc_status.log"
[[ ! -s $LOGFILE ]] && touch $LOGFILE

PROCESS="$1"  # Process to Monitor
SCRIPT_NAME=$(basename $0) # Script Name w/o the PATH
TTY=$(tty)    # Current tty or pty

####################################################
############# DEFINE FUNCTIONS HERE ################
####################################################

usage ()
{
    echo "\nUSAGE:  $SCRIPT_NAME  process_to_monitor\n"
}

####################################################

trap_exit ()
{
    # Log an ending time for process monitoring
    TIMESTAMP=$(date +%D@%T) # Get a new time stamp...
    echo "MON_STOP: Monitoring for $PROCESS ended ==> $TIMESTAMP" \
        | tee -a $LOGFILE

    # Kill all functions
```

Listing 8.5 proc_watch.ksh shell script listing.

```
    kill -9 $(jobs -p) 2>/dev/null
}


####################################################

mon_proc_end ()
{
    END_RC="0"
    until (( END_RC != 0 ))
    do
        ps -ef | grep -v "grep $PROCESS" | grep -v $SCRIPT_NAME \
                | grep $PROCESS >/dev/null 2>&1

        END_RC=$? # Check the Return Code!!
        sleep 1   # Needed to reduce CPU load!
    done

    print 'N' # Turn the RUN flag off

    # Grab a TimeStamp
    TIMESTAMP=$(date +%D@%T)

    echo "END PROCESS: $PROCESS ended ==> $TIMESTAMP" >> $LOGFILE &
    echo "END PROCESS: $PROCESS ended ==> $TIMESTAMP" > $TTY
}


####################################################

mon_proc_start ()
{
    START_RC="-1"  # Initialize to -1
    until (( START_RC == 0 ))
    do
        ps -ef | grep -v "grep $PROCESS" | grep -v $SCRIPT_NAME \
                | grep $PROCESS >/dev/null 2>&1

        START_RC=$? # Check the Return Code!!!
        sleep 1     # Needed to reduce CPU load!
    done

    print 'Y' # Turn the RUN flag on

    # Grab the Timestamp
    TIMESTAMP=$(date +%D@%T)

    echo "START PROCESS: $PROCESS began ==> $TIMESTAMP" >> $LOGFILE &
```

Listing 8.5 proc_watch.ksh shell script listing. *(continues)*

```
        echo "START PROCESS: $PROCESS began ==> $TIMESTAMP" > $TTY
}

######################################################
############## START OF MAIN #########################
######################################################

### SET A TRAP ####

trap 'trap_exit; exit 0' 1 2 3 15

# Check for the Correct Command Line Argument - Only 1

if (( $# != 1 ))
then
     usage
     exit 1
fi

# Get an Initial Process State and Set the RUN Flag

ps -ef | grep -v "grep $PROCESS" | grep -v $SCRIPT_NAME \
       | grep $PROCESS >/dev/null

PROC_RC=$?  # Check the Return Code!!

# Give some initial feedback before starting the loop

if (( PROC_RC == 0 ))
then
     echo "The $PROCESS process is currently running...Monitoring..."
     RUN="Y"      # Set the RUN Flag to YES
else
     echo "The $PROCESS process is not currently running...Monitoring..."
     RUN="N"      # Set the RUN Flag to NO
fi

TIMESTAMP=$(date +%D@%T) # Grab a timestamp for the log

# Use a "tee -a $#LOGFILE" to send output to both standard output
# and to the file referenced by $LOGFILE

echo "MON_START: Monitoring for $PROCESS began ==> $TIMESTAMP" \
     | tee -a $LOGFILE

# Loop Forever!!

while :
```

Listing 8.5 proc_watch.ksh shell script listing. *(continued)*

```
do

    case $RUN in
    'Y') # Loop Until the Process Ends
        RUN=$(mon_proc_end)
        ;;

    'N') # Loop Until the Process Starts
        RUN=$(mon_proc_start)
        ;;

    esac
done

# End of Script
```

Listing 8.5   proc_watch.ksh shell script listing. *(continued)*

The shell script in Listing 8.5 is a nice, modular shell script. The actual monitoring loop is the final **while** loop. The loop is short and tight, with all of the work being done within the two functions, `proc_mon_start` and `proc_mon_end`. Notice that in both functions we remain in the loop until there is a transition from run to stop or not running to process startup. On each transition we return updated run status information back to the calling shell script with a **print** command, as opposed to a return code. For the concurrent display to the screen and logging to the file we use `tee -a $LOGFILE` within the shell script body, and in the functions we redirect output to the `tty` device that we assigned to the `$TTY` variable. We use the `tty` device to ensure that the screen output will go to the terminal, or pseudo-terminal, that we are currently looking at. Otherwise we cannot be assured where standard output is pointing within the function. We again did all numeric tests with the double parentheses method. Notice that we do *not* use a $ with a user-defined variable! For the **while** loop we are looping forever. The No-Op character (**while :**) allows this to work (**true** would also work). The `proc_watch.ksh` shell script will continue to run until it is interrupted—for example, **CTRL-C** is pressed.

We have improved our script, but it does not let us know how many processes are active. There is no timing mechanism for the shell script; it just runs until interrupted. We are next going to expand on our script to do a few things differently. First, we want to be able to time the monitoring to execute for a specific period of time. We also want to let the user know how many processes are currently active and the PID of each process. In addition, we want to time stamp *each* process startup and end time. To time stamp each process we can count the number of processes that are running during each loop iteration, and if the count changes we will grab a new time stamp and update the PID list for the currently running processes. We also will give the option to run some pre, startup, and/or post event before the process starts, as the process starts, or after the process has ended.

```
[root:yogi]@/scripts/WILEY/PROC_MON# ./proc_watch.ksh xcalc

The xcalc process is currently running...Monitoring...
MON_START: Monitoring for xcalc began ==> 09/27/01@21:09:41
END PROCESS: xcalc ended ==> 09/27/01@21:09:56
START PROCESS: xcalc began ==> 09/27/01@21:10:06
END PROCESS: xcalc ended ==> 09/27/01@21:10:25
^C
MON_STOP: Monitoring for xcalc ended ==> 09/27/01@21:10:31
```

Listing 8.6   proc_watch.ksh shell script in action.

Timed Execution for Process Monitoring, Showing each PID, and Time Stamp with Event and Timing Capability

Sound like a lot? After we get through this section, each step will be intuitively obvious. In all of the previous three scripts, we had no ability to monitor *each* process that matched the grepped pattern or to execute the monitoring for a specific amount of time. Because we are using the **grep** command we may get multiple matches to a pattern. In case of multiple matches we need to know (1) how many matches we have and (2) *each* process that was matched. This information can be very beneficial if you are monitoring a specific user's activities or anything where we are interested in the exact process IDs that are running.

We also want a good timing mechanism that will allow for easy, flexible timing of the duration of the monitoring activity. Because we have no way of knowing what user requirements may be, we want to allow for as much flexibility as possible. Let's go to the far side and allow timing from seconds to days, and anything in between. The easiest way to handle timing, but not the most accurate, is to add up all of the seconds and count down from the total seconds to zero while sleeping for one second between counts. We could continuously check the date/time using the **date** command for a very accurate time, or—even better—we can kick off an **at** job to kill the script at some specific time in the future. The Korn shell variable SECONDS is also useful. For this script we are going to use **getopts** to parse the command line for seconds, minutes, hours, days, and the process to monitor. Then we add up the seconds and count down to zero and quit. Alternatively, if the total seconds and a process are the only arguments, the user will be able to enter these directly—for only a process and total seconds **getopts** will not be used. The usage function will list two ways to use our new script.

Another nice option is the capability to run pre, startup, and/or post events. By pre, startup, and post events we are talking about running some command, script, or function before the process starts, as the process starts, or after the process stops, or in any combination. As an example, we may want to reboot the machine after a backup program ends, or we may want to set up environment variables before some process starts up. For the event options we also need to be as flexible as possible. For flexibility we will just add a function for each event that contains only the no-op character, **:** (colon), as a place holder. A colon does not execute anything; it does nothing and has a return code of 0, zero. Anything that a user may want to run before startup, at startup, or after the process has ended can be added into the appropriate function. We will use flags, or variables, to enable and disable the pre, startup, and post events individually.

In this section we are going to do two things that may be new, using **getopts** to process the command-line arguments and executing a function in the background as a *co-process*. The **getopts** functionality is an easy and efficient way to parse through mixed command-line arguments, and the command switches can be with or without switch arguments. A co-process is an easy way to set up a communication link with a *background* script or function and the foreground.

Let's first look at how to use **getopts** to parse the command line. The **getopts** command is built in to Korn shell. The command parses the command line for valid options specified by a single character, following a – (minus sign) or a + (plus sign). To specify that a command switch requires an argument, the switch character must be followed by a **:** (colon). If the switch does not require any argument, then the : should be omitted. All of the switch options put together are called the OptionString, and this is followed by some variable name that we define. The argument for each switch is stored in a variable called $OPTARG as the arguments are parsed in a loop one at a time. If the *entire* OptionString is *preceded* by a **:** (colon), then any unmatched switch option causes a ? to be loaded into the variable that we defined in the **getopts** command. The form of the command follows:

```
getopts OptionString Name [ Argument ... ]
```

The easiest way to explain the **getopts** command is with an example. For our script we need seconds, minutes, hours, days, and a process to monitor. For each one we want to supply an argument—for example, -s 5 -m10 -p my_backup. In this example we are specifying 5 seconds, 10 minutes, and the process is my_backup. Notice that there does not have to be a space between the switch and the argument. This is what makes **getopts** so great! The code to set up our example looks like the following example in Listing 8.7.

```
SECS=0          # Initialize all to zero
MINUTES=0
HOURS=0
DAYS=0
PROCESS=          # Initialize to null

while getopts ":s:m:h:d:p:" TIMED 2>/dev/null
do
    case $TIMED in
      s) SECS=$OPTARG
```

Listing 8.7 Example getopts command usage. *(continues)*

```
            ;;
     m) (( MINUTES = $OPTARG * 60 ))
            ;;
     h) (( HOURS = $OPTARG * 3600 ))
            ;;
     d) (( DAYS = $OPTARG * 86400 ))
            ;;
     p) PROCESS=$OPTARG
            ;;
     \?) usage
         exit 1
            ;;
   esac
done

(( TOTAL_SECONDS = SECS + MINUTES + HOURS + DAYS ))
```

Listing 8.7 Example getopts command usage. *(continued)*

There are a few things to note in Listing 8.7. The **getopts** command needs to be part of a **while** loop with a **case** statement within the loop. On each option we specified, -s,-m,-h,-d, and -p, and we added a : (colon) after each switch character. This tells **getopts** that an argument is required for that particular switch character. The : (colon) *before* the OptionString list tells **getopts** that if an unspecified option is given on the command line, to set the $TIMED variable to the ? character. The ? allows us to call the usage function and **exit** with a return code of 1 for an incorrect command-line option. The only thing to be careful of is that **getopts** does not care what arguments it receives so it is *our* responsibility to check each argument to ensure that it meets our expectations; then we have to take action if we want to exit. The last thing to note in Listing 8.7 is that the first line of the **while** loop has redirection of the standard error (file descriptor 2) to the bit bucket. Any time an unexpected argument is encountered, **getopts** sends a message to standard error, but it is not considered an error, just informational. Because we expect that incorrect command-line arguments may be entered, we can just ignore the messages and discard them with redirection to /dev/null, a.k.a. the bit bucket.

We also need to cover setting up a co-process. A co-process is a communications link between a foreground and a background process. The most common question is, "*Why is this needed?*" In our next script we are going to call a function that will handle all of the monitoring for us while we do the timing control in the main script. The problem arises because *we need to run this function in the background*. Within the background process monitoring function there are two loops in which one loop is always executing. Without the ability to tell the loop to break out of the internal loop, it will continue to execute on its own after the main script, and function, have exited due to an interrupt. We know what this causes—*one or more defunct processes!* From the main script we need a way to communicate with the loop in the background function to tell it to break out of the loop or exit the function cleanly when the countdown is complete and if the script is interrupted—for example, with **CTRL-C**. To solve this little problem we kick off our background `proc_watch` function as a **co-process**. "How do we do this?" you ask. "*Pipe it to the background*" is the simplest way to put it, and that is also what it looks like. Look at the next example in Listing 8.8.

```
function proc_watch
{
# This function is started as a co-process!!!

    while :        # Loop forever
    do
         Some Code Here

         read BREAK_OUT  # Do NOT need a "-p" to read!
         if [[ $BREAK_OUT = 'Y' ]]
         then
              return 0
         fi
    done
}
############################
##### Start of Main ########
############################

### Set a Trap ###

trap 'BREAK='Y'; print -p $BREAK; exit 2' 1 2 3 15

TOTAL_SECONDS=300
BREAK_OUT='N'

proc_watch |&        # Start proc_watch as a co-process!!!!

until (( TOTAL_SECONDS == 0 ))
do
    (( TOTAL_SECONDs = TOTAL_SECONDS - 1 ))
    sleep 1
done

BREAK_OUT='Y'

# Use "print -p" to communicate with the co-process variable

print -p $BREAK_OUT

exit 0
```

Listing 8.8 Example using a co-process.

In the code block in Listing 8.8 we defined the `proc_watch` function, which is the function that we want to start as a *background* process. As you can see, the `proc_watch` function has an infinite loop. If the main script, is interrupted, then without a means to exit the loop within the `proc_watch` background function, the loop alone will continue to execute! To solve this we start the `proc_watch` as a co-process by "piping it to the background" using *pipe ampersand*, **|&**, as a suffix. Now when we want to communicate with the function from the main script, we use `print  -p` `$BREAK_OUT`. Inside the function we just use the standard **read** command, `read BREAK_OUT`. The co-process is the mechanism that we are going to use to break out of the loop if the main script is interrupted on a trapped signal, and for normal countdown termination at the end of the script. Of course, we can never catch **kill -9** with a trap.

Try setting up the scenario just described, without a co-process, with a background function that has an infinite loop. Then press the **CTRL-C** key sequence to kill the main script and do a **ps -ef | more**. You will see that the background *loop* is still executing! Get the PID, and do a **kill -9** to kill it. Of course, if the loop's exit criteria is ever met, the loop will exit on its own.

Now take a look at the entire script, and see how we handled all of these extra requirements. Pay close attention to the highlighted code in Listing 8.9.

```ksh
#!/bin/ksh
#
# SCRIPT: proc_watch_timed.ksh
# AUTHOR: Randy Michael
# DATE: 09-14-2001
# REV: 1.0.P
# PLATFORM: Not Platform Dependent
#
# PURPOSE: This script is used to monitor and log
#          the status of a process as it starts and stops.
#          Command line options are used to identify the target
#          process to monitor and the length of time to monitor.
#          Each event is logged to the file defined by the
#          $LOGFILE variable. This script also has the ability
#          to execute pre, startup, and post events. These are
#          controlled by the $RUN_PRE_EVENT, $RUN_STARTUP_EVENT, and
#          $RUN_POST_EVENT variables. These variables control execution
#          individually. Whatever is to be executed is to be placed in
#          either the "pre_event_script", startup_event_script, or the
#          "post_event_script" functions, or in any combination. Timing
#          is controlled on the command line.
#
#          USAGE:  $SCRIPT_NAME  total_seconds  target_process
#
#          Will monitor the specified process for the
```

Listing 8.9 proc_watch_timed.ksh shell script listing.

```
#              specified number of seconds.
#
#         USAGE:   $SCRIPT_NAME   [-s|-S seconds] [-m|-M minutes]
#                                 [-h|-H hours] [-d|-D days]
#                                 [-p|-P process]
#
#         Will monitor the specified process for number of
#         seconds specified within -s seconds, -m minutes,
#         -h hours, and -d days.  Any combination of command
#         switches can be used.
#
# REV LIST:
#
# set -x # Uncomment to debug this script
# set -n # Uncomment to check syntax without ANY execution
#
###################################################
######### DEFINE FILES AND VARIABLES HERE #########
###################################################

typeset -u RUN_PRE_EVENT  # Force to UPPERCASE
typeset -u RUN_STARTUP_EVENT  # Force to UPPERCASE
typeset -u RUN_POST_EVENT # force to UPPERCASE

RUN_PRE_EVENT='N'  # A 'Y' will execute, anything else will not
RUN_STARTUP_EVENT='Y' # A 'Y' will execute, anything else will not
RUN_POST_EVENT='Y' # A 'Y' will execute, anything else will not

LOGFILE="/tmp/proc_status.log"
[[ ! -s $LOGFILE ]] && touch $LOGFILE

SCRIPT_NAME=$(basename $0)
TTY=$(tty)
INTERVAL="1" # Seconds between sampling
JOBS=

###################################################
############# DEFINE FUNCTIONS HERE ###############
###################################################
usage ()
{
echo "\n\n\t*****USAGE ERROR*****"
echo "\n\nUSAGE:  $SCRIPT_NAME  seconds  process"
echo "\nWill monitor the specified process for the"
echo "specified number of seconds."
echo "\nUSAGE:  $SCRIPT_NAME  [-s|-S seconds] [-m|-M minutes]"
echo "          [-h|-H hours] [-d|-D days] [-p|-P process]\n"
```

Listing 8.9 proc_watch_timed.ksh shell script listing. *(continues)*

```
echo "\nWill monitor the specified process for number of"
echo "seconds specified within -s seconds, -m minutes,"
echo "-h hours and -d days.  Any combination of command"
echo "switches can be used.\n"
echo "\nEXAMPLE: $SCRIPT_NAME  300  dtcalc"
echo "\n\nEXAMPLE: $SCRIPT_NAME  -m 5 -p dtcalc"
echo "\nBoth examples will monitor the dtcalc process"
echo "for 5 minutes.  Can specify days, hours, minutes"
echo "and seconds, using -d, -h, -m and -s\n\n"
}
#####################################################
trap_exit ()
{
# set -x # Uncommant to debug this function
# Log an ending time for process monitoring
echo "INTERRUPT: Program Received an Interrupt...EXITING..." > $TTY
echo "INTERRUPT: Program Received an Interrupt...EXITING..." >> $LOGFILE
TIMESTAMP=$(date +%D@%T) # Get a new time stamp...
echo "MON_STOPPED: Monitoring for $PROCESS ended ==> $TIMESTAMP\n" \
     >> $TTY
echo "MON_STOPPED: Monitoring for $PROCESS ended ==> $TIMESTAMP\n" \
     >> $LOGFILE
echo "LOGFILE: All Events are Logged ==> $LOGFILE \n" > $TTY

# Kill all functions
JOBS=$(jobs -p)
if [[ ! -z $JOBS && $JOBS != '' && $JOBS != '0' ]]
then
     kill $(jobs -p) 2>/dev/null 1>&2
fi
return 2
}
#####################################################
pre_event_script ()
{
# Put anything that you want to execute BEFORE the
# monitored process STARTS in this function

: # No-OP - Needed as a place holder for an empty function
# Comment Out the Above colon, ':'

PRE_RC=$?
return $PRE_RC
}
#####################################################
startup_event_script ()
{
```

Listing 8.9 proc_watch_timed.ksh shell script listing. *(continued)*

```
# Put anything that you want to execute WHEN, or AS, the
# monitored process STARTS in this function

: # No-OP - Needed as a place holder for an empty function
# Comment Out the Above colon, ':'

STARTUP_RC=$?
return $STARTUP_RC
}
#####################################################
post_event_script ()
{
# Put anything that you want to execute AFTER the
# monitored process ENDS in this function

: # No-OP - Need as a place holder for an empty function
# Comment Out the Above colon, ':'

POST_RC=$?
return $POST_RC
}
#####################################################
# This function is used to test character strings

test_string ()
{
if (( $# != 1 ))
then
    echo 'ERROR'
    return
fi

C_STRING=$1
# Test the character string for its composition

case $C_STRING in

    +([0-9])) echo  'POS_INT' # Integer >= 0
            ;;
    +([-0-9])) echo 'NEG_INT' # Integer < 0
            ;;
    +([a-z])) echo  'LOW_CASE'   # lower case text
            ;;
    +([A-Z])) echo  'UP_CASE'    # UPPER case text
            ;;
    +([a-z]|[A-Z])) echo 'MIX_CASE' # MIxed CAse text
            ;;
```

Listing 8.9   proc_watch_timed.ksh shell script listing. *(continues)*

```
                    *) echo 'UNKNOWN'  # Anything else
esac
}
####################################################
proc_watch ()
{
# set -x # Uncomment to debug this function
# This function does all of the process monitoring!

while :      # Loop Forever!!
do
    case $RUN in
    'Y')
            # This will run the startup_event_script, which is a function

            if [[ $RUN_STARTUP_EVENT = 'Y' ]]
            then
                echo "STARTUP EVENT: Executing Startup Event Script..."\
                    > $TTY
                echo "STARTUP EVENT: Executing Startup Event Script..."\
                    >> $LOGFILE

                startup_event_script # USER DEFINED FUNCTION!!!
                RC=$?  # Check the Return Code!!
                if (( "RC" == 0 ))
                then
                    echo "SUCCESS: Startup Event Script Completed RC -
${RC}" > $TTY
                    echo "SUCCESS: Startup Event Script Completed RC -
${RC}" >> $LOGFILE

                else
                    echo "FAILURE: Startup Event Script FAILED RC -
${RC}" > $TTY
                    echo "FAILURE: Startup Event Script FAILED RC -
${RC}" >> $LOGFILE
                fi
            fi
            integer PROC_COUNT='-1' # Reset the Counters
            integer LAST_COUNT='-1'
            # Loop until the process(es) end(s)

            until (( "PROC_COUNT" == 0 ))
            do
                # This function is a Co-Process. $BREAK checks to see if
                # "Program Interrupt" has taken place. If so BREAK will
                # be 'Y' and we exit both the loop and function.

                read BREAK
```

Listing 8.9   proc_watch_timed.ksh shell script listing. *(continued)*

```
                            if [[ $BREAK = 'Y' ]]
                            then
                                    return 3
                            fi
                            PROC_COUNT=$(ps -ef | grep -v "grep $PROCESS" \
                                         | grep -v $SCRIPT_NAME \
                                         | grep $PROCESS | wc -1) >/dev/null 2>&1

                            if (( "LAST_COUNT" > 0 && "LAST_COUNT" != "PROC_COUNT" ))
                            then
                                    # The Process Count has Changed...
                                    TIMESTAMP=$(date +%D@%T)
                                    # Get a list of the PID of all of the processes
                                    PID_LIST=$(ps -ef | grep -v "grep $PROCESS" \
                                                 | grep -v $SCRIPT_NAME \
                                                 | grep $PROCESS | awk '{print $2}')

                                    echo "PROCESS COUNT: $PROC_COUNT $PROCESS\
Processes Running ==> $TIMESTAMP" >> $LOGFILE &
                                    echo "PROCESS COUNT: $PROC_COUNT $PROCESS\
Processes Running ==> $TIMESTAMP" > $TTY

                                    echo ACTIVE PIDS: $PID_LIST >> $LOGFILE &
                                    echo ACTIVE PIDS: $PID_LIST > $TTY
                            fi
                            LAST_COUNT=$PROC_COUNT
                            sleep $INTERVAL # Needed to reduce CPU load!
                    done

                    RUN='N' # Turn the RUN Flag Off

            TIMESTAMP=$(date +%D@%T)
            echo "ENDING PROCESS: $PROCESS END time  ==>\
$TIMESTAMP" >> $LOGFILE &
            echo "ENDING PROCESS: $PROCESS END time  ==>\
$TIMESTAMP" > $TTY

                    # This will run the post_event_script, which is a function

                    if [[ $RUN_POST_EVENT = 'Y' ]]
                    then
                        echo "POST EVENT: Executing Post Event Script..."\
                            > $TTY
                        echo "POST EVENT: Executing Post Event Script..."\
                            >> $LOGFILE &

                    post_event_script # USER DEFINED FUNCTION!!!
                    integer RC=$?
                    if (( "RC" == 0 ))
```

Listing 8.9   proc_watch_timed.ksh shell script listing. *(continues)*

```
                then
                        echo "SUCCESS: Post Event Script Completed RC -
${RC}" > $TTY
                        echo "SUCCESS: Post Event Script Completed RC -
${RC}" >> $LOGFILE
                else
                        echo "FAILURE: Post Event Script FAILED RC - ${RC}"\
                             > $TTY
                        echo "FAILURE: Post Event Script FAILED RC - ${RC}"\
                                >> $LOGFILE
                fi
        fi
    ;;


    'N')
        # This will run the pre_event_script, which is a function

        if [[ $RUN_PRE_EVENT = 'Y' ]]
        then
            echo "PRE EVENT: Executing Pre Event Script..." > $TTY
            echo "PRE EVENT: Executing Pre Event Script..." >> $LOGFILE

            pre_event_script # USER DEFINED FUNCTION!!!
            RC=$?    # Check the Return Code!!!
            if (( "RC" == 0 ))
            then
                    echo "SUCCESS: Pre Event Script Completed RC - ${RC}"\
                         > $TTY
                    echo "SUCCESS: Pre Event Script Completed RC - ${RC}"\
                            >> $LOGFILE
            else
                    echo "FAILURE: Pre Event Script FAILED RC - ${RC}"\
                         > $TTY
                    echo "FAILURE: Pre Event Script FAILED RC - ${RC}"\
                            >> $LOGFILE
            fi
        fi

        echo "WAITING: Waiting for $PROCESS to
startup...Monitoring..."

        integer PROC_COUNT='-1' # Initialize to a fake value

        # Loop until at least one process starts

        until (( "PROC_COUNT" > 0 ))
```

Listing 8.9 proc_watch_timed.ksh shell script listing. *(continued)*

```
        do
                # This is a Co-Process. This checks to see if a "Program
                # Interrupt" has taken place. If so BREAK will be 'Y' and
                # we exit both the loop and function

                read BREAK
                if [[ $BREAK = 'Y' ]]
                then
                        return 3
                fi

                PROC_COUNT=$(ps -ef | grep -v "grep $PROCESS" \
                        | grep -v $SCRIPT_NAME | grep $PROCESS | wc -l) \
                        >/dev/null 2>&1

                sleep $INTERVAL # Needed to reduce CPU load!
        done

        RUN='Y' # Turn the RUN Flag On

        TIMESTAMP=$(date +%D@%T)

        PID_LIST=$(ps -ef | grep -v "grep $PROCESS" \
                        | grep -v $SCRIPT_NAME \
                        | grep $PROCESS | awk '{print $2}')

        if (( "PROC_COUNT" == 1 ))
        then
                echo "START PROCESS: $PROCESS START time ==>
$TIMESTAMP" >> $LOGFILE &
                echo ACTIVE PIDS: $PID_LIST >> $LOGFILE &
                echo "START PROCESS: $PROCESS START time ==>
$TIMESTAMP" > $TTY
                echo ACTIVE PIDS: $PID_LIST > $TTY
        elif (( "PROC_COUNT" > 1 ))
        then
                echo "START PROCESS: $PROC_COUNT $PROCESS
Processes Started: START time ==> $TIMESTAMP" >> $LOGFILE &
                echo ACTIVE PIDS: $PID_LIST >> $LOGFILE &
                echo "START PROCESS: $PROC_COUNT $PROCESS
Processes Started: START time ==> $TIMESTAMP" > $TTY
                echo ACTIVE PIDS: $PID_LIST > $TTY
        fi
    ;;
  esac
done
```

Listing 8.9   proc_watch_timed.ksh shell script listing. *(continues)*

```
}

#####################################################
############## START OF MAIN #######################
#####################################################

### SET A TRAP ####

trap 'BREAK='Y';print -p $BREAK 2>/dev/null;trap_exit\
 2>/dev/null;exit 0' 1 2 3 15

BREAK='N'  # The BREAK variable is used in the co-process proc_watch
PROCESS=    # Initialize to null
integer TOTAL_SECONDS=0

# Check commnand line arguments

if (( $# > 10 || $# < 2 ))
then
     usage
     exit 1
fi

# Check to see if only the seconds and a process are
# the only arguments

if [[ ($# -eq 2) && ($1 != -*) && ($2 != -*) ]]
then
     NUM_TEST=$(test_string $1)  # Is this an Integer?
     if [[ "$NUM_TEST" = 'POS_INT' ]]
     then
          TOTAL_SECONDS=$1  # Yep - It's an Integer
          PROCESS=$2        # Can be anything
     else
          usage
          exit 1
     fi
else
     # Since getopts does not care what arguments it gets lets
     # do a quick sanity check to make sure that we only have
     # between 2 and 10 arguments and the first one must start
     # with a -* (hyphen and anything), else usage error

     case "$#" in
     [2-10]) if [[ $1 != -* ]]; then
                usage; exit 1
            fi
        ;;
```

Listing 8.9 proc_watch_timed.ksh shell script listing. *(continued)*

```
        esac

        HOURS=0    # Initialize all to zero
        MINUTES=0
        SECS=0
        DAYS=0

        # Use getopts to parse the command line arguments

        # For each $OPTARG for DAYS, HOURS, MINUTES and DAYS check to see
        # that each one is an integer by using the check_string function

        while getopts ":h:H:m:M:s:S:d:D:P:p:" OPT_LIST 2>/dev/null
        do
          case $OPT_LIST in
          h|H) [[ $(test_string $OPTARG) != 'POS_INT' ]] && usage && exit 1
               (( HOURS = $OPTARG * 3600 )) # 3600 seconds per hour
               ;;
          m|H) [[ $(test_string $OPTARG) != 'POS_INT' ]] && usage && exit 1
               (( MINUTES = $OPTARG * 60 )) # 60 seconds per minute
               ;;
          s|S) [[ $(test_string $OPTARG) != 'POS_INT' ]] && usage && exit 1
               SECS="$OPTARG"              # seconds are seconds
               ;;
          d|D) [[ $(test_string $OPTARG) != 'POS_INT' ]] && usage && exit 1
               (( DAYS = $OPTARG * 86400 )) # 86400 seconds per day
               ;;
          p|P) PROCESS=$OPTARG                # process can be anything
               ;;
           \?) usage                          # USAGE ERROR
               exit 1
               ;;
            :) usage
               exit 1
               ;;
            *) usage
               exit 1
               ;;
          esac
        done
fi

# We need to make sure that we have a process that
# is NOT null or empty! - sanity check - The double quotes are required!

if [[ -z "$PROCESS" || "$PROCESS" = '' ]]
then
        usage
```

Listing 8.9   proc_watch_timed.ksh shell script listing. *(continues)*

```
        exit 1
fi

# Check to see that TOTAL_SECONDS was not previously set

if (( TOTAL_SECONDS == 0 ))
then
        # Add everything together if anything is > 0

        if [[ $SECS -gt 0 || $MINUTES -gt 0 || $HOURS -gt 0 \
              || $DAYS -gt 0 ]]
        then
                (( TOTAL_SECONDS = SECS + MINUTES + HOURS + DAYS ))
        fi
fi

# Last Sanity Check!

if (( TOTAL_SECONDS <= 0 )) || [ -z $PROCESS ]
then
        # Either There are No Seconds to Count or the
        # $PROCESS Variable is Null...USAGE ERROR...

        usage
        exit 1
fi

########## START MONITORING HERE!##########

echo "\nCurrently running $PROCESS processes:\n" > $TTY
ps -ef | grep -v "grep $PROCESS" | grep -v $SCRIPT_NAME \
        | grep $PROCESS > $TTY

PROC_RC=$? # Get the initial state of the monitored function

echo >$TTY # Send a blank line to the screen

(( PROC_RC != 0 )) && echo "\nThere are no $PROCESS processes running\n"

if (( PROC_RC == 0 )) # The Target Process(es) is/are running...
then
        RUN='Y' # Set the RUN flag to true, or yes.

        integer PROC_COUNT # Strips out the "padding" for display

        PROC_COUNT=$(ps -ef | grep -v "grep $PROCESS" | grep -v \
                     $SCRIPT_NAME | grep $PROCESS | wc -l) >/dev/null 2>&1
        if (( PROC_COUNT == 1 ))
```

Listing 8.9   proc_watch_timed.ksh shell script listing. *(continued)*

```
        then
                echo "The $PROCESS process is currently
    running...Monitoring...\n"
            elif (( PROC_COUNT > 1 ))
            then
                print "There are $PROC_COUNT $PROCESS processes currently
    running...Monitoring...\n"
            fi
    else
            echo "The $PROCESS process is not currently running...monitoring..."
            RUN='N' # Set the RUN flag to false, or no.
    fi


    TIMESTAMP=$(date +%D@%T) # Time that this script started monitoring

    # Get a list of the currently active process IDs

    PID_LIST=$(ps -ef | grep -v "grep $PROCESS" \
                      | grep -v $SCRIPT_NAME  \
                      | grep $PROCESS | awk '{print $2}')

    echo "MON_STARTED: Monitoring for $PROCESS began ==> $TIMESTAMP" \
          | tee -a $LOGFILE
    echo ACTIVE PIDS: $PID_LIST | tee -a $LOGFILE


    ##### NOTICE ####
    # We kick off the "proc_watch" function below as a "Co-Process"
    # This sets up a two way communications link between the
    # "proc_watch" background function and this "MAIN BODY" of
    # the script.  This is needed because the function has two
    # "infinite loops", with one always executing at any given time.
    # Therefore we need a way to break out of the loop in case of
    # an interrupt, i.e. CTRL-C, and when the countdown is complete.
    # The "pipe appersand", |&, creates the background Co-Process
    # and we use "print -p $VARIABLE" to transfer the variable's
    # value back to the background co-process.
    ####################################

    proc_watch |&  # Create a Background Co-Process!!
    WATCH_PID=$!   # Get the process ID of the last background job!

    # Start the Count Down!

    integer SECONDS_LEFT=$TOTAL_SECONDS

    while (( SECONDS_LEFT > 0 ))
    do
```

Listing 8.9 proc_watch_timed.ksh shell script listing. *(continues)*

```
         # Next send the current value of $BREAK to the Co-Process
         # proc_watch, which was piped to the background...

         print -p $BREAK 2>/dev/null

         (( SECONDS_LEFT = SECONDS_LEFT - 1 ))
         sleep 1 #  1 Second Between Counts
done

# Finished - Normal Timeout Exit...

TIMESTAMP=$(date +%D@%T) # Get a new time stamp...
echo "MON_STOPPED: Monitoring for $PROCESS ended ==> $TIMESTAMP\n" \
     | tee -a $LOGFILE

echo "LOGFILE: All Events are Logged ==> $LOGFILE \n"

# Tell the proc_watch function to break out of the loop and die

BREAK='Y'
print -p $BREAK 2>/dev/null

kill $WATCH_PID 2>/dev/null

exit 0

# End of Script
```

Listing 8.9   proc_watch_timed.ksh shell script listing. *(continued)*

The most important things to note in Listing 8.9 are the communication link used between the foreground main script and the background co-process function, proc_watch, and the use of **getopts** to parse the command-line arguments. Some other things to look at are the integer tests using the string_test function and the way that the user is notified of a new process either starting or stopping by time stamp. The updated process count and the listing of all of the PIDs and how text is sent to the tty display within the function. As usual, we use the double parentheses numerical test method in the control structures. (Notice again that the $ is not used to reference the user defined variables!) This shell script is also full of good practices for using different control structures and the use of the logical AND and logical OR (&& and ||), which reduces the need for **if..then..else..** and **case** structures. One *very important* test needs to be pointed out—the "null/empty" test for the PROCESS variable just after **getopts** parses the command line. This test is so important because the **getopts** command does not care what arguments it is parsing;, nothing will "error out." For this reason, *we need to verify* all of the variables ourselves. The only thing **getopts** is doing is matching the command switches to the appropriate arguments, *not* the validity of the command-line argument! If this test is left out and invalid command line arguments are present, then **grep** command errors will cover the screen during the script's execution—bad, very bad!

A good review of Listing 8.9 is needed to point out some other interesting aspects. Let's start at the top:

In the definitions of the files and variables there are three variables that control the execution of the pre, startup, and post events. The variables are RUN_PRE_EVENT, RUN_STARTUP_EVENT, and RUN_POST_EVENT, and for ease of testing, the variables are **typeset** to UPPERCASE. A 'Y' will enable the execution of the function, in which a user can put anything that he or she wants to run. The *functions* are called pre_event_script, startup_event_script, and post_event_script, but don't let the names fool you. We also identify the LOGFILE variable and test to see if a log file exists. If the file does not exist, we **touch** the $LOGFILE variable, which creates an empty file with the filename that the $LOGFILE variable points to. This script section also grabs the SCRIPT_NAME using the **basename $0** command, and we define the current tty device for display purposes. An important variable is INTERVAL. This variable defines the number of seconds between sampling the process list. It is *very* important that this value is greater than 0, zero! If the INTERVAL value is set to 0, zero, then the CPU load will be extreme and will produce a noticeable load, to say the least.

The next section in Listing 8.9 defines all of the functions used in this script. We have a usage function that is displayed for usage errors. Then there is the trap_exit function. The trap_exit function will execute on exit codes 1, 2, 3, and 15, which we will see in the **trap** statement later at "Start of Main" in the script. Next are the pre_event_script, startup_event_script, and post_event_script functions. You may ask why a function would have a name indicating it is a script. It is done this way to encourage the use of an external script, or program, for any pre, startup, or post event activity, rather than editing this script and debugging an internal function. The next function is used to test character strings, thus the name test_string. If you have ever wondered how to test a string (the entire string!) for its composition, test_string will do the trick. We just use a regular expression test for a range of characters. The preceding + (plus sign) is required in this regular expression to specify that all characters are of the specified type.

Then comes the main function in the script that does all of the work, proc_watch. This function is also the one that is executed as the co-process that we have been talking so much about. The proc_watch function is an infinite loop that contains two internal loops, where one internal loop is always executing at any given time. During both of these internal loops we check the variable BREAK to see if the value is 'Y'. The 'Y' value indicates that the function should exit immediately. The BREAK variable is updated, or changed, from the main script and is "transferred" to this *co-process background function* using the **print -p $BREAK** command within the main script. This variable is reread, in the function, on each loop iteration using the standard **read BREAK** command. This is what enables the clean exit from the *background* function's loop. The word *background* is key to understanding the need for the co-process. If the main script is interrupted, then the *innermost* loop will continue to execute even after both the function and script end execution. It will exit on its own when the loop's exit parameters are met, but if they are never met we end up with a defunct process. To get around this problem we start the `proc_watch` function as a background co-process using |**&** as a suffix to the function—for example, `proc_watch` |&. An easy way to think of a co-process is a *pipe to the background*, and through this pipe we have a communications link.

For the main part of the shell script, at the START OF MAIN, we first set a **trap**. In the **trap** command we set the BREAK variable to 'Y', to indicate that the `proc_watch` co-process should exit, and we make the new BREAK value known to the co-process with the **print -p $BREAK 2>/dev/null** command. This command sometimes sends error notification to the standard error, file descriptor 2, but we want all error notification suppressed. Otherwise, the error messages would go to the screen during the script's execution, which is highly undesirable.

Next are the standard things of initializing a few variables and checking for the correct number of arguments. There are two ways to run this script: (1) only specifying the total seconds and the process to monitor or (2) using the command-line switches to specify the seconds, minutes, hours, days, and process to monitor. The latter method will use the **getopts** command to parse the arguments, but we do not need **getopts** for the first method. We first check to see if we are given only seconds and a process. We use the `test_string` function to ensure that the $1 argument is a positive integer. The second argument could be anything except a string that begins with a - (hyphen) or a null string. Otherwise, we will use the **getopts** command to parse the command line.

Using the **getopts** command makes life much easier when we need to process command-line arguments; however, **getopts** does have its limitations. The command is parsing the command-line arguments, but it really does not care what the arguments are. Therefore, we need to do a sanity check on each and every argument to ensure that it meets the criteria that is expected. If the argument fails, then we just run the usage function and **exit** with a return code of 1, one. Two tests are conducted on each argument. We test the PROCESS variable to make sure that it is not null, or empty, and we check all of the numeric variables used for timing to make sure they are positive integers, or 0, zero. The positive integer test is to ensure that at least one of the numeric variables, SECS, MINUTES, HOURS, and DAYS, has an integer value greater than 0, zero. If we get past this stage we assume we have creditable data to start monitoring.

The monitoring starts by getting an initial state of the process, either currently running or not running. With this information we initialize the RUN variable, which is used as a control mechanism for the rest of the script. Once the initialization text is both logged and sent to the screen, the `proc_watch` function is started as a background co-process, again using `proc_watch` |&. The main script just does a countdown to 0, zero, and exits. To make the `proc_watch` function exit cleanly we assign 'Y' to the BREAK variable and make this new value known to the co-process with the **print -p $BREAK** command. Then we **kill** the background PID that we saved in the WATCH_PID variable and then **exit** the script with a return code of 0, zero. If the script is interrupted, then the **trap** will handle stopping the co-process and exiting. See Listing 8.10.

```
[root:yogi]@/scripts/WILEY/PROC_MON# ./proc_watch_timed.ksh -m 5 -pxcalc

Currently running xcalc processes:

There are no xcalc processes running

The xcalc process is not currently running...monitoring...
MON_STARTED: Monitoring for xcalc began ==> 09/27/01@21:15:02
ACTIVE PIDS:
START PROCESS: xcalc START time ==> 09/27/01@21:15:19
ACTIVE PIDS: 26190
STARTUP EVENT: Executing Startup Event Script...
SUCCESS: Startup Event Script Completed RC - 0
PROCESS COUNT: 2 xcalc Processes Running ==> 09/27/01@21:15:46
ACTIVE PIDS: 13060 26190
PROCESS COUNT: 3 xcalc Processes Running ==> 09/27/01@21:16:04
ACTIVE PIDS: 13060 18462 26190
PROCESS COUNT: 4 xcalc Processes Running ==> 09/27/01@21:16:27
ACTIVE PIDS: 13060 18462 22996 26190
PROCESS COUNT: 3 xcalc Processes Running ==> 09/27/01@21:16:39
ACTIVE PIDS: 18462 22996 26190
PROCESS COUNT: 4 xcalc Processes Running ==> 09/27/01@21:16:56
ACTIVE PIDS: 18462 22996 24134 26190
PROCESS COUNT: 3 xcalc Processes Running ==> 09/27/01@21:17:31
ACTIVE PIDS: 22996 24134 26190
PROCESS COUNT: 2 xcalc Processes Running ==> 09/27/01@21:17:41
ACTIVE PIDS: 22996 24134
PROCESS COUNT: 3 xcalc Processes Running ==> 09/27/01@21:18:39
ACTIVE PIDS: 21622 22996 24134
PROCESS COUNT: 2 xcalc Processes Running ==> 09/27/01@21:18:58
ACTIVE PIDS: 21622 22996
PROCESS COUNT: 3 xcalc Processes Running ==> 09/27/01@21:19:04
ACTIVE PIDS: 18180 21622 22996
PROCESS COUNT: 4 xcalc Processes Running ==> 09/27/01@21:19:10
ACTIVE PIDS: 18180 21622 22758 22996
PROCESS COUNT: 6 xcalc Processes Running ==> 09/27/01@21:19:17
ACTIVE PIDS: 18180 21622 22758 22996 23164 26244
PROCESS COUNT: 5 xcalc Processes Running ==> 09/27/01@21:19:37
ACTIVE PIDS: 18180 22758 22996 23164 26244
PROCESS COUNT: 4 xcalc Processes Running ==> 09/27/01@21:19:47
ACTIVE PIDS: 18180 22996 23164 26244
PROCESS COUNT: 3 xcalc Processes Running ==> 09/27/01@21:19:53
ACTIVE PIDS: 18180 22996 26244
```

Listing 8.10 proc_watch_times.ksh shell script in action. *(continues)*

```
PROCESS COUNT: 2 xcalc Processes Running ==> 09/27/01@21:19:55
ACTIVE PIDS: 18180 26244
PROCESS COUNT: 1 xcalc Processes Running ==> 09/27/01@21:20:05
ACTIVE PIDS: 18180
PROCESS COUNT: 0 xcalc Processes Running ==> 09/27/01@21:20:09
ACTIVE PIDS:
ENDING PROCESS: xcalc END time  ==> 09/27/01@21:20:11
POST EVENT: Executing Post Event Script...
SUCCESS: Post Event Script Completed RC - 0
MON_STOPPED: Monitoring for xcalc ended ==> 09/27/01@21:20:23

LOGFILE: All Events are Logged ==> /tmp/proc_status.log
```

Listing 8.10   proc_watch_times.ksh shell script in action. *(continued)*

Other Options to Consider

The `proc_watch_timed.ksh` shell script is thorough, but it may need to be tailored to a more specific need. Some additional considerations are listed next.

Common Uses

These scripts are suited for things like monitoring how long a process runs, logging a process as it starts and stops, restarting a process that has terminated prematurely, and monitoring a problem user or contractor. We can also monitor activity on a particular `tty` port and send an email as a process starts execution. Use your imagination.

We can start the monitoring script on the command line, or as a cron or **at** job, and run it during the work day. A cron table entry might look like the following:

```
0 7 * * 1-5 /usr/local/bin/proc_watch_timed.ksh -h9 -p fred >/dev/null
```

This cron table entry would monitor any process in the process table that contained "fred" from 7:00 A.M. Monday through Friday for nine hours. Note: The nine hours may be much longer due to the system's load during the day as the script counts down to zero.

Anything in the system's process list can be monitored from seconds to days.

Modifications to Consider

These scripts are generic, and you may want to make modifications. One option to consider is to list the actual lines in the process list instead of only the PID and a process count with a time stamp. You may have a different **ps** command that is preferred—for example, **ps aux**. For a more accurate timing you may want to check the date/time at longer intervals (as opposed to counting down); checking the time would also reduce the CPU load. Another good idea is to get the timing data and run an **at** command to kill the script at the specified time. Also, consider using the Korn shell built-in variable SECONDS. First initialize the SECONDS variable to 0, zero and it will automatically increment each second as long as the parent process is executing. The pre, startup, and post events are something else to look at, the startup in particular. The startup_event_script currently executes only when (1) the monitoring starts and the target process is running and (2) when the very first, if more than one, process starts, not as *each* process starts. You may want to modify this function's execution to run only as each individual process starts and not to execute when monitoring starts and the target process is already running. Additionally, depending on what is to be executed for any of these events, some **sleep** time might be needed to allow for things to settle down. As we can see, there are many ways to do all of this, and everyone has different expectations and requirements. Just remember that we never have a *final script*; we just try to be flexible!

Summary

In this chapter we started with a very basic idea of monitoring for a process to start or stop. We quickly built on user options to monitor the process state for a specified period of time and added time stamps. We also allowed the user to specify pre, startup, and post events to execute as an option. Never try to do everything at once. Build a short shell script that does the basic steps of your target goal and expand on the base shell script to build in the nice-to-have things. I use the **proc_mon.ksh** and **proc_wait.ksh** shell scripts almost daily for monitoring system events and they sure do save a lot of time reentering the same command over-and-over again.

In the next chapter we are going to expand on our monitoring to include applications. We always want to know if an application or database has gone down during the day. As you watch the heads popping up above all of the cubicles it is always nice to be proactively informed and not be surprised by the application group.

Monitoring Processes and Applications

The most critical part of any business is ensuring that applications continue to run without error. In this chapter, we are going to look at several techniques for monitoring applications and critical processes that the applications rely on. The problem with trying to write this chapter is that there are so many applications in the corporate world that the techniques to monitor them vary widely.

From the lowest level we can **ping** the machine to see if it is up. A **ping**, though, is not an operating system response, but rather a machine response to confirm that the network adapter is configured. At a higher level, we can look at the processes that are required for the application to run properly, but this too does not completely confirm, 100 percent, that the application is working properly. The only way to ensure the application is working properly is to interact with the application. As an example, if we have a database that the application requires we can do a simple SQL query to ensure that the database is working properly. For interactive applications we can try to use a *here* document to log in to the application and maybe even perform a small task. Applications work differently, so the solution to ensure that the application is up and running properly will vary widely.

We are going to look at monitoring local processes, remote monitoring using Secure Shell (SSH), checking for active Oracle databases, and checking an application URL and HTTP server status in this chapter.

Monitoring Local Processes

Above pinging a host machine, the most common application monitoring technique is to look for the critical processes that are required for the application to work properly. This is also a good practice when we have a flaky application that has a process that dies intermittently. The basic technique is to use the **ps -ef | grep** *target_process* **| grep -v grep** command syntax. If you have more than one required process, then this command statement needs to be executed for each of the processes individually. We do not want to use **egrep** in place of **grep** in this case. If **egrep** is used, then we get a positive result if *any* of the processes are currently running.

The key to making this technique work is to find a *unique* string pattern that represents the target process. The PID is no good because the process may have a child or parent process that has the same PID somewhere in the **ps -ef** output. Finding a unique string pattern that works with the **grep** command is key. This is easily tested by using the following command syntax on the command line.

```
ps -ef | grep Appserver | grep -v grep
```

This command statement assumes that we are looking for a process called **Appserver**. Notice that we always pipe (|) the last pipe's output to **| grep -v grep**. This last **grep** on **grep** is needed so that the system will not report on the **grep Appserver** process. In the process table each part of the command statement that has a pipe will have a separate PID.

Then there is another thing to consider if this command is executed in a shell script. The shell script name may show up in the **grep** output, depending on how the shell script is written. To get around this little problem we need to query the system to capture the shell script's filename and add a third **grep** to the **ps -ef** command statement using the following syntax:

```
SCRIPT_NAME=$(basename $0)

ps -ef | grep target_process | grep -v grep | grep -v $SCRIPT_NAME
```

Now we have a command that will work if, *and only if*, a unique character string can be found that separates the target process from all other processes. This usually takes a few tries for each application that we want to monitor.

In Listing 9.1 we have a code segment from a shell script that monitors an application service, using a unique character string. This particular application service is defined by the APPSVC variable. If this service is not currently running, there is an attempt to restart the application service and an email is sent to my text pager and my regular email account. Follow the code segment in Listing 9.1.

```
#######################################################
############# DEFINE VARIABLES HERE #################
#######################################################

APPSVC="/usr/local/sbin/appstrt_u1"
MAILLIST="1234567890@mypage.provider.abc randy@my.domain.com"
MAILFILE="/tmp/mailfile.out"
TIMESTAMP=$(date +%m%d%y%H%M%S)
APPS_LOG="/usr/local/log/appsvc.log
[ -s $APP_LOG ] || touch $APP_LOG


#######################################################
################ START OF MAIN #####################
#######################################################

# Check to see if the APPSVC process(es) is/are running

APPSVC_COUNT=$(ps -ef | grep $APPSVC | grep -v grep \
                     | grep -v $SCRIPT_NAME | wc -1)

# If the count is zero then we need to attempt to restart the service

if (( $APPSVC_COUNT == 0 ))
then
    # Need to attempt an Application server restart.
    echo "SVC-A1 - APPSVC: Attempting Restart" > $MAILFILE
    # Send email notification
    sendmail -f rmichael@my.domain.com $MAILLIST < $MAILFILE
    # Make a log entry
    echo "ERROR: $TIMESTAMP - Appsvc DOWN - Attempting Restart">>
$APP_LOG
    # Make another log entry
    echo "STARTING APPLICATION SERVER - $TIMESTAMP" >>$APPS_LOG

    # Attempt the restart!!!
    su - appsvc -c '/usr/local/sbin/appsvc start 2>&1' >> $APP_LOG
fi
```

Listing 9.1   Code segment to monitor an application process.

In the code segment in Listing 9.1 notice that we defined a unique string for the process, which in this case is the fully qualified pathname, to the APPSVC variable. Because this application server can have multiple instances running at the same time, we need to get a count of how many of these processes are running. If the process count is 0, zero, a restart of the application server is attempted.

During the restart effort an email notification is sent to reflect that the application service is down and the script is attempting a restart. This information is also logged in the $APP_LOG file *before* the restart command. Notice the restart command at the end of the script segment. This monitoring script is executed from the **root** crontab every 10 minutes. Because the script is running as **root** it is easy to use the **su** (switch user) command to execute a single command as the **appsvc** user for the restart. If you are not familiar with this technique, then study the syntax in Listing 9.1 and study the **man** page for the **su** command.

Remote Monitoring with Secure Shell

In the previous section we studied a "local" shell script. No one said, though, that you could not run this same script from a remote machine. This is where Open Secure Shell (OpenSSH) comes into play.

Open Secure Shell is a freeware encryption replacement for **telnet**, **ftp**, and **rsh**, for the most part. When we use the **ssh** command we establish a connection between two machines, and a secure *tunnel* allows encrypted communication between two *trusted* machines. Using **ssh** we can log in to another trusted machine in the network, we can copy files between the machines in an encrypted state, and we can run commands on a remote trusted machine. OpenSSH can be downloaded at the following URL:

```
http://www.openssh.com
```

To establish *password-free* encrypted connections, an encryption key pair must be created on both machines. This encryption key is located on both machines in the user's $HOME/.ssh directory. All of the details to set up the password-free encrypted connections are shown in great detail in the **ssh** man page (**man ssh**).

Let's look at a couple of examples of using **ssh**. The first example shown in Listing 9.2 shows a simple login without the key pair created.

```
# ssh randy@dino
The authenticity of host 'dino (10.10.10.6)' can't be established.
RSA key fingerprint is c5:19:37:b9:59:ad:3a:18:6b:45:57:2d:ab:b8:df:bb.
Are you sure you want to continue connecting (yes/no)? yes
Warning: Permanently added 'dino (10.10.10.6)' (RSA) to the list of
known
hosts.
randy@dino's password:
Last unsuccessful login: Tue Jul 2 13:58:18 EDT 2002 on /dev/pts/24 from
bambam
```

Listing 9.2   Sample secure shell login.

```
Last login: Wed Aug  7 10:28:00 EDT 2002 on /dev/pts/18 from bambam

*************************************************************************
*
*
*  Welcome to dino!
*
*
*  Please see the README file in /usr/lpp/bos for information pertinent
*  to this release of the AIX Operating System.
*
*
*
*************************************************************************
[YOU HAVE NEW MAIL]
[randy@dino] $
```

Listing 9.2   Sample secure shell login. *(continued)*

Notice in Listing 9.2 that the login to **dino** required a password, which indicates that the systems do not have the encryption key pairs set up. This does get a bit annoying when you are trying to run a command on a remote machine using an **ssh** tunnel. With the key pairs created on both machines we can monitor remote machines using encryption, and no password is required. As an example, suppose I need to check the filesystem usage on **dino** and I am logged into **yogi**. By adding the command that we want to execute on **dino** to the end of the **ssh** login statement, we establish a trusted connection between the two machines, and the command executes on the remote machine with the output going to the local machine. Of course, this is equivalent to a remote shell, **rsh**, except that the information is encrypted using **ssh** in place of **rsh**. A simple example of this technique is shown in Listing 9.3.

```
[randy@yogi] ssh randy@dino df -k

Filesystem    1024-blocks      Free %Used    Iused %Iused Mounted on
/dev/hd4           196608     66180   67%     2330     3% /
/dev/hd2          1441792    488152   67%    29024     9% /usr
/dev/hd9var       2162688   1508508   31%      868     1% /var
/dev/hd3           131072    106508   19%      361     2% /tmp
```

Listing 9.3   Example of running a remote command. *(continues)*

```
/dev/hd1          589824    235556   61%    15123    11% /home
/dev/local_lv     393216     81384   80%     2971     4% /usr/local
/dev/oracle_lvx  1507328    307388   80%     5008     2% /oracle
/dev/arch_lvx   13631488   8983464   35%       44     1% /oradata
```

Listing 9.3   Example of running a remote command. *(continued)*

Notice in the output in Listing 9.3 that there was no prompt for a password and that the result was presented back to the local terminal. Once the key pairs are set up you can do remote monitoring with ease, as long as your security staff does not find any bugs in the **ssh** code. Let's move on to Oracle now.

Checking for Active Oracle Databases

I wanted to have at least one example of interacting with an application in this chapter, and I picked an Oracle database as the example using a SQL+ database query. We will look at three steps to check the Oracle database status. The first step is to list all of the Oracle instances defined in the /etc/oratab file. This file is colon-separated (:) with the Oracle instance name(s) in the first field, **$1**. The function shown in Listing 9.4 first checks to see if a /etc/oratab file exists. If the file is not found, then a notification message is displayed on the user's terminal and the function returns a 3 for a return code. Otherwise, the /etc/oratab file is parsed to find the Oracle instance name(s). Removing all of the lines that begin with comments, specified by beginning with a hash mark (#), in the file is done using a **sed** statement in combination with the ^# notation. Removing the comment lines is easy using the **sed** statement, as shown here with a /etc/hosts file as an example.

```
cat /etc/hosts | sed /^#/b > /etc/hosts.without_beginning_comments
```

The output of the previous command shows all of the IP address and hostname entries, except that the commented-out lines have been removed. The ^# is the key to finding the commented lines, which translates to *begins with a #*.

Check out the function in Listing 9.4 to see how we use this technique to parse the Oracle instances from the /etc/oratab file.

```
function show_oratab_instances
{
if [ ! -f "$ORATAB" ]
then
    echo "\nOracle instance file $ORATAB does not exist\n"
    return 3
else
    cat $ORATAB | sed /^#/b | awk -F: '{print $1}'
fi
}
```

Listing 9.4   show_oratab_instances function listing.

The output of the `show_oratab_instances` function in Listing 9.4 is a list of all of the Oracle instances defined on the system. We have already removed the lines that are comments; next comes the **awk** statement that extracts the first field, specified by `awk -F: '{print $1}'`. In this **awk** statement the **-F:** specifies that the line is field separated by colons (`:`). Once we know the field separator we just extract the first field (**$1**), which is the Oracle instance name.

Now we are going to use the same function shown in Listing 9.4 to get the status of all of the defined Oracle instances by checking for the process for each instance. This technique is shown in Listing 9.5.

```
function show_all_instances_status
{
for INSTANCE in $(show_oratab_instances)
do
    ps -ef | grep ora | grep $INSTANCE | grep -v grep >/dev/null 2>&1
    if (($? != 0))
    then
        echo "\n$INSTANCE is NOT currently running $(date)\n"
    else
        echo "\n$INSTANCE is currently running OK $(date)\n"
    fi
done
}
```

Listing 9.5   show_all_instances_status function listing.

Notice in Listing 9.5 that we use the function from Listing 9.4 to get the list of Oracle instances to query the system for. In this case, all we are doing is using the **ps -ef** command again. This time we narrow the list down with a **grep** on the string **ora**. This output is piped (`|`) to another **grep** statement, where we are looking for the instance name for the current loop iteration, specified by `$INSTANCE`. Of course, we need to strip out any grep processes from the output so we add one more **grep -v grep**. If the return code of the entire **ps -ef** statement is 0, zero, then the instance is running; if the return is anything other than 0, zero, then the instance is not running.

We are still looking at the process level. I have seen cases when the instance processes are running, but I still could not log in to the database. For a final test we need to do an actual SQL query of the database to interact with Oracle. This just needs to be a very simple query to prove that we can interact with the database and get data back.

To actually query the Oracle database we can use a simple SQL+ statement, as shown in Listing 9.6. This two-line SQL script is used in the function `simple_SQL_query`, shown in Listing 9.6 using the **sqlplus** command.

```
select * from user_users;
exit
```

Listing 9.6   my_sql_query.sql SQL script listing.

As you can see in Listing 9.6, this is not much of a query, but it is all that we need. This SQL script, `my_sql_query.sql`, is used in the **sqlplus** function in Listing 9.7. Notice in this function, `simple_SQL_query`, that the **sqlplus** command statement requires a username, password, and an Oracle SID name to work. See the function code in Listing 9.7.

```
function simple_SQL_query
{
USER=oracle
PASSWD=oracle
SID=yogidb

sqlplus ${USER}/${PASSWD}@$SID @my_sql_query.sql
}
```

Listing 9.7   simple_SQL_query function listing.

The function shown in Listing 9.7 can be shortened further, *if* you are logged in to the system as the **oracle** user or executing a script as the **oracle** user. If these conditions are met then you can run a simpler version of the previous **sqlplus**, as shown in Listing 9.8, with the output of the query; however, the Oracle Listener is not tested as in the previous **sqlplus** statement in Listing 9.7. The **sqlplus** command in Listing 9.8 should be run on the local machine.

```
[oracle@yogi] sqlplus / @/usr/local/bin/mysql_query.sql

SQL*Plus: Release 8.1.7.0.0 - Production on Wed Aug 7 16:07:30 2002

(c) Copyright 2000 Oracle Corporation.  All rights reserved.


Connected to:
Oracle8i Enterprise Edition Release 8.1.7.4.0 - Production
With the Partitioning option
JServer Release 8.1.7.4.0 - Production


USERNAME                               USER_ID ACCOUNT_STATUS
------------------------------------ ---------- --------------------------------
LOCK_DATE   EXPIRY_DATE DEFAULT_TABLESPACE
----------- ----------- -------------------------------
TEMPORARY_TABLESPACE             CREATED      INITIAL_RSRC_CONSUMER_GROUP
```

Listing 9.8   Example of an SQL+ Oracle query.

```
---------------------------------  -----------  -----------------------------
EXTERNAL_NAME
---------------------------------------------------------------------------
---
OPS$ORACLE                                    940 OPEN
                            USERS
TEMP                                    18-APR-2002



Disconnected from Oracle8i Enterprise Edition Release 8.1.7.4.0 -
Production
With the Partitioning option
JServer Release 8.1.7.4.0 - Production
```

Listing 9.8   Example of an SQL+ Oracle query. *(continued)*

This is about as simple as it gets! You can check the return code from the **sqlplus** command shown in Listing 9.8. If it is zero, then the query worked. If the return code is nonzero, then the query failed and the database should be considered down. In any case, the Database Administrator needs to be notified of this condition.

Checking If the HTTP Server/Application Is Working

Some applications use a Web browser interface. For this type of application we can use a command-line browser, such as **linx**, to attempt to reach a specific URL, which in turn should bring up the specified application Web page. The function shown in Listing 9.9 utilizes the **linx** command-line browser to check both the HTTP server and the Web page presented by the specified URL, which is passed to the function in the **$1** argument.

```
check_HTTP_server ()
{
LINX="/usr/local/bin/lynx"    # Define the location of the linx program
URL=$1                        # Capture the target URL in the $1 position
URLFILE=/tmp/HTTP.$$          # Define a file to hold the URL output


###########################################

$LINX "$URL" > $URLFILE       # Attempt to reach the target URL

if (($? != 0))                # If the URL is unreachable - No Connection
```

Listing 9.9   check_HTTP_server function listing. *(continues)*

```
then
        echo "\n$URL - Unable to connect\n"
        cat $URLFILE
else                            # Else the URL was found

        while read VER RC STATUS  # This while loop is fed from the bottom
                                  # after the "done" using input
redirection
        do
            case $RC in           # Check the return code in the $URLFILE

            200|401|301|302)    # These are valid return codes!

                                echo "\nHTTP Server is OK\n"
                                ;;
                  *)  # Anything else is not a valid return code

                                echo "\nERROR: HTTP Server Error\n"
                                ;;

            esac

        done < $URLFILE
fi

rm -f $URLFILE
}
```

Listing 9.9   check_HTTP_server function listing. *(continued)*

This is a nice function in Listing 9.9 for checking the status of a Web server and also to see if an application URL is accessible. You should test this function against doing the same task manually using a graphical browser. This has been tested on an application front-end, and it works as expected; however, a good test is recommended before implementing this, or any other code, in this book. You know all about the disclaimer stuff. (I am really not even here writing this book, or so the disclaimer says.)

Other Things to Consider

As with any code that is written, it can always be improved. Each of the functions and code segments presented in this chapter are just that, code segments. When you are monitoring applications, code like this is only one part of a much bigger shell script, at least it should be. The monitoring should start at the lowest level, which is sending a **ping** to the application host to ensure that the machine is powered on and booted. Then we apply more layers as we try to build a script that will allow us to debug the problem. I have presented only a few ideas; it is your job to work out the details for your environment.

Application APIs and SNMP Traps

Most enterprise management tools come with application program interfaces (APIs) for the more common commercial applications; however, we sometimes must write shell scripts to fill in the gaps. This is where SNMP traps come in. Because the enterprise management tool *should* support SNMP traps, the APIs allow the application to be monitored using the SNMP MIB definitions on both the management server and the client system.

When an enterprise management tool supports SNMP traps, you can usually write your own shell scripts that can use the tool's MIB and SNMP definitions to get the message out from your own shell scripts. As an example, the command shown here utilizes a well-known monitoring tool's SNMP and MIB data to allow a trap to be sent.

```
/usr/local/bin/trapclient $MON_HOST $MIB_NUM $TRAP_NUM $TRAP_TEXT
```

In the previous command the MON_HOST variable represents the enterprise management workstation. The MIB_NUM variable represents the specific code for the MIB parameter. The TRAP_NUM variable represents the specific trap code to send, and the TRAP_TEXT is the text that is sent with the trap. This type of usage varies depending on the monitoring tool that you are using. At any rate, there are techniques that allow you to write shell scripts to send traps. The methods vary, but the basic syntax remains the same for SNMP.

Summary

This is one of those chapters where it is useless to write a bunch of shell scripts. I tried to show some of the techniques of monitoring applications and application processes, but the details are too varied to cover in a single chapter. I have laid down a specific process that you can utilize to build a very nice tool to monitor your systems and applications. Always start with a **ping**! If the box is unpingable, then your first job is to get the machine booted or to call hardware support.

In the next steps you have several options, including interacting with the application, as we did with a SQL+ query of an Oracle database. We also covered monitoring specific processes that are a little flaky and die every once in a while. I have two applications that I have to monitor this way, and I have not had even one phone call since I put this tool in place. The key is to keep the business in business, and the best way to do that is to be very proactive. This is where good monitoring and control shell scripts make you look like gold.

Remember, no one *ever* notices an application except when it is down!

In the next chapter, we move on to study creating pseudo-random passwords. The scripts include the use of arrays in shell scripts and a practical use for computer-generated pseudo-random numbers in a shell script. See you in the next chapter!

Creating Pseudo-Random Passwords

Got security? Most of the user community does not know how to create secure passwords that are not easy to guess. Users tend to have several passwords that they rotate. The problem with these "rotating" passwords is that they are usually easy to guess. For example, users find that birth dates, social security numbers, addresses, department names/numbers, and so on make good passwords that are easy to remember. Sometimes they even use words found in any dictionary, which is a starting point for any cracker. In this chapter we are going to create a shell script that creates *pseudo-random passwords*.

Randomness

If you look at Chapter 21, " *Pseudo-Random Number Generator*," you can see the exercise that we used to create pseudo-random numbers. These numbers are not true random numbers because of the cyclical nature of how "random numbers" are created on a computer system. For example, if you always start a random number sequence with the same *seed*, or first number, you will always have the same sequence of numbers. In Chapter 21 we used the process ID (PID) of the current process, which was the shell script, as the seed for creating pseudo-random numbers. This use of the PID is good because PIDs are created by the system in a somewhat random nature. Now that I have lost you in random numbers you are asking, "What does a random number have to do with a password?" As we proceed, the answer will be intuitively obvious.

Creating Pseudo-Random Passwords

We started this chapter with a discussion on randomness because we are going to use computer-generated pseudo-random numbers, then use these generated numbers as pointers to specific array elements of keyboard characters, which are stored in the array KEYS. In this chapter you get a practical use for generating random numbers, and you thought Chapter 21 was a waste of time!

The script idea goes like this: We use an external file that contains keyboard characters, one character per line. You can put any keyboard characters in this file that you want. I just went down the rows on the keyboard from left to right, starting on the top row of keys with numbers. As I went through all of the keyboard keys I then added a second set of numbers from the number keypad, as well as all of the uppercase and lowercase characters. The nice thing about this strategy is that you have the ability to specify the exact group of characters that make a valid password in your shop. Country-specific keyboards, which use characters other than those of the U.S. keyboards, also benefit from this strategy.

Once we have the keyboard file created, we load the keyboard data into an *array*. Don't panic! Korn shell arrays are easy to work with, as you will see in the scripting section as well as in the array introduction section. When we have all of the array elements loaded, then we know how many total elements we have to work with. Using techniques described in Chapter 21, we create pseudo-random numbers between one and the total number of array elements, *n*. With an array *pointer*, which is nothing more than a pseudo-random number, pointing to an individual character, we add the specific character to build a text string. The default length of this character string, which is the password we are creating, is eight characters; however, this can be changed on the command line to make the password longer or shorter by adding an integer value specifying the new password length.

The final step is to print the password to the screen. We also add two command-line switch options, -n and -m. The -n switch specifies that the user wants to create a new keyboard data file. The -m switch specifies that the user wants to print a *password page*. In our shop we are required to put some passwords, such as **root**, in multiple security envelopes to be locked in a safe, just in case. To remove the risk of typos, I print the password page, which has three copies of the password data on the same page, and cut the sheet up into three pieces. I then fold each of the three slips of paper and seal each one in a security envelope and give them to my Admin Manager.

As you can see, creating passwords is not something that I take lightly! Weak passwords make for a real security risk, and as a Systems Administrator you need to take a proactive approach to create secure passwords that are as random as you can make them. This chapter is a valuable asset to any security team as well as for the common user.

Syntax

As with any of our scripting sessions we first need the correct syntax for the primary commands that we are going to use in the shell script. In this case we need to introduce arrays and the commands that are used to work with the array and the array elements. There is a lot more than loading an array to creating this shell script. When we get to the scripting section you will see the other tasks that I have in mind, and you can pick up a pointer or two from the chapter.

Arrays

In a Korn shell we can create one-dimensional *arrays*. A one-dimensional array contains a sequence of *array elements*, which are like the boxcars connected together on a train track. An array element can be just about anything, except for another array. I know, you're thinking that you can use an array to access an array to create two- and three-dimensional arrays. If this can be done, it is beyond the scope of this book.

For our task we are going to load our array with single-character array elements that are loaded into the array from an external file. An array element can be a text string, number, line of text, print queue name, or just about anything you can list.

Loading an Array

An array can be loaded in two ways. You can define and load the array in one step with the **set -A** command, or you can load the array one element at a time. Both techniques are shown here.

Defining and Loading Array "KEYS" in One Step

```
set -A KEYS q w e r t y u i o p \[ \] a s d f g h j k l \$
```

Notice in this preceding list that the characters [,], and $ have been *escaped* to remove their special function by adding a *backslash* character. If we had not escaped these characters, then errors, and *strange* behavior, may occur as you tried to load or display the array elements. You will see this on a larger scale in the shell script. Also remember that if you enclose a list in double quotes or single tic marks it is treated as a single array element, not as individual array elements.

Loading Array "KEYS" One Array Element at a Time

The second option for loading the array KEYS is to use a **while read** loop and use a file as input to the **while** loop. In this example we load the array elements one at a time using a counter to index the KEYS array.

```
X=0
while read ARRAY_ELEMENT
do
      ((X = X + 1))

          KEYS[$X]=$ARRAY_ELEMENT

done < $ARRAY_ELEMENT_FILE
```

The first loading option, which uses the **set -A** command, requires that you hard-code the keyboard layout into the shell script, which removes much of the flexibility that you want when restricting or expanding password content. Using the **while** loop method we can use an external file and load this file with any characters that we want, and we can have as many or as few characters defined for passwords as we like. We can also duplicate characters and change the order of the characters any way we wish.

As the counter is incremented on each **while** loop iteration, we load the array elements in sequential order, starting with array elements 1, KEYS[1]. When we get to the end of the file, we know how many elements we have loaded in the array by the value of the array counter, $X. To see the specific value of array element 22, you can use the following syntax:

```
# echo ${KEYS[22]}
;
```

As you can see from the response, the 22nd array element that was loaded is a semi-colon character (;). We can also display the number of array elements using either of the following two options:

```
# echo ${#KEYS[*]}
# echo ${#KEYS[@]}
```

Notice that we started with array element 1, one. The Korn shell also supports array element 0, zero, but the pseudo-random numbers we create start with one, not zero. We will look at arrays more closely as we write our shell script.

Building the Password Creation Script

I want to explain this shell script one step at a time, and we have a lot to cover, so let's get started. First, you need to understand the order of execution and each task that is involved in this script.

Order of Appearance

As usual, we start out by defining the variables that are required for this script. The following section shows the variables that are defined for this shell script.

Define Variables

LENGTH=8   # Default password length.

NOTIFICATION_LIST=<Manager notification list>   # Persons to notify if the password is revealed or the "glass has been broken."

DEFAULT_PRINTER=<printer or queue name>   # Default printer to print the password report.

```
SCRIPT=$(basename $0)   # The name of this shell script with the directory
```
path removed.

```
OUTFILE=/tmp/tmppwd.out   # Temporary hold file for the printer report.
```

```
KEYBOARD_FILE=/scripts/keyboard.keys   # File containing keyboard
```
characters.

```
PRINT_PASSWORD_MANAGER_REPORT=<TRUE or Anything else>   # Print
```
report flag.

```
RANDOM=$$   # Initializes the random seed to the PID of the shell script, which is
```
pretty random.

The purpose of each of these variables is shown after the pound sign (#) on each line.

Define Functions

We have six functions to go through in this section. The functions described here are listed in their order of appearance in the shell script, mk_passwd.ksh. In each of the function descriptions there is a function listing for you to follow through.

in_range_random_number Function Description

The Korn shell provides an environment variable called—you guessed it—RANDOM. This pseudo-random number generator uses a *seed* as a starting point to create all future numbers in the sequence. The initial seed is used to create a pseudo-random number. This resulting number is used for the next seed to create the next random number, and so on. As you would expect, if you always start generating your numbers with the same seed each time, you will get the exact same number sequence each time. To change the repeatability we need to have a mechanism to vary the initial seed each time we start generating numbers. I like to use the current process ID (PID) of the shell script because this number will vary widely and is an easy way to change the seed value each time we start generating numbers.

We often want to limit the range of numbers not to exceed a user-defined maximum. An example is creating lottery numbers between 1 and the maximum number, which might be 36. We are going to use the modulo arithmetic operator to reduce all numbers to a fixed set of numbers between [0..N-1], which is called *modulo N arithmetic*. We are going to use this pseudo-random number to index array elements in the KEYS array.

For our number range we need a script-defined maximum value, which we will assign to a variable called UPPER_LIMIT. This UPPER_LIMIT variable is defined when the KEYS array has been loaded because it represents the total number of elements that are contained in the KEYS array. The modulo operator is the percent sign (%), and we use this operator the same way that you use the forward slash (/) in division. We still use the RANDOM Korn shell variable to get a new pseudo-random number. This time, though, we are going to use the following equation to limit the number to not exceed the script-defined maximum.

```
RANDOM_NUMBER=$(($RANDOM % $UPPER_LIMIT + 1))
```

Notice that we added one to the result. Using the preceding equation will produce a pseudo-random number between 1 and the script-defined $UPPER_LIMIT, which is the total number of elements in the KEYS array. The function using this equation is in_range_random_number and is shown in Listing 10.1.

```
function in_range_random_number
{
# Create a pseudo-random number less than or equal
# to the $UPPER_LIMIT value, which is defined in the
# main body of the shell script.

RANDOM_NUMBER=$(($RANDOM % $UPPER_LIMIT + 1))

echo "$RANDOM_NUMBER"
}
```

Listing 10.1   in_range_random_number function listing.

The function in Listing 10.1 assumes that the RANDOM variable seed has been initialized in the main body of the shell script and that a script-defined UPPER_LIMIT variable has been set. This function will produce numbers between 1 and the script-defined maximum value.

load_default_keyboard Function Description

As it turns out, you can add as many, or as few, characters to the $KEYBOARD_FILE file. What if the user wants a quick startup and an easy way to create this required file? This is the reason why I added this function to the mk_passwd.ksh shell script.

There are two mechanisms for loading a *default* keyboard layout. The first way is when the shell script is unable to locate the $KEYBOARD_FILE on the system. In this case the user is prompted to load the default keyboard layout. The second option is to add -n as a command-line switch. We will get to parsing command-line switches later in this chapter. In either of the two situations the user is still prompted before the $KEYBOARD_FILE is loaded with default keyboard layout.

Other than prompting the user to load the default keyboard layout, we need to supply a list of keyboard characters to load into the file. At this point let's look at the function code in Listing 10.2 and cover the details at the end.

```
function load_default_keyboard
{
# If a keyboard data file does not exist then the user
# is prompted to load the standard keyboard data into the
# $KEYBOARD_FILE, which is defined in the main body of
```

Listing 10.2   load_default_keyboard function listing.

```
# the shell script.

clear  # Clear the screen

echo "\nLoad the default keyboard data file? (Y/N): \c"
read REPLY

case $REPLY in
y|Y) :
     ;;
  *) echo "\nSkipping the load of the default keyboard file...\n"
     return
     ;;
esac

cat /dev/null > $KEYBOARD_FILE

echo "\nLoading the Standard Keyboard File...\c"

# Loop through each character in the following list and
# append each character to the $KEYBOARD_FILE file. This
# produces a file with one character on each line.

for CHAR in \` 1 2 3 4 5 6 7 8 9 0 \- \= \\ q w e r t y u i o \
            p \[ \] a s d f g h j k l \; \' z x c v b n m \, \
            \. \/ \\ \~ \! \@ \# \$ \% \^ \& \* \( \) _ \+ \| \
            Q W E R T Y U I O P \{ \} A S D F G H J K L \: \" \
            Z X C V B N M \< \> \? \| \. 0 1 2 3 4 5 6 7 8 9 \/ \
            \* \- \+
do
     echo "$CHAR" >> $KEYBOARD_FILE
done
echo "\n\n\t...Done...\n"

sleep 1
```

Listing 10.2   load_default_keyboard function listing. *(continued)*

Now I want to direct your attention to the **for** loop in Listing 10.2, which is in bold-face text. The idea is to loop through each character one at a time and append the character to the $KEYBOARD_FILE. The result is a file that contains the keyboard layout, listed one character per line. The file shows one character per line to make it easier to load the file and the KEYS array.

In the list of characters please notice that most of the nonalphanumeric characters are preceded by a backslash (\), not just the Korn shell special characters. As we discussed previously, this backslash is used to *escape* the special meaning of these characters.

When you precede a special character with the backslash, you are able to use the character as a literal character, just like the alphanumeric characters, and if a backslash precedes the other non-alphanumeric characters, it is ignored. The list of characters that are escaped is shown here:

```
` ! @ # $ % ^ & * ( ) _ - = + [ ] { }
```

On each loop iteration one character is appended to the $KEYBOARD_FILE using the following command:

```
echo "$CHAR" >> $KEYBOARD_FILE
```

When the file is loaded, which happens extremely fast, we notify the user that the load is complete and then **sleep** for one second. I added this **sleep 1** at the end of this function because the load happened so fast that the user needed a second to see the message.

check_for_and_create_keyboard_file Function Description

Is this function name descriptive enough? I like to know exactly what a function is used for by reading the name of the function.

The purpose of this function is to check for the existence of the $KEYBOARD_FILE and to prompt the user to load the default keyboard layout into the $KEYBOARD_FILE. The user has the option to load the default data or not to load it. If the user declines to load the keyboard data file, then this script will not work. To get around this little problem, we just notify the user of this ERROR and exit the shell script.

When the user gets the error message, he or she is also informed of the name of the missing file and a description of what the script expects in the file—specifically, one keyboard character per line. The full function is shown in Listing 10.3.

```
function check_for_and_create_keyboard_file
{
# If the $KEYBOARD_FILE does not exist then
# ask the user to load the "standard" keyboard
# layout, which is done with the load_default_keyboard
# function.

if [ ! -s $KEYBOARD_FILE ]
then
     echo "\n\nERROR: Missing Keyboard File"
     echo "\n\nWould You Like to Load the"
     echo "Default Keyboard Layout?"
     echo "\n\t(Y/N): \c"
     typeset -u REPLY=FALSE
     read REPLY
     if [[ $REPLY != Y ]]
     then
```

Listing 10.3   check_for_and_create_keyboard_file function listing.

```
               echo "\n\nERROR: This shell script cannot operate"
               echo "without a keyboard data file located in"
               echo "\n==>  $KEYBOARD_FILE\n"
               echo "\nThis file expects one character per line."
               echo "\n\t...EXITING...\n"
               exit 3
       else

               load_default_keyboard
               echo "\nPress ENTER when you are you ready to continue: \c"
               read REPLY
               clear
       fi
  fi
  }
```

Listing 10.3 check_for_and_create_keyboard_file function listing. *(continued)*

To check for the existence of the $KEYBOARD_FILE, we use the **-s** test in an **if** statement, an shown here:

```
if [ ! -s $KEYBOARD_FILE ]
then

      ...
fi
```

Notice that we negated the test by adding an exclamation point (! -s). This is actually a test to see if the file is *not* greater than zero bytes in size *or* that the $KEYBOARD_FILE does not exist. If either of these conditions is met, then we display some messages to the user and ask the user if the default keyboard layout should be loaded.

If the user acknowledges the question with a "Y" or a "y," then we execute the load_default_keyboard function, which we studied in the last section, "load_default_keyboard Function Description." After the keyboard data is loaded into the $KEYBOARD_FILE, we stop and ask the user to press ENTER to continue. Once the user presses ENTER, the script creates a pseudo-random password, which we will cover in a later section.

build_manager_password_report Function Description

You may be asking, "Why do you want to *print* a password?" There are a lot of reasons to print a password, but only *one* of the answers is valid! *For security reasons*. Now, I really lost you! How can a printed password be good for security? It's simple: The **root** password needs to be protected at all costs. Our machines do not have direct login access to **root**, but we use an auditing script that captures every keystroke of the **root** user. If a machine has failed and you need to log on to the system on the console, you are definitely going to need access to the **root** password. For this reason we keep three copies of the **root** password in secure envelopes, and they get locked up for safe keeping.

The `build_manager_password_report` function creates a file, pointed to by the `$OUTFILE` variable, that has three copies of the same information on a single page. Look at the function shown in Listing 10.4 to see the message.

```
function build_manager_password_report
{
# Build a file to print for the secure envelope
(
echo "\n                  RESTRICTED USE!!!"
echo "\n\n\tImmediately send an e-mail to:\n"

echo "     $NOTIFICATION_LIST"

echo "\n\tif this password is revealed!"
echo "\n\tAIX root password:  $PW\n"

echo "\n\n"

echo "\n                  RESTRICTED USE!!!"
echo "\n\n\tImmediately send an e-mail to:\n"

echo "     $NOTIFICATION_LIST"

echo "\n\tif this password is revealed!"
echo "\n\tAIX root password:  $PW\n"

echo "\n\n"

echo "\n                  RESTRICTED USE!!!"
echo "\n\n\tImmediately send an e-mail to:\n"

echo "     $NOTIFICATION_LIST"

echo "\n\tif this password is revealed!"
echo "\n\tAIX root password:  $PW\n"

    ) > $OUTFILE

}
```

Listing 10.4 build_manager_password_report function listing.

Notice that the entire message is enclosed in parentheses, with the final output redirected to the `$OUTFILE` file using the following syntax:

```
( echo statements.... ) > $OUTFILE
```

This method runs all of the **echo** commands as a separate shell and sends the resulting output to the $OUTFILE using output redirection.

Also notice the $NOTIFICATION_LIST variable. This variable is set in the main body of the script. This variable contains the list of people who must be notified if the password is ever released, as stated in the message in the function.

When I get one of these printouts, I always run to get it as soon as the page comes out of the printer. This is an extremely important piece of paper! I take it to my desk and cut the page into three pieces and seal each one in a secure envelope and have it locked up for safe keeping.

A sample manager's password report is shown in Listing 10.5.

```
                    RESTRICTED USE!!!


        Immediately send an e-mail to:

    Donald Duck, Yogi Bear, and Mr. Ranger

        if this password is revealed!

        AIX root password:  E-,6Kc11




                    RESTRICTED USE!!!


        Immediately send an e-mail to:

    Donald Duck, Yogi Bear, and Mr. Ranger

    Immediately send an e-mail to:

    Donald Duck, Yogi Bear, and Mr. Ranger

        if this password is revealed!

        AIX root password:  E-,6Kc11




                    RESTRICTED USE!!!
```

Listing 10.5 Password report printout. *(continues)*

```
        Immediately send an e-mail to:

    Donald Duck, Yogi Bear, and Mr. Ranger

        if this password is revealed!

        AIX root password:  E-,6Kc11
```

Listing 10.5 Password report printout. *(continued)*

You need to edit this function and change the message to suit your environment. If you do not need this functionality, then never use the –m switch, or reply "No" when asked to confirm the printing.

usage Function Description

It is always a good idea to show the user a USAGE: statement when incorrect or insufficient input is detected (we will get to detecting input errors later in this chapter). For our mk_passwd.ksh shell script we have four options and several combinations.

We can execute the mk_passwd.ksh script with no arguments, and you can execute the mk_passwd.ksh shell script with the –n and –m command-line switches. The –n switch loads the default keyboard layout into the $KEYBOARD_FILE file. We can also change the length of the password, which is defined as eight characters by default. Any combination of these command options can be executed. Please look closely at the USAGE: statement shown in Listing 10.6.

```
function usage
{
echo "\nUSAGE: $SCRIPT [-m] [-n]  [password_length]\n"
echo "  Where:

    -m  Creates a password printout for Security

    -n  Loads the default keyboard data keys file

    password_length   Integer value that overrides
                      the default 8 character
                      password length.\n"
}
```

Listing 10.6 usage function listing.

When a usage error is detected, the script executes the usage function that displays the following message:

```
USAGE: $SCRIPT [-m] [-n]   [password_length]
 Where:

     -m  Creates a password printout for Security

     -n  Loads the default keyboard data keys file

     password_length   Integer value that overrides
                       the default 8 character
                       password length.\n"
```

trap_exit Function Description

This function, `trap_exit`, is executed only when an exit signal is *trapped*. You will see how to set a **trap** a little later. The purpose of this function is to execute any command(s) that are listed in the function. In our case, we want to remove the `$OUTFILE` before exiting the shell script. Additionally, we do not want to see any messages sent to `stderr` if the file does not exist. The statement is shown in the following code.

```
function trap_exit
{
rm -f $OUTFILE >/dev/null 2>&1
}
```

Notice that we redirect the `stderr` output to `stdout`, which is specified by the `2>&1` notation, but not before we send everything to the bit bucket, specified by `>/dev/null`.

That is it for the functions. The next section covers the testing and parsing required for the command arguments.

Testing and Parsing Command-Line Arguments

Because this shell script has command-line options to control execution, we need to test the validity of each command-line argument and then parse through each one to set up how the script is to be executed. We have four tests that need to be performed to validate each argument.

Validating the Number of Command-Line Arguments

The first step is to ensure that the number of command-line arguments is what we are expecting. For this script we are expecting no more than three arguments. To test the number of arguments, we use the **echo $#** command to display the number of command-line arguments. The result is greater than or equal to 0, zero. This test code is shown here.

```
# Check command line arguments - $# < 3

if (($# > 3))
then
    usage
    exit 1
fi
```

Notice that we used the mathematical test here. One thing to note about the syntax of this test is that for user-, or script-defined variables we do not use the dollar sign ($) in front of the variable. For shell variables you must use the shell notation here, too. If the number of arguments on the command line exceeds three, then we display the usage function and **exit** the shell script with a return code of 1, one.

Test for Valid Command-Line Arguments

We really have only three valid command-line arguments. Because –n and –m are lowercase alphabetic characters, we may as well add their uppercase counterparts for people who love to type uppercase characters. Now we have only five valid command-line arguments:

- Any Integer
- -n and -N to indicate creating a new $KEYBOARD_FILE
- -m and -M to indicate that the manager's password report is to be printed

This seems easy enough to test for using a **case** statement to parse through the command-line arguments using the $@ values, which is a list of the command-line arguments separated by a single space. Look at the block of code in Listing 10.7 for details.

```
# Test for valid command line arguments -
# Valid auguments are "-n, -N, -m, -M, and any integer

if (($# != 0))
then
    for CMD_ARG in $@
    do
        case $CMD_ARG in
        +([-0-9]))
                # The '+([-0-9]))' test notation is looking for
                # an integer. Any integer is assigned to the
                # length of password variable, LENGTH

                LENGTH=$CMD_ARG
                ;;
        -n|-N)      :     # The colon (:) is a no-op, which does nothing
                ;;
```

Listing 10.7   Code for testing for command-line arguments.

```
        -m|-M)    :   # The colon (:) is a no-op, which does nothing
              ;;
           *)         # Invalid Command-Line Argument, show usage and
exit
              usage
              exit 1
              ;;
        esac
   done
fi
```

Listing 10.7 Code for testing for command-line arguments. *(continued)*

Before we test the validity of each argument, we ensure that there is at least one command-line argument to test. If we have some arguments to test, we start a **case** statement to parse through each argument on the command line. As the arguments are parsed, the value is assigned to the CMD_ARG variable.

Notice the very first test, +([0-9]). This regular expression is testing for an integer value. When we add this integer test to the **case** statement, we need to add the last close parentheses ,), for the **case** statement. If the test is true, we know that an integer has been supplied that overrides the default eight-character password length, specified by the LENGTH variable.

The tests for -n, -N, -m, and -M are do nothings, or no-ops in this case. A no-op is specified by the colon character (:). The no-op does not do anything, but it always has a 0, zero, return code. When our valid command options are found, the **case** statement goes to the next argument on the command line.

When an invalid command-line option is detected, the function displays the usage message and exits the script with a return code of 1, one, which is defined as a usage error.

Ensuring the $LENGTH Variable Is an Integer

As a final sanity check of the $LENGTH variable, I added this extra step to ensure that it is assigned an integer value. This test is similar to the test in the previous section, but it is restricted to testing the LENGTH variable assignment. This test code is shown in Listing 10.8.

```
#
# Ensure that the $LENGTH variable is an integer
#
case $LENGTH in
+([0-9])) : # The '+([0-9]))' test notation is looking for
            # an integer. If it is an integer then the
```

Listing 10.8 Testing $LENGTH for an integer value. *(continues)*

```
            # no-op, specified by a colon, (Do Nothing)
            # command is executed, otherwise this script
            # exits with a return code of 1, one, after
            # displaying the usage message
         ;;
*) usage
   exit 1
;;
esac
```

Listing 10.8 Testing $LENGTH for an integer value. *(continued)*

If the LENGTH variable does not have an integer assignment, then the usage message function is shown, and the script exits with a return code of 1, which is defined as
a usage error.

Parsing Command-Line Arguments with getopts

The **getopts** function is the best tool for parsing through command-line arguments.
With the **getopts** function we can take direct action or set variables as a valid
command-line arguments is found. We can also find invalid command-line arguments,
if they are preceded with a minus sign (–).

The **getopts** function is used with a **while** loop that contains a **case** statement. The
basic syntax is shown in Listing 10.9.

```
while getopts ":n N V: m M" AUGEMENT 2>/dev/null 2>&1
do
     case $ARGUMENT in
     n|N) # Do stuff for -n and -N
      ;;
     m|M) # Do stuff for -m and -M
      ;;
       V) # The colon (:) after the V, V:, specifies
          # that -V must have an option attached on the command line.
      ;;
      \?) # The very first colon (:n) specifies that any unknown
          # argument (-A, for example) produces a question mark (?) as
          # output. For these unknown arguments we show the usage
          # message and exit with a return code of 1, one.
      ;;
     esac
done
```

Listing 10.9 Basic syntax for using the getopts function.

As you can see, using **getopts** to parse command-line arguments is an easy way to catch invalid command-line arguments and also to assign values or tasks to specific arguments. The nice thing about this method is that we do not have to worry about the order of the arguments on the command line.

Let's look at the code for parsing the command line for this shell script, as shown in Listing 10.10.

```
# Use the getopts function to parse the command-
# line arguments.

while getopts ":n N m M" ARGUMENT 2>/dev/null
do
    case $ARGUMENT in
    n|N)
        # Create a new Keyboard Data file
        load_default_keyboard
        echo "\nPress ENTER when you are you ready to continue: \c"
        read REPLY
        clear
        ;;
    m|M)
        # Print the Manager Password Report
        PRINT_PASSWORD_MANAGER_REPORT=TRUE
        ;;
    \?) # Show the usage message
        usage
        exit 1
    esac
done
```

Listing 10.10   getops command line parsing.

In our **getopts** statement, located on the line with the **while** loop, notice that there is only one colon (:) in the listing. This specifies that any invalid option is to be assigned the question mark (?), specifying an unknown option. We do not have any colons after any options so we are not expecting any values to be assigned to any arguments.

In the case of the -n and -N options the `load_default_keyboard` function is executed. For the -m and -M options the printer variable is set to TRUE. Any other options result in the script exiting with a return code of 1, one.

Beginning of Main

Now that we have defined all of the variables and functions and verified all of the command-line arguments, we are ready to start the main part of the `mk_passwd.ksh` shell script.

Setting a Trap

The first thing to do is to set a trap. A **trap** allows us to take action before the shell script or function exits, if an exit signal is trappable and defined. We can *never* **trap** a **kill -9** exit. This **kill** option does not do anything graceful; it just removes the process from the system process table, and it no longer exists. The more common exit signals are 1, 2, 3, and 15. For a complete list of exit signals see Chapter 1, or enter **kill -l** (that's ell) on the command line.

Our **trap** is shown here:

```
trap 'trap_exit; exit 2' 1 2 3 15
```

When a trapped exit signal is detected, in this case signals 1, 2, 3, or 15, the **trap** executes the two commands enclosed within the single tic marks, (' commands '). The commands include running the `trap_exit` function that removes the `$OUTFILE` file; then the script exits with a return code of 2, which has been defined as a trap exit for this shell script.

Checking for the Keyboard File

This shell script is useless without a keyboard data file and cannot execute anything. To check for the existence of the `$KEYBOARD_FILE`, we execute the `check_for_` `and_create_keyboard_file` function. As we previously saw, this function checks to see if a keyboard data file is on the system. If the file is not found, then the user is prompted to automatically load the default keyboard layout, which is a standard 109 key QWERT keyboard. This functionality allows for a quick start for new users and an easy recovery if the file is deleted. When we want to load a custom keyboard layout, all that is needed is to replace the default keyboard file with a new keyboard layout file.

Loading the "KEYS" Array

Once we have a `$KEYBOARD_FILE` we are ready to load the KEYS array with the keyboard characters. For this shell script we are loading the KEYS array with file data. The easiest way to do this is to use a **while** loop to read each line of the file, which in this case is a single character, while feeding the loop from the bottom, as shown in Listing 10.11.

```
X=0 # Initialize the array counter to zero

# Load the array called "KEYS" with keyboard elements
# located in the $KEYBOARD_FILE.

while read ARRAY_ELEMENT
do
```

Listing 10.11 Code to load the KEYS array.

```
     ((X = X + 1)) # Increment the counter by 1

     # Load an array element in the array

     KEYS[$X]=$ARRAY_ELEMENT

done < $KEYBOARD_FILE


UPPER_LIMIT=$X  # Random Number Upper Limit
```

Listing 10.11 Code to load the KEYS array. *(continued)*

In Listing 10.11 we initialize a loop counter, X, to zero. This counter is used to index each array element in sequential order. Next we start the **while** loop to read each line of data, a single character, and assign the value to the ARRAY_ELEMENT variable on each loop iteration.

Inside of the **while** loop the counter is incremented as the loop progresses, and the KEYS array is assigned a new array element on each loop iteration until all of the file data is loaded into the KEYS array. Notice the command syntax we use to load an array element.

```
KEYS[$X]=$ARRAY_ELEMENT
```

At the bottom of the **while** loop after **done**, notice the *input* redirection into the loop. This is one of the fastest ways to parse a file line by line. For more information on this and other file parsing methods, see Chapter 2. The last task is to define the UPPER_LIMIT variable. This variable is used to create the pseudo-random numbers that are used to point to the KEYS array elements when creating a new pseudo-random password.

Using the LENGTH Variable to Build a Loop List

A **for** loop needs a list of something to loop through, which is defined on the **for** loop declaration line. This next section of code uses the $LENGTH value to create a list of numbers to loop through. This list of numbers represents the length of the password. The default list is 1 2 3 4 5 6 7 8. The code to build this list is shown in Listing 10.12.

```
# Produce the "for" loop list of elements that represent
# the length of the password: '1 2 3 4 5 6 7 8' is
# the default "for" loop list.

FOR_COUNT=$(
```

Listing 10.12 Code to build a for loop list of numbers. *(continues)*

```
X=0
while ((X < LENGTH))
do
    # Build the list here

    ((X = X + 1))
    echo "$X "
done
)
```

Listing 10.12   Code to build a for loop list of numbers. *(continued)*

Notice how the command substitution is used in Listing 10.12. The entire **while** loop is enclosed within a command substitution, specified by the MY_LIST=$(all of my commands) syntax.

The **while** loop is interesting. This is a good way to build a list. The process consists of incrementing a counter and then using an **echo** or **print** command to print the character, followed by a blank space. The result is a list of characters separated by a single space.

Building a New Pseudo-Random Password

The code to build a new password is short and relatively easy to understand. The code is shown in Listing 10.13. After the code listing, we will cover the details.

```
# Create the pseudo-random password in this section

clear    # Clear the screen

PW=       # Initialize the password to NULL

# Build the password using random numbers to grab array
# elements from the KEYS array.

for i in $FOR_COUNT
do
        PW=${PW}${KEYS[$(in_range_random_number $UPPER_LIMIT)]}
done

# Done building the password
```

Listing 10.13   Building a new pseudo-random password code.

We first initialize the password variable (PW) to a null value, specified by PW= , when you make a variable assign to nothing, then you set the variable to NULL. Next we use a **for** loop to loop through the numbers we previously created and assigned to the FOR_COUNT variable. The default value for this variable is 1 2 3 4 5 6 7 8.

Inside the **for** loop we use a single command to build the password by adding a new pseudo-random character as we go through each loop iteration. Building the password works like this. We start with a NULL variable, PW. On each loop iteration we assign the PW variable the previous PW assignment, which it had from the last loop iteration. Then we add to this current character string a new character, which we generate using the in_range_random_number function inside the KEYS array element assignment using command substitution. The in_range_random_number function expects as input the $UPPER_LIMIT value, which is 109 keys for the default keyboard layout in this script. Using this method we use the function directly in the KEY array element assignment. This is a good way to build a list.

Printing the Manager's Password Report for Safe Keeping

This last section of code will create a temporary report file for printing purposes. The only time this section of code is executed is when the –m or –M command-line arguments are present. In the **getops** command-line parsing section, the PRINT_PASSWORD_ MANAGER_REPORT variable is assigned the value TRUE. Any other value disables the printing option.

This section of code, shown in Listing 10.14, tests the printing variable and if TRUE, executed the build_manager_password_report function. The user is then prompted to print to the default printer, which is listed in the text. The user has a chance to change the printer/queue at this point or to cancel the printing completely. If the $OUTFILE is printed, the **lp** command adds the **-c** switch to make a copy of the file in the spooler. This method allows us to immediately delete the password report file from the system. We just do not want this report file sitting on the system for very long.

```
# Print the Manager's password report, if specified
# on the command with the -m command switch.

if [ $PRINT_PASSWORD_MANAGER_REPORT = TRUE ]
then

  typeset -u REPLY=N

  echo "\nPrint Password Sheet for the Secure Envelope? (Y/N)? \c"
```

Listing 10.14 Code to create and print the password report. *(continues)*

```
    read REPLY

    if [[ $REPLY = 'Y' ]]
    then
        build_manager_password_report

        REPLY=       # Set REPLY to NULL

        echo "\nPrint to the Default Printer ${DEFAULT_PRINTER} (Y/N)? \c"
        read REPLY
        if [[ $REPLY = 'Y' ]]
        then
            echo "\nPrinting to $DEFAULT_PRINTER\n"
            lp -c -d $DEFAULT_PRINTER $OUTFILE

        else
            echo "\nNEW PRINT QUEUE: \c"
            read DEFAULT_PRINTER
            echo "\nPrinting to $DEFAULT_PRINTER\n"
            lp -c -d $DEFAULT_PRINTER $OUTFILE
        fi
    else
        echo "\n\n\tO.K. - Printing Skipped..."
    fi
fi


#####################################################
#
# Remove the $OUTFILE, if it exists and has a size
# greater than zero bytes.

[ -s $OUTFILE ] && rm -f $OUTFILE
```

Listing 10.14   Code to create and print the password report. *(continued)*

The last two things that are done at the end of this shell script are to remove the $OUTFILE, if it exists, and then prompt the user to press ENTER to clear the screen and exit. We do not want to leave a password on the screen for anyone to read.

That is it for the steps involved to create the mk_passwd.ksh shell script. The entire shell script is shown in Listing 10.15. Pay particular attention to the boldface text throughout the mk_passwd.ksh shell script.

```
#!/usr/bin/ksh
#
# AUTHOR: Randy Micahel
# SCRIPT: mk_passwd.ksh
```

Listing 10.15   mk_passwd.ksh shell script listing.

```
# DATE: 11/12/2001
# REV: 1.2.P
#
# PLATFORM: Not Platform Dependent
#
# PURPOSE: This script is used to create pseudo-random passwords.
#          An external keyboard data file is utilized, which is
#          defined by the KEYBOARD_FILE variable. This keyboard
#          file is expected to have one character on each line.
#          These characters are loaded into an array, and using
#          pseudo-random numbers generated, the characters are
#          "randomly" put together to form a string of characters.
#          By default, this script produces eight-character passwords,
#          but this length can be changed on the command line by
#          adding an integer value after the script name. There are
#          two command-line options, -n, which creates the default
#          KEYBOARD_FILE, and -m, which prints the manager's
#          password report. This password report is intended
#          to be locked in a safe for safe keeping.
#
# EXIT CODES:
#                0 - Normal script execution
#                1 - Usage error
#                2 - Trap exit
#                3 - Missing Keyboard data file
#
# REV LIST:
#          6/26/2002: Added two command-line options, -n, which
#          creates a new $KEYBOARD_FILE, and -m, which prints
#          the manager's password report.
#
# set -x # Uncomment to debug
# set -n # Uncomment to check syntax without any command execution
#
#####################################################
########### DEFINE SOME VARIABLES HERE ############
#####################################################

LENGTH=8 # Default Password Length

# Notification List for Printing the Manager's
# Password Report for Locking Away Passwords
# Just in Case You Are Unavaliable.

NOTIFICATION_LIST="Donald Duck, Yogi Bear, and Mr. Ranger"

# Define the Default Printer for Printing the Manager's
# Password Report. The user has a chance to change this
```

Listing 10.15 mk_passwd.ksh shell script listing. *(continues)*

```
# printer at execution time.

DEFAULT_PRINTER="hp4@yogi"

SCRIPT=$(basename $0)

OUTFILE="/tmp/tmppdw.file"

KEYBOARD_FILE=/scripts/keyboard.keys

PRINT_PASSWORD_MANAGER_REPORT="TO_BE_SET"

RANDOM=$$    # Initialize the random number seed to the
             # process ID (PID) of this shell script.

#####################################################
########## DEFINE FUNCTIONS HERE ###################
#####################################################

function in_range_random_number
{
# Create a pseudo-random number less than or equal
# to the $UPPER_LIMIT value, which is defined in the
# main body of the shell script.

RANDOM_NUMBER=$(($RANDOM % $UPPER_LIMIT + 1))

echo "$RANDOM_NUMBER"
}
#
#####################################################
#
function load_default_keyboard
{
# If a keyboard data file does not exist then the user
# prompted to load the standard keyboard data into the
# $KEYBOARD_FILE, which is defined in the main body of
# the shell script.

clear  # Clear the screen

echo "\nLoad the default keyboard data file? (Y/N): \c"
read REPLY

case $REPLY in
y|Y) :
     ;;
  *) echo "\nSkipping the load of the default keyboard file...\n"
```

Listing 10.15 mk_passwd.ksh shell script listing. *(continued)*

```
        return
        ;;
esac

cat /dev/null > $KEYBOARD_FILE

echo "\nLoading the Standard Keyboard File...\c"

# Loop through each character in the following list and
# append each character to the $KEYBOARD_FILE file. This
# produces a file with one character on each line.

for CHAR in \` 1 2 3 4 5 6 7 8 9 0 - = \\ q w e r t y u i o \
            p \[ \] a s d f g h j k l \; \' z x c v b n m \, \
            \. \/ \\ \~ \! \@ \# \$ \% \^ \& \* \( \) _ \+ \| \
            Q W E R T Y U I O P \{ \} A S D F G H J K L \: \" \
            Z X C V B N M \< \> \? \| \. 0 1 2 3 4 5 6 7 8 9 \/ \
            \* \- \+
do
    echo "$CHAR" >> $KEYBOARD_FILE
done
echo "\n\n\t...Done...\n"

sleep 1
}
#
#######################################################
#
function check_for_and_create_keyboard_file
{
# If the $KEYBOARD_FILE does not exist then
# ask the user to load the "standard" keyboard
# layout, which is done with the load_default_keyboard
# function.

if [ ! -s $KEYBOARD_FILE ]
then
    echo "\n\nERROR: Missing Keyboard File"
    echo "\n\nWould You Like to Load the"
    echo "Default Keyboard Layout?"
    echo "\n\t(Y/N): \c"
    typeset -u REPLY=FALSE
    read REPLY
    if [ $REPLY != Y ]
    then
        echo "\n\nERROR: This shell script cannot operate"
        echo "without a keyboard data file located in"
        echo "\n==>  $KEYBOARD_FILE\n"
```

Listing 10.15   mk_passwd.ksh shell script listing. *(continues)*

```
                echo "\nThis file expects one character per line."
                echo "\n\t...EXITING...\n"
                exit 3
        else
                load_default_keyboard
                echo "\nPress ENTER when you are you ready to continue: \c"
                read REPLY
                clear
        fi
fi
}
#
#######################################################
#
function build_manager_password_report
{
# Build a file to print for the secure envelope
(
echo "\n                    RESTRICTED USE!!!"
echo "\n\n\tImmediately send an e-mail to:\n"

echo "    $NOTIFICATION_LIST"

echo "\n\tif this password is revealed!"
echo "\n\tAIX root password:  $PW\n"

echo "\n\n"

echo "\n                    RESTRICTED USE!!!"
echo "\n\n\tImmediately send an e-mail to:\n"

echo "    $NOTIFICATION_LIST"

echo "\n\tif this password is revealed!"
echo "\n\tAIX root password:  $PW\n"

echo "\n\n"

echo "\n                    RESTRICTED USE!!!"
echo "\n\n\tImmediately send an e-mail to:\n"

echo "    $NOTIFICATION_LIST"

echo "\n\tif this password is revealed!"
```

Listing 10.15 mk_passwd.ksh shell script listing. *(continued)*

```
echo "\n\tAIX root password:  $PW\n"

    ) > $OUTFILE

}
#
####################################################
#
function usage
{
echo "\nUSAGE: $SCRIPT [-m] [-n]  [password_length]\n"
echo "   Where:

    -m  Creates a password printout for Security

    -n  Loads the default keyboard data keys file

    password_length - Interger value that overrides
                      the default 8 character
                      password length.\n"
}
#
####################################################
#
function trap_exit
{
rm -f $OUTFILE >/dev/null 2>&1
}


####################################################
########## END OF FUNCTION DEFINITIONS #############
####################################################


####################################################
####### VALIDATE EACH COMMAND LINE ARGUMENT ########
####################################################

# Check command line arguments - $# < 3

if (($# > 3))
then
    usage
    exit 1
fi
```

Listing 10.15   mk_passwd.ksh shell script listing. *(continues)*

```
##################################################
#
# Test for valid command line arguments -
# Valid auguments are "-n, -N, -m, -M, and any integer

if (($# != 0))
then
    for CMD_ARG in $@
    do
        case $CMD_ARG in
        +([-0-9]))
                # The '+([-0-9]))' test notation is looking for
                # an integer. Any integer is assigned to the
                # length of password variable, LENGTH

                LENGTH=$CMD_ARG
                ;;
        -n) :
                ;;
        -N) :
                ;;
        -m) :
                ;;
        -M) :
                ;;
        *)
                usage
                exit 1
                ;;
        esac
    done
fi


##################################################
#
# Ensure that the $LENGTH variable is an integer

case $LENGTH in
+([0-9])) : # The '+([-0]))' test notation is looking for
            # an integer. If an integer then the
            # no-op, specified by a colon, (Do Nothing)
            # command is executed, otherwise this script
            # exits with a return code of 1, one.
        ;;
*) usage
```

Listing 10.15   mk_passwd.ksh shell script listing. *(continued)*

```
    exit 1
    ;;
esac


#####################################################
#
# Use the getopts function to parse the command-
# line arguments.

while getopts ":n N m M" ARGUMENT 2>/dev/null
do
     case $ARGUMENT in
     n|N)
         # Create a new Keyboard Data file
         load_default_keyboard
         echo "\nPress ENTER when you are you ready to continue: \c"
         read REPLY
         clear
         ;;
     m|M)
         # Print the Manager Password Report
         PRINT_PASSWORD_MANAGER_REPORT=TRUE
         ;;
     \?) # Show the usage message
         usage
         exit 1
     esac
done


#####################################################
################ START OF MAIN ######################
#####################################################


# Set a trap

trap 'trap_exit;exit 2' 1 2 3 15


#####################################################
#
# Check for a keyboard data file

check_for_and_create_keyboard_file


#####################################################
############### LOAD THE ARRAY ######################
```

Listing 10.15   mk_passwd.ksh shell script listing. *(continues)*

```
#####################################################

X=0 # Initialize the array counter to zero

# Load the array called "KEYS" with keyboard elements
# located in the $KEYBOARD_FILE.

while read ARRAY_ELEMENT
do
      ((X = X + 1)) # Increment the counter by 1

      # Load an array element in the the array

      KEYS[$X]=$ARRAY_ELEMENT

done < $KEYBOARD_FILE


UPPER_LIMIT=$X   # Random Number Upper Limit

#####################################################
#
# Produce the "for" loop list of elements that represent
# the length of the password: '1 2 3 4 5 6 7 8' is
# the default "for" loop list.

FOR_COUNT=$(
X=0
while ((X < LENGTH))
do
    # Build the list here

    ((X = X + 1))
    echo "$X "
done
)

#####################################################
#
# Create the pseudo-random password in this section

clear   # Clear the screen

PW=     # Initialize the password to NULL

# Build the password using random numbers to grab array
```

Listing 10.15 mk_passwd.ksh shell script listing. *(continued)*

```
# elements from the KEYS array.

for i in $FOR_COUNT
do
        PW=${PW}${KEYS[$(in_range_random_number $UPPER_LIMIT)]}
done

# Done building the password

######################################################
#
# Display the new pseudo-random password to the screen

echo "\n\n       The new $LENGTH character password is:\n"
echo "\n            ${PW}\n"

######################################################
#
# Print the Manager's password report, if specified
# on the command with the -m command switch.

if [ $PRINT_PASSWORD_MANAGER_REPORT = TRUE ]
then

    typeset -u REPLY=N

    echo "\nPrint Password Sheet for the Secure Envelope? (Y/N)? \c"
    read REPLY

    if [[ $REPLY = 'Y' ]]
    then
       build_manager_password_report

       REPLY=    # Set REPLY to NULL

       echo "\nPrint to the Default Printer ${DEFAULT_PRINTER} (Y/N)? \c"
       read REPLY
       if [[ $REPLY = 'Y' ]]
       then
           echo "\nPrinting to $DEFAULT_PRINTER\n"
           lp -c -d $DEFAULT_PRINTER $OUTFILE

       else
           echo "\nNEW PRINT QUEUE: \c"
           read DEFAULT_PRINTER
           echo "\nPrinting to $DEFAULT_PRINTER\n"
```

Listing 10.15   mk_passwd.ksh shell script listing. *(continues)*

```
          lp -c -d $DEFAULT_PRINTER $OUTFILE
    fi
  else
     echo "\n\n\tO.K. - Printing Skipped..."
  fi
fi


######################################################
#
# Remove the $OUTFILE, if it exists and has a size
# greater than zero bytes.

[ -s $OUTFILE ] && rm -f $OUTFILE


######################################################
#
# Clear the screen and exit

echo "\n\nPress ENTER to Clear the Screen and EXIT: \c"
read X
clear


# End of mk_passwd.ksh shell script
```

Listing 10.15 mk_passwd.ksh shell script listing. *(continued)*

This was an interesting shell script to create. I hope you picked up some pointers in this chapter. I tried to add as many script options to this script as desirable but not make the script too difficult to understand.

Other Options to Consider

As with any script, improvements can be made. I cannot think of anything to add to the script, but you may want to remove some of the functionality for the common user community.

Password Reports?

Do you need to create password reports for your Manager and Directors? If not, you should disable the ability to create any file that contains any password and disable printing any passwords. This is easy to disable by commenting out the **getopts** parsing for the -m and -M command-line options.

Which Password?

You certainly do not have to accept the first password that is produced by this script. It usually takes me 5 to 10 tries to get a password that I may be able to remember. Don't stop at the first one—keep going until you get a password that you like but is not guessable.

Other Uses?

Sure, there are other uses for this shell script. Any time that you need a pseudo-random list of keyboard characters, you can use this shell script to create the list. License key is the first thing that comes to mind. If you are selling software and you need to create some unguessable keys, run the script and specify the length of the key as an integer value.

Summary

This was an excellent exercise in creating pseudo-random numbers and using a function directly in a command assignment. We used arrays to store our keyboard data so that any element is directly accessible. This chapter goes a long way in making any task intuitively obvious to solve. We love a good challenge.

In the next chapter we are going to study how to monitor for stale disk partitions on an AIX system. I'll see you in the next chapter!

Monitor for Stale Disk Partitions

Monitoring for stale disk partitions is an AIX thing. To understand this chapter you need to be familiar with the Logical Volume Manager (LVM) that is at the heart of the AIX operating system. We will get to the LVM in the next section. At the high level a stale disk partition means that the mirrored disks are not in sync. Sometimes when you find stale disks partitions you can resync the mirrors, and all is well. If the mirrors will not sync up, you may be seeing the first signs of a failing disk.

In this chapter we are going to look at three methods of monitoring for stale partitions:

- Monitoring at the Logical Volume (LV) level
- Monitoring at the Physical Volume (PV), or disk, level
- Monitoring at the Volume Group (VG), PV, and LV levels to get the full picture

All three methods will report the number of stale disk partitions, but it is nice to know the VG, PV, and the LV that are involved in the unsynced mirrors. We are going to step through the entire process of building these shell scripts, starting with the command syntax required to query the system. Before we start our scripting effort, I want to give you a high-level overview of the AIX LVM and the commands we are going to use.

AIX Logical Volume Manager (LVM)

Unlike most Unix operating systems, IBM manages disk resources using a program called the Logical Volume Manager (LVM). The LVM consists of the following components, starting with the smallest.

Each Physical Volume (PV), or disk, in the system is broken down into small partitions called Physical Partitions (PP). The default size of a PP is 4MB, but it can be larger depending on the size of the disk.

The LVM uses groups of these PPs to create a *logical map* to point to the actual PPs on the disk. These mapped partitions are called Logical Partitions (LP). The sizes of an LP and PP are exactly the same because an LP is just a pointer to a PP.

At the next level we have the Logical Volume (LV). An LV consists of one or more LPs. The LV can span multiple PVs, and this is what differentiates AIX from other flavors of Unix. This is the level at which the Systems Administrator creates the mirrors. When an LV is first created, the LV is considered *raw*, meaning that it does not have a Filesystem mount point. Raw LVs are commonly used for databases.

On top of an LV we can create a Filesystem, which has a mount point—for example, /scripts. The LV does not require a Filesystem if you want the LV to remain raw, but you can create one.

Volume Group (VG) is a collection of one or more Physical Volumes (PV), or disks. A PV is listed on the system as an **hdisk#**, where **#** is an integer value. A VG is the largest component of the LMV. The VG contains one or more LVs, so this is the mechanism that allows an LV to span multiple PVs.

That is the high-level overview of the LVM and its components. For this chapter we are going to focus our attention at the VG, PV, LV, and PP levels, and we are concerned only with disks in a mirrored configuration. If you want more information on the AIX LVM there are plenty of books that go into great detail about AIX system management.

The Commands and Methods

As usual, we need the command syntax before we can write a shell script. We will work with three LVM commands in this chapter. Each of these commands queries the system for specific information on the components and status of the disk subsystem. Before we proceed, it is important to know what each of these commands is used for and what type of information can be gathered from the system.

Disk Subsystem Commands

The **lsvg** command queries the system for VG information. To see which VGs are *varied-on*, or active, we add the **-o** switch to the **lsvg** command. We also have the **-l** flag that allows the **lsvg** command to query the system for the contents of a specific VG. We are interested in one of the fields in the **lsvg** <*VG_name*> command output called STALE_PPs:, which has a value representing the number of stale PVs in the target VG. Ideally we want this number to be zero.

Then we move to the LV command, **lslv**. The **lslv** command will query the system for the status information of a specific LV, which is entered as a command parameter. One of the fields in the output of the **lslv <LV_name>** command is STALE PP:. This output shows the number of stale PPs for the LV specified on the command line. Ideally, we want this number to be 0, zero. If we add the **-l** flag to the **lslv** command, we can see which PVs are associated with the LV in the first column of the command output.

Next we can move down to the PV, or disk, level. The **lspv** command queries the system for information on a specific PV, which is passed as a command parameter to the **lspv** command. Like **lslv**, the **lspv** command also reports the number of STALE PARTITIONS: as a field in the output.

You will see the output of each of these commands as we write the scripts for this chapter. We have the commands defined so we are now ready to start creating our first shell script to monitor for stale disk partitions.

Method 1: Monitoring for Stale PPs at the LV Level

The easiest, but not always the quickest, method of checking for stale disk partitions is to work at the LV level of the LVM structure. Querying the system for LV stale partition information gives the high-level overview for each LV. If however, the LV spans more than one PV, or disk, then another step must be taken to find the actual mirrored disks that are not in sync. We will get to this finer granularity of monitoring in the next section of this chapter.

We start our monitoring by issuing an LVM query to find each of the active VGs on the system, or the VGs that are *varied online*. For this step we use the **lsvg -o** command. The **-o** flag tells the **lsvg** command to list only the volume groups that are *currently* varied online. Many more VGs may exist on the system, but if they are not varied online we cannot check the status of any of the logical volumes that reside within the VG because the entire VG is inactive. Let's assign the VG list to a variable called ACTIVE_VG_LIST.

```
ACTIVE_VG_LIST=$(lsvg -o)
```

My test machine has two VGs, and both are active:

```
rootvg
appvg2
```

The previous command saves the active Volume Groups in a variable. Using the ACTIVE_VG_LIST variable contents we next create a list of active LVs on the system. Each VG will have one or more LVs that may or may not be active, or *open*. Using the $ACTIVE_VG_LIST data we can query the system to list each active LV within each active VG. The **lsvg -l $VG** command queries the system at the VG level to display the contents. Listing 11.1 shows the output of **lsvg -l appvg2 rootvg** command on my test machine.

```
appvg2:
LV NAME            TYPE     LPs    PPs    PVs    LV STATE       MOUNT POINT
tel_lv             jfs      2      2      1      open/syncd     /usr/telalert
oracle_lv          jfs      128    128    1      open/syncd     /oracle
oradata_lv         jfs      128    128    1      open/syncd     /oradata
ar_lv              jfs      16     16     1      open/syncd     /usr/ar
remp_tmp01         jfs      128    128    1      open/syncd     /remd_tmp01
export_lv          jfs      100    100    1      open/syncd     /export
loglv00            jfslog   1      1      1      open/syncd     N/A
remp2_ctl01        jfs      1      1      1      open/syncd     /remd_ctl01
remp2_ctl02        jfs      1      1      1      open/syncd     /remd_ctl02
remp2_ctl03        jfs      1      1      1      open/syncd     /remd_ctl03
rempR2_dat01       jfs      192    192    1      open/syncd     /remd_dat01
R2remedy_lv        jfs      10     10     1      open/syncd     /usr/remedy
remp2_log1a        jfs      1      1      1      open/syncd     /remd_log1a
remp2_log1b        jfs      1      1      1      open/syncd     /remd_log1b
remp2_log2a        jfs      1      1      1      open/syncd     /remd_log2a
remp2_log2b        jfs      1      1      1      open/syncd     /remd_log2b
remp2_log3a        jfs      1      1      1      open/syncd     /remd_log3a
remp2_log3b        jfs      1      1      1      open/syncd     /remd_log3b
remp2_log4a        jfs      1      1      1      open/syncd     /remd_log4a
remp2_log4b        jfs      1      1      1      open/syncd     /remd_log4b
remp2_log5a        jfs      1      1      1      open/syncd     /remd_log5a
remp2_log5b        jfs      1      1      1      open/syncd     /remd_log5b
remp2_rbs01        jfs      47     47     1      open/syncd     /remd_rbs01
remp2_sys01        jfs      4      4      1      open/syncd     /remd_sys01
arlogs_lv          jfs      35     35     1      open/syncd     /usr/ar/logs
remp2_usr01        jfs      6      6      1      open/syncd     /remd_usr01
rootvg:
LV NAME            TYPE     LPs    PPs    PVs    LV STATE       MOUNT POINT
hd5                boot     1      2      2      closed/syncd   N/A
hd6                paging   80     160    2      open/syncd     N/A
hd8                jfslog   1      2      2      open/syncd     N/A
hd4                jfs      4      8      2      open/syncd     /
hd2                jfs      40     80     2      open/syncd     /usr
hd9var             jfs      10     20     2      open/syncd     /var
hd3                jfs      10     20     2      open/syncd     /tmp
hd1                jfs      3      6      2      open/syncd     /home
local_lv           jfs      9      18     2      open/syncd     /usr/local
```

Listing 11.1 Output of the `lsvg -l appvg2 rootvg` command.

The list of LVs is shown in column one. Notice the sixth column in the output in Listing 11.1, LV STATE. Most of the LVs are **open/synced**, but one LV, **hd5**, is **closed/
synced**. The **hd5** LV that is closed is the *boot logical volume* and is active only when the
system is booting up. Because we want only active LVs all we need to do is to **grep** on

the string **open** and then **awk** out the first column. The next command saves the list of currently active LVs in a variable called `ACTIVE_LV_LIST`.

```
ACTIVE_LV_LIST=$(lsvg -l $ACTIVE_VG_LIST | grep open | awk '{print $1}')
```

In the previous command, we use our $ACTIVE_VG_LIST as a command parameter for the **lsvg -l** command. Then we pipe (|) to **grep** the **lsvg** output for only the rows that contain the string **open**. Next, another pipe is used to **awk** out the first column, specified by **awk '{print $1}'**. The result is a list of currently active LV names. If you think about an array, the **grep** command works on the *rows* and the **awk** command works on the *columns*.

The only thing left to do is to query each LV for the number of stale PPs, specified by the `STALE PP:` field. To check every LV we need to set up a **for** loop to run the same command on each LV in the active list. The command we use to query the LV is **lslv -L $LV_NAME**. The output for a single LV is shown in Listing 11.2.

```
LOGICAL VOLUME:     remp_tmp01          VOLUME GROUP:    appvg2
LV IDENTIFIER:      00011151b819f83a.5  PERMISSION:      read/write
VG STATE:           active/complete     LV STATE:        opened/syncd
TYPE:               jfs                 WRITE VERIFY:    off
MAX LPs:            512                 PP SIZE:         32
megabyte(s)
COPIES:             1                   SCHED POLICY:    parallel
LPs:                128                 PPs:             128
STALE PPs:          0                   BB POLICY:       relocatable
INTER-POLICY:       minimum             RELOCATABLE:     yes
INTRA-POLICY:       middle              UPPER BOUND:     32
MOUNT POINT:        /remd_tmp01         LABEL:           /remd_tmp01
MIRROR WRITE CONSISTENCY: on
EACH LP COPY ON A SEPARATE PV ?: yes
```

Listing 11.2 LV statistics for the remp_tmp01 logical volume.

Notice in the command output in Listing 11.2 the ninth row, where the field `STALE PP:` is listed. The second column of this row contains the number of stale partitions in the logical volume. Ideally, we want this value to be zero, 0. If the value is greater than zero we have a problem. Specifically, the mirrored disks associated with this LV are not in sync, which translates to a worthless mirror. Looking at this output, how are we supposed to get the number of stale disk partitions? It turns out that this is a very simple combination of **grep** and **awk**. Take a look at the following command statement.

```
NUM_STALE_PP=$(lslv -L $LV | grep "STALE PP" | awk '{print $3}'
```

The previous statement saves the number of stale PPs into the `NUM_STALE_PP` variable. We accomplish this feat by command substitution, specified by the `VARIABLE=$( commands )` notation. The way to make this task easy is to do the parsing one step at a time. First, the row containing the STALE PP string is extracted and is provided as input to the next command in the pipe. The next command in the pipe is an **awk** statement that extracts only the third field, specified by '{print $3}'. At this point you may be asking why we used the third field instead of the second. By default, **awk** uses white space as a field separator, and because STALE PPs: 0 contains two areas of white space, we need the third field instead of the second.

Now that we have all of the commands, all we need to do is set up a loop to run the previous command against each logical volume stored in the $ACTIVE_LV_LIST variable. A little **for** loop will work just fine for this script. The loop is shown in Listing 11.3.

```
THIS_HOST=$(hostname)

for LV in $(echo $ACTIVE_LV_LIST)
do
        NUM_STALE_PP=$(lslv -L $LV | grep "STALE PP" | awk '{print $3}'
        if ((NUM_STALE_PP > 0))
        then
                echo "\n${THIS_HOST}: $LV has $NUM_STALE_PP stale PPs"
        fi
done
```

Listing 11.3   Loop to show the number of stale PPs from each LV.

I want to point out several things in Listing 11.3. First, notice that we save the hostname of the machine in a variable called THIS_HOST. When creating any type of report we need to know which machine we are reporting on. When you have more than 100 machines, things can get a little confusing if you do not have a **hostname** to go with the report.

A **for** loop needs a list of items to loop through. To get the list of active LVs, we use command substitution to **echo** the contents of the $ACTIVE_LV_LIST to provide our **for** loop with a list. Actually, the **echo** is not necessary, but I wanted to show you a varied approach. The next step is to run the **lslv -L** command for each LV listed and extract the field that shows the number of stale PPs. For this command we again use command substitution to assign the value to a variable called NUM_STALE_PP. Using this saved value we do a numeric test in the **if** statement. Notice that we did not add a dollar sign ($) in front of the NUM_STALE_PP variable. Because we used the double parentheses numeric test method, the command assumes that every nonnumeric string is a variable so the dollar sign ($) is not needed; in fact, the test may give an error if the $ was added.

If we find that the number of stale PPs is greater than zero, then we use an **echo** statement to show the **hostname** of the machine followed by the LV name that has stale partitions and, last, the number of stale partitions that were found. These steps are followed for every active LV in every active VG on the entire system. The full shell script is shown in Listing 11.4.

```
#!/bin/ksh
#
# SCRIPT: stale_LV_mon.ksh
#
# AUTHOR: Randy Michael
# DATE: 01/22/2002
# REV: 1.1.P
#
# PLATFORM: AIX only
#
# PURPOSE: This shell script is used to query the system
#         for stale PPs in every active LV within every active
#         VG.
#
# REVISION LIST:
#
#
# set -x # Uncomment to debug this script
# set -n # Uncomment to check command syntax without any execution

THIS_HOST=`hostname`   # Hostname of this machine
STALE_PP_COUNT=0       # Initialize to zero

# Find all active VGs
echo "\nGathering a list of active Volume Groups"
ACTIVE_VG_LIST=$(lsvg -o)

# Find all active LVs in every active VG.
echo "\nCreating a list of all active Logical Volume"
ACTIVE_LV_LIST=$(lsvg -l $ACTIVE_VG_LIST | grep open | awk '{print $1}')

# Loop through each active LV and query for stale disk partitions
echo "\nLooping through each Logical Volume searching for stale PPs"
echo "...Please be patient; this may take several minutes to
complete..."

for LV in $(echo $ACTIVE_LV_LIST)
do
    # Extract the number of STALE PPs for each active LV
    NUM_STALE_PP=`lslv -L $LV | grep "STALE PP" | awk '{print $3}'`
    # Check for a value greater than zero
    if ((NUM_STALE_PP > 0))
    then
        # Increment the stale PP counter
        (( STALE_PP_COUNT = $STALE_PP_COUNT + 1))
        # Report on all LVs containing stale disk partitions
        echo "\n${THIS_HOST}: $LV has $NUM_STALE_PP PPs"
```

Listing 11.4 stale_LV_mon.ksh shell script listing. *(continues)*

```
      fi
done


# Give some feedback if no stale disk partitions were found

if ((STALE_PP_COUNT == 0))
then
      echo "\nNo stale PPs were found in any active LV...EXITING...\n"
fi
```

Listing 11.4   stale_LV_mon.ksh shell script listing. *(continued)*

Notice in the script in Listing 11.4 that we added notification at each step in the process. As always, we need to let the user know what is going on. Before each command I added an **echo** statement to show the user how we progress through the shell script. I also added a STALE_PP_COUNT variable to give feedback if no stale PPs were found. Now let's move on to searching for stale PPs at the PV level instead of the LV level.

Method 2: Monitoring for Stale PPs at the PV Level

Checking for stale disk partitions at the LV level will let you know that one or more LVs have stale PPs. To get a better picture of where the unsynced mirrors reside we need to look at the hdisk level. In this section we are going to change the query point for searching for stale Physical Partitions, or PPs, from the Logical Volume to the Physical Volume, or disk level. The time saving in execution time between these two methods is threefold in favor of working directly with the disks by my measurements. On my test machine, an H-80 RS/6000, the LV query took 40.77 seconds in real time, 0.36 seconds of system time, and 0.02 seconds of user time. Using the PV query method I reduced the execution time to 12.77 seconds in real time and 0.17 seconds of system time, and I had the same 0.02 seconds for user time. To understand the LV and PV configuration I have 18 mirrored disks, which are 9 mirror pairs of 9.1GB disk drives, and a total of 32 LVs. Because an LV query takes longer to execute than a PV query, it is understandable that the PV query won. Depending on the system configuration, this timing advantage may not always hold.

In the PV monitoring method we still are concerned only with the hdisks that are in currently varied-on Volume Groups (VGs), as we did in the LV method using the **lsvg -o** command. Using this active VG list we can query each active VG and extract all of the hdisks that belong to each VG. Once we have a complete list of all of the hdisks we can start a loop and query each of the PVs independently. The output of a PV query is similar to the LV query statistics in Listing 11.2. Take a look at the PV query of **hdisk5** using the **lspv -l hdisk5** command in Listing 11.5.

```
PHYSICAL VOLUME:     hdisk5                    VOLUME GROUP:      appvg2
PV IDENTIFIER:       00011150e33c3f14 VG IDENTIFIER      00011150e33ce9bb
PV STATE:            active
STALE PARTITIONS:    0                         ALLOCATABLE:     yes
PP SIZE:             16 megabyte(s)            LOGICAL VOLUMES: 2
TOTAL PPs:           542 (8672 megabytes)      VG DESCRIPTORS:  1
FREE PPs:            397 (6352 megabytes)
USED PPs:            145 (2320 megabytes)
FREE DISTRIBUTION:   89..00..91..108..109
USED DISTRIBUTION:   20..108..17..00..00
```

Listing 11.5   PV statistics for the hdisk5 physical volume.

In the output in Listing 11.5 the STALE PARTITIONS: field in row four and its value are the third field in the row. If the stale partition value ever exceeds zero, then we use the same type of reporting technique that we used in the LV query in Method 1. If no stale partitions are found, then we can give the "all is well" message and exit the script.

Because we have the basic idea of the process, let's take a look at the shell script in Listing 11.6. We will explain the technique in further detail at the end of the code listing.

```ksh
#!/usr/bin/ksh
#
# SCRIPT: stale_PP_mon.ksh
#
# AUTHOR: Randy Michael
# DATE: 01/29/02
# REV: 1.2.P
#
# PLATFORM: AIX only
#
# PURPOSE: This shell script is used to query the system for stale PPs.
#          The method queries the system for all of the currently
#          varied-on volume groups and then builds a list
#          of the PVs to query. If a PV query detects any stale
#          partitions notification is sent to the screen. Each step in
#          the process has user notification
#
# REVISION LIST:
#
#
```

Listing 11.6   stale_PP_mon.ksh shell script listing. *(continues)*

```
# set -x # Uncomment to debug this shell script
# set -n # Uncomment to check command syntax without any execution

THIS_HOST=$(hostname)     # Hostname of this machine
HDISK_LIST=               # Initialize to NULL
STALE_PP_COUNT=0          # Initialize to zero

# Inform the user at each step
echo "\nGathering a list of hdisks to query\n"

# Loop through each currently varied-on VG

for VG in $(lsvg -o)
do
    # Build a list of hdisks that belong to currently varied-on VGs
    echo "Querying $VG for a list of disks"
    HDISK_LIST="$HDISK_LIST $(lsvg -p $VG |grep disk \
                                        | awk '{print $1}')"
done

echo "\nStarting the hdisk query on individual disks\n"

# Loop through each of the hdisks found in the previous loop

for HDISK in $(echo $HDISK_LIST)
do
    # Query a new hdisk on each loop iteration

    echo "Querying $HDISK for stale partitions"
    NUM_STALE_PP=$(lspv -L $HDISK | grep "STALE PARTITIONS:" \
            | awk '{print $3}')
    # Check to see if the stale partition count is greater than zero
    if ((NUM_STALE_PP > 0))
    then
        # This hdisk has at least one stale partition - Report it!
        echo "\n${THIS_HOST}: $HDISK has $NUM_STALE_PP Stale
Partitions"

        # Build a list of hdisks that have stale disk partitions
        STALE_HDISK_LIST=$(echo $STALE_HDISK_LIST; echo $HDISK)
    fi
done

# If no stale partitions were found send an "all is good" message

((NUM_STALE_PP > 0)) \
   || echo "\n${THIS_HOST}: No Stale PPs have been found...EXITING...\n"
```

Listing 11.6   stale_PP_mon.ksh shell script listing. *(continued)*

We totally changed our viewpoint in our search for stale disk partitions. Instead of working at each LV we are scanning each disk, or PV, independently. The search time on my test machine was three times faster, but my machine configuration does not mean that your system query will be as fast. I want to start at the top of our `stale_PP_mon.ksh` shell script in Listing 11.6 and work to the bottom.

We start off the script by initializing three variables, `THIS_HOST` (the hostname of the reporting machine), `HDISK_LIST` (the list of PVs to query, which we initialize to NULL), and `STALE_PP_COUNT` (the total number of stale disk partitions on all disks, which is initialized to zero). We will show how each of these variables is used as we progress through the script.

The next step is to use the list of currently varied-on VGs (using the **lsvg -o** command) to create a list of currently available hdisks—at least they should be available. We do this in a **for** loop by appending to the `HDISK_LIST` variable during each loop iteration. Once we have a list of available system disks, we start a **for** loop to query each hdisk individually. During the query statement:

```
NUM_STALE_PP=$(lspv -L $HDISK | grep "STALE PARTITIONS:" \
               | awk '{print $3}')
```

we capture the number of stale disk partitions by using **grep** and **awk** together in the same statement. Just remember that the **grep** command acts on the *rows* and the **awk** statement acts on the *columns*. On each loop iteration we check the value of the `$NUM_STALE_PP` variable. If the count is greater than zero we do two things: report the disk to the screen, and append to the `STALE_HDISK_LIST` variable. Notice how we append to a variable that currently has data in it. By initializing the variable to NULL (specified by `VARIABLE=`), by creating an assignment to nothing, we can always append to the variable using the following syntax:

```
VARIABLE="$VARIABLE $NEW_VALUE"
```

Because the `$VARIABLE` has an initial value of nothing, NULL, then the first value assigned is a new value, and all subsequent values are appended to the `VARIABLE` variable on each loop iteration.

At the end of the script we test the `$NUM_STALE_PP` variable, which has a running count of all stale disk partitions. If the value is zero, then we let the end user know that everything is OK. Notice how we do the test. We do a numerical test on the `$NUM_STALE_PP` variable to see if it is greater than zero. If the value is one or more, then the statement is true. On a true statement the logical OR (`||`) passes control to the second part of the statement, which states "No stale PPs have been found." The logical OR saves an **if** statement and is faster to execute than an **if** statement.

Now that was a fun little script. We can improve on both scripts that have been presented thus far. There is a procedure to attempt to resync the disks containing stale partitions. In the next section we are going to combine the LV and PP query methods and add in a VG query as the top-level query to search for stale disk partitions. We will also attempt to resync all of the stale LVs that we find, if the `ATTEMPT_RESYNC` variable is set to `TRUE`.

Method 3: VG, LV, and PV Monitoring with a resync

We have looked at stale disk mirrors from two angles, but we can look for stale disk partitions at a higher level, the VG level. By using the **lsvg** command we can find which VG has disks that have stale PPs. Using the **lsvg** *<VG_name>* command we can shorten our queries to a limited number of disks, although with Murphy's Law working, it just might be the largest VG on the planet!

The strategy that we want to follow is first to query each active VG for stale PVs, which we find using the **lsvg** *<VG_name>* command. Then, for each VG that has the STALE PV: field greater than zero, we query the current VG in the loop to get a list of associated PV, or disks. Using a list of all of the PVs that we found, we conduct a query of each disk to find both the list of LVs the PV is associated with and the value of the STALE PARTITIONS: field. For each PV found to have at least one stale partition, we query the PV for a list of LVs that reside on the current PV. Please don't get confused now! The steps involved are a natural progression through the food chain to the source. The final result of all of these queries is that we know which VG, PV, and LV have unsynced mirrors, which is the complete picture that we want.

The process that we follow in this section is faster to execute and easier to follow, so let's start. The commands we are going to use are shown in Listing 11.7.

```
lsvg -o              Produces a list of active VGs
lsvg $VG_NAME        Queries the target VG for status information
lsvg -p $VG_NAME     Produces a list of hdisks that belong to the VG
lspv $PV_NAME        Queries the hdisk specified by $PV_NAME
lspv -l $PV_NAME     Produces a list of LVs on the target hdisk
lslv $LV_NAME        Queries the target LV for status information
syncvg $HDISK_LIST   Synchronizes the mirrors at the hdisk level
syncvg -l $LV_LIST   Synchronizes the mirrors at the LV level
varyonvg             Synchronizes only the stale partitions
```

Listing 11.7 Command summary for the Method 3 shell script.

Using the nine commands in Listing 11.7 we can produce a fast-executing shell script that produces the full picture of exactly where all of the unsynced mirrors reside, and we can even attempt to fix the problem!

For this shell script I want to present you with the entire script; then we will step through and explain the philosophy behind the techniques used. In studying Listing 11.8 pay close attention to the bold text.

```
#!/usr/bin/ksh
#
# SCRIPT: stale_VG_PV_LV_PP_mon.ksh
#
# AUTHOR: Randy Michael
```

Listing 11.8 stale_VG_PV_LV_PP_mon.ksh shell script listing.

```
# DATE: 01/29/02
# REV: 1.2.P
#
# PLATFORM: AIX only
#
# PURPOSE: This shell script is used to query the system for stale PPs.
#          The method queries the system for all of the currently
#          varied-on volume groups and then builds a list of the PVs to
#          query. If a PV query detects any stale partitions notification
#          is sent to the screen. Each step in the process has user
#          notification.
#
# REVISION LIST:
#
#
# set -x # Uncomment to debug this shell script
# set -n # Uncomment to check command syntax without any execution
#
# EXIT CODES: 0 ==> Normal execution or no stale PP were found
#             1 ==> Trap EXIT
#             2 ==> Auto resyncing failed
#
##############################################################################
######### DEFINE VARIABLES HERE ####################

ATTEMPT_RESYNC=FALSE      # Flag to enable auto resync, "TRUE" will resync

LOGFILE="/tmp/stale_PP_log" # Stale PP logfile
THIS_HOST=$(hostname)       # Hostname of this machine
STALE_PP_COUNT=0            # Initialize to zero
STALE_PV_COUNT=0            # Initialize to zero
HDISK_LIST=                 # Initialize to NULL
INACTIVE_PP_LIST=           # Initialize to NULL
STALE_PV_LIST=              # Initialize to NULL
STALE_LV_LIST=              # Initialize to NULL
STALE_VG_LIST=              # Initialize to NULL
RESYNC_LV_LIST=             # Initialize to NULL
PV_LIST=                    # Initialize to NULL


########################################
#### INITIALIZE THE LOG FILE ####

>$LOGFILE         # Initialize the log file to empty
date >> $LOGFILE  # Date the log file was created
echo "\n$THIS_HOST \n" >> $LOGFILE # Hostname for this report


#### DEFINE FUNCTIONS HERE ############
```

Listing 11.8 stale_VG_PV_LV_PP_mon.ksh shell script listing. *(continues)*

```
# Trap Exit function

function trap_exit
{
     echo "\n\t...EXITING on a TRAPPED signal...\n"
}


#########################################

# Set a trap...

trap 'trap_exit; exit 1' 1 2 3 5 15

#########################################
######### BEGINNING OF MAIN ###########
#########################################

# Inform the user at each step

# Loop through each currently varied-on VG and query VG for stale PVs.
# For any VG that has at least one stale PV we then query the VG
# for the list of associated PV and build the $PV_LIST

echo "\nSearching each Volume Group for stale Physical Volumes...\c" \
      | tee -a $LOGFILE

# Search each VG for stale PVs, then build a list of VGs and PVs
# that have stale disk partitions

for VG in $(lsvg -o)
do
     NUM_STALE_PV=$(lsvg $VG | grep 'STALE PVs:' | awk '{print $3}')

     if ((NUM_STALE_PV > 0))
     then
          STALE_VG_LIST="$STALE_VG_LIST $VG"
          PV_LIST="$PV_LIST $(lsvg -p $VG | tail +3 | awk '{print $1}')"
          ((STALE_PV_COUNT = STALE_PV_COUNT + 1))
     fi
done

# Test to see if any stale PVs were found, if not then
# exit with return code 0

if ((STALE_PV_COUNT == 0))
```

Listing 11.8 stale_VG_PV_LV_PP_mon.ksh shell script listing. *(continued)*

```
then
     echo "\nNo Stale Disk Mirrors Found...EXITING...\n" | tee -a
$LOGFILE
     exit 0
else
     echo "\nStale Disk Mirrors Found!...Searching each hdisk for stale
PPs...\c" \
            | tee -a $LOGFILE
fi

# Now we have a list of PVs from every VG that reported stale PVs
# The next step is to query each PV to make sure each PV is in
# an "active" state and then query each PV for stale PPs.
# If a PV is found to be inactive then we will not query
# the PV for stale partitions, but move on to the next PV in
# the $PV_LIST.

for HDISK in $(echo $PV_LIST)
do
    PV_STATE=$(lspv $HDISK | grep 'PV STATE:' | awk '{print $3}')
    if [[ $PV_STATE != 'active' ]]
    then
        INACTIVE_PV_LIST="$INACTIVE_PV_LIST $HDISK"
    fi
    if ! $(echo $INACTIVE_PV_LIST | grep $HDISK) >/dev/null 2>&1
    then
        NUM_STALE_PP=$(lspv $HDISK | grep 'STALE PARTITIONS:' \
                       | awk '{print $3}')
        if ((NUM_STALE_PP > 0))
        then
            STALE_PV_LIST="$STALE_PV_LIST $HDISK"
            ((STALE_PP_COUNT = $STALE_PP_COUNT + 1))
        fi
    fi
done

# Now we have the list of PVs that contain the stale PPs.
# Next we want to get a list of all of the LVs affected.

echo "\nSearching each disk with stale PPs for associated LVs\c" \
       | tee -a $LOGFILE

for PV in $(echo $STALE_PV_LIST)
do
    STALE_LV_LIST="$STALE_LV_LIST $(lspv -l $PV | tail +3 \
                   | awk '{print $1}')"
```

Listing 11.8 stale_VG_PV_LV_PP_mon.ksh shell script listing. *(continues)*

```
done

# Using the STALE_LV_LIST variable list we want to query
# each LV to find which ones need to be resynced

echo "\nSearch each LV for stale partitions to build a resync LV list\c" \
        | tee -a $LOGFILE

for LV in $(echo $STALE_LV_LIST)
do
    LV_NUM_STALE_PP=$(lslv $LV | grep "STALE PPs:" | awk '{print $3}')
    (($LV_NUM_STALE_PP == 0)) & RESYNC_LV_LIST="$RESYNC_LV_LIST $LV"
done

# If any inactive PVs were found we need to inform the user
# of each inactive PV

# Check for a NULL variable

if [[ -n "$INACTIVE_PV_LIST" && "$INACTIVE_PV_LIST" != '' ]]
then
    for PV in $(echo $INACTIVE_PV_LIST)
    do
        echo "\nWARNING: Inactive Physical Volume Found:" | tee -a
$LOGFILE
        echo "\n$PV is currently inactive:\n" | tee -a $LOGFILE
        echo "\nThis script is not suitable to to correct this
problem..." \
                | tee -a $LOGFILE
        echo "        ...CALL IBM SUPPORT ABOUT ${PV}..." | tee -a
$LOGFILE
    done
fi

echo "\nStale Partitions have been found on at least one disk!" \
        | tee -a $LOGFILE
echo "\nThe following Volume Group(s) have stale PVs:\n" \
        | tee -a $LOGFILE
echo $STALE_VG_LIST | tee -a $LOGFILE
echo "\nThe stale disk(s) involved include the following:\n" \
        | tee -a $LOGFILE
echo $STALE_PV_LIST | tee -a $LOGFILE
echo "\nThe following Logical Volumes need to be resynced:\n" \
        | tee -a $LOGFILE
echo $RESYNC_LV_LIST | tee -a $LOGFILE

if [[ $ATTEMPT_RESYNC = "TRUE" ]]
```

Listing 11.8 stale_VG_PV_LV_PP_mon.ksh shell script listing. *(continued)*

```
then
      echo "\nAttempting to resync the LVs on $RESYNC_PV_LIST ...\n" \
            | tee -a $LOGFILE
      syncvg -l $RESYNC_LV_LIST | tee -a $LOGFILE 2>&1
      if (( $? == 0))
      then
            echo "\nResyncing all of the LVs SUCCESSFUL...EXITING..." \
                  | tee -a $LOGFILE
      else
            echo "\nResyncing FAILED...EXITING...\n" | tee -a $LOGFILE
            exit 2
      fi
else
      echo "\nAuto resync is not enabled...set to TRUE to automatically
resync\n" \
            | tee -a $LOGFILE
      echo "\n\t...EXITING...\n" | tee -a $LOGFILE
fi

echo "\nThe log file is: $LOGFILE\n"
```

Listing 11.8   stale_VG_PV_LV_PP_mon.ksh shell script listing. *(continued)*

The shell script in Listing 11.8 is interesting because of the techniques used. As we start at the top of the shell script, notice the first variable definition, ATTEMPT_ RESYNC. I initialize this variable to FALSE because resyncing at the LV level can cause a significant system load. A better method is to run the **varyonvg** command without any arguments. This method will only resync the stale partitions. Because of the possibility of loading the system down and slowing production response time, I initialize this variable to FALSE. If I am working on a test/development or sandbox machine, I usually set the ATTEMPT_RESYNC variable to TRUE, in uppercase. The TRUE setting will attempt to resync, at the LV level, of every stale LV.

The remaining variables initialize the LOGFILE and THIS_HOST variables to the log filename and hostname, respectively. A couple of counters are initialized to zero, and seven other variables are initialized to NULL. In the next section we initialize the $LOGFILE with header information.

The only function in this script is the trap_exit function. The trap_exit function displays only to the screen **...EXITING on a TRAPPED signal...** when a trap is captured. The **trap** is set for exit codes 1, 2, 3, 5, and 15 and then the script exits with return code 1. This functionality is just a notification measure for the user. Now we are at BEGINNING OF MAIN in our script.

At each step through this shell script we want to give the user feedback so that he or she will know what is going on. When writing shell scripts you need to do two things: Comment *everything* and give your users feedback so that they know what is going on. In our first query we inform the users that we are searching each VG for stale PVs. For this step we use the **lsvg -o** command to get a list of currently varied-on volume groups. Using this active VG list, we use a **for** loop to loop through each active VG and query for the STALE PVs: field using the **lsvg $VG** command to extract the number of stale PVs in each VG using both **grep** and **awk**. When any stale PVs are detected, the VG is added to the STALE_VG_LIST variable, all of the PVs in the VG are then added to the PV_LIST variable, specified by the **lsvg -p $VG** command. Next the STALE_PV_COUNT variable is incremented by one for each PV using the math notation ((STALE_PV_COUNT = STALE_PV_COUNT + 1)). At this point we have a list of all of the volume groups that have stale physical volumes and a list of all of the PVs in all of the VGs that have stale PVs identified.

If the STALE_PV_COUNT variable is zero, there are no stale disk partitions to report in the system for the currently varied-on volume groups. If the count is zero, we inform the user that no stale disk mirrors were found, and we exit the script with a return code of 0, zero. If no stale disk partitions exist, this shell script executes in seconds. If the count is greater than zero, then we inform the user that stale disk mirrors were found, and we continue to the next step, which is to query each PV in the $PV_LIST searching for stale disk partitions.

To query each PV that is part of a VG that has stale PVs identified, we use a **for** loop to loop through each hdisk assigned to the $PV_LIST variable. Before we can query the disk, we need to ensure that the PV is in an *active* state. If the disk is inactive, then we cannot query that disk. In this section of the shell script we use the **lspv $HDISK** command within the **for** loop twice. The first time we are ensuring that the disk is active, and in the second step we query the disk for value of the STALE PARTITIONS: field. If the disk is found to be inactive, then we just add the disk to the INACTIVE_PV_LIST variable. If the disk is in an active state and the query detects any stale partitions, we add the hdisk to the STALE_PV_LIST variable. Notice in this section the **if** statement syntax that is used to check for inactive PVs before the disk query is initiated:

```
if ! $(echo $INACTIVE_PV_LIST | grep $HDISK) >/dev/null 2>&1
```

The previous test ensures that the disk is not listed in the $INACTIVE_PV_LIST variable. The nice thing about using this syntax is that we use the **if** statement to check the return code of the enclosed command. We also negate the response so that we are testing for the disk not being listed in the variable by using the ! operator. To stop any screen output, the command is redirected to the bit bucket, and standard error is redirected to standard output, specified by the 2>&1 notation. Through the process of this **for** loop we populate the STALE_PV_LIST variable, which is a list of each of the active disks on the system that have stale disk partitions. We also keep a running count of the stale PPs found.

In the next section we use the populated $STALE_PV_LIST variable to get a list of all of the logical volumes that are part of each disk in the stale disk list. In this step we use another **for** loop to loop through each stale PV and populate the STALE_LV_LIST variable using the **lspv -l $PV** command. Then we use this newly populated $STALE_LV_LIST to query each LV to find which ones have stale PPs. For this section we query each LV using the **lslv $LV** command and extract the value of the STALE

PP: field using a combination of **grep** and **awk** commands in a pipe. Each LV found to have at least one stale PP is added to the RESYNC_LV_LIST variable, which is used later to resync each of the LVs, if enabled, and in the log report.

Now we use the list of inactive PVs, using the $INACTIVE_PV_LIST variable, to produce notification to the user of each inactive PV found on the system. We start with an **if** statement and test for the $INACTIVE_PV_LIST variable being NULL, or empty. If the variable is not NULL, then we loop through each PV in the list and issue a warning message to the user for each inactive PV. This information is also logged in the $LOGFILE using a pipe to the **tee -a** command to append to the $LOGFILE and display the information to the screen at the same time.

In the next step, we give the user a list of each VG, PV, and LV that is affected by the stale disk partitions. After this notification is both logged and displayed we attempt to resync the mirrors at the LV level. Sometimes there are just one or two LVs on a PV that have stale disk partitions, so the LV is where we want to attempt to resync. We will attempt a resync only if the $ATTEMPT_RESYNC variable is initialized to TRUE. Any other value will cause this step to be skipped, but the user is notified that the resync option is disabled. If a resync is enabled, the **syncvg -l $RESYNC_LV_LIST** command is executed. The return code is checked for a zero value, indicating a successful resync operation. If the return code is not zero, you need to call IBM support and replace the disk before it goes dead on you. The steps involved in replacing a disk are beyond the scope of this book. We can also use the **varyonvg** command to resync only the stale partitions.

Other Options to Consider

As usual, any shell script can be improved, and this set of shell scripts is no exception.

SSA Disks

The **ssaxlate** command is used with a type of disk developed by IBM known as Serial Storage Architecture (SSA). The SSA disks not only use the **hdisk#** but also have an associated **pdisk#**. Normally the **hdisk#** and the **pdisk#** differ on the system. The **ssaxlate** command gives a cross-reference between the two disk representations. It is always a good idea to have this extra information if we are dealing with SSA disks, especially if you are replacing an SSA disk. To use the **ssaxlate** command, you need to know the specific **hdisk#** to translate to the corresponding **pdisk#**, or vice versa. As an example, we want to know what **pdisk#** translates to **hdisk36**. The command syntax to do the translation is shown here:

```
# ssaxlate -l hdisk36
pdisk32
```

In this example, **hdisk36** translates to **pdisk32**. From this you can imply that **hdisk0** through **hdisk3** are not SSA disks. Usually the first few disks on an AIX system are

SCSI disk drives. You can also translate a **pdisk#** into the corresponding **hdisk#** by running the **ssaxlate** command against the **pdisk#**.

Log Files

In the first two shell scripts in this chapter we did not use a log file as we did in Method 3. It is always nice to have a log file to look at after the fact when you are running any type of system query. Creating a log file is a simple process of defining a variable to point to a filename that you want to use for a log file and appending output to the log file variable. If your system tends to fill up the **/tmp** filesystem, then I recommend creating a log directory, maybe in **/usr/local/logs**, or creating a separate filesystem just for log files. You can still have the mount point **/usr/local/logs**, or anything you want. If **/tmp** fills up, then you will not be able to write anything to the log file. You may also want to keep a month's worth of log files to review in case of system problems. To do this you can add a date stamp as a filename extension and remove all files older than 30 days with the **find** command.

Automated Execution

You can make a cron entry in the root cron table to execute this shell script to automate running the script daily. A sample cron table entry is shown here:

```
05 23 * * * /usr/local/bin/stale_PP_mon.ksh >/dev/null 2>&1
```

The previous cron table entry will execute the `stale_PP_mon.ksh` shell script every day at 11:05 P.M., 365 days a year. The output is redirected to the bit bucket, but the log file will be created for review the next day.

Event Notification

If you use the previous cron table entry to execute the shell script every day, you may want to get some kind of notification by way of an email or a page. The easiest way is to email the log file to yourself every day. You can also modify the shell script to produce a very short message as a page. As an example, you could send one of the following text messages to an alphanumeric pager:

```
$THIS_HOST: stale PP check OK

$THIS_HOST: stale PP check FAILED
```

These are short messages to get the point across, and you will know which machine the page came from.

Summary

In this chapter we looked at a logical progression of creating a shell script by starting at the basics. I hope you have gained at least some knowledge of the AIX Logical Volume Manager (LVM) through this experience. As you can see in this chapter, the first attempt to solve a challenge may not always be the best, or fastest, method; but this is how we learn. If we take these small steps and work up a full-blown shell script with all of the bells and whistles, we have learned a great deal. I know a lot of you do not work on AIX systems but this is still a valuable exercise.

In the next chapter we look at some techniques of automating the **ping** process to ensure that the machines can communicate, at least at the lowest level of a **ping**. This is just another step toward being proactive and looking like gold. See you in the next chapter!

Automated Hosts Pinging with Notification

In every shop there is a critical need to keep the servers serving. For system availability, the quicker you know that a system is unreachable, the quicker you can act to resolve the problem and reduce company losses. At the lowest level of system access we can **ping** each machine in the "critical machine" list. If the **ping** works it will tell you if the network adapter is working, but it does not guarantee that the machine and applications are working. For this level of checks you need to actually access the application or operating system.

In this chapter we are going to create a shell script that will **ping** hosts using a list of machines, which is stored in a separate file that is easily edited. Other options to this scenario include pinging all of the machines in the /etc/hosts file, using **ftp** to transfer a file, and querying the database, to name a few. Our interest in this chapter is to work at the lowest level and use the **ping** command to ensure that the machines are reachable from the network. When a machine is found unreachable we send notification to alert staff that the machine is down. Due to the fact that in some shops the network can become saturated with network traffic, we are going to add an extra level of testing on a failed **ping** test, which we will get into later in this chapter. But before we go any further let's look at the command syntax for each of our operating systems (AIX, HP-UX, Linux, and Solaris) to see if we can find a command syntax that will produce the same output for all of the operating systems that we are working with.

Syntax

As always, we need the correct command syntax before we can write a shell script. Our goal is to find the command syntax for each operating system that produces the same output. For this shell script we want to **ping** each host multiple times to ensure that the node is reachable; the default is three pings. The standard output we want to produce on each OS is shown here.

```
# ping -c3 dino
PING dino: (10.10.10.4): 56 data bytes
64 bytes from 10.10.10.4: icmp_seq=0 ttl=255 time=2 ms
64 bytes from 10.10.10.4: icmp_seq=1 ttl=255 time=1 ms
64 bytes from 10.10.10.4: icmp_seq=2 ttl=255 time=1 ms

----dino PING Statistics----
3 packets transmitted, 3 packets received, 0% packet loss
round-trip min/avg/max = 1/1/2 ms
```

This is the command, and the output is from an AIX machine. Notice the PING Statistics at the bottom of the command output, where I have highlighted **3 packets received**. This is the output line that we are interested in for every operating system. Now, how do we produce the same output for each OS? Instead of leaving you in the dark I am just going to list each one in Table 12.1, showing you how to **ping** the host **dino**.

In Table 12.1, notice that AIX and Linux have the same command syntax. For HP-UX and Solaris notice the two numbers, 56 and 3. The 56 specifies the packet size to send on each ping, and the 3 is the number of times to try to reach the host. For a packet size 56 is a standard packet, and we are not going to change from this standard. It is important to know the differences in command structure for each operating system because we are creating one shell script and we will **ping** each node using a function, which selects the correct command to execute based on the Unix flavor. To find the OS we use the **uname** command. Using the output of the **uname** command in a **case** statement we are assured that the correct command is executed on any of the four operating systems. This is really all we have for the syntax, but we need to do some checks and create some variables, so we are going to build the shell script around these commands listed in Table 12.1.

Table 12.1 Ping Command for Each Operating System

OPERATING SYSTEM	PING COMMAND
AIX	# ping -c3 dino
HP-UX	# ping dino 56 3
Linux	# ping -c3 dino
Solaris	# ping -s dino 56 3

Creating the Shell Script

In scripting this solution we want to add a couple of options for convenience. The first option is to have a means of stopping the pinging without interrupting the scheduled script execution, which is usually executed through a cron table entry. The second option is to have a means of stopping the *notification* for nodes that are unreachable. For each of these we can use a flag variable that must have a value of TRUE to enable the option. There are many times where you want to disable these two options, but the main reason is during a maintenance window when many of the machines are unreachable at the same time. If you have only one or two machines that are down, then commenting out the node name(s) in the ping.list file, which contains a list of nodes to **ping**, is preferable. You can also comment out the cron table entry to disable the test alogether.

Now we need to define the pinging technique that we want to use. I like to use a two-level approach in checking for a system's reachability. In a two-level testing scenario, when a node is unreachable we go to sleep for a few seconds and try the test again. We do this to eliminate "false positives" due to a heavy network load. This is a major concern at some shops where I have worked, and finger pointing back and forth between the network team and the Systems Administrators always happens, and I try to stay out of this argument. This second-level test adds just a few seconds to the testing window for each unreachable node. This is a relatively simple shell script to create, so keep reading!

Define the Variables

The first thing that we want to do in almost any shell script is to define the variables and files that are used in the script. We have already discussed two variables, which enable pinging and notification. For pinging we use the PINGHOSTS variable and MAILOUT as the variable to permit or disable notification. Additionally, for ease of testing we are going to **typeset** both of these variables to force all text assignments to these variables to uppercase, as shown here.

```
typeset -u PINGHOSTS
typeset -u MAILOUT
PINGHOSTS=TRUE
MAILOUT=TRUE
```

We can also **typeset** the variables and assign the values in the same step, as shown here.

```
typeset -u PINGHOSTS=true
typeset -u MAILOUT=true
```

Notice that I assign a lowercase "true" to both variables, but when you print or test the variables you will see that the assignments have been changed to uppercase characters.

```
# echo $MAILOUT
TRUE
```

There are a few more variables that we also need to define, including PING_COUNT and PACKET_SIZE that specify the number of times to **ping** the target host and the packet size for each packet, which we discussed earlier.

```
integer PING_COUNT=3
integer PACKET_SIZE=56
```

Notice the **integer** notation used to define these variables as integers. This notation produces the exact same results that the **typeset -i** command produces.

Next we need the Unix flavor that this shell script is running. This shell script recognizes AIX, HP-UX, Linux, and Solaris. For this step we use the **uname** command, as shown here.

```
UNAME=$(uname)
```

In this UNAME assignment we used command substitution to assign the result of the **uname** command to the variable UNAME.

The next two steps in this definition section involve defining the PINGFILE and MAILFILE file assignments. The PINGFILE contains a list of nodes that we want to **ping**. The shell script is expecting one node, or hostname, per line. If you no longer want to **ping** a node in the list file, then you can comment the node out using a pound sign (#). For this shell script I specified that the ping list is located in /usr/local/bin/ping.list. Similarly, the MAILFILE has a list of email addresses that are to be notified when a node is not reachable. This email list is located in /usr/local/bin/mail.list. The variable assignments are shown here.

```
PINGFILE="/usr/local/bin/ping.list" # List of nodes to ping
MAILFILE="/usr/local/bin/mail.list" # List of persons to notify
```

For these two files we are going to check for a nonzero length file, which implies the file exists and its size is greater than zero bytes. If the $PINGFILE does not exist, then we need to send an ERROR message to the user and exit the shell script because we do not have a list of nodes to **ping**. If the $MAILFILE does not exist we are just going to notify the user that there will not be any email notification sent for unreachable nodes.

We also need a file to hold the data that is emailed out when a node is unreachable. The file is located in /tmp/pingfile.out and is assigned to the PING_OUTFILE variable.

```
PING_OUTFILE="/tmp/pingfile.out" # File for e-mailed notification
>$PING_OUTFILE  # Initialize to an empty file
```

Notice how we created an empty file by redirecting nothing to the file, which is pointed to by the $PING_OUTFILE variable. You could also use **cat /dev/null** to accomplish the same task, as shown here.

```
cat /dev/null > $PING_OUTFILE
```

Next we need three variables that are to hold numeric values—at least we hope they are numeric. The first variable is called INTERVAL, and it contains a value specifying the number of seconds to **sleep** before trying to **ping** an unreachable node for the second time. I like to use three seconds.

```
integer INTERVAL="3" # Number of seconds to sleep between retries
```

As we discussed before, in our standard **ping** output we are interested in the PING Statistics line of output. Specifically, we want to extract the numeric value for the **"3 packets received"**, which should be greater than zero if the node is reachable. To hold the value for the number of pings received back we need two variables, one for the first try and one for the second attempt, in case the node is unreachable the first time. These two variables are PINGSTAT and PINGSTAT2 and are initialized to NULL, as shown here.

```
PINGSTAT=    # Number of pings received back from pinging a node
PINGSTAT2=   # Number of pings received back on the second try
```

The last variable we need to assign is the **hostname** of the machine that is running this script. We need the **hostname** because we may have two nodes pinging each node in case one pinging node fails. For this variable we again use command substitution, as shown here.

```
THISHOST=`hostname`      # The hostname of this machine
```

Notice that this time we used the back tics (`command`) instead of the dollar-double parentheses method ($(command)) for command substitution. Both command substitution options produce the same result, which is **yogi** on this machine.

Creating a Trap

To start out our shell script we are going to set a **trap**, which allows us to take some kind of action when an exit signal is captured, such as a user pressing **CTRL-C**. We can capture most exit signals *except* for **kill -9**. The only *action* that we want to take in this shell script is to inform the user that the shell script has detected an **exit** signal and the script is exiting. This **trap** is added in this shell script so that you get used to putting traps in all of your shell scripts. We are going to capture **exit** signals 1, 2, 3, 5, and 15 only. You can add many more, but it is overkill in this case. For a complete list of signals use the **kill -l** (-ell) command. The command syntax for the trap is shown here.

```
trap 'echo "\nExiting on a trapped signal...\n";exit 1' 1 2 3 5 15
```

Using this **trap** command statement, the following message is displayed before the shell script exits with **exit** signal 1.

```
Exiting on a trapped signal...
```

The Whole Shell Script

We have all of the initializations complete and know what the **ping** syntax is for each operating system, so let's look at the whole shell script and cover some other issues at the end of Listing 12.1. Pay close attention to the boldface text.

```ksh
#!/usr/bin/ksh
#
#
# SCRIPT: pingnodes.ksh
#
# AUTHOR: Randy Michael
#
# DATE: 02-20-2001
#
# PURPOSE: This script is used to ping a list of nodes and
# send email notification (or alphanumeric page) of any unreachable
# nodes.
#
#
# REV: 1.0.A
#
# REV.LIST:
#
#
# set -x # Uncomment to debug this script
# set -n # Uncomment to check command syntax without any execution
#
########################################################

# Set a trap and clean up before a trapped exit...
# REMEMBER: you CANNOT trap "kill -9"

trap 'echo "\n\nExiting on trapped signal...\n" \
      ;exit 1' 1 2 3 15


########################################################

# Define and initialize variables here...

PING_COUNT="3"         # The number of times to ping each node
PACKET_SIZE="56"  # Packet size of each ping

typeset -u PINGNODES    # Always use the UPPERCASE value for $PINGNODES
PINGNODES="TRUE"        # To enable or disable pinging FROM this node -
"TRUE"

typeset -u MAILOUT      # Always use the UPPERCASE value for $MAILOUT
```

Listing 12.1   pingnodes.ksh shell script listing.

```
MAILOUT="TRUE"              # TRUE enables outbound mail notification of
events

UNAME=$(uname)              # Get the Unix flavor of this machine

PINGFILE="/usr/local/bin/ping.list" # List of nodes to ping

if [ -s $PINGFILE ]
then
        # Ping all nodes in the list that are not commented out and blank
        PINGLIST=$(cat $PINGFILE | grep -v '^#')
else
        echo "\nERROR: Missing file - $PINGFILE"
        echo "\nList of nodes to ping is unknown...EXITING...\n"
        exit 2
fi


MAILFILE="/usr/local/bin/mail.list" # List of persons to notify

if [ -s $MAILFILE ]
then
        # Ping all nodes in the list that are not commented out and
blank
        MAILLIST=$(cat $MAILFILE | egrep -v '^#')
else
        echo "\nERROR: Missing file - $MAILFILE"
        echo "\nList of persons to notify is unknown...\n"
        echo "No one will be notified of unreachable nodes...\n"
fi

PING_OUTFILE="/tmp/pingfile.out" # File for emailed notification
>$PING_OUTFILE  # Initialize to an empty file

integer INTERVAL="3" # Number of seconds to sleep between retries

# Initialize the next two variables to NULL

PINGSTAT=     # Number of pings received back from pinging a node
PINGSTAT2=    # Number of pings received back on the second try

THISHOST=`hostname`      # The hostname of this machine

#####################################################
########### DEFINE FUNCTIONS HERE ###################
#####################################################

function ping_host
{
```

Listing 12.1   pingnodes.ksh shell script listing. *(continues)*

```
# This function pings a single node based on the Unix flavor

# set -x # Uncomment to debug this function
# set -n # Uncomment to check the syntax without any execution

# Look for exactly one argument, the host to ping

if (( $# != 1 ))
then
     echo "\nERROR: Incorrect number of arguments - $#"
     echo "       Expecting exactly one argument\n"
     echo "\t...EXITING...\n"
     exit 1
fi

HOST=$1 # Grab the host to ping from ARG1.

# This next case statement executes the correct ping
# command based on the Unix flavor

case $UNAME in

AIX|Linux)
          ping -c${PING_COUNT} $HOST 2>/dev/null
          ;;
HP-UX)
          ping $HOST $PACKET_SIZE $PING_COUNT 2>/dev/null
          ;;
SunOS)
          ping -s $HOST $PACKET_SIZE $PING_COUNT 2>/dev/null
          ;;
*)
          echo "\nERROR: Unsupported Operating System - $(uname)"
          echo "\n\t...EXITING...\n"
          exit 1
esac
}

#######################################################

function ping_nodes
{
#######################################################
#
# Ping the other systems check
#
# This can be disabled if you do not want every node to be pinging all
```

Listing 12.1   pingnodes.ksh shell script listing. *(continued)*

```
# of the other nodes.  It is not necessary for all nodes to ping all
# other nodes although you do want more than one node doing the pinging
# just in case the pinging node is down.  To activate pinging the
# "$PINGNODES" variable must be set to "TRUE".  Any other value will
#  disable pinging from this node.
#

# set -x # Uncomment to debug this function
# set -n # Uncomment to check command syntax without any execution

if [[ $PINGNODES = "TRUE" ]]
then
     echo      # Add a single line to the output

     # Loop through each node in the $PINGLIST

     for HOSTPINGING in $(echo $PINGLIST) # Spaces between nodes in the
                                          # list are assumed
     do
          # Inform the user what is going on

          echo "Pinging --> ${HOSTPINGING}...\c"

          # If the pings received back is equal to "0" then you have a
          # problem.

          # Ping $PING_COUNT times, extract the value for the pings
          # received back.


          PINGSTAT=$(ping_host $HOSTPINGING | grep transmitted \
                    | awk '{print $4}')

          # If the value of $PINGSTAT is NULL, then the node is
          # unknown to this host

          if [[ -z "$PINGSTAT" && "$PINGSTAT" = '' ]]
          then
               echo "Unknown host"
               continue
          fi
          if (( PINGSTAT == 0 ))
          then    # Let's do it again to make sure it really is
unreachable

               echo "Unreachable...Trying one more time...\c"
               sleep $INTERVAL
```

Listing 12.1   pingnodes.ksh shell script listing. (continues)

```
                    PINGSTAT2=$(ping_host $HOSTPINGING | grep transmitted \
                        | awk '{print $4}')

                    if (( PINGSTAT2 == 0 ))
                    then # It REALLY IS unreachable...Notify!!
                        echo "Unreachable"
                        echo "Unable to ping $HOSTPINGING from $THISHOST" \
                            | tee -a $PING_OUTFILE
                    else
                        echo "OK"
                    fi
                else
                    echo "OK"
                fi

        done
fi
}


#######################################################

function send_notification
{
if [ -s $PING_OUTFILE -a  "$MAILOUT" = "TRUE" ];
then

        case $UNAME in
        AIX|HP-UX|Linux) SENDMAIL="/usr/sbin/sendmail"
        ;;
        SunOS) SENDMAIL="/usr/lib/sendmail"
        ;;
        esac

        echo "\nSending e-mail notification"
        $SENDMAIL -f randy@$THISHOST $MAILLIST < $PING_OUTFILE
fi
}

#################################################
############ START of MAIN ######################
#################################################


ping_nodes
send_notification


# End of script
```

Listing 12.1 pingnodes.ksh shell script listing. *(continued)*

Now we get to the fun stuff! Let's start out with the three functions because they do all of the work anyway. The first function is `ping_host`. The idea here is to set up a **case** statement, and based on the response from the **uname** command, which was assigned to the `UNAME` variable in the definitions section, we execute the specific **ping** command for the particular Unix flavor. If an unlisted Unix flavor is given, an ERROR message is given to the user, and this shell script exits with a return code 1. We must do this because we have no idea what the correct syntax for a **ping** command should be for an unknown operating system.

The `ping_host` function is called from the `ping_nodes` function on every loop iteration. Inside the `ping_nodes` function we first ensure that the $`PINGNODES` variable is set to `TRUE`; otherwise, the pinging of nodes is disabled.

We use the $`PINGFILE` file to load a variable, `PINGLIST`, with a list of nodes that we want to **ping**. This extra step is done to give the user the ability to comment out specific node(s) in the $`PINGFILE`. Without this ability you would leave the user in a state of annoyance for all of the notifications because of a single node being down for a period of time. The command to strip out the commented lines and leave the remaining nodes in the list is shown here.

```
PINGLIST=$(cat $PINGFILE | grep -v '^#')
```

Notice how this command substitution works. We **cat** the $`PINGFILE` and pipe the output to a **grep** command. In the **grep** part of the statement we use the **-v** switch. The **-v** switch tells **grep** to list everything *except* for the following pattern, which is "`^#`" in this case. Now let's look at the `^#` part. When you put a carat character (`^`) in front of a pattern in this **grep** statement, we are ignoring any line that *begins* with a pound sign (#). The carat (`^`) means *begins with*.

A **for** loop is started using the $`PINGLIST` variable as a list, which contains each node in the `/usr/local/bin/ping.list` file that is *not* commented out. For each node in the listing we **echo** to the screen the target node name and call the `ping_host` function inside of a command substitution statement on each loop iteration, which is shown here.

```
echo "Pinging --> ${HOSTPINGING}...\c"
PINGSTAT=$(ping_host $HOSTPINGING | grep transmitted | awk '{print $4}')
```

For each node in the $`PINGLIST` the **echo** statement and the command substitution statement are executed. There are three possible results for the command substitution statement, and we test for two; the last one is assumed. (1) The `PINGSTAT` value is 0, zero. If the packets received are 0, zero, then we sleep for $`INTERVAL` seconds and try to reach the node again, this time assigning the packets received to the `PINGSTAT2` variable. (2) The `PINGSTAT` value is NULL. This results when you try to **ping** a node that is unknown to the system. In this case we **echo** to the screen Unknown host and continue to the next node in the list. (3) The `PINGSTAT` value is nonzero and non-NULL, which means that the **ping** was successful. Please study each of these tests in the `ping_nodes` function.

Notice the tests used in the **if** statements. Each of these is a mathematical test so we use the double parentheses method of testing, as shown here.

```
if (( PINGSTAT == 0 ))
```

There are two things to notice in this **if** statement. The first is that there is no dollar sign ($) in front of the PINGSTAT variable. The dollar sign is not needed in a mathematical test when using the double parentheses method because the shell assumes that any nonnumeric string is a variable for this type of mathematical test. I have had cases where I added the dollar sign ($) in front of the variable, and it took me four days to figure out why the script was failing. In other cases I have seen the dollar sign used and the script worked without error. I always remove the dollar sign, just in case. This problem is extremely hard to find should an error occur.

The second point I want to make in the previous **if** statement is the use of the double equal signs (==). Using this type of mathematical test, a single equal sign is an *assignment*, not an equality test. This sounds a little strange, but you can actually assign a value to a variable in a test. To test for equality, always use double equal signs (==) with this test method.

The last function in this shell script is the send_notification function. This function is used to send an email notification to each address listed in the /usr/local/bin/mail.list file, which is pointed to by the MAILFILE variable. Before attempting any notification the function tests to see if the $PING_OUTFILE file has anything in it or if its size is greater than zero bytes. The second test is to ensure that the MAILOUT variable is set to TRUE. If the $PING_OUTFILE has some data and the MAILOUT variable is set to TRUE, then the function will attempt to notify each email address in the $MAILFILE.

In the send_notification function notice that I am using the **sendmail** command, as opposed to the **mail** or **mailx** commands. I use the **sendmail** command because I worked at a shop where I had a lot of trouble getting mail through the firewall because I was sending the mail as **root**. I found a solution by using the **sendmail** command because I can specify a valid nonroot user as the person who *sent* the email. The command I use is shown here.

```
sendmail -f randy@$THISHOST $MAILLIST < $PING_OUTFILE
```

In this statement the **-f <user@host>** specifies who is sending the e-mail. The $MAILLIST is the list of persons who should receive the email, and the < $PING_OUTFILE input redirection is the body text of the email, which is stored in a file. I still have one little problem, though. The **sendmail** command is not always located in the same directory, and sometimes it is not in the $PATH. On AIX, HP-UX, and Linux the **sendmail** command is located in /usr/sbin. On Solaris the **sendmail** command is located in the /usr/lib directory. To get around this little problem we need a little **case** statement that utilizes the $UNAME variable that we used in the ping_host function. With a little modification we have the function shown in Listing 12.2.

```
function send_notification
{
if [ -s $PING_OUTFILE -a  "$MAILOUT" = "TRUE" ];
then

        case $UNAME in
        AIX|HP-UX|Linux) SENDMAIL="/usr/sbin/sendmail"
        ;;
        SunOS) SENDMAIL="/usr/lib/sendmail"
        ;;
        esac

        echo "\nSending e-mail notification"
        $SENDMAIL -f randy@$THISHOST $MAILLIST < $PING_OUTFILE
fi
}
```

Listing 12.2   send_notification function listing.

Notice that we used a single line for AIX, HP-UX, and Linux in the **case** statement. At the end of the function we use the $SENDMAIL variable to point to the correct full path of the **sendmail** command for the specific operating system.

Let's not forget to look at the pingnodes.ksh shell script in action! In the following output, shown in Listing 12.3, the node **dino** is unknown to the system, and the **mrranger** node is powered down so there is no response from the **ping** to the system.

```
# ./pinghostfile.ksh.new

Pinging --> yogi...OK
Pinging --> bambam...OK
Pinging --> booboo...OK
Pinging --> dino...Unknown host
Pinging --> wilma...OK
Pinging --> mrranger...Unreachable...Trying one more time...Unreachable
Unable to ping mrranger from yogi

Sending e-mail notification
```

Listing 12.3   pingnodes.ksh shell script in action.

From the output in Listing 12.3, notice the result of pinging the node **dino**. I commented out the hostname **dino** in the /etc/hosts file. By doing so I made the node unknown to the system because DNS is not configured on this system. The **mrranger** node is powered down so it is known but not reachable. Notice the difference in the outputs for these two similar, but very different, situations. Please study the code related to both of these tests in the ping_nodes function.

Other Options to Consider

As always, we can improve on any shell script, and this one is no exception. I have listed some options that you may want to consider.

$PINGLIST Variable Length Limit Problem

In this scripting solution we gave the user the capability to comment out specific nodes in the $PINGFILE. We assigned the list of nodes, which is a list without the comments, to a variable. This is fine for a relatively short list of nodes, but a problem arises when the maximum variable length, which is usually 2048 characters, is exceeded. If you have a long list of nodes that you want to **ping** and you notice that the script never gets to the end of the ping list, you have a problem. Or if you see a funny-looking node name, which is probably a hostname that has been cut off by the variable limit and associated with a system error message, then you have a problem. To resolve this issue, define a new file to point to the PINGLIST variable, and then we will use the *file* to store the ping list data instead of a *variable*. To use PINGLIST as a file, add/ change the following lines:

ADD THIS LINE:

```
PINGLIST=/tmp/pinglist.out
```

CHANGE THIS LINE:

```
PINGLIST=$(cat $PINGFILE | grep -v '^#')
```

TO THIS LINE:

```
cat $PINGFILE | grep -v '^#' > $PINGLIST
```

CHANGE THIS LINE:

```
for HOSTPINGING in $(echo $PINGLIST)
```

TO THIS LINE:

```
for HOSTPINGING in $(cat $PINGLIST)
```

Using the file to store the ping list data changes the limit to the maximum file size that the system supports or when the filesystem fills up, which should be plenty of space for anyone. This modified shell script is located on this book's companion Web site. The script name is `pingnodes_using_a_file.ksh`.

Ping the /etc/hosts File Instead of a List File

This may be overkill for any large shop, but it is easy to modify the shell script to accomplish this task. You want to make the following change to the shell script after completing the tasks in the previous section "`$PINGLIST` Variable Length Limit Problem" to the shell script shown in Listing 12.1.

CHANGE THESE LINES:

```
if [ -s $PINGFILE ]
then
PINGLIST=$(cat $PINGFILE | grep -v '^#')
```

TO THESE LINES:

```
if [ -s /etc/hosts ]
then
      # Ping all nodes in the /etc/hosts file
cat /etc/hosts | sed /^#/d | sed /^$/d | grep -v 127.0.0.1 \
               | awk '{print $2}' > $PINGLIST
```

In this changed code we **cat** the `/etc/hosts` file and pipe the output to a **sed** statement, `sed /^#/d`. This **sed** statement removes every line in the `/etc/hosts` file that begins with a pound sign (#). The output of this **sed** statement is then piped to another **sed** statement, `sed /^$/d`, which removes all of the blank lines in the `/etc/hosts` file (the blank lines are specified by the **^$**). This **sed** output is sent to a **grep** command that removes the **loopback** address from the list. Finally, the remaining output is piped to an **awk** statement that extracts the **hostname** out of the second field. The resulting output is redirected to the `$PINGLIST` file. This modified shell script to ping the `/etc/hosts` file is included on the Web site that accompanies the book. The filename is `pinghostsfile.ksh`.

Logging

I have not added any logging capability to this shell script. Adding a log file, in addition to user notification, can help you find trends of when nodes are unreachable. Adding a log file is not too difficult to do. The first step is to define a unique log filename in the definitions section and assign the filename to a variable, maybe `LOGFILE`. In the script test for the existence of the file, using a test similar to the following statement will work.

ADD THESE LINES:

```
LOGPATH=/usr/local/log
LOGFILE=${LOGPATH}/pingnodes.log
if [ ! -s $LOGFILE ]
then
     if [ ! -d $LOGPATH ]
     then
          echo "\nCreating directory ==> $LOGPATH\c"
          mkdir /usr/local/log
          if (( $? != 0 ))
          then
               echo "\nUnable to create the $LOGPATH directory...EXITING
\n"
               exit 1
          fi
          chown $USER /usr/local/log
          chmod 755 $LOGPATH
          echo
     fi
     echo "\nCreating Logfile ==> $LOGFILE\c"
     cp /dev/null > $LOGFILE
     chown $USER $LOGFILE
     echo
fi
```

After adding these lines of code, use the **tee -a $LOGFILE** command in a pipe to both display the text on the screen and log the data in the $LOGFILE.

Notification of "Unknown Host"

You may want to add notification, and maybe logging too, for nodes that are not known to the system. This usually occurs when the machine cannot resolve the node name into an IP address. This can be caused by the node not being listed in the /etc/hosts file or failure of the DNS lookup. Check both conditions when you get the Unknown host message. Currently, this shell script only echoes this information to the screen. You may want to add this message to the notification.

Notification Method

In this shell script we use email notification. I like email notification, but if you have a network failure this is not going to help you. To get around the network down problem with email, you may want to set up a modem, for *dial-out* only, to dial your alpha-numeric pager number and leave you a message. At least you will always get the message. I have had times, though, when I received the message two hours later due to a message overflow to the modem.

You may just want to change the notification to another method, such as SNMP traps. If you execute this shell script from an enterprise management tool, then the response required back to the program is usually an SNMP trap. Refer to the documentation of the program you are using for details.

Automated Execution Using a Cron Table Entry

I know you do not want to execute this shell script from the command line every 15 minutes yourself! I use a **root** cron table entry to execute this shell script every 15 minutes, 24 hours a day, Monday through Saturday, and 8:00 A.M. to midnight on Sunday; of course, this requires two cron table entries. Because weekly backups and reboots happen early Sunday morning, I do not want to be awakened every Sunday morning when a machine reboots, so I have a special cron entry for Sunday. Both root cron table entries shown execute this script every 15 minutes.

```
5,20,35,50 * * * 1-6 /usr/local/bin/pingnodes.ksh >/dev/null 2>&1
5,20,35,50 8-23 * * 0  /usr/local/bin/pingnodes.ksh </dev/null 2>&1
```

The first entry executes the `pingnodes.ksh` shell script at 5, 20, 35, and 50 minutes of every hour from Monday through Saturday. The second entry executes the `ping-nodes.ksh` shell script at 5, 20, 35, and 50 minutes from 8:00 A.M. until 11:59 P.M., with the last **ping** test running at 11:50 P.M. Sunday night.

Summary

In this chapter we took a different approach than that of some other shell scripts in this book. Instead of creating a different function for each operating system, we created a single shell script and then used a separate function to execute the correct command syntax for the specific operating system. The **uname** command is a very useful tool for shell scripting solutions for various Unix flavors in a single shell script.

I hope you enjoyed this chapter. I think we covered some unique ways to solve the scripting problems that arise when programming for multiple Unix flavors in the same script. In the next chapter we will dive into the task of taking a system *snapshot*. The idea is to get a point-in-time system configuration for later comparison if a system problem has you puzzled. See you in the next chapter!

CHAPTER

13

Taking a System Snapshot

Have you ever rebooted a system and it came up in an unusual state? Any time you reboot a system you run a risk that the system will not come back up properly. When problems arise it is nice to have before and after pictures of the state of the machine. In this chapter we are going to look at some options for shell scripts that execute a series of commands to take a *snapshot* of the state of the machine. Some of the things to consider for this system snapshot include filesystems that are mounted, NFS mounts, processes that are running, network statistics and configuration, and a list of defined system resources, just to name a few. This is different from gathering a snapshot of performance statistics, which is gathered over a period of time. All we are looking for is system configuration data and the system's state at a point in time, specifically before the system is rebooted or when it is running in a normal state with all of the applications running properly.

With this information captured before a system reboot, you have a better chance of fixing a reboot problem quickly and reducing down time. I like to store snapshot information in a directory called `/usr/local/reboot` with the command names used for filenames. For this shell script all of the system information is stored in a single file with a section header added for each command output. Overall, this is not a difficult shell script to write, but gathering the list of commands that you want to run can sometimes be a challenge. For example, if you want to gather an application's configuration you need to find the commands that will produce the desired output. I always prefer having too much information, rather than not enough information, to troubleshoot a problem.

337

In this chapter I have put together a list of commands and created a bunch of functions to execute in the shell script. The commands selected are the most critical for troubleshooting an AIX machine; however, you will need to tailor this set of commands to suit your particular needs, operating system, and environment. Every shop is different, but they are all the same in some sense, especially when it comes to troubleshooting a problem. Let's look at some commands and the syntax that is required.

Syntax

As always, we need the commands and the proper syntax for these commands before we can write a shell script. The commands presented in this section are just a sample of the information that you can gather from the system. This set of commands is for an AIX system, but most apply to other Unix flavors with modified syntax. The list of AIX commands is shown in Listing 13.1.

```
# Hostname of the machine
hostname
OR
uname -n
# Unix flavor
uname -s
# AIX OS version
oslevel
# AIX maintenance level patch set
instfix -i | grep AIX_ML
OR
oslevel -r
# Time zone for this system
cat /etc/environment | grep TZ | awk -F'=' '{print $2}'
# Real memory in the system
echo "$(bootinfo -r)KB"
OR
lsattr -El -a realmem | awk '{print $2}'
# Machine type/architecture
uname -M
OR - Depending on the architecture
uname -p
# List of defined system devices
lsdev -C
# Long directory listing of /dev
ls -l /dev
# List of all defined disks
lsdev -Cc disk
# List of all defined pdisks for SSA disks
lsdev -Cc pdisk
# List of defined tape drives
```

Listing 13.1 System snapshot commands for AIX.

```
lsdev -Cc tape
# List of defined CD-ROMs
lsdev -Cc cdrom
# List of all defined adapters
lsdev -Cc adapter
# List of network routes
netstat -rn
# Network adapter statistics
netstat -i
# Filesystem Statistics
df -k
AND
mount
# List of defined Volume Groups
lsvg | sort -r
# List of varied-on Volume Groups
lsvg -o | sort -r
# List of Logical Volumes in each Volume Group
for VG in $(lsvg -o | sort -r)
do
     lsvg -l $VG
done
# Paging space definitions and usage
lsps -a
AND
lsps -s
# List of all hdisks in the system
lspv
# Disk drives listed by Volume Group assignment
for VG in $(lsvg -o | sort -r)
do
     lsvg -p $VG
done
# List the HACMP configuration, if installed
if [ -x /usr/sbin/cluster/utilities/cllsif ]
then
     /usr/sbin/cluster/utilities/cllsif
     echo "\n"
fi

if [ -x /usr/sbin/cluster/utilities/clshowres ]
then
     /usr/sbin/cluster/utilities/clshowres
fi
# List of all defined printers
lpstat -W | tail +3
AND
cat /etc/qconfig
```

Listing 13.1   System snapshot commands for AIX. *(continues)*

```
# List of active processes
ps -ef
# Show SNA configuration, if installed
sna -d s
if (($? != 0))
then
     lssrc -s sna -l
fi
# List of udp and x25 processes, if any
ps -ef | egrep 'udp|x25' | grep -v grep
# Short listing of the system configuration
lscfg
# Long listing of the system configuration
lscfg -vp
# List of all system installed filesets
lslpp -L
# List of broken or inconsistant filesets
lppchk -v 2>&1
# List of the last 100 users to log in to the system
last | tail -100
```

Listing 13.1   System snapshot commands for AIX. *(continued)*

As you can see in Listing 13.1, we can add anything that you want to the snapshot shell script to get as much detail as needed to troubleshoot a problem. Every environment is different, so this list of commands should be modified, or added to, to suit the needs of your shop. Additional tests include a list of databases that are running, application configurations, specific application processes that are critical, and a **ping** list of machines that are critical to the operation of any applications. You can add anything that you want or need here. Always try to gather more information than you think you may need to troubleshoot a problem.

Using this snapshot technique allows us to go back and look at what the system looked like under normal conditions and load. By looking at the snapshot script output file, the problem usually stands out when comparing it to the currently running system that has a problem.

Creating the Shell Script

For this shell script we are going to take the commands shown in Listing 13.1 and create a function for each one. Using functions greatly simplifies both creating and modifying the entire shell script. When we want to add a new test, or configuration output, we just create a new function and add the function-name in the main body of the shell script exactly where we want it to run. In this shell script all of the function definitions use the C-like function statement, as shown here.

```
get_last_logins ()
{
Commands to execute
}
```

A lot of script programmers like this function definition technique. I prefer defining a function using the *function* statement method, as shown here.

```
function get_last_logins
{
Commands to execute
}
```

This last method of defining a function is more intuitive to understand for the people who will follow in your footsteps and modify this shell script. I hope you noticed the use of the word *will* in the last sentence. No matter what the shell script does, there is always someone who will come along, after you have moved on to bigger and better things, who will modify the shell script. It is usually not because there is a problem with the script coding, but more likely a need for added functionality. For the people who follow me, I like to make sure that the shell script is easy to follow and understand. Use your own judgment and preference when defining functions in a shell script; just be consistent.

Because we have all of the commands listed in Listing 13.1 let's look at the entire shell script in Listing 13.2 and see how we created all of these functions.

```
#!/bin/ksh
#
# SCRIPT: AIXsysconfig.ksh
# AUTHOR: Randy Michael
# REV: 2.1.P
# DATE: 06/14/2002
#
# PLATFORM: AIX only
#
# PURPOSE:  Take a snapshot of the system for later comparision in the
#       event of system problems. All data is stored in
#             /usr/local/reboot in the file defined to the $SYSINFO_FILE
#             variable below.
#
#
# REV LIST:
#             7/11/2002: Changed this script to use a single output file
#                        that receives data from a series of commands
#                        within a bunch of functions.
#
#
```

Listing 13.2 AIXsysconfig.ksh shell script listing. *(continues)*

```
# set -x  # Uncomment to debug this script
# set -n  # Uncomment to verify command syntax without execution
#
#################################################
######### DEFINE VARIABLES HERE ################
#################################################

THISHOST=$(/usr/bin/hostname)
DATETIME=$(/usr/bin/date +%m%d%y_%H%M%S)
WORKDIR="/usr/local/reboot"
SYSINFO_FILE="${WORKDIR}/sys_snapshot.${THISHOST}.$DATETIME"

#################################################
############ DEFINE FUNCTIONS HERE #############
#################################################

get_host ()
{
# Hostname of this machine

hostname

# uname -n works too
}
#################################################

get_OS ()
{
# Operating System - AIX or exit

uname -s
}
#################################################

get_OS_level ()
{
# Query for the operating system release and version level

oslevel
}
#################################################

get_ML_for_AIX ()
{
# Query the system for the maintenance level patch set

instfix -i | grep AIX_ML
```

Listing 13.2 AIXsysconfig.ksh shell script listing. *(continued)*

```
echo "\n"
oslevel -r
}
###################################################

get_TZ ()
{
# Get the time zone that the system is operating in.

cat /etc/environment | grep TZ | awk -F'=' '{print $2}'
}
###################################################

get_real_mem ()
{
# Query the system for the total real memory

echo "$(bootinfo -r)KB"

# lsattr -El sys0 -a realmem | awk '{print $2}'  Works too
}
###################################################

get_arch ()
{
# Query the system for the hardware architecture. Newer
# machines use the -M switch, and the older Micro-Channel
# architecture (MCA) machines use the -p option for
# the "uname" command.

ARCH=$(uname -M)
if [[ -z "$ARCH" && "$ARCH" = '' ]]
then
     ARCH=$(uname -p)
fi

echo "$ARCH"
}
###################################################

get_devices ()
{
# Query the system for all configured devices

lsdev -C
}
###################################################
```

Listing 13.2 AIXsysconfig.ksh shell script listing. *(continues)*

```
get_long_devdir_listing ()
{
# Long listing of the /dev directory. This shows the
# device major and minor numbers and raw device ownership

ls -l /dev
}

##################################################
get_defined_disks ()
{
# List of all defined disks

lsdev -Cc disk
}
##################################################
get_defined_pdisks ()
{
# List of all defined pdisks for SSA disks
lsdev -Cc pdisk
}
##################################################

get_tape_drives ()
{
# Query the system for all configured tape drives

lsdev -Cc tape
}
##################################################

get_cdrom ()
{
# Query the system for all configured CD-ROM devices

lsdev -Cc cdrom
}
##################################################

get_adapters ()
{
# List all configured adapters in the system

lsdev -Cc adapter
}
```

Listing 13.2 AIXsysconfig.ksh shell script listing. *(continued)*

```
##################################################

get_routes ()
{
# Save the network routes defined on the system

netstat -rn
}
##################################################

get_netstats ()
{
# Save the network adapter statistics

netstat -i
}
##################################################

get_fs_stats ()
{
# Save the file system statistics

df -k
echo "\n"
mount
}
##################################################

get_VGs ()
{
# List all defined Volume Groups

lsvg | sort -r
}
##################################################

get_varied_on_VGs ()
{
# List all varied-on Volume Groups

lsvg -o | sort -r
}
##################################################

get_LV_info ()
{
```

Listing 13.2 AIXsysconfig.ksh shell script listing. *(continues)*

```
# List the Logical Volumes in each varied-on Volume Group

for VG in $(get_varied_on_VGs)
do
     lsvg -l $VG
done
}
##################################################

get_paging_space ()
{
# List the paging space definitions and usage

lsps -a
echo "\n"
lsps -s
}
##################################################

get_disk_info ()
{
# List of all "hdisk"s (hard drives) on the system

lspv
}
##################################################

get_VG_disk_info ()
{
# List disks by Volume Group assignment

for VG in $(get_varied_on_VGs)
do
     lsvg -p $VG
done
}
##################################################

get_HACMP_info ()
{
# If the System is running HACMP then save the
# HACMP configuration

if [ -x /usr/sbin/cluster/utilities/cllsif ]
then
     /usr/sbin/cluster/utilities/cllsif
     echo "\n\n"
```

Listing 13.2 AIXsysconfig.ksh shell script listing. *(continued)*

```
fi

if [ -x /usr/sbin/cluster/utilities/clshowres ]
then
     /usr/sbin/cluster/utilities/clshowres
fi
}
####################################################

get_printer_info ()
{
# Wide listing of all defined printers

lpstat -W | tail +3
echo "\nPrint Queue Configuration File Listing\n"
cat /etc/qconfig | grep -v ^*
}
####################################################

get_process_info ()
{
# List of all active processes

ps -ef
}
####################################################

get_sna_info ()
{
# If the system is using SNA save the SNA configuration

sna -d s                  # Syntax for 2.x SNA
if (( $? != 0 ))
then
     lssrc -s sna -l    # must be SNA 1.x
fi
}
####################################################

get_udp_x25_procs ()
{
# Listing of all "udp" and "x25" processes, if
# any are running

ps -ef | egrep 'udp|x25' | grep -v grep
}
####################################################
```

Listing 13.2 AIXsysconfig.ksh shell script listing. *(continues)*

```
get_sys_cfg ()
{
# Short listing of the system configuration

lscfg
}
#################################################

get_long_sys_config ()
{
# Long detailed listing of the system configuration

lscfg -vp
}
###################################################

get_installed_filesets ()
{
# Listing of all installed LPP filesets (system installed)

lslpp -L
}
###################################################

check_for_broken_filesets ()
{
# Check the system for broken filesets

lppchk -v 2>&1
}
###################################################

last_logins ()
{
# List the last 100 system logins

last | head -100
}
###################################################
############## START OF MAIN  ###################
###################################################

# Check for AIX as the operating system

if [[ $(get_OS) != 'AIX' ]]
then
```

Listing 13.2   AIXsysconfig.ksh shell script listing. *(continued)*

```
        echo "\nERROR: Incorrect operating system. This
          shell script is written for AIX.\n"
        echo "\n\t...EXITING...\n"
        exit 1
fi


##################################################
#
# Define the working directory and create this
# directory if it does not exist.

if [ ! -d $WORKDIR ]
then
     mkdir -p $WORKDIR >/dev/null 2>&1
     if (($? != 0))
     then
          echo "\nERROR: Permissions do not allow you to create the
         $WORKDIR directory. This script must exit.
         Please create the $WORKDIR directory and
         execute this script again.\n"
          echo "\n\t...EXITING...\n"
          exit 2
     fi
fi


##################################################

{   # Everything enclosed between this opening bracket and the
    # later closing bracket is both displayed on the screen and
    # also saved in the log file defined as $SYSINFO_FILE.


echo "\n\n[ $(basename $0) - $(date) ]\n"

echo "Saving system information for $THISHOST..."

echo "\nSystem:\t\t\t$(get_host)"
echo "Time Zone:\t\t$(get_TZ)"
echo "Real Memory:\t\t$(get_real_mem)"
echo "Machine Type:\t\t$(get_arch)"
echo "Operating System:\t$(get_OS)"
echo "OS Version Level:\t$(get_OS_level)"
echo "\nCurrent OS Maintenance Level:\n$(get_ML_for_AIX)"

echo "\n##################################################\n"
echo "Installed and Configured Devices\n"
get_devices
```

Listing 13.2 AIXsysconfig.ksh shell script listing. *(continues)*

```
echo "\n###################################################\n"
echo "Long Device Directory Listing - /dev\n"
get_long_devdir_listing
echo "\n###################################################\n"
echo "\nSystem Defined Disks\n"
get_defined_disks
echo "\n###################################################\n"
echo "\nSystem Defined SSA pdisks\n"
get_defined_pdisks
echo "\n###################################################\n"
echo "System Tape Drives\n"
get_tape_drives
echo "\n###################################################\n"
echo "System CD-ROM Drives\n"
get_cdrom
echo "\n###################################################\n"
echo "Defined Adapters in the System\n"
get_adapters
echo "\n###################################################\n"
echo "Network Routes\n"
get_routes
echo "\n###################################################\n"
echo "Network Interface Statistics\n"
get_netstats
echo "\n###################################################\n"
echo "Filesystem Statistics\n"
get_fs_stats
echo "\n###################################################\n"
echo "Defined Volume Groups\n"
get_VGs
echo "\n###################################################\n"
echo "Varied-on Volume Groups\n"
get_varied_on_VGs
echo "\n###################################################\n"
echo "Logical Volume Information by Volume Group\n"
get_LV_info
echo "\n###################################################\n"
echo "Paging Space Information\n"
get_paging_space
echo "\n###################################################\n"
echo "Hard Disks Defined\n"
get_disk_info
echo "\n###################################################\n"
echo "Volume Group Hard Drives\n"
get_VG_disk_info
echo "\n###################################################\n"
echo "HACMP Configuration\n"
get_HACMP_info
```

Listing 13.2   AIXsysconfig.ksh shell script listing. *(continued)*

```
echo "\n#################################################\n"
echo "Printer Information\n"
get_printer_info
echo "\n#################################################\n"
echo "Active Process List\n"
get_process_info
echo "\n#################################################\n"
echo "SNA Information\n"
get_sna_info
echo "\n#################################################\n"
echo "x25 and udp Processes\n"
get_udp_x25_procs
echo "\n#################################################\n"
echo "System Configuration Overview\n"
get_sys_cfg
echo "\n#################################################\n"
echo "Detailed System Configuration\n"
get_long_sys_config
echo "\n#################################################\n"
echo "System Installed Filesets\n"
get_installed_filesets
echo "\n#################################################\n"
echo "Looking for Broken Filesets\n"
check_for_broken_filesets
echo "\n#################################################\n"
echo "List of the last 100 users to log in to $THISHOST\n"
last_logins

echo "\n\nThis report is save in: $SYSINFO_FILE \n"

# Send all output to both the screen and the $SYSINFO_FILE
# using a pipe to the "tee -a" command"

} | tee -a $SYSINFO_FILE
```

Listing 13.2   AIXsysconfig.ksh shell script listing. *(continued)*

As you can see in Listing 13.2, we have a lot of functions in this shell script. When I created these functions I tried to place each one in the order that I want to execute in the shell script. This is not necessary as long as you do *not* try to use a function before it is defined. Because a Korn shell script is interpreted, as opposed to compiled, the flow goes from the top to the bottom. It makes sense that you have to define a function in the code above where the function is used. If we slip up and the function is defined *below* where it is used, then we may or may not get an error message. Getting an error message depends on what the function is supposed to do and how the function is executed in the shell script.

From the top of the shell script in Listing 13.2 we first define the variables that we need. The **hostname** of the machine is always nice to know, and it is required for the report-file definition and in the report itself. Next we create a date/time stamp. This $DATATIME variable is used in the report-file definition as well. We want the date *and* time because this script may be executed more than once in a single day. Next we define the working directory. I like to use /usr/local/reboot, but you can use any directory that you want. Finally, we define the report-file, which is assigned to the $SYSINFO_FILE variable.

The next section is where all of the functions are defined. Notice that some of these functions contain only a single command, and some have a bit more code. In a shell script like this one it is a good idea to place every command in a separate function. Using this method allows you to change the commands to a different operating system simply by editing some functions and leaving the basic shell script operation intact. There are too many functions in this shell script to go over them one at a time, but an output of this shell script is shown in Listing 13.3. For details on the specific AIX commands please refer to the AIX documentation and **man** pages on an AIX system.

At START OF MAIN we begin the real work. The first step is to ensure that the operating system is AIX. If this shell script is executed on another Unix flavor, then a lot of the commands will fail. If a non-AIX Unix flavor is detected, then the user receives an error message and the script exits with a return code of 1, one. Step two is to test for the existence of the $WORKDIR directory, which is defined as /usr/local/reboot in this shell script. If the directory does not exist, an attempt is made to create the directory. Not all users will have permission to create a directory here. If the directory creation fails, then the user receives an error message and is asked to create the directory manually and run the shell script again.

If the operating system is AIX and the $WORKDIR exists, then we create the report-file and begin creating the report. Notice that the entire list of functions and commands for the report is enclosed in braces, { code }. Then, after the final brace, at the end of the shell script, all of the output is piped to the **tee -a** command. Using this pipe to the **tee -a** command allows the user to see the report as it is being created and the output is written to the $SYSINFO_FILE file. Enclosing *all* of the code for the report within the braces saves a lot of effort to get the output to the screen and to the report file. The basic syntax is shown here.

```
{

report command
report command
    .

    .

    .

report command

} | tee -a $SYSINFO_FILE
```

Within the braces we start by setting up the report header information, which includes the hostname, time zone, real memory, machine type, operating system, operating system version, and the maintenance level patch set of the operating system version.

When the header is complete then the script executes the functions listed in the DEFINE FUNCTIONS HERE section. As I stated before, I tried to define the functions in the order of execution. Before each function is executed, a line of hash marks is written out to separate each report section, and then some section header information is written for the specific task. At the end, and just before the ending brace, the report filename is shown to the user to indicate where the report file is located.

Let's take a look at an abbreviated report output in Listing 13.3.

```
[ AIXsysconfig.ksh - Thu Jul 25 09:46:58 EDT 2002 ]

Saving system information for yogi...

System:              yogi
Time Zone:           EST5EDT
Real Memory:         131072KB
Machine Type:        powerpc
Operating System:    AIX
OS Version Level:    5.1.0.0

Current OS Maintenance Level:
    Not all filesets for 5.0.0.0_AIX_ML were found.
    Not all filesets for 5.1.0.0_AIX_ML were found.


##################################################

Installed and Configured Devices

sys0        Available 00-00         System Object
sysplanar0  Available 00-00         System Planar
ioplanar0   Available 00-00         I/O Planar
sio0        Available 00-00         Standard I/O Planar
hdisk0      Available 00-00-0S-0,0  2.0 GB SCSI Disk Drive
hdisk1      Available 00-00-0S-1,0  2.0 GB SCSI Disk Drive
rmt0        Available 00-00-0S-5,0  5.0 GB 8mm Tape Drive
cd0         Available 00-00-0S-6,0  SCSI Multimedia CD-ROM Drive
proc0       Available 00-00         Processor
mem0        Available 00-0A         32 MB Memory SIMM
mem1        Available 00-0B         32 MB Memory SIMM
mem2        Available 00-0C         32 MB Memory SIMM
mem3        Available 00-0D         32 MB Memory SIMM
fd0         Available 00-00-0D-00   Diskette Drive
lvdd        Available               LVM Device Driver
tty0        Available 00-00-S1-00   Asynchronous Terminal
rootvg      Defined                 Volume group
hd5         Defined                 Logical volume
hd6         Defined                 Logical volume
.
```

Listing 13.3 AIXsysconfig.ksh shell script in action. *(continues)*

```
.
.

##################################################

Long Device Directory Listing - /dev

total 24
crw-rw-rw-    1 root      system    19,  0 Jun 23 15:23 rmt0
crw-rw-rw-    1 root      system    19,  1 Mar 29 13:49 rmt0.1
crw-rw-rw-    1 root      system    19,  2 Jul 26 2001 rmt0.2
crw-rw-rw-    1 root      system    19,  3 Jul 26 2001 rmt0.3
crw-rw-rw-    1 root      system    19,  4 Jul 26 2001 rmt0.4
crw-rw-rw-    1 root      system    19,  5 Jul 26 2001 rmt0.5
crw-rw-rw-    1 root      system    19,  6 Jul 26 2001 rmt0.6
crw-rw-rw-    1 root      system    19,  7 Jul 26 2001 rmt0.7
crw-rw----    1 root      system    10,  0 Jul 26 2001 rootvg
crw-rw----    1 root      system    10, 10 Jul 29 2001 rscripts_lv
crw-rw-rw-    1 root      system    13, 14 Jul 26 2001 sad
brw-rw----    1 root      system    10, 10 Jul 29 2001 scripts_lv
crw-rw-rw-    1 root      system    11,  0 Jul 26 2001 scsi0
crw-rw-rw-    1 root      system    13, 15 Jul 26 2001 slog
crw-rw-rw-    1 root      system    13, 30 Jul 26 2001 spx
crw-------    1 root      system     7,  0 Jul 26 2001 sysdump
crw-------    1 root      system     7,  1 Jul 26 2001 sysdumpctl
crw-------    1 root      system     7,  3 Jul 26 2001 sysdumpfile
crw-------    1 root      system     7,  2 Jul 26 2001 sysdumpnull
crw-rw-rw-    1 root      system     5,  0 Jul 26 2001 systrace
crw-rw-rw-    1 root      system     5,  1 Jul 26 2001 systrctl
crw-rw-rw-    1 root      system     1,  0 Jul 24 17:53 tty
crw--w--w-    1 root      system    18,  0 Jul 24 17:58 tty0
crw-rw-rw-    1 root      system    18,  1 Jun 23 15:18 tty1
crw-rw-rw-    1 root      system    26,  0 Jul 26 2001 ttyp0
crw-rw-rw-    1 root      system    26,  1 Jul 26 2001 ttyp1
crw-rw-rw-    1 root      system     2,  3 Jul 26 2001 zero
.
.
.

##################################################

System Defined Disks

hdisk0 Available 00-00-0S-0,0 2.0 GB SCSI Disk Drive
hdisk1 Available 00-00-0S-1,0 2.0 GB SCSI Disk Drive

##################################################
```

Listing 13.3   AIXsysconfig.ksh shell script in action. *(continued)*

```
System Defined SSA pdisks


####################################################

System Tape Drives

rmt0 Available 00-00-0S-5,0 5.0 GB 8mm Tape Drive

####################################################

System CD-ROM Drives

cd0 Available 00-00-0S-6,0 SCSI Multimedia CD-ROM Drive

####################################################

Defined Adapters in the System

sio0    Available 00-00    Standard I/O Planar
fda0    Available 00-00-0D Standard I/O Diskette Adapter
sioka0  Available 00-00-0K Keyboard Adapter
sa0     Available 00-00-S1 Standard I/O Serial Port 1
sa1     Available 00-00-S2 Standard I/O Serial Port 2
scsi0   Available 00-00-0S Standard SCSI I/O Controller
siota0  Available 00-00-0T Tablet Adapter
sioma0  Available 00-00-0M Mouse Adapter
ppa0    Available 00-00-0P Standard I/O Parallel Port Adapter
ent0    Available 00-03    Ethernet High-Performance LAN Adapter (8ef5)
.
.
.

####################################################

Network Routes

Routing tables
Destination     Gateway        Flags  Refs    Use  If  PMTU Exp
Groups

Route Tree for Protocol Family 2 (Internet):
default         10.10.10.2     UGc      0       0  en0   -   -
10.10/16        10.10.10.1     U       37  135807  en0   -   -
127/8           127.0.0.1      U        5     264  lo0   -   -

Route Tree for Protocol Family 24 (Internet v6):
```

Listing 13.3   AIXsysconfig.ksh shell script in action. *(continues)*

```
::1                    ::1              UH         0        0  lo0 16896     -

##################################################

Network Interface Statistics

Name  Mtu   Network  Address          Ipkts Ierrs   Opkts Oerrs  Coll
en0   1500  link#2   2.60.8c.2d.75.b1  112330    0  108697      0     0
en0   1500  10.10    yogi              112330    0  108697      0     0
lo0   16896 link#1                      28302    0   28304      0     0
lo0   16896 127      loopback           28302    0   28304      0     0
lo0   16896 ::1                         28302    0   28304      0     0


##################################################

Filesystem Statistics

Filesystem      1024-blocks      Free %Used   Iused %Iused Mounted on
/dev/hd4            32768       10924  67%     1854   12% /
/dev/hd2          1449984       61680  96%    40941   12% /usr
/dev/hd9var         53248       10568  81%      673    6% /var
/dev/hd3           106496       70184  35%      223    1% /tmp
/dev/hd1             4096        3892   5%       55    6% /home
/proc                  -           -    -        -     -  /proc
/dev/hd10opt       655360       16460  98%    16260   10% /opt
/dev/scripts_lv    102400       25296  76%      887    4% /scripts
/dev/lv_temp       409600      350456  15%       26    1% /tmpfs


  node        mounted         mounted over    vfs        date
options
--------  ------------    ------------    ------  ------------  ----------------
          /dev/hd4          /              jfs    Jul 23 18:56 rw,log=/dev/hd8
          /dev/hd2          /usr           jfs    Jul 23 18:56 rw,log=/dev/hd8
          /dev/hd9var       /var           jfs    Jul 23 18:56 rw,log=/dev/hd8
          /dev/hd3          /tmp           jfs    Jul 23 18:56 rw,log=/dev/hd8
          /dev/hd1          /home          jfs    Jul 23 18:57 rw,log=/dev/hd8
          /proc             /proc          procfs Jul 23 18:57 rw
          /dev/hd10opt      /opt           jfs    Jul 23 18:57 rw,log=/dev/hd8
          /dev/scripts_lv   /scripts       jfs    Jul 23 18:57 rw,log=/dev/hd8
          /dev/lv_temp      /tmpfs         jfs    Jul 23 18:57 rw,log=/dev/hd8


##################################################

Defined Volume Groups

rootvg
```

Listing 13.3   AIXsysconfig.ksh shell script in action. *(continued)*

```
##################################################

Varied-on Volume Groups

rootvg

##################################################

Logical Volume Information by Volume Group

rootvg:
LV NAME             TYPE      LPs   PPs   PVs  LV STATE      MOUNT
POINT
hd5                 boot      2     2     1    closed/syncd  N/A
hd6                 paging    84    84    1    open/syncd    N/A
hd8                 jfslog    1     1     1    open/syncd    N/A
hd4                 jfs       8     8     1    open/syncd    /
hd2                 jfs       354   354   2    open/syncd    /usr
hd9var              jfs       13    13    2    open/syncd    /var
hd3                 jfs       26    26    1    open/syncd    /tmp
hd1                 jfs       1     1     1    open/syncd    /home
hd10opt             jfs       160   160   2    open/syncd    /opt
scripts_lv          jfs       25    25    1    open/syncd    /scripts
lv_temp             jfs       100   100   1    open/syncd    /tmpfs

##################################################

Paging Space Information

Page Space   Physical Volume  Volume Group  Size  %Used Active Auto  Type
hd6          hdisk0           rootvg        336MB  10    yes    yes   lv


Total Paging Space   Percent Used
     336MB                10%

##################################################

Hard Disks Defined

hdisk0          00003677cf068b62                rootvg
hdisk1          000125608a48c132                rootvg

##################################################

Volume Group Hard Drives
```

Listing 13.3 AIXsysconfig.ksh shell script in action. *(continues)*

```
rootvg:
PV_NAME              PV STATE    TOTAL PPs   FREE PPs    FREE DISTRIBUTION
hdisk0               active      479         0           00..00..00..00..00
hdisk1               active      479         184         92..00..00..00..92


##################################################

HACMP Configuration


##################################################

Printer Information

hp4                  lp0              READY
hp4-ps               lp0              READY
hp4-gl               lp0              READY
yogi_hp4_1           lp0              READY
yogi_hp4_1ps         lp0              READY


Print Queue Configuration File Listing

hp4:
        device = lp0
lp0:
        file = /dev/lp0
        header = never
        trailer = never
        access = both
        backend = /usr/lib/lpd/piobe
hp4-ps:
        device = lp0
lp0:
        file = /dev/lp0
        header = never
        trailer = never
        access = both
        backend = /usr/lib/lpd/piobe
hp4-gl:
        device = lp0
lp0:
        file = /dev/lp0
        header = never
        trailer = never
        access = both
```

Listing 13.3   AIXsysconfig.ksh shell script in action. *(continued)*

```
backend = /usr/lib/lpd/piobe
yogi_hp4_1:
        device = lp0
lp0:
        file = /dev/lp0
        header = never
        trailer = never
        access = both
        backend = /usr/lib/lpd/piobe
yogi_hp4_1ps:
        device = lp0
lp0:
        file = /dev/lp0
        header = never
        trailer = never
        access = both
        backend = /usr/lib/lpd/piobe


####################################################

Active Process List

    UID   PID  PPID   C    STIME    TTY  TIME CMD
    root     1     0   0   Jul 23    -   0:17 /etc/init
    root  1950     1   0   Jul 23    -   0:00 /usr/sbin/srcmstr
    root  2672     1   0   Jul 23    -   0:00 /usr/lib/errdemon
    root  3140     1   0   Jul 23    -   2:04 /usr/sbin/syncd 60
    root  3642  4644   0 17:11:20    -   0:00 rpc.ttdbserver 100083 1
    root  3882  1950   0   Jul 23    -   0:04 sendmail: accepting
connections
    root  4168  1950   0   Jul 23    -   0:00 /usr/sbin/syslogd
    root  4388  1950   0   Jul 23    -   0:00 /usr/sbin/portmap
    root  4644  1950   0   Jul 23    -   0:00 /usr/sbin/inetd
  nobody  4906  5418   0   Jul 23    -   0:01 /usr/sbin/tftpd -n
  daemon  8798  1950   0   Jul 23    -   0:00 /usr/sbin/rpc.statd
    root  9034  1950   0   Jul 23    -   0:00 /usr/sbin/biod 6
    root  9296  1950   0   Jul 23    -   0:00 /usr/sbin/nfsd 3891
    root  9554  1950   0   Jul 23    -   0:00 /usr/sbin/rpc.mountd
    root  9814  1950   0   Jul 23    -   0:00 /usr/sbin/rpc.lockd
    root 10336     1   0   Jul 23    -   0:00 /usr/sbin/uprintfd
    root 10588  1950   0   Jul 23    -   0:00 qdaemon
    root 10842     1   0   Jul 23    -   0:02 /usr/sbin/cron
    root 11360  1950   0   Jul 23    -   0:00 /usr/sbin/writesrv
    root 11616     1   0   Jul 23    -   0:00
/usr/lpp/diagnostics/bin/diagd
    root 16820 15772   0 17:11:39  pts/0 0:03 dtfile
```

Listing 13.3   AIXsysconfig.ksh shell script in action. *(continues)*

```
     root 17540 16538   0 21:16:59  pts/3   0:00 /usr/bin/ksh
       .
       .
       .


###################################################

SNA Information

0513-085 The sna Subsystem is not on file.


###################################################

x25 and udp Processes


###################################################

System Configuration Overview

INSTALLED RESOURCE LIST

The following resources are installed on the machine.
+/- = Added or deleted from Resource List.
*   = Diagnostic support not available.

* sys0              00-00            System Object
+ sysplanar0        00-00            System Planar
+ ioplanar0         00-00            I/O Planar
+ hdisk0            00-00-0S-0,0     2.0 GB SCSI Disk Drive
+ hdisk1            00-00-0S-1,0     2.0 GB SCSI Disk Drive
+ rmt0              00-00-0S-5,0     5.0 GB 8mm Tape Drive
+ cd0               00-00-0S-6,0     SCSI Multimedia CD-ROM Drive (650
+ proc0             00-00            Processor
+ mem0              00-0A            32 MB Memory SIMM
+ mem1              00-0B            32 MB Memory SIMM
+ mem2              00-0C            32 MB Memory SIMM
+ mem3              00-0D            32 MB Memory SIMM
* sysunit0          00-00            System Unit
       .
       .
       .


###################################################

Detailed System Configuration
```

Listing 13.3 AIXsysconfig.ksh shell script in action. *(continued)*

```
INSTALLED RESOURCE LIST WITH VPD

The following resources are installed on your machine.

   sys0              00-00              System Object
   sysplanar0        00-00              System Planar

          Part Number................065G8317
          EC Level...................00D28027
          Processor Identification....00012560
          ROS Level and ID...........IPLVER1.3 LVL3.01,065G8318
          Processor Component ID......0800004800000050
          Device Specific.(Z0)........000000
          Device Specific.(Z1)........000000
          Device Specific.(Z2)........000000
          Device Specific.(Z3)........000000
          Device Specific.(Z4)........000000
          Device Specific.(Z5)........000000
          Device Specific.(Z6)........000000
          Device Specific.(Z7)........000000
          Device Specific.(Z8)........000000
          Device Specific.(Z9)........000000
          ROS Level and ID...........OCS(00000C54)
          ROS Level and ID...........SEEDS(28040203)

   hdisk0            00-00-0S-0,0     2.0 GB SCSI Disk Drive

          Manufacturer...............IBMRISC
          Machine Type and Model......0664M1H
          Part Number................86F0101
          ROS Level and ID...........5 5A
          Serial Number..............00221833
          EC Level...................895186
          FRU Number.................86F0118
          Device Specific.(Z0)........000002029F00001E
          Device Specific.(Z1)........75G3644
          Device Specific.(Z2)........0983
          Device Specific.(Z3)........95123
          Device Specific.(Z4)........0002
          Device Specific.(Z5)........22
          Device Specific.(Z6)........895172

   rmt0              00-00-0S-5,0     5.0 GB 8mm Tape Drive

          Manufacturer...............EXABYTE
```

Listing 13.3   AIXsysconfig.ksh shell script in action. *(continues)*

```
            Machine Type and Model......IBM-8505
            Device Specific.(Z1).......807A
            Part Number................8191044
            Serial Number..............082737
            Device Specific.(LI).......00000001
            EC Level...................D48098
            FRU Number.................59H3159
            Device Specific.(Z0).......0180020283000010


   cd0             00-00-0S-6,0     SCSI Multimedia CD-ROM Drive (650
                                    MB)


            Manufacturer...............IBM
            Machine Type and Model......CDRM00203
            ROS Level and ID...........8B08
            Device Specific.(Z0).......058002028F000018
            Part Number................73H2600
            EC Level...................D75458A
            FRU Number.................73H2601


   siota0          00-00-0T         Tablet Adapter
   sa0             00-00-S1         Standard I/O Serial Port 1
   tty0            00-00-S1-00      Asynchronous Terminal
   sa1             00-00-S2         Standard I/O Serial Port 2
   tty1            00-00-S2-00      Asynchronous Terminal
   proc0           00-00            Processor
   mem0            00-0A            32 MB Memory SIMM

            Size.......................32
            Device Specific.(Z3).......90000000
            EC Level...................00


   mem1            00-0B            32 MB Memory SIMM

            Size.......................32
            Device Specific.(Z3).......90000000
            EC Level...................00




    .
    .
    .


   ################################################

   System Installed Filesets

     Fileset                    Level  State  Type  Description
   (Uninstaller)
   -----------------------------------------------------------------
```

Listing 13.3 AIXsysconfig.ksh shell script in action. *(continued)*

```
           .
           .

           .
    Tivoli_Management_Agent.client.rte
                             3.2.0.0    C      F      Management Agent
runtime"
    X11.Dt.ToolTalk          5.1.0.0    C      F      AIX CDE ToolTalk
Support
    X11.Dt.adt               5.1.0.0    C      F      AIX CDE Application
Developers'
                                                      Toolkit
    X11.Dt.bitmaps           5.1.0.0    C      F      AIX CDE Bitmaps
    X11.Dt.compat            5.1.0.0    C      F      AIX CDE Compatibility
    X11.Dt.helpinfo          5.1.0.0    C      F      AIX CDE Help Files
and Volumes
    X11.Dt.helpmin           5.1.0.0    C      F      AIX CDE Minimum Help
Files
    X11.Dt.helprun           5.1.0.0    C      F      AIX CDE Runtime Help
    X11.Dt.lib               5.1.0.0    C      F      AIX CDE Runtime
Libraries
    X11.Dt.rte               5.1.0.0    C      F      AIX Common Desktop
Environment
                                                      (CDE) 1.0
    X11.Dt.xdt2cde           5.1.0.0    C      F      AIX CDE Migration
Tool
    X11.adt.bitmaps          5.1.0.0    C      F      AIXwindows
Application
                                                      Development Toolkit
Bitmap Files
    X11.adt.imake            5.1.0.0    C      F      AIXwindows
Application
                                                      Development Toolkit
imake
    X11.adt.include          5.1.0.0    C      F      AIXwindows
Application
                                                      Development Toolkit
Include
                                                      Files
    X11.adt.lib              5.1.0.0    C      F      AIXwindows
Application
                                                      Development Toolkit
Libraries
    X11.adt.motif            5.1.0.0    C      F      AIXwindows
Application
                                                      Development Toolkit
Motif
    X11.apps.xterm           5.1.0.0    C      F      AIXwindows xterm
Application
```

Listing 13.3   AIXsysconfig.ksh shell script in action. *(continues)*

```
    X11.base.common          5.1.0.0    C    F    AIXwindows Runtime
Common
                                                  Directories
    X11.base.lib             5.1.0.0    C    F    AIXwindows Runtime
Libraries
    X11.base.rte             5.1.0.1    A    F    AIXwindows Runtime
Environment
    bos.acct                 5.1.0.0    C    F    Accounting Services
    bos.adt.base             5.1.0.1    A    F    Base Application
Development
                                                  Toolkit
    bos.adt.debug            5.1.0.1    A    F    Base Application
Development
                                                  Debuggers
    bos.adt.include          5.1.0.1    A    F    Base Application
Development
                                                  Include Files
    bos.adt.lib              5.1.0.0    C    F    Base Application
Development
                                                  Libraries
    bos.adt.libm             5.1.0.0    C    F    Base Application
Development
                                                  Math Library
    bos.alt_disk_install.boot_images
                             5.1.0.0    C    F    Alternate Disk
Installation Disk
                                                  Boot Images
    bos.alt_disk_install.rte 5.1.0.0    C    F    Alternate Disk
Installation
                                                  Runtime
    bos.diag.com             5.1.0.0    C    F    Common Hardware
Diagnostics
    bos.diag.rte             5.1.0.0    C    F    Hardware Diagnostics
    bos.diag.util            5.1.0.1    A    F    Hardware Diagnostics
Utilities
    bos.msg.en_US.net.tcp.client
                             5.1.0.0    C    F    TCP/IP Messages -
U.S. English
    bos.msg.en_US.rte        5.1.0.0    C    F    Base Operating System
Runtime
                                                  Msgs - U.S. English
    bos.msg.en_US.svprint    5.1.0.0    C    F    System V Print
Subsystem
                                                  Messages - U.S.
English
    bos.msg.en_US.sysmgt.nim.master_gui
                             4.3.0.0    C    F    NIM GUI Messages -
U.S. English
```

Listing 13.3   AIXsysconfig.ksh shell script in action. *(continued)*

```
   bos.msg.en_US.txt.tfs      5.1.0.0     C     F     Text Formatting
Services
                                                      Messages - U.S.
English
   bos.net.ate                5.1.0.0     C     F     Asynchronous Terminal
Emulator
   bos.net.ipsec.rte          5.1.0.0     C     F     IP Security
   bos.net.ncs                5.1.0.0     C     F     Network Computing
System 1.5.1
   bos.net.nfs.adt            5.1.0.0     C     F     Network File System
Development
                                                      Toolkit
   bos.net.nfs.cachefs        5.1.0.0     C     F     CacheFS File System
   bos.net.nfs.client         5.1.0.1     A     F     Network File System
Client
   bos.net.nfs.server         5.1.0.0     C     F     Network File System
Server
   bos.net.nis.client         5.1.0.0     C     F     Network Information
Service
   .
   .
   .


State codes:
 A -- Applied.
 B -- Broken.
 C -- Committed.
 O -- Obsolete.   (partially migrated to newer version)
 ? -- Inconsistent State...Run lppchk -v.


Type codes:
 F -- Installp Fileset
 P -- Product
 C -- Component
 T -- Feature
 R -- RPM Package


##################################################

Looking for Broken Filesets

lppchk: The following filesets need to be installed or corrected to
bring the system to a consistent state:

  vac.C.readme.ibm 4.4.0.1         (not installed; requisite fileset)

##################################################
```

Listing 13.3 AIXsysconfig.ksh shell script in action. *(continues)*

```
       List of the last 100 users to log in to yogi

  root        ftp           booboo        Jul 25 13:28 - 13:29  (00:00)
  root        ftp           booboo        Jul 25 12:17 - 12:18  (00:00)
  root        tty0                        Jul 24 17:35   still logged in.
  root        ftp           booboo        Jul 24 17:35 - 17:35  (00:00)
  root        pts/1         mrranger      Jul 24 17:11   still logged in.
  root        pts/0         mrranger      Jul 24 17:11   still logged in.
  root        pts/0         mrranger      Jul 24 17:09 - 17:11  (00:01)
  root        ftp           booboo        Jul 23 21:53 - 21:53  (00:00)
  shutdown    tty0                        Jul 10 00:25
  root        ftp           booboo        Jul 09 23:41 - 23:41  (00:00)
  reboot      ~                           Jul 09 19:38
  reboot      ~                           Jun 27 16:07
  root        pts/3         mrranger      Jun 26 20:55 - 20:56  (00:00)
  root        pts/2         mrranger      Jun 26 20:55 - 20:56  (00:00)
  root        pts/1         mrranger      Jun 26 20:55 - 20:56  (00:00)
  .
  .
  .

  wtmp begins      Jul 31 18:20



  This report is saved in:
  /usr/local/reboot/sys_snapshot.yogi.072502_094658
```

Listing 13.3   AIXsysconfig.ksh shell script in action. *(continued)*

From Listing 13.3 you can see that we collected a lot of information about the system configuration. This is just a sample of what you can collect, and I will leave the specifics of the information you gather up to you. For each function that you add or change, be sure to test the response. Sometimes you may be surprised that you do not see any output. Some of the command output shown in Listing 13.3 does not have any output because my little system does not have the hardware that the query is looking for. If you expect output and there is not any, try redirecting standard error to standard output by using the following syntax:

```
command 2>&1
```

Many commands send information type output to standard error, specified by file descriptor 2, instead of standard output, specified by file descriptor 1. First try the command without this redirection.

Other Options to Consider

There can always be improvements to any shell script. The shell script presented in this chapter is intended to be an example of the process of gathering system information. You always want to query the system for as much information as you can. Notice that I did not add any database or application configuration/statistics gathering here. The amount of information gathered is up to you. As I said before, every shop is different, but they are all the same when troubleshooting a problem. The AIXsysconfig.ksh shell script looks only at system-level statistics and configuration, so there is a large gap that you need to fill in. This gap is where your specific application comes into play. Look at your database and application documentation for the best method of gathering information about these products. By running the configuration gathering script at least once a week, you will save yourself a lot of effort *when* a problem arises.

Summary

In this chapter we strictly looked at AIX. The process is the same for any Unix flavor, but the information gathered will vary in each shop. No rocket science is needed here, but you do need a good understanding of how your system is configured. You need to understand the applications and databases and what determines a failed application. You may be looking for a set of processes, or it could be a database query with an SQL statement. These are the things that need research on your part to make this type of shell script really beneficial.

In the next chapter we are going to move on to installing, configuring, and using **sudo**. The **sudo** program stands for *super user do*, and it allows us to set up specific commands that a user can execute as **root**. I hope you enjoyed this chapter, and I'll see you in the next chapter!

CHAPTER 14

Compiling, Installing, Configuring, and Using sudo

The main job of any good Systems Administrator is to protect the *root* password. No matter how firm and diligent we are about protecting the root password we always have the application support group and DBAs wanting root access for one reason or another. But, alas, there is a way to give specific users the ability to run selected commands as the root user without the need to know the root password. Facilitating this restricted root access is a *free software* program called **sudo**, which stands for *superuser do*. In this chapter we are going to show how to compile, install, configure, and use the **sudo** program. The current distribution can be downloaded by following the link on the Web site that accompanies the book, and I will list some Web other sites where you can download the program in this chapter.

Because **sudo** is not a shell script you may be asking, "Why is **sudo** included in *this* book?" I am including the **sudo** chapter because I have not found any reference to **sudo** in any scripting book, and it is a nice tool to use. We will cover a short shell script at the end of this chapter showing how to use **sudo** in a shell script.

The Need for sudo

In Unix the root user is almighty and has absolutely no restrictions. All security is bypassed, and anyone with root access can perform any task, with some possibly resulting in major damage to the system, without any restrictions at all. Unix systems do *not* ask "Are you sure?"; they just run the command specified by the root user and assume you know what you are doing. The **sudo** program allows the Systems Administrator to set up specific commands (or all commands) to be executed as the root user and specify only certain users (or groups of users) to execute the individual commands. In addition, all commands and command arguments are logged either to a defined file or the system *syslog*. The logging allows the Systems Administrator to have an audit trail and to monitor user **sudo** activities as well as failed **sudo** attempts! The user executes a restricted command by preceding the command with the word **sudo**. For example:

```
sudo chmod 600 /etc/sudoers
Password:
```

When a user executes the preceding command, a password prompt is displayed. The password that the **sudo** program is asking for is **not** the root password but the *user's* password that wants root access. When the password is entered, the /etc/sudoers file is searched to determine if root authority should be granted to run the specified command. If both the system password is correct and the /etc/sudoers search grants access, then the command will execute with root authority. After this initial **sudo** command, the user may submit more **sudo** commands without the need for a password until a **sudo** timeout, typically five minutes without issuing another **sudo** command. After the timeout period the user will again be prompted for his or her password when a **sudo** command is entered.

Downloading and Compiling sudo

The **sudo** program is included on the Web site that accompanies the book and can be downloaded from various FTP mirror sites. The main **sudo** Web site is located at **www.courtesan.com/sudo**. The **sudo** program is *free software* and is distributed under a BDS-style license. As of this writing the current version of **sudo** is 1.6.6 and was released April 25, 2002. Todd Miller currently maintains the **sudo** program, and if you would like to tip Todd for his fine work you may do so at PayPal, which can be accessed from a link on the **sudo** main page. You can download **sudo** from any of the Web sites shown in Listing 14.1.

```
http://www.courtesan.com/sudo/dist/ (Main site in Boulder, Colorado USA)
http://www.rge.com/pub/admin/sudo/  (Rochester, New York USA)
http://sudo.stikman.com/  (Los Angeles, California USA)
http://www.c0r3dump.com/sudo/  (Edmonton, Canada)
http://core.ring.gr.jp/archives/misc/sudo/  (Japan)
http://www.ring.gr.jp/archives/misc/sudo/  (Japan)
http://sudo.cdu.elektra.ru/  (Russia)
```

Listing 14.1 Web sites to download the sudo program.

There are two ways to download the files. You can download the precompiled binaries for your Unix flavor and version or download the source code distribution and compile the **sudo** program for your particular machine. I always download the source code and compile it on each individual system. The process takes just a few minutes, and you can be assured that it will run on your system. If you have a boatload of systems to install, you may want to consider using the precompiled binaries and pushing the binaries out to each system, or writing a shell script to push and install the product! Either way you choose, you will need only about 4MB of free space to work with. Once **sudo** is installed you can remove the downloaded files if you need to regain the disk space. In this chapter we are going to download the source code and compile **sudo** for a particular system.

Compiling sudo

You will need a C compiler; **cc** is preferred but **gcc** normally works fine and is free to download. I say **gcc** *normally* works fine because I have found instances where **gcc** had compiler errors and **cc** did not have any problems. The source code distribution is in a compressed **tar** format, where **gzip** is used for compression. The **gzip** file has a **.gz** extension—for example, sudo-1.6.6.tar.gz. When you download the file, put the software distribution in a directory that has about 4MB of free space. In our example we will use /usr/local, which is a separate filesystem from /usr on my machine. You *must* have **root** access to compile, install, and configure **sudo**!

After the **sudo** distribution file is placed in a work directory, the first step is to unzip the compressed file. The **gunzip** command uncompresses a gzipped file, as shown in the next example:

```
gunzip sudo-1.6.6.tar.gz
```

After the file is uncompressed, you are left with the following **tar** archive file:

```
sudo-1.6.6.tar
```

When we *untar* the archive, a subdirectory will be created called sudo-1.6.6 that will contain all of the source code, LICENSE, README, manuals, **configure**, and Makefile. In the directory containing the sudo-1.6.6.tar file, in our case /usr/local, issue the following command:

```
tar xvf sudo-1.6.6.tar
```

After the program distribution file is uncompressed and untarred we can proceed to the installation process. This is not a difficult process so if you have never worked with the **make** command and Makefile before, don't worry. The first step is to configure the Makefile for your system. As you might expect, this is done with the **configure** command. First change directory to where the source code is located, in our example /usr/local/sudo-1.6.6, and run the **configure** command.

```
cd /usr/local/sudo-1.6.6
./configure
```

The **configure** command goes through system checks and builds a `Makefile` and the `config.h` file used to build **sudo** for your system. The **configure** command output for my system is shown in Listing 14.2.

```
Configuring Sudo version 1.6.6
checking whether to lecture users the first time they run sudo... yes
checking whether sudo should log via syslog or to a file by default...
syslog
checking which syslog facility sudo should log with... local2
checking at which syslog priority to log commands... notice
checking at which syslog priority to log failures... badpri
checking how long a line in the log file should be... 80
checking whether sudo should ignore '.' or '' in $PATH... no
checking whether to send mail when a user is not in sudoers... yes
checking whether to send mail when user listed but not for this host...
no
checking whether to send mail when a user tries a disallowed command...
no
checking who should get the mail that sudo sends... root
checking for bad password prompt... Password:
checking for bad password message... Sorry, try again.
checking whether to expect fully qualified hosts in sudoers... no
checking for umask programs should be run with... 0022
checking for default user to run commands as... root
checking for editor that visudo should use... vi
checking whether to obey EDITOR and VISUAL environment variables... no
checking number of tries a user gets to enter their password... 3
checking time in minutes after which sudo will ask for a password
again... 5
checking time in minutes after the password prompt will time out... 5
checking whether to use per-tty ticket files... no
checking whether to include insults... no
checking whether to override the user's path... no
checking whether to get ip addresses from the network interfaces... yes
checking whether to do user authentication by default... yes
checking whether to disable running the mailer as root... no
checking whether to disable use of POSIX saved ids... no
checking whether to disable shadow password support... no
checking whether root should be allowed to use sudo... yes
checking whether to log the hostname in the log file... no
checking whether to invoke a shell if sudo is given no arguments... no
checking whether to set $HOME to target user in shell mode... no
checking whether to disable 'command not found' messages... no
checking for egrep... egrep
```

Listing 14.2 Command output—./configure.

```
checking for gcc... no
checking for cc... cc
checking for C compiler default output... a.out
checking whether the C compiler works... yes
checking whether we are cross compiling... no
checking for executable suffix...
checking for object suffix... o
checking whether we are using the GNU C compiler... no
checking whether cc accepts -g... (cached) no
checking for POSIXized ISC... no
checking for cc option to accept ANSI C... none needed
checking how to run the C preprocessor... cc -E
checking for uname... uname
checking for tr... tr
checking for sed... sed
checking for nroff... nroff
checking build system type... powerpc-ibm-aix5.1.0.0
checking host system type... powerpc-ibm-aix5.1.0.0
checking for getspnam... no
checking for getspnam in -lgen... no
checking for getprpwnam... no
checking for an ANSI C-conforming const... yes
checking for working volatile... yes
checking for bison... no
checking for byacc... no
checking for mv... /usr/bin/mv
checking for bourne shell... /bin/sh
checking for sendmail... /usr/sbin/sendmail
checking for vi... /usr/bin/vi
checking for ANSI C header files... yes
checking for dirent.h that defines DIR... yes
checking for opendir in -ldir... no
checking for malloc.h... yes
checking for paths.h... yes
checking for utime.h... yes
checking for netgroup.h... no
checking for sys/sockio.h... no
checking for sys/bsdtypes.h... no
checking for sys/select.h... yes
checking POSIX termios... yes
checking for sys/types.h... yes
checking for sys/stat.h... yes
checking for stdlib.h... yes
checking for string.h... yes
checking for memory.h... yes
checking for strings.h... yes
checking for inttypes.h... yes
```

Listing 14.2 Command output–./configure. *(continues)*

```
checking for stdint.h... no
checking for unistd.h... yes
checking for mode_t... yes
checking for uid_t in sys/types.h... yes
checking for sig_atomic_t... yes
checking for sigaction_t... no
checking for size_t... yes
checking for ssize_t... yes
checking for dev_t... yes
checking for ino_t... yes
checking for full void implementation... yes
checking max length of uid_t... 10
checking for long long support... yes
checking for sa_len field in struct sockaddr... yes
checking return type of signal handlers... void
checking for strchr... yes
checking for strrchr... yes
checking for memchr... yes
checking for memcpy... yes
checking for memset... yes
checking for sysconf... yes
checking for tzset... yes
checking for seteuid... yes
checking for setegid... yes
checking for strftime... yes
checking for setrlimit... yes
checking for initgroups... yes
checking for fstat... yes
checking for setreuid... yes
checking for getifaddrs... no
checking for getcwd... yes
checking for lockf... yes
checking for waitpid... yes
checking for innetgr... yes
checking for getdomainname... yes
checking for lsearch... yes
checking for utime... yes
checking for POSIX utime... yes
checking for working fnmatch with FNM_CASEFOLD... no
checking for isblank... yes
checking for strerror... yes
checking for strcasecmp... yes
checking for sigaction... yes
checking for snprintf... yes
checking for vsnprintf... yes
checking for asprintf... no
checking for vasprintf... no
```

Listing 14.2   Command output—./configure. *(continued)*

```
checking for crypt... yes
checking for socket... yes
checking for inet_addr... yes
checking for syslog... yes
checking for log file location... /var/adm/sudo.log
checking for timestamp file location... /tmp/.odus
configure: creating ./config.status
config.status: creating Makefile
config.status: creating sudo.man
config.status: creating visudo.man
config.status: creating sudoers.man
config.status: creating config.h
config.status: creating pathnames.h
```

Listing 14.2   Command output—./configure. *(continued)*

After the **configure** command completes without error, you have a customized `Makefile` for your system. You can, if you need to, edit the `Makefile` and change the default paths and the compiler to use. Now that we have a new customized `Makefile` we can now compile the **sudo** program on the system. Issue the following command, assuming you are still in the `/usr/local/sudo-1.6.6` directory:

```
make
```

The **make** command is located in `/usr/bin/make` on most systems, and it uses the `Makefile` in the current directory to compile, in our case `/usr/local/sudo-1.6.6`. The **make** command output is shown in Listing 14.3. Notice that my system uses the **cc** compiler.

```
    cc -c -I. -I.  -D_XOPEN_EXTENDED_SOURCE  -
D_PATH_SUDOERS=\"/etc/sudoers\" -D_PATH_SUDOERS_TMP=\"/etc/sudoers.tmp\"
-DSUDOERS_UID=0 -DSUDOERS_GID=0 -DSUDOERS_MODE=0440  check.c
    cc -c -I. -I.  -D_XOPEN_EXTENDED_SOURCE  -
D_PATH_SUDOERS=\"/etc/sudoers\" -D_PATH_SUDOERS_TMP=\"/etc/sudoers.tmp\"
-DSUDOERS_UID=0 -DSUDOERS_GID=0 -DSUDOERS_MODE=0440  env.c
    cc -c -I. -I.  -D_XOPEN_EXTENDED_SOURCE  -
D_PATH_SUDOERS=\"/etc/sudoers\" -D_PATH_SUDOERS_TMP=\"/etc/sudoers.tmp\"
-DSUDOERS_UID=0 -DSUDOERS_GID=0 -DSUDOERS_MODE=0440  getspwuid.c
    cc -c -I. -I.  -D_XOPEN_EXTENDED_SOURCE  -
D_PATH_SUDOERS=\"/etc/sudoers\" -D_PATH_SUDOERS_TMP=\"/etc/sudoers.tmp\"
-DSUDOERS_UID=0 -DSUDOERS_GID=0 -DSUDOERS_MODE=0440  goodpath.c
```

Listing 14.3   Command output—make command. *(continues)*

```
     cc -c -I. -I.  -D_XOPEN_EXTENDED_SOURCE  -
D_PATH_SUDOERS=\"/etc/sudoers\" -D_PATH_SUDOERS_TMP=\"/etc/sudoers.tmp\"
-DSUDOERS_UID=0 -DSUDOERS_GID=0 -DSUDOERS_MODE=0440  fileops.c
     cc -c -I. -I.  -D_XOPEN_EXTENDED_SOURCE  -
D_PATH_SUDOERS=\"/etc/sudoers\" -D_PATH_SUDOERS_TMP=\"/etc/sudoers.tmp\"
-DSUDOERS_UID=0 -DSUDOERS_GID=0 -DSUDOERS_MODE=0440  find_path.c
     cc -c -I. -I.  -D_XOPEN_EXTENDED_SOURCE  -
D_PATH_SUDOERS=\"/etc/sudoers\" -D_PATH_SUDOERS_TMP=\"/etc/sudoers.tmp\"
-DSUDOERS_UID=0 -DSUDOERS_GID=0 -DSUDOERS_MODE=0440  interfaces.c
     cc -c -I. -I.  -D_XOPEN_EXTENDED_SOURCE  -
D_PATH_SUDOERS=\"/etc/sudoers\" -D_PATH_SUDOERS_TMP=\"/etc/sudoers.tmp\"
-DSUDOERS_UID=0 -DSUDOERS_GID=0 -DSUDOERS_MODE=0440  logging.c
     cc -c -I. -I.  -D_XOPEN_EXTENDED_SOURCE  -
D_PATH_SUDOERS=\"/etc/sudoers\" -D_PATH_SUDOERS_TMP=\"/etc/sudoers.tmp\"
-DSUDOERS_UID=0 -DSUDOERS_GID=0 -DSUDOERS_MODE=0440  parse.c
     cc -c -I. -I.  -D_XOPEN_EXTENDED_SOURCE  -
D_PATH_SUDOERS=\"/etc/sudoers\" -D_PATH_SUDOERS_TMP=\"/etc/sudoers.tmp\"
-DSUDOERS_UID=0 -DSUDOERS_GID=0 -DSUDOERS_MODE=0440  set_perms.c
     cc -c -I. -I.  -D_XOPEN_EXTENDED_SOURCE  -
D_PATH_SUDOERS=\"/etc/sudoers\" -D_PATH_SUDOERS_TMP=\"/etc/sudoers.tmp\"
-DSUDOERS_UID=0 -DSUDOERS_GID=0 -DSUDOERS_MODE=0440  sudo.c
     cc -c -I. -I.  -D_XOPEN_EXTENDED_SOURCE  -
D_PATH_SUDOERS=\"/etc/sudoers\" -D_PATH_SUDOERS_TMP=\"/etc/sudoers.tmp\"
-DSUDOERS_UID=0 -DSUDOERS_GID=0 -DSUDOERS_MODE=0440  tgetpass.c
     cc -c -I. -I.  -D_XOPEN_EXTENDED_SOURCE  -
D_PATH_SUDOERS=\"/etc/sudoers\" -D_PATH_SUDOERS_TMP=\"/etc/sudoers.tmp\"
-DSUDOERS_UID=0 -DSUDOERS_GID=0 -DSUDOERS_MODE=0440  ./auth/sudo_auth.c
     cc -c -I. -I.  -D_XOPEN_EXTENDED_SOURCE  -
D_PATH_SUDOERS=\"/etc/sudoers\" -D_PATH_SUDOERS_TMP=\"/etc/sudoers.tmp\"
-DSUDOERS_UID=0 -DSUDOERS_GID=0 -DSUDOERS_MODE=0440  ./auth/passwd.c
     cc -c -I. -I.  -D_XOPEN_EXTENDED_SOURCE  -
D_PATH_SUDOERS=\"/etc/sudoers\" -D_PATH_SUDOERS_TMP=\"/etc/sudoers.tmp\"
-DSUDOERS_UID=0 -DSUDOERS_GID=0 -DSUDOERS_MODE=0440  sudo.tab.c
     cc -c -I. -I.  -D_XOPEN_EXTENDED_SOURCE  -
D_PATH_SUDOERS=\"/etc/sudoers\" -D_PATH_SUDOERS_TMP=\"/etc/sudoers.tmp\"
-DSUDOERS_UID=0 -DSUDOERS_GID=0 -DSUDOERS_MODE=0440  lex.yy.c
     cc -c -I. -I.  -D_XOPEN_EXTENDED_SOURCE  -
D_PATH_SUDOERS=\"/etc/sudoers\" -D_PATH_SUDOERS_TMP=\"/etc/sudoers.tmp\"
-DSUDOERS_UID=0 -DSUDOERS_GID=0 -DSUDOERS_MODE=0440  alloc.c
     cc -c -I. -I.  -D_XOPEN_EXTENDED_SOURCE  -
D_PATH_SUDOERS=\"/etc/sudoers\" -D_PATH_SUDOERS_TMP=\"/etc/sudoers.tmp\"
-DSUDOERS_UID=0 -DSUDOERS_GID=0 -DSUDOERS_MODE=0440  defaults.c
     cc -c -I. -I.  -D_XOPEN_EXTENDED_SOURCE  -
D_PATH_SUDOERS=\"/etc/sudoers\" -D_PATH_SUDOERS_TMP=\"/etc/sudoers.tmp\"
-DSUDOERS_UID=0 -DSUDOERS_GID=0 -DSUDOERS_MODE=0440  fnmatch.c
     cc -c -I. -I.  -D_XOPEN_EXTENDED_SOURCE  -
D_PATH_SUDOERS=\"/etc/sudoers\" -D_PATH_SUDOERS_TMP=\"/etc/sudoers.tmp\"
-DSUDOERS_UID=0 -DSUDOERS_GID=0 -DSUDOERS_MODE=0440  snprintf.c
```

Listing 14.3 Command output—make command. *(continued)*

```
     cc -o sudo check.o env.o getspwuid.o goodpath.o fileops.o
find_path.o  interfaces.o logging.o parse.o set_perms.o sudo.o
tgetpass.o  sudo_auth.o  passwd.o sudo.tab.o lex.yy.o alloc.o defaults.o
fnmatch.o snprintf.o  -Wl,-bI:./aixcrypt.exp
     cc -c -I. -I.  -D_XOPEN_EXTENDED_SOURCE  -
D_PATH_SUDOERS=\"/etc/sudoers\" -D_PATH_SUDOERS_TMP=\"/etc/sudoers.tmp\"
-DSUDOERS_UID=0 -DSUDOERS_GID=0 -DSUDOERS_MODE=0440  visudo.c
     cc -o visudo visudo.o fileops.o goodpath.o find_path.o sudo.tab.o
lex.yy.o alloc.o defaults.o fnmatch.o snprintf.o
Target "all" is up to date.
```

Listing 14.3   Command output—make command. *(continued)*

After the **make** command completes, we have custom compiled code for your
system, but we still have one more installation step to complete before we are ready to
configure **sudo**. This last step is to install the compiled files created with the **make**
command. The next command handles the installation of **sudo**:

```
make install
```

Remember that the **make** command is usually located in /usr/bin and should be
in your $PATH. The output of the **make install** command for my machine is shown in
Listing 14.4.

```
     /bin/sh ./mkinstalldirs /usr/local/bin  /usr/local/sbin /etc
/usr/local/man/man8 /usr/local/man/man5
     /bin/sh ./install-sh -c -O 0 -G 0 -M 4111 -s sudo
/usr/local/bin/sudo
     /bin/sh ./install-sh -c -O 0 -G 0 -M 0111 -s visudo
/usr/local/sbin/visudo
     test -f /etc/sudoers ||  /bin/sh ./install-sh -c -O 0 -G 0 -M 0440
./sudoers /etc/sudoers
     /bin/sh ./install-sh -c -O 0 -G 0 -M 0444 ./sudo.man
/usr/local/man/man8/sudo.8
     /bin/sh ./install-sh -c -O 0 -G 0 -M 0444 ./visudo.man
/usr/local/man/man8/visudo.8
     /bin/sh ./install-sh -c -O 0 -G 0 -M 0444 ./sudoers.man
/usr/local/man/man5/sudoers.5
Target "install" is up to date.
```

Listing 14.4   Command output—make install.

If you did not have any failures during the compilation and installation processes,
then **sudo** is installed but not yet configured. In the next section we will look at two
sample configuration files.

Configuring sudo

Configuring **sudo** is where a lot of people get a bit confused. The configuration is not too difficult if you take small steps and test each part as you build the configuration file. If you look in /etc after the installation is complete, you will see a file called sudoers. The sudoers file is used to configure the commands and users for the **sudo** program. Be very careful to *never directly edit* the sudoers file! A special program is supplied that has a wrapper around the **vi** editor called **visudo**, or *vi sudo*.

The **visudo** program resides in /usr/local/sbin by default. The nice thing about **visudo** is that it checks the /etc/sudoers file for any errors before saving the file. If errors are detected, the **visudo** program will tell you exactly what the error is and in most cases the line the error is on. If you directly edit the /etc/sudoers file and you make a mistake, the editor will just let you save the file, with the mistake, and it can be difficult to find the error. The **visudo** program checks for the correct file format and ensures that the command/user references are consistent. If you make a mistake with a user name, the **visudo** editor will not catch the mistake, but this type of error should be easy to find and correct after an initial run.

I am enclosing two samples of a /etc/sudoers file for you to use as a template in Listings 14.5 and 14.6.

NOTE The sudoers file in Listing 14.5 is used with the permission of Todd Miller at **www.courtesan.com** and is included in the sudo distribution as a sample. Thank you, Todd!

```
#
# Sample /etc/sudoers file.
#
# This file MUST be edited with the 'visudo' command as root.
#
# See the sudoers man page for the details on how to write a sudoers
file.
#


##
# User alias specification
##
User_Alias      FULLTIMERS = millert, mikef, dowdy
User_Alias      PARTTIMERS = bostley, jwfox, crawl
User_Alias      WEBMASTERS = will, wendy, wim


##
# Runas alias specification
##
```

Listing 14.5 Sample /etc/sudoers file #1.

```
Runas_Alias  OP = root, operator
Runas_Alias  DB = oracle, sybase


##
# Host alias specification
##
Host_Alias   SPARC = bigtime, eclipse, moet, anchor:\
             SGI = grolsch, dandelion, black:\
             ALPHA = widget, thalamus, foobar:\
             HPPA = boa, nag, python
Host_Alias   CUNETS = 128.138.0.0/255.255.0.0
Host_Alias   CSNETS = 128.138.243.0, 128.138.204.0/24, 128.138.242.0
Host_Alias   SERVERS = master, mail, www, ns
Host_Alias   CDROM = orion, perseus, hercules


##
# Cmnd alias specification
##
Cmnd_Alias   DUMPS = /usr/sbin/dump, /usr/sbin/rdump, /usr/sbin/restore,
\
                     /usr/sbin/rrestore, /usr/bin/mt
Cmnd_Alias   KILL = /usr/bin/kill
Cmnd_Alias   PRINTING = /usr/sbin/lpc, /usr/bin/lprm
Cmnd_Alias   SHUTDOWN = /usr/sbin/shutdown
Cmnd_Alias   HALT = /usr/sbin/halt, /usr/sbin/fasthalt
Cmnd_Alias   REBOOT = /usr/sbin/reboot, /usr/sbin/fastboot
Cmnd_Alias   SHELLS = /usr/bin/sh, /usr/bin/csh, /usr/bin/ksh, \
                      /usr/local/bin/tcsh, /usr/bin/rsh, \
                      /usr/local/bin/zsh
Cmnd_Alias   SU = /usr/bin/su
Cmnd_Alias   VIPW = /usr/sbin/vipw, /usr/bin/passwd, /usr/bin/chsh, \
                    /usr/bin/chfn


##
# Override builtin defaults
##
Defaults              syslog=auth
Defaults:FULLTIMERS   !lecture
Defaults:millert      !authenticate
Defaults@SERVERS      log_year, logfile=/var/log/sudo.log


##
# User specification
##


# root and users in group wheel can run anything on any machine
# as any user
```

Listing 14.5 Sample /etc/sudoers file #1. *(continues)*

```
root          ALL = (ALL) ALL
%wheel        ALL = (ALL) ALL

# full time sysadmins can run anything on any machine without a password
FULLTIMERS    ALL = NOPASSWD: ALL

# part time sysadmins may run anything but need a password
PARTTIMERS    ALL = ALL

# jack may run anything on machines in CSNETS
jack          CSNETS = ALL

# lisa may run any command on any host in CUNETS (a class B network)
lisa          CUNETS = ALL

# operator may run maintenance commands and anything in /usr/oper/bin/
operator      ALL = DUMPS, KILL, PRINTING, SHUTDOWN, HALT, REBOOT,\
              /usr/oper/bin/

# joe may su only to operator
joe           ALL = /usr/bin/su operator

# pete may change passwords for anyone but root on the hp snakes
pete          HPPA = /usr/bin/passwd [A-z]*, !/usr/bin/passwd root

# bob may run anything on the sparc and sgi machines as any user
# listed in the Runas_Alias "OP" (ie: root and operator)
bob           SPARC = (OP) ALL : SGI = (OP) ALL

# jim may run anything on machines in the biglab netgroup
jim           +biglab = ALL

# users in the secretaries netgroup need to help manage the printers
# as well as add and remove users
+secretaries  ALL = PRINTING, /usr/bin/adduser, /usr/bin/rmuser

# fred can run commands as oracle or sybase without a password
fred          ALL = (DB) NOPASSWD: ALL

# on the alphas, john may su to anyone but root and flags are not
allowed
john          ALPHA = /usr/bin/su [!-]*, !/usr/bin/su *root*

# jen can run anything on all machines except the ones
# in the "SERVERS" Host_Alias
```

Listing 14.5 Sample /etc/sudoers file #1. *(continued)*

```
jen          ALL, !SERVERS = ALL


# jill can run any commands in the directory /usr/bin/, except for
# those in the SU and SHELLS aliases.
jill         SERVERS = /usr/bin/, !SU, !SHELLS


# steve can run any command in the directory /usr/local/op_commands/
# as user operator.
steve        CSNETS = (operator) /usr/local/op_commands/


# matt needs to be able to kill things on his workstation when
# they get hung.
matt         valkyrie = KILL


# users in the WEBMASTERS User_Alias (will, wendy, and wim)
# may run any command as user www (which owns the web pages)
# or simply su to www.
WEBMASTERS   www = (www) ALL, (root) /usr/bin/su www


# anyone can mount/unmount a CD-ROM on the machines in the CDROM alias
ALL          CDROM = NOPASSWD: /sbin/umount /CDROM,\
             /sbin/mount -o nosuid\,nodev /dev/cd0a /CDROM
```

Listing 14.5   Sample /etc/sudoers file #1. *(continued)*


```
# sudoers file.
#
# This file MUST be edited with the 'visudo' command as root.
#
# See the sudoers man page for the details on how to write a sudoers
file.
#
# Users Identification:
#
# All ROOT access:
#
# d7742 - Michael
#
# Restricted Access to: mount umount and exportfs
#
#
```

Listing 14.6   Sample /etc/sudoers file #2. *(continues)*

```
# Restricted Access to: Start and stop Fasttrack Web Server
#
# d3920 - Park
# d7525 - Brinker
# d7794 - Doan
#
# Restricted OPERATIONS access
#
# d6331 - Sutter
# d6814 - Martin
# d8422 - Smith
# d9226 - Milando
# d9443 - Summers
# d0640 - Lawson
# d2105 - Fanchin
# d2188 - Grizzle
# d3408 - Foster
# d3551 - Dennis
# d3883 - Nations
# d6290 - Alexander
# d2749 - Mayo
# d6635 - Wright
# d3916 - Chatman
# d6782 - Scott
# d6810 - Duckery
# d6811 - Wells
# d6817 - Gilliam
# d5123 - Crynick
# d7504 - Davis
# d7505 - McCaskey
# d7723 - Rivers
#
# Host alias specification

Host_Alias    LOCAL=yogi

# User alias specification

User_Alias    NORMAL=d7742,d7537,d7526,d6029,d7204,d1076,d7764,d7808
User_Alias    ADMIN=e17742,d7211,d6895,d8665,d7539,b003
User_Alias    ORACLE=d7742
User_Alias    SAP=d7742
User_Alias OPERATOR=d7742,d6895,d6331,d6814,d8422,d9226,d9443,d0640,
d2105,d2188,d3408,d3551,d3883,d6290,d2749,d6635,d3916,d6782,d6810,
```

Listing 14.6   Sample /etc/sudoers file #2. *(continued)*

```
d6811,d6817,d5123,d7504,d7505,d7723
User_Alias FASTTRACK=d3920,d7525,d7794

# Cmnd alias specification

Cmnd_Alias    MNT=/usr/bin/mount
Cmnd_Alias    UMNT=/usr/bin/umount
Cmnd_Alias    EXP_FS=/usr/bin/exportfs
Cmnd_Alias    KILL=/usr/bin/kill
Cmnd_Alias    ROOT_SU=/usr/bin/su -
Cmnd_Alias    SU_ROOT=/usr/bin/su - root
Cmnd_Alias    SUROOT=/usr/bin/su root
Cmnd_Alias    ORACLE_SU=/usr/bin/su - oracle
Cmnd_Alias    SAP_SU=/usr/bin/su - sap
Cmnd_Alias    TCPDUMP=/usr/sbin/tcpdump
Cmnd_Alias    ERRPT=/usr/bin/errpt
Cmnd_Alias    SVRMGRL=/oracle/product/8.0.5/bin/svrmgrl
Cmnd_Alias    RSH_UPDATE=/usr/local/bin/rsh_update.ksh
Cmnd_Alias    START_FT_YOGI=/usr/netscape/httpd-yogi/start
Cmnd_Alias    STOP_FT_YOGI=/usr/netscape/httpd-yogi/stop
Cmnd_Alias    START_FT_DINO=/usr/netscape/httpd-dino/start
Cmnd_Alias    STOP_FT_DINO=/usr/netscape/httpd-dino/stop
Cmnd_Alias    START_WSADM=/usr/netscape/start-admin
Cmnd_Alias    STOP_WSADM=/usr/netscape/stop-admin

# User privilege specification

# FULL ROOT ACCESS!!!!!! (BE CAREFUL GRANTING FULL ROOT!!!!!!!)
root  ALL=(ALL) ALL
d7742 ALL=(ALL) ALL # Michael

# Only mount, umount and exportfs
NORMAL        LOCAL=MNT,UMNT,EXP_FS

# Some Limited Sys Admin Functions
ADMIN LOCAL=MNT,UMNT,KILL,ORACLE_SU,SAP_SU,TCPDUMP,ERRPT,ROOT_SU: \
      LOCAL=SU_ROOT,SUROOT,EXP_FS

# Some Operator Functions
OPERATOR LOCAL=RSH_UPDATE

# Some FastTrack/WebAdm Functions
FASTTRACK
LOCAL=START_FT_E1,STOP_FT_E1,START_FT_E2,STOP_FT_E2,START_WSADM,
```

Listing 14.6   Sample /etc/sudoers file #2. *(continues)*

```
STOP_WSADM

# Override Defaults

# Change the default location of the SUDO log file
Defaults       logfile=/var/adm/sudo.log
```

Listing 14.6   Sample /etc/sudoers file #2. *(continued)*

As you can see by the two sample /etc/sudoers files, you can get as detailed as you want. As you look at these files, notice that there are four kinds of aliases: User_Alias, Runas_Alias, Host_Alias, and Cmd_Alias. The use of each alias type is listed next.

A User_Alias is a list that can contain any combination of usernames, UID (with a "#" prefix), system groups (with a "%" prefix), netgroups (with a "+" prefix), and other user-defined aliases. Any of these can be prefixed with the NOT operator, "!", to negate the entry.

A Runas_Alias can contain any of the same elements as the User_Alias; the only difference is that you use Runas_Alias instead of User_Alias in the configuration. The Runas_Alias allows execution of a command as a user other than **root**.

A Host_Alias is a list of hostnames, IP addresses, or netgroups (with a "+" prefix). The Host_Alias also supports the NOT operator, "!", to negate an entry. You will need to use the fully qualified DNS name if the **hostname** command on any machine returns the name of the machine in a fully qualified DNS format. The **visudo** editor will not catch this "error."

A Cmnd_Alias is list of one or more commands specified by a *full pathname*, not just the filename. You can also specify directories and other aliases to commands. The command alone will allow command arguments to the command, but you can disable command arguments using double quotes (" "). If a directory is specified a user can execute any command within that directory, but *not* any subdirectories. Wildcards are allowed, but be very careful to ensure that the wildcard is working as expected.

I am not going to discuss every piece of **sudo** because very detailed documentation is included with the **sudo** distribution, and I need to limit my page count in this book. Our next step is to look at how to use **sudo** and how to use **sudo** in a shell script.

Using sudo

We use **sudo** by preceding the command that we want to run with the word **sudo**. As an example, if my user ID is **rmichael** and I want to gain **root** access for the first time, I will follow these steps:

```
PATH=$PATH:/usr/local/bin
export PATH
sudo su - root

We trust you have received the usual lecture from the local System
Administrator. It usually boils down to these two things:

        #1) Respect the privacy of others.
        #2) Think before you type.

Password:
yogi@/#
```

Listing 14.7   Using sudo for the first time.

Notice the short lecture that is displayed in Listing 14.7. This lecture message is displayed only the first time that **sudo** is used by each user. In the password field the user responds with his or her normal user account password, *not* the **root** password. You should be careful granting full **root** permission like this. Allowing a user to **su** to root via the **sudo** program does not leave an audit trail of what the user did as root! You should still have the root history file if the user did not delete or edit the file. Also notice in Listing 14.7 that I added /usr/local/bin to my **$PATH**. By default the **sudo** command is located in the /usr/local/bin directory, but most shops do not add this directory to the **$PATH** environment variable as a normal path when setting up user accounts. Just make sure that *all sudo users* have the **sudo** command in the **$PATH** or that they need to provide the full pathname to the **sudo** command.

Using sudo in a Shell Script

We can also use **sudo** in a shell script. As you create the shell script add the **sudo** command as a prefix to each command that you want to execute as **root**. The script in Listing 14.8 uses the **sudo** command to allow our Operations Team to reset passwords.

On an AIX system you can manage user passwords with the **pwdadm** command. In this particular shell script we want our Operations Team to be able to change a user's password from a menu selection in a shell script. The bold text shown in Listing 14.8 points out the use of **sudo** and also the use of the **tput** command for reverse video, which we will study further in Chapter 15.

```
#!/usr/bin/ksh
#
# SCRIPT: chpwd_menu.ksh
# AUTHOR: Randy Michael
# DATE: 11/05/2001
# PLATFORM: AIX
# REV: 1.1.P
#
# PURPOSE: This script was created for the Operations Team
#          to change user passwords. This shell script uses
#          "sudo" to execute the "pwdadm" command as root.
#          Each member of the Operations Team needs to be
#          added to the /etc/sudoers file. CAUTION: When
#          editing the /etc/sudoers file always use the
#          /usr/local/sbin/visudo program editor!!!
#          NEVER DIRECTLY EDIT THE sudoers FILE!!!!
#
# REV LIST:
#
# set -x # Uncomment to debug this script
# set -n # Uncomment to check syntax without any execution
#
#######################################################
#         DEFINE FUNCTIONS HERE
#######################################################

function chg_pwd
{
USER_NAME="$1"

echo "\nThe next password prompt is for YOUR NORMAL PASSWORD"
echo "NOT the new password..."

# The next command turns off the checking of the password history

/usr/local/bin/sudo /usr/bin/pwdadm -f NOCHECK $USER_NAME
if [ $? -ne 0 ]
then
        echo "\nERROR: Turning off password history failed..."
        usage
        exit 1
fi

# The next command changes the user's password

/usr/local/bin/sudo /usr/bin/pwdadm $USER_NAME
```

Listing 14.8 chpwd_menu.ksh shell script listing.

```
if [ $? -ne 0 ]
then
        echo "\nERROR: Changing $USER_NAME password failed..."
        usage
        exit 1
fi

# The next command forces the user to change his or her password
# at the next login.

/usr/local/bin/sudo /usr/bin/pwdadm -f ADMCHG $USER_NAME

return 0
}


##########################################################
#                    START OF MAIN
##########################################################

OPT=0       # Initialize to zero

clear       # Clear the screen

while [[ $OPT != 99 ]] # Start a loop
do

# Draw reverse image bar across the top of the screen
# with the system name.

clear
tput smso
echo "                           $(hostname)                           "
tput sgr0
echo ""

# Draw menu options.

echo "\n\n\n\n\n\n\n"

print "10. Change Password"

echo "\n\n\n\n\n\n\n\n\n"

print "99. Exit Menu"

# Draw reverse image bar across bottom of screen,
```

Listing 14.8   chpwd_menu.ksh shell script listing. *(continues)*

```
# with error message, if any.

tput smso
echo "              $MSG                    "
tput sgr0

# Prompt for menu option.

read OPT

# Assume invalid selection was taken.  Message is always
# displayed, so blank it out when a valid option is selected.

MSG="       Invalid option selected            "
# Option 10 - Change Password

if [ $OPT -eq 10 ]
then
        echo "\nUsername for password change? \c"
        read USERNAME
        grep $USERNAME /etc/passwd >/dev/null 2>&1
        if [ $? -eq 0 ]
        then
                chg_pwd $USERNAME
                if [ $? -eq 0 ]
                then
                        MSG="$USERNAME password successfully changed"
                else
                        MSG="ERROR: $USERNAME password change failed"
                fi
        else
                MSG="   ERROR: Invalid username $USERNAME      "
        fi
fi

# End of Option 99 Loop

done

# Erase menu from screen upon exiting.

clear
```

Listing 14.8 chpwd_menu.ksh shell script listing. *(continued)*

The chpwd_menu.ksh shell script in Listing 14.8 displays a menu on the screen that has only two options, change a user's password or exit. This shell script uses the **sudo** program to execute the **pwdadm** command as the **root** user. The **pwdadm** command is used for password administration in AIX and has options to turn password history checking off and to force password changes on the next login attempt. The **pwdadm** command is executed three times in the chg_pwd function within the shell script. The first time **pwdadm** is executed as **root** we turn off the checking of the password history. Notice that I added a comment to the staff that the next password prompt is for *their normal user password*, not the new user password. I turn off the history checking because the password that the Operation Team is going to enter is a temporary password. The next time the user logs in, the system will prompt for a new password, and at this stage the password history will be checked. The second time that **pwdadm** is executed, the password is actually changed by the Operations Team member. The third time **pwdadm** is executed, the user is forced to change his or her password the next time they log in. Each time **sudo** is used to execute **pwdadm** as **root**.

Also notice the **tput** commands. The **tput** command has many options to control the cursor and the terminal. In this script we are using reverse video to display the hostname of the machine in the menu title bar at the top and to display messages at the bottom of the menu. There is much more on the **tput** command options in Chapter 15.

The sudo Log File

Before we end this chapter I want to show you what the **sudo** log file looks like. Each time that **sudo** is executed, an entry is made in the specified log. Logging can be to a file or to the system syslog. I specify a log file in the /etc/sudoers, but you may prefer the syslog. A short version of my **sudo** log file is shown in Listing 14.9.

```
Nov  9 10:07:44 : d7742 : TTY=pts/2 ; PWD=/usr/local ; USER=root ;
    COMMAND=/usr/bin/ftp bambam
Nov  9 10:09:13 : d7742 : TTY=pts/2 ; PWD=/usr/local ; USER=root ;
    COMMAND=/usr/bin/ftp dino
Nov 13 10:10:48 : d7742 : TTY=pts/0 ; PWD=/home/guest ; USER=root ;
    COMMAND=/usr/bin/whoami
Jul 23 17:35:47 : d7996 : TTY=pts/3 ; PWD=/home/guest ; USER=root ;
    COMMAND=/usr/sbin/mount /usr/local/common
Oct  2 09:29:33 : d7742 : TTY=pts/1 ; PWD=/home/d7742 ; USER=root ;
    COMMAND=/usr/bin/su -
Nov 14 16:01:31 : d7742 : TTY=pts/0 ; PWD=/home/d7742 ; USER=root ;
    COMMAND=/usr/bin/su - root
Nov 14 16:03:58 : rmichael : TTY=pts/0 ; PWD=/home/rmichael ; USER=root
;
    COMMAND=/usr/bin/su - root
Nov 15 11:31:32 : d7742 : TTY=pts/0 ; PWD=/scripts ; USER=root ;
    COMMAND=/usr/bin/pwdadm -f NOCHECK rmichael
Nov 15 11:31:32 : d7742 : TTY=pts/0 ; PWD=/scripts ; USER=root ;
    COMMAND=/usr/bin/pwdadm rmichael
Nov 15 11:31:32 : d7742 : TTY=pts/0 ; PWD=/scripts ; USER=root ;
```

Listing 14.9   Sample sudo log file. *(continues)*

```
    COMMAND=/usr/bin/pwdadm -f ADMCHG rmichael
Nov 15 14:58:49 : root : TTY=pts/0 ; PWD=/usr/local/sudo-1.6.3p7 ;
    USER=root ; COMMAND=/usr/bin/errpt
Nov 15 14:59:50 : d7742 : 3 incorrect password attempts ; TTY=pts/0 ;
    PWD=/home/d7742 ; USER=root ; COMMAND=/usr/bin/errpt
```

Listing 14.9 Sample sudo log file. *(continued)*

In Listing 14.9 notice the last line of output. This line shows three incorrect password attempts. You can set up **sudo** to send an email on each password failure if you want immediate notification of misuse. The shell script in Listing 14.8 produced three log entries on each password change. I have highlighted several other entries for **ftp** and **su** to root to show you how the log entries look.

Summary

Through this chapter we have shown how to compile, install, configure, and use the **sudo** program. We all know that protecting the **root** password is one of our main tasks as a Systems Administrator, and **sudo** makes the job a little less difficult. When you use **sudo** in a shell script, it is important that each user is familiar with **sudo** and has used it at least once from the command line. Remember that on the first use the lecture message is displayed and you do not want a lecture in the middle of a menu! In the **sudo** distribution there are several files that you should review. The README file has valuable information in installation and a lot of OS-specific problems and workarounds. The FAQ file answers the most frequently asked questions. The Sudoers Manual is a must read! This manual describes the many options in configuring your `sudoers` file. Finally, we have the Visudo Manual that explains how to use the **visudo** editor and lists the command options and possible error conditions. Again, I want to thank Todd Miller at **www.courtesan.com** for allowing me to use his material in this chapter.

In the next chapter we are going to create a *highlight grep* script. If you have ever wanted to find a text string in a large file, you will really appreciate this script! The command syntax is exactly the same as the **grep** command, but instead of extracting the line that the **grep** command pattern matched on, we display the entire file and use reverse video to highlight the text within the file.

## CHAPTER 15

hgrep: Highlighted grep Script

Ever want to find text in a large file easily? The larger the text file, the more you will appreciate this shell script. We can use reverse video in shell scripts for more than just making pretty menus. What about highlighting text in a file or in a command's output? In this chapter we are going to show an example of using reverse video in a shell script that works similar to the **grep** command. Instead of displaying the line(s) that match the pattern, we are going to display the entire file, or command output, with the matched pattern highlighted in reverse video. I like to call this **hgrep**.

In the process of creating this shell script, an initial test script was developed that ended up being very complicated. It started by grepping each line for the specified pattern. If the pattern was found in the line, then a scan of the line, character by character, was started to locate the exact pattern in the line for highlighting, then we grepped again for the pattern in remaining line of text, and so on. This initial code had quite a few problems, other than the complicated nature of the script, caused by Unix special characters making the output do some very interesting things when scanning shell script code. Regular text files worked fine, but the script was *very* slow to execute.

Then there was the revelation that **sed** should somehow be able to handle the pattern matching—and do so a lot faster than parsing the file with a shell script. A Korn shell script is really not meant to work on a file line by line and *character by character*; it can be done, but this is what Perl is for! The problem to resolve using **sed** was how to add in the highlighting control within a **sed** command statement. After thinking about using **sed** and command substitution for a while, I had a working script in about 15 minutes (we might have a record!), and the following is what I came up with.

Reverse Video Control

There are two commands that control reverse video: **tput smso** turns *soft* reverse video on, and **tput rmso** turns highlighting back off. The **tput** command has many other options to control the terminal, but **tput sgr0** (sgr-zero) will turn every **tput** option off. To highlight text we turn reverse video on, print whatever we want highlighted, and then turn reverse video off. We can also save this output, with the highlighted text, in a file. To display the file with highlighted text we can use **pg**, or **page**, and on some operating systems **more** will work. The **more** command did not work on either AIX or HP-UX operating systems. Instead, the **more** command displayed the characters that make up the *escape sequence* for the highlighted text, not the highlighted text itself. You would see the same result using the **vi** editor. On Solaris both commands displayed the highlighted text, but not all operating systems have the **pg** and **page** commands.

There is one common mistake that will prevent this shell script from working, not double quoting the variables, for example `"$STRING"`. The double quotes have no effect on a single-word pattern match, but for multiword string patterns the variables *must* be double quoted or standard error will produce command usage errors within the script. The errors are due to the fact that each word that makes up the string pattern will be interpreted as a separate argument instead of one entity. The double quotes are very important when working with string variables. Forgetting the double quotes is a very hard error to find when troubleshooting code!

The **sed** command is next. Remember the basic **sed** syntax that we use in this book:

```
cat $FILENAME | sed s/current_string/new_string/g
```

In our script we want to take the **sed** command statement and redirect output to a file, then display the file with **pg**, **page**, or **more**.

```
cat $FILENAME | sed s/current_string/new_string/g > $OUTPUT_FILE

pg $OUTPUT_FILE
    --verse--
more $OUTPUT_FILE
```

To add in the reverse video piece we have to do some command substitution within the **sed** statement using the **tput** commands—this is the part that had to be worked out. Where we specify the `new_string` we will add in the control for reverse video using command substitution, one to turn highlighting on and one to turn it back off. When the command substitution is added, our **sed** statement will look like the following:

```
sed s/current_string/$(tput smso)new_string$(tput rmso)/g
```

In our case, the `current_string` and `new_string` will be the same because we only want to highlight existing text without changing it. We also want the string to be assigned to a variable, as in the next command:

```
sed s/"$STRING"/$(tput smso)"$STRING"$(tput rmso)/g
```

Notice the double quotes around the string variable, `"$STRING"`. Do not forget to add the double quotes around variables!

As an experiment using command substitution, try this next command statement on any Unix machine:

```
cat /etc/hosts | sed s/`hostname`/$(tput smso)`hostname`$(tput rmso)/g
```

In the preceding command statement notice that we used both types of command substitution, enclosing the command within back tics, `` `command` ``, and the dollar parentheses method, `$(command)`. The previous statement will **cat** the `/etc/hosts` file and highlight the machine's **hostname** in reverse video each time it appears in the file. Now try the same command, but this time pipe the command to **more**. Try the same command again using **pg** and **page** instead of **more**, if your machine supports the **page** commands. If your machine does not have the **pg** command, then the **more** command should work. If your operating system has both **pg** and **more**, notice that using **more** may not display the string pattern in reverse video—it will display the characters that make up the escape sequence that the **tput** commands create, but Solaris is an exception. We will need to consider this when we display the result on different operating systems.

To make this script have the same look and feel as the **grep** command, we want to be able to supply input via a file, as a command-line argument, or as standard input from a command pipe. When supplying a filename to the script as a command-line argument, we need to ensure that the file exists, its size is greater than zero bytes, it is readable by this script, and the string pattern is matched in the file. We could leave out the last step, but if the pattern is not in the file then it would be nice to let the user know. If we are getting input from standard input instead of a file specified as an argument— for example, `cat /etc/hosts | hgrep.ksh `` `hostname` `` `—then we need to check for the string pattern in the output file instead of the input file. Then we can still inform the user if the pattern is not found.

Building the hgrep.ksh Shell Script

Now that we have the basic command syntax, let's build the `hgrep.ksh` shell script. There are two types of input for this script, file input and standard input. For the file input we need to do some sanity checks so that we don't get standard error messages from the system. We also want to give the user some feedback if there is something that will cause an error using the specified file as input—for example, the file does not exist or is not readable by the script because of file permissions. The command syntax using the `hgrep.ksh` script should be the same as the **grep** command, which is:

```
grep pattern [filename]
```

By looking at this we can determine that we will sanity-check the file only when we have two command-line arguments; otherwise, we are using piped-in standard input, which implies that we check the file only when `$#` is equal to 2. We begin with checking the command-line arguments and making assignments of the arguments to variables.

```
if [ $# -eq 1 ]
then

    # Input coming from standard input

    PATTERN="$1" # Pattern to highlight
    FILENAME=    # Assign NULL to FILENAME

elif [ $# -eq 2 ]
then

    # Input coming from $FILENAME file

    PATTERN="$1"  # Pattern to highlight
    FILENAME="$2" # File to use as input
else
    # Incorrect number of command-line arguments

    usage
    exit 1
fi
```

We should now have enough to get us started. If we have a single command-line argument, then we assign $1 to PATTERN and assign the FILENAME variable a NULL value. If there are two command-line arguments, then we assign $1 to PATTERN and $2 to FILENAME. If we have zero or more than two arguments, then we display the usage message and exit with a return code of 1, one. The function for correct usage is listed here:

```
function usage
{
 echo "\nUSAGE: $SCRIPT_NAME  pattern  [filename]\n"
}
```

Follow through the hgrep.ksh script in Listing 15.1, and the process will be explained at the end of the shell script.

```
#!/usr/bin/ksh
#
# SCRIPT: hgrep.ksh
# AUTHOR: Randy Michael
# DATE: 03/09/2001
# REV 2.1.P
#
# PLATFORM: Not Platform Dependent...(Not very platform dependent)
#           There is a slight "more" command issue that has been
#           resolved
#
# PURPOSE: This script is used to highlight text in a file or standard
```

Listing 15.1 hgrep.ksh shell script.

```
#       input. Given a text string and a file, or standard input, the
#       script will search for the specified string and highlight each
#       occurrence of the string using command substitution within a
#       sed statement to turn on and off the reverse video. "tput smso"
#       turns on reverse video and "tput rmso" will turn it off.  This
#       script is a "highlighted grep" command.
#
# set -x         # Uncomment to debug
# set -n         # Uncomment to check command syntax without execution
#
# EXIT CODES:
#
#       0 ==> Script exited normally
#       1 ==> Usage error
#       2 ==> Input file error
#       3 ==> Pattern not found in the file
#
# REV LIST:
#          03/12/2001 - Randy Michael - Sr. Sys. Admin.
#          Added code to just exit if the string is not in
#          the target file.
#
#          03/13/2001 - Randy Michael - Sr. Sys. Admin.
#          Added code to ensure the target file is a readable "regular"
#          non-zero file.
#
#          03/13/2001 - Randy Michael - Sr. Sys. Admin.
#          Added code to highlight the text string and filename
#          in the error and information messages.
#
#          08-22-2001 - Randy Michael - Sr. Sys. Admin
#          Changed the code to allow this script to accept standard
#          input from a pipe.  This makes the script work more like the
#          grep command

SCRIPT_NAME=`basename $0`


##############################################
########## DEFINE FUNCTIONS HERE ############
##############################################


function usage
{
     echo "\nUSAGE: $SCRIPT_NAME  pattern  [filename]\n"
}


##############################################
########## CHECK COMMAND SYNTAX ############
```

Listing 15.1   hgrep.ksh shell script. *(continues)*

```
##############################################

if [ $# -eq 1 ]
then

    # Input coming from standard input

    PATTERN="$1" # Pattern to highlight
    FILENAME=    # Assign NULL to FILENAME

elif [ $# -eq 2 ]
then

    # Input coming from $FILENAME file

    PATTERN="$1"  # Pattern to highlight
    FILENAME="$2" # File to use as input

    # Perform sanity checks on the file!!!

    # Does the file exist as a "regular" file?

    if [[ ! -f $FILENAME ]]
    then
       echo "\nERROR: \c"
       tput smso
       echo "${FILENAME}\c" # Highlight the filename
       tput rmso
       echo " does not exist as a regular file...\n"
       usage
       exit 2
    fi

    # Is the file empty?

    if [[ ! -s $FILENAME ]]
    then
       echo "\nERROR: \c"
       tput smso
       echo "${FILENAME}\c" # Highlight the filename
       tput rmso
       echo " file size is zero...nothing to search\n"
       usage
       exit 2
    fi

    # Is the file readable by this script?

    if [[ ! -r $FILENAME ]]
    then
```

Listing 15.1   hgrep.ksh shell script. *(continued)*

```
            echo "\nERROR: \c"
            tput smso
            echo "${FILENAME}\c" # Highlight the filename
            tput rmso
            echo " is not readable to this program...\n"
            usage
            exit 2
    fi

    # Is the pattern anywhere in the file?

    grep "$PATTERN" $FILENAME >/dev/null 2>&1
    if [ $? -ne 0 ]
    then
            echo "\nSORRY: The string \c"
            tput smso
            echo "${PATTERN}\c" # Highlight the pattern
            tput rmso
            echo " was not found in \c"
            tput smso
            echo "${FILENAME}\c" # Highlight the filename
            tput rmso
            echo "\n\n....EXITING...\n"
            exit 3
    fi
else
    # Incorrect number of command line arguments

    usage
    exit 1
fi


#############################################
########### DEFINE VARIABLES HERE ###########
#############################################

OUTPUT_FILE="/tmp/highlightfile.out"
>$OUTPUT_FILE


#############################################
############ START OF MAIN ##################
#############################################

# If the $FILENAME varaible is NULL then input is from a command pipe
# Testing for NULL assigned to $FILENAME.

if [[ ! -z "$FILENAME" && "$FILENAME" != '' ]]
then
```

Listing 15.1   hgrep.ksh shell script. *(continues)*

```
        # Using $FILENAME as input


# MUST USE DOUBLE QUOTES AROUND $PATTERN!!! -> "$PATTERN"

    cat "$FILENAME" \
    | sed s/"${PATTERN}"/$(tput smso)"${PATTERN}"$(tput rmso)/g \
      > $OUTPUT_FILE
else
    # Input is from standard input...
    # MUST USE DOUBLE QUOTES AROUND $PATTERN!!! -> "$PATTERN"

    sed s/"${PATTERN}"/$(tput smso)"${PATTERN}"$(tput rmso)/g \
        > $OUTPUT_FILE

    # Check to see if the pattern was in the standard input
    grep "$PATTERN" $OUTOUT_FILE >/dev/null 2>&1
    if [ $? -ne 0 ]
    then
        echo "\nSORRY: The string \c"
        tput smso
        echo "${PATTERN}\c"
        tput rmso
        echo " was not found in standard input \c"
        echo "\n\n....EXITING...\n"
        exit 3
    fi
fi

# Check the operating system, on AIX and HP-UX we need to
# use the "pg", or "page" command.  The "more" command does
# not work to highlight the text, it will show only the
# characters that make up the escape sequence.  All
# other operating systems use the "more" command.

case $(uname) in
AIX|HP-UX)

    # This is a fancy "pg" command.  It acts similarly to the
    # "more" command but instead of showing the percentage
    # displayed it shows the page number of the file

    /usr/bin/cat $OUTPUT_FILE | /usr/bin/pg -csn -p"Page %d:"
  ;;
*)
```

Listing 15.1   hgrep.ksh shell script. *(continued)*

```
        /usr/bin/cat $OUTPUT_FILE | /usr/bin/more
    ;;
esac


rm -f $OUTPUT_FILE  # End of Script Cleanup
```

Listing 15.1   hgrep.ksh shell script. *(continued)*

In the shell script in Listing 15.1 we first check for the correct number of command-line arguments; either one or two arguments are valid. Otherwise, the script usage message is displayed, and the script will exit with a return code 1. If we have the correct number of arguments, then we assign the arguments to variables. If we have two command-line arguments, then an input file is specified in $2—at least it is supposed to be a file. We need to do some sanity checking on this second command-line argument by first checking to see that the file exists as a regular file. We do not want to do anything with the file if it is a block or character special file, a directory, or any other *nonregular* file. Next we make sure that the file is not empty. Then we ensure that the script can read the file, and finally we **grep** for the pattern in the file to see if we have anything to highlight. If all of the tests are passed, then we can proceed.

By checking if the $FILENAME variable is null, or empty, we know which type of input we are dealing with. A null or empty $FILENAME variable means we use standard input, which is input from a pipe in this case. If $FILENAME is not null, then we have a file specified as input to the script on the command line. The only difference in handling an input file versus standard input is that we will supply the "cat $FILENAME |" if there is an input file specified. Otherwise, the input is already coming in from a pipe directly into the **sed** statement—it's that simple. We have one more check before displaying the output. If we are using piped-in standard input, then we **grep** for "$PATTERN" in the $FILENAME to see if it exists. If not, we display a *string not found* message and exit.

The output display is interesting because **more** will not work on HP-UX or AIX to display the highlighted text. For HP-UX and AIX we use **pg** instead of **more**. To determine which flavor of Unix we are running, we use the **uname** command in a **case** statement. If the OS is either AIX or HP-UX, we used a *fancy* **pg** command, which has output that appears similar to the **more** output. Using **pg -csn -p"Page %d:"** will display the page number of the file, where **more** displays the percentage of file. All other Unix flavors will use **more** to display the output file.

The script in Listing 15.1 is a good example of how a little ingenuity can greatly simplify a challenge. We sometimes make things more complicated than they need to be, as in my initial test script that parsed through the file line by line and character by character, searching for the pattern. We live and learn!

Other Options to Consider

As with every script there is room for improvement or customization, however you want to look at it.

Other Options for the tput Command

The only **tput** command option that we worked with was the **tput smso** command, which is used to turn on highlighting. The **tput** command has many other options to control terminal display. In our example we did a highlight of not only the text but also the surrounding *block* for *each* character. We could also highlight only the text piece, double video the entire text block, underline with other options—for example, we could have underlined bold text. The **tput** command is fun to play with. The short list of command options is shown in Table 15.1.

Table 15.1 Options for the tput Command

tput bell	Ring the bell
tput blink	Start blinking mode
tput bold	Start double intensity (much brighter than reverse video)
tput civis	Turn the cursor off (make the cursor invisible)
tput cnorm	Make the cursor normal again
tput cr	Send a carriage to the terminal
tput cvvis	Make the cursor very bright
tput dim	Start one-half intensity mode
tput ed	Clear to the end of the display
tput el	Clear to the end of the line
tput flash	Send a visible bell (good to send a flash to someone's screen)
tput invis	Start invisible text mode
tput prot	Start protected mode
tput rc	Restore the last saved cursor position (paved by tput sc)
tput rev	Begin reverse video mode (bright!)
tput rmso	End the standout mode (reverses tput smso)
tput rmul	Ends the underline (underscore) mode
tput sc	Save the cursor position

Table 15.1   *(Continued)*

tput sgr0	Turn off all video modes
tput smso	Start the standout mode (soft reverse video we used in this chapter)
tput smul	Start the underline (underscore) mode
tput	Underscore one character and move to the next character

Table 15.1 is only an abbreviated listing of the **tput** command options. As you can see, we can do a lot with the text on the screen. Use your imagination, and play around with the commands.

Summary

In this chapter we introduced using reverse video to highlight text within our output. Also we showed how to do command substitution inside a **sed** command statement. There are many more options for the **tput** command to control the terminal; for example, we could have underlined the matching pattern. The nice thing about the **tput** command is that it will let you mix things up, too.

In the next chapter we are going to look at how to keep the printers in the landscape printing. If you do not automate this function you could spend all of your time doing printer management instead of doing any real work. See you in the next chapter!

## CHAPTER 16

Print Queue Hell: Keeping the Printers Printing

If you have worked in a large systems environment for very long you already know how frustrating it can be to keep the printer farm happy. In my contracting days I worked in several shops that consistently had problems with the printers. In most cases, the print queues went down because of network timeouts and extended device waits. In this kind of environment you have two choices: keep answering the calls from the help desk or write a shell script to monitor the printer queues and reenable the queues as they drop offline.

I prefer the second method. Like every other Systems Administrator, I like to be proactive in my approach to solving the little problems as well as the big ones. The shop I remember the best was a hospital. This hospital has more than 30 satellite clinics around town and only one 100MB/Sec pipe coming in to the hospital from the outside world. Most of the clinics have between three and five printers, with at least one printer active most of the day. When I came on board, the first problem I encountered was the huge volume of calls to the help desk about printer problems. What caught my eye was the fact that all of the calls came from the clinics, not from inside the hospital. I knew immediately that a shell script was in order! In this chapter we are going to look at two methods of bringing up the print queues, enabling individual queues and bringing up the whole lot. Because Unix flavors vary on handling printers and queues, we first will look at the differences between the Unix flavors.

System V versus BSD Printer Subsystems

Depending on the Unix flavor, the commands vary to control the printers and queues because some use the System V subsystem and others use BSD. With AIX you have an ever more confusing situation beginning with AIX 5L. Starting with this release, AIX now supports both the "classic" AIX printer subsystem *and* the System V printer service. Another problem is that some commands do not provide the full print queue name if the queue name exceeds seven characters. I have come up with some ways to get around the long queue names, and on most systems you do not have to worry about long queue names too much if you want to control *all* of the printers at once.

In this book we are covering AIX, HP-UX, Linux, and Solaris. For no other reason that I can think of, let's cover the printer systems in alphabetical order.

AIX Print Control Commands

AIX is the most interesting of the bunch with its new support for the System V printer service starting with AIX 5L. Although the AIX classic printer subsystem will still be supported for many years, the move seems to be going to System V for printing service.

Classic AIX Printer Subsystem

Most AIX Systems Administrators still prefer to use the classic AIX printer subsystem. This is the primary printing that I have supported for years. With the AIX printer subsystem you do not have the detailed control that the System V service offers. For example, you do not control forms and user priorities at a granular level, and you cannot manage the printers independently of the print queues easily. With this printer subsystem anyone can print on any printer, and the print queue is either UP, allowing you to print, or DOWN, disabling all printing. The shell scripts we are going to write for the classic AIX printer subsystem work at the print queue level.

The two commands we are going to use are **lpstat** and **enq -A**. Both commands produce the same output, but some administrators seem to like one over the over. As I stated earlier, we need to be aware that sometimes print queues are created with queue names longer than seven characters, which is the default that can be displayed with both of these commands. I guess IBM noticed this little problem and added the **-W** switch to give a wide character output. Look at Listings 16.1 and 16.2 to see the different outputs.

```
# lpstat

Queue    Dev    Status     Job Files      User         PP  %   Blks  Cp Rnk
-------- -----  ---------- --- ----------- ----------- ---- -- ----- --- ---
hp4      lp0    READY
hp4-ps   lp0    READY
hp4-gl   lp0    READY
yogi_hp  lp0    DOWN
yogi_hp  lp0    DOWN
```

Listing 16.1   Output using lpstat or enq -A.

```
# lpstat -W
Queue               Dev     Status   Job   Files      User    PP   %   Blks Cp   Rnk
----------------    -----   -------- ----  --------   ------  ---  --  ---- ---   ---
hp4                 lp0     READY
hp4-ps              lp0     READY
hp4-gl              lp0     READY
yogi_hp4_1          lp0     DOWN
yogi_hp4_1ps        lp0     DOWN
```

Listing 16.2   Output using lpstat -W or enq -AW.

As you can see in Listing 16.1, the long queue names are cut off at the seventh character when using the **lpstat** or **enq -A** commands. By adding the **-W** switch to these commands we see the entire long queue name. This is important because you cannot control a print queue if you do not have the exact, and full, queue name.

There are two methods to script using either **lpstat -W** or **enq -AW**. One method is to loop through each queue that is reported DOWN; the other is to use one long compound command. We are first going to look at the looping method.

A little **for** loop can be used to extract out the queue names of the printers in a DOWN state. The list used for the for loop comes from either of the following command statements:

```
lpstat -W | tail +3 | grep DOWN | awk '{print $1}'
```

or

```
enq -AW | tail +3 | grep DOWN | awk '{print $1}'
```

Both of the previous statements produce the same output. Notice that **tail +3** is the second command in pipe, just after the **lpstat** and **enq** commands. We use **tail +3** in this statement to remove the two lines of header information. This method is much cleaner than trying to **grep** out some unique character in both of the header lines.

Notice that the number of lines, specified by **+3**, is one larger than the actual number of lines that we want to remove. Using the **tail** command this way, we are telling **tail** to start listing at the third line, so two lines are removed at the top of the output.

The third command in the pipe is where we **grep** for DOWN, looking for disabled printers, as shown in Listing 16.2. The output from this stage of the command is only the lines of the **enq** and **lpstat** output that contains the word DOWN. Using these lines as input for the next command in the pipe, we are ready to extract the actual queue name(s) of the disabled printers, as shown in the output here.

```
yogi_hp4_1          lp0     DOWN
yogi_hp4_1ps        lp0     DOWN
```

The **awk** command, as we use it, is used to extract the field that we want to work with, which is the first field, the queue name. Using the previous output as input to our **awk** statement we extract out the first field using the following syntax:

```
command | awk '{print $1}'
```

You can extract any valid field using **awk** as well as different fields at the same time. For example, if we want to extract fields 1 and 3, specified by **$1** and **$3**, the following **awk** statement will take care of the task.

```
command | awk '{print $1, $3}'
```

Notice that I added a comma between **$1** and **$3**. If the comma is omitted, then there will *not* be a space between the two strings. Instead the output will be two strings appended together without a space.

For our **for** loop we can first send the **lpstat** and **enq** command output to a file and process the file in a loop, or we can use command substitution to add the statement directly into the **for** loop to create the list of objects to loop through. Let's look at our **for** loop structure.

```
for Q in $( enq -AW | tail +3 | grep DOWN | awk '{print $1}' )
do
      # Do something here.
done
```

Using this loop command statement, the **for** loop will loop through yogi_hp4_1 and yogi_hp4_1ps print queue names, which is equivalent to the following **for** loop structure:

```
for Q in yogi_hp4_1 yogi_hp4_1ps
do
      # Do something here.
done
```

Because we never know which queues may be down, we need to parse through the output of the actual queue names of the printers in a disabled state. The shell script in its entirety is shown in Listing 16.3.

```
#!/bin/ksh
#
# SCRIPT: enable_AIX_classic.ksh
#
# AUTHOR: Randy Michael
# DATE: 03/14/2002
# REV: 1.1.P
```

Listing 16.3   For loop to enable "classic" AIX print queues.

```
#
# PLATFORM: AIX Only
#
# PURPOSE: This script is used to enable print queues on AIX systems.
#
# REV LIST:
#
# set -x # Uncomment to debug this script
# set -n # Uncomment to check syntax without any execution
#

for Q in $( enq -AW | tail +3 | grep DOWN | awk '{print $1}')
do
     enable $Q
     (( $? == 0 )) || echo "\n$Q print queue FAILED to enable.\n"
done
```

Listing 16.3 For loop to enable "classic" AIX print queues. *(continued)*

Inside the **for** loop we attempt to enable each print queue individually. If the return code of the **enable** command is not zero we **echo** an error message indicating that the queue could not be enabled. Notice the highlighted lines in Listing 16.3. We use the mathematical test, specified by the double parentheses, ((math test)). Using this math test you normally do not add a dollar sign, $, in front of a numeric variable. When the variable is produced by the system, such as $?, the dollar sign is required. Testing for equality also requires using the double equal signs, ==, because the single equal sign, =, is meant as an assignment, not a test.

After the test to check for a zero return code, we use a logical OR, specified by the double pipes, ||. This logical OR will execute the next command only if the return code of the **enable $Q** command is nonzero, which means that the command failed. There is also a logical AND that is used by placing double ampersands, &&, in a command statement. A logical AND does just the opposite; it would execute the succeeding command if the test is true, instead of false. Both the logical OR and logical AND are used as replacements for **if..then..else..** statements.

We can also accomplish this task by using a single compound command statement. Just as we used command substitution in the **for** loop, we can use command substitution to produce command parameters. For example, we can use our **for** loop command to create command parameters to the enable command. To see this more clearly, look at the following two commands.

```
enable $(enq -AW | tail +3 | grep DOWN | awk '{print $1}') 2>/dev/null
```

or

```
enable $(lpstat -W | tail +3 | grep DOWN | awk '{print $1}') 2>/dev/null
```

Both of the previous compound command statements produce the same result, enabling all of the print queues on the system. The only problem with using this technique is that if you execute this command and all of the printers are already enabled, then you will get the following output from standard error:

```
usage: enable PrinterName ...
             Enables or activates printers.
```

As you can see, I sent this output to the bit bucket by adding 2>/dev/null to the end of the statement, but the return code is still nonzero if all of the printers are already enabled. This should not be a problem unless you want to create some notification that a printer failed to enable. In our **for** loop in Listing 16.3 we used the return code from the **enable** command to produce notification. I will leave the technique that you use up to you. If you do not want to see any output, then you could add the single compound statement as a cron table entry or use the **for** loop technique in a shell script to redirect the failure notification to a log file. If you use a log file you may want to add a date stamp.

System V Printing on AIX

Beginning with AIX 5L, IBM supports System V printing. I find that Solaris has the closest command usage and output. With only a few differences between AIX and Solaris System V printing in the output produced, you could use the shell scripts interchangeably. Because people tend to read only the parts of a technical book that they need to, I will devote this entire section to AIX System V printing.

To switch your AIX system from the "classic" AIX printer subsystem to System V printing, refer to your AIX reference manual. This section expects that you are already running System V printing.

Like Solaris, AIX uses the System V **lpc** (line printer control) command to control the printers and print queues. The nice thing about this print service is that you can control the queues and the printers independently. The main commands that we are interested in for AIX queuing and printing include the following options and parameters to the **lpc** command, as shown in Table 16.1.

Table 16.1 AIX lpc Command Options

LPC COMMAND	COMMAND RESULT
disable (printer[@host] | all)	Disables queuing
stop (printer[@host] | all)	Disables printing
down (printer[@host] | all)	Disables printing and queuing
enable (printer[@host] | all)	Enables queuing
start (printer[@host] | all)	Enables printing
up (printer[@host] | all)	Enables printing and queuing

As you can see in Table 16.1, the granularity of printer control is excellent, which gives us several options when creating shell scripts. To control *all* of the printing and queuing at one time you really do not need a shell script. The following two commands can start and stop *all* printing and queuing on *all* print queues at the same time.

```
lpc down all      # Disable all printing and queuing

lpc up all        # Enable all printing and queuing
```

To keep all of the printers printing and queuing you only need the **lpc up all** command entered into a cron table. I placed an entry in my root cron table to execute this **lpc** command every 10 minutes, as shown here:

```
5,15,25,35,45,55 * * * * /usr/sbin/lpc up all >/dev/null 2>&1
```

This cron table entry enables all printing and queuing on all printers on the 5s, 24 hours a day, 7 days a week. With AIX System V printing, the data we are interested in is separated on three lines of output when we use the **lpc status all** command to monitor the printer service. The same command executed on AIX , Linux, and Solaris is shown here.

AIX SYSTEM V OUTPUT

```
# lpc status all

hp4V:
        queueing is enabled
        printing is disabled
        5 entries in spool area
```

LINUX SYSTEM V OUTPUT

```
# lpc status
 Printer              Printing Spooling Jobs  Server Subserver Redirect
Status/(Debug)
hp4@localhost        enabled  disabled   0    none   none
```

SOLARIS SYSTEM V OUTPUT

```
# lpc status all

bambam_hp4:
        queueing is enabled
        printing is enabled
        no entries
```

Of these three outputs Linux is the one that differs. With the data we are interested in for AIX residing on three separate lines for each print queue, we need a different strategy to get the exact data the we want. First notice that at the beginning of each stanza a queue name has a colon, :, appended to the name of the queue. Because this character occurs only in the queue name, we can use the colon character as a tag for a **grep** statement. Following the queue name entry, the next two lines contain the data that we are interested in pertaining to the status of the queuing and printing.

Because we have some unique tag for each entry, it is easy to extract the lines of data that we are interested in by using an *extended* **grep**, or **egrep**, statement, as shown here:

```
lpc status all | egrep ':|printing|queueing' | while read LINE
```

The **egrep** command works the same way as the **grep** command except that you can specify multiple patterns to match. Each pattern is separated by a pipe *without any spaces*! If you add spaces on either side of the search pattern, the **egrep** statement will fail to make a match. The entire list of patterns is then enclosed within single forward tic marks, 'pattern1|pattern2|pattern3'. The output produced has the queue name on the first line, the printing status on the second line, and the queuing status on the third line.

The last part of the previous command is where the output is piped to a **while** loop. On each **read** the entire line of data is loaded into the variable LINE. Inside of the **while** loop we use the following **case** statement to assign the data to the appropriate variable.

```
case $LINE in
    *:) Q=$(echo $LINE | cut -d ':' -f1)
        ;;
    printing*)
        PSTATUS=$(echo $LINE | awk '{print $3}')
        ;;
    queueing*)
        QSTATUS=$(echo $LINE | awk '{print $3}')
        ;;
esac
```

Notice that if $LINE begins with *: then we load the Q variable. If $LINE begins with printing* we load the PSTATUS variable with the third field, which should be either enabled or disabled. We do the same thing in loading the QSTATUS variable with the third field of the value that the $LINE variable points to.

The trick in this script is how to load and process three lines of data and then load and process three more lines of data, and so on. The most intuitive approach is to have a loop counter. Each time the loop counter reaches three we process the data and reset the loop counter back to zero. Take a look at the entire script in Listing 16.4 to see how this loop count works. Pay close attention to the bold type.

```ksh
#!/bin/ksh
#
# SCRIPT: print_UP_SYSV_AIX.ksh
#
# AUTHOR: Randy Michael
# DATE: 03/14/2002
# REV: 1.1.P
#
# PLATFORM: AIX System V Printing
#
# PURPOSE: This script is used to enable printing and queuing separately
#          on each print queue on AIX and Solaris systems.
#
# REV LIST:
#
# set -x # Uncomment to debug this script
# set -n # Uncomment to check syntax without any execution
#
##################################################

LOOP=0       # Loop Counter - To grab three lines at a time

lpc status all | egrep ':|printing|queueing' | while read LINE
do
     # Load three unique lines at a time
     case $LINE in
     *:) Q=$(echo $LINE | cut -d ':' -f1)
          ;;
     printing*)
          PSTATUS=$(echo $LINE | awk '{print $3}')
          ;;
     queueing*)
          QSTATUS=$(echo $LINE | awk '{print $3}')
          ;;
     esac

     # Increment the LOOP counter
     (( LOOP = LOOP + 1 ))
     if ((LOOP == 3))  # Do we have all three lines of data?
     then
          # Check printing status
          case $PSTATUS in
```

Listing 16.4   print_UP_AIX.ksh shell script listing. *(continues)*

```
            disabled) lpc start $Q >/dev/null
                      (($? == 0)) && echo "\n$Q printing re-started\n"
                      ;;
            enabled|*) :  # No-Op - Do Nothing
                      ;;
            esac


            # Check queuing status
            case $QSTATUS in
            disabled) lpc enable $Q >/dev/null
                      (($? == 0)) && echo "\n$Q queueing re-enabled\n"
                      ;;
            enabled|*) :  # No-Op - Do Nothing
                      ;;
            esac
            LOOP=0  # Reset the loop counter to zero
      fi
done
```

Listing 16.4   print_UP_AIX.ksh shell script listing. *(continued)*

Notice that we grab three lines at a time. The reason that I say that we are grabbing three lines at a time is because I use the **case** statement to specify unique tags for each line of data. I know that the queue name will have a colon, :, as a suffix. I know that the printing status line will begin with printing*, and I know that the queuing line will begin with queueing*. We load only one variable on each loop iteration. So, to get three pieces of data (queue name, printing status, and queuing status), we need to go through the **while** loop three times for each printer queue. Once we pass the initial **case** statement, we increment the LOOP counter by one. If the $LOOP variable is equal to 3 then we have all of the data that we need to process a single printer queue. After processing the data for this printer queue, we reset the LOOP variable to zero, 0, and start gathering data for the next printer queue.

Sounds simple enough? This same technique works for any fixed set of lines of data in command output or in a file. The only changes that are needed to use this method include creating unique tags for the data you are interested in and setting the $LOOP equality statement to reflect the number of lines in each set of data.

More System V Printer Commands

We have been looking at only the **lpc** command thus far. We also need to look at two command parameters to the **lpstat** command in this section. The **-a** parameter lists the status of queuing, and the **-p** command parameter lists the status of printing. The nice thing about these two command options is that the output for each queue is on a single line, which makes the data easier to parse through. See Table 16.2.

Table 16.2 System V `lpstat` Command Options

COMMAND	DESCRIPTION
lpstat -a	Show status of queuing on all printers
lpstat -p	Show status of printing on all printers

Other than having to query the printer service twice, having to use separate commands for monitoring printing and queuing is not so bad. The separation is built in because the **-a** and **-p** command parameters are mutually exclusive, which means that you cannot use **-a** and **-p** at the same time. Output from each command option is shown here:

```
# lpstat -a

hp4 accepting requests since May 07 07:02 2002
yogi_hp4_1ps accepting requests since May 07 07:02 2002
long_queue not accepting requests since Tue May  7 07:02:23 EDT 2002 -

s_q_nam not accepting requests since Tue May  7 07:02:23 EDT 2002 -

# lpstat -p

printer long_queue disabled since Tue May  7 07:02:01 EDT 2002.
available.
        stopped by user
printer s_q_nam disabled since Tue May  7 07:02:01 EDT 2002. available.
        stopped by user
printer hp4 unknown state. enabled since May 07 07:30 2002. available.
printer yogi_hp4_1ps unknown state. enabled since May 07 07:30 2002.
available.
```

Listing 16.5 lpstat -a and lpstat -p command output.

Notice in Listing 16.5 that the output from each command option has a unique set of status information for each printer on each line of output. We want to use the uniqueness of the status information as tags in a **grep** statement. The terms make sense, too. A queue is either *accepting* new requests or is *not accepting* new requests, and a printer is either *enabled* for printing or is *disabled* from printing. Because we are interested only in the disabled and not-accepting states, we can create a simple script or a one-liner.

We need to know two things to enable printing and to bring up a print queue to accept new requests, the printer/queue name and the state of the queue or printer. The first step is to **grep** out the lines of output that contain our tag. The second step is to extract the printer/queue name from each line of output. Let's first look at using a while loop to bring everything up, as shown in the Listing 16.6.

```
lpstat -a | grep 'not accepting' | while read LINE
do
     Q=$(echo $LINE | awk '{print $1}')
     lpc enable $Q
done


lpstat -p | grep disabled | while LINE
do
     P=$(echo $LINE | awk '{print $2}')
     lpc start $P
done
```

Listing 16.6   Scripting the lpstat command using -a and -p.

Notice in Listing 16.6 that we have to work on the print queues and printers separately, by using two separate loops. In the first **while** loop all of the queuing is started. In the second loop we enable printing for each of the printers. The down side to this method occurs when you have hundreds of printers and scanning through all of the printers twice can take quite a while. Of course, if you have hundreds of printers you should use **lpc up all** to bring everything up at once.

As I said before, we can also make a one-liner out of the two loops in Listing 16.6. We can combine the **grep** and **awk** commands on the same line and use command substitution to execute the **lpc** command. The following two commands replace the two **while** loops.

```
lpc enable $(lpstat -a | grep 'not accepting' | awk '{print $1}')

lpc start $( lpstat -p | grep disabled | awk '{print $2}')
```

The first command enables queuing, and the second command starts printing. The command substitution, specified by the $(command) notation, executes the appropriate **lpstat** command, then greps on the tag and extracts the printer/queue name out. The resulting output is used as the parameter to the **lpc** commands.

HP-UX Print Control Commands

Of the Unix operating systems, HP-UX has a unique **lpstat** command output. We do not have to do anything special to see the full print queue names, and if a queuing is disabled or printing is stopped, we get a *Warning:* message. With a warning message for each printer on a single line we can use **grep** and **awk** to find the printer/queue name and the status in a **case** statement. Let's first look at the **lpstat** output when both printing and queuing is up, as shown here:

```
# lpstat

printer queue for hp4_yogi_1


printer queue for yogi_hp4_1ps
```

If print requests were queued up they would be listed below the queue name. Now let's **disable** printing on the hp4_yogi_1 print queue.

```
# disable hp4_yogi_1

printer "hp4_yogi_1" now disabled
```

Now look at the output of the **lpstat** command:

```
# lpstat

printer queue for hp4_yogi_1
dino: Warning: hp4_yogi_1 is down


printer queue for yogi_hp4_1ps
```

The warning message tells us that the printer is down; however, notice that the queue status is not listed here. Now let's bring down the hp4_yogi_1 print queue and see what this does.

```
# reject hp4_yogi_1

destination "hp4_yogi_1" will no longer accept requests
```

To see only queuing status we use the **lpstat -a** command, as shown here:

```
# lpstat -a

hp4_yogi_1 not accepting requests since Oct  1 05:45 -
        reason unknown
yogi_hp4_1ps accepting requests since Sep 26 04:23
```

Because hp4_yogi_1 now has printing disabled and queuing stopped, I would expect that we should see some queue status output in the **lpstat** command output for the first time.

```
# lpstat

printer queue for hp4_yogi_1
```

```
dino: Warning: hp4_yogi_1 queue is turned off
dino: Warning: hp4_yogi_1 is down


printer queue for yogi_hp4_1ps
```

Just what we expected. From this little exercise we have determined that queuing is reported only when the queuing is stopped on the queue using the **lpstat** command alone. For our scripting effort let's stick to the **lpstat** output. We want to use the word Warning as a tag for our **grep** statement. Then we can further **grep** this extracted line to check printing and queuing status. If the string `'queue is turned off'` is present we know that queuing is turned off, and if the string `'is down'` appears on the line we know that printing is disabled. The only thing left to extract is the printer/queue name, which is always located in the third field.

To script this we can use the code in Listing 16.7. Pay attention to the bold type, and we will cover the script at the end.

```ksh
#!/bin/ksh
#
# SCRIPT: print_UP_HP-UX.ksh
#
# AUTHOR: Randy Michael
# DATE: 03/14/2002
# REV: 1.1.P
#
# PLATFORM: HP-UX Only
#
# PURPOSE: This script is used to enable printing and queuing separately
#          on each print queue on an HP-UX system.
#
# REV LIST:
#
# set -x # Uncomment to debug this script
# set -n # Uncomment to check syntax without any execution

lpstat | grep Warning: | while read LINE
do
     if (echo $LINE | grep 'is down') > /dev/null
     then
          enable $(echo $LINE | awk '{print $3}')
     fi

     if (echo $LINE | grep 'queue is turned off') >/dev/null
     then
          accept $(echo $LINE | awk '{print $3}')
     fi
done
```

Listing 16.7   print_UP_HP-UX.ksh shell script listing.

I want to point out a nice little trick in the shell script in Listing 16.7. In both of the **if..then..fi** statements, notice that we execute a command inside parentheses. What this technique allows us to do is execute a command in a *sub-shell* and use the command's resulting return code directly in the **if..then..fi** structure. We really could not care less about seeing the line that we are grepping on; however, if the return code from the command is zero, then the pattern is present.

In the first half of the script in Listing 16.7 we check the status of printing. If a printer is found to be disabled, then we use command substitution to produce the printer name for the **enable** command. Likewise, we check for the status of queuing in the second half of the script. Again, using command substitution we have the queue name to provide as a parameter to the **accept** command. Notice that I added the redirection to the bit bucket, specified by >/dev/null, after the command in the **if** statement. I add this redirection to /dev/null to suppress the output of the **grep** statement.

That is it for HP-UX printing. HP did a good job of keeping everything pretty straightforward in the printing arena.

Linux Print Control Commands

Linux uses the System V **lpc** (line printer control) command to control the printers and print queues, as most System V Unix does. The nice thing about this print service is that you can control the queues and the printers independently. The main commands that we are interested in for Linux queuing and printing include the options to the **lpc** command listed in Table 16.3.

As you can see in Table 16.3, the granularity of printer control is excellent, which gives up several options when creating shell scripts. To control *all* of the printing and queuing at one time you really do not need a shell script. The following two commands can start and stop all printing and queuing on all print queues at the same time.

```
lpc down all      # Disable all printing and queuing

lpc up all        # Enable all printing and queuing
```

Table 16.3 Linux lpc Command Options

LPC COMMAND	COMMAND RESULT
disable (printer[@host] | all)	Disables queuing
stop (printer[@host] | all)	Disables printing
down (printer[@host] | all)	Disables printing and queuing
enable (printer[@host] | all)	Enables queuing
start (printer[@host] | all)	Enables printing
up (printer[@host] | all)	Enables printing and queuing

To keep all of the printers printing and queuing you need just the **lpc up all** command entered into a cron table. I placed an entry in my root cron table to execute this command every 10 minutes. My cron table entry is shown here:

```
5,15,25,35,45,55 * * * * /usr/sbin/lpc up all >/dev/null 2>&1
```

This cron table entry enables all printing and queuing on all printers on the 5s, 24 hours a day, 7 days a week.

If you do want a little more control and if you keep a log of what is going on on a per queue/printer basis, then we have to do a little scripting. The script that follows searches all of the queues and reports on the individual status of printing and queuing and then enables each one independently.

For this script we are going to use *arrays* to load the variables on each loop iteration. Array can be created and elements assigned values in two ways. The first technique is to use **set -A** to define the array and all of its elements. For example, if I want an array called QUEUE to contain the values for printing and queuing for a specified queue, I can set it up this way:

```
PQueue=yogi_hp4
Print_val=enabled
Queue_val=disabled


set -A QUEUE $PQueue $Print_val $Queue_val
```

We could have assigned the values directly in the **set -A** statement, but this time we used variables for the assignments. This statement defines an array named QUEUE that contains three array elements. The elements loaded into the array are the values that the variables $PQueue, $Print_val, and $Queue_val point to. For example, we assigned PQueue the value yogi_hp4, Print_val is assigned the value enabled, and Queue_val is assigned the value disabled. The result is that the first array element, 0 (zero) contains the value yogi_hp4, the second array element, 1 (one), has the value enabled, and the third array element, 2, contains the value disabled, which is what the $Queue_val variable points to. Using this technique requires that you access the array elements starting with 0, zero.

To address the array elements you use the following syntax:

```
${QUEUE[0]} # Points to value assigned to the first array element,
              yogi_hp4
${QUEUE[1]} # Points to value assigned to the second array element,
              enabled
${QUEUE[2]} # Points to the value assigned to the third array element,
              disabled
```

To address all of the array's elements at the same time use the following syntax:

```
# print "${QUEUE[*]}"

    ----OR----
```

```
# print "${QUEUE[@]}"
```

```
yogi_hp4 enabled disabled
```

Now, before I lose you, let's take a look at a more intuitive way of working with arrays and array elements. Instead of using the **set -A** command to define and load an array, we can define an array and load its elements at the same time using the following syntax:

```
QUEUE[1]=yogi_hp4
QUEUE[2]=enabled
QUEUE[3]=disabled
```

Notice that the first array element is now referenced by 1, one. These commands create an array named QUEUE and load the first three array elements, referenced by 1, 2, and 3, into array QUEUE. Now you can use the array directly in a command statement by pointing to the array element that you want to use. For example, if I want to print the *printing* status of the yogi_hp4 print queue, I use the following syntax:

```
echo "\nPrinter ${QUEUE[1]} has print status ${QUEUE[2]}\n"
```

The previous command produces the following output:

```
Printer yogi_hp4 has print status enabled
```

Now that we have seen the basics of working with arrays, let's look at a shell script to handle keeping the printing and queuing enabled on all of the printers individually. The first step is to load an array in a **while** loop. This is a little different from what we did before with arrays. In this case I want to use the **lpc status all** command to find printers that have either printing or queuing disabled. The output of the **lpc status all** command is shown below.

```
# lpc status all
  Printer           Printing Spooling Jobs  Server Subserver Redirect
Status/(Debug)
hp4@localhost       enabled  disabled   0    none   none
```

This is an easy output to deal with because all of the data for each queue is on a single line. The output that we are interested in is the printer name, the printing status, and the spooling status—the first three fields on the second line. We are not interested in the first line at all so we can get rid of it with a pipe to the **tail** command. When we add to our command we get the following output:

```
# lpc status all | tail +2
yogi_hp4@localhost  enabled  disabled   0    none   none
```

I currently have only one printer defined on this system, so the output is the status of a single printer. Now we want to load the first three fields into an array using a

while loop. Look at the next command line to see how we are directly loading an array called pqstat with array elements of the first three fields on each line.

```
lpc status all | tail +2 | while read pqstat[1] pqstat[2] pqstat[3] junk
```

Because I want just the first three fields in the output, notice that the fourth variable in the **read** part of the **while** statement is junk. The junk variable is a catch-all variable to capture any remaining strings on the line of output in a single variable. It is a *requirement* that you take care of this remaining text because if you neglect adding a variable to catch any remaining characters on the line, you will **read** the characters in as strings on the next loop iteration! This type of error produces some strange output that is hard to find and troubleshoot.

Notice that in the output of the **lpc status all** command the printer has queuing disabled, which is the third field. The easiest way to handle the two status fields is to use two **case** statements, with each tagging on a separate field. Look at the full script code in Listing 16.8, and we will cover the technique at the end.

```
#!/bin/ksh
#
# SCRIPT: print_UP_Linux.ksh
#
# AUTHOR: Randy Michael
# DATE: 03/14/2002
# REV: 1.1.P
#
# PLATFORM: Linux Only
#
# PURPOSE: This script is used to enable printing and queuing separately
#          on each print queue on a Linux system. Logging can be
#          enabled.
#
# REV LIST:
#
# set -x # Uncomment to debug this script
# set -n # Uncomment to check syntax without any execution
#
#################################################
# Initial Variables Here
#################################################

LOGILE=/usr/local/log/PQlog.log
[ -f $LOGFILE ] || echo /dev/null > $LOGFILE


#################################################

lpc status | tail +2 | while read pqstat[1] pqstat[2] pqstat[3] junk
```

Listing 16.8   print_UP_Linux.ksh shell script listing.

```
do
      # First check the status of printing for each printer
      case ${pqstat[2]} in
      disabled)
              # Printing is disabled - print status and restart printing
              echo "${pqstat[1]} Printing is ${pqstat[2]}" \
                  | tee -a$LOGFILE
              lpc start ${pqstat[1]} | tee -a $LOGFILE
              (($? == 0)) && echo "${pqstat[1]} Printing Restarted" \
                              | tee -a $LOGFILE
              ;;
      enabled|*) : # No-Op - Do Nothing
              ;;
      esac
      # Next check the status of queueing for each printer
      case ${pqstat[3]} in
      disabled)
              echo "${pqstat[1]} Queueing is ${pqstat[3]}" \
                  | tee -a $LOGFILE
              lpc enable ${pqstat[1]} | tee -a $LOGFILE
              (($? == 0)) && echo "${pqstat[1]} Printing Restarted" \
                              | tee -a $LOGFILE
              ;;
      enabled|*) :    # No-Op - Do Nothing
              ;;
      esac
done
```

Listing 16.8   print_UP_Linux.ksh shell script listing. *(continued)*

We start off this script in Listing 16.8 by defining the $LOGFILE. Notice that the following command, after the log file definition, checks to see if the log file exists. If the $LOGFILE does not exist, then the result of the test is a nonzero return code. We use a logical OR, specified by the double pipes, ||, to execute the succeeding command to create a zero length $LOGFILE because it does not exist if the return code of the test is nonzero.

Next, we start our **while** loop to load the pqstat array on each loop iteration, which in our case is a single loop iteration for a single printer. This means that we load a one-dimensional array with new data on each loop iteration (one-dimensional arrays are all that the Korn shell can use). Again, notice the junk variable that is added as the last variable in the **while** loop statement. This extra variable is required to catch the remaining text in a single variable.

With the array loaded we proceed with two **case** statements to test for the status of printing and queuing on each print queue. Notice that we use the array element directly in the case statement, as shown here:

```
case ${pqstat[2]} in
```

We use the same technique with the print queuing array element in a separate `case` statement. We have only two possible results for the array elements, `enabled` and `disabled`. The only result we are concerned about is any `disabled` value. If we receive any `disabled` values we attempt to reenable the printing or queuing on the printer. Notice that the second option in both case statements includes `enabled` and anything else, specified by the wildcard, *, as shown here:

```
enabled|*)
```

We could have just used the wildcard to cover everything, but it is clearer to the reader of the script to see actual expected results in a **case** statement than just a catchall asterisk.

When a reenabling task is completed successfully, notice the use of the logical AND to test the return code and give notification on a zero return code value, as shown here:

```
(($? == 0)) && echo "${pqstat[1]} Printing Restarted"
```

The second part of the command will execute only if the test for a zero return code is true. Otherwise, the system will report an error, so there is no need for us to add any failure notification.

To see everything that is happening on the screen and to log everything at the same time we use the **tee -a** command. This command works with a pipe and prints all of the output to the screen; at the same time it sends the exact same output to the file specified after **tee -a**. An example is shown here.

```
lpc start ${pqstat[1]} | tee -a $LOGFILE
```

The previous command attempts to restart printing on the print queue specified by the array element `pqstat[1]` and sends any resulting output to the screen and to the `$LOGFILE` simultaneously.

Controlling Queuing and Printing Individually

Depending on the situation, you may not always want to enable printing and queuing at the same time. We can break up the shell script in Listing 16.8 and pull out the individual **case** statements to start either printing or queuing. Because printing is controlled by array element 2 we can extract the first case statement to create a new shell script. Let's call this shell script `printing_only_UP_Linux.ksh`. You can see the modifications in Listing 16.9.

```
#!/bin/ksh
#
# SCRIPT: printing_only_UP_Linux.ksh
#
```

Listing 16.9 printing_only_UP_Linux.ksh shell script listing.

```
# AUTHOR: Randy Michael
# DATE: 03/14/2002
# REV: 1.1.P
#
# PLATFORM: Linux Only
#
# PURPOSE: This script is used to enable printing on each printer
#          on a Linux system. Logging is enabled.
#
# REV LIST:
#
# set -x # Uncomment to debug this script
# set -n # Uncomment to check syntax without any execution
#
#################################################
# Initial Variables Here
#################################################

LOGILE=/usr/local/log/PQlog.log
[ -f $LOGFILE ] || echo /dev/null > $LOGFILE


#################################################

lpc status | tail +2 | while read pqstat[1] pqstat[2] pqstat[3] junk
do
    # Check the status of printing for each printer
    case ${pqstat[2]} in
    disabled)
              # Printing is disabled - print status and restart
printing
              echo "${pqstat[1]} Printing is ${pqstat[2]}" \
                   | tee -a$LOGFILE
              lpc start ${pqstat[1]} | tee -a $LOGFILE
              (($? == 0)) && echo "${pqstat[1]} Printing Restarted" \
                            | tee -a $LOGFILE
           ;;
    enabled|*) : # No-Op - Do Nothing
           ;;
    esac
done
```

Listing 16.9   printing_only_UP_Linux.ksh shell script listing. *(continued)*

Notice that the only thing that was changed is that the second **case** statement structure was removed from the script and the name was changed. We can do the same thing to create a shell script that only enables queuing, as shown in Listing 16.10.

```
#!/bin/ksh
#
# SCRIPT: queuing_only_UP_Linux.ksh
#
# AUTHOR: Randy Michael
# DATE: 03/14/2002
# REV: 1.1.P
#
# PLATFORM: Linux Only
#
# PURPOSE: This script is used to enable printing and queuing separately
#          on each print queue on a Linux system. Logging can be
#          enabled.
#
# REV LIST:
#
# set -x # Uncomment to debug this script
# set -n # Uncomment to check syntax without any execution
#
##################################################
# Initial Variables Here
##################################################

LOGILE=/usr/local/log/PQlog.log
[ -f $LOGFILE ] || echo /dev/null > $LOGFILE


##################################################

lpc status | tail +2 | while read pqstat[1] pqstat[2] pqstat[3] junk
do
     # check the status of queueing for each printer
     case ${pqstat[3]} in
     disabled)
               echo "${pqstat[1]} Queueing is ${pqstat[3]}" \
                    | tee -a $LOGFILE
               lpc enable ${pqstat[1]} | tee -a $LOGFILE
               (($? == 0)) && echo "${pqstat[1]} Printing Restarted" \
                              | tee -a $LOGFILE
               ;;
     enabled|*) :    # No-Op - Do Nothing
               ;;
     esac
done
```

Listing 16.10   queuing_only_UP_Linux.ksh shell script listing.

Notice that the only thing that was changed this time is the first **case** statement structure was removed from the script and the name of the shell script was changed.

You could also modify the shell script in Listing 16.8 to add a command-line parameter to let you control queuing and printing individually from the same shell script. I am going to leave this as an exercise for you to complete.

As a hint for this exercise: Expect only zero or one command-line parameters. If $#$ is equal to zero, then enable both queuing and printing. If there is one parameter and the value of $1 is "all", then enable both printing and queuing. If the $1 parameter is equal to "printing", then enable only printing. If $1 is equal to "queuing", then enable only queuing. You need to add a usage function to show how to use the shell script if the given value does not match what you are expecting.

Arrays are good to use in a lot of situations where you want to address certain output fields directly and randomly. All Korn shell arrays are one-dimensional arrays, but using the array in a loop gives the *appearance* of a two-dimensional array.

Solaris Print Control Commands

Solaris uses the System V **lpc** (line printer control) command to control the printers and print queues, as most System V Unix does. The nice thing about this print service is that you can control the queues and the printers independently. The main commands that we are interested in for Solaris queuing and printing include the following options and parameters to the **lpc** command, as shown in Table 16.4.

As you can see in Table 16.4, the granularity of printer control is excellent, which gives several options when creating shell scripts. To control *all* of the printing and queuing at one time you really do not need a shell script. The following two commands can start and stop all printing and queuing on all print queues at the same time.

```
lpc down all      # Disable all printing and queuing

lpc up all        # Enable all printing and queuing
```

To keep all of the printers printing and queuing you need only the **lpc up all** command entered into a cron table. I placed an entry in my root cron table to execute this command every 10 minutes. My cron table entry is shown here:

```
5,15,25,35,45,55 * * * * /usr/sbin/lpc up all >/dev/null 2>&1
```

Table 16.4   Solaris lpc Command Options

LPC COMMAND	COMMAND RESULT
disable (printer[@host] | all)	Disables queuing
stop (printer[@host] | all)	Disables printing
down (printer[@host] | all)	Disables printing and queuing
enable (printer[@host] | all)	Enables queuing
start (printer[@host] | all)	Enables printing
up (printer[@host] | all)	Enables printing and queuing

This cron table entry enables all printing and queuing on all printers on the 5s, 24 hours a day, 7 days a week.

We have a nice situation here because we can use the same shell script that we used for the AIX System V printing on Solaris. Unlike Linux, where all of the data that we want is on a single line of output, with Solaris and AIX System V printing, the data we are interested in is separated on three lines of output. You can see the difference in the output here.

AIX SYSTEM V OUTPUT

```
# lpc status all
hp4V:
        queueing is enabled
        printing is disabled
        5 entries in spool area
```

LINUX SYSTEM V OUTPUT

```
# lpc status
 Printer             Printing Spooling Jobs  Server Subserver Redirect
Status/(Debug)
hp4@localhost       enabled disabled    0   none    none
```

SOLARIS SYSTEM V OUTPUT

```
# lpc status all

bambam_hp4:
        queueing is enabled
        printing is enabled
        no entries
```

Of these three outputs, Linux is the one that differs. With the data we are interested in for Solaris residing on three separate lines for each print queue, we need a different strategy to get the exact data the we want. First notice that the beginning of the stanza for the queue name there is a colon, :, appended to the name of the queue. Because this character occurs only in the queue name, we can use the colon character as a tag for a **grep** statement. Following the queue name entry the next two lines contain the data pertaining to the status of the queuing and printing.

Because we have some unique tag for each entry, it is easy to extract the lines of data that we are interested in by using an *extended* **grep**, or **egrep**, statement, as shown here:

```
lpc status all | egrep ':|printing|queueing' | while read LINE
```

The **egrep** command works the same way as the **grep** command except that you can specify multiple patterns to match. Each pattern is separated by a pipe *without any* *spaces*! If you add spaces on either side of the search pattern the **egrep** statement will fail to make a match. The entire list of patterns is then enclosed within single forward tic marks, `'pattern1|pattern2|pattern3'`. The output produced has the queue name on the first line, the printing status on the second line, and the queuing status on the third line.

The last part of the previous command is where the output is piped to a **while** loop. On each **read**, the entire line of data is loaded into the variable LINE. Inside of the **while** loop we use the following **case** statement to assign the data to the appropriate variable.

```
case $LINE in
     *:) Q=$(echo $LINE | cut -d ':' -f1)
         ;;
     printing*)
         PSTATUS=$(echo $LINE | awk '{print $3}')
         ;;
     queueing*)
         QSTATUS=$(echo $LINE | awk '{print $3}')
         ;;
esac
```

Notice that if $LINE begins with `*:` then we load the Q variable. If $LINE begins with `printing*` we load the PSTATUS variable with the third field, which should be either `enabled` or `disabled`. We do the same thing in loading the QSTATUS variable with the third field of the value that the $LINE variable points to.

The trick in this script is how to load and process three lines of data and then load and process three more lines of data, and so on. The most intuitive approach is to have a loop counter. Each time the loop counter reaches three we process the data and reset the loop counter back to zero. Take a look at the entire script in Listing 16.11 to see how this loop count works. Pay close attention to the bold type.

```
#!/bin/ksh
#
# SCRIPT: print_UP_Solaris.ksh
#
# AUTHOR: Randy Michael
# DATE: 03/14/2002
# REV: 1.1.P
#
# PLATFORM: Solaris Only
#
# PURPOSE: This script is used to enable printing and queuing separately
#          on each print queue on Solaris systems.
#
#
# REV LIST:
```

Listing 16.11 print_UP_SUN.ksh shell script listing. *(continues)*

```
#
# set -x # Uncomment to debug this script
# set -n # Uncomment to check syntax without any execution
#
##################################################

LOOP=0        # Loop Counter - To grab three lines at a time

lpc status all | egrep ':|printing|queueing' | while read LINE
do
     # Load three unique lines at a time
     case $LINE in
     *:) Q=$(echo $LINE | cut -d ':' -f1)
         ;;
     printing*)
         PSTATUS=$(echo $LINE | awk '{print $3}')
         ;;
     queueing*)
         QSTATUS=$(echo $LINE | awk '{print $3}')
         ;;
     esac


     # Increment the LOOP counter
     (( LOOP = LOOP + 1 ))
     if ((LOOP == 3))  # Do we have all three lines of data?
     then
         # Check printing status
         case $PSTATUS in
         disabled) lpc start $Q >/dev/null
                   (($? == 0)) && echo "\n$Q printing re-started\n"
                   ;;
         enabled|*) :  # No-Op - Do Nothing
                   ;;
         esac

         # Check queuing status
         case $QSTATUS in
         disabled) lpc enable $Q >/dev/null
                   (($? == 0)) && echo "\n$Q queueing re-enabled\n"
                   ;;
         enabled|*) :  # No-Op - Do Nothing
                   ;;
         esac
         LOOP=0  # Reset the loop counter to zero
    fi
done
```

Listing 16.11 print_UP_SUN.ksh shell script listing. *(continued)*

Table 16.5   System V `lpstat` Command Options

COMMAND	DESCRIPTION
lpstat -a	Show status of queuing on all printers
lpstat -p	Show status of printing on all printers

Within this **while** loop we are grabbing three lines of data at a time to process. I say that we are grabbing three lines at a time in Listing 16.11 because I use the **case** statement to specify unique tags for each line of data. I know that the queue name will have a colon, `:`, as a suffix. I know that the printing status line will begin with `printing*`, and I know that the queuing line will begin with `queueing*`. We load only one variable on each loop iteration, though. To get three pieces of data (queue name, printing status, and queuing status), we need to go through the **while** loop three times for each printer queue. Once we pass the initial case statement we increment the `LOOP` counter by one. If the `$LOOP` variable is equal to `3`, then we have all data that we need to process a single printer queue. After processing the data for this printer queue we reset the `LOOP` variable to zero, `0`, and start gathering data for the next printer queue.

Sounds simple enough? This same technique works for any fixed set of lines of data in command output or in a file. The only changes that are needed to use this method include creating unique tags for the data you are interested in and setting the `$LOOP` equality statement to reflect the number of lines that are in each set of data.

More System V Printer Commands

We have been looking only at the **lpc** command thus far. We also need to look at two command parameters to the **lpstat** command in this section. The **-a** parameter lists the status of queuing, and the **-p** command parameter lists the status of printing. The nice thing about these two command options is that the output for each queue is on a single line, which makes the data easier to parse through. The **lpstat** command options are shown in Table 16.5.

Other than having to query the printer subsystem twice, having to use separate commands for monitoring printing and queuing is not so bad. The separation is built in because the **-a** and **-p** command parameters are mutually exclusive, which means that you cannot use **-a** and **-p** at the same time. Output from each command option is shown here:

```
# lpstat -a

hp4 accepting requests since May 07 07:02 2002
yogi_hp4_1ps accepting requests since May 07 07:02 2002
```

Listing 16.12   lpstat -a and lpstat -p command output. *(continues)*

```
long_queue not accepting requests since Tue May  7 07:02:23 EDT 2002 -

s_q_nam not accepting requests since Tue May  7 07:02:23 EDT 2002 -

# lpstat -p

printer long_queue disabled since Tue May  7 07:02:01 EDT 2002.
available.
        stopped by user
printer s_q_nam disabled since Tue May  7 07:02:01 EDT 2002. available.
        stopped by user
printer hp4 unknown state. enabled since May 07 07:30 2002. available.
printer yogi_hp4_1ps unknown state. enabled since May 07 07:30 2002.
available.
```

Listing 16.12   lpstat -a and lpstat -p command output. *(continued)*

Notice in Listing 16.12 that the output from each command option has a unique set of status information for each printer on each line of output. We want to use the uniqueness of the status information as tags in a **grep** statement. The terms make sense, too. A queue is either *accepting* new requests or *not accepting* new requests, and a printer is either *enabled* for printing or *disabled* from printing. Because we are interested in only the disabled and not accepting states, we can create a simple script or a one-liner.

We need to know two things to enable printing and to bring up a print queue to accept new requests, the printer/queue name and the state of the queue or printer. The first step is to **grep** out the lines of output that contain our tag. The second step is to extract the printer/queue name from each line of output. Let's first look at using a **while** loop to bring everything up, as shown in Listing 16.13.

```
lpstat -a | grep 'not accepting' | while read LINE
do
     Q=$(echo $LINE | awk '{print $1}')
     lpc enable $Q
done

lpstat -p | grep disabled | while LINE
do
     P=$(echo $LINE | awk '{print $2}')
     lpc start $P
done
```

Listing 16.13   Scripting the lpstat command using -a and -p.

Notice in Listing 16.13 that we have to work on the print queues and printers separately, by using two separate loops. In the first **while** loop all of the queuing is started. In the second loop we enable printing for each of the printers. The down side to this method is where you have hundreds of printers. The time it takes to scan through all of the printers once and then rescan the printer service can be quite long. Of course, if you have hundreds of printers, you should use **lpc up all** to bring everything up at once.

As I said before, we can also make a one-liner out of the two loops in Listing 16.13. We can combine the **grep** and **awk** commands on the same line and use command substitution to execute the **lpc** command. The following two commands replace the two **while** loops.

```
lpc enable $(lpstat -a | grep 'not accepting' | awk '{print $1}')

lpc start $( lpstat -p | grep disabled | awk '{print $2}')
```

The first command enables queuing, and the second command starts printing. The command substitution, specified by the `$(command)` notation, executes the appropriate **lpstat** command, then greps on the tag and extracts the printer/queue name. The resulting output is used as the parameter to the **lpc** commands.

Putting It All Together

Now we need to combine the shell scripts for each of the different Unix flavors so that one script does it all. Please do not think that taking several shell scripts, making functions out of them, and combining the new functions into a new script are difficult tasks. To make one script out of this chapter we are going to take the best of our scripts and extract the code. For each shell script we make a new function, which requires only the word **function**, a function name, and the code block surrounded by curly braces, `function function_name { code stuff here }`. Let's take a look at the entire combined shell script in Listing 16.14 and cover the functions at the end.

```
#!/bin/ksh
#
# SCRIPT: PQ_all_in_one.ksh
#
# AUTHOR: Randy Michael
# DATE: 03/14/2002
# REV: 1.1.P
#
# PLATFORM: AIX, HP-UX, Linux and Solaris
```

Listing 16.14 PQ_all_in_one.ksh shell script listing. *(continues)*

```
#
# PURPOSE: This script is used to enable printing and queuing on
#          AIX, HP-UX, Linux and Solaris
#
# REV LIST:
#
# set -x # Uncomment to debug this script
# set -n # Uncomment to check syntax without any execution
#
##################################################
############## DEFINE FUNCTIONS HERE ################

function AIX_classic_printing
{
for Q in $( enq -AW | tail +3 | grep DOWN | awk '{print $1}')
do
     enable $Q
     (( $? == 0 )) || echo "\n$Q print queue FAILED to enable.\n"
done
}


#######################################################

function AIX_SYSV_printing
{
LOOP=0      # Loop Counter - To grab three lines at a time

lpc status all | egrep ':|printing|queueing' | while read LINE
do
     # Load three unique lines at a time
     case $LINE in
     *:) Q=$(echo $LINE | cut -d ':' -f1)
          ;;
     printing*)
          PSTATUS=$(echo $LINE | awk '{print $3}')
          ;;
     queueing*)
          QSTATUS=$(echo $LINE | awk '{print $3}')
          ;;
     esac

     # Increment the LOOP counter
     (( LOOP = LOOP + 1 ))
     if ((LOOP == 3))  # Do we have all three lines of data?
     then
          # Check printing status
          case $PSTATUS in
```

Listing 16.14 PQ_all_in_one.ksh shell script listing. *(continued)*

```
                 disabled) lpc start $Q >/dev/null
                             (($? == 0)) && echo "\n$Q printing re-started\n"
                             ;;
                 enabled|*) :  # No-Op - Do Nothing
                             ;;
                 esac

                 # Check queuing status
                 case $QSTATUS in
                 disabled) lpc enable $Q >/dev/null
                             (($? == 0)) && echo "\n$Q queueing re-enabled\n"
                             ;;
                 enabled|*) :  # No-Op - Do Nothing
                             ;;
                 esac
                 LOOP=0  # Reset the loop counter to zero
        fi
done


}


#######################################################

function HP_UX_printing
{
lpstat | grep Warning: | while read LINE
do
        if (echo $LINE | grep 'is down') > /dev/null
        then
              enable $(echo $LINE | awk '{print $3}')
        fi

        if (echo $LINE | grep 'queue is turned off') >/dev/null
        then
              accept $(echo $LINE | awk '{print $3}')
        fi
done
}


#######################################################

function Linux_printing
{
lpc status | tail +2 | while read pqstat[1] pqstat[2] pqstat[3] junk
do
        # First check the status of printing for each printer
        case ${pqstat[2]} in
```

Listing 16.14   PQ_all_in_one.ksh shell script listing. *(continues)*

```
        disabled)
                  # Printing is disabled - print status and restart
printing
                  echo "${pqstat[1]} Printing is ${pqstat[2]}"
                  lpc start ${pqstat[1]}
                  (($? == 0)) && echo "${pqstat[1]} Printing Restarted"
              ;;
      enabled|*) : # No-Op - Do Nothing
                  ;;
      esac
      # Next check the status of queueing for each printer
      case ${pqstat[3]} in
      disabled)
                  echo "${pqstat[1]} Queueing is ${pqstat[3]}"
                  lpc enable ${pqstat[1]}
                  (($? == 0)) && echo "${pqstat[1]} Printing Restarted"
              ;;
      enabled|*) :   # No-Op - Do Nothing
                  ;;
      esac
done
}


#########################################################

function Solaris_printing
{
LOOP=0     # Loop Counter - To grab three lines at a time

lpc status all | egrep ':|printing|queueing' | while read LINE
do
      # Load three unique lines at a time
      case $LINE in
      *:) Q=$(echo $LINE | cut -d ':' -f1)
          ;;
      printing*)
          PSTATUS=$(echo $LINE | awk '{print $3}')
          ;;
      queueing*)
          QSTATUS=$(echo $LINE | awk '{print $3}')
          ;;
      esac

      # Increment the LOOP counter
      (( LOOP = LOOP + 1 ))
      if ((LOOP == 3))  # Do we have all three lines of data?
      then
```

Listing 16.14   PQ_all_in_one.ksh shell script listing. *(continued)*

```
          # Check printing status
          case $PSTATUS in
          disabled) lpc start $Q >/dev/null
                    (($? == 0)) && echo "\n$Q printing re-started\n"
                    ;;
          enabled|*) :  # No-Op - Do Nothing
                    ;;
          esac

          # Check queuing status
          case $QSTATUS in
          disabled) lpc enable $Q >/dev/null
                    (($? == 0)) && echo "\n$Q queueing re-enabled\n"
                    ;;
          enabled|*) :  # No-Op - Do Nothing
                    ;;
          esac
          LOOP=0  # Reset the loop counter to zero
     fi
done
}


#########################################################
############### BEGINNING OF MAIN ####################
#########################################################

# What OS are we running?

# To start with we need to know the Unix flavor.
# This case statement runs the uname command to
# determine the OS name. Different functions are
# used for each OS to restart printing and queuing.

case $(uname) in

AIX) # AIX okay...Which printer subsystem?
     # Starting with AIX 5L we support System V printing also!

     # Check for an active qdaemon using the SRC lssrc command

     if (ps -ef | grep '/usr/sbin/qdaemon' | grep -v grep) \
         >/dev/null 2>&1
     then
          # Standard AIX printer subsystem found
          AIX_PSS=CLASSIC
     elif (ps -ef | grep '/usr/lib/lp/lpsched' | grep -v grep) \
         >/dev/null 2>&1
```

Listing 16.14   PQ_all_in_one.ksh shell script listing. *(continues)*

```
        then
                # AIX System V printer service is running
                AIX_PSS=SYSTEMV
        fi

        # Call the correct function for Classic AIX or SysV printing

        case $AIX_PSS in
        CLASSIC)  # Call the classic AIX printing function
                AIX_classic_printing
                ;;
        SYSTEMV)  # Call the AIX SysV printing function
                AIX_SYSV_printing
                ;;
        esac


    ;;
HP-UX)  # Call the HP-UX printing function
        HP_UX_printing


    ;;
Linux)  # Call the Linux printing function
        Linux_printing


    ;;
SunOS)  # Call the Solaris printing function
        Solaris_printing


    ;;
*)      # Anything else is unsupported.
        echo "\nERROR: Unsupported Operating System: $(uname)\n"
          echo "\n\t\t...EXITING...\n"
        ;;
esac
```

Listing 16.14   PQ_all_in_one.ksh shell script listing. *(continued)*

For each of the operating systems and, in the case of AIX, each printer service we took the previously created shell scripts, extracted the code, and placed it between function function_name { and the function ending character }. We now have the following functions:

```
AIX_classic_printing
AIX_SYSV_printing
HP_UX_printing
Linux_printing
Solaris_printing
```

To execute the correct function for a specific operating system, we need to know the Unix flavor. The **uname** command returns the following output for each of our target operating systems:

OS	uname Output
AIX	AIX
HP-UX	HP-UX
Linux	Linux
Solaris	SunOS

With the exception of AIX, this information is all that is needed to execute the correct function. But with AIX we have to determine which printer service is running on the server. Both types of print services have a process controlling them so we can **grep** for each of the processes using the **ps -ef** command to find the currently running printer service. When the classic AIX printer subsystem is running, there is a /usr/sbin/qdaemon process running. When the System V printer service is running, there is a /usr/lib/lp/lpsched process running. With this information we have everything needed to make a decision on the correct function to run.

We added at the end of the script all of the function execution control in the **case** statement that is shown in Listing 16.15.

```
case $(uname) in

AIX)   # AIX okay...Which printer subsystem?
       # Starting with AIX 5L we support System V printing also!

       # Check for an active qdaemon using the SRC lssrc command

       if (ps -ef | grep '/usr/sbin/qdaemon' | grep -v grep) \
          >/dev/null 2>&1
       then
              # Standard AIX printer subsystem found
              AIX_PSS=CLASSIC
       elif (ps -ef | grep '/usr/lib/lp/lpsched' | grep -v grep) \
          >/dev/null 2>&1
       then
              # AIX System V printer service is running
              AIX_PSS=SYSTEMV
       fi

       # Call the correct function for Classic AIX or SysV printing

       case $AIX_PSS in
       CLASSIC)  # Call the classic AIX printing function
                 AIX_classic_printing
              ;;
```

Listing 16.15 Controlling case statement listing to pick the OS. *(continues)*

```
        SYSTEMV)  # Call the AIX SysV printing function
                AIX_SYSV_printing
                ;;
        esac


        ;;
HP-UX)  # Call the HP-UX printing function
        HP_UX_printing


        ;;
Linux)  # Call the Linux printing function
        Linux_printing


        ;;
SunOS)  # Call the Solaris printing function
        Solaris_printing


        ;;
*)        # Anything else is unsupported.
        echo "\nERROR: Unsupported Operating System: $(uname)\n"
            echo "\n\t\t...EXITING...\n"
        ;;
esac
```

Listing 16.15   Controlling case statement listing to pick the OS. *(continued)*

I hope by now that the code in the **case** statement is intuitively obvious to read and understand. If not, the first line of the **case** block of code is the **uname** command. At this point we know what the OS flavor is. For HP-UX, Linux, and Solaris we execute the target OS printing function. For AIX we make an additional test to figure out which one of the supported printing services is running. The two options are System V and the Classic AIX printer subsystem.

Notice that I removed all of the logging functionality from the functions. With this type of setup, where you have the functions doing the work, you can move the logging out to the main body of the shell script. This means that you can capture all of the output data of the function to save to a log file, use the **tee** command to view the data while logging at the same time, or just point it to the bit bucket by redirection to `/dev/null`.

Other Options to Consider

As usual, we can always improve on a shell script, and these shell scripts are no exception. Some options that you may want to consider are listed next.

Logging

You may want to add logging with date/time stamps. If you are having a lot of trouble keeping certain print queues up, studying the log may give you a trend that can help you find the cause of the problem. Some queues may drop in a particular location more than others. This can indicate network problems to the site. Any time you start logging do not forget to keep an eye on the log files! I often see that a script is added to a production machine, and the next thing you know, the log file has grown so large that it has filled up the filesystem. Don't forget to prune the log files. Trimming the log files is another little shell script for you to write.

Exceptions Capability

In a lot of shops you do not want to enable every single printer and print queue. In this case you can create an *exceptions* file, which contains the queue/printer names that you want to exclude from enabling. You also may have special considerations if your shop uses specific forms at different times on some of the *floating* printers. Some shops are just print queue hell! Having the capability to keep the majority of the printers active all of the time and exclude a few is a nice thing to have.

Maintenance

During maintenance windows and other times when you want to stop all printing, you may want to comment out any cron table entries that are executing the enabling scripts. You usually find this out after the fact.

Scheduling

I keep a script running 24×7 to keep all of the printers available. You may want to tailor the monitoring scheduling to fit business hours (my requirement is 24×7). Users' loading up on print jobs during the middle of the day is always a problem, so we try to hold big jobs for times of low activity. Low activity times are the times when you want to be at home so make sure you are keeping the printers printing during these hours, or the next morning you will have the same problem.

Summary

In this chapter we covered some unique techniques to handle the data from command output. In the Linux script we used arrays to hold the data as array elements. In other cases we read in a line at a time and used tags to grab the data we needed. We learned how to process a specific number of lines of data in groups by using a loop counter within a **while** loop.

The techniques in this chapter are varied, but the solutions are readable and can be easily maintained. Someone will follow in your footsteps and try to figure out what you did when you wrote the shell script. Do not play the "job security" game because you are you own worst enemy when it comes to documenting your shell scripts. If you comment when you write the script and make a note in the REV section when you edit it, you will have a long, happy life using your shell script.

In the next chapter we are going to move into the world of FTP. The object of the next chapter is to automate file transfers between systems using FTP, or file transfer protocol.

CHAPTER

17

Automated FTP Stuff

In many shops the business relies on nightly, or even hourly, file transfers of data that is to be processed. Due to the importance of this data, the data movement must be automated. The extent of automation in the **ftp** world is threefold. We want the ability to move outbound files to another site, move inbound files from a remote location to your local machine, and check a remote site on a regular basis for files that are ready to download. In this chapter we are going to create some shell scripts to handle each of these scenarios.

Most businesses that rely on this type of data movement also require some pre-**ftp** and post-**ftp** processing to ready the system for the files before the transfer takes place and to verify the data integrity or file permissions after the transfer. For this pre and post processing we need to build into the shell script the ability to either hard-code the pre and post processing events or point to a file that performs these tasks. Now we are up to five pieces of code that we need to create. Before we go any further let's look at the syntax for the **ftp** connections.

Syntax

Normally when we **ftp** a file, the remote machine's hostname is included as an argument to the **ftp** command. We are prompted for the password and, if it is entered correctly, we are logged into the remote machine. We then can move to the local directory

441

containing the file we want to upload, then to the directory that is to receive the upload from our local machine. In either case we are working with an interactive program. A typical **ftp** session looks like the output shown in Listing 17.1.

```
[root:yogi]@/# cd /scripts/download
[root:yogi]@/scripts/download# ftp wilma
Connected to wilma.
220 wilma FTP server (SunOS 5.8) ready.
Name (wilma:root): randy
331 Password required for randy.
Password:
230 User randy logged in.
ftp> cd /scripts
250 CWD command successful.
ftp> get auto_ftp_xfer.ksh
200 PORT command successful.
150 ASCII data connection for auto_ftp_xfer.ksh (10.10.10.1,32787) (227
bytes).
226 ASCII Transfer complete.
246 bytes received in 0.0229 seconds (10.49 Kbytes/s)
local: auto_ftp_xfer.ksh remote: auto_ftp_xfer.ksh
ftp> bye
221 Goodbye.
[root:yogi]@/scripts/download#
```

Listing 17.1 Typical FTP file download.

As you can see in Listing 17.1 the **ftp** command requires interaction with the user to make the transfer of the file from the remote machine to the local machine. How do we automate this interactive process? If you have been studying other chapters, then you know the answer is a *here document*. A here document is a coding technique that allows us to place all of the required interactive command input between two *labels*. Let's look at an example of coding a simple **ftp** transfer using this automation technique in Listing 17.2.

```
#!/bin/ksh
#
# SCRIPT: tst_ftp.ksh
# AUTHOR: Randy Michael
# DATE: 6/12/2002
# REV: 1.1.A
# PLATOFRM: Not platform dependent
```

Listing 17.2 Simple here document for FTP transfer in a script.

```
#
# PURPOSE: This shell script is a simple demonstration of
#          using a here document in a shell script to automate
#          an FTP file transfer.
#

# Connect to the remote machine and begin a here document.

ftp -i -v -n wilma <<END_FTP

user randy mypassword
binary
lcd /scripts/download
cd /scripts
get auto_ftp_xfer.ksh
bye

END_FTP
```

Listing 17.2   Simple here document for FTP transfer in a script. *(continued)*

Notice in Listing 17.2 where the beginning and ending labels are located. The first label, <<END_FTP, begins the here document and is located just after the interactive command that requires input, which is the **ftp** command in our case. Next comes all of the input that a user would have to supply to the interactive command. In this example we log in to the remote machine, **wilma**, using the user randy mypassword syntax. This **ftp** command specifies that the user is randy and the password is mypassword. Once the user is logged in, we set up the environment for the transfer by setting the transfer mode to binary, locally changing directory to /scripts/ download, then changing directory on the remote machine to /scripts. The last step is to get the auto_ftp_xfer.ksh file. To exit the **ftp** session we use bye; quit also works. The last label, END_FTP, ends the here document, and the script exits.

Also notice the **ftp** command switches used in Listing 17.2. The **-i** command switch turns off interactive prompting during multiple file transfers so there is no prompt for the username and password. See the FTP **man** pages for **prompt, mget, mput**, and **mdelete** subcommands for descriptions of prompting during multiple file transfers. The **-n** switch prevents an automatic login on the initial connection. Otherwise, the **ftp** command searches for a $HOME/.netrc entry that describes the login and initialization process for the remote host. See the **user** subcommand in the **man** page for **ftp**. The **-v** switch was added to the **ftp** command to set *verbose* mode, which allows us to see the commands as the **ftp** sessions runs. The tst_ftp.ksh shell script from Listing 17.2 is shown in action in Listing 17.3.

```
[root:yogi]@/scripts# ./tst_ftp.ksh
Connected to wilma.
220 wilma FTP server (SunOS 5.8) ready.
331 Password required for randy.
230 User randy logged in.
200 Type set to I.
Local directory now /scripts/download
250 CWD command successful.
200 PORT command successful.
150 Binary data connection for auto_ftp_xfer.ksh (10.10.10.1,32793)
(227 bytes).
226 Binary Transfer complete.
227 bytes received in 0.001092 seconds (203 Kbytes/s)
local: auto_ftp_xfer.ksh remote: auto_ftp_xfer.ksh
221 Goodbye.
[root:yogi]@/scripts#
```

Listing 17.3   Simple automated FTP file transfer using a script.

Using these techniques we are going to create shell scripts to tackle some of the common needs of a business that depends on either receiving data from or transferring data to a remote host.

Automating File Transfers and Remote Directory Listings

We have the basic idea of automating an **ftp** file transfer, but what do we want to accomplish? We really want to do three things: download one or more files with **get** or **mget**, upload one or more files with **put** or **mput**, and get a directory listing from a remote host. The first two items are standard uses for any **ftp** script, but getting a remote directory listing has not been explained in any of the documentation of a scripting technique that I have seen.

Additionally, we need to add the ability of pre-event and post-event processing. For example, a pre-**ftp** event may be getting a directory listing from a remote host. A post-**ftp** event may be changing the ownership and file permissions on a newly downloaded file. This last example brings up another point. When you **ftp** a file that has the execute bit set, the file will be received with the execute bit *unset*. Any time you **ftp** a file, the execution bit is stripped out of the file permissions.

Let's look at these topics one at a time.

Using FTP for Directory Listings on a Remote Machine

To save a remote directory listing from a remote system to a local file, we use the **ftp** subcommand **nlist**. The **nlist** subcommand has the following form:

```
nlist [RemoteDirectory][LocalFile]
```

The **nlist** subcommand writes a listing of the contents of the specified remote directory (RemoteDirectory) to the specified local file (LocalFile). If the RemoteDirectory parameter is not specified, the **nlist** subcommand lists the contents of the current remote directory. If the LocalFile parameter is not specified or is a - (hyphen), the **nlist** subcommand displays the listing on the local terminal.

Let's create a little shell script to test this idea. We can use most of the shell script contents shown in Listing 17.2, but we remove the **get** command and replace it with the **nlist** subcommand. Take a look at Listing 17.4.

```
#!/bin/ksh
#
# SCRIPT: get_remote_dir_listing.ksh
# AUTHOR: Randy Michael
# DATE: July 15, 2002
# REV: 1.1.P
#
# PLATFORM: Not Platform Dependent
#
# PURPOSE: This shell script uses FTP to get a remote directory listing
#          and save this list in a local file.
#
# set -n # Uncomment to check the script syntax without any execution
# set -x # Uncomment to debug this shell script
#
####################################################################
################## DEFINE VARIABLES HERE ###########################
####################################################################

RNODE="wilma"
USER="randy"
UPASSWD="mypassword"
LOCALDIR="/scripts/download"
REMOTEDIR="/scripts"
DIRLISTFILE="${LOCALDIR}/${RNODE}.$(basename ${REMOTEDIR}).dirlist.out"
cat /dev/null > $DIRLISTFILE


####################################################################
##################### BEGINNING OF MAIN ############################
####################################################################

ftp -i -v -n $RNODE <<END_FTP
user $USER $UPASSWD
nlist $REMOTEDIR $DIRLISTFILE
bye

END_FTP
```

Listing 17.4   get_remote_dir_listing.ksh shell script listing.

There are several things to point out in Listing 17.4. We start out with a variable definition section. In this section we define the remote node, the username and password for the remote node, a local directory, a remote directory, and finally the local file that is to hold the remote directory listing. Notice that we had to create this file. If the local file does not already exist, then the remote listing to the local file will fail. To create the file you can use either of the following techniques:

```
cat /dev/null > $DIRLISTFILE
>$DIRLISTFILE
touch $DIRLISTFILE
```

The first two examples create an empty file or will make an existing file empty. The **touch** command will update the time stamp for the file modification for an existing file and will create the file if it does not exist.

At the BEGINNING OF MAIN we have our five lines of code that obtain the directory listing from the remote node. We use the same technique as we did in Listing 17.2 except that we use variables for the remote node name, username, and password. Variables are also used for the directory name on the remote machine and for the local filename that holds the directory listing from the remote machine using the **ftp** subcommand **nlist**.

Notice that the password is hard-coded into this shell script. This is a security nightmare! In a later section in this chapter we will cover a technique of replacing hard-coded passwords with hidden password variables.

Getting One or More Files from a Remote System

Now we get to some file transfers. Basically we are going to combine the shell scripts in Listings 17.1 and 17.4. We are also going to add the functionality to add pre- and post-**ftp** events. Let's start by looking at the shell script in Listing 17.5, get_ftp_files.ksh.

```
#!/bin/ksh
#
# SCRIPT: get_ftp_files.ksh
# AUTHOR: Randy Michael
# DATE: July 15, 2002
# REV: 1.1.P
#
# PLATFORM: Not Platform Dependent
#
# PURPOSE: This shell script uses FTP to get a list of one or more
#          remote files from a remote machine.
#
# set -n # Uncomment to check the script syntax without any execution
```

Listing 17.5   get_ftp_files.ksh shell script listing.

```
# set -x # Uncomment to debug this shell script
#
######################################################################
################## DEFINE VARIABLES HERE ##########################
######################################################################


REMOTEFILES=$1

THISSCRIPT=$(basename $0)
RNODE="wilma"
USER="randy"
UPASSWD="mypassword"
LOCALDIR="/scripts/download"
REMOTEDIR="/scripts"


######################################################################
################## DEFINE FUNCTIONS HERE ##########################
######################################################################


pre_event ()
{
# Add anything that you want to execute in this function. You can
# hard-code the tasks in this function or create an external shell
# script and execute the external function here.

:  # no-op: The colon (:) is a no-op character. It does nothing and
   # always produces a 0, zero, return code.
}


######################################################################

post_event ()
{
# Add anything that you want to execute in this function. You can
# hard-code the tasks in this function or create an external shell
# script and execute the external function here.

:  # no-op: The colon (:) is a no-op character. It does nothing and
   # always produces a 0, zero, return code.
}


######################################################################

usage ()
{
echo "\nUSAGE: $THISSCRIPT \"One or More Filenames to Download\" \n"
exit 1
```

Listing 17.5   get_ftp_files.ksh shell script listing. *(continues)*

```
}

################################################################

usage_error ()
{
echo "\nERROR: This shell script requires a list of one or more
       files to download from the remote site.\n"

usage
}

################################################################
#################### BEGINNING OF MAIN #########################
################################################################

# Test to ensure that the file(s) is/are specified in the $1
# command-line argument.

(($# != 1)) && usage_error

pre_event

# Connect to the remote site and begin the here document.

ftp -i -v -n $RNODE <<END_FTP

user $USER $UPASSWD
binary
lcd $LOCALDIR
cd $REMOTEDIR
mget $REMOTEFILES
bye

END_FTP

post_event
```

Listing 17.5 get_ftp_files.ksh shell script listing. *(continued)*

We made a few changes in Listing 17.5. The major change is that we get the list of files to download from the **$1** command-line argument. If more than one file is listed on the command line, then they must be enclosed in quotes, "file1 file2 file3 file*n*", so they are interpreted as a single argument in the shell script. A blank space is assumed when separating the filenames in the list.

Notice that the local and remote directories are hard-coded into the shell script. If you want, you can modify this shell script and use **getopts** to parse through some command-line switches. This is beyond the basic concept of this chapter.

Because we are now requiring a single argument on the command line, we also need to add a `usage` function to this shell script. We are looking for exactly one command-line argument. If this is not the case, then we execute the `usage_error` function, which in turn executes the `usage` function.

Because we may have more than one filename specified on the command line, we need to use the **ftp** subcommand **mget**, as opposed to **get**. We have already turned off interactive prompting by adding the **-i** switch to the **ftp** command so there will not be any prompting when using **mget**.

Pre and Post Events

Notice in Listing 17.5 that we added two new functions, `pre_event` and `post_event`. By default, both of these functions contain only the no-op character, `:` (colon). A `:` does nothing but always has a return code of 0, zero. We are using this as a placeholder to have something in the function.

If you have a desire to perform a task before or after the **ftp** activity, then enter the tasks in the `pre_event` and/or the `post_event` functions. It is a good idea to enter only a filename of an external shell script rather than editing this shell script and trying to debug a function in an already working shell script. An external shell script filename, that is executable, is all that is needed to execute the pre and post events.

In the external shell script enter everything that needs to be done to set up the environment for the **ftp** file transfers. Some things that you may want to do include removing the old files from a directory before downloading new files or getting a directory listing of a remote host to see if there is anything to even download. You can make the code as long or as short as needed to accomplish the task at hand.

Script in Action

To see the shell script in Listing 17.5 in action, look at Listing 17.6 where we are transferring the shell script to another host in the network.

```
[root:yogi]@/scripts# ./get_ftp_files.ksh get_ftp_files.ksh
Connected to wilma.
220 wilma FTP server (SunOS 5.8) ready.
331 Password required for randy.
230 User randy logged in.
200 Type set to I.
Local directory now /scripts/download
250 CWD command successful.
200 PORT command successful.
```

Listing 17.6   get_ftp_files.ksh shell script in action. *(continues)*

```
150 Binary data connection for get_ftp_files.ksh (10.10.10.1,32808)
(1567 bytes)
.
226 Binary Transfer complete.
1567 bytes received in 0.001116 seconds (1371 Kbytes/s)
local: get_ftp_files.ksh remote: get_ftp_files.ksh
221 Goodbye.
[root:yogi]@/scripts#
```

Listing 17.6   get_ftp_files.ksh shell script in action. *(continued)*

In this example the transfer is taking place between a local AIX machine called **yogi** and the remote SunOS machine called **wilma**.

Putting One or More Files to a Remote System

Uploading files to another machine is the same as downloading the files except we now use the **put** and **mput** commands. Let's slightly modify the shell script in Listing 17.5 to make it into an upload script. This script modification is shown in Listing 17.7.

```
#!/bin/ksh
#
# SCRIPT: put_ftp_files.ksh
# AUTHOR: Randy Michael
# DATE: July 15, 2002
# REV: 1.1.P
#
# PLATFORM: Not Platform Dependent
#
# PURPOSE: This shell script uses FTP to put a list of one or more
#          local files to a remote machine.
#
# set -n # Uncomment to check the script syntax without any execution
# set -x # Uncomment to debug this shell script
#
#################################################################
################ DEFINE VARIABLES HERE #########################
#################################################################

LOCALFILES=$1

THISSCRIPT=$(basename $0)
RNODE="wilma"
```

Listing 17.7   put_ftp_files.ksh shell script listing.

```
USER="randy"
UPASSWD="mypassword"
LOCALDIR="/scripts"
REMOTEDIR="/scripts/download"


##################################################################
################# DEFINE FUNCTIONS HERE #########################
##################################################################

pre_event ()
{
# Add anything that you want to execute in this function. You can
# hard-code the tasks in this function or create an external shell
# script and execute the external function here.

:   # no-op: The colon (:) is a no-op character. It does nothing and
    # always produces a 0, zero, return code.
}


##################################################################

post_event ()
{
# Add anything that you want to execute in this function. You can
# hard-code the tasks in this function or create an external shell
# script and execute the external function here.

:   # no-op: The colon (:) is a no-op character. It does nothing and
    # always produces a 0, zero, return code.
}


##################################################################

usage ()
{
echo "\nUSAGE: $THISSCRIPT \"One or More Filenames to Download\" \n"
exit 1
}


##################################################################

usage_error ()
{
echo "\nERROR: This shell script requires a list of one or more
       files to download from the remote site.\n"

usage
```

Listing 17.7   put_ftp_files.ksh shell script listing. *(continues)*

```
}

####################################################################
#################### BEGINNING OF MAIN #############################
####################################################################

# Test to ensure that the file(s) is/are specified in the $1
# command-line argument.

(($# != 1)) && usage_error

pre_event

# Connect to the remote site and begin the here document.

ftp -i -v -n $RNODE <<END_FTP

user $USER $UPASSWD
binary
lcd $LOCALDIR
cd $REMOTEDIR
mput $LOCALFILES
bye

END_FTP

post_event
```

Listing 17.7 put_ftp_files.ksh shell script listing. *(continued)*

The script in Listing 17.7 uses the same techniques as the get_ftp_files.ksh shell script in Listing 17.5. We have changed the **$1** variable assignment to LOCAL-FILES instead of REMOTEFILES and changed the **ftp** transfer mode to **mput** to upload the files to a remote machine. Other than these two changes the scripts are identical.

In all of the shell scripts in this chapter we have a security nightmare with hard-coded passwords. In the next section is a technique that allows us to remove these hard-coded passwords and replace them with hidden password variables. Following the next section we will use this technique to modify each of our shell scripts to utilize hidden password variables.

Replacing Hard-Coded Passwords with Variables

Traditionally when a password is required in shell script it has been hard-coded into the script. Using this hard-coded technique presents us with a lot of challenges, ranging from a security nightmare to the inability to change key passwords on a regular basis. The variable technique presented in this section is very easy to implement with only minor changes to *each* shell script.

NOTE Important: *Each* shell script must be changed in order to properly implement the technique throughout the infrastructure.

The variable replacement technique consists of a single file that contains unique variable assignments for each password required for shell scripts on the system. A sample password file looks like the following:

```
DBORAPW=alpha
DBADMPW=beta
BACKUPW=gamma
RANDY=mypassword
```

Some of the considerations of implementing this variable replacement technique include the following:

- The scope of where the variable containing the password can be seen
- The file permission of the password variable file that contains the hard-coded passwords

To limit the scope of the variable it is extremely important that the variable *not* be exported in the password variable file. If the variable is exported, then you will be able to see the password *in plain text* in the process environment of the shell script that is using the password variable. Additionally, with all of these passwords in a single file, the file must be locked down to *read-only* by root ideally.

The best illustration of this technique is a real example of how it works. In the following code sections, shown in Listings 17.8, 17.9, and 17.10, there is a password file that contains the password variable assignments that has the name setpwenv.ksh (notice this file is a shell script!). In the first file, the password variable *is* exported. In the second file, the password variable is *not* exported. Following these two files is a shell script, mypwdtest.ksh, that executes the password environment file, setpwenv.ksh, and tests to see if the password is visible in the environment.

NOTE Test results of using each technique are detailed in the next section of this chapter.

Example of Detecting Variables in a Script's Environment

We start the examples with a setpwenv.ksh file that exports the password variable in Listing 17.8.

```
#!/bin/ksh
#
# SCRIPT: setpwenv.ksh
#
# PURPOSE: This shell script is executed by other shell
```

Listing 17.8 Password file with the password variable exported. *(continues)*

```
#               scripts that need a password contained in
#               a variable
#
#
# This password is NOT exported

# MYPWDTST=bonehead

# This password IS exported

MYPWDTST=bonehead
export MYPWDTST
```

Listing 17.8   Password file with the password variable exported. *(continued)*

Notice in Listing 17.8 that the password *is* exported. As you will see, this export of the password variable will cause the password to be visible in plain text in the calling shell script's environment.

The password file in Listing 17.9 shows an example of *not* exporting the password variable.

```
#!/bin/ksh
#
# SCRIPT: setpwenv.ksh
#
# PURPOSE: This shell script is executed by other shell
#          scripts that need a password contained in
#          a variable
#
#
# This password is NOT exported

MYPWDTST=bonehead

# This password IS exported

# MYPWDTST=bonehead
# export MYPWDTST
```

Listing 17.9   Password file showing the variable *not* exported.

Notice in Listing 17.9 that the password is *not* exported. As you will see, this variable assignment without exporting the password variable will cause the password to *not* be visible in the calling shell script's environment, which is the result that we are looking for.

The shell script shown in Listing 17.10 performs the test of the visibility of the password assigned for each of the password environment files.

```
#!/usr/bin/ksh
#
# SCRIPT: mypwdtest.ksh
#
# PURPOSE: This shell script is used to demonstrate the
#          use of passwords hidden in variables.
#
# set -x # Uncomment to debug this script
# set -n # Uncomment to check syntax without any execution

# Set the BIN directory
BINDIR=/usr/local/bin

# Execute the shell script that contains the password variable
# assignments.

. ${BINDIR}/setpwenv.ksh

echo "\n\nPASS is $MYPWDTST"  # Display the password contained in
                              # the variable
echo "\nSearching for the password in the environment..."
env | grep $MYPWDTST
if (($? == 0))
then
     echo "\nERROR: Password was found in the environment\n\n"
else
     echo "\nSUCCESS: Password was NOT found in the environment\n\n"
fi
```

Listing 17.10   Shell script to demonstrate the scope of a variable.

The shell script shown in Listing 17.10, `mypwdtest.ksh`, tests the environment using each of the `setpwenv.ksh` shell scripts, one with the password environment exported and the second file that does not do the export. You can see the results of the tests here.

Example with the Password Variable Exported

```
PASS is bonehead

Searching for the password in the environment...
MYPWDTST=bonehead

ERROR: Password was found in the environment
```

Notice in the previous example that the password is visible in the shell script's environment. When the password is visible you can run the **env** command while the `mypwdtest.ksh` shell script is executing and see the password in plain text. Therefore, anyone could conceivably get the passwords very easily. Notice in the next output that the password is hidden.

Example with the Password Variable *Not* Exported

```
PASS is bonehead

Searching for the password in the environment...

SUCCESS: Password was NOT found in the environment
```

> **WARNING** As you can see, it is extremely important never to export a password variable.

To implement this variable password substitution into your shell scripts you only need to add the password to the password environment file using a unique variable name. Then inside the shell script that requires the password you execute the password file, which is `setpwenv.ksh` in our case. After the password file is executed the password variable(s) is/are ready to use.

> **NOTE** The preceding content uses this technique for passwords; however, this practice can also be utilized for usernames, hostnames, and application variables. The main purpose of this exercise is to have a central point of changing passwords on a regular basis and to eliminate hard-coded passwords in shell scripts.

Modifying Our FTP Scripts to Use Password Variables

As you saw in the previous section, *Replacing Hard-Coded Passwords with Variables,* it is an easy task to modify a shell script to take advantage of hidden password variables. Here we make the two lines of modifications to our **nlist**, **get**, and **put** shell scripts.

The first thing that we need to do is create a password environment file. Let's use a name that is a little more obscure than `setpwenv.ksh`. How about `setlink.ksh`? Also, let's hide the `setlink.ksh` shell script in `/usr/sbin` for a little more security. Next let's set the file permissions to 400, *read-only* by the owner (**root**). Now you may be asking how can we execute a shell script that is read-only. All we need to do is to *dot* the filename. An example of dotting the file is shown here.

```
. /usr/sbin/setlink.ksh
```

The dot just says to execute the filename that follows. Now let's set up the password environment file. This example assumes that the user is **root**.

```
echo "RANDY=mypassword" >> /usr/sbin/setlink.ksh
chown 400 /usr/sbin/setlink.ksh
```

Now in each of our shell scripts we need to *dot* the /usr/sbin/setlink.ksh file and replace the hard-coded password with the password variable defined in the external file, /usr/sbin/setlink.ksh, which is $RANDY in our case.

Listings 17.11, 17.12, and 17.13 show the modified shell scripts with the hard-coded passwords removed.

```
#!/bin/ksh
#
# SCRIPT: get_remote_dir_listing_pw_var.ksh
# AUTHOR: Randy Michael
# DATE: July 15, 2002
# REV: 1.1.P
#
# PLATFORM: Not Platform Dependent
#
# PURPOSE: This shell script uses FTP to get a remote directory listing
#          and save this list in a local file. This shell script uses
#          remotely defined passwords.
#
# set -n # Uncomment to check the script syntax without any execution
# set -x # Uncomment to debug this shell script
#
######################################################################
################## DEFINE VARIABLES HERE ###########################
######################################################################

RNODE="wilma"
USER="randy"
LOCALDIR="/scripts/download"
REMOTEDIR="/scripts"
DIRLISTFILE="${LOCALDIR}/${RNODE}.$(basename ${REMOTEDIR}).dirlist.out"
cat /dev/null > $DIRLISTFILE

######################################################################
#################### BEGINNING OF MAIN ###########################
######################################################################

# Get a password
```

Listing 17.11   get_remote_dir_listing_pw_var.ksh script listing. *(continues)*

```
. /usr/sbin/setlink.ksh

ftp -i -v -n $RNODE <<END_FTP

user $USER $RANDY
nlist $REMOTEDIR $DIRLISTFILE
bye

END_FTP
```

Listing 17.11   get_remote_dir_listing_pw_var.ksh script listing. *(continued)*

In Listing 17.11 the only modifications that we made to the original shell script include a script name change, the removal of hard-coded passwords, adding the execution of the `/usr/sbin/setlink.ksh` shell script, and adding the `$RANDY` remotely defined password variable.

```
#!/bin/ksh
#
# SCRIPT: get_ftp_files_pw_var.ksh
# AUTHOR: Randy Michael
# DATE: July 15, 2002
# REV: 1.1.P
#
# PLATFORM: Not Platform Dependent
#
# PURPOSE: This shell script uses FTP to get one or more remote
#          files from a remote machine. This shell script uses a
#          remotely defined password variable.
#
# set -n # Uncomment to check the script syntax without any execution
# set -x # Uncomment to debug this shell script
#
##################################################################
################# DEFINE VARIABLES HERE ##########################
##################################################################

REMOTEFILES=$1

THISSCRIPT=$(basename $0)
RNODE="wilma"
USER="randy"
LOCALDIR="/scripts/download"
```

Listing 17.12   get_ftp_files_pw_var.ksh shell script listing.

```
REMOTEDIR="/scripts"

######################################################################
################## DEFINE FUNCTIONS HERE ##########################
######################################################################

pre_event ()
{
# Add anything that you want to execute in this function. You can
# hard-code the tasks in this function or create an external shell
# script and execute the external function here.

:   # no-op: The colon (:) is a no-op character. It does nothing and
    # always produces a 0, zero, return code.
}


####################################################################

post_event ()
{
# Add anything that you want to execute in this function. You can
# hard-code the tasks in this function or create an external shell
# script and execute the external function here.

:   # no-op: The colon (:) is a no-op character. It does nothing and
    # always produces a 0, zero, return code.
}


####################################################################

usage ()
{
echo "\nUSAGE: $THISSCRIPT \"One or More Filenames to Download\" \n"
exit 1
}


####################################################################

usage_error ()
{
echo "\nERROR: This shell script requires a list of one or more
      files to download from the remote site.\n"

usage
}


####################################################################
##################### BEGINNING OF MAIN ##########################
```

Listing 17.12   get_ftp_files_pw_var.ksh shell script listing. *(continues)*

```
##################################################################

# Test to ensure that the file(s) is/are specified in the $1
# command-line argument.

(($# != 1)) && usage_error

# Get a password

. /usr/sbin/setlink.ksh

pre_event

ftp -i -v -n $RNODE <<END_FTP

user $USER $RANDY
binary
lcd $LOCALDIR
cd $REMOTEDIR
mget $REMOTEFILES
bye

END_FTP

post_event
```

Listing 17.12   get_ftp_files_pw_var.ksh shell script listing. *(continued)*

In Listing 17.12 the only modifications that we made to the original shell script include a script name change, the removal of hard-coded passwords, adding the execution of the /usr/sbin/setlink.ksh shell script, and adding the $RANDY remotely defined password variable.

```
#!/bin/ksh
#
# SCRIPT: put_ftp_files_pw_var.ksh
# AUTHOR: Randy Michael
# DATE: July 15, 2002
# REV: 1.1.P
#
# PLATFORM: Not Platform Dependent
#
# PURPOSE: This shell script uses FTP to put a list of one or more
#          local files to a remote machine. This shell script uses
```

Listing 17.13   put_ftp_files_pw_var.ksh shell script listing.

```
#          remotely defined password variables
#
# set -n # Uncomment to check the script syntax without any execution
# set -x # Uncomment to debug this shell script
#
###################################################################
################## DEFINE VARIABLES HERE #########################
###################################################################

LOCALFILES=$1

THISSCRIPT=$(basename $0)
RNODE="wilma"
USER="randy"
LOCALDIR="/scripts"
REMOTEDIR="/scripts/download"


###################################################################
################## DEFINE FUNCTIONS HERE #########################
###################################################################

pre_event ()
{
# Add anything that you want to execute in this function. You can
# hard-code the tasks in this function or create an external shell
# script and execute the external function here.

:  # no-op: The colon (:) is a no-op character. It does nothing and
   # always produces a 0, zero, return code.
}


###################################################################

post_event ()
{
# Add anything that you want to execute in this function. You can
# hard-code the tasks in this function or create an external shell
# script and execute the external function here.

:  # no-op: The colon (:) is a no-op character. It does nothing and
   # always produces a 0, zero, return code.
}


###################################################################

usage ()
{
echo "\nUSAGE: $THISSCRIPT \"One or More Filenames to Download\" \n"
```

Listing 17.13   put_ftp_files_pw_var.ksh shell script listing. *(continues)*

```
exit 1
}

####################################################################

usage_error ()
{
echo "\nERROR: This shell script requires a list of one or more
        files to download from the remote site.\n"

usage
}

####################################################################
##################### BEGINNING OF MAIN #########################
####################################################################

# Test to ensure that the file(s) is/are specified in the $1
# command-line argument.

(($# != 1)) && usage_error

# Get a password

. /usr/sbin/setlink.ksh

pre_event

# Connect to the remote site and begin the here document.

ftp -i -v -n $RNODE <<END_FTP

user $USER $RANDY
binary
lcd $LOCALDIR
cd $REMOTEDIR
mput $LOCALFILES
bye

END_FTP

post_event
```

Listing 17.13 put_ftp_files_pw_var.ksh shell script listing. *(continued)*

In Listings 17.11–17.13 the only modifications that we made to the original shell scripts include a script name change, the removal of hard-coded passwords, adding the execution of the /usr/sbin/setlink.ksh shell script, and adding the $RANDY remotely defined password variable.

Other Things to Consider

This set of shell scripts is very useful to a lot of businesses, but you will need to tailor the shell scripts to fit your environment. Some options that you may want to consider are listed in the following sections.

Use Command-Line Switches to Control Execution

By using **getopts** to parse command-line options you can modify these shell scripts to have all of the variables assigned on the command line with switches and switch-arguments. This modification can allow you to specify the target host, the local and remote working directories, and the file(s) to act on. We have used **getopts** a lot in this book, so look at some of the other chapters that use **getopts** to parse the command-line switches and try making some modifications as an exercise.

Keep a Log of Activity

It is a very good idea to keep a log of each connection and check the return codes. If you use the **ftp** switch **-v** you will have a detailed account of the connection activity of each transaction. Remember to add a date stamp to each log entry, and also remember to trim the log file periodically so the filesystem does not fill up.

Add a Debug Mode to the Scripts

If a connection fails you could put the script into debug mode by adding a function called debug. In this function the first thing to do is to **ping** the remote machine to see if it is reachable. If the machine is not reachable by pinging, then attempting to **ftp** to the remote node is useless.

You can also issue the **ftp** command with the debug option turned on, specified by the **-d** switch. For more information on **ftp** debug mode see the **man** pages for the **ftp** command.

Summary

This chapter is meant to form a basis for creating larger shell scripts that require the transfer of files between machines. The set of shell scripts presented in this chapter can be modified or made onto functions to suit your needs. There are too many variables for the use of **ftp** to follow each path to its logical end, so in this case you get the building blocks. If you have trouble with a shell script, always try to do the same thing the shell script is doing, except do it on the command line. Usually you can find where the problem is very quickly. If you cannot reach a remote node, then try to **ping** the machine. If you cannot **ping** the machine, then network connectivity or name resolution is the problem.

In the next chapter we are moving on to finding large files on the system. This is a nice tool to clean up filesystems and to look for files that have filled up a filesystem. You start from the current top-level directory, and the search traverses from the current directory to all subdirectories below. I hope you found this chapter useful, and I'll see you in the next chapter!

Finding "Large" Files

Filesystem alert! We all hate to get full filesystem alerts, especially at quitting time on Friday when the developers are trying to meet a deadline. The usual culprit is one or more *large* files that were just created, compiled, or loaded. Determining the definition of a large file varies by system environment, but a "large" file can fill up a filesystem quickly, especially in a development shop. To find these large files we need a flexible tool that will search for files larger than a user-defined value. The **find** command is your friend when a filesystem search is needed.

The **find** command is one of the most flexible and powerful commands on the system. Before we get started, print out the manual page for the **find** command. Enter the following command:

```
man find | lp -d print_queue_name
```

The previous command will print the manual page output to the printer defined by `print_queue_name`. By studying the **find** command manual page you can see that the **find** command is the most flexible command on the system. You can find files by modification/creation time, last access time, exact size, greater-than size, owner, group, permission, and a boatload of other options. You can also execute a command to act on the file(s) using the **-exec** command switch. For this chapter we are going to concentrate on finding files larger that an integer value specified on the command line. As with all of our shell scripts, we first need to get the correct command syntax for our task.

Syntax

We are going to use the **-size** option for the **find** command. There are two things to consider when using the **-size** command switch. We must supply an argument for this switch, and the argument must be an integer. But the integer number alone as an argument to the **-size** switch specifies an *exact* value, and the value is expressed, by default, in 512-byte blocks instead of measuring the file size in bytes. For a more familiar measurement we would like to specify our search value in megabytes (MB). To specify the value in bytes instead of 512-byte blocks we add the character **c** as a suffix to the integer value, and to get to MB we can just add six zeros. We also want to look at values *greater than* the command-line integer value. To specify greater than we add a + (plus sign) as a prefix to the integer value. With these specifications the command will look like the following:

```
find $SEARCH_PATH -size +integer_valuec  -print
```

To search for files greater than 5MB we can use the following command:

```
find $SEARCH_PATH -size +5000000c -print
```

The + (plus sign) specifies greater than, and the **c** denotes bytes. Also notice in the previous command that we specified a path to search using the variable $SEARCH_PATH. The **find** command requires a search path to be defined in the first argument to the command. We also added the **-print** switch at the end of the command line. If you omit the **-print**, then you cannot guarantee that any output will be produced. The command will return the appropriate return code but may not give any output, even if the files were found! I have found this to be operating system dependent by both Unix flavor and release. Just always remember to add the **-print** switch to the **find** command, and you will not be surprised.

For ease of using this shell script we are going to assume that the search will always begin in the current directory. The **pwd** command, or *print working directory* command, will display the full pathname of the current directory. Using our script this way requires that the shell script is located in a directory that is in the user's $PATH, or you must use the full script pathname any time you use the shell script. I typically put all of my scripts in the /usr/local/bin directory and add this directory to my $PATH environment. You can add a directory to your path using the following command syntax:

```
PATH=$PATH:/usr/local/bin
export PATH
```

Creating the Script

We have the basic idea of the **find** command syntax, so let's write a script. The only argument that we want from the user is a positive integer representing the number of megabytes (MB) to trigger the search on. We will add the extra six zeros inside the shell script. As always, we need to confirm that the data supplied on the command line is valid and usable. For our search script we are expecting exactly one argument; therefore, $# must equal one. We are also expecting the argument to be an integer so the regular expression +([0-9]) should be true. We will use this regular expression in a **case** statement to confirm that we have an integer. The integer specified must also be a positive value so the value given must be greater than zero. If all three tests are true, then we have a valid value to trigger our search.

I can envision this script producing a daily report at some shops. To facilitate the reporting we need some information from the system. I would like to know the hostname of the machine that the report represents. The **hostname** command will provide this information. A date and time stamp would be nice to have also. The **date** command has plenty of options for the time stamp, and because this is going to be a report, we should store the data in a file for printing and future review. We can just define a $OUTPUT file to store our report on disk.

Everyone needs to understand that this script always starts the search from the *current working directory*, defined by the system environment variable $PWD and the **pwd** command. We are going to use the **pwd** command and assign the output to the SEARCH_PATH script variable. The only other thing we want to do before starting the search is to create a header for the $OUTFILE file. For the header information we can append all of the pertinent system data we have already gathered from the system to the $OUTFILE.

We are now ready to perform the search starting from the current directory. Starting a search from the current directory implies, again, that this script filename must be in the $PATH for the user who is executing the script, or the full pathname to the script must be used instead.

Study the findlarge.ksh shell script in Listing 18.1, and pay attention to the bold type.

```
#!/usr/bin/ksh
#
# SCRIPT: findlarge.ksh
#
# AUTHOR: Randy Michael
#
# DATE: 11/30/2000
#
# REV: 1.0.A
#
# PURPOSE: This script is used to search for files that
# are larger than $1 Meg. Bytes.  The search starts at
# the current directory that the user is in, `pwd`, and
# includes files in and below the user's current directory.
# The output is both displayed to the user and stored
# in a file for later review.
#
# REVISION LIST:
```

Listing 18.1   findlarge.ksh shell script listing. *(continues)*

```
#
#
# set -n   # Uncomment to check syntax without ANY execution
# set -x   # Uncomment to debug this script

SCRIPT_NAME=$(basename $0)

##############################################

function usage
{
echo "\n*****************************************"
echo "\nUSAGE:    $SCRIPT_NAME   [Number_Of_Meg_Bytes]"
echo "\nEXAMPLE:  $SCRIPT_NAME   5"
echo "\n\nWill Find Files Larger Than 5 Mb in, and below"
echo "the Current Directory..."
echo "\n\n\t...EXITING..."
echo "\n*****************************************"
}

##############################################

function trap_exit
{
echo "\n***********************************************"
echo "\n\n     EXITING ON A TRAPPED SIGNAL..."
echo "\n\n***********************************************\n"
}

##############################################

# Set a trap to exit.  REMEMBER - CANNOT TRAP ON kill -9

trap 'trap_exit; exit 2' 1 2 3 15

##############################################
# Check for the correct number of arguments

if [ $# -ne 1 ]
then
        usage
        exit 1
fi

#######################################
# Check for an integer

case $1 in
```

Listing 18.1   findlarge.ksh shell script listing. *(continued)*

```
+([0-9])) :  # no-op -- Do Nothing!
         ;;
      *) usage
         exit 1
         ;;
esac

######################################
# Check for an integer greater than zero

if [ $1 -lt 1 ]
then
     usage
     exit 1
fi

############################################

# Define and initialize files and variables here...

THISHOST=`hostname`       # Hostname of this machine

DATESTAMP=$(date +"%h%d:%Y:%T") # Date/Time Stamp

SEARCH_PATH=$(pwd)        # Top-level directory to search (CURRENT DIR!)

MEG_BYTES=$1              # Number of MB for file size trigger

OUTFILE="/tmp/largefiles.out" # Output user file
cat /dev/null > $OUTFILE       # Initialize to a null file

HOLDFILE="/tmp/temp_hold_file.out" # Temporary storage file
cat /dev/null > $HOLDFILE       # Initialize to a null file

#############################################
# Prepare the Output File Header

echo "\nSearching for Files Larger Than ${MEG_BYTES}Mb Starting in:"
echo "\n==> $SEARCH_PATH"
echo "\nPlease Standby for the Search Results..."
echo "\nLarge Files Search Results:" >> $OUTFILE
echo "\nHostname of Machine: $THISHOST" >> $OUTFILE
echo "\nTop Level Directory of Search:" >> $OUTFILE
echo "\n==> $SEARCH_PATH" >> $OUTFILE
echo "\nDate/Time of Search: `date`" >> $OUTFILE
echo "\nSearch Results Sorted by File Modification Time" >> $OUTFILE

#############################################
```

Listing 18.1   findlarge.ksh shell script listing. *(continues)*

```
# Search for files > $MEG_BYTES starting at the $SEARCH_PATH
#

find $SEARCH_PATH -type f -size +${MEG_BYTES}000000c \
        -print > $HOLDFILE

# How many files were found?

if [ -s $HOLDFILE ] # File greater than zero bytes?
then
    NUMBER_OF_FILES=`cat $HOLDFILE | wc -1`

    echo "\nNumber of Files Found: ==> $NUMBER_OF_FILES\n\n" >> $OUTFILE

    # Append to the end of the Output File...

    ls -lt `cat $HOLDFILE` >> $OUTFILE

    # Display the Time Sorted Output File...

    more $OUTFILE

    echo "\nThese Search Results are Stored in ==> $OUTFILE"
    echo "\nSearch Complete...EXITING...\n"
else
    cat $OUTFILE    # Show the header information!
    echo "\n\nNo Files were Found in the Search Path that"
    echo "are Larger than ${MEG_BYTES}Mb\n"
    echo "\n\t...EXITING...\n"
fi

rm -f $HOLDFILE  # Remove the temp. file

# End of the findlarge.ksh Script
```

Listing 18.1   findlarge.ksh shell script listing. *(continued)*

Let's review the findlarge.ksh shell script in Listing 18.1 in a little more detail. We added two functions to our script. We always need a usage function, and in case **CTRL-C** is pressed we added a trap_exit function. The trap_exit function is executed by the **trap** for exit signals 1, 2, 3, and 15 and will display EXITING ON A TRAPPED SIGNAL before exiting with a return code of 2. The usage function is executed if any of our three previously discussed data tests fail and the script exits with a return code of 1, one, indicating a script usage error.

In the next block of code we query the system for the hostname, date/time stamp, and the search path (the current directory!) for the **find** command. All of this system data is used in the file header for the $OUTFILE. For the search path we could have just used a dot to specify the current directory, but this short notation would result in a *relative pathname* in our report. The *full pathname*, which begins with a forward slash (/), provides much clearer information and results in an easier-to-read file report. To get the full pathnames for our report, we use the **pwd** command output assigned to the SEARCH_PATH variable.

We define two files for processing the data. The $HOLDFILE holds the search results of the **find** command's output. The $OUTFILE contains the header data, and the search results of the **find** command are appended to the end of the $OUTFILE file. If the $HOLDFILE is zero-sized, then the **find** command did not find any files larger than $MEG_BYTES, which is the value specified in $1 on the command line. If the $HOLDFILE is not empty, we count the lines in the file with the command NUMBER_OF_LINES=`cat $HOLDFILE | wc -l`. Notice that we used back tics for command substitution, `command`. This file count is displayed along with the report header information in our output file. The search data from the **find** command, stored in $HOLDFILE, consists of full pathnames of each file that has exceeded our limit. In the process of appending the $HOLDFILE data to our $OUTFILE, we do a long listing sorted by the modification time of each file. This long listing is produced using the ls -lt $(cat $HOLDFILE) command. A long listing is needed in the report so that we can see not only the modification date/time but also the file owner and group as well as the size of each file.

All of the data in the $OUTFILE is displayed by using the **more** command so that we display the data one page at a time. The findlarge.ksh shell script is in action in Listing 18.2.

```
Searching for Files Larger Than 1Mb starting in:

==> /scripts

Please Standby for the Search Results...

Large Files Search Results:

Hostname of Machine: yogi

Top Level Directory of Search:

==> /scripts

Date/Time of Search: Thu Nov  8 10:46:21 EST 2001

Search Results Sorted by File Modification Time:

Number of Files Found: ==>      4

-rwxrwxrwx   1 root   sys      3490332 Oct 25 10:03
/scripts/sling_shot621.tar
```

Listing 18.2   findlarge.ksh shell script in action. *(continues)*

```
-rwxrwxrwx   1 root   sys      1280000 Aug 27 15:33 /scripts/sudo/sudo-
1.6.tar
-rw-r--r--   1 root   sys     46745600 Jul 27 09:48 /scripts/scripts.tar
-rw-r--r--   1 root   system 10065920 Apr 20 2001
/scripts/exe/exe_files.tar



These Search Results are Stored in ==> /tmp/largefiles.out



Search Complete...EXITING...
```

Listing 18.2   findlarge.ksh shell script in action. *(continued)*

The output in Listing 18.2 is a listing of the entire screen output, which is also the contents of the $OUTFILE. The user is informed of the trigger threshold for the search, the top-level directory for the search, the hostname of the machine, the date and time of the search, and the number of files found to exceed the threshold. The long listing of each file is displayed that has the file owner and group, the size of the file in bytes, the modification time, and the full path to the file. The long listing is very helpful in large shops with thousands of users!

Other Options to Consider

The `findlarge.ksh shell` script is simple and does all of the basics for the system reporting, but it can be improved and customized for your particular needs. I think you will be interested in the following ideas:

1. The first thing you probably noticed is that the script uses the current directory as the top-level directory for the search path. You may want to add a second command-line argument so that you can specify a search path other than the current directory. You could add this user-supplied search path as an option, and if a search path is omitted you use the current directory to start the search. This adds a little more flexibility to the shell script.

2. Each time we run the `findlarge.ksh` shell script, we overwrite the $OUTFILE. You may, however, want to keep a month's worth of reports on the system. An easy way to keep one month of reports is to use the **date** command and extract the day of the month, and then add this value as a suffix to the $OUTFILE file name definition. The following command will work:

   ```
   OUTFILE="/tmp/largefiles.out.$(date +%d)"
   ```

   Over time our script will result in filenames `largefile.out.01` through `largefiles.out.31`.

3. When searching large filesystems the search may take a very long time to complete. To give the user feedback that the search process is continuing you may want to add one of the progress indicators studied in Chapter 4. Two of the studied progress indicators would be appropriate, the rotating line and the series of dots. Look in Chapter 4 for details.

4. When we specify our search value we are just adding six zeros to the user-supplied integer value. But we are back to a basic question: Is one MB equal to 1,000,000 or 1,024,000? Because a System Administrator may not be the one reading the report, maybe a manager, I used the mathematical 1,000,000 and not the system-reported power-of-2 value. This is really a toss-up, so you make the decision on the value you want to use. The value is easy to change by doing a little math to multiply the user-supplied value by 1,024,000.

5. If you need to look for newly created files when a filesystem has just filled up, you can add the following command as a cross reference to find the true cause of the filesystem filling up:

```
find $SEARCH_PATH -mtime 1 -print
```

This command will find all files that have been modified, or created, in the last 24 hours. You can redirect this output to a file and do a cross-reference to discover the files, and users, that actually caused the filesystem to fill up.

Summary

In this chapter we have shown how to search the system for large files and create a machine-specific report. As stated in the previous section, there are many ways to do the same task, and as always we have other options to consider. This chapter, along with filesystem monitoring in Chapter 5, can help keep filesystem surprises to a minimum.

In the next chapter we are going to study techniques to capture a user's keystrokes. Capturing keystrokes has many uses, from giving you an audit trail of all root access to keeping track of a problem contractor or user. I use this technique to keep an audit trail of all root access to the systems. I hope you gained some knowledge in this chapter, and I will see you in the next chapter!

## CHAPTER 19

Monitoring and Auditing User Key Strokes

In most large shops there is a need, at least occasionally, to monitor a user's actions. You may even want to audit the keystrokes of anyone with **root** access to the system or other administration type accounts, such as **oracle**. Contractors on site can pose a particular security risk. Typically when a new application comes into the environment one or two contractors are on site for a period of time for installation, troubleshooting, and training personnel on the product. I always set up contractors in **sudo** (see Chapter 14 for more details on **sudo**) to access the new application account, after I change the password. **sudo** tracks only the commands that were entered with a date/time stamp. The detail of the command output from stdout and stderr does not get logged so you do not have a complete audit trail of exactly what happened if a problem arises.

To get around this dilemma you can track a user's keystrokes from the time he or she accesses a user account until the time he or she exits the account, if you have the space for the log file. This little feat is accomplished using the **script** command. The idea is to use **sudo** to kick off a shell script that starts a **script** session. When the script session is running, all of the input and output on the terminal is captured in the log file. Of course, if the user goes into some menus or programs the log file gets a little hard to read, but we at least have an idea what happened. This monitoring is not done surreptitiously because I always want everyone to know that the monitoring is taking place. When a **script** session starts, output from the **script** command informs the user that a session is running and gives the name of the session's log file. We can also set up monitoring to take place from the time a user logs in until the user logs out. For this monitoring we do not need sudo, but we do need to edit the $HOME/.profile or other login configuration file for the particular user.

Syntax

Using the **script** command is straightforward, but we want to do a few more things in the shell script. Giving a specific command prompt is one option. If you are auditing **root** access you need to have a timeout set so that after about five minutes (see the TMOUT environment variable) the shell times out and the **root** access ends. On a shell timeout, the session is terminated and the user is either logged out or presented with a command prompt, but we can control this behavior. We have many options for this set of shell scripts. You are going to need to set up **sudo**, *super-user-do*, on your machine. The full details for installing and configuring **sudo** are in Chapter 14. We want **sudo** to be configured with the names of each of the shell scripts that are used for this monitoring effort, as well as the specific users that you will allow to execute them. We will get to these details later.

The **script** command works by making a typescript of everything that appears on the terminal. The **script** command is followed by a filename that will contain the captured typescript. If no filename is given the typescript is saved in the current directory in a file called typescript. For our scripting we will specify a filename to use. The script session ends when the forked shell is exited, which means that there are two exits required to completely log out of the system. The script command has the following syntax:

```
script [filename]
```

As the **script** session starts, notification is shown on the terminal and a time stamp is placed at the top of the file, indicating the start time of the session. Let's look at a short **script** session as used on the command line in Listing 19.1.

```
[root:yogi]@/# more /usr/local/logs/script/script_example.out

Script command is started on Wed May  8 21:35:27 EDT 2002.
[root:yogi]@/# cd /usr/spool/cron/crontabs
[root:yogi]@/usr/spool/cron/crontabs# ls
adm    root  sys   uucp
[root:yogi]@/usr/spool/cron/crontabs# ls -al
total 13
drwxrwx---    2 bin      cron           512 Feb 10 21:36 .
drwxr-xr-x    4 bin      cron           512 Jul 26 2001  ..
-rw-r--r--    1 adm      cron          2027 Feb 10 21:36 adm
-rw-------    1 root     cron          1125 Feb 10 21:35 root
-rw-r--r--    1 sys      cron           864 Jul 26 2001  sys
```

Listing 19.1 Command-line script session.

```
-rw-r--r--   1 root     cron           703 Jul 26 2001  uucp
[root:yogi]@/usr/spool/cron/crontabs# cd ../..
[root:yogi]@/usr/spool# ls -l
total 12
drwxrwsrwt   2 daemon   staff          512 Sep 17 2000  calendar
drwxr-xr-x   4 bin      cron           512 Jul 26 2001  cron
drwxrwxr-x   7 lp       lp             512 Mar 23 15:21  lp
drwxrwxr-x   5 bin      printq         512 May 01 20:32  lpd
drwxrwxr-x   2 bin      mail           512 May 06 17:36  mail
drwxrwx---   2 root     system         512 May 06 17:36  mqueue
drwxrwxr-x   2 bin      printq         512 Apr 29 11:52  qdaemon
drwxr-xr-x   2 root     system         512 Jul 26 2001  rwho
drwxrwsrwx   2 bin      staff          512 Jul 26 2001  secretmail
drwxr-xr-x  11 uucp     uucp           512 Mar 13 20:43  uucp
drwxrwxrwx   2 uucp     uucp           512 Sep 08 2000  uucppublic
drwxrwxr-x   2 root     system         512 Apr 16 2001  writesrv
[root:yogi]@/usr/spool# exit

Script command is complete on Wed May  8 21:36:11 EDT 2002.

[root:yogi]@/#
```

Listing 19.1 Command-line script session. *(continued)*

Notice that every keystroke is logged as well as all of the command output. At the beginning and end of the log file a **script** command time stamp is produced. These lines of text are also displayed on the screen as the script session starts and stops. These are the user notifications given as the monitoring starts and stops.

Scripting the Solution

There are three different situations in which you want to use this type of monitoring/auditing. In this first instance we have users that you want to monitor the entire session. In the next situation you want to monitor activity only when a user wants **root** access to the system. Our systems have direct, remote, and **su root** login disabled, so to gain **root** access the user must use **sudo** to switch to **root** using the `broot` script. The third script is a catch-all for other administrative user accounts that you want to audit. The first script is covering end-to-end monitoring with the script execution starting at login through the user's $HOME/.profile.

Before we actually start the script session, there are some options to consider. Because we are executing a shell script from the user's .profile we need to ensure that the script is the last entry in the file. If you do not want the users to edit any .profile files, then you need to set the ownership of the file to **root** and set the user to read-only access.

Logging User Activity

We are keeping log files so it is a good idea to have some kind of standard format for the log filenames. You have a lot of options for filenames, but I like to keep it simple. Our log files use the following naming convention:

```
[hostname].[user $LOGNAME].[Time Stamp]
```

We want the hostname because most likely you are monitoring users on multiple systems and using a central repository to hold all of the log files. When I write a shell script I do not want to execute a command more times than necessary. The **hostname** command is a good example. Assigning the system's hostname to a variable is a good idea because it is not going to change, or it should not change, during the execution of the script. To assign the **hostname** of the system to a variable use the following syntax:

```
THISHOST=$(hostname)
```

For the date/time stamp a simple integer representation is best. The following **date** command gives two digits for month, day, year, hour, minute, and second:

```
TS=$(date +%m%d%y%H%M%S)
```

Now we have to reference only the $TS variable for the date/time stamp. Because the user may change we can find the active username with either of the following environment variables:

```
echo $LOGNAME
```

```
echo $USER
```

```
echo $LOGIN
```

As you change user IDs by using the switch user command (**su**), all of these environment variables change accordingly. However, if a user does a switch user using **sudo**, then the $LOGIN environment variable carries over to the new user while the $LOGNAME and $USER environment variables gain the new user ID. Now we have everything to build a log filename. A good variable name for a log file is LOGFILE, unless this variable is used by your system or another application. On my systems the LOGFILE variable is not used. Not only do we need to create the name of the $LOGFILE, but we need to create the file and set the permissions on the file. The initial permissions on the file need to be set to read/write by the owner, chmod 600 $LOGFILE. The following commands set up the log file:

```
TS=$(date +%m%d%y%H%M%S)              # Create a time stamp
THISHOST=$(hostname)                  # Query the system for the hostname
LOGFILE=${THISHOST}.${LOGNAME}.$TS # Name the log file
touch ${LOGDIR}/$LOGFILE              # Create an empty log file
chmod 600 ${LOGDIR}/${LOGFILE}        # Set the file permissions
```

A sample filename is shown here:

```
yogi.randy.05110274519
```

The filename is good, but where do we want to store the file on the system? I like to use a separate variable to hold the directory name. With two separate variables representing the directory and filename, you can move the log directory to another location and have to change just one entry in the script. I set up a log directory on my system in /usr/local/logs. For these script log files I added a subdirectory called script. Then I set a LOGDIR variable to point to my logging directory, as shown here:

```
LOGDIR=/usr/local/logs/script
```

Starting the Monitoring Session

With the logging set up we are ready to start a **script** session. We start the session using the following syntax:

```
script ${LOGDIR}/${LOGFILE}
```

When the **script** session starts, a message is displayed on the screen that informs the user that a **script** session has started and lists the name of the script log file, as shown here:

```
Script command is started. The file is
/usr/local/logs/script/yogi.randy.051102174519.
```

If the user knows that monitoring is going on and also knows the name of the file, what is to keep the user from editing or deleting the log? Usually directory permissions will take care of this little problem. During the **script** session the actual log file is an open file—that is, actually a system temporary file that cannot be accessed directly by the user. But if the user is able to delete the $LOGFILE then you have lost the audit trail. This is one problem that we will discuss later.

Where Is the Repository?

So far here is the scenario. A user has logged into the system. As the user logs in, a monitoring session is started using the **script** command, which logs all of the terminal output in a log file that we specify. During the time that the session is active the log file is open as a system temporary file. When the session ends, by a user typing **exit** or **CTRL-D** or by an exit signal, the log file is closed and the user is notified of the session ending, and again the name of the log file is displayed.

For security and auditing purposes we need to have a central repository for the logs. The method I like to use is email. When the session ends we want to set the file permissions on the log file to *read only* by the owner. Then we email the log to another machine, ideally, which is where the repository is located. Once the email is sent I compress the local file and exit the script.

With two copies of the user session existing on two different machines, an audit will easily detect any changes. In fact, if a user tries to change the log these commands will also be logged. You may have different ideas on handling the repository, but I set up a user on a remote machine that I use as a log file manager, with a name **logman**. The **logman** user's email is the repository on the audit machine. For simplicity in this shell script we are going to email the logs to the local **logman** user. To send mail, I use the **mailx** command on all Unix flavors except Linux, where I use the **mail** command, as shown here:

```
mailx -s "$TS - $LOGNAME Audit Report" $LOG_MANAGER <
${LOGDIR}/${LOGFILE}
```

In the shell script the $LOG_MANAGER is defined as **logman**. The nice thing about having a variable hold the mail recipients is that you can add a second repository or other people to receive email notifications. By using the local **logman** account you have other options. You can set up mail aliases; one of my favorites is to use the **logman** account as a *bounce account*. By adding a .forward file in the $HOME directory for the **logman** user, you can redirect all of the email sent to the **logman** user to other destinations. If a .forward file exists in the user's home directory, the mail is not delivered to the user but instead is sent to each email address and alias listed in the .forward file. A sample .forward file is shown here.

```
yogibear@cave.com
booboo@cave.com
dino@flintstones.org
admin
```

With the previous entries in the $HOME/.forward file for the **logman** user, all mail directed to **logman** is instead sent to the three email address and all of the addresses pointed to by the **admin** email alias.

The Scripts

We have covered all of the basics for the shell scripts. We have three different shell scripts that are used in different ways. The first script is intended to be executed at login time by being the last entry in the user's $HOME/.profile. The second shell script is used only when you want to gain **root** access, which is done through **sudo**, and the third script is a catch-all for any other administration-type accounts that you want to audit, which also use **sudo**. Let's first look at the login script called log_keystrokes.ksh, shown in Listing 19.2.

```
#!/bin/ksh
#
# SCRIPT: log_keystrokes.ksh
#
# AUTHOR: Randy Michael
```

Listing 19.2   log_keystrokes.ksh shell script listing.

```
# DATE: 05/08/2002
# REV: 1.0.P
# PLATFOEM: Any Unix
#
# PURPOSE: This shell script is used to monitor a login session by
#          capturing all of the terminal data in a log file using
#          the script command. This shell script name should be
#          the last entry in the user's $HOME/.profile. The log file
#          is both kept locally and emailed to a log file
#          administrative user either locally or on a remote machine.
#
# REV LIST:
#
#
# set -n # Uncomment to check syntax without any execution
# set -x # Uncomment to debug this shell script
#
############# DEFINE AUDIT LOG MANAGER ##################
#
# This user receives all of the audit logs by email. This
# Log Manager can have a local or remote email address. You
# can add more than one email address if you want by separating
# each address with a space.

LOG_MANAGER="logman"        # List to email audit log

##########################################################
################ DEFINE FUNCTIONS HERE ##################
##########################################################


cleanup_exit ()
{
# This function is executed on any type of exit except of course
# a kill -9, which cannot be trapped. The script log file is
# emailed either locally or remotely, and the log file is
# compressed. The last "exit" is needed so the user does not
# have the ability to get to the command line without logging.

if [[ -s ${LOGDIR}/${LOGFILE} ]]
then
    case `uname` in
    Linux)  # Linux does not have "mailx"
    mail -s "$TS - $LOGNAME Audit Report" $LOG_MANAGER <
${LOGDIR}/${LOGFILE}
    ;;
    *)
    mailx -s "$TS - $LOGNAME Audit Report" $LOG_MANAGER <
${LOGDIR}/${LOGFILE}
    ;;
```

Listing 19.2 log_keystrokes.ksh shell script listing. *(continues)*

```
        esac

        compress ${LOGDIR}/${LOGFILE} 2>/dev/null
fi

exit
}

# Set a trap

trap 'cleanup_exit'1 2 3 4 5 6 7 8 9 10 11 12 13 14 15 16 17 18 19 20 26

############################################################
############### DEFINE VARIABLES HERE ###################
############################################################

TS=$(date +%m%d%y%H%M%S)           # File time stamp
THISHOST=$(hostname|cut -f1-2 -d.) # Host name of this machine
LOGDIR=/usr/local/logs/script      # Directory to hold the logs
LOGFILE=${THISHOST}.${LOGNAME}.$TS # Creates the name of the log file
touch $LOGDIR/$LOGFILE             # Creates the actual file
set -o vi 2>/dev/null              # Previous commands recall
stty erase ^?                      # Set the backspace key

# Set the command prompt
export PS1="[$LOGNAME:$THISHOST]@"'$PWD> '

#################### RUN IT HERE ########################

chmod 600 ${LOGDIR}/${LOGFILE}     # Change permission to RW for the owner

script ${LOGDIR}/${LOGFILE}        # Start the script monitoring session

chmod 400 ${LOGDIR}/${LOGFILE}     # Set permission to read-only for
                                   # the owner

cleanup_exit                       # Execute the cleanup and exit function
```

Listing 19.2   log_keystrokes.ksh shell script listing. *(continued)*

The `log_keystrokes.ksh` script in Listing 19.2 is not difficult when you look at it. At the top we define the `cleanup_exit` function that is used when the script exits to email and compress the log file. In the next section we set a **trap** and define and set some variables. Finally we start the logging activity with a **script** session.

In the `cleanup_exit` function notice the list of exit codes that the **trap** command will exit on. This signal list ensures that the log file gets emailed and the file gets compressed.

The only exit signal we cannot do anything about is a **kill -9** signal because you cannot trap **kill -9**. There are more exit signals if you want to add more to the list in the **trap** statement, but I think the most captured are listed.

The last command executed in this shell script is **exit** because in every case the `cleanup_exit` function must execute. If **exit** is not the last command, then the user will be placed back to a command prompt without any logging being done. The reason for this behavior is that the **script** session is really a **fork** of the original shell. Therefore, when the **script** command stops executing, one of the shells in the fork terminates, but not the original shell. This last **exit** logs out of the original shell. You may want to replace this last **exit**, located in the `cleanup_exit` function, with **logout**, which will guarantee the user is logged out of the system.

Logging root Activity

In some shops there is a need to log the activity of the **root** user. If you log the root activity, then you have an audit trail, and it is much easier to do root cause analysis on a **root** user booboo. We can use the same type of shell that we used in the previous sections, but this time we will use **sudo** instead of a `.profile` entry. I call this script `broot` because it is a short name for "I want to *be* **root**". In this section let's look at the shell script in Listing 19.3 and go through the details at the end.

```
#!/bin/ksh
#
# SCRIPT: broot
#
# AUTHOR: Randy Michael
# DATE: 05/08/2002
# REV: 1.0.P
# PLATFOEM: Any Unix
#
# PURPOSE: This shell script is used to monitor all root access by
#          capturing all of the terminal data in a log file using
#          the script command. This shell script is executed from the
#          command line using sudo (Super User Do). The log file
#          is kept locally and emailed to a log file administrative
#          user either locally or on a remote machine. Sudo must be
#          configured for this shell script. Refer to your sudo notes.
#
# USAGE:  sudo  broot
#
# REV LIST:
#
#
# set -n # Uncomment to check syntax without any execution
# set -x # Uncomment to debug this shell script
#
```

Listing 19.3   broot shell script listing. *(continues)*

```
############# DEFINE AUDIT LOG MANAGER ##################

# This user receives all of the audit logs by email. This
# Log Manager can have a local or remote email address. You
# can add more than one email address if you want by separating
# each address with a space.

LOG_MANAGER="logman"       # List to email audit log

#########################################################
################ DEFINE FUNCTIONS HERE ##################
#########################################################

cleanup_exit ()
{
# This function is executed on any type of exit except of course
# a kill -9, which cannot be trapped. The script log file is
# emailed either locally or remotely, and the log file is
# compressed. The last "exit" is needed so the user does not
# have the ability to get to the command line without logging.

if [[ -s ${LOGDIR}/${LOGFILE} ]]
then
    case `uname` in
    Linux)  # Linux does not have "mailx"
    mail -s "$TS - $LOGNAME Audit Report" $LOG_MANAGER <
${LOGDIR}/${LOGFILE}
    ;;
    *)
    mailx -s "$TS - $LOGNAME Audit Report" $LOG_MANAGER <
${LOGDIR}/${LOGFILE}
    ;;
    esac

    nohup compress ${LOGDIR}/${LOGFILE} 2>/dev/null &
fi

exit
}

# Set a trap

trap 'cleanup_exit'1 2 3 4 5 6 7 8 9 10 11 12 13 14 15 16 17 18 19 20 26

#########################################################
################ DEFINE VARIABLES HERE ##################
#########################################################

TS=$(date +%m%d%y%H%M%S)              # File time stamp
```

Listing 19.3 broot shell script listing. *(continued)*

```
THISHOST=$(hostname)              # Host name of this machine
LOGDIR=/usr/local/logs/script     # Directory to hold the logs
LOGFILE=${THISHOST}.${LOGNAME}.$TS # Creates the name of the log file
touch $LOGDIR/$LOGFILE            # Creates the actual file
TMOUT=300                         # Set the root shell timeout!!!
export TMOUT                      # Export the TMOUT variable
set -o vi                         # To recall previous commands
stty erase _                      # Set the backspace key


# Run root's .profile if one exists

if [[ -f $HOME/.profile ]]
then
     . $HOME/.profile
fi


# set path to include /usr/local/bin
echo $PATH|grep -q ':/usr/local/bin' || PATH=$PATH:/usr/local/bin

# Set the command prompt to override the /.profile default prompt

PS1="$THISHOST:broot> "
export PS1


#################### RUN IT HERE ##########################


chmod 600 ${LOGDIR}/${LOGFILE}   # Change permission to RW for the owner

script ${LOGDIR}/${LOGFILE}      # Start the script monitoring session

chmod 400 ${LOGDIR}/${LOGFILE}   # Set permission to read-only for the
owner

cleanup_exit                     # Execute the cleanup and exit function
```

Listing 19.3   broot shell script listing. *(continued)*

There is one extremely important difference between this script and the script in Listing 19.2. In the broot script in Listing 19.3 we execute the .profile for **root**, if there is a .profile for **root**. You may ask why we did not execute the profile last time. The answer involves the recursive nature of running a file onto itself. In the previous case we had the following entry in the $HOME/.profile file:

```
. /usr/local/bin/log_keystrokes.ksh
```

We add this entry beginning with a "dot", which means to execute the following file, as the last entry in the $HOME/.profile. If you added execution of $HOME/.profile into the *shell script* you end up executing the log_keystrokes.ksh shell script recursively. When you run the script like this you fill up the buffers and you get an error message similar to the following output:

```
ksh: .: 0403-059 There cannot be more than 9 levels of recursion.
```

For monitoring **root** access with the `broot` script we are not executing from the `.profile`, but we use **sudo** to run this `broot` script, so we have no worries about recursion. At the top of the script in Listing 19.3 we define a `LOG_MANAGER`. This list of one or more email addresses is where the log files are going to be emailed. You may even want real-time notification of **root** activity. I like to send the log files off to my audit box for safe keeping using my **logman** user account. This email notice in the `cleanup_exit` function uses two different e-mail commands, depending on the Unix flavor. The only machine that does not support the **mailx** command is Linux, which supports only the **mail** command. This is not a problem, but I had to use the mix email commands to add a subject heading in the email; not all **mail** commands on all systems allow a subject heading so I used **mailx** instead.

The next step is to set a **trap**. If the script exits on signals 1 2 3 4 5 6 7 8 9 10 11 12 13 14 15 16 17 18 19 20 26, the `cleanup_exit` function is executed. This **trap** ensures that the log file gets emailed and the file gets compressed locally. In the next section we define and set the variables that we use. Notice that we added a shell timeout, specified by the `TMOUT` environment variable. If someone with **root** access is not typing for five minutes the shell times out. You can set the `TMOUT` variable to anything you want or even comment it out if you do not want a shell timeout. The measurement is in seconds. The default is 300 seconds, or 5 minutes, for this script.

After the variable definitions we execute the root `.profile`. We run the profile here because we are not running the `broot` script from a login `$HOME/.profile`, as we did with the `log_keystrokes.ksh` script in Listing 19.2. Next we add `/usr/local/bin` to root's `$PATH`, if it is not already present. And, finally, before we are ready to execute the **script** command we set a command prompt.

The final four things we do are (1) set the permissions on the log file so we can write to it; (2) run the **script** command using the log filename as a parameter; (3) set the file permissions on the log file to read-only; and (4) execute the `cleanup_exit` function to email the log and compress the file locally.

Some sudo Stuff

I have inserted a short `/etc/sudoers` file for Listing 19.4 to show entries that need to be made. The entire task of setting up and using **sudo** is shown in Chapter 14. Pay attention to the bold type in Listing 19.4.

```
# sudoers file.
#
# This file MUST be edited with the 'visudo' command as root.
#
# See the sudoers man page for the details on how to write a
```

Listing 19.4 Example /etc/sudoers file.

```
# sudoers file.
#
#
# Users Identification:
#
# All access:
#
# randy - Randy Michael
# terry - Admin
#
# Restricted Access to: mount umount and exportfs
#
# oracle - Oracle Admin
# operator - operator access
#
# Host alias specification

Host_Alias   LOCAL=yogi

# User alias specification

User_Alias      ROOTADMIN=randy,terry
User_Alias      NORMAL=randy,operator,terry
User_Alias      ADMIN=randy,terry
User_Alias      ORACLE=oracle
User_Alias      DB2=db2adm
User_Alias      OPERATOR=operator

# Runas alias specification

Runas_Alias     ORA=oracle

# Cmnd alias specification

Cmnd_Alias      BROOT=/usr/local/bin/broot
Cmnd_Alias      MNT=/usr/bin/mount
Cmnd_Alias      UMNT=/usr/bin/umount
Cmnd_Alias      EXP_FS=/usr/bin/exportfs
Cmnd_Alias      KILL=/usr/bin/kill
Cmnd_Alias      ORACLE_SU=/usr/bin/su - oracle
Cmnd_Alias      TCPDUMP=/usr/sbin/tcpdump
Cmnd_Alias      ERRPT=/usr/bin/errpt
Cmnd_Alias      SVRMGRL=/oracle/product/8.0.5/bin/svrmgrl

# User privilege specification
root      ALL=(ALL) ALL
ROOTADMIN      LOCAL=BROOT
NORMAL      LOCAL=MNT,UMNT,EXP_FS
```

Listing 19.4   Example /etc/sudoers file. *(continues)*

```
ADMIN
      LOCAL=BROOT,MNT,UMNT,KILL,ORACLE_SU,TCPDUMP,ERRPT: \
      LOCAL=EXP_FS
ORACLE        LOCAL=SVRMGRL

# Override Defaults

Defaults    logfile=/var/adm/sudo.log
```

Listing 19.4   Example /etc/sudoers file. *(continued)*

Three entries need to be added to the /etc/sudoers file. Do *not* ever edit the sudoers file directly with **vi**. There is a special program called **visudo**, in the /usr/local/sbin directory, that has a wrapper around the **vi** editor that does a thorough check for mistakes in the file before the file is saved. If you make a mistake the **visudo** program will tell you where the error is located in the /etc/sudoers file.

The three entries that need to be added to the /etc/sudoers are listed next and are highlighted in bold text in Listing 19.4.

Define the User_Alias, which is where you give a name to a group of users. For this file let's name the list of users who can get **root** access ROOTADMIN, as shown here:

```
User_Alias      ROOTADMIN=randy,terry
```

Next we need to define the Cmnd_Alias, which is where you define the full pathname to the command, as shown here.

```
Cmnd_Alias      BROOT=/usr/local/bin/broot
```

The last step is to define the exact commands that the User_Alias group of users can execute. In our case we have a separate User_Alias group only for the users who can use the broot script. Notice that the definition also specifies the machine where the command can be executed. I always let **sudo** execution take place only on a single machine at a time, specified by LOCAL here.

```
ROOTADMIN       LOCAL=BROOT
```

Once the /etc/sudoers file is set up, you can change the **root** password and allow **root** access only by using the broot script. Using this method you have an audit trail of **root** access to the system.

Monitoring Other Administration Users

More often than not, you will want add to the list of auditing that can be done. This next script is rewritten to allow you to quickly set up a `broot` type shell script by changing only the user name and the script name. The method that we use to execute the **script** command is what makes this script different—and easy to modify.

For ease of use we can use a lot of variables throughout the script. We have already been doing this to some extent. Now we will call the monitored user the *effective user*, which fits our new variable $EFF_USER. For this script I have set the username to **oracle**. You can make it any user that you want to. Take a look at this shell script in Listing 19.5, and pay particular attention to the boldface type.

```ksh
#!/bin/ksh
#
# SCRIPT: "Banybody"    boracle - This time
#
# AUTHOR: Randy Michael
# DATE: 05/08/2002
# REV: 1.0.P
# PLATFOEM: Any Unix
#
# PURPOSE: This shell script is used to capture all "$EFF_USER"
#          access by capturing all of the terminal data in a log
#          file using the script command. This shell script is
#          executed from the command line using sudo (Super User Do).
#          The log file is kept locally and emailed to a log file
#          administrative user either locally or on a remote
#          machine. Sudo must be configured for this shell script.
#          Refer to your sudo notes. The effective user, currently
#          oracle, can be changed by setting the "EFF_USER" variable
#          to another user, and changing the name of the script.
#          This is why the original name of the script is called
#          "Banybody".
#
# ORIGINAL USAGE:  sudo  Banybody
#
# THIS TIME USAGE ==> USAGE: sudo boracle
#
#
# REV LIST:
#          5/10/2002: Modified the script to replace the hard-coded
#                     username with the variable $EFF_USER. This
#                     allows flexibility to add auditing of more
```

Listing 19.5   boracle shell script listing. *(continues)*

```
#                           accounts by just changing the EFF_USER variable
#                           and the script name.
#
# set -n # Uncomment to check syntax without any execution
# set -x # Uncomment to debug this shell script
#
#
################ DEFINE EFFECTIVE USER #################

# This EFF_USER is the username you want to be to execute
# a shell in. An su command is used to switch to this user.

EFF_USER=oracle

############# DEFINE AUDIT LOG MANAGER ###################

# This user receives all of the audit logs by email. This
# Log Manager can have a local or remote email address. You
# can add more than one email address if you want by separating
# each address with a space.

LOG_MANAGER="logman"      # List to email audit log


#############################################################
################ DEFINE FUNCTIONS HERE ##################
#############################################################

cleanup_exit ()
{
# This function is executed on any type of exit except of course
# a kill -9, which cannot be trapped. The script log file is
# emailed either locally or remotely, and the log file is
# compressed. The last "exit" is needed so that the user does not
# have the ability to get to the command line without logging.

if [[ -s ${LOGDIR}/${LOGFILE} ]] # Is it greater than zero bytes?
then
    case `uname` in
    Linux)
    mail -s "$TS - $LOGNAME Audit Report" $LOG_MANAGER <
${LOGDIR}/${LOGFILE}
    ;;
    *)
    mailx -s "$TS - $LOGNAME Audit Report" $LOG_MANAGER <
${LOGDIR}/${LOGFILE}
```

Listing 19.5   boracle shell script listing. *(continued)*

```
        ;;
        esac

        compress ${LOGDIR}/${LOGFILE} 2>/dev/null
fi

exit
}


################# SET A TRAP ############################

trap 'cleanup_exit' 1 2 3 5 15


###########################################################
################# DEFINE VARIABLES HERE ##################
###########################################################

TS=$(date +%m%d%y%H%M%S)          # File time stamp
THISHOST=$(hostname)              # Hostname of this machine
LOGDIR=/usr/local/logs/script     # Directory to hold the logs
LOGFILE=${THISHOST}.${EFF_USER}.$TS # Creates the name of the log file
touch $LOGDIR/$LOGFILE            # Creates the actual file
TMOUT=300                         # Set the root shell timeout!!!
export TMOUT                      # Export the TMOUT variable
set -o vi                         # To recall previous commands
stty erase ^?                     # Set the backspace key

# set path to include /usr/local/bin
echo $PATH|grep -q ':/usr/local/bin' || PATH=$PATH:/usr/local/bin

# Set the command prompt to override the /.profile default prompt

PS1="$THISHOST:b${EFF_USER}> "
export PS1


#################### RUN IT HERE ##########################

chmod 666 ${LOGDIR}/${LOGFILE}      # Set permission to read/write

# To get the script session to work we have to use the switch user (su)
# command with the -c flag, which means execute what follows. Sudo is
# also used just to ensure that root is executing the su command.
# We ARE executing now as root because this script was started with
# sudo. If a nonconfigured sudo user tries to execute this command
# then it will fail unless sudo was used to execute this script as root.
```

Listing 19.5   boracle shell script listing. *(continues)*

```
# Notice we are executing the script command as "$EFF_USER". This
# variable is set at the top of the script. A value such as
# "EFF_USER=oracle" is expected.

sudo su - $EFF_USER -c "script ${LOGDIR}/${LOGFILE}"

chmod 400 ${LOGDIR}/${LOGFILE}   # Set permission to read-only for
                                 # the owner

cleanup_exit                     # Execute the cleanup and exit function
```

Listing 19.5 boracle shell script listing. *(continued)*

The most important line to study in Listing 19.5 is the third line from the bottom:

```
sudo su - $EFF_USER -c "script ${LOGDIR}/${LOGFILE}"
```

There are several points to make about this command. Notice that we start the command with **sudo**. Because you must use **sudo** to execute the boracle script, and you are already executing as **root**, then why use **sudo** here? We use **sudo** here to ensure that the boracle script was indeed started with **sudo**. If any old user runs the boracle command we want it to fail if **sudo** was not used.

The second command in the previous statement is su - $EFF_USER. The significance of the hyphen, -, is important here. Using the hyphen, -, with a space on both sides tells the **su** command to switch to the user pointed to by the $EFF_USER, **oracle** in our case, and run that user's .profile. If the hyphen is omitted or the spaces are not around the hyphen, then the user .profile is not executed, which is a bad thing in this case.

The last part of this command is where we start our **script** session. When you switch users with **su**, you can specify that you want to run a command as this user by adding the **-c** switch followed by the command enclosed in single or double quotes. Do not forget the quotes around the command.

The only other real change is the use of the EFF_USER variable. This variable is set at the top of the script, and changing this variable changes who you want to "be." If you want to create more admin auditing scripts, copy the boracle file to a new filename and edit the file to change the name at the top of the script and modify the EFF_USER variable. That's it!

Other Options to Consider

Through this chapter we have covered some interesting concepts. You may have quite a few things that you want to add to these scripts. I have come up with a few myself.

Emailing the Audit Logs

Depending on the extent of monitoring and auditing you need to do, you may want to send the files to several different machines. I selected using email for the transport, but you may have some other techniques, such as automated FTP. You may also want to compress the files before you email, or whatever, the log files. To email a compressed file you will need some type of mail tool like **metasend** or a tool that does a type of *uuencoding*. This is needed sometimes because the mail program will think that some of the characters, or control characters, are mail commands. This can cause some strange things to happen. You should be able to find some mail tools on the Web.

Watch the disk space! When you start logging user activity you need to keep a close check on disk space. Most systems store email in /var. If you fill up /var for an extended period of time you may crash the box. For my log files I create a large dedicated filesystem called /usr/local/logs. With a separate filesystem I do not have to worry about crashing the system if I fill up the filesystem. You can probably think of other methods to move the files around as the emails are received.

Compression

For all of these scripts we used the **compress** command. This compression algorithm is okay, but we can do better. I find that **gzip** has a much better compression algorithm, and the compression ratio is tunable for your needs. The tuning is done using numbers as a parameter to the **gzip** command, as shown here:

```
# gzip -9 $LOGFILE
```

The valid numbers are 1 to 9, with 9 indicating the best compression. This extra compression does come at a price—time! The higher the number, the longer it takes to compress the file. By omitting the number you use **gzip** in default mode, which is **-5**. For our needs you will still see a big increase in compression over **compress** at about the same amount of time.

Need Better Security?

Another option for this keystroke auditing is to use open secure shell and keep a real time encrypted connection to the log server by creating a *named pipe*. This can be done but it, too, has some potential problems. This first major problem is that you introduce a dependency for the logging to work. If the connection is lost then the script session ends. For auditing **root** activities, and especially when all other **root** access has been disabled, you can have a real nightmare. I will leave this idea for you to play around with because it is beyond the scope of this book.

Inform the Users

I did not add this chapter to the book for everyone to start secretly monitoring everyone's keystrokes. Always be up-front with the user community, and let them know that an audit is taking place. I know for a fact that Systems Administrators do not like to have the **root** password taken away from them. I know first hand about the reaction.

If you are going to change the user password, please place the **root** password in a safe place where, in case of emergency, you can get to the password without delay. Your group will have to work out how this is accomplished.

Sudoers File

If you start running these scripts and you have a problem, first check your **sudo** configuration by looking at the /etc/sudoers file. There are some things to look for that the **visudo** editor will not catch:

- Check the **LOCAL** line. This variable should have the hostname of your machine assigned.
- Check for exact pathnames of the files.
- Ensure that the correct users are assigned to the correct commands.

The **visudo** editor does catch most errors, but there are some things that are not so easy to test for.

Summary

I had a lot of fun writing this chapter and playing with these scripts. I hope you take these auditing scripts and use them in a constructive way. The information gathered can be immense if you do not have a mechanism for pruning the old log files. The following command works pretty well:

```
find /directory -mtime +30 -print -exec rm {}  \;
```

This command will remove all the files in /directory that have not been modified in 30 days. You may want to add a -name parameter to limit what you delete. As with any type of monitoring activity that creates logs, you need to watch the filesystem space very closely, especially at first, to see how quickly logs are being created and how large the log files grow.

Another topic that comes up a lot is the shell timeout. The only place I use the TMOUT environment is in the broot script. If you add a shell timeout to your other administrative accounts you may find that a logout happens during a long processing job. With these users I expect them to just lock the terminal when they leave.

In the next chapter we are going to look at Serial Storage Architecture (SSA) disk drives and how to physically identify them. These drives normally come in a rack of 18 drives, and we have a ton of racks! In this mess it is hard to locate a specific drive or a group of drives. We have a script that turns the identification lights on and off, with a lot of different options. See you in the next chapter!

## chapter 20

Turning On/Off SSA Identification Lights

On any system that utilizes the Serial Storage Architecture (SSA) disk subsystem from IBM you understand how difficult it is to find a specific failed disk in the hundreds of disks that populate the racks. Other needs for SSA disk identification include finding all of the drives attached to a particular system. Then you may also want to see only the drives that are in currently varied-on volume groups or a specific group of disks. In this chapter we will work through all of these areas of identification.

In identifying hardware components in a system you usually have a set of tools for this function. This chapter is going to concentrate on AIX systems. The script presented in this chapter is valid only for AIX, but with a few modifications it can run on other Unix flavors that utilize the SSA subsystem. I am sticking to AIX because this script has an option to query *volume groups*, which not all Unix flavors support. If your systems are running the Veritas filesystem, then only a few commands need to be modified for my identification script to work because Veritas supports the concept of a volume group.

In identifying an SSA disk you have two ways of referencing the disk. In AIX all disks are represented as an *hdisk#*. As an example, **hdisk0** almost always contains the operating system, and it is part of the *rootvg* volume group. It is not often an SSA disk; it is usually an internal SCSI disk. If an hdisk is an SSA disk, then it has a second disk name that is used within the SSA subsystem, which is called the *pdisk#*. Not often are the **hdisk#** and the **pdisk#** the same number because the first couple of disks are usually SCSI drives. We need to be able to translate an hdisk to its associated pdisk, and vice versa.

Syntax

As always, we need to start out with the commands to accomplish the task. With the SSA subsystem we are concerned about two commands that relate to hdisks and pdisks. The first command, **ssaxlate**, translates an **hdisk#** into a **pdisk#**, or vice versa. The second command we use is the **ssaidentify** command, which requires a pdisk representation of the SSA disk drive. This command is used to turn the SSA disk identification lights on and off. We want the script to identify the SSA disks to recognize either disk format, hdisk and pdisk. With the **ssaxlate** command this is not a problem.

To use these commands you need to know only the SSA disk to act on and add the appropriate command switch. Let's look at both commands here.

Translating an hdisk to a pdisk

```
# ssaxlate -l hdisk43

pdisk41
```

In this example hdisk43 translates to pdisk41. This tells me that the hdisk to pdisk offset is 2, which I have to assume means that hdisk0 and hdisk1 are both SCSI disks, and hdisk3 through, at least, hdisk43 are all SSA disks. This is not always the case. It depends on how the AIX configuration manager discovered the disks in the first place, but my statement is a fair assumption. We could just as easily translate pdisk41 to hdisk43 by specifying pdisk41 in the **ssaxlate** command.

The next step is to actually turn on the identification light for hdisk43, which we discovered to be pdisk41. The **ssaidentify** command wants the disks represented as pdisks, so we need to use pdisk41 for this command.

Identifying an SSA Disk

```
# ssaidentify -l pdisk41 -y
```

The **ssaidentify** command will just return a return code of success or failure, but no text is returned. If the return code is 0, zero, then the command was successful. If the return code is nonzero, then the command failed for some reason and a message is sent to standard error, which is file descriptor 2. All we are interested in is if the return code is zero or not.

Table 20.1   SSA Identification Functions

FUNCTION NAME	PURPOSE
usage	Shows the user how to use the shell script
man_page	Shows detailed information on how to use the shell script
cleanup	Executes when a trapped exit signal is detected
twirl	Used to give the user feedback that processing continues
all_defined_pdisks	Controls SSA identification lights for all system SSA disks
all_varied_on_pdisks	Controls SSA disks only in currently varied-on volume groups
list_of_disks	Controls SSA identification of a list of one or more disks

The Scripting Process

In the SSA identification script we are going to use a lot of functions. These functions perform the work so we just need the logic to decide which function to execute. An important thing you need to understand about functions is that the function *must* be declared, or written, in the code previous to when you want to execute the function. This makes sense if you think about it: You have to write the code before you can use it! The functions involved in this shell script are listed in Table 20.1 for your convenience.

Usage and User Feedback Functions

As you can see, we have our work cut out for us, so let's get started. The first function is the usage function. When a user input error is detected you want to give the user some feedback on how to properly use the shell script. Always create a usage function. I want to show you this function because I did something you may not know that you can do. I used a single **echo** command and have 15 separate lines of output. Take a look at the function in Listing 20.1 to see the method.

```
function usage
{
echo "\nUSAGE ERROR...
\nMAN PAGE ==> $SCRIPTNAME  -?
\nTo Turn ALL Lights Either ON or OFF:
\nUSAGE: SSAidentify.ksh [-v] [on] [off]
EXAMPLE: SSAidentify.ksh -v  on
\nWill turn ON ALL of the system's currently VARIED ON
SSA identify lights. NOTE: The default is all DEFINED SSA disks
\nTo Turn SPECIFIC LIGHTS Either ON or OFF Using EITHER
the pdisk#(s) AND/OR the hdisk#(s):
\nUSAGE: SSAidentify.ksh [on] [off] pdisk{#1} [hdisk{#2}]...
EXAMPLE: SSAidentify.ksh on hdisk36 pdisk44 pdisk47
\nWill turn ON the lights to all of the associated pdisk#(s)
that hdisk36 translates to and PDISKS pdisk44 and pdisk47.
\nNOTE: Can use all pdisks, all hdisks or BOTH hdisk
and pdisk together if you want..."

exit 1
}
```

Listing 20.1 Usage function with a single echo command.

As you can see in Listing 20.1, I enclose the entire text that I want to **echo** to the screen within double quotes, `"usage text"`. To place text on the next line, just press the **ENTER** key. If you want an extra blank line or a **TAB**, then use one or more of the many cursor functions available with the **echo** command, as shown in Table 20.2.

There are many more in the **man** pages on your system. When incorrect usage of the shell script is detected, which you have to build in to the script, the proper usage message in Listing 20.2 is displayed on the screen.

Table 20.2 Cursor Control Commands for the echo Command

ECHO FUNCTION	PURPOSE
\n	Insert a new line with a carriage return
\t	Tab over on TAB length characters for each \t entered
\b	Back the cursor up one space for each \b entered
\c	Leaves the cursor at the current position, without a carriage return or line feed

```
USAGE ERROR...

MAN PAGE ==> SSAidentify.ksh  -?

To Turn ALL Lights Either ON or OFF:

USAGE: SSAidentify.ksh [-v] [on] [off]
EXAMPLE: SSAidentify.ksh -v  on

Will turn ON ALL of the system's currently VARIED ON
SSA identify lights. NOTE: The default is all DEFINED SSA disks

To Turn SPECIFIC LIGHTS Either ON or OFF Using EITHER
the pdisk#(s) AND/OR the hdisk#(s):

USAGE: SSAidentify.ksh [on] [off] pdisk{#1} [hdisk{#2}]...
EXAMPLE: SSAidentify.ksh on hdisk36 pdisk44 pdisk47

Will turn ON the lights to all of the associated pdisk#(s)
that hdisk36 translates to and PDISKS pdisk44 and pdisk47.

NOTE: Can use all pdisks, all hdisks or BOTH hdisk
and pdisk together if you want...
```

Listing 20.2   Example of cursor control using the echo command.

By using cursor control with the **echo** command, we can eliminate using a separate **echo** command on every separate line of text we want to display. I do the same thing in the man_page function. You can see this function in its entirety in the full shell script shown in Listing 20.9.

Before I show you the cleanup function, I want to show you the twirl function. The twirl function is used to give feedback to the user, which you saw back in Chapter 4. As a brief review, the twirl function displays the appearance of a line rotating. And this is accomplished through? You guess it, cursor control using the **echo** command. I like the twirl function because it is not too hard to understand and it is very short. This function works by starting an infinite **while** loop, which is done using the : (colon) no-op operator. A no-op does nothing and always has a zero return code so it is perfect to create an infinite loop. The next step is to have a counter that counts only from 0 to 4. When the counter reaches 4 it is reset back to 0, zero. At each count a **case** statement is used to decide which of the four lines, -, \, |, and /, is to be displayed. At the same time, the cursor is backed up so it is ready to overwrite the previous line character with a new one. There is a sleep for one second on each loop iteration. You must leave the **sleep** statement in the code or you will see a big load on the system by all of the continuous updates to the screen. I use this function for giving user feedback when a time-consuming job is executing. When the job is finished I **kill** the `twirl` function and move on. The easiest way to **kill** a background function is to capture the PID just after kicking off the background job, which is assigned to the `$!` shell variable. This is similar to the way `$?` is used to see the return code of the last command. The `twirl` function is shown in Listing 20.3.

```
function twirl
{
TCOUNT="0"        # For each TCOUNT the line twirls one increment

while :           # Loop forever...until you break out of the loop
do
      TCOUNT=$(expr ${TCOUNT} + 1) # Increment the TCOUNT

      case ${TCOUNT} in
          "1")     echo '-'"\b\c"
                   sleep 1
                   ;;
          "2")     echo '\\'"\b\c"
                   sleep 1
                   ;;
          "3")     echo "|\b\c"
                   sleep 1
                   ;;
          "4")     echo "/\b\c"
                   sleep 1
                   ;;
          *)       TCOUNT="0" ;;  # Reset the TCOUNT to "0", zero.
      esac
done
# End of twirl function
}
```

Listing 20.3 Twirl function listing.

When I have a time-consuming job starting, I start the `twirl` function with the following commands:

```
twirl &

TWIRL_PID=$!
```

This leads into the next function, `cleanup`. In normal operation the `twirl` function is killed in the main body of the script, or in the function that it is called in, by using the

kill command and the previously saved PID, which is pointed to by the TWIRL_PID variable. Life, though, is not always normal. In the top of the main body of the shell script we set a **trap**. The **trap** is used to execute one or more commands, programs, or shell scripts when a specified exit code is captured. Of course, you cannot **trap** a **kill -9**! In this shell script we execute the cleanup function on exit codes 1, 2 ,3, 5, and 15. You can add more exit codes if you want. This cleanup function displays a message on the screen that a **trap** has occurred and runs the **kill -9 $TWIRL_PID** command before exiting the shell script. If you omit the **trap** and the twirl function is running in the background, it will continue to run in the background! You cannot miss it—you always have a twirling line on your screen. Of course, you can **kill** the PID if you can find it in the process table with the **ps** command. The cleanup function is shown in Listing 20.4.

```
function cleanup
{
echo "\n...Exiting on a trapped signal...EXITING STAGE LEFT...\n"

kill -9 $TWIRL_PID

# End of cleanup function
}
```

Listing 20.4 Cleanup function listing.

When an exit code is captured the user is informed that the shell script is exiting, and then the **kill** command is executed on the PID saved in the $TWIRL_PID variable.

Control Functions

Now we get into the real work of turning on and off the SSA identification lights starting with the all_defined_pdisks function. This function is the simplest of the SSA identification functions in this chapter. The goal is to get a list of every SSA disk on the system and use the pdisk# to control the identification lights by turning all lights on or off in sequence.

To understand this function you need to understand an AIX command called **lsdev** and the switches we use to extract only the pdisk information. The **lsdev** command is used to display devices in the system and the characteristics of devices. The **-C** switch tells the **lsdev** command to look at only the currently defined devices. Then the **-c** command switch is added to specify the particular *class* of device; in our case the device class is **pdisk**. So far our **lsdev** command looks like the following statement:

```
# lsdev -Cc pdisk
```

But we want to drill down a little deeper in the system. We can also specify a *subclass* to the previously defined class by adding the **-s** switch with our subclass **ssar**. We also want to have a formatted output with column headers so we add the **-H** switch. These headers just help ensure that we have good separation between fields. Now we have the following command:

```
# lsdev -Cc pdisk -s ssar -H
```

Using this command on a system with SSA disks you see an output similar to the one in Listing 20.5.

```
name     status    location          description

pdisk0   Available 34-08-5B91-01-P SSA160 Physical Disk Drive
pdisk1   Available 34-08-5B91-02-P SSA160 Physical Disk Drive
pdisk2   Available 34-08-5B91-03-P SSA160 Physical Disk Drive
pdisk3   Available 34-08-5B91-04-P SSA160 Physical Disk Drive
pdisk4   Available 24-08-5B91-05-P SSA160 Physical Disk Drive
pdisk5   Available 24-08-5B91-07-P SSA160 Physical Disk Drive
pdisk6   Available 24-08-5B91-06-P SSA160 Physical Disk Drive
pdisk7   Available 24-08-5B91-08-P SSA160 Physical Disk Drive
pdisk8   Available 24-08-5B91-09-P SSA160 Physical Disk Drive
pdisk9   Available 24-08-5B91-10-P SSA160 Physical Disk Drive
pdisk10  Available 24-08-5B91-11-P SSA160 Physical Disk Drive
pdisk11  Available 24-08-5B91-12-P SSA160 Physical Disk Drive
pdisk12  Available 34-08-5B91-13-P SSA160 Physical Disk Drive
pdisk13  Available 34-08-5B91-14-P SSA160 Physical Disk Drive
pdisk14  Available 34-08-5B91-16-P SSA160 Physical Disk Drive
pdisk15  Available 34-08-5B91-15-P SSA160 Physical Disk Drive
```

Listing 20.5 lsdev listing of pdisks.

In Listing 20.5 we have more information than we need. The only part of this **lsdev** command output that we are interested in is in the first column, and only the lines that have "pdisk" in the first column. To filter this output we need to expand our **lsdev** command by adding **awk** and **grep** to filter the output. Our expanded command is shown here:

```
# lsdev -Cc pdisk -s ssar -H | awk '{print $1}' | grep pdisk
```

In this command statement we extract the first column using the **awk** statement in a pipe, while specifying the first column with the `'{print $1}'` notation. Then we use **grep** to extract only the lines that contain the pattern **pdisk**. The result is a list of all currently defined pdisks on the system.

To control the identification lights for the pdisks in this list we use a **for** loop and use our **lsdev** command to create the list of pdisks with command substitution. These steps are shown in Listing 20.6.

```
function all_defined_pdisks
{
   # TURN ON/OFF ALL LIGHTS:
   # Loop through each of the system's pdisks by using the "lsdev"
   # command with the "-Cc pdisk" switch while using "awk" to extract
   # out the actual pdisk number.  We will either
   # turn the identifier lights on or off specified by the $SWITCH
   # variable:
   #
   #    Turn lights on:  -y
   #    Turn lights off: -n
   #
   # as the $SWITCH value to the "ssaidentify" command, as used below...

echo "\nTurning $STATE ALL of the system's pdisks...Please Wait...\n"

for PDISK in $(lsdev -Cc pdisk -s ssar -H | awk '{print $1}' \
            | grep pdisk)
do
    echo "Turning $STATE ==> $PDISK"
    ssaidentify -l $PDISK -${SWITCH} \
    || echo "Turning $STATE $PDISK Failed"
done
echo "\n...TASK COMPLETE...\n"
}
```

Listing 20.6   all_defined_pdisks function listing.

In Listing 20.6 notice the command substitution used in the **for** loop, which is in bold text. The command substitution produces the list arguments that are assigned to the $PDISK variable on each loop iteration. As each pdisk is assigned, the **ssaidentify** command is executed using the $PDISK definition as the target and uses the –$SWITCH as the action to take, which can be either **-y** for light on or **-n** for light off. These values are defined in the main body of the shell script. As each light is being turned on or off the user is notified. If the action fails the user is notified of the failure also. This failure notification is done using a logical OR, specified by the double pipes, ||.

The next function is all_varied_on_pdisks. This function is different in that we must approach the task of getting a list of SSA disks to act on using completely different strategy. The result we want is the ability to control the SSA disks that are in volume groups that are currently varied-on. To get this list we must first get a list of the varied-on volume groups using the **lsvg -o** command. This command gives a list of varied-on volume groups directly without any added text so we are okay with this command's output. Using this list of volume groups we can now use the **lspv** command to get a full listing of defined hdisks. From this list we use **grep** to extract the hdisks that are in currently varied-on volume groups. Notice that all of this activity so far is at the hdisk level. We need to have pdisks to control the identification lights. To build a list of hdisks to convert we use a **for** loop tagging on the volume groups with the VG variable. For each $VG we run the following command to build a list.

```
# lspv | grep $VG >> $HDISKFILE
```

Notice that we use a file to store this list. A file is needed because if a variable were used we might exceed the character limit for a variable, which is 2048 on most systems. As you know, most large shops have systems with hundreds, if not thousands, of SSA disks. To be safe we use a file for storage here.

Using this list of hdisks we are going to use another **for** loop to translate each of the hdisks into the associated pdisk. Because we may still have a huge list containing pdisks we again use a file to hold the list. The translation takes place using the **ssaxlate** command, but what if some of these hdisks are not SSA disks? Well, the translation will fail! To get around this little problem we first test each translation and send all of the output to the bit bucket and check the return code of the **ssaxlate** command. If the return code is 0, zero, then the hdisk is an SSA disk. If the return code is nonzero, then the hdisk is not an SSA disk. The result is that only pdisks are added to the new pdisk list file, which is pointed to by the PDISKFILE variable. Because this translation may take quite a while we start the `twirl` function, which is our progress indicator, in the background before the translation begins. As soon as the translation process ends, the `twirl` function is killed using the saved PID.

The only thing left to do is to perform the desired action on each of the pdisk identification lights. We do this by starting yet another **for** loop. This time we use command substitution to produce a list of pdisks by listing the pdisk list file with the **cat** command. On each loop iteration the **ssaidentify** command is executed for each pdisk in the list file. The all_varied_on_pdisk function is shown in Listing 20.7.

```
function all_varied_on_pdisks
{
trap 'kill -9 $TWIRL_PID; return 1' 1 2 3 15

cat /dev/null > $HDISKFILE
cat /dev/null > $PDISKFILE

echo "\nGathering a list of Varied on system SSA disks...Please
wait...\c"

VG_LIST=$(lsvg -o) # Get the list of Varied ON Volume Groups

for VG in $(echo $VG_LIST)
```

Listing 20.7 all_varied_on_pdisks function listing.

```
do
        lspv | grep $VG >> $HDISKFILE # List of Varied ON PVs
done


twirl & # Gives the user some feedback during long processing times...


TWIRL_PID=$!

echo "\nTranslating hdisk(s) into the associated pdisk(s)
        ...Please Wait...\c"

for DISK in $(cat $HDISKFILE) # Translate hdisk# into pdisk#(s)
do
    # Checking for an SSA disk
    /usr/sbin/ssaxlate -l $DISK # 2>/dev/null 1>/dev/null
    if (($? == 0))
    then
        /usr/sbin/ssaxlate -l $DISK >> $PDISKFILE # Add to pdisk List
    fi
done

kill -9 $TWIRL_PID # Kill the user feedback function...
echo "\b  "     # Clean up the screen by overwriting the last character

echo "\nTurning $STATE all VARIED ON system pdisks...Please Wait...\n"


# Act on each pdisk individually...


for PDISK in $(cat $PDISKFILE)
do
   echo "Turning $STATE ==> $PDISK"
   /usr/sbin/ssaidentify -l $PDISK -${SWITCH} \
        ||echo "Turning $STATE PDISK Failed"
done
echo "\n\t...TASK COMPLETE...\n"
}
```

Listing 20.7 all_varied_on_pdisks function listing. *(continued)*

Notice that there is a **trap** at the beginning of this function in Listing 20.7. Because we are using the `twirl` function for user feedback we need a way to kill off the rotating line so we added a **trap** inside the function. In the next step we initialized both of the list files to empty files. Then the fun starts. This is where we filter through all of the hdisks to find the ones that are in currently varied-on volume groups. With this hdisk list we loop through each of the disks looking for SSA disks. As we find each hdisk it is translated into a pdisk and added to the pdisk list. With all of the pdisks of interest found we loop through each one and turn on/off the SSA identification lights.

The last function is `list_of_disks`, which acts on one or more hdisks or pdisks that are specified on the command line when the shell script is executed. In the main body of the shell script we do all of the parsing of the command-line arguments because if you tried to parse the command line inside a function the parsing would act on the *function's* argument, not the shell script's arguments. Therefore this is a short function.

In the main body of the shell script a variable, PDISKLIST, is populated with a list of pdisks. Because the user can specify either hdisks or pdisks, or both, on the command line the only verification that has been done is on the hdisks only, when they were translated to pdisks. We need do a sanity check to make sure that each of the pdisks we act on has a character special file in the /dev filesystem. This is done using the **-c** switch in an **if...then** test. If the pdisk listed has a character special file associated with it, then an attempt is made to turn the SSA identification light on/off, otherwise, the user is notified that the specified pdisk is not defined on the system. The `list_of_disks` function is shown in Listing 20.8.

```
function list_of_disks
{
    # TURN ON/OFF INDIVDUAL LIGHTS:
    # Loop through each of the disks that was passed to this script
    # via the positional parameters greater than $1, i.e., $2, $3, $4...
    # We first determine if each of the parameters is a pdisk or an
    # hdisk. For each hdisk passed to the script we first need to
    # translate the hdisk definition into a pdisk definition.  This
    # script has been set up to accept a combinition of hdisks and
    # pdisks.
    #
    # We will either turn the identifier lights on or off specified by
    # the $SWITCH variable for each pdisk#:
    #
    #    Turn lights on:  -y
    #    Turn lights off: -n
    #
    # as the $SWITCH value to the "ssaidentify" command, as used below...

    echo "\n"

    # The disks passed to this script can be all hdisks, all pdisks,
    # or a combination of pdisks and hdisks; it just does not matter.
    # We translate each hdisk into the associated pdisk(s).


    echo "\nTurning $STATE individual SSA disk lights...\n"

    for PDISK in $(echo $PDISKLIST)
    do
```

Listing 20.8 list_of_disks function listing.

```
        # Is it a real pdisk??
        if [ -c /dev/${PDISK} ] 2>/dev/null
        then # Yep - act on it...

               /usr/sbin/ssaidentify -l $PDISK -${SWITCH} >/dev/null
               if (($? == 0))
               then
                      /usr/bin/ssaxlate -l $PDISK -${SWITCH}
                      if (($? == 0))
                      then
                             echo "Light on $PDISK is $STATE"
                      else
                             echo "Turning $STATE $PDISK Failed"
                      fi
               fi
        else
else
               echo "\nERROR: $PDISK is not a defined device on $THISHOST\n"
        fi
done

echo "\n...TASK COMPLETE...\n"
}
```

Listing 20.8   list_of_disks function listing. *(continued)*

Notice in the boldface text in Listing 20.8 where we do the test to see if the pdisk listed is a real pdisk by using the **-c** switch in the **if** statement. We have covered the rest of the function, so let's move on to the main body of the shell script.

The Full Shell Script

This is a good point to show the entire shell script and go through the details at the end of the listing. The SSAidentify.ksh shell script is shown in Listing 20.9.

```
#!/bin/ksh
#
# SCRIPT: SSAidentify.ksh
#
# AUTHOR: Randy Michael
#
# DATE: 11/7/2000
```

Listing 20.9   SSA identify.ksh shell script listing. *(continues)*

```
#
# REV: 2.5.A
#
# PURPOSE: This script is used to turn on, or off, the
# identify lights on the system's SSA disks
#
# REV LIST:
#    11/27/2000: Added code to allow the user to turn on/off
#    individual pdisk lights
#
#    12/10/2000: Added code to accept a combination of pdisks
#    and hdisks.  For each hdisk passed the script translates
#    the hdisk# into the associated pdisk#(s).
#
#    12/10/2000: Added code to ALLOW using the currently VARIED ON
#    Volume Group's disks (-v switch), as opposed to ALL DEFINED
#    SSA disks, which is the default behavior.  Very helpful in an
#    HACMP environment.
#
#    12/11/2000: Added the "twirl" function to give the user feedback
#    during long processing periods, i.e., translating a few hundred
#    hdisks into associated pdisks.  The twirl function is just a
#    rotating cursor, and it twirls during the translation processing.
#
# set -n   # Uncomment to check syntax without any execution
# set -x   # Uncomment to debug this script

SCRIPTNAME=$(basename $0)


#################################################


function usage
{
echo "\nUSAGE ERROR...
\nMAN PAGE ==> $SCRIPTNAME   -?
\nTo Turn ALL Lights Either ON or OFF:
\nUSAGE: SSAidentify.ksh [-v] [on] [off]
EXAMPLE: SSAidentify.ksh -v  on
\nWill turn ON ALL of the system's currently VARIED ON
SSA identify lights. NOTE: The default is all DEFINED SSA disks
\nTo Turn SPECIFIC LIGHTS Either ON or OFF Using EITHER
the pdisk#(s) AND/OR the hdisk#(s):
\nUSAGE: SSAidentify.ksh [on] [off] pdisk{#1} [hdisk{#2}]...
EXAMPLE: SSAidentify.ksh on hdisk36 pdisk44 pdisk47
\nWill turn ON the lights to all of the associated pdisk#(s)
that hdisk36 translates to and PDISKS pdisk44 and pdisk47.
\nNOTE: Can use all pdisks, all hdisks or BOTH hdisk
```

Listing 20.9   SSA identify.ksh shell script listing. *(continued)*

```
and pdisk together if you want..."

exit 1
}


##############################################

function man_page
{
MAN_FILE="/tmp/man_file.out"
>$MAN_FILE

# Text for the man page...

echo "\n\t\tMAN PAGE FOR SSAidentify.ksh SHELL SCRIPT\n
This script is used to turn on, or off, the system's SSA disk drive
identification lights.  You can use this script in the following ways:\n
To turn on/off ALL DEFINED SSA drive identification lights, ALL VARIED-
ON SSA
drive identification lights (-v switch), AN INDIVIDUAL SSA drive
identification
light or A LIST OF SSA drive identification lights.\n
SSA disk drives can be specified by EITHER the pdisk OR the hdisk, or
a COMBINATION OF BOTH.  The script translates all hdisks into the
associated pdisk(s) using the system's /usr/sbin/ssaxlate command and
turns
the SSA identification light on/off using the system's
/usr/sbin/ssaidentify
command.\n

This script has four switches that control its action:\n
-? - Displays this man page.\n
on - Turns the SSA identify light(s) ON.\n
off - Turns the SSA identify light(s) OFF.\n
-v - Specifies to only act on SSA disks that are in currently varied-on
volume groups.  The default action is to act on ALL DEFINED SSA disks.\n
NOTE: This switch is ignored for turning on/off individual SSA drive
lights,
only valid when turning on/off ALL lights.  This option is very helpful
in an
HACMP environment because ALL DEFINED, the default action, will turn
on/off all
of the SSA drive lights even if the SSA disk is in a volume group that
is not
currently varied-on.  This can be confusing in an HA cluster.\n
Using this script is very straight forward.  The following examples show
the
```

Listing 20.9   SSA identify.ksh shell script listing. *(continues)*

```
correct use of this script:\n" >> $MAN_FILE
echo "\nUSAGE: SSAidentify.ksh [-v] [on] [off] [pdisk#/hdisk#]
[pdisk#/hdisk# list]
\n\nTo Turn ALL Lights Either ON or OFF:
\nUSAGE: SSAidentify.ksh [-v] [on] [off]
\nEXAMPLE: $SCRIPTNAME  on
\nWill turn ON ALL of the system's DEFINED SSA identify lights.
This is the default.
EXAMPLE: SSAidentify.ksh -v  on
\nWill turn ON ALL of the system's currently VARIED-ON
SSA identify lights.  OVERRIDES THE DEFAULT ACTION OF ALL DEFINED SSA
DISKS
\nTo Turn SPECIFIC LIGHTS Either ON or OFF Using EITHER
the pdisk#(s) AND/OR the hdisk#(s):
\nUSAGE: $SCRIPTNAME [on] [off] pdisk{#1} [hdisk{#2}]...
\nEXAMPLE: $SCRIPTNAME on hdisk36 pdisk44 pdisk47
\nWill turn ON the lights to all of the associated pdisk#(s)
that hdisk36 translates to and PDISKS pdisk44 and pdisk47.
\nNOTE: Can use all pdisks, all hdisks or BOTH hdisk
and pdisk together if you want...\n\n" >> $MAN_FILE

more $MAN_FILE

# End of man_page function
}

################################################

function cleanup
{
echo "\n...Exiting on a trapped signal...EXITING STAGE LEFT...\n"

kill $TWIRL_PID

# End of cleanup function
}

################################################

function twirl
{
TCOUNT="0"      # For each TCOUNT the line twirls one increment

while :         # Loop forever...until you break out of the loop
do
       TCOUNT=$(expr ${TCOUNT} + 1) # Increment the TCOUNT

       case ${TCOUNT} in
```

Listing 20.9 SSA identify.ksh shell script listing. *(continued)*

```
        "1")    echo '-'"\b\c"
                sleep 1
                ;;
        "2")    echo '\\'"\b\c"
                sleep 1
                ;;
        "3")    echo "|\b\c"
                sleep 1
                ;;
        "4")    echo "/\b\c"
                sleep 1
                ;;
        *)      TCOUNT="0" ;;  # Reset the TCOUNT to "0", zero.
    esac
done
# End of twirl function
}


##############################################

function all_defined_pdisks
{
    # TURN ON/OFF ALL LIGHTS:
    # Loop through each of the system's pdisks by using the "lsdev"
    # command with the "-Cc pdisk" switch while using "awk" to extract
    # out the actual pdisk number.  We will either
    # turn the identifier lights on or off specified by the
    # $SWITCH variable:
    #
    #    Turn lights on:  -y
    #    Turn lights off: -n
    #
    # as the $SWITCH value to the "ssaidentify" command, as used below...

echo "\nTurning $STATE ALL of the system's pdisks...Please Wait...\n"

for PDISK in $(lsdev -Cc pdisk -s ssar -H | awk '{print $1}' | grep
pdisk)
do
    echo "Turning $STATE ==> $PDISK"
    ssaidentify -l $PDISK -${SWITCH} || echo "Turning $STATE $PDISK
Failed"
done
echo "\n...TASK COMPLETE...\n"


}

##############################################
```

Listing 20.9 SSA identify.ksh shell script listing. *(continues)*

```
function all_varied_on_pdisks
{
trap 'kill -9 $TWIRL_PID; return 1' 1 2 3 15

cat /dev/null > $HDISKFILE

echo "\nGathering a list of Varied on system SSA disks...Please
wait...\c"

VG_LIST=$(lsvg -o) # Get the list of Varied ON Volume Groups

for VG in $(echo $VG_LIST)
do
        lspv | grep $VG >> $HDISKFILE # List of Varied ON PVs
done

twirl & # Gives the user some feedback during long processing times...

TWIRL_PID=$!

echo "\nTranslating hdisk(s) into the associated pdisk(s)...Please
Wait... \c"

for DISK in $(cat $HDISKFILE) # Translate hdisk# into pdisk#(s)
do
    # Checking for an SSA disk
    /usr/sbin/ssaxlate -l $DISK # 2>/dev/null 1>/dev/null

    if (($? == 0))
    then
            /usr/sbin/ssaxlate -l $DISK >> $PDISKFILE # Add to pdisk List
    fi
done

kill -9 $TWIRL_PID # Kill the user feedback function...
echo "\b  "


echo "\nTurning $STATE all VARIED-ON system pdisks...Please Wait...\n"

for PDISK in $(cat $PDISKFILE)
do # Act on each pdisk individually...
    echo "Turning $STATE ==> $PDISK"
    /usr/sbin/ssaidentify -l $PDISK -${SWITCH} || echo "Turning $STATE
$PDISK Failed"
```

Listing 20.9   SSA identify.ksh shell script listing. *(continued)*

```
done

echo "\n\t...TASK COMPLETE...\n"


}


###############################################


function list_of_disks
{
# TURN ON/OFF INDIVDUAL LIGHTS:
# Loop through each of the disks that was passed to this script
# via the positional parameters greater than $1, i.e., $2, $3, $4...
# We first determine if each of the parameters is a pdisk or an hdisk.
# For each hdisk passed to the script we first need to translate
# the hdisk definition into a pdisk definition.  This script has
   # been set up to accept a combination of hdisks and pdisks.
#
# We will either turn the identifier lights on or off specified by
# the $SWITCH variable for each pdisk#:
#
#    Turn lights on:  -y
#    Turn lights off: -n
#
# as the $SWITCH value to the "ssaidentify" command.

echo "\n"

# The disks passed to this script can be all hdisks, all pdisks
# or a combination of pdisks and hdisks; it just does not matter.
# We translate each hdisk into the associated pdisk(s).


echo "\nTurning $STATE individual SSA disk lights...\n"

for PDISK in $(echo $PDISKLIST)
do
     # Is it a real pdisk??
     if [ -c /dev/${PDISK} ] 2>/dev/null
     then # Yep - act on it...

          /usr/sbin/ssaidentify -l $PDISK -${SWITCH}
          if [ $? -eq 0 ]
          then
               /usr/bin/ssaxlate -l $PDISK -${SWITCH}
               if (($? == 0))
```

Listing 20.9   SSA identify.ksh shell script listing. *(continues)*

```
                  then
                        echo "Light on $PDISK is $STATE"
                  else
                        echo "Turning $STATE $PDISK Failed"
                  fi
            fi
      else
            echo "\nERROR: $PDISK is not a defined device on $THISHOST\n"
      fi
done

echo "\n...TASK COMPLETE...\n"
}


###############################################
############# BEGINNING OF MAIN ############
###############################################

# Set a trap...

# Remember...Cannot trap a "kill -9" !!!

trap 'cleanup;exit 1' 1 2 3 15


###############################################

# Check for the correct number of arguments (1)

if (($# == 0))
then
      usage
fi


###############################################

# See if the system has any pdisks defined before proceeding

PCOUNT=$(lsdev -Cc pdisk -s ssar | grep -c pdisk)

if ((PCOUNT == 0))
then
      echo "\nERROR: This system has no SSA disks defined\n"
      echo "\t\t...EXITING...\n"
```

Listing 20.9   SSA identify.ksh shell script listing. *(continued)*

```
        exit 1
fi


##############################################

# Make sure that the ssaidentify program is
# executable on this system...

if [ ! -x /usr/sbin/ssaidentify ]
then
        echo "\nERROR: /usr/sbin/ssaidentify is NOT an executable"
        echo "program on $THISHOST"
        echo "\n...EXITING...\n"
        exit 1
fi


###############################################

# Make sure that the ssaxlate program is
# executable on this system...

if [ ! -x /usr/sbin/ssaxlate ]
then
        echo "\nERROR: /usr/sbin/ssaxlate is NOT an executable"
        echo "program on $THISHOST"
        echo "\n...EXITING...\n"
        exit 1
fi


##############################################
##############################################
#
# Okay, we should have valid data at this point
# Let's do a light show.
#
##############################################
##############################################

# Always use the UPPERCASED value for the $STATE, $MODE,
# and $PASSED variables...


typeset -u MODE
```

Listing 20.9   SSA identify.ksh shell script listing. *(continues)*

```
MODE="DEFINED_DISKS"
typeset -u STATE
STATE=UNKNOWN
typeset -u PASSED

# Use lowercase for the argument list
typeset -l ARGUMENT

# Grab the system hostname

THISHOST=$(hostname)

# Define the hdisk and pdisk FILES

HDISKFILE="/tmp/disklist.out"
>$HDISKFILE
PDISKFILE="/tmp/pdisklist.identify"
>$PDISKFILE

# Define the hdisk and pdisk list VARIABLES

HDISKLIST=
PDISKLIST=

# Use getopts to parse the command-line arguments

while getopts ":v V" ARGUMENT 2>/dev/null
do
      case $ARGUMENT in

            v|V)      MODE="VARIED_ON"
                      ;;
            \?)       man_page
                      ;;
      esac
done

###############################################

# Decide if we are to turn the lights on or off...

(echo $@ | grep -i -w on  >/dev/null) && STATE=ON
(echo $@ | grep -i -w off >/dev/null) && STATE=OFF


case $STATE in

ON)
```

Listing 20.9 SSA identify.ksh shell script listing. *(continued)*

```
  # Turn all of the lights ON...
    SWITCH="y"
    ;;
OFF)
    # Turn all of the lights OFF...
    SWITCH="n"
    ;;
*)
    # Unknown Option...
    echo "\nERROR: Please indicate the action to turn lights ON or
OFF\n"
    usage
      exit 1
    ;;
esac


#################################################
#################################################
########## PLAY WITH THE LIGHTS ##############
#################################################
#################################################

if (($# == 1)) && [[ $MODE = "DEFINED_DISKS" ]]
then
    # This function will turn all lights on/off

    all_defined_pdisks

elif [[ $MODE = "VARIED_ON" ]] && (($# = 2))
then
    # This function will turn on/off SSA disk lights
    # in currently varied-on volume groups only

    all_varied_on_pdisks

# Now check for hdisk and pdisk arguments

elif [ $MODE = DEFINED_DISKS ] && (echo $@ | grep disk >/dev/null) \
                            && (($# >= 2))
then
    # If we are here we must have a list of hdisks
    # and/or pdisks

    # Look for hdisks and pdisks in the command-line arguments

    for DISK in $(echo $@ | grep disk)
    do
        case $DISK in
```

Listing 20.9   SSA identify.ksh shell script listing. *(continues)*

```
        hdisk*)  HDISKLIST="$HDISKLIST $DISK"
              ;;
        pdisk*)  PDISKLIST="$PDISKLIST $DISK"
              ;;
        *)       :  # No-Op - Do nothing
              ;;
     esac
done


if [[ ! -z "$HDISKLIST" ]] # Check for hdisks to convert to pdisks
then

# We have some hdisks that need to be converted to pdisks
# so start converting the hdisks to pdisks

     # Give the user some feedback

     echo "\nConverting hdisks to pdisk definitions"
     echo "\n     ...Please be patient...\n"

     # Start converting the hdisks to pdisks

     for HDISK in $(echo $HDISKLIST)
     do
          PDISK=$(ssaxlate -l $HDISK)
          if (($? == 0))
          then
                  echo "$HDISK translates to ${PDISK}"
          else
                  echo "ERROR: hdisk to pdisk translation FAILED
for $HDISK"
          fi
          # Build a list of pdisks
                                        # Add pdisk to the pdisk
list
          PDISKLIST="$PDISKLIST $PDISK"
        done
     fi


if [[ -z "$PDISKLIST" ]]
then
     echo "\nERROR: You must specify at least one hdisk or
pdisk\n"
     man_page
     exit 1
```

Listing 20.9   SSA identify.ksh shell script listing. *(continued)*

```
        else
                # Turn on/off the SSA identification lights

                list_of_disks
        fi
fi


###############################################
#            END OF SCRIPT                    #
###############################################
```

Listing 20.9   SSA identify.ksh shell script listing. *(continued)*

Let's start at the "Beginning of Main" in Listing 20.9. The very first thing that we do is set a **trap**. This **trap** is set for exit codes 1, 2, 3, 5, and 15. On any of these captured signals the cleanup function is executed, and then the shell script exits with a return code of 1. It is nice to be able to clean up before the shell script just exits.

In the next series of tests we first make sure that there is at least one argument present on the command line. If no arguments are given, then the script presents the usage function, which displays proper usage and exits. If we pass the argument test then I thought it would be a good idea to see if the system has any SSA disks defined on the system. For this step we use the **PCOUNT=$(lsdev -Cc pdisk -s ssar | grep -c pdisk)**. The **grep -c** returns the count of SSA disks found on the system and assigns the value to the **PCOUNT** variable. If the value is zero there are no SSA disks, so inform the user and **exit**. If we do have some SSA disks, the next thing we do is make sure that the **ssaidentify** and **ssaxlate** commands exist and are executable on this system. At this point we know we are in an SSA environment so we define and initialize all of the script's variables.

Then we get to use the **getopts** function to parse the command-line arguments. We expect and recognize just two arguments, **-v** and **-V**, to specify varied-on volume groups only. Any other argument, specified by a preceding hyphen, **-**, displays the man_page function. Anything else on the command line is ignored by the **getopts** function, which is a shell built-in function.

On the command line we **must** have either **on** or **off** present, or we do not have enough information to do anything. We check the command-line arguments by echoing out the full list and grepping for **on** and **off**. At the next **case** statement the $STATE variable is tested. If on or off was not found, the usage function is displayed and the script exits. If we get past this point we know that we have the minimal data to do some work.

When we start playing with the lights we have to do some tests to decide what action we need to take and on what set of SSA disks. The first one is simple. If we have only one command-line argument and it is either **on** or **off**, then we know to turn on or off all defined SSA disk identification lights on the system without regard to volume group status. So, here we run the `all_defined_pdisks` function. If we have two arguments on the command line and one of them is **-v** or **-V**, then we know to act only on SSA disks in currently varied-on volume groups by turning every one of the SSA identification lights on or off.

The last option is to have hdisks or pdisks listed on the command line. For this option we know to act on only the disks that the user specified and to turn on or off only these disks. Because we allow both hdisks and pdisks we need to convert everything to pdisk definitions before we call the `list_of_disks` function. To do this we **echo** the entire list of command-line arguments and **grep** for the word **disk**. Using this list in a **case** statement, we can detect the presence of an hdisk or a pdisk. For each one found it is added to either the HDISKLIST or the PDISKLIST variables. After the test we check to see if the HDISKLIST variable has anything assigned, which means that the variable is not null. If there are entries, then we convert each hdisk to its associated pdisk and build up the pdisk list in the PDISKLIST variable. When the list is complete, and it is not an empty list, we call the `list_of_disks` function. That is it for this shell script.

Other Things to Consider

I cannot always fit all of the options into a chapter, and this chapter is no exception. Here are a few things to consider to modify this shell script.

Error Log

When I created this shell script it was for a personal need because I have so many SSA disk trays. For my purposes I did not need an error log, but you may find one necessary. In the places that I sent everything to the bit bucket, especially standard error, or file descriptor 2, redirect this output to append to an error log. This may help you find something in the system that you missed.

Cross-Reference

Because it is rare for the hdisk and pdisk associations to match by numbers you may find that a shell script to cross-reference the numbers beneficial. You should be able to knock this out in about one hour. Look through the code where I first test the hdisk to see if it is an SSA disk and then do the translation. Using these few lines of code you can build a nice little cross-reference sheet for your staff.

Root Access and sudo

Both of the SSA commands need root privilege to execute. If your systems have strict root access rules you may just want to define this shell script in your /etc/sudoers file. Please *never* directly edit this file! There is a special wrapper program around the vi editor in the `/usr/local/sbin` directory called **visudo**. This command starts a **vi** session and opens up the `/etc/sudoers` file automatically. When you are finished editing and save the file, this program checks the `/etc/sudoers` file for errors.

Summary

In this chapter we learned a few new things about controlling the SSA subsystem on an AIX machine. These principles apply to any other Unix system utilizing SSA. As always, there are many different ways to write a shell script, and some are lean and mean with no comments. I like to make the shell scripts easier to understand and maintain. But I do have a few things that you may want to consider.

I hope you learned something in this chapter. In the next chapter we will look at pseudo-random number generators. See you in the next chapter!

## CHAPTER 21

Pseudo-Random
Number Generation

In writing shell scripts we sometimes run into a situation where we are creating files faster than we can make the filenames unique. Most of the time a date/time stamp can be added as a suffix to the filename to make the filename unique, but if we are creating more than one file per second we end up overwriting the same file during a single second. To get around this problem we can create *pseudo-random numbers* to append to the filename after the date/time stamp. You may recall that in Chapter 10 we studied creating pseudo-random passwords by using the computer generated numbers as pointers to array elements that contained keyboard characters. A more thorough discussion of randomness is presented in this chapter.

What Makes a Random Number?

It is very difficult to create a true random number in a computer system. The problem is repeatability and predictability of the number. When you start researching random numbers you quickly enter the realm of heavy mathematical theory, and many of the researchers have varying opinions of randomness. The only *true* random numbers that I know of are the frequency variations of radioactive decay events and the frequency variations of white noise. Radioactive decay events would have to be detected in some way, and because we do not want to have any radioactive material hanging around we can use built-in computer programs called pseudo-random number generators. Some computer techniques are able to create numbers that are suitable for encryption keys and for cryptographic secure communication links. Some of these techniques include measuring the time between keystrokes and use this measured value as a memory address to read the contents.

A popular Unix technique is to use a special Unix character device called /dev/ random. If you search the Internet for /dev/random you will find more information than you could imagine on the topic of randomness. Randomness is a discussion topic with many experts in the field having widely varying viewpoints. I am not an expert on randomness, and this topic is beyond the scope of this book. We are going to concentrate on creating pseudo-random numbers to make unique filenames in this chapter.

The numbers that we will create are not sufficiently random for any type of encryption because they are repeatable and cyclical in nature, but they will create unique filenames. The Korn shell provides an environment variable called—you guessed it— RANDOM. This pseudo-random number generator uses a *seed* as a starting point to create all future numbers in the sequence. After the initial seed is used to create a pseudo-random number, this resulting number is used for the next seed to create the next random number, and so on. As you would expect, if you always start generating your numbers with the same seed each time, you will get the exact same number sequence each time. To change the repeatability we need to have a mechanism to vary the initial seed each time we start generating numbers. I like to use the current process ID (PID) because this number will vary widely and is an easy way to change the seed value each time we start generating numbers.

The Methods

In this chapter we are going to look at three techniques to generate pseudo-random numbers:

- Create numbers between zero and the maximum number allowed by the system (32,767)
- Create numbers between one and a user-defined maximum
- Create fixed-length numbers between one and a user-defined maximum with leading zeros added if needed

Each method is valid for a filename extension, but you may have other uses that require either a range of numbers or a fixed number of digits with leading zeros. In any case the basic concept is the same.

We start out by initializing the RANDOM environment variable to the current PID:

```
RANDOM=$$
```

The double dollar signs ($$) specify the PID of the current system process. The PID will vary, so this is a good way to initialize the RANDOM variable so that we do not always repeat the same number sequence. Once the RANDOM environment variable is initialized we can use RANDOM just like any other variable. Most of the time we will use the **echo** command to print the next pseudo-random number. An example of using the RANDOM environment variable is shown in Listing 21.1.

```
# RANDOM=$$
# echo $RANDOM
23775
# echo $RANDOM
3431
# echo $RANDOM
12127
# echo $RANDOM $RANDOM
2087 21108
```

Listing 21.1   Using the RANDOM environment variable.

By default the RANDOM variable will produce numbers between 0 and 32767. Notice the last entry in Listing 21.1. We can produce more than one number at a time if we need to by adding more $RANDOM entries to our **echo** command. In showing our three methods in this chapter we are going to create three functions and then create a shell script that will use one of the three methods depending on the user-supplied input. The last step is to write a shell script that will create unique filenames using a date/time stamp and a random number.

Method 1: Creating Numbers between 0 and 32,767

Creating pseudo-random numbers using this default method is the simplest way to use the RANDOM environment variable. The only thing that we need to do is to initialize the RANDOM environment variable to an initial seed value and use the **echo** command to display the new number. The numbers will range from 0 to 32767, which is the maximum for the RANDOM variable. You do not have control over the number of digits, except that the number of digits will not exceed five, and you cannot specify a maximum value for the number in this first method. The function get_random_number is shown in Listing 21.2.

```
function get_random_number
{
# This function gets the next random number from the
# $RANDOM variable. The range is 0 to 32767.

echo "$RANDOM"
}
```

Listing 21.2   get_random_number function listing.

As you can see, the function is just one line, and we are assuming that the RANDOM environment variable is initialized in the main body of the calling shell script.

Method 2: Creating Numbers between 1 and a User-Defined Maximum

We often want to limit the range of numbers to not exceed a user-defined maximum. An example is creating lottery numbers between 1 and the maximum number, which might be 36. We are going to use the modulo arithmetic operator to reduce all numbers to a fixed set of numbers between [0..N-1], which is called *modulo N arithmetic*.

For our number range we need a user-supplied maximum value, which we will assign to a variable called UPPER_LIMIT. The modulo operator is the percent sign (%), and we use this operator the same way that you use the forward slash (/) in division. We still use the RANDOM environment variable to get a new pseudo-random number. This time, though, we are going to use the following equation to limit the number to not exceed the user-defined maximum *modulo N arithmetic*.

```
RANDOM_NUMBER=$(($RANDOM % $UPPER_LIMIT + 1))
```

Notice that we added one to the equation.

Using the preceding equation will produce a pseudo-random number between 1 and the user-defined $UPPER_LIMIT. The function using this equation is in_range_random_number and is shown in Listing 21.3.

```
function in_range_random_number
{
# Create a pseudo-random number less than or equal
# to the $UPPER_LIMIT value, which is user defined

RANDOM_NUMBER=$(($RANDOM % $UPPER_LIMIT + 1))

echo "$RANDOM_NUMBER"
}
```

Listing 21.3   in_range_random_number function listing.

The function in Listing 21.3 assumes that the RANDOM variable seed has been initialized in the main body of the calling shell script and that a user-defined UPPER_LIMIT variable has been set. This function will produce numbers between 1 and the user-defined maximum value, but the number of digits will vary as the numbers are produced.

Method 3: Fixed-Length Numbers between 1 and a User-Defined Maximum

In both of the previous two examples we had no way of knowing how many digits the new number would contain. When we are creating unique filenames it would be nice to have filenames that are consistent in length. We can produce fixed-length numbers by padding the number with leading zeros for each missing digit. As an example we want all of our numbers to have four digits. Now let's assume that the number that is produced is 24. Because we want 24 to have four digits, we need to pad the number with two leading zeros, which will make the number 0024. To pad the number we need to know the length of the character string that makes up the number. The Korn shell uses the pound operator (#) preceding the variable enclosed within curly braces ({}), as shown here.

```
RN_LENGTH=$(echo ${#RANDOM_NUMBER})
```

If the RANDOM_NUMBER variable has 24 assigned as an assigned value, then the result of the previous command is 2 (this RN_LENGTH variable points to the value 2), indicating two digits. We will also need the length of the UPPER_LIMIT value, and we will use the difference to know how many zeros to use to pad the pseudo-random number output. Take a close look at the code in Listing 21.4 where you will find the function in_range_fixed_length_random_number.

```
function in_range_fixed_length_random_number
{
# Create a pseudo-random number less than or equal
# to the $UPPER_LIMIT value, which is user defined.
# This function will also pad the output with leading
# zeros to keep the number of digits consistent.

RANDOM_NUMBER=$(($RANDOM % $UPPER_LIMIT + 1))

# Find the length of each character string

RN_LENGTH=$(echo ${#RANDOM_NUMBER})
UL_LENGTH=$(echo ${#UPPER_LIMIT})

# Calculate the difference in string length

(( LENGTH_DIFF = UL_LENGTH - RN_LENGTH ))

# Pad the $RANDOM_NUMBER value with leading zeros
```

Listing 21.4 in_range_fixed_length_random_number function. *(continues)*

```
# to keep the number of digits consistent.

case $LENGTH_DIFF in
0)   echo "$RANDOM_NUMBER"
     ;;
1)   echo "0$RANDOM_NUMBER"
     ;;
2)   echo "00$RANDOM_NUMBER"
     ;;
3)   echo "000$RANDOM_NUMBER"
     ;;
4)   echo "0000$RANDOM_NUMBER"
     ;;
5)   echo "00000$RANDOM_NUMBER"
     ;;
*)   echo "$RANDOM_NUMBER"
     ;;
esac
}
```

Listing 21.4   in_range_fixed_length_random_number function. *(continued)*

In Listing 21.4 we use the same technique from Listing 21.3 to set an upper limit to create our numbers, but we add in code to find the string length of both the UPPER_LIMIT and RANDOM_NUMBER values. By knowing the length of both strings we subtract the random-number length from the upper-limit length and use the difference in a **case** statement to add the correct number of zeros to the output.

Because this is a function, we again need to assume that the UPPER_LIMIT is defined and the RANDOM environment variable is initialized in the main body of the calling shell script. The resulting output is a fixed-length pseudo-random number padded with leading zeros if the output string length is less than the upper limit string length. Example output is shown in Listing 21.5 for an UPPER_LIMIT value of 9999.

```
0024
3145
9301
0328
0004
4029
2011
0295
0159
4863
```

Listing 21.5   Sample output for fixed-length random numbers.

Why Pad the Number with Zeros the Hard Way?

An easier, and much cleaner, way to pad a number with leading zeros is to **typeset** the variable to a fixed length. The following command works for any length number:

```
typeset -Z5 FIXED_LENGTH
FIXED_LENGTH=25
echo $FIXED_LENGTH
00025
```

Listing 21.6   Using the typeset command to fix the length of a variable.

In the example in Listing 21.6 we used the **typeset** command to set the length of the FIXED_LENGTH variable to five digits. Then we assigned the value 25 to it. When we use the **echo** command to show the value assigned to the variable the result is 00025, which is fixed to five digits. Let's modify the function in Listing 21.4 to use this technique as shown in Listing 21.7.

```
function in_range_fixed_length_random_number_typeset
{
# Create a pseudo-random number less than or equal
# to the $UPPER_LIMIT value, which is user defined.
# This function will also pad the output with leading
# zeros to keep the number of digits consistent using
# the typeset command.

# Find the length of each character string

UL_LENGTH=$(echo ${#UPPER_LIMIT})

# Fix the length of the RANDOM_NUMBER variable to
# the length of the UPPER_LIMIT variable, specified
# by the $UL_LENGTH variable.

typeset -Z$UL_LENGTH  RANDOM_NUMBER

# Create a fixed length pseudo-random number

RANDOM_NUMBER=$(($RANDOM % $UPPER_LIMIT + 1))

# Return the value of the fixed length $RANDOM_NUMBER

echo $RANDOM_NUMBER
}
```

Listing 21.7   Using the typeset command in a random number function.

As you can see in Listing 21.7, we took all of the complexity out of fixing the length of a number. The only value we need to know is the length of the UPPER_LIMIT variable assignment. As an example, if the upper limit is 9999 then the length is 4. We use 4 to **typeset** the RANDOM_NUMBER variable to four digits.

Now that we have four functions that will create pseudo-random numbers, we can proceed with a shell script that will use one of the three methods depending on the command-line arguments supplied to the shell script.

Shell Script to Create Pseudo-Random Numbers

Using the three functions from Listings 21.2, 21.3, and 21.7 we are going to create a shell script that, depending on the command-line arguments, will use one of these three functions. We first need to define how we are going to use each function.

With the usage definitions from Table 21.1 let's create a shell script. We already have the functions to create the numbers so we will start with BEGINNING OF MAIN in the shell script.

For the usage function we will need the name of the shell script. We never want to hard-code the name of a shell script because someone may rename the shell script for one reason or another. To query the system for the actual name of the shell script we use the **basename $0** command. This command will return the name of the shell script, specified by the **$0** argument, with the directory path stripped out. I like to use either of the following commands to create a SCRIPT_NAME variable.

```
SCRIPT_NAME=`basename $0`
```

or

```
SCRIPT_NAME=$(basename $0)
```

Table 21.1   random_number.ksh Shell Script Usage

SHELL SCRIPT USAGE	FUNCTION USED TO CREATE THE NUMBER
random_number.ksh	Without argument will use get_random_number
random_number.ksh 9999	With one numeric argument will use in_range_random_number
random_number.ksh -f 9999	With **-f** as the first argument followed by a numeric argument will use in_range_fixed_length_random_number_typeset

The result of both command substitution commands is the same. Next we need to initialize the RANDOM environment variable. As we described before, we are going to use the current process ID as the initial seed for the RANDOM variable.

```
RANDOM=$$
```

The SCRIPT_NAME and the RANDOM variables are the only initialization needed for this shell script. The rest of the script is a **case** statement that uses the number of command-line arguments ($#) as a value to decide which random number function we will use. We also do some numeric tests to ensure that "numbers" are actually numeric values. For the numeric tests we use the regular expression +([0-9]) in a **case** statement. If the value is a number, then we do nothing, which is specified by the no-op character, colon (:).

The entire shell script is shown in Listing 21.8.

```
#!/usr/bin/ksh
#
# AUTHOR: Randy Michael
# SCRIPT: random_number.ksh
# DATE: 11/12/2001
# REV: 1.2.P
#
# PLATFORM: Not Platform Dependent
#
# EXIT CODES:
#          0 - Normal script execution
#          1 - Usage error
#
# REV LIST:
#
#
# set -x # Uncomment to debug
# set -n # Uncomment to check syntax without any command execution
#
####################################################
######### DEFINE FUNCTIONS HERE ###################
####################################################

function usage
{
echo "\nUSAGE: $SCRIPT_NAME [-f] [upper_number_range]"
echo "\nEXAMPLE: $SCRIPT_NAME"
echo "Will return a random number between 0 and 32767"
echo "\nEXAMPLE: $SCRIPT_NAME 1000"
echo "Will return a random number between 1 and 1000"
echo "\nEXAMPLE: $SCRIPT_NAME -f 1000"
```

Listing 21.8 random_number.ksh shell script listing. *(continues)*

```
echo "Will add leading zeros to a random number from"
echo "1 to 1000, which keeps the number of digits consistant\n"
}

####################################################

function get_random_number
{
# This function gets the next random number from the
# $RANDOM variable. The range is 0 to 32767.

echo "$RANDOM"
}

####################################################

function in_range_random_number
{
# Create a pseudo-random number less than or equal
# to the $UPPER_LIMIT value, which is user defined

RANDOM_NUMBER=$(($RANDOM % $UPPER_LIMIT + 1))

echo "$RANDOM_NUMBER"
}

####################################################

function in_range_fixed_length_random_number_typeset
{
# Create a pseudo-random number less than or equal
# to the $UPPER_LIMIT value, which is user defined.
# This function will also pad the output with leading
# zeros to keep the number of digits consistent using
# the typeset command.

# Find the length of each character string

UL_LENGTH=$(echo ${#UPPER_LIMIT})

# Fix the length of the RANDOM_NUMBER variable to
# the length of the UPPER_LIMIT variable, specified
```

Listing 21.8   random_number.ksh shell script listing. *(continued)*

```
# by the $UL_LENGTH variable.

typeset -Z$UL_LENGTH  RANDOM_NUMBER

# Create a fixed length pseudo-random number

RANDOM_NUMBER=$(($RANDOM % $UPPER_LIMIT + 1))

# Return the value of the fixed length $RANDOM_NUMBER

echo $RANDOM_NUMBER
}


####################################################
############## BEGINNING OF MAIN ###################
####################################################

SCRIPT_NAME=`basename $0`

RANDOM=$$  # Initialize the RANDOM environment variable
           # using the PID as the initial seed

case $# in
0)   get_random_number
;;

1)   UPPER_LIMIT="$1"

     # Test to see if $UPPER_LIMIT is a number

     case $UPPER_LIMIT in
     +([0-9])) :      # Do Nothing...It's a number
                      # NOTE: A colon (:) is a no-op in Korn shell
          ;;
     *)       echo "\nERROR: $UPPER_LIMIT is not a number..."
              usage
              exit 1
          ;;
     esac

     # We have a valid UPPER_LIMIT. Get the number.

     in_range_random_number
```

Listing 21.8   random_number.ksh shell script listing. *(continues)*

```
;;

2)   # Check for the -f switch to fix the length.

     if [[ $1 = '-f' ]] || [[ $1 = '-F' ]]
     then

          UPPER_LIMIT="$2"

          # Test to see if $UPPER_LIMIT is a number

          case $UPPER_LIMIT in
          +([0-9])) :      # Do Nothing...It's a number
                           # NOTE: A colon (:) is a no-op in Korn shell
               ;;
          *)        echo "\nERROR: $UPPER_LIMIT is not a number..."
                    usage
                    exit 1
               ;;
          esac

          in_range_fixed_length_random_number_typeset

     else
          echo "\nInvalid argument $1, see usage below..."
          usage
          exit 1
     fi
;;

*)   usage
     exit 1
;;
esac

# End of random_number.ksh Shell Script
```

Listing 21.8   random_number.ksh shell script listing. *(continued)*

Notice in Listing 21.8 that we will allow only zero, one, or two command-line arguments. More than three arguments produces an error, and nonnumeric values, other than **-f** or **-F** in argument one, will produce a usage error. Output using the random_number.ksh shell script is shown in Listing 21.9.

```
yogi@/scripts# random_number.ksh 32000
10859
yogi@/scripts# random_number.ksh -f 32000
14493
yogi@/scripts# ./random_number.ksh -f 32000
05402
yogi@/scripts# ./random_number.ksh -f

ERROR: -f is not a number...

USAGE: random_number.ksh [-f] [upper_number_range]

EXAMPLE: random_number.ksh
Will return a random number between 0 and 32767

EXAMPLE: random_number.ksh 1000
Will return a random number between 1 and 1000

EXAMPLE: random_number.ksh -f 1000
Will add leading zeros to a random number from
1 to 1000, which keeps the number of digits consistent
```

Listing 21.9   random_number.ksh shell script in action.

The last part of Listing 21.9 is a usage error. Notice that we give an example of each of the three uses for the random_number.ksh shell script as well as state why the usage error occurred.

Now that we have the shell script to produce pseudo-random numbers, we need to move on to creating unique filenames.

Creating Unique Filenames

The goal of this chapter is to write a shell script that will produce unique filenames using a date/time stamp with a pseudo-random number as an extended suffix. When I create these unique filenames I like to keep the length of the filenames consistent so we are going to use only one of the random number functions, in_range_fixed_length_random_number_typeset.

We have a few new pieces to put into this new shell script. First we have to assume that there is some program or shell script that will be putting data into each of the unique files. To take care of executing the program or shell script we can add a function that will call the external program, and we will redirect our output to the new unique filename on each loop iteration. The second piece is that we need to ensure that we never use the same number during the same second. Otherwise, the filename is not unique and the data will be overwritten. We need to keep a list of each number that we use during each second and reset the USED_NUMBERS list to null on each new second. In addition we need to **grep** the list each time we create a new number to see if it has already been used. If the number has been used we just create a new number and check for previous usage again.

The procedure to step through our new requirements is not difficult to understand once you look at the code. The full shell script is shown in Listing 21.10, and an example of using the shell script is shown in Listing 21.11. Please study the script carefully, and we will go through the details at the end.

```ksh
#!/usr/bin/ksh
#
# AUTHOR: Randy Micahel
# SCRIPT: mk_unique_filename.ksh
# DATE: 11/12/2001
# REV: 1.2.P
#
# PLATFORM: Not Platform Dependent
#
# EXIT CODES:
#               0 - Normal script execution
#               1 - Usage error
#
# REV LIST:
#
#
# set -x # Uncomment to debug
# set -n # Uncomment to debug without any execution
#
##################################################
########## DEFINE FUNCTIONS HERE #################
##################################################

function usage
{
echo "\nUSAGE: $SCRIPT_NAME base_file_name\n"
exit 1
}

##################################################

function get_date_time_stamp
{
DATE_STAMP=$(date +'%m%d%y.%H%M%S')
```

Listing 21.10   mk_unique_filename.ksh shell script listing.

```
echo $DATE_STAMP
}


#####################################################

function get_second
{
THIS_SECOND=$(date +%S)
echo $THIS_SECOND
}


######################################################


function in_range_fixed_length_random_number_typeset
{
# Create a pseudo-random number less than or equal
# to the $UPPER_LIMIT value, which is user defined.
# This function will also pad the output with leading
# zeros to keep the number of digits consistent using
# the typeset command.

# Find the length of each character string

UL_LENGTH=$(echo ${#UPPER_LIMIT})

# Fix the length of the RANDOM_NUMBER variable to
# the length of the UPPER_LIMIT variable, specified
# by the $UL_LENGTH variable.

typeset -Z$UL_LENGTH  RANDOM_NUMBER

# Create a fixed length pseudo-random number

RANDOM_NUMBER=$(($RANDOM % $UPPER_LIMIT + 1))

# Return the value of the fixed length $RANDOM_NUMBER

echo $RANDOM_NUMBER
}



#####################################################

function my_program
{
```

Listing 21.10   mk_unique_filename.ksh shell script listing. *(continues)*

```
# Put anything you want to process in this function. I
# recommend that you specify an external program of shell
# script to execute.

echo "HELLO WORLD - $DATE_ST" > $UNIQUE_FN &

#    :  # No-Op - Does nothing but has a return code of zero
}


#######################################################
############### BEGINNING OF MAIN ###############
#######################################################

SCRIPT_NAME=$(basename $0) # Query the system for this script name

# Check for the correct number of arguments - exactly 1

if (( $# != 1 ))
then
     echo "\nERROR: Usage error...EXITING..."
     usage
fi

# What filename do we need to make unique?

BASE_FN=$1      # Get the BASE filename to make unique

RANDOM=$$       # Initialize the RANDOM environment variable
                # with the current process ID (PID)

UPPER_LIMIT=32767 # Set the UPPER_LIMIT

CURRENT_SECOND=99 # Initialize to a nonsecond
LAST_SECOND=98    # Initialize to a nonsecond

USED_NUMBERS=     # Initialize to null

PROCESSING="TRUE" # Initialize to run mode

while [[ $PROCESSING = "TRUE" ]]
do
    DATE_ST=$(get_date_time_stamp) # Get the current date/time
    CURRENT_SECOND=$(get_second)   # Get the current second

    RN=$(in_range_fixed_length_random_number_typeset) # Get a new number

    # Check to see if we have already used this number this second

    if (( CURRENT_SECOND == LAST_SECOND ))
```

Listing 21.10   mk_unique_filename.ksh shell script listing. *(continued)*

```
    then
          UNIQUE=FALSE # Initialize to FALSE
          while [[ "$UNIQUE" != "TRUE" ]] && [[ ! -z "$UNIQUE" ]]
          do
              # Has this number already been used this second?
              echo $USED_NUMBERS | grep $RN >/dev/null 2>&1
              if (( $? == 0 ))
              then
                  # Has been used...Get another number
                  RN=$(in_range_fixed_length_random_number)
              else
                  # Number is unique this second...
                  UNIQUE=TRUE
                  # Add this number to the used number list
                  USED_NUMBERS="$USED_NUMBERS $RN"
              fi
          done
    else
          USED_NUMBERS=    # New second...Reinitialize to null
    fi
    # Assign the unique filename to the UNIQUE_FN variable

    UNIQUE_FN=${BASE_FN}.${DATE_ST}.$RN

    # echo $UNIQUE_FN # Comment out this line!!

    LAST_SECOND=$CURRENT_SECOND # Save the last second value

    # We have a unique filename...
    #
    # PROCESS SOMETHING HERE AND REDIRECT OUTPUT TO $UNIQUE_FN
    #
    my_program
    #
    # IF PROCESSING IS FINISHED ASSIGN "FALSE" to the
    # PROCESSING VARIABLE
    #
    # if [[ $MY_PROCESS = "done" ]]
    # then
    #        PROCESSING="FALSE"
    # fi
done
```

Listing 21.10   mk_unique_filename.ksh shell script listing. *(continued)*

We need five functions in this shell script. As usual, we need a function for correct usage. We are expecting exactly one argument to this shell script, the *base filename* to make into a unique filename. The second function is used to get a date/time stamp.

The **date** command has a lot of command switches that allow for flexible date/time stamps. We are using two digits for month, day, year, hour, minute, and second with a period (.) between the date and time portions of the output. This structure is the first part that is appended to the base filename. The **date** command has the following syntax: **date +/%m%d%y.%H%M%S'**.

We also need the current second of the current minute. The current second is used to ensure that the pseudo-random number that is created is unique to each second, thus a unique filename. The **date** command is used again using the following syntax: **date +%S**.

The `in_range_fixed_length_random_number_typeset` function is used to create our pseudo-random numbers in this shell script. This function keeps the number of digits consistent for each number that is created. With the base filename, date/time stamp, and the unique number put together, we are assured that every filename has the same number of characters.

One more function is added to this shell script. The `my_program` function is used to point to the program or shell script that needs all of these unique filenames. It is better to point to an external program or shell script than trying to put everything in the internal `my_program` function and debugging the internal function on an already working shell script. Of course, I am making an assumption that you will execute the external program once during each loop iteration, which may not be the case. At any rate, this script will show the concept of creating unique filenames while remaining in a tight loop.

At the BEGINNING OF MAIN in the main body of the shell script we first query the system for name of the shell script. The script name is needed for the usage function. Next we check for exactly one command-line argument. This single command-line argument is the base filename that we use to create further unique filenames. The next step is to assign our base filename to the variable BASE_FN for later use.

The RANDOM environment variable is initialized with an initial seed, which we decided to be the current process ID (PID). This technique helps to ensure that the initial seed changes each time the shell script is executed. For this shell script we want to use the maximum value as the UPPER_LIMIT, which is 32767. If you need a longer or shorter pseudo-random number, you can change this value to anything you want. If you make this number longer than five digits the extra preceding digits will be zeros. There are four more variables that need to be initialized. We initialize both CURRENT_SECOND and LAST_SECOND to nonsecond values 99 and 98, respectively. The USED_NUMBERS list is initialized to null, and the PROCESSING variable is initialized to TRUE. The PROCESSING variable allows the loop to continue creating unique filenames and to keep calling the my_process function. Any non-TRUE value stops the loop and thus ends execution of the shell script.

A **while** loop is next in our shell script, and this loop is where all of the work is done. We start out by getting a new date/time stamp and the current second on each loop iteration. Next a new pseudo-random number is created and is assigned to the RN variable. If the current second is the same as the last second, then we start another loop to ensure that the number that we created has not been previously used during the current second. It is highly unlikely that a duplicate number would be produced in such a short amount of time, but to be safe we need to do a sanity check for any duplicate numbers.

When we get a unique number we are ready to put the new filename together. We have three variables that together make up the filename: $BASE_FN, $DATE_ST, and $RN. The next command puts the pieces together and assigns the filename to the variable to the UNIQUE_FN variable.

```
UNIQUE_FN=${BASE_FN}.${DATE_ST}.$RN
```

Notice the use of the curly braces ({}) around the first two variables, BASE_FN and DATE_ST. The curly braces are needed because there is a character that is not part of the variable name without a space. The curly braces separate the variable from the character to ensure that we do not get unpredictable output. Because the last variable, $RN, does not have any character next to its name, the curly braces are not needed, but it is *not* a mistake to add them.

The only thing left is to assign the $CURRENT_SECOND value to the LAST_SECOND value and to execute the my_program function, which actually uses the newly created filename. I have commented out the code that would stop the script's execution. You will need to edit this script and make it suitable for your particular purpose. The mk_unique_filename.ksh shell script is in action in Listing 21.11.

```
yogi@/scripts# ./mk_unique_filename.ksh /tmp/myfilename
/tmp/myfilename.120601.131507.03038
/tmp/myfilename.120601.131507.15593
/tmp/myfilename.120601.131507.11760
/tmp/myfilename.120601.131508.08374
/tmp/myfilename.120601.131508.01926
/tmp/myfilename.120601.131508.07238
/tmp/myfilename.120601.131509.07554
/tmp/myfilename.120601.131509.12343
/tmp/myfilename.120601.131510.08496
/tmp/myfilename.120601.131510.18285
/tmp/myfilename.120601.131510.18895
/tmp/myfilename.120601.131511.16618
/tmp/myfilename.120601.131511.30612
/tmp/myfilename.120601.131511.16865
/tmp/myfilename.120601.131512.01134
/tmp/myfilename.120601.131512.19362
/tmp/myfilename.120601.131512.04287
/tmp/myfilename.120601.131513.10616
/tmp/myfilename.120601.131513.08707
/tmp/myfilename.120601.131513.27006
/tmp/myfilename.120601.131514.15899
/tmp/myfilename.120601.131514.18913
/tmp/myfilename.120601.131515.27120
/tmp/myfilename.120601.131515.23639
/tmp/myfilename.120601.131515.13096
/tmp/myfilename.120601.131516.19111
/tmp/myfilename.120601.131516.05964
```

Listing 21.11   mk_unique_filename.ksh shell script in action. *(continues)*

```
/tmp/myfilename.120601.131516.07809
/tmp/myfilename.120601.131524.03831
/tmp/myfilename.120601.131524.21628
/tmp/myfilename.120601.131524.19801
/tmp/myfilename.120601.131518.13556
/tmp/myfilename.120601.131518.24618
/tmp/myfilename.120601.131518.12763

# Listing of newly created files

yogi@/tmp# ls -ltr /tmp/myfilename.*
-rw-r--r-- root  system  Dec 06 13:15
/tmp/myfilename.120601.131507.15593
-rw-r--r-- root  system  Dec 06 13:15
/tmp/myfilename.120601.131507.03038
-rw-r--r-- root  system  Dec 06 13:15
/tmp/myfilename.120601.131508.08374
-rw-r--r-- root  system  Dec 06 13:15
/tmp/myfilename.120601.131508.01926
-rw-r--r-- root  system  Dec 06 13:15
/tmp/myfilename.120601.131507.11760
-rw-r--r-- root  system  Dec 06 13:15
/tmp/myfilename.120601.131509.12343
-rw-r--r-- root  system  Dec 06 13:15
/tmp/myfilename.120601.131509.07554
-rw-r--r-- root  system  Dec 06 13:15
/tmp/myfilename.120601.131508.07238
-rw-r--r-- root  system  Dec 06 13:15
/tmp/myfilename.120601.131510.18285
-rw-r--r-- root  system  Dec 06 13:15
/tmp/myfilename.120601.131510.08496
-rw-r--r-- root  system  Dec 06 13:15
/tmp/myfilename.120601.131511.30612
-rw-r--r-- root  system  Dec 06 13:15
/tmp/myfilename.120601.131511.16618
-rw-r--r-- root  system  Dec 06 13:15
/tmp/myfilename.120601.131510.18895
-rw-r--r-- root  system  Dec 06 13:15
/tmp/myfilename.120601.131512.19362
-rw-r--r-- root  system  Dec 06 13:15
/tmp/myfilename.120601.131512.01134
-rw-r--r-- root  system  Dec 06 13:15
/tmp/myfilename.120601.131511.16865
-rw-r--r-- root  system  Dec 06 13:15
/tmp/myfilename.120601.131513.10616
-rw-r--r-- root  system  Dec 06 13:15
/tmp/myfilename.120601.131513.08707
```

Listing 21.11   mk_unique_filename.ksh shell script in action. *(continued)*

```
-rw-r--r-- root  system  Dec 06 13:15
/tmp/myfilename.120601.131512.04287
-rw-r--r-- root  system  Dec 06 13:15
/tmp/myfilename.120601.131514.18913
-rw-r--r-- root  system  Dec 06 13:15
/tmp/myfilename.120601.131514.15899
-rw-r--r-- root  system  Dec 06 13:15
/tmp/myfilename.120601.131513.27006
-rw-r--r-- root  system  Dec 06 13:15
/tmp/myfilename.120601.131515.27120
-rw-r--r-- root  system  Dec 06 13:15
/tmp/myfilename.120601.131515.23639
-rw-r--r-- root  system  Dec 06 13:15
/tmp/myfilename.120601.131515.13096
-rw-r--r-- root  system  Dec 06 13:15
/tmp/myfilename.120601.131516.19111
-rw-r--r-- root  system  Dec 06 13:15
/tmp/myfilename.120601.131516.05964
-rw-r--r-- root  system  Dec 06 13:15
/tmp/myfilename.120601.131524.21628
-rw-r--r-- root  system  Dec 06 13:15
/tmp/myfilename.120601.131524.03831
-rw-r--r-- root  system  Dec 06 13:15
/tmp/myfilename.120601.131516.07809
-rw-r--r-- root  system  Dec 06 13:15
/tmp/myfilename.120601.131518.24618
-rw-r--r-- root  system  Dec 06 13:15
/tmp/myfilename.120601.131518.13556
-rw-r--r-- root  system  Dec 06 13:15
/tmp/myfilename.120601.131524.19801
-rw-r--r-- root  system  Dec 06 13:15
/tmp/myfilename.120601.131518.12763
```

Listing 21.11   mk_unique_filename.ksh shell script in action. *(continued)*

Summary

In this chapter we stepped through some different techniques of creating pseudo-random numbers and then used this knowledge to create unique filenames. Of course these numbers are *not* suitable for any security-related projects because of the predictability and cyclical nature of computer generated numbers using the RANDOM variable. Play around with these shell scripts and functions and modify them for your needs. In Chapter 10 we used pseudo-random numbers to create pseudo-random passwords. If you have not already studied Chapter 10, I suggest that you break out of sequence and study this chapter next.

In the next chapter we move into a little floating point mathematics and introduce you to the **bc** utility. Floating point math is not difficult if you use some rather simple techniques. Of course you can make mathematics as difficult as you wish. I hope you gained a lot of knowledge in this chapter and I will see you in the next chapter!

## CHAPTER 22

Floating-Point Math and the bc Utility

Have you ever had a need to do some floating-point math in a shell script? If the answer is yes, then you're in luck. On Unix machines there is a utility called **bc** that is an interpreter for arbitrary-precision arithmetic language. The **bc** command is an interactive program that provides arbitrary-precision arithmetic. You can start an interactive **bc** session by typing **bc** on the command line. Once in the session you can enter most complex arithmetic expressions as you would in a calculator. The **bc** utility can handle more than I can cover in this chapter, so we are going to keep the scope limited to simple floating-point math in shell scripts.

In this chapter we are going to create shell scripts that add, subtract, multiply, divide, and average a list of numbers. With each of these shell scripts the user has the option of specifying a *scale*, which is the number of significant digits to the right of the decimal point. If no scale is specified, then an integer value is given in the result. Because the **bc** utility is an interactive program, we are going to use a *here document* to supply input to the interactive **bc** program. We will cover using a here document in detail throughout this chapter.

Syntax

By now you know the routine: We need to know the syntax before we can create a shell script. Depending on what we are doing we need to create a mathematical statement to present to **bc** for a here document to work. A here document works kind of like a *label* in other programming languages. The syntax that we are going to use in this chapter will have the following form:

```
VARIABLE=$(bc <<LABEL
scale=$SCALE
($MATH_STATEMENT)
LABEL)
```

The way a here document works is some label name, in this case LABEL, is added just after the **bc** command. This LABEL has double redirection for input into the interactive program, bc <<LABEL. From this starting label until the same label is encountered again everything in between is used as input to the **bc** program. By doing this we are automating an interactive program. We can also do this automation using another technique. We can use **echo**, **print**, and **printf** to print all of the data for the math statement and pipe the output to **bc**. It works like the following commands.

```
VARIABLE=$(print 'scale = 10; 104348/33215' | bc)
```

or

```
VARIABLE=$(print 'scale=$SCALE; ($MATH_STATEMENT)' | bc)
```

In either case we are automating an interactive program. This is the purpose of a here document. It is called a here document because the required input is *here*, as opposed to somewhere else, such as user input from the keyboard. When all of the required input is supplied *here*, it is a here document.

Creating Some Shell Scripts Using bc

We have the basic syntax, so let's start with a simple shell script to add numbers together. The script is expecting a list of numbers as command-line arguments. Additionally, the user may specify a *scale* if the user wants the result calculated as a floating-point number to a set precision. If a floating point number is *not* specified, then the result is presented as an integer value.

Creating the float_add.ksh Shell Script

The first shell script that we are going to create is float_add.ksh. The idea of this shell script is to add a list of numbers together that the user provides as command-line arguments. The user also has the option of setting a scale for the precision of floating-point numbers. Let's take a look at the float_add.ksh shell script in Listing 22.1, and we will go through the details at the end.

```ksh
#!/usr/bin/ksh
#
# SCRIPT: float_add.ksh
# AUTHOR: Randy Michael
# DATE: 03/01/2001
# REV: 1.1.A
#
# PURPOSE: This shell script is used to add a list of numbers
#          together. The numbers can be either integers or floating-
#          point numbers. For floating-point numbers the user has
#          the option of specifying a scale of the number of digits to
#          the right of the decimal point. The scale is set by adding
#          a -s or -S followed by an integer number.
#
# EXIT CODES:
#       0 ==> This script completed without error
#       1 ==> Usage error
#       2 ==> This script exited on a trapped signal
#
# REV. LIST:
#
#
# set -x # Uncomment to debug this script
# set -n # Uncomment to debug without any command execution
#
#######################################################
############## DEFINE VARIABLE HERE ####################
#######################################################

SCRIPT_NAME=$(basename $0)  # The name of this shell script
SCALE="0"       # Initialize the scale value to zero
NUM_LIST=       # Initialize the NUM_LIST variable to NULL
COUNT=0         # Initialize the counter to zero
MAX_COUNT=$#    # Set MAX_COUNT to the total number of
                # command-line arguments.

#######################################################
############### FUNCTIONS ##############################
#######################################################

function usage
{
echo "\nPURPOSE: Adds a list of numbers together\n"
echo "USAGE: $SCRIPT_NAME [-s scale_value]  N1 N2...Nn"
```

Listing 22.1   float_add.ksh shell script listing. *(continues)*

```
echo "\nFor an integer result without any significant decimal places..."
echo "\nEXAMPLE: $SCRIPT_NAME 2048.221 65536 \n"
echo "OR for 4 significant decimal places"
echo "\nEXAMPLE: $SCRIPT_NAME -s 4  8.09838 2048 65536 42.632"
echo "\n\t...EXITING...\n"
}

########################################################

function exit_trap
{
echo "\n...EXITING on trapped signal...\n"
}

########################################################
################# START OF MAIN #######################
########################################################

###### Set a Trap ######

trap 'exit_trap; exit 2' 1 2 3 15

########################################################

# Check for at least two command-line arguments

if [ $# -lt 2 ]
then
     echo "\nERROR: Please provide a list of numbers to add"
     usage
     exit 1
fi

# Parse the command-line arguments to find the scale value, if present.

while getopts ":s:S:" ARGUMENT
do
    case $ARGUMENT in
        s|S) SCALE=$OPTARG
            ;;
          \?) # Because we may have negative numbers we need
              # to test to see if the ARGUMENT that begins with a
              # hyphen (-) is a number, and not an invalid switch!!!

              for TST_ARG in $*
              do
                  if [[ $(echo $TST_ARG | cut -c1) = '-' ]] \
```

Listing 22.1 float_add.ksh shell script listing. *(continued)*

```
                      && [ $TST_ARG != '-s' -a $TST_ARG != '-S' ]
                   then
                      case $TST_ARG in
                      +([-0-9])) : # No-op, do nothing
                          ;;
                      +([-0-9].[0-9]))
                          : # No-op, do nothing
                          ;;
                      +([-.0-9])) : # No-op, do nothing
                          ;;
                      *) echo "\nERROR: Invalid argument on the command
line"
                         usage
                         exit 1
                         ;;
                      esac
                   fi
             done
             ;;
     esac
done


##########################################################

# Parse through the command-line arguments and gather a list
# of numbers to add together and test each value.

while ((COUNT < MAX_COUNT))
do
     ((COUNT = COUNT + 1))
     TOKEN=$1    # Grab a command line argument on each loop iteration
     case $TOKEN in    # Test each value and look for a scale value.
             -s|-S) shift 2
                    ((COUNT = COUNT + 1))
                    ;;
          -s${SCALE}) shift
                    ;;
          -S${SCALE}) shift
                    ;;
             *) # Add the number ($TOKEN) to the list
                NUM_LIST="${NUM_LIST} $TOKEN"
                ((COUNT < MAX_COUNT)) && shift
                    ;;
     esac
done


##########################################################
```

Listing 22.1 float_add.ksh shell script listing. *(continues)*

```
# Ensure that the scale is an integer value

case $SCALE in
                # Test for an integer
    +([0-9])) : # No-Op - Do Nothing
             ;;
         *) echo "\nERROR: Invalid scale - $SCALE - Must be an
integer"
             usage
             exit 1
             ;;
esac


############################################################

# Check each number supplied to ensure that the "numbers"
# are either integers or floating-point numbers.

for NUM in $NUM_LIST
do
    case $NUM in
    +([0-9])) # Check for an integer
             : # No-op, do nothing.
             ;;
    +([-0-9])) # Check for a negative whole number
             : # No-op, do nothing
             ;;
    +([0-9]|[.][0-9]))
             # Check for a positive floating point number
             : # No-op, do nothing
             ;;
    +(+[0-9][.][0-9]))
             # Check for a positive floating point number
             # with a + prefix
             : # No-op, do nothing
             ;;
    +(-[0-9][.][0-9]))
             # Check for a negative floating point number
             : # No-op, do nothing
             ;;
    +([-.0-9]))
             # Check for a negative floating point number
             : # No-op, do nothing
             ;;
    +([+.0-9]))
             # Check for a positive floating point number
```

Listing 22.1 float_add.ksh shell script listing. *(continued)*

```
                  : # No-op, do nothing
                  ;;
       *) echo "\nERROR: $NUM is NOT a valid number"
          usage
          exit 1
          ;;
       esac
done


#########################################################

# Build the list of numbers to add

ADD=     # Initialize the ADD variable to NULL
PLUS=    # Initialize the PLUS variable to NULL

# Loop through each number and build a math statement that
# will add all of the numbers together.

for X in $NUM_LIST
do
       # If the number has a + prefix, remove it!
       if [[ $(echo $X | cut -c1) = '+' ]]
       then
             X=$(echo $X | cut -c2-)
       fi
       ADD="$ADD $PLUS $X"
       PLUS="+"
done


#########################################################

# Do the math here by using a here document to supply
# input to the bc command. The sum of the numbers is
# assigned to the SUM variable.

SUM=$(bc <<EOF
scale = $SCALE
(${ADD})
EOF)


#########################################################

# Present the result of the addition to the user.

echo "\nThe sum of: $ADD"
echo "\nis: ${SUM}\n"
```

Listing 22.1   float_add.ksh shell script listing. *(continued)*

Let's take it from the top. We start the shell script in Listing 22.1 by defining some variables. These five variables, SCRIPT_NAME, SCALE, NUM_LIST, COUNT, and MAX_COUNT are predefined for later use. The SCRIPT_NAME variable assignment extracts the filename of the script from the system using the **basename $0** command, and SCALE is used to define the precision of floating-point numbers that are calculated. The NUM_LIST variable is used to hold valid numbers that are to be calculated, where the command switch and the switch-argument are removed from the list. The COUNT and MAX_COUNT variables are used to scan all of the command-line arguments to find the numbers..

In the next section we define the functions. This shell script has two functions, usage and exit_trap. The usage function shows the user how to use the script, and the exit_trap function is executed only when a trapped exit signal is captured. Of course, you cannot trap a **kill -9**. At the START OF MAIN the first thing that we do is to set a **trap**. A **trap** allows us to take some action when the trapped signal is captured. For example, if the user presses CTRL-C we may want to clean up some temporary files before the script exits. A **trap** allows us to do this.

A **trap** has the form of **trap '{command; command; ... ; exit 2' 1 2 3 15**. We first enclose the commands that we want to execute within tic marks (single quotes) and then give a list of **exit** signals that we want to capture. As I said before, it is not possible to capture a **kill -9** signal because the system really just yanks the process out of the process table and it ceases to exist.

After setting the **trap** we move on to verifying that each of the command-line arguments is valid. To do this verification we do five tests. These five tests consist of checking for at least two command-line arguments, using **getopts** to parse the command-line switches, test for invalid switches, and assign switch-arguments to variables for use in the shell script. The next step is to scan each argument on the command line and extract the numbers that we need to do our calculations. Then the $SCALE value is checked to ensure that it points to an integer value, and the final test is to check the "numbers" that we gathered from the command-line scan and ensure that each one is either an integer or a floating-point number.

Testing for Integers and Floating-Point Numbers

I want to go over the integer and floating-point test before we move on. At this point in the script we have a list of "numbers"—at least they are supposed to be numbers—and this list is assigned to the NUM_LIST variable. Our job is to verify that each value in the list is either an integer or a floating-pointing number. Look at the code segment shown in Listing 22.2.

```
# Check each number supplied to ensure that the "numbers"
# are either integers or floating-point numbers.

for NUM in $NUM_LIST
do
      case $NUM in
```

Listing 22.2 Testing for integers and floating-point numbers.

```
        +([0-9])) # Check for an integer
                : # No-op, do nothing.
                ;;
        +(-[0-9])) # Check for a negative whole number
                : # No-op, do nothing
                ;;
        +([0-9]|[.][0-9]))
                # Check for a positive floating point number
                : # No-op, do nothing
                ;;
        +(+[0-9]|[.][0-9]))
                # Check for a positive floating point number
                # with a + prefix
                : # No-op, do nothing
                ;;
        +(-[0-9][.][0-9]))
                # Check for a negative floating point number
                : # No-op, do nothing
                ;;
        +([-.0-9]))
                # Check for a negative floating point number
                : # No-op, do nothing
                ;;
        +([+.0-9]))
                # Check for a positive floating point number
                : # No-op, do nothing
                ;;
        *) echo "\nERROR: $NUM is NOT a valid number"
           usage
           exit 1
           ;;
        esac
    done
```

Listing 22.2   Testing for integers and floating-point numbers. *(continued)*

We use a **for** loop to test each value in the NUM_LIST. On each loop iteration the current value in the $NUM_LIST is assigned to the NUM variable. Within the **for** loop we have set up a **case** statement. For the tests we use regular expressions to indicate a range, or type of value, that we are expecting. If the value does not meet the criteria that we defined, the * is matched and we execute the usage function before exiting the shell script.

The regular expressions for testing for integers and floating point numbers include +([0-9]), +(-[0-9]), +([0-9]|.[0-9], +(+[0-9].[0-9], +(-[0-9].[0-9], +([-.0-9]), +([+.0-9]). The first two tests are for integers and negative whole numbers. The last five tests are for positive and negative floating point numbers.

Notice the use of the plus sign (+), minus sign (-), and the decimal point (.). The placement of the plus sign, minus sign, and the decimal point are important when testing the string. Because a floating point number, both positive and negative, can be represented in many forms we need to test for all combinations. Floating point numbers are one of the more difficult tests to make as you can see by the number of tests that are required.

Building a Math Statement for the bc Command

Once we are sure that all of the data is valid we proceed to building the actual math statement that we are sending to the **bc** utility. To build this statement we are going to loop through our newly confirmed $NUM_LIST of numbers and build a string with a plus sign (+) between each of the numbers in the $NUM_LIST. This is a neat trick. We first initialize two variables to NULL, as shown here.

```
ADD=
PLUS=
```

As we build the math statement, the ADD variable will hold the entire statement as it is added to. The PLUS variable will be assigned the + character inside of the **for** loop on the first loop iteration. This action prevents the + sign showing up as the first character in the string we are building. Let's look at this code segment here.

```
ADD=     # Initialize the ADD variable to NULL
PLUS=    # Initialize the PLUS variable to NULL

# Loop through each number and build a math statement that
# will add all of the numbers together.

for X in $NUM_LIST
do
        if [[ $(echo $X | cut -c1) = '+' ]]
        then
              X=$(echo $X | cut -c2-)
        fi
        ADD="$ADD $PLUS $X"
        PLUS="+"
done
```

On the first loop iteration only the first number in the $NUM_LIST is assigned to the ADD variable. On each of the following loop iterations a plus sign (+) is added followed by the next number in the $NUM_LIST, specified by the X variable on each loop iteration, until all of the numbers and plus signs have been assigned to the ADD variable. As an example, we have the following list of numbers:

```
12   453.766   223.6   3.145927   22
```

Also notice that we added a test for the number beginning with a + sign. We need to strip this character out so that we do not have two plus signs together when we present the equation to the **bc** program or an error will occur. As we build the math statement the following assignments are made to the ADD variable on each loop iteration:

```
ADD="12"
ADD="12 + 453.766"
ADD="12 + 453.766 + 223.6"
ADD="12 + 453.766 + 223.6 + 3.145927"
ADD="12 + 453.766 + 223.6 + 3.145927 + 22"
```

Using a Here Document

When the looping finishes we have built the entire math statement and have it assigned to the ADD variable. Now we are ready to create the here document to add all of the numbers together with the **bc** utility. Let's take a look at the here document shown here.

```
# Do the math here by using a here document to supply
# input to the bc command. The sum of the numbers is
# assigned to the SUM variable.

SUM=$(bc <<EOF
scale=$SCALE
(${ADD})
EOF)
```

For this here document the label is the EOF character string (you will see this used a lot in shell scripts). The **bc** command has its input between the first EOF and the ending EOF. The first EOF label starts the here document, and the second EOF label ends the here document. Each line between the two labels is used as input to the **bc** command. There are a couple of requirements for a here document. The first requirement is that the starting label *must* be preceded by double input redirection (<<EOF). The second requirement is that there are *never* any blank spaces at the beginning of *any* line in the here document. If even one blank space is placed in column one, then strange things may begin to happen. Depending on what you are doing, and the interactive program you are using, the here document may work, but it may not! This is one of the most difficult programming errors to find when you are testing, or using, a shell script with a here document. To be safe, just leave out any beginning spaces.

The final step is to display the result to the user. Listing 22.3 shows the float_add.ksh shell script in action.

```
[root:yogi]@/scripts# ./float_add.ksh -s 8 2 223.545 332.009976553

The sum of: 2 + 223.545 + 332.009976553

to a scale of 8 is 557.554976553
```

Listing 22.3 float_add.ksh shell script in action.

Notice that the scale is set to 8, but the output has 9 decimal places. For this shell script the scale has absolutely no impact on the final result. This is just how the **bc** program works. It is not an error to add in a scale but the result does not use it in this case. The **man** page for the **bc** program can provide you with more details on this effect. We will see how the scale works in some of the other shell scripts later in this chapter.

That is it for the addition shell script, but we still have four more shell scripts to go in this chapter. Each of the following shell scripts is very similar to the script in Listing 22.1. With this being the case I am going to cover different aspects of each of the following scripts and also show where the differences lie. Please keep reading to catch a few more shell programming tips.

Creating the float_subtract.ksh Shell Script

As the `float_add.ksh` shell script performed addition on a series of numbers, this section studies the technique of subtraction. Because this shell script is very similar to the shell script in Listing 22.1 we are going to show the shell script and study the details at the end. The `float_subtract.ksh` shell script is shown in Listing 22.4.

```
#!/usr/bin/ksh
#
# SCRIPT: float_subtract.ksh
# AUTHOR: Randy Michael
# DATE: 02/23/2001
# REV: 1.1.A
#
# PURPOSE: This shell script is used to subtract a list of numbers.
#          The numbers can be either integers or floating- point
#          numbers. For floating- point numbers the user has the
#          option to specify a scale of the number of digits to
#          the right of the decimal point. The scale is set by
#          adding a -s or -S followed by an integer number.
#
# EXIT STATUS:
#       0 ==> This script completed without error
#       1 ==> Usage error
#       2 ==> This script exited on a trapped signal
#
# REV. LIST:
#
#
# set -x # Uncomment to debug this script
# set -n # Uncomment to debug without any command execution
#
#######################################################
############## DEFINE VARIABLE HERE ###################
#######################################################
```

Listing 22.4 float_subtract.ksh shell script listing.

```
SCRIPT_NAME=`basename $0` # The name of this shell script
SCALE="0"       # Initialize the scale value to zero
NUM_LIST=       # Initialize the NUM_LIST to NULL
COUNT=0         # Initialize the counter to zero
MAX_COUNT=$#    # Set MAX_COUNT to the total number of
                # command-line arguments


#########################################################
############### FUNCTIONS ############################
#########################################################


function usage
{
echo "\nPURPOSE: Subtracts a list of numbers\n"
echo "USAGE: $SCRIPT_NAME [-s scale_value]  N1 N2...Nn"
echo "\nFor an integer result without any significant decimal places..."
echo "\nEXAMPLE: $SCRIPT_NAME 2048.221 65536 \n"
echo "OR for 4 significant decimal places"
echo "\nEXAMPLE: $SCRIPT_NAME -s 4  8.09838 2048 65536 42.632"
echo "\n\t...EXITING...\n"
}


#########################################################


function exit_trap
{
        echo "\n...EXITING on trapped signal...\n"
}


#########################################################
############### START OF MAIN #########################
#########################################################


###### Set a Trap ######

trap 'exit_trap; exit 2' 1 2 3 15

#######################

# Check for at least two command-line arguments

if (($# < 2))
then
        echo "\nERROR: Please provide a list of numbers to subtract"
        usage
        exit 1
fi
```

Listing 22.4 float_subtract.ksh shell script listing. *(continues)*

```
# Parse the command-line arguments to find the scale value, if present.

while getopts ":s:S:" ARGUMENT
do
    case $ARGUMENT in
        s|S) SCALE=$OPTARG
            ;;
        \?) # Because we may have negative numbers we need
            # to test to see if the ARGUMENT that begins with a
            # hyphen (-) is a number, and not an invalid switch!!!

            for TST_ARG in $*
            do
                if [[ $(echo $TST_ARG | cut -c1) = '-' ]] \
                   && [ $TST_ARG != '-s' -a $TST_ARG != '-S' ]
                then
                    case $TST_ARG in
                    +([-0-9])) : # No-op, do nothing
                                ;;
                    +([-0-9].[0-9]))
                                : # No-op, do nothing
                                ;;
                    +([-.0-9])) : # No-op, do nothing
                                ;;
                    *) echo "\nERROR: Invalid argument on the command
line"
                        usage
                        exit 1
                        ;;
                    esac
                fi
            done
            ;;
    esac
done

##########################################################

# Parse through the command-line arguments and gather a list
# of numbers to subtract.

while ((COUNT < MAX_COUNT))
do
    ((COUNT = COUNT + 1))
    TOKEN=$1
    case $TOKEN in
        -s|-S) shift 2
            ((COUNT = COUNT + 1))
            ;;
```

Listing 22.4 float_subtract.ksh shell script listing. *(continued)*

```
                -s${SCALE}) shift
                        ;;
            -S${SCALE}) shift
                        ;;
                *) NUM_LIST="${NUM_LIST} $TOKEN"
                   ((COUNT < MAX_COUNT)) && shift
                   ;;
    esac
done

########################################################

# Ensure that the scale is an integer value

case $SCALE in
    +([0-9])) :  # No-Op - Do Nothing
            ;;
        *) echo "\nERROR: Invalid scale - $SCALE - Must be an
integer"
            usage
            exit 1
            ;;
esac

########################################################

# Check each number supplied to ensure that the "numbers"
# are either integers or floating- point numbers.


for NUM in $NUM_LIST
do
    case $NUM in
    +([0-9])) # Check for an integer
            : # No-op, do nothing.
            ;;
    +([-0-9])) # Check for a negative whole number
            : # No-op, do nothing
            ;;
    +([0-9]|[.][0-9]))
            # Check for a positive floating point number
            : # No-op, do nothing
            ;;
    +(+[0-9]|[.][0-9]))
            # Check for a positive floating point number
            # with a + prefix
            : # No-op, do nothing
            ;;
    +([-0-9]|.[0-9]))
```

Listing 22.4   float_subtract.ksh shell script listing. *(continues)*

```
                        # Check for a negative floating point number
                        : # No-op, do nothing
                        ;;
        +(-[.][0-9]))
                        # Check for a negative floating point number
                        : # No-op, do nothing
                        ;;
        +([+.0-9]))
                        # Check for a positive floating point number
                        : # No-op, do nothing
                        ;;
        *) echo "\nERROR: $NUM is NOT a valid number"
           usage
           exit 1
           ;;
        esac
done


#######################################################

# Build the list of numbers to subtract

SUBTRACT=        # Initialize the SUBTRACT variable to NULL
MINUS=           # Initialize the MINUS variable to NULL

# Loop through each number and build a math statement that
# will subtract the numbers in the list.

for X in $NUM_LIST
do
        # If the number has a + prefix, remove it!
        if [[ $(echo $X | cut -c1) = '+' ]]
        then
                X=$(echo $X | cut -c2-)
        fi
        SUBTRACT="$SUBTRACT $MINUS $X"
        MINUS='-'
done


#######################################################

# Do the math here by using a here document to supply
# input to the bc command. The difference of the numbers is
# assigned to the DIFFERENCE variable.

DIFFERENCE=$(bc <<EOF
scale=$SCALE
(${SUBTRACT})
```

Listing 22.4   float_subtract.ksh shell script listing. *(continued)*

```
EOF)

#########################################################

# Present the result of the subtraction to the user.

echo "\nThe difference of: $SUBTRACT"
echo "\nis: ${DIFFERENCE}\n"
```

Listing 22.4   float_subtract.ksh shell script listing. *(continued)*

The parts of the `float_subtract.ksh` shell script, shown in Listing 22.4, that remain unchanged from Listing 22.1 include the following sections: variable definitions and the `usage` function, which is unchanged except that the references to addition are changed to subtraction. Additionally, all of the same tests are performed on the user-provided data to ensure the data integrity. When we get to the end of the shell script where the math statement is created and the here document performs the calculation, we get into some changes.

Using getopts to Parse the Command Line

Let's first cover parsing the command line for the **-s** and **-S** switches and these switch-arguments that we use to define the floating-point precision with the **getopts** command. Using **getopts** for command-line parsing is the simplest method. It sure beats trying to program all of the possibilities inside the shell script. The first thing to note about **getopts** is that this command does not care *what* is on the command line! The **getopts** is interested in only command switches, which must begin with a hyphen (-), such as **-s** and **-S** for this shell script. Let's look at the **getopts** code segment and see how it works.

```
# Parse the command-line arguments to find the scale value, if present.

while getopts ":s:S:" ARGUMENT
do
    case $ARGUMENT in
        s|S) SCALE=$OPTARG
            ;;
        \?)  # Because we may have negative numbers we need
             # to test to see if the ARGUMENT that begins with a
             # hyphen (-) is a number, and not an invalid switch!!!

             for TST_ARG in $*
             do
                if [[ $(echo $TST_ARG | cut -c1) = '-' ]] \
                    && [ $TST_ARG != '-s' -a $TST_ARG != '-S' ]
```

```
            then
                case $TST_ARG in
                +([-0-9])) : # No-op, do nothing
                            ;;
                +([-0-9].[0-9]))
                            : # No-op, do nothing
                            ;;
                +([-.0-9])) : # No-op, do nothing
                            ;;
                *) echo "\nERROR: $TST_ARG is an invalid argument\n"
                   usage
                   exit 1
                   ;;
                esac
            fi
        done
    esac
done
```

A **getopts** statement starts with a **while** loop. To define valid command-line switches for a shell script you add the list of characters that you want to use for command-line switches just after the **while getopts** part of the **while** statement. It is a good practice to enclose the list of command-line switches in double quotes (`"list"`). The next thing that you need to notice is the use of the colons (`:`) in the list of valid switches. The placement and usage of the colons is important. Specifically, if the list *starts* with a colon, then any undefined command-line switch that is located will be assigned the question mark (?) character. The question mark character is then assigned to the ARGUMENT variable (which can actually be any variable name). Whenever the ? is matched it is a good idea to **exit** the script or send an error message to the user, and show the user the correct usage of the shell script before exiting. This ability of catching usage errors is what makes **getopts** a very nice and powerful tool to use.

But, in our case when we encounter the ? we may just have a negative number! Therefore, any time we encounter a hyphen (-) on the command line we need to test for a negative number before we tell the user that the input is invalid. This piece of code is in the **case** statement after the ?.

The other colon (`:`) used in the list specifies that the switch character that appears immediately *before* the colon requires a switch-argument. Looking at the following **getopts** example statement may help to clarify the colon usage.

```
while getopts ":s:S:rtg:" ARGUMENT
```

In this **getopts** statement the list begins with a colon so any command-line switch other than -s, -S, -r, -t, and -g will cause the ARGUMENT variable to be assigned the ? character, indicating a usage error. When any *defined* command-line argument is located on the command line it is assigned to the ARGUMENT variable (you can use any variable name here). When any *undefined* command-line switch is located, and the valid switch list *begins* with a colon, then the question mark character is assigned to the ARGUMENT variable. If the switch list does *not* begin with a colon, then the undefined switch is ignored. In our shell script we do not want to ignore any invalid command-line argument but we also do not want a negative number to be considered invalid input. This is where we do the extra test on the command-line.

Looking at each of the individually defined switches in the previous example, **-s**, and **-S** each require a switch-argument. The **-r** and **-g** switches do *not* have an argument because they do not have a colon after them in the definition list. When a switch is encountered that requires a switch-argument, the switch-argument is assigned to a variable called OPTARG. In our case the switch-argument to **-s** or **-S** is the value of the scale for precision floating-point arithmetic, so we make the following assignment: SCALE=$OPTARG in the **case** statement inside the **while** loop. As with the float_add.ksh shell script, the scale does not give the results that you expect. The use of the scale is in this shell script as a learning experience and you will see expected results in the following shell scripts in this chapter.

Just remember when using **getopts** to parse command-line arguments for valid switches that **getopts** could care less what is on the command line. It is up to you to verify that all of the data that you use is valid for your particular purpose. This is why we make so many tests of the data that the user inputs on the command line.

Building a Math Statement String for bc

Next we move on to the end of the shell script where we build the math statement for the **bc** command. In building the math statement that we use in the here document we now use the SUBTRACT and MINUS variables in the **for** loop. Take a look at the code segment listed here to build the math statement.

```
# Build the list of numbers to subtract

SUBTRACT=     # Initialize the SUBTRACT variable to NULL
MINUS=        # Initialize the MINUS variable to NULL

# Loop through each number and build a math statement that
# will subtract the numbers in the list.

for X in $NUM_LIST
do
      # If the number has a + prefix, remove it!
      if [[ $(echo $X | cut -c1) = '+' ]]
      then
            X=$(echo $X | cut -c2-)
      fi

      SUBTRACT="$SUBTRACT $MINUS $X"
      MINUS='-'
done
```

Notice that we initialize the SUBTRACT and MINUS variables to NULL. We do this because on the first loop iteration we do not want a minus sign (–) included. The minus sign is defined within the **for** loop. The SUBTRACT variable is initialized to NULL because we want to begin with an empty statement string. As we start the **for** loop, using the valid list of numbers that we so painstakingly verified, we add only the first number in the $NUM_LIST. On the second loop iteration, and continuing until all of the numbers in the $NUM_LIST have been exhausted, we add a minus sign to the math statement, followed by the next number in the list. Additionally, we took the extra step of removing any plus sign (+) that may be a prefix to any positive number. This step is required because we do not want the + in the equation or an error will occur because there will be a - *and* a + between two numbers. During this **for** loop the entire math statement is assigned to the SUBTRACT variable. The statement is built in the following manner, assuming that we have the following numbers to work with.

```
12  453.766  -223.6  3.145927  22
```

As we build the math statement the following assignments are made to the SUBTRACT variable:

```
SUBTRACT="12"
SUBTRACT="12 - 453.766"
SUBTRACT="12 - 453.766 - -223.6"
SUBTRACT="12 - 453.766 - -223.6 - 3.145927"
SUBTRACT="12 - 453.766 - -223.6 - 3.145927 - 22"
```

Here Document and Presenting the Result

I want to cover a here document one more time because it is important to know what you can and cannot do with this technique. With the math statement created we are ready to create the here document to add all of the numbers together with the **bc** utility. Let's take a look at the here document shown here.

```
# Do the math here by using a here document to supply
# input to the bc command. The difference of the numbers is
# assigned to the DIFFERENCE variable.

DIFFERENCE=$(bc <<EOF
scale=$SCALE
(${SUBTRACT})
EOF)
```

Just like the here document in Listing 22.1, float_add.ksh, this here document label is the EOF character string. The **bc** command has its input between the starting EOF label and the ending EOF label. The first label starts the here document, and the second EOF label ends the here document. Each line between the two labels is used as input to the **bc** command. There are a couple of requirements for a here document. The first requirement is that the starting label *must* be preceded by double input redirection (<<EOF). The second requirement is that there are *never* any blank spaces at the beginning of *any* line in the here document. If even one blank space is placed in column one, then strange things may begin to happen with the calculation. This is the cause of a lot of frustration when programming here documents. This blank-space problem is one of the most difficult programming errors to find when you are testing, or using, a shell script with a here document.

The final step is to display the result to the user. Listing 22.5 shows the `float _subtract.ksh` shell script in action.

```
[root:yogi]@/scripts# float_subtract.ksh -s 4  8.09838 2048 65536 42.632

The difference of: 8.09838 - 2048 - 65536 - 42.632

to a scale of 4 is -67618.53362
```

Listing 22.5 float_subtract.ksh shell script in action.

The `float_subtract.ksh` shell script is very similar to the `float_add.ksh` shell script. Again, notice that the scale had no effect on the result of this calculation. The **man** page for **bc** has more information on using scale. The next three shell scripts have some variations also. With this commonality I am going to deviate and cover some of the different aspects of each of the following scripts and show where the differences lie.

Creating the float_multiply.ksh Shell Script

This time we are going to multiply a list of numbers. Using the same front end, for the most part, this shell script changes the building of the math statement and has a new here document. I want to cover the technique that we use to scan the command-line arguments to find the nonswitch-arguments and their associated switch-arguments. What remains after the command-line argument scan should be only a list of numbers, which is assigned to the `NUM_LIST` variable. Of course, we test each number with regular expressions just as before. Let's look at the `float_multiply.ksh` shell script shown in Listing 22.6 and study the details at the end.

```
#!/usr/bin/ksh
#
# SCRIPT: float_multiply.ksh
# AUTHOR: Randy Michael
# DATE: 02/23/2001
# REV: 1.1.P
#
# PURPOSE: This shell script is used to multiply a list of numbers
#          together. The numbers can be either integers or floating-
#          point numbers. For floating-point numbers the user has
#          the option of specifying a scale of the number of digits to
#          the right of the decimal point. The scale is set by adding
#          a -s or -S followed by an integer number.
#
# EXIT STATUS:
```

Listing 22.6 float_multiply.ksh shell script listing. *(continues)*

```
#         0 ==> This script/function exited normally
#         1 ==> Usage or syntax error
#         2 ==> This script/function exited on a trapped signal
#
# REV. LIST:
#
#
# set -x # Uncomment to debug this script
# set -n # Uncomment to debug without any command execution
#
#########################################################
############## DEFINE VARIABLE HERE ####################
#########################################################

SCRIPT_NAME=$(basename $0)  # The name of this shell script
SCALE="0"       # Initialize the scale value to zero
NUM_LIST=       # Initialize the NUM_LIST to NULL
COUNT=0         # Initialize the counter to zero
MAX_COUNT=$#    # Set MAX_COUNT to the total number of
                # command-line arguments


#########################################################
################ FUNCTIONS #############################
#########################################################

function usage
{
echo "\nPURPOSE: Multiplies a list of numbers together\n"
echo "USAGE: $SCRIPT_NAME [-s scale_value]  N1 N2...Nn"
echo "\nFor an integer result without any significant decimal places..."
echo "\nEXAMPLE: $SCRIPT_NAME 2048.221 65536 \n"
echo "OR for 4 significant decimal places"
echo "\nEXAMPLE: $SCRIPT_NAME -s 4   8.09838 2048 65536 42.632"
echo "\n\t...EXITING...\n"
}


#########################################################

function exit_trap
{
echo "\n...EXITING on trapped signal...\n"
}


#########################################################
################# START OF MAIN ########################
#########################################################


###### Set a Trap ######
```

Listing 22.6   float_multiply.ksh shell script listing. *(continued)*

```
trap 'exit_trap; exit 2' 1 2 3 15

#######################################################

# Check for at least two command-line arguments

if (($# < 2))
then
        echo "\nERROR: Please provide a list of numbers to multiply"
    usage
    exit 1
fi

#######################################################

# Parse the command-line arguments to find the scale value, if present.

while getopts ":s:S:" ARGUMENT
do
    case $ARGUMENT in
        s|S) SCALE=$OPTARG
            ;;
        \?) # Because we may have negative numbers we need
            # to test to see if the ARGUMENT that begins with a
            # hyphen (-) is a number, and not an invalid switch!!!

            for TST_ARG in $*
            do
                if [[ $(echo $TST_ARG | cut -c1) = '-' ]] \
                    && [ $TST_ARG != '-s' -a $TST_ARG != '-S' ]
                then
                    case $TST_ARG in
                    +([-0-9])) : # No-op, do nothing
                            ;;
                    +([-0-9].[0-9]))
                            : # No-op, do nothing
                            ;;
                    +([-.0-9])) : # No-op, do nothing
                            ;;
                    *) echo "\nERROR: $TST_ARG is an invalid argument\n"
                        usage
                        exit 1
                        ;;
                    esac
                fi
            done
            ;;
    esac
```

Listing 22.6 float_multiply.ksh shell script listing. *(continues)*

```
done

##########################################################

# Parse through the command-line arguments and gather a list
# of numbers to multiply together.

while ((COUNT < MAX_COUNT))
do
     ((COUNT = COUNT + 1))
     TOKEN=$1
     case $TOKEN in
               -s|-S) shift 2
                      ((COUNT = COUNT + 1))
                      ;;
          -s${SCALE}) shift
                      ;;
          -S${SCALE}) shift
                      ;;
                  *) NUM_LIST="${NUM_LIST} $TOKEN"
                     ((COUNT < MAX_COUNT)) && shift
                     ;;
     esac
done

##########################################################

# Ensure that the scale is an integer value

case $SCALE in
     +([0-9])) :   # No-Op - Do Nothing
               ;;
          *) echo "\nERROR: Invalid scale - $SCALE - Must be an
integer"
               usage
               exit 1
               ;;
esac

##########################################################

# Check each number supplied to ensure that the "numbers"
# are either integers or floating-point numbers.

for NUM in $NUM_LIST
do
case $NUM in
     +([0-9])) # Check for an integer
               : # No-op, do nothing.
```

Listing 22.6   float_multiply.ksh shell script listing. *(continued)*

```
                          ;;
      +([-0-9]))  # Check for a negative whole number
                : # No-op, do nothing
                ;;
      +([0-9]|[.][0-9]))
                # Check for a positive floating point number
                : # No-op, do nothing
                ;;
      +(+[0-9]|[.][0-9]))
                # Check for a positive floating point number
                # with a + prefix
                : # No-op, do nothing
                ;;
      +([-0-9]|.[0-9]))
                # Check for a negative floating point number
                : # No-op, do nothing
                ;;
      +(-.[0-9]))
                # Check for a negative floating point number
                : # No-op, do nothing
                ;;
      +([+.0-9]))
                # Check for a positive floating point number
                : # No-op, do nothing
                ;;
      *) echo "\nERROR: $NUM is NOT a valid number"
         usage
         exit 1
         ;;
      esac
done


############################################################

# Build the list of numbers to multiply

MULTIPLY=  # Initialize the MULTIPLY variable to NULL
TIMES=     # Initialize the TIMES variable to NULL

# Loop through each number and build a math statement that
# will multiply all of the numbers together.

for X in $NUM_LIST
do
      # If the number has a + prefix, remove it!
      if [[ $(echo $X | cut -c1) = '+' ]]
      then
           X=$(echo $X | cut -c2-)
      fi
```

Listing 22.6 float_multiply.ksh shell script listing. *(continues)*

```
        MULTIPLY="$MULTIPLY $TIMES $X"
        TIMES='*'
done


########################################################

# Do the math here by using a here document to supply
# input to the bc command. The product of the multiplication
# of the numbers is assigned to the PRODUCT variable.

PRODUCT=$(bc <<EOF
scale=$SCALE
$MULTIPLY
EOF)


########################################################

# Present the result of the multiplication to the user.

echo "\nThe product of: $MULTIPLY"
echo "\nto a scale of $SCALE is ${PRODUCT}\n"
```

Listing 22.6   float_multiply.ksh shell script listing. *(continued)*

As you can see in Listing 22.6, most of the previous two shell scripts have been carried over for use here. Now I want to cover in a little more detail how the scanning of the command-line arguments works when we extract the command switches, and the associated switch-arguments, from the entire list of arguments.

Parsing the Command Line for Valid Numbers

To start the extraction process we use the two previously initialized variables, COUNT and MAX_COUNT. The COUNT variable is incremented during the processing of the **while** loop, and the MAX_COUNT has been initialized to the value of $#, which specifies the total number of command-line arguments given by the user. The **while** loop runs until the COUNT variable is greater than or equal to the MAX_COUNT variable.

Inside of the **while** loop the COUNT variable is incremented by one, so on the first loop iteration the COUNT equals 1, one, because it was initialized to 0, zero. Next is the TOKEN variable. The TOKEN variable always points to the $1 positional parameter throughout the **while** loop execution. Using the current value of the $1 positional parameter, which is pointed to by the TOKEN variable, as the **case** statement argument we test to see if $TOKEN points to a known value. The current known values on the command line are the **-s** and **-S** switches that are used to define the scale for floating-point arithmetic, if a scale was given, and the integer value of the SCALE. There are only two options for the value of the scale:

```
-s{Scale Integer}
```

```
-s  {Scale Integer}
```

Because these are the only possible scale values (we also allow an uppercase -S) for the command line, we can test for this condition easily in a **case** statement. Remember that I said the $TOKEN variable always points to the **$1** positional parameter? To move the other positional parameters to the **$1** position we use the **shift** command. The **shift** command alone will shift the **$2** positional parameter to the **$1** position. What if you want to move the **$3** positional parameter to the **$1** position? We have two options: Use two **shift** commands in series, or add an integer as an argument to the **shift** command. Both of the following commands move the **$3** positional parameter to the **$1** position.

```
shift; shift
```

OR

```
shift 2
```

Now you may be wondering what happens to the previous **$1**, and in this case **$2**, positional parameter values. Well, anything that is shifted from the **$1** position goes to the bit bucket! But this is the result that we want here.

If the value of the positional parameter in the **$1** position is the **-s** or **-S** switch alone, then we **shift** two positions. We do this double **shift** because we know that there should be an integer value after the **-s** or **-S** switch, which is the integer switch-argument that defines the scale. On the other hand, if the user did *not* place a space between the **-s** or **-S** switch and the switch-argument, then we shift only once. Let's say that the user entered either of the following command statements on the command line:

```
[root:yogi]@/scripts# float_multiply.ksh -s 4  8.09838 2048 65536 42.632
```

OR

```
[root:yogi]@/scripts# float_multiply.ksh -s4  8.09838 2048 65536 42.632
```

Notice in the first command the user added a space between the switch and the switch-argument (**-s 4**). In this situation our test will see the **-s** as a single argument so we need to **shift** two places to move past the switch-argument, which is **4**. In the second command statement the user did *not* add a space between the switch and the switch-argument (**-s4**). This time we shift only one position because the switch and the switch-argument are together in the **$1** positional parameter, which is what $TOKEN points to.

There is one more thing that I want to point out. On each loop iteration the COUNT is incremented by 1, one, as you would expect. But if we **shift** two times, then we need to increment the COUNT by 1, one, a second time so we do not count past the number of arguments on the command line. This is very important! If you leave this extra counter incrementation out, the shell script errors out. Every little piece of this loop has a reason for being there. Speaking of the loop, please study the **while** loop in the code segment shown in Listing 22.7.

```
# Parse through the command-line arguments and gather a list
# of numbers to multiply together.

while ((COUNT < MAX_COUNT))
do
     ((COUNT = COUNT + 1))
     TOKEN=$1
     case $TOKEN in
               -s|-S) shift 2
                      ((COUNT = COUNT + 1))
                      ;;
          -s${SCALE}) shift
                      ;;
          -S${SCALE}) shift
                      ;;
                   *) NUM_LIST="${NUM_LIST} $TOKEN"
                      ((COUNT < MAX_COUNT)) && shift
                      ;;
     esac
done
```

Listing 22.7   Code to parse numbers from the command line.

The techniques to build the math statement and to do the calculations with a here document using the **bc** command are changed only slightly. Of course, because we are multiplying a string of numbers instead of adding or subtracting, we changed the build code to add a *, instead of a + or −. The here document is exactly the same except that the result is assigned to the PRODUCT variable. Please look closely at the float_multiply.ksh shell script shown in Listing 22.6 and study the subtle changes from the previous two shell scripts in Listing 22.1 and Listing 22.3.

The float_multiply.ksh shell script is shown in action in Listing 22.8. Notice in this output that the scale setting still has no effect on the output.

```
[root:yogi]@/scripts# float_multiply.ksh -s 4  8.09838 2048 65536 42.632

The product of:   8.09838 * 2048 * 65536 * 42.632

is 46338688867.08584
```

Listing 22.8   float_multiply.ksh shell script in action.

In the next section we move on to study division. We had to do some creative engineering to change the previous shell script to work with only two numbers. Keep reading—I think you will pick up a few more pointers.

Creating the float_divide.ksh Shell Script

For the division script we had to do some changes because we are dealing with only two numbers, as opposed to an unknown string of numbers. The `float_divide` `.ksh` shell script starts out the same as the previous three scripts, with the same variables and a modified `usage` function. The first test is for the correct number of command-line arguments. In this shell script we can handle from two to four arguments, with the option to specify a scale value for precision of floating-point numbers, which by the way *does* work for division.

In the **getopts** statement we perform the same test to parse out the scale switch, **-s** or **-S**, and the switch-argument. When however, we get to parsing the entire list of command-line arguments to gather the numbers for the division, we do things a little differently. The **while** loop is the same with the counter and the `TOKEN` variable always pointing to the **$1** positional parameter, which we use as we **shift** command-line arguments to the **$1** position. It is in the **case** statement that we do our modification. For division we need a *dividend* and a *divisor*, which has the form in a division statement of `((QUOTIENT = $DIVIDEND / $DIVISOR))`. As we parse the command-line arguments we assign the first number to the `DIVIDEND` variable and the second number to the `DIVISOR`. Look at the code segment in Listing 22.9, and we will go into the details at the end.

```
# Parse through the command-line arguments and gather a list
# of numbers to subtract.

TOTAL_NUMBERS=0

while ((COUNT < MAX_COUNT))
do
    ((COUNT = COUNT + 1))
    TOKEN=$1
    case $TOKEN in
            -s|-S) shift 2
                   ((COUNT = COUNT + 1))
                   ;;
        -s${SCALE}) shift
                   ;;
        -S${SCALE}) shift
                   ;;
              *) ((TOTAL_NUMBERS = TOTAL_NUMBERS + 1))
                 if ((TOTAL_NUMBERS == 1))
                 then
                     DIVIDEND=$TOKEN
                 elif ((TOTAL_NUMBERS == 2))
                 then
                     DIVISOR=$TOKEN
                 else
                     echo "ERROR: Too many numbers to divide"
                     usage
```

Listing 22.9   Code to extract the dividend and divisor. *(continues)*

```
                        exit 1
            fi
            NUM_LIST="$NUM_LIST $TOKEN"
            ((COUNT < MAX_COUNT)) && shift
            ;;
      esac
done
```

Listing 22.9 Code to extract the dividend and divisor. *(continued)*

In the **case** statement in Listing 22.9 notice the boldface text. When a number is encountered we use a variable called TOTAL_NUMBERS to keep track of how many numbers are on the command-line. If $TOTAL_NUMBERS is equal to 1, one, we assign the value of the $TOKEN variable to the DIVIDEND variable, the number on the top in a division math statement. When $TOTAL_NUMBERS is equal to 2 we assign the value of the $TOKEN variable to the DIVISOR variable. If the $TOTAL_NUMBERS counter variable exceeds 2, then we print an error message to the screen, execute the usage function, and **exit** the script with a return code of 1, which is a normal usage error for this shell script.

Notice that we are also keeping the NUM_LIST variable. We use the $NUM_LIST to verify that each "number" is actually an integer or a floating-point number by using the regular expressions that we covered previously in this chapter.

Notice in the shell script in Listing 22.10 that we omitted the step of building the math statement. In this script it is not necessary because we have the dividend and divisor captured in the code segment in Listing 22.9. Check out the shell script in Listing 22.10, and pay close attention to the boldface text.

```
#!/usr/bin/ksh
#
# SCRIPT: float_divide.ksh
# AUTHOR: Randy Michael
# DATE: 02/23/2001
# REV: 1.1.A
#
# PURPOSE: This shell script is used to divide two numbers.
#          The numbers can be either integers or floating point
#          numbers. For floating point numbers the user has the
#          option to specify a scale of the number of digits to
#          the right of the decimal point. The scale is set by
#          adding a -s or -S followed by an integer number.
```

Listing 22.10 float_divide.ksh shell script listing.

```
#
# EXIT STATUS:
#      0 ==> This script exited normally
#      1 ==> Usage or syntax error
#      2 ==> This script exited on a trapped signal
#
# REV. LIST:
#
#
# set -x # Uncomment to debug this script
# set -n # Uncomment to debug without any command execution
#
#########################################################
############## DEFINE VARIABLE HERE ###################
#########################################################

SCRIPT_NAME=`basename $0`
SCALE="0"       # Initialize the scale value to zero
NUM_LIST=       # Initialize the NUM_LIST to NULL
COUNT=0         # Initialize the counter to zero
MAX_COUNT=$#    # Set MAX_COUNT to the total number of
                # command-line arguments


#########################################################
############### FUNCTIONS #############################
#########################################################

function usage
{
echo "\nPURPOSE: Divides two numbers\n"
echo "USAGE: $SCRIPT_NAME [-s scale_value]  N1 N2"
echo "\nFor an integer result without any significant decimal places..."
echo "\nEXAMPLE: $SCRIPT_NAME 2048.221 65536 \n"
echo "OR for 4 significant decimal places"
echo "\nEXAMPLE: $SCRIPT_NAME -s 4  2048.221 65536"
echo "\n\t...EXITING...\n"
}


#######################################################


function exit_trap
{
        echo "\n...EXITING on trapped signal...\n"
}


#########################################################
############### START OF MAIN ########################
#########################################################
```

Listing 22.10   float_divide.ksh shell script listing. *(continues)*

```
###### Set a Trap ######

trap 'exit_trap; exit 2' 1 2 3 15

#######################

# Check for at least two command-line arguments
# and not more than four

if (($# < 2))
then
        echo "\nERROR: Too few command line arguments"
        usage
        exit 1

elif (($# > 4))
then
        echo "\nERROR: Too many command line arguments"
        usage
        exit 1
fi

# Parse the command-line arguments to find the scale value, if present.

while getopts ":s:S:" ARGUMENT
do
    case $ARGUMENT in
        s|S) SCALE=$OPTARG
             ;;
         \?) # Because we may have negative numbers we need
             # to test to see if the ARGUMENT that begins with a
             # hyphen (-) is a number, and not an invalid switch!!!

             for TST_ARG in $*
             do
               if [[ $(echo $TST_ARG | cut -c1) = '-' ]] \
               && [ $TST_ARG != '-s' -a $TST_ARG != '-S' ]
               then
                 case $TST_ARG in
                 +([-0-9])) : # No-op, do nothing
                         ;;
                 +([-0-9].[0-9]))
                             : # No-op, do nothing
                         ;;
                 +([-.0-9])) : # No-op, do nothing
                         ;;
                 *) echo "\nERROR: $TST_ARG is an invalid argument\n"
                    usage
```

Listing 22.10   float_divide.ksh shell script listing. *(continued)*

```
                        exit 1
                        ;;
                esac
            fi
        done
        ;;
    esac
done

##########################################################

# Parse through the command-line arguments and gather a list
# of numbers to subtract.

TOTAL_NUMBERS=0

while ((COUNT < MAX_COUNT))
do
    ((COUNT = COUNT + 1))
    TOKEN=$1
    case $TOKEN in
            -s|-S) shift 2
                   ((COUNT = COUNT + 1))
                   ;;
        -s${SCALE}) shift
                   ;;
        -S${SCALE}) shift
                   ;;
            *) ((TOTAL_NUMBERS = TOTAL_NUMBERS + 1))
               if ((TOTAL_NUMBERS == 1))
               then
                   DIVIDEND=$TOKEN
               elif ((TOTAL_NUMBERS == 2))
               then
                   DIVISOR=$TOKEN
               else
                   echo "ERROR: Too many numbers to divide"
                   usage
                   exit 1
               fi
               NUM_LIST="$NUM_LIST $TOKEN"
               ((COUNT < MAX_COUNT)) && shift
               ;;
    esac
done

##########################################################

# Ensure that the scale is an integer value
```

Listing 22.10 float_divide.ksh shell script listing. *(continues)*

```
case $SCALE in
    +([0-9])) :  # No-op - Do Nothing
            ;;
    *) echo "\nERROR: Invalid scale - $SCALE - Must be an integer"
            usage
            exit 1
            ;;
esac

#########################################################

# Check each number supplied to ensure that the "numbers"
# are either integers or floating point numbers.

for NUM in $NUM_LIST
do
    case $NUM in
    +([0-9])) # Check for an integer
            : # No-op, do nothing.
            ;;
    +([-0-9])) # Check for a negative whole number
            : # No-op, do nothing
            ;;
    +([0-9]|[.][0-9]))
            # Check for a positive floating point number
            : # No-op, do nothing
            ;;
    +(+[0-9]|[.][0-9]))
            # Check for a positive floating point number
            # with a + prefix
            : # No-op, do nothing
            ;;
    +([-0-9]|.[0-9]))
            # Check for a negative floating point number
            : # No-op, do nothing
            ;;
    +(-.[0-9]))
            # Check for a negative floating point number
            : # No-op, do nothing
            ;;
    +([+.0-9]))
            # Check for a positive floating point number
            : # No-op, do nothing
            ;;
    *) echo "\nERROR: $NUM is NOT a valid number"
            usage
            exit 1
            ;;
```

Listing 22.10 float_divide.ksh shell script listing. *(continued)*

```
      esac
done


#######################################################

# Do the math here by using a here document to supply
# input to the bc command. The quotient of the division is
# assigned to the QUOTIENT variable.

QUOTIENT=$(bc <<EOF
scale=$SCALE
$DIVIDEND / $DIVISOR
EOF)


#######################################################

# Present the result of the division to the user.

echo "\nThe quotient of: $DIVIDEND / $DIVISOR"
echo "\nto a scale of $SCALE is ${QUOTIENT}\n"
```

Listing 22.10   float_divide.ksh shell script listing. *(continued)*

Let's look at the here document that we feed input into the **bc** utility at the end of Listing 22.10. We already have extracted the dividend and divisor directly from the command line so we skipped building the math statement. Using command substitution we use double input redirection with a label (<<EOF), which defines the beginning of a here document, to set the scale of the precision of floating-point numbers and to divide the two numbers. If no scale was given on the command line, then the scale is 0, zero. The here document ends with the final label (EOF) to end the here document and exit the **bc** utility, which is an interactive program. The final step is to present the result to the user. In Listing 22.11 you can see the float_divide.ksh shell script in action.

```
[root:yogi]@/scripts# float_divide.ksh -s 6 .3321 -332.889

The quotient of: .3321 / -332.889

to a scale of 6 is -.000997
```

Listing 22.11   float_divide.ksh shell script in action.

Notice that the scale worked with the division script! We have completed shell scripts for addition, subtraction, multiplication, and division. I want to present one more variation in the next section.

Creating the float_average.ksh Shell Script

Using the addition shell script from Listing 22.1 we can make a couple of minor modifications and take the average of a series of numbers. I am not going to show the entire shell script, only the modifications that I made to the `float_add.ksh` shell script to average the series of numbers.

The first addition to Listing 22.1 is the addition of the variable TOTAL_NUMBERS. To average a list of numbers we need to know how many numbers are in the list so we can divide the SUM by the total number of numbers. The counter is added in the sanity check of the $NUM_LIST numbers, where we are ensuring that the numbers are either integers or floating point. This modification is shown in Listing 22.12.

```
TOTAL_NUMBERS=0

for NUM in $NUM_LIST
do
    ((TOTAL_NUMBERS = TOTAL_NUMBERS + 1))
    case $NUM in
    +([0-9])) # Check for an integer
            : # No-op, do nothing.
            ;;
    +([-0-9])) # Check for a negative whole number
            : # No-op, do nothing
            ;;
    +([0-9]|[.][0-9]))
            # Check for a positive floating point number
            : # No-op, do nothing
            ;;
    +(+[0-9]|[.][0-9]))
            # Check for a positive floating point number
            # with a + prefix
            : # No-op, do nothing
            ;;
    +([-0-9]|.[0-9]))
            # Check for a negative floating point number
            : # No-op, do nothing
            ;;
    +(-.[0-9]))
            # Check for a negative floating point number
            : # No-op, do nothing
            ;;
    +([+.0-9]))
            # Check for a positive floating point number
            : # No-op, do nothing
            ;;
    *) echo "\nERROR: $NUM is NOT a valid number"
        usage
        exit 1
```

Listing 22.12   Code segment to keep a running total of numbers.

```
        ;;
    esac

done
```

Listing 22.12 Code segment to keep a running total of numbers. *(continued)*

The two lines of modification are highlighted in boldface text in Listing 22.12. The only other modifications are with the here document, where we added a division to the $ADD by the $TOTAL_NUMBERS, and the code to present the result to the user. This code modification is shown in the code segment in Listing 22.13.

```
# Do the math with a here document for the bc command

AVERAGE=$(bc <<EOF
scale=$SCALE
(${ADD}) / $TOTAL_NUMBERS
EOF)

# Present the result to the user

echo "\nThe average of: $(echo $ADD | sed s/+//g)"
echo "\nto a scale of $SCALE is ${AVERAGE}\n"
```

Listing 22.13 Code segment to average a list of numbers.

In Listing 22.13 notice how the averaging of the numbers is done. In a previous code section an addition math statement was created and assigned to the ADD variable. Now we use this ADD variable as input to the **bc** command in the here document and divide the result of the addition by the total number of numbers given on the command line, $TOTAL_NUMBERS. The result is an average of the numbers.

In the next step we present the result to the user. Notice the **sed** statement that is in boldface text. This **sed** statement is replacing every occurrence of the plus sign (+) with a blank space. The result is a list of the numbers only. We could have just as easily used the $NUM_LIST variable, but I wanted to slip a **sed** statement into this chapter somewhere. The float_average.ksh shell script is in action in Listing 22.14.

```
[root:yogi]@/scripts# float_average.ksh -s 8 .22389 65 -32.778 -.221
The average of: .22389  65  -32.778  -.221

to a scale of 8 is 8.05622250
```

Listing 22.14 float_average.ksh shell script in action.

The `float_average.ksh` shell script listing is not shown in the book, but it is on the Web site that accompanies this book.

Other Options to Consider

As always, these scripts can be improved, just as any shell script can be improved. As you saw in each of the shell scripts in this chapter, we did a lot of tests to verify the integrity of the data the user entered on the command-line. You may be able to combine some of these tests, but I still like to separate each piece so that whoever comes along in the future can follow the shell script easily. Sure, some of these can be done in three lines of code, but this does not allow for data verification, and the user would have to rely on the cryptic system error messages that do not always tell *where* the data error is located.

Remove the Scale from Some of the Shell Scripts

Since the scale was only valuable when we did division you may as well remove all of scale references in the addition, subtraction, and multiplication shell scripts. The division and average shell scripts use the scale since both use division to get the answer.

Create More Functions

As an exercise for this chapter, replace each of the data tests with functions. This is easy to do! All that is required is that the function must be defined before it can be used. So, put these new functions at the top of the shell scripts in the DEFINE FUNCTIONS HERE section. When you extract a code segment, from the main body of the shell script, make a comment to yourself that "XYZ Function goes here." Then use one of the following techniques to make the code segment into a function.

```
function my_new_function_name
{
Place Code Segment Here
}

OR

my_new_function_name ()
{
Place Code Segment Here
}
```

Both techniques produce the same result, but I prefer the first method because it is more intuitive to new shell programmers. Remember where the scope of your variables can be seen. A variable in the main body of the shell script is a *global* variable, which can be seen by all functions. A variable inside of a function has limited scope and can be seen in the function and any function that the current function calls, but not in the calling shell script. There are techniques that we have covered in this book to get around these scope limitations, so I hope you have read the whole book. Experiment! That is how you learn.

I hope you enjoyed studying this chapter. Please explore the other options that are available in the **bc** command; you will be surprised by what you can do.

Summary

We have covered a lot of material in this chapter. I hope that you will now find that math is not difficult in a shell script and that it can be done to the precision required. The **bc** command is very powerful, and we only touched the surface of the ability of **bc** here. For more information on **bc** look at the **man** page, **man bc**.

In the next chapter we are moving on to changing numbers between numbers bases. We start with the basics and move to a shell script that converts any number in any number base to any other number base. See you in the next chapter!

## CHAPTER 23

Scripts for Number Base Conversions

On many occasions in computer science you need to convert numbers between different number bases. For example, you may need to translate a hexadecimal number into an octal representation, or if you are a software developer you may want to license the software you create for a specific machine. One way of creating a machine-specific license key is to use the IP address of the machine to create a hexadecimal character string, which will allow the software to execute only on that specific machine. The first example here is a common occurrence, but the latter one is a little more obscure.

In this chapter we are going to present some number base conversion techniques and also show how to create a shell script that produces a license key, as in our second example. Converting between number bases is very straightforward, and we are going to go through each step. Before we can write a shell script we need the correct command syntax. In this case we add setting up the proper environment for the system to do all of the hard work automatically.

Syntax

By far, the easiest way to convert a number from one base to another is to use the **typeset** command with the **-ibase** option. The **typeset** command is used a lot in this book, mostly to force a character string to uppercase or lowercase and to classify a variable as an integer value. This time we are adding to the integer setting, specified by **typeset -i VAR_NAME**, by adding the number base that the variable is to maintain. For example, if the variable BASE_16_NUM is to always contain a hexadecimal number, then the next command will set the variable's environment:

```
typeset -i16 BASE_16_NUM
```

After the BASE_16_NUM variable is **typeset** to base 16, then any value assigned to this variable is automatically converted to hexadecimal. We can also **typeset** a variable *after* a number has been assigned. This applies not only to base 10 numbers, but also to *any* base number up to the system limit, which is at least base 36. Let's look at some examples of converting between bases.

Example 23.1: Converting from Base 10 to Base 16

```
[root@yogi:/scripts]> typeset -i16 BASE_16_NUM
[root@yogi:/scripts]> BASE_16_NUM=47295
[root@yogi:/scripts]> echo $BASE_16_NUM

16#b8bf
```

Notice the output in Example 23.1. The output starts out by setting the number base that is represented, which is base 16 here. The string after the pound sign (#) is the hexadecimal number, b8bf. Next we want to convert from base 8, octal, to base 16, hexadecimal. We use the same technique, except this time we must specify the number base of the octal number in the assignment, as shown in Example 23.2.

Example 23.2: Converting from Base 8 to Base 16

```
[root@yogi:/scripts]> typeset -i16 BASE_16_NUM
[root@yogi:/scripts]> BASE_16_NUM=8#472521
[root@yogi:/scripts]> echo $BASE_16_NUM

16#735c9
```

In Example 23.2 notice that we assigned the octal number 472521 to the BASE_16_NUM variable by specifying the number base followed by the base 8 number, BASE_16_NUM=8#472521. When this base 8 number is assigned to the BASE_16_NUM variable it is automatically converted to base 16. As you can see, the system can do the hard work for us.

In Unix there is never just one way to accomplish a task, and number base conversions are no exception. We can also use the **printf** command to convert between number bases. The **printf** command accepts base 10 integer values and converts the number to the specified number base. The following options are available:

- o   Accepts a base 10 integer and prints the number in octal
- x   Accepts a base 10 integer and prints the number in hexadecimal

Let's look at two examples of using the **printf** command.

Example 23.3 Converting Base 10 to Octal

```
[root@yogi:/scripts]> printf %o 20398

47656
```

In Example 23.3 notice the added percent sign (%) before the **printf** command option. This % tells the **printf** command that the following lowercase o is a number base conversion to octal.

Example 23.4 Converting Base 10 to Hexadecimal

```
[root@yogi:/scripts]> printf %x 20398

4fae
```

Although not as flexible as the **typeset** command the **printf** command allows you to do base conversions from base 10 to base 8 and base 16. I like the extra flexibility of the **typeset** command, so this is the conversion method that we are going to use in this chapter.

Scripting the Solution

The most common number base conversion that computer science people use is conversions between base 2, 8, 10, and 16. We want to be able to convert back and forth between these, and other, bases in this chapter. To do this conversion we are going to create four shell scripts to show the flexibility, and use, of number base conversions. The following shell scripts are covered:

- Base 2 (binary) to base 16 (hexadecimal) shell script
- Base 10 (decimal) to base 16 (hexadecimal) shell script
- Script to create a software key based on the hexadecimal representation of an IP address
- Script to translate between *any* number base

We have a lot to cover in this chapter, but these shell scripts are not too difficult to follow. I hope you pick up a few tips and techniques in this chapter, as well as the whole book.

Base 2 (Binary) to Base 16 (Hexadecimal) Shell Script

This is the first conversion that most computer science students learn in school. It is easy enough to do this conversion with a pencil and paper, but, hey, we want *automation*! This shell script to convert from binary to hexadecimal uses the **typeset** technique, as all of these scripts use. You know the basic principle of the conversion, so let's present the shell script and cover the details at the end. The equate_base_2_to_16 .ksh shell script is shown in Listing 23.1.

```
#!/usr/bin/ksh
#
# SCRIPT: equate_base_2_to_16.ksh
# AUTHOR: Randy Michael
# DATE: 07/07/2002
# REV: 1.2.P
#
# PURPOSE: This script is used to convert a base 2 number
#          to a base 16 hexadecimal representation.
#          This script expects that a base 2 number
#          is supplied as a single argument.
#
# EXIT CODES:
#                 0 - Normal script execution
#                 1 - Usage error
#
# REV LIST:
#
#
# set -x # Uncomment to debug this script
# set -n # Uncomment to check command syntax without any execution
#
SCRIPT_NAME=`basename $0`

function usage
{
        echo "\nUSAGE: $SCRIPT_NAME {base 2 number}"
        echo "\nEXAMPLE: $SCRIPT_NAME 1100101101"
        echo "\nWill return the hexadecimal base 16 number 32d"
        echo "\n\t ...EXITING...\n"
}

# Check for a single command-line argument

if (($# != 1))
then
        echo "\nERROR: A base 2 number must be supplied..."
        usage
        exit 1
fi

# Check that this single command-line argument is a binary number!

case $1 in
        +([0-1])) BASE_2_NUM=$1
                  ;;
              *) echo "\nERROR: $1 is NOT a base 2 number"
                  usage
                  exit 1
```

Listing 23.1   equate_base_2_to_16.ksh shell script listing.

```
                         ;;

esac


# Assign the base 2 number to the BASE_16_NUM variable


BASE_16_NUM=$((2#${BASE_2_NUM}))


# Now typeset the BASE_16_NUM variable to base 16.
# This step converts the base 2 number to a base 16 number.


typeset -i16 BASE_16_NUM


# Display the resulting base 16 representation


echo $BASE_16_NUM
```

Listing 23.1   equate_base_2_to_16.ksh shell script listing. *(continued)*

In Listing 23.1 all of the real work is done with three commands. The rest of the code is for testing the user input and providing the correct usage message when an error is detected. Two tests are performed on the user input. First, the number of command-line arguments is checked to ensure that exactly one argument is supplied on the command line. The second test is to ensure that the single command-line argument is a binary number. Let's look at these two tests.

The **$#** shell variable shows the total number of command-line arguments, with the command itself being in the **$0** position, and the single command-line argument represented by the positional parameter **$1**. For this shell script the value **$#** shell variable must be equal to 1, one. This test is done using the mathematical test shown here.

```
if (($# != 1))
then
        echo "\nERROR: A base 2 number must be supplied..."
        usage
        exit 1
fi
```

The second test is to ensure that a base 2 number is given on the command line. For this test we use a good ole regular expression. You have to love the simplicity of making this type of test. Because a binary number can consist only of 0, zero, or 1, one, it is an easy test with a regular expression. The idea is to specify a valid range of *characters* that can make up a binary number. The tests for decimal and hexadecimal are similar. The regular expression that we use is used in the **case** statement shown here.

```
case $1 in
        +([0-1])) BASE_2_NUM=$1
            ;;
```

```
                          *) echo "\nERROR: $1 is NOT a base 2 number"
                             usage
                             exit 1
                             ;;

     esac
```

The regular expression shown here has the form +([0-1]) and is used as a test for the specified valid range of numbers 0 through 1. If the range is valid, then we assign the binary number to the BASE_2_NUM variable. We will look at more regular expressions later in this chapter.

When we are satisfied that we have valid data we are ready to do the number base conversion. The first step is to assign the binary number that was supplied on the command line to the BASE_16_NUM variable. Notice that thus far we have not **typeset** any of the variables, so the variable can contain any *character string*. It is *how* we assign the binary number to the BASE_16_NUM variable that is important. When the binary value is assigned to the variable the current number base is specified, as shown here.

```
     BASE_16_NUM=$((2#${BASE_2_NUM}))
```

Notice in this assignment that the BASE_2_NUM variable is preceded by the number base, which is base 2 in this case. This allows for the number to be assigned to the BASE_16_NUM as a base 2 number. The base translation takes place in the next step where we **typeset** the variable to base 16, as shown here.

```
     typeset -i16 BASE_16_NUM
```

With the BASE_16_NUM variable **typeset** to base 16, specified by the -i16 argument, the binary number is translated to hexadecimal. We could just as easily **typeset** the BASE_16_NUM variable at the top of the shell script, but it really does not matter.

Base 10 (Decimal) to Base 16 (Hexadecimal) Shell Script

This shell script is very similar to the shell script in the previous section. We are really changing just the tests and the conversion values. Other than these few changes the two shell scripts are identical. Again, I want to present the shell script and cover the details at the end. The equate_base_10_to_16.ksh shell script is shown in Listing 23.2.

```
#!/usr/bin/ksh
#
# SCRIPT: equate_base_10_to_16.ksh
# AUTHOR: Randy Michael
# DATE: 07/07/2002
# REV: 1.2.P
#
# PURPOSE: This script is used to convert a base 10 number
#          to a base 16 hexadecimal representation.
```

Listing 23.2 equate_base_10_to_16.ksh shell script listing.

```
#              This script expects that a base 10 number
#              is supplied as a single argument.
#
# EXIT CODES:
#              0 - Normal script execution
#              1 - Usage error
#
# REV LIST:
#
#
# set -x # Uncomment to debug this script
# set -n # Uncomment to check command syntax without any execution
#
#
SCRIPT_NAME=`basename $0`

function usage
{
        echo "\nUSAGE: $SCRIPT_NAME {base 10 number}"
        echo "\nEXAMPLE: $SCRIPT_NAME 694"
        echo "\nWill return the hexadecimal number 2b6"
        echo "\n\t...EXITING...\n"
}

# Check for a single command-line argument

if (($# != 1))
then
        echo "\nERROR: A base 10 number must be supplied..."
        usage
        exit 1
fi

# Check that this single command-line argument is a base 10 number!

case $1 in
        +([0-9])) BASE_10_NUM=$1
                        ;;
                    *) echo "\nERROR: $1 is NOT a base 10 number"
                        usage
                        exit 1
                        ;;
esac

# Assign the base 10 number to the BASE_16_NUM variable

BASE_16_NUM=$((10#${BASE_10_NUM}))

# Now typeset the BASE_16_NUM variable to base 16.
```

Listing 23.2 equate_base_10_to_16.ksh shell script listing. *(continues)*

```
# This step converts the base 10 number to a base 16 number.

typeset -i16 BASE_16_NUM

# Display the resulting base 16 number representation

echo $BASE_16_NUM

# This following code is optional. It removes the number base
# prefix. This may be helpful if using this script with
# other programs and scripts.
#
# Strip out the base prefix and the pound sign (#). (Optional)
#
# echo $BASE_16_NUM | grep -q "#"
#
# if (($? == 0))
# then
#         echo $BASE_16_NUM | awk -F '#' '{print $2}'
# else
#         echo $BASE_16_NUM
# fi
```

Listing 23.2   equate_base_10_to_16.ksh shell script listing. *(continued)*

In Listing 23.2 we have a few things to point out. First, notice the usage function and how we use the extracted name of the shell script directly from the system, specified by SCRIPT_NAME=`basename $0`. This is command substitution using *back tics*, which are located in the upper left corner of a standard keyboard under the ESC-key. Using this technique is equivalent to using the *dollar parentheses* method, specified by $(command), as we use in most chapters in this book. Notice in the assignment that the **basename $0** command holds the name of the shell script. We always want to query the system for a script name in the main body of the shell script, before it is used in a usage function. If we use the **basename $0** command in the function the response would be the name of the *function*, not the name of the shell script. We never want to hard-code the script name because someone may change the name of the shell script in the future.

The next thing that I want to point out is the change made to the regular expression. Before, we were testing for a binary number, which can consist of only 0 and 1. This time we are testing for a decimal number, which can consist of only numbers 0 through 9. The new regular expression is shown here.

```
case $1 in
        +([0-9])) BASE_10_NUM=$1
                ;;
                *) echo "\nERROR: $1 is NOT a base 10 number"
                usage
```

```
                    exit 1
                    ;;
    esac
```

In this **case** statement we are testing the ARG[1] variable, represented by the **$1** positional parameter. This regular expression will assign **$1** to the BASE_10_NUM variable only if the characters are numbers between 0 and 9. If any other character is found in this character string, then an ERROR message is displayed and the **usage** function is called before the script exits with a return code of 1, one.

In the assignment of the base 10 number to the BASE_16_NUM variable notice the change in the variable assignment as shown here.

```
BASE_16_NUM=$((10#${BASE_10_NUM}))
```

Notice that the ${BASE_10_NUM} variable is preceded by number base representation, 10#. Because this is a decimal number we really did not need to do this, but to be consistent it was added.

The last thing that I want to point out is the optional code at the end of the shell script in Listing 23.2. If you are using this shell script with other programs or shell scripts to produce number base conversions, then this optional code strips out the number base prefix. Look at the code segment shown here.

```
# Strip out the base prefix and the pound sign (#). (Optional)
#
# echo $BASE_16_NUM | grep -q "#"
#
# if (($? == 0))
# then
#          echo $BASE_16_NUM | awk -F '#' '{print $2}'
# else
#          echo $BASE_16_NUM
# fi
```

This code is commented out, but let's look at what it does. The purpose is to remove the base number prefix and leave only the number alone, which implies that you must have some built-in logic to know the number base in which the number is represented. The first step is to test for the existence of a pound sign (#). We do this by printing the variable with the **echo** command and piping the output to a **grep** statement, using the quiet option **-q**. This command does not produce any output to the screen, but we test the return code to see if a pattern match was made. If the return code is 0, zero, then a match was made and there is a pound sign in the string. Because we want to display everything *after* the pound sign (#) we use this pound sign as a field separator. To split the string and leave only the number, which will be in the second field now, we can use either **cut** or **awk**. Let's use **awk** for a change of pace. To do field separation with **awk** we use the **-F** switch, followed by the character(s) that represent a separation of the fields, which is the # here. Then we just print the second field, specified by the **$2** positional parameter, and we are left with the number alone. If you use this optional code segment, always remember to keep track of the current number base and comment out the **echo** statement that precedes this code block.

Script to Create a Software Key Based on the Hexadecimal Representation of an IP Address

With the techniques learned in the last two shell scripts let's actually do something that is useful. In this section we are going to create a shell script that will create a software license key based on the IP address of the machine. To tie the license key to the machine and the software we are going to convert each set of numbers in the machine's IP address from decimal to hexadecimal. Then we are going to combine all of the hexadecimal numbers together to make a license key string. This is pretty primitive, but it is a good example for using base conversions. Again, let's look at the code and go through the details at the end. The mk_swkey.ksh shell script is shown in Listing 23.3.

```
#!/usr/bin/ksh
#
# SCRIPT: mk_swkey.ksh
# AUTHOR: Randy Michael
# DATE: 07/07/2002
# REV: 1.2.P
#
# PURPOSE: This script is used to create a software
#          license key based on the IP address of the
#          system that this shell script is executed on.
#          The system is queried for the system's IP
#          address. The IP address is stripped of the
#          dots (.), and each number is converted to
#          hexadecimal. Then each hex string is combined
#          into a single hex string, which is the software
#          license key.
#
# REV LIST:
#
#
# set -x # Uncomment to debug this script
# set -n # Uncomment to check command syntax without any execution
#
##############################################################
############### DEFINE FUNCTIONS HERE #######################
##############################################################

function convert_base_10_to_16
{
# set -x # Uncomment to debug this function

typeset -i16 BASE_16_NUM

BASE_10_NUM=$1

BASE_16_NUM=$((10#${BASE_10_NUM}))
```

Listing 23.3 mk_swkey.ksh shell script listing.

```
# Strip the number base prefix from the hexadecimal
# number. This prefix is not needed here.

echo $BASE_16_NUM | grep -q '#'
if (($? == 0))
then
        echo $BASE_16_NUM | awk -F '#' '{print $2}'
else
        echo $BASE_16_NUM
fi
}


################################################################
################# BEGINNING OF MAIN #######################
################################################################

# Query the system for the IP address using the "host $(hostname)"
# command substitution.

IP=$(host $(hostname) | awk '{print $3}' | awk -F ',' '{print $1}')

# Field delimit the IP address on the dots (.) and assign each
# number to a separate variable in a "while read" loop.

echo $IP | awk -F '.' '{print $1, $2, $3, $4}' | while read a b c d junk
do
     # Convert each of the numbers in the IP address
     # into hexadecimal by calling the "convert_base_10_to 16"
     # function.

     FIRST=$(convert_base_10_to_16 $a)
     SECOND=$(convert_base_10_to_16 $b)
     THIRD=$(convert_base_10_to_16 $c)
     FORTH=$(convert_base_10_to_16 $d)
done

# Combine all of the hexadecimal strings into a single
# hexadecimal string, which represents the software key.

echo "${FIRST}${SECOND}${THIRD}${FORTH}"
```

Listing 23.3   mk_swkey.ksh shell script listing. *(continued)*

In the script in Listing 23.3 we are actually doing something useful—at least if you license your own software this script is useful. To start this shell script off we converted the base 10 to base 16 code into a function called convert_base_10_to_16. This allows us to call the function four times, one for each piece of the IP address. In this function I want you to notice that we **typeset** the BASE_16_NUM variable to base 16 at the top of the function, as opposed to the bottom in the previous shell script. It does not make any difference *where* it is set as long as it is set before the value is returned to the main body of the shell script, or displayed.

Also, the optional code segment that was commented out on Listing 23.2 is now used in this shell script. In this case we know that we are converting to a hexadecimal number, and we do not want the number base prefix to appear in the software license key. We use the following code segment to remove the prefix from the output.

```
# Strip the number base prefix from the hexadecimal
# number. This prefix is not needed here.

echo $BASE_16_NUM | grep -q '#'
if (($? == 0))
then
        echo $BASE_16_NUM | awk -F '#' '{print $2}'
else
        echo $BASE_16_NUM
fi
```

Notice the silent execution of the **grep** command using the **-q** command switch. Then, if a pound sign is found, the **awk** statement uses the # as a field delimiter by specifying the -F '#' switch, and then the second field is extracted. This is the value that is returned back to the main body of the shell script from the conversion function.

At the BEGINNING_OF_MAIN we start out by querying the system for the system's IP address using the following command:

```
IP=$(host $(hostname) | awk '{print $3}' | awk -F ',' '{print $1}')
```

Let's step through each part of this command. On my system I pulled an IP address out of the air for this demonstration. On the **yogi** machine the command substitution **host $(hostname)** results in the following output:

```
[root:yogi]@/scripts# host $(hostname)
yogi is 163.155.204.42,
```

From this output you can see that the fictional IP address is located in the third field, 163.155.204.42,. Notice that I have an extra comma (,) tacked on to the end of the IP address, which we do not want included. After we extract the third field from the command output we pipe this result to an **awk** statement (the **cut** command will do the same thing here). In the **awk** part of the statement we set the field delimiter to the comma (,) that we want to get rid of, using the -F ',' notation. Now that the string is field delimited on the comma we just extract the first field, which is the IP address alone. This result is then assigned to the IP variable using command substitution.

Now that we have the whole IP address we can chop it up into a series of four numbers. Once we have four individual numbers we can convert each of the decimal numbers into their hexadecimal equivalent. To separate the IP address into separate individual numbers we can use **cut, sed,** or **awk.** For consistency let's keep using **awk.** This time we field delimit the string, which is an IP address, using the dots (.) and then use the **print** argument for the **awk** command to print each of the four fields. At this point we are left with the following four numbers:

```
163 155 204 42
```

Now we have some numbers to work with. Because we want to work on each number individually, we pipe this output to a **while read** loop and assign each of the four numbers to a separate variable. Then, inside of the loop, we convert each decimal number into hexadecimal. The entire command statement is shown here.

```
echo $IP | awk -F '.' '{print $1, $2, $3, $4}' | while read a b c d junk
```

Notice the final variable at the end of the **while** statement, junk. I added this as a catch-all for anything that may be tacked on to the previous pipe outputs. It does not matter if there is anything to capture, but if there are "extra" field(s) the junk variable will catch everything remaining in the output. Other than this, each of the four fields is stored in the variables a, b, c, and d.

Inside of the **while read** loop we call the conversion function four times, once for each variable, as shown here:

```
FIRST=$(convert_base_10_to_16 $a)
SECOND=$(convert_base_10_to_16 $b)
THIRD=$(convert_base_10_to_16 $c)
FOURTH=$(convert_base_10_to_16 $d)
```

The result of these four function calls is the assignment of the hexadecimal values to four new variables, FIRST, SECOND, THIRD, and FOURTH. Now that we have the hexadecimal values all we need to do now is combine the hex strings into a single string. The combination is shown here.

```
echo "${FIRST}${SECOND}${THIRD}${FOURTH}"
```

The resulting output from the IP address that I pulled out of the air for temporary use (163.155.204.42) is shown next.

```
[root:yogi]@/scripts# ./mk_swkey.ksh
a39bcc2a
```

This hexadecimal string is the software license that is tied to the IP address.

Script to Translate between *Any* Number Base

So far we have been working in a restricted environment with limited ability to switch between number bases. This script will convert *any* number to *any* number base within the limits of the system. The base conversions availability is to base 36 at least, and some systems may go higher. I am not sure what you would do with a base 36 number, but you can make one if you want to.

In this script we rely on two command-line switches, each requiring an argument, and the "number" to convert. The two switches are **-f {Starting Number Base, or**

From:} and **-t {Ending Number Base, or To:}**. These two parameters tell the shell script what number base we are converting *from* and what number base we want to convert the number *to*, which is where the **-f** and **-t** command-line switches came from. This is another shell script that needs to be presented first, and we will cover the details at the end. The equate_any_base.ksh shell script is shown in Listing 23.4.

```ksh
#!/usr/bin/ksh
#
# SCRIPT: equate_any_base.ksh
# AUTHOR: Randy Michael
# DATE: 07/07/2002
# REV: 1.2.P
#
# PURPOSE: This script is used to convert a number to any
#          supported number base, which is at least base 36.
#          This script requires that two command-line
#          arguments and the "number" to be converted
#          are present on the command line. An example
#          number base conversion is shown here:
#
#          equate_any_base.ksh -f16 -t2 e245c
#          2#11100010010001011100
#
#          This example converts the base 16 number, e245c, to
#          the base 2 equivalent, 2#11100010010001011100.
#          The 2#, which precedes the binary number, shows
#          the base of the number represented.
#
# EXIT CODES:
#              0 - Normal script execution
#              1 - Usage error
#
# set -x # Uncomment to debug this shell script
# set -n # Uncomment to check syntax without any execution
#
########################################################
############## DEFINE VARIABLES HERE ################
########################################################

SCRIPT_NAME=$(basename $0)
COUNT=0
MAX_COUNT=$#


########################################################
############## DEFINE FUNCTIONS HERE ################
########################################################

function usage
{
```

Listing 23.4   equate_any_base.ksh shell script listing.

```
echo "\n\t***USAGE ERROR***"
echo "\nPURPOSE: This script converts between number bases"
echo "\nUSAGE: $SCRIPT_NAME -f{From base#} -t{To base#} NUMBER"
echo "\nEXAMPLE: $SCRIPT_NAME -f16 -t10 fc23"
echo "\nWill convert the base 16 number fc23 to its"
echo "decimal equivalent base 10 number 64547"
echo "\n\t ...EXITING...\n"
}


#######################################################
######### CHECK COMMAND LINE ARGUMENTS HERE ##########
#######################################################

# The maximum number of command line arguments is five
# and the minimum number is three.

if (($# > 5))
then
        echo "\nERROR: Too many command line arguments\n"
        usage
        exit 1
elif (($# < 3))
then
        echo "\nERROR: Too few command line arguments\n"
        usage
        exit 1
fi

# Check to see if the command line switches are present

echo $* | grep -q '\-f' || (usage; exit 1)
echo $* | grep -q '\-t' || (usage; exit 1)

# Use getopts to parse the command line arguments

while getopts ":f:t:" ARGUMENT
do
  case $ARGUMENT in
    f) START_BASE="$OPTARG"
       ;;
    t) END_BASE="$OPTARG"
       ;;
    \?) usage
        exit 1
        ;;
  esac
done


# Ensure that the START_BASE and END_BASE variables
```

Listing 23.4   equate_any_base.ksh shell script listing. *(continues)*

```
# are not NULL.

if [ -z "$START_BASE" ] || [ "$START_BASE" = '' ] \
   || [ -z "$END_BASE" ] || [ "$END_BASE" = '' ]
then
     echo "\nERROR: Base number conversion fields are empty\n"
     usage
     exit 1
fi

# Ensure that the START_BASE and END_BASE variables
# have integer values for the number base conversion.

case $START_BASE in
+([0-9)) : # Do nothing - Colon is a no-op.
          ;;
       *) echo "\nERROR: $START_BASE is not an integer value"
          usage
          exit 1
          ;;
esac

case $END_BASE in
+([0-9)) : # Do nothing - Colon is a no-op.
          ;;
       *) echo "\nERROR: $END_BASE is not an integer value"
          usage
          exit 1
          ;;
esac

#####################################################
############### BEGINNING OF MAIN ###################
#####################################################

# Begin by finding the BASE_NUM to be converted.

# Count from 1 to the max number of command line arguments

while ((COUNT < MAX_COUNT))
do
   ((COUNT == COUNT + 1))
   TOKEN=$1
   case $TOKEN in
      -f) shift; shift
          ((COUNT == COUNT + 1))
          ;;
      -f${START_BASE}) shift
          ;;
```

Listing 23.4   equate_any_base.ksh shell script listing.

```
        -t) shift; shift
            ((COUNT == COUNT + 1))
            ;;
        -t${END_BASE}) shift
                ;;
        *) BASE_NUM=$TOKEN
           break
           ;;
    esac
done


# Typeset the RESULT variable to the target number base

typeset -i$END_BASE RESULT

# Assign the BASE_NUM variable to the RESULT variable
# and add the starting number base with a pound sign (#)
# as a prefix for the conversion to take place.

# NOTE: If an invalid number is entered a system error
# will be displayed. An example is inputting 1114400 as
# a binary number, which is invalid for a binary number.

RESULT="${START_BASE}#${BASE_NUM}"

# Display the result to the user or calling program.

echo "$RESULT"

# End of script...
```

Listing 23.4 equate_any_base.ksh shell script listing. *(continued)*

Please stay with me here! This script in Listing 23.4 is really not as difficult as it looks. Because we are requiring the user to provide command-line arguments we need to do a lot of testing to ensure that we have good data to work with. We also need to give the user good and informative feedback if a usage error is detected. Remember, always let the user know what is going on. Keeping the user informed is just good script writing!

Let's start at the top of the equate_any_base.ksh shell script and work our way through the details. The first thing we do is to define three variables. The $SCRIPT_NAME variable points to the name of this shell script. We need to query the system for this script name for two reasons. First, the name of the script may change in the future; second, the SCRIPT_NAME variable is used in the usage function. If we had executed the **basename $0** command inside of the usage function we would get the name of the *function* instead of the name of the shell script. This is an important point to make. We need to know where the scope lies when referring to positional parameters,

$0 in this case. When we refer to positional parameters in the main body of a shell script then the position parameters are command-line arguments, including the name of the shell script. When we refer to positional parameters inside of a function then the scope of the positional parameters lies with the arguments supplied to the function, not the shell script. In either case, the name of the shell script, or function, can be referenced by the **basename $0** command.

The next two variables definitions, COUNT=0 and MAX_COUNT=$#, are to be used to parse through each of the shell scripts command-line arguments, where $# represents the total number of command-line arguments of the shell script. We will go into more detail on these two variables a little later.

In the next section we define any functions that we need for this shell script. For this shell script we need just a usage function. If you look at this usage function, though, we have a good deal of information to describe how to use the shell script in Listing 23.4. We state the purpose of the shell script followed by the USAGE statement. Then we supply an example of using the shell script. This really helps users who are not familiar with running this script.

As I stated before, we need to do a lot of checking because we are relying on the user to supply command-line arguments for defining the execution behavior. We are going to do seven independent tests to ensure that the data we receive is good data that we can work with.

The first two tests are to ensure that we have the correct number of command-line arguments. For the equate_any_base.ksh shell script the user may supply as few as three arguments and as many as five arguments. This variation may sound a little strange, but when we go to the **getopts** command it will be intuitively obvious. For testing the number of arguments we just use an **if..then..elif..fi** structure where we test the $# shell parameter to make sure that the value is not greater than five and is not less than three, as shown here.

```
if (($# > 5))
then
        echo "\nERROR: Too many command-line arguments\n"
        usage
        exit 1
elif (($# < 3))
then
        echo "\nERROR: Too few command-line arguments\n"
        usage
        exit 1
fi
```

Using getopts to Parse the Command Line

Now we get to use **getopts** to parse through each command-line switch and its arguments. The **getopts** command recognizes a command switch as any character that is preceded by a hyphen (–)—for example, **-f** and **-t**. The **getopts** command really does not care *what* is on the command line, unless it is a command switch or its argument. Let's look at a couple of examples of command-line arguments so I can clear the mud.

Example 23.5 Correct Usage of the equate_any_base.ksh Shell Script

```
[root:yogi]@/scripts# ./equate_any_base.ksh -f 2 -t16 10110011110101
```

Notice in Example 23.5 the use of the two command switches, -f 2 and -t16. Both of these are valid because **getopts** does not care if there is a space or no space between the switch and the switch-argument, and the order of appearance does not matter either. As you can see in Example 23.5, we can have as few as three command-line arguments if no spaces are used or as many as five if both command switches have a space between the command switch and the switch-argument.

Example 23.6 Incorrect Usage of the equate_any_base.ksh Shell Script

```
[root:yogi]@/scripts# ./equate_any_base.ksh -i -f 2 -t 16 10110011110101
```

In Example 23.6 we have an error condition in two different ways. The first error is that there are six command-line arguments given to the equate_any_base.ksh shell script. The second error is that there is an undefined command switch, **-i**, given on the command line. This is a good place to go through using **getopts** to parse a defined set of command-line switches and arguments.

The purpose of the **getopts** command is to process command-line arguments and check for valid options. The **getopts** command is used with a **while** loop and has an enclosed **case** statement to let you take action for each correct and incorrect argument found on the command line. We can define command-line switches to require an argument, or the switch can be defined as a standalone command switch. The order of the switch does not matter, but if the switch is defined to require an argument then the switch-argument must follow the switch, either with or without a space. When **getopts** finds a switch that requires an argument, the argument is always assigned to a variable called OPTARG. This variable allows you to assign the switch argument value to a useful variable name to use in the shell script. Let's look at the **getopts** definition that is used in this shell script.

```
while getopts ":f:t:" ARGUMENT
do
   case $ARGUMENT in
      f) START_BASE="$OPTARG"
         ;;
      t) END_BASE="$OPTARG"
         ;;
      \?) usage
         exit 1
         ;;
   esac
done
```

There are two parts to the **getopts** definition. The first is the **while** loop that contains the **getopts** statement, and the second is the **case** statement that allows you to do something when a valid or invalid switch is found. In the **while** loop we have defined two valid command switches, **-f** and **-t**. When you define these you do not add the hyphen (–) in the **case** statement, but it is required on the command-line. Notice the colons (:) in the definitions. The beginning colon specifies that when an undefined switch is found—for example, **-i**—then the invalid switch is matched with the question mark (?) in the **case** statement. In our case we always run the usage function and immediately **exit** the shell script with a return code of 1, one. Also notice that we *escaped* the ? with a backslash (\?). By escaping the ? character (\?) we can use the ? as a regular character without any special meaning or function.

When a colon (:) is present *after* a switch definition it means that the switch must have an argument associated with it. If the switch definition does *not* have a colon after it, then the switch has no argument. For example, the statement **getopts ":t:f:i"** defines **-t** and **-f** as command-line switches that require an argument and **-i** as a switch that has no argument associated with it.

When a switch is found, either defined or undefined, it is assigned to the ARGUMENT variable (you can use any variable name here), which is used by the **case** statement. For defined variables we need a matching match in the **case** statement, but for undefined switches the ARGUMENT is assigned ? *if* the **getopts** definition begins with a colon (:). Additionally, when a defined switch is found that requires an argument then the argument to the switch is assigned to the OPTARG variable (you cannot change this variable name) during the current loop iteration. This is the mechanism that we use to get our *from* and *to* number base definitions, START_BASE and END_BASE, for the equate_any_base.ksh shell script.

Continuing with the Script

As I stated before, **getopts** does not care what is on the command line if it is not a command switch or a switch argument. So, we need more sanity checks. The next test is to ensure that both **-f** and **-t** command-line switches are present on the command-line as arguments. We must also check to ensure that the START_BASE and END_BASE variables are not empty and also make sure that the values are integers. We can do all of these sanity checks with the code segment in Listing 23.5.

```
# Check to see if the command line switches are present

echo $* | grep -q '\-f' || (usage; exit 1)
echo $* | grep -q '\-t' || (usage; exit 1)


# Use getopts to parse the command line arguments

while getopts ":f:t:" ARGUMENT
do
   case $ARGUMENT in
```

Listing 23.5   Code segment to verify number base variables.

```
        f)  START_BASE="$OPTARG"
            ;;
        t)  END_BASE="$OPTARG"
            ;;
       \?)  usage
            exit 1
            ;;
   esac
done


# Ensure that the START_BASE and END_BASE variables
# are not NULL.

if [ -z "$START_BASE" ] || [ "$START_BASE" = '' ] \
   || [ -z "$END_BASE" ] || [ "$END_BASE" = '' ]
then
       echo "\nERROR: Base number conversion fields are empty\n"
       usage
       exit 1
fi

# Ensure that the START_BASE and END_BASE variables
# have integer values for the number base conversion.

case $START_BASE in
+([0-9])) : # Do nothing - Colon is a no-op.
            ;;
       *) echo "\nERROR: $START_BASE is not an integer value"
            usage
            exit 1
            ;;
esac

case $END_BASE in
+([0-9])) : # Do nothing - Colon is a no-op.
            ;;
       *) echo "\nERROR: $END_BASE is not an integer value"
            usage
            exit 1
            ;;
esac
```

Listing 23.5 Code segment to verify number base variables. *(continued)*

Starting at the top in Listing 23.5 we first check to ensure that both **-f** and **-t** are present as command-line arguments. Next the **getopts** statement parses the command line and populates the START_BASE and END_BASE variables. After **getopts** we test the START_BASE and END_BASE variables to ensure that they are not NULL. When you do have NULL value tests always remember to use double quotes ("$VAR_NAME") around the variable names, or you will get an error if they are actually empty. This is one of those hard-to-find errors that can take a long time to track down.

In the next two **case** statements we use a regular expression to ensure that the $START_BASE and $END_BASE variables are pointing to integer values. If either one of these variables is not an integer we give the user an informative error message, show the correct usage by running the usage function, and **exit** the shell script with a return code of 1, one.

Beginning of Main

At this point we have confirmed that the data that was entered on the command line is valid so let's do our number base conversion. Because we have all of the command switches and switch-arguments on the command line, we actually need to *find* the "number" that is to be converted between bases. To find our number to convert we need to scan all of the command-line arguments starting with the argument at **$1** and continuing until the number is found, or until the last argument, which is pointed to by the **$#** shell variable.

Scanning the command-line arguments and trying to find the "number" is a little tricky. First the "number" may be in any valid number base that the system supports, so we may have alphanumeric characters. But we do have one thing going for us: We know the command switches and the integer values of the $START_BASE and $END_BASE variables. We still need to consider that there may or may not be spaces between the command switches and the switch-arguments. Let's think about this a minute. If a single command-line argument is one of the command switches, then we know that the user placed a space between the command switch and the switch-argument. On the other hand, if a single command-line argument is a command-line switch *and* its switch-argument, then we know that the user does *not* place a space between the command switch and the switch-argument. By using this logic we can use a simple **case** statement to test for these conditions. When we get to a command-line argument that does not fit this logic test we have found the "number" that we are looking for.

Look at the code segment in Listing 23.6, and we will go into a little more detail at the end.

```
# Count from 1 to the max number of command-line arguments

while ((COUNT  < MAX_COUNT))
do
   ((COUNT == COUNT + 1))
   TOKEN=$1
   case $TOKEN in
      -f) shift; shift
          ((COUNT == COUNT + 1))

              ;;
      -f${START_BASE}) shift
              ;;
```

Listing 23.6 Code segment to parse the command line. *(continues)*

```
    -t) shift; shift
        ((COUNT == COUNT + 1))
            ;;
    -t${END_BASE}) shift
            ;;
    *) BASE_NUM=$TOKEN
        break
        ;;
    esac
done
```

Listing 23.6   Code segment to parse the command line. *(continued)*

Remember that at the beginning of the shell script we defined the variables COUNT=0 and MAX_COUNT=$#. Now we get a chance to use them. I also want to introduce the **shift** command. This Korn shell built-in allows us to always reference the **$1** command-line argument to access *any* argument on the command line. To go to the next command-line argument we use the **shift** command to make the next argument, which is **$2** here, shift over to the **$1** position parameter. If we want to **shift** more than one position then we can either execute multiple **shift** commands or just add an integer value to the **shift** command to indicate how many positions that we want to shift to the **$1** position. Both of the following commands shift positional parameters two positions to the **$1** argument.

```
shift; shift

shift 2
```

The idea in our **case** statement is to do *one* **shift** if a command-line switch *with* its switch-argument is found at **$1** and to **shift** *two* positions if a command-line switch is found alone. We start with a **while** loop and increment a counter by one. Then we use the TOKEN variable to always grab the value in the **$1** position. We make the test to check for a command-line switch alone or a command-line switch plus its switch argument. If the **$1** positional parameter contains either of these, then we **shift** accordingly. If the test is not matched, then we have found the number that we are looking for. So, this is really not that difficult a test when you know what the goal is.

When we have found the "number," which is assigned to the BASE_NUM variable, we are ready to do the conversion between number bases. We do the conversion as we did in the previous shell scripts in this chapter except that this time we use the variable assignments of the START_BASE and END_BASE variable as number bases to start at and to end with, as shown in the next command statement.

```
RESULT="${START_BASE}#${BASE_NUM}"
```

Let's assume that the $START_BASE variable points to the integer 2, and the $BASE_NUM variable points to the binary number 1101101011. Then the following command statement is equivalent to the previous statement.

```
RESULT="2#1101101011"
```

The next step is to **typeset** the BASE_TO variable to the target number base. This is also accomplished using the previously defined variable END_BASE, as shown here.

```
typeset -i$END_BASE RESULT
```

Now let's assume that the target number base, $END_BASE, is 16. The following command statement is equivalent to the preceding variable statement.

```
typeset -i16 RESULT
```

The only thing left to do is print the result to the screen. You can use **echo**, **print**, or **printf** to display the result. I still like to use **echo**, so this is the final line of the shell script.

```
echo $RESULT
```

Other Options to Consider

As with all of the scripts in this book, we can always make some changes to any shell script to improve it or to customize the script to fit a particular need.

Software Key Shell Script

To make a software key more complicated you can hide the hexadecimal representation of the IP address within some pseudo-random numbers, which we studied in Chapters 10 and 21. As an example, add five computer-generated pseudo-random numbers as both a prefix and a suffix to the hexadecimal IP address representation. Then to verify the license key in your software program you can extract the hex IP address from the string. There are several techniques to do this verification, and I am going to leave the details up to you as a little project.

This is the only modification that I can think of for this chapter.

Summary

We went through a lot of variations in this chapter, but we did hit the scripts from different angles. Number base conversion can be used for many purposes, and we wrote one script that takes advantage of the translation. Software keys are usually more complicated than this script example, but I think you get the basic idea.

In the next chapter we are going to look at creating a menu that is suitable for your operations staff because you rarely want the Operators to have access to the command line. See you in the next chapter!

Menu Program Suitable for Operations Staff

Oh yes, we can never forget about the Operations staff! A lot of us traveled along this road in the beginning; I know I did back in the 1980s. These guys still do the grunt work, but most of the time you do not want a beginning Operator to get near a command prompt for everyday tasks. The chance for small mistakes is too great with the newcomers, but we must give them the ability to do their job.

This ability is easily given to the Operators by a menu that has all of the functionality that they need to get the job done, and we might as well make it a nice-looking menu. Some of the more common operations tasks include managing the print queues, managing the backup tapes, and changing user passwords. There are many more tasks, but this short list will get us started.

First, let's set some expectations. Normally, this type of shell script is put in the user's $HOME/.profile or other login configuration file, and when the user logs in the menu is presented. When the user exits the menu the user is logged out immediately. Using this method we do our best not to let the user gain access to a command prompt. Be careful! If a program like **vi** is in the menu, then all a user has to do is escape out to a shell with a couple of key strokes and the user is at a command prompt. Of course, if your Operators can find a way to get a command prompt, then just give it to them!

The techniques used in this chapter involve using reverse video, as we last saw in Chapter 15 when we created the hgrep shell script. This time we will use reverse video in a menu interface, again using the **tput** command options.

Reverse Video Syntax

To start off we want to give the menu a reverse video *title bar* across the top of the screen. To refresh your memory, to turn on reverse video we use **tput smso** and to turn off the highlight we use **tput rmso**. For this title bar we will use the system's hostname in the title. After the script is started we will remain in the menu until 99 (exit) is entered as a menu selection. We also would like to highlight the menu options next to the option label. The title bar is first.

```
clear          # Clear the screen first
tput smso      # Turn on reverse video
echo "                                    $(hostname)\c" # 33 spaces
echo "                                    "        # 39 spaces
tput rmso      # Turn off reverse video
```

In the preceding code block we first clear the screen for the menu using the **clear** command. The second line will turn on the reverse video using the **tput smso** command. An **echo** statement that executes the Unix command **hostname**, as command substitution, follows this. In both **echo** statements the *blank spaces are highlighted*, which results in a bar across the top of the screen with the system's hostname in the middle, displayed in reverse video. Notice that before the hostname there are 33 spaces and after the hostname there are 39 more spaces. This allows up to 8 characters for the hostname in the middle of the title bar. You can adjust this spacing easily to suit your needs.

Creating the Menu

The next thing we want to do is display the menu options. For this step we want to make the selection options appear in reverse video to the left of the option label. We will again use command substitution, but this time to turn on and off the highlight within an **echo** statement. The block of code shown in Listing 24.1 will handle this nicely.

```
echo "$(tput smso)1$(tput rmso) - Tape Management"
echo "$(tput smso)2$(tput rmso) - Initialize New Tapes"
echo "$(tput smso)3$(tput rmso) - Dismount Tape Volume"
echo "$(tput smso)4$(tput rmso) - Query Volumes in Library"
echo "$(tput smso)5$(tput rmso) - Query Tape Volumes"
echo "$(tput smso)6$(tput rmso) - Audit Library/Check-in Scratch
Volumes"
echo "$(tput smso)7$(tput rmso) - Print Tape Volume Audit Report"

echo "\n\n" # Print two blank lines
```

Listing 24.1   Reverse video menu options.

```
echo "$(tput smso)10$(tput rmso) - Change Password"

echo "$(tput smso)11$(tput rmso) - Enable all Print Queues

echo "\n\n\n\n\n\n"

echo "$(tput smso)99$(tput rmso) - Logout\n"
```

Listing 24.1   Reverse video menu options. *(continued)*

Notice how the command substitution works in the **echo** statements. Highlighting is turned on, the menu selection number is displayed, and reverse video is turned off, then the selection label is printed in plain text.

Creating a Message Bar for Feedback

Another nice thing to have in our menu is a *message bar*. This can be used to display a message for an *invalid option* selection and also can be used to display a message if we want to disable a menu option. For this we want to set the message up to *assume* an invalid selection, and we will blank the message variable out if we have valid input. In case we want to disable an option in the menu we can comment out the commands that we want to disable and put a *disabled option* comment in the message variable. The next few lines of code, shown in Listing 24.2, will work to display the message bar.

```
# Draw a reverse video message bar across bottom of screen,
# with the error message displayed, if there is a message.

tput smso  # Turn on reverse video

echo "                              ${MSG}\c" # 30 spaces
echo "                          "              # 26 spaces

tput rmso  # Turn off reverse video

# Prompt for menu option.

echo "Selection: \c"
read OPTION

# Assume the selection was invalid. Because a message is always
# displayed we need to blank it out when a valid option
# is selected.

MSG="Invalid Option Selected."              # 24 spaces
```

Listing 24.2   Setting up the reverse video message bar.

This message bar works the same as the title bar. The text message pointed to by $MSG is displayed in the middle of the message bar. Notice that we are assuming an invalid option was entered as the default. If we have valid input we need to replace the text in the $MSG variable with 24 blank spaces, for a total of 80 characters. This way we have only a highlighted bar, without any text, across the screen. We do this in each option of the **case** statement that is used to process the menu selections. The entire shell script is shown in Listing 24.3. See how menu option 5 is disabled in the **case** statement.

```ksh
#!/usr/bin/ksh
#
# SCRIPT: operations_menu.ksh
# AUTHOR: Randy Michael
# DATE: 09-06-2001
# REV 2.0.P
#
# PLATFORM: Any Unix OS, with modifications
#
# PURPOSE: This script gives the operations staff an easy-
#          to-follow menu to handle daily tasks, such
#          as managing the backup tapes and changing
#          their password
#
# REV LIST:
#
#
# set -n # Uncomment to check script syntax without any execution
# set -x # Uncomment to debug this script
#
###############################################
####### DEFINE FILES AND VARIABLES HERE #######
###############################################


BINDIR="/usr/local/bin"
PASSWORD_SERVER="yogi"
THIS_HOST=$(hostname)


###############################################
########## INITIALIZE VARIABLES HERE ##########
###############################################


MSG="                        "
OPT=" " # Variable for menu selection


###############################################
############## SET A TRAP HERE ################
```

Listing 24.3   operations_menu.ksh shell script listing.

```
##############################################

trap 'echo "\nEXITING on a TRAPPED SIGNAL\n"; \
     exit 1' 1 2 3 15

##############################################
############ BEGINNING OF MAIN ###############
##############################################

# Loop until option 99 is Selected

# We use 99 as a character instead of an integer
# in case a user enters a non-integer selection,
# which would cause the script to fail.

while [[ $OPT != 99 ]]
do

    # Display a reverse video image bar across the top
    # of the screen with the hostname of the machine.

    clear         # Clear the screen first
    tput smso     # Turn on reverse video
    echo "                              ${THIS_HOST}\c"
    echo "                                          "
    tput rmso     # Turn off reverse video
    echo "\n"     # Add one blank line of output

    # Show the menu options available to the user with the
    # numbered options highlighted in reverse video
    #
    # $(tput smso) Turns ON reverse video
    # $(tput rmso) Turns OFF reverse video

    echo "$(tput smso)1$(tput rmso) - Tape Management"
    echo "$(tput smso)2$(tput rmso) - Label Tapes"
    echo "$(tput smso)3$(tput rmso) - Query Volumes in Library"
    echo "$(tput smso)4$(tput rmso) - Query Tape Volumes"
    echo "$(tput smso)5$(tput rmso) - Audit/Check-in Scratch Volumes"
    echo "$(tput smso)6$(tput rmso) - Print Tape Volume Audit Report"

    echo "\n\n" # Print two new lines

    echo "$(tput smso)7$(tput rmso) - Change Password"

    echo "$(tput smso)8$(tput rmso) - Enable all Print Queues"


    echo "\n\n\n\n"
```

Listing 24.3 operations_menu.ksh shell script listing. *(continues)*

```
echo "$(tput smso)99$(tput rmso) - Logout\n"

# Draw a reverse video message bar across bottom of screen,
# with the error message displayed, if there is a message.

tput smso  # Turn on reverse video

echo "                                    ${MSG}\c"
echo "                          "

tput rmso  # Turn off reverse video

# Prompt for menu option.

echo "Selection: \c"
read OPT

# Assume the selection was invalid. Because a message is always
# displayed we need to blank it out when a valid option
# is selected.

MSG="Invalid option selected."

# Process the Menu Selection

case $OPT in
1)
     # Option 1 - Tape Management

     ${BINDIR}/manage_tapes.ksh
     MSG="                          "
     ;;
2)
     # Option 2 - Tape Labeling

     ${BINDIR}/label_tapes.ksh
     MSG="                          "
     ;;
3)
     # Option 3 - Query Tape Volumes in Library

     dsmadmc -ID=admin -Password=pass query libvol
     print "Press ENTER to continue"
     read
     MSG="                             "
     ;;
4)
```

Listing 24.3   operations_menu.ksh shell script listing.

```
        # Option 4 - Query Tape Volumes

        clear # Clear the screen
        print "Enter Tape Volume to Query:"
        read ANSWER
        dsmadmc -ID=admin -PAssword=pass query vol $ANSWER \
                format=detailed
        if (($? == "11")) # Check for "Not Found"
        then
            print "Tape Volume $ANSWER not found in database."
            print "Press ENTER to continue."
            read
        fi
        MSG="                        "
        ;;
    5)
        # Option 5 - Audit/Checkin Scratch Volumes

#         dsmadmc -ID=admin -PAssword=pass audit library mainmount
#         dsmadmc -ID=admin -PAssword=pass checkin libvol mainmount\
#               status=scratch search=yes

        # Not for Operations anymore!!!

        MSG=" Option is disabled.   "
        ;;
    6)
        # Option 6 - Print Tape Volume Audit Report

        ${BINDIR}/print_audit_report.ksh
        MSG="                        "
        ;;
    7)
        # Option 7 - Change Password

        echo "Remote Shell into $PASSWORD_SERVER for Password Change"
        echo "Press ENTER to continue: \c"
        read KEY
        rsh $PASSWORD_SERVER passwd
        # ssh $PASSWORD_SERVER passwd
        MSG="                        "
        ;;
    8)
        # Option 8 - Enable all print queues

        echo "Attempting to Enable all print queues...\c"
        ${BINDIR}/enable_all_queues.ksh
        echo "\nQueue Enable Attempt Complete\n"
```

Listing 24.3 operations_menu.ksh shell script listing. *(continues)*

```
        sleep 1
        MSG="                        "
        ;;
    esac

    # End of Loop until 99 is selected

done

# Erase menu from screen upon exiting with the "clear" command

clear

# End of Script
```

Listing 24.3   operations_menu.ksh shell script listing. *(continued)*

From the Top

Let's look at this script from the top. The first step is to define files and variables. In this section we define three variables, our BINDIR directory, which is the location of all of the shell scripts and programs that we call from the menu. The second variable is the hostname of the *password server*. I use a single server to hold the master password list, and every 15 minutes this master password file is pushed out to all of the other servers in the landscape. This method just makes life much easier when you have a lot of machines to manage. Of course you may use NIS or NIS+ for this functionality. The last variable is the **hostname** of the machine running the menu, THIS_HOST.

Next we initialize two variables; one is for the message bar, and the other is for the menu options, $MSG and $OPT. After initializing these two variables we *set a trap*. This **trap** is just informational. All that we want to do if this shell script receives a trapped signal is to let the user know that this program exited on a trapped signal, nothing more.

Now comes the fun stuff at the BEGINNING OF MAIN. For the menu we stay in a loop until the user selects 99 as a menu option. Only an exit signal or a 99 user selection will exit this loop. The easiest way to create this loop is to use a **while** loop specifying 99 as the exit criteria. Each time through the loop we first clear the screen. Then we display the title bar, which has the hostname of this machine, specified by the $THIS_HOST variable. Next we display the menu options. This current menu has 8 options, plus the 99 exit selection.

We preset the message bar to always assume an incorrect entry. If the entry is valid, then we overwrite the $MSG variable with blank spaces. After the message bar is displayed we prompt the user for a menu selection. When a valid selection is made we jump down to the **case** statement, which executes the selected menu option.

Notice that the message string, $MSG, is always the same length, 24 characters. This is a requirement to ensure that the message bar and the title bar are the same length; assuming an eight character hostname. This is also true for the hostname in the title bar. In each of the **case** statement options we process the menu selection and make the $MSG all blank spaces, with the exception of item number 5. We disabled menu option 5 by commenting out all of the code and changing the $MSG to read **Option is Disabled**. This is an easy way to remove a menu option from being executed temporarily. The $MSG will always be displayed in the message bar, whether the "message" is all blank spaces or an actual text message. Both the title and message bars are always 80 characters long, assuming a hostname of 8 characters. You may want to add some code to ensure that the title bar is always 80 characters. This is a little project for you to resolve.

The 8 menu options include the following:

- Tape management

- Tape labeling

- Query tape volumes in the library

- Query tape volumes

- Audit/check-in scratch volumes

- Print tape volume audit report

- Change password

- Enable all print queues

- 99—exit

For each valid menu selection in this script either a local command is executed or an external program or shell script is executed. You will have to modify this menu script to suit your needs. Do not assume that the TSM commands listed as menu options in this script will work without modification. These menu entries are just an example of the types of tasks that you *may* want your operations staff to handle. Every environment is different and some operations staff members are more capable than others.

For safety I recommend that you add this shell script name to the end of the users' $HOME/.profile and follow this script name with the **exit** command as the last entry in the user's .profile. This method allows the Operators to log in to run the tasks in the menu. When 99 is selected the menu is exited and the user is logged out of the system due to the exit command, without ever seeing a command prompt.

Other Options to Consider

This script, like any other shell script, can be improved. I can think of only a couple of things that I might add depending on the environment. You may have better ideas on how a menu should look and work, but this is one way to get the job done in an easily readable script.

Shelling Out to the Command Line

Be extremely careful about the commands that you put into the menu. Some programs are very easy to get to a shell prompt. The example I mentioned earlier was the **vi** editor. With a couple of key strokes you can suspend **vi** and get to a shell prompt. You can do this with many other programs, too.

Good Candidate for Using sudo

In Chapter 14 we went through installing and configuring **sudo**, which stands for *super user do*. A menu is an excellent place to use **sudo**. One of the major advantages is that you keep an audit trail of who did what and when the commands were executed. If a problem arises this **sudo** log should be one of the first places to look.

Summary

In this chapter we covered the creation of a moderately complex menu shell script. This one is not too difficult to read and understand, and I like to keep it that way. Some administrators will try to put everything in a couple of lines of code that they understand. When the menu needs to be modified, though, you really need an easy-to-understand script. It is not *if* you will modify this shell script but *when* you will have to modify the script.

You can place just about any task in a menu by using the proper method. As I mentioned before, **sudo** is excellent for keeping an audit trail. You can also add a logging facility into this menu script by using the **tee -a $LOGFILE** command in a pipe after each command. The **tee -a $LOGFILE** command displays everything on the screen and also appends the output data to the specified file.

In the next chapter we are going to look at a technique to send pop-up messages to Windows desktop using Samba. See you in the next chapter!

## CHAPTER 25

Sending Pop-Up Messages from Unix to Windows

There is a need in every shop for quick communications to the users in your environment. Getting a message out quickly when an application has failed is a good example. In this chapter we are going to look at a method of sending "pop-up" messages to Windows desktops. The only requirement for the Unix machines is that Samba must be configured and running on the Unix sever. Samba is a freeware product with a lot of uses; however, our focus in this chapter is sending pop-up messages using the **smbclient** command.

I really like this shell script, and I use it a lot to tell my users of impending maintenance, to notify users when a problem is to be corrected, and to give the status of an ongoing maintenance procedure. In this chapter we will look at setting up a master broadcast list and setting up individual *group* lists for sending messages, as well as specifying where the message is to be sent as the script is executing.

About Samba and the smbclient Command

Samba is a suite of programs that allows for the sharing of resources between various operating systems. We are interested in only the Unix-to-Windows part of Samba. The part of the Samba suite of programs that we use in this chapter to broadcast a message to one or more Windows clients is the **smbclient** command. The **smbclient** command is a client that allows nodes to *talk,* and in our case to send messages. This chapter focuses on sending *pop-up* messages to Windows clients from our Unix machine. The **smbclient** command has a lot more functionality than is covered in this chapter; so if you want to know what else the **smbclient** command can do, see the Samba documentation and the **man** pages.

We use a single switch in this chapter with the **smbclient** command. The **-M** switch allows us to send messages using the *Winpopup* protocol. The receiving computer must be running the Winpopup protocol, however, or the message is lost and no error notification is given. Even if we check the return code, which we always do, it is only a nonzero return code when a node name cannot be resolved. For the Windows machines in the following list, the receiving machine must copy Winpopup into the startup group if the machine is to always have pop-up messages available:

- Windows for Workgroups
- Windows 95 and 98

Most other versions of Windows will accept pop-up messages by default. It is always a good idea to work with the System Administrators in your Windows team to test the correct usage and functionality; all Windows networks are not created equally. The **-M** option of the **smbclient** command is expecting a NetBios name, which is the standard in a Windows network. You can also use the **-R** command to set the name resolution order to search. We also have the option of specifying an IP address by using the **-I** option.

This shell script has been tested on the following Windows operating systems, and the script delivered the message without any modification to the Windows systems:

- Windows NT
- Windows XP
- Windows 2000

Because this is the last chapter in the book, I'm sure that you know we are going to cover the syntax for the proper usage.

Syntax

To send messages from Unix to Windows we need only the **smbclient -M** command. The basic use of the command, especially for testing, is shown here.

```
NODELIST="winhostA winhostB winhostC"

MESSAGE="Hello World"

for NODE in $NODELIST
do
     echo $MESSAGE | smbclient -M $NODE
done
```

The only thing that we need is a list of nodes to send the message to and a message to send. When we have these two elements then all that is required is echoing the messaging and piping it to the **smbclient** command. Normally the **smbclient** command is an interactive command. By using the piped-in input we have the input ready, which is the same result that a here document produces for interactive programs.

Building the broadcast.ksh Shell Script

When I started this chapter it was going to be about five pages. I kept coming up with more ideas and options for broadcasting messages so I just had to expand this chapter to fit these ideas into the mix. The basic idea is to send a message from a Unix system to a specific Windows machine in the network. I started thinking about sending messages to selected groups of users that all have a related purpose. For example, we can have the following list of individual groups: Unix, DBA, ORACLE, DB2, APPLICATION, and so on. Then we have a default list of ALL Windows machines in the business, or at least in a department.

With all of these options in mind I started rewriting an already working shell script. In the next sections we are going to put the pieces together and make a very flexible shell script that you can tailor to suit your needs very easily. Let's start with the default behavior of sending a message to all users.

Sending a Message to All Users

The basics of the original shell script has a *master* list of nodes, which may be represented by a username in some shops and a node name in others. This list of nodes or users is read one at a time in a **for** loop. As each node name is read it is placed in the **smbclient** command statement. The message is sent to all nodes in a series of loop iterations until all of the target nodes have been processed. For this basic functionality we need only a file that contains the names of the nodes (or users) and a **for** loop to process each node name in the file. This one is the simple version and forms the basis for sending messages in this chapter. Study Listing 25.1, and pay attention to the boldface text.

```
# Define the list file containing the list of nodes/users.

WINNODEFILE="/usr/local/bin/WINlist"

# Load the node list into the WINLIST variable, but ignore
# any line in the file that begins with a pound sign (#).

WINLIST=$(cat $WINNODEFILE | grep -v ^# | awk '{print $1}' | uniq)
# Ask the user for the message to send
```

Listing 25.1   Code segment to broadcast a message. *(continues)*

```
echo "\nEnter the message to send (Press ENTER when finished)"

echo "\n\nMessage ==> \c"
read MESSAGE

for NODE in $WINLIST
do
     echo "$MESSAGE" | smbclient -M $NODE
done
```

Listing 25.1 Code segment to broadcast a message. *(continued)*

In the code segment in Listing 25.1 we first define the list file containing the nodes (or users) for which the message is intended. After the node list file is defined we load the file's contents into the WINLIST variable. We want to give the user the ability to comment out entries in the $WINNODEFILE with a pound sign (#). We also want the user to be able to make comments in the list file after the node/user name. With this increased flexibility we added some filtering in the WINLIST variable assignment. Notice in this assignment that we used **grep** and **awk** to do the filtering. First comes the **grep** command. In this statement we have the entry:

```
grep -v ^#
```

The **-v** tells the **grep** command to list everything *except* what **grep** is pattern matching on. The ^# is the notation for *begins with a* #. The caret (^) is a nice little option that lets us do filtering on lines of data that begin with the specified pattern. To ignore blank lines in a file use the cat $FILE | grep -v ^$ command statement.

Also notice the use of the **uniq** command. This command removes any duplicate line in the file. Any time you need to remove exact duplicate entries you can pipe the output to the **uniq** command.

In the next section we prompt the user for the message to send and **read** the entire message into the MESSAGE variable. Because we are using a variable for the message the length can not exceed 2048 characters. The **smbclient** command will truncate the text string to 1600 characters, which should be more than enough for a pop-up message.

Now that we have the message and the destination nodes/users, we are ready to loop through each destination in the $WINLIST using the **for** loop. Usually the **smbclient** command is an interactive program. The method that we use to supply the message is to **echo** the $MESSAGE and pipe the output to the **smbclient** command. The full command statement for sending the message is shown here:

```
echo "$MESSAGE" | smbclient -M $NODE
```

The **-M** switch expects a NetBios node name, which is a typical Windows protocol.

Sending Pop-Up Messages from Unix to Windows

Adding Groups to the Basic Code

The code segment in Listing 25.1 forms the basis for the entire shell script. We are going to build on the base code to allow us to send messages to specific groups of users by defining the GROUPLIST variable. Each group that is added to the group list is a variable in itself that points to a filename that contains a list of nodes/users, just like the WINNODEFILE variable. By adding this new ability we need a way to tell the shell script that we want the message sent to a particular group. This is where we need to use the **getopts** command to parse the command line for command switches and switch-arguments. We have used **getopts** in other chapters in this book so we will get to the details in a moment.

There are three steps in defining a group for this shell script. The first step is to add the new group to the GROUPLIST variable assignment statement, which is toward the top of the script. For this example we are adding three groups: UNIX, DBA, and APP-A. The first step looks like the statement shown here.

```
GROUPLIST="UNIX DBA APP-A"
```

The second step is to define a filename for each newly defined group. I like to define a variable to point to the top-level directory, which is /usr/local/bin on my machines. This method makes moving the location of the list files easy with a one-line edit. The code segment is shown here.

```
GRP_DIR="/usr/local/bin"

UNIX="${GRP_DIR}/UNIXlist"
DBA="${GRP_DIR}/DBAlist"
APP-A="${GRP_DIR}/APPAlist"
```

Notice the use of the curly braces (${VAR}) in this code segment. The curly braces are used to separate the variable from the next character if there is no space between the variable name and the next character.

The third and final step is to create each of the files and enter the destination nodes in the file with one entry on each line. The code in this shell script allows for you to comment out entries with a pound sign (#) and to add comments after the node/user definition in the file.

To use a group the user must specify one or more groups on the command line with the **-G** switch, followed by one or more groups that are defined in the script. If more than one group is specified, then the group list *must* be enclosed in double quotes. To send a message to everyone in the Unix and DBA groups use the following command:

```
# broadcast.ksh -G "UNIX DBA"
```

Adding the Ability to Specify Destinations Individually

With the code described thus far we are restricted to the users/nodes that are defined in the list files that we created. Now let's add the ability for a user to specify one or more message destinations on the command line or by prompting the user for the destination list. These two options require more command-line switches and, in one case, a switch-argument.

We are going to add the following command-line switches to this script:

-M, -m   Prompts the user for the message destination(s) and the message.

-H, -h, -N, -n   Expects a destination list as a switch-argument. Each switch does the same thing here.

The first switch, **-M** and **-m**, is the *message* switch. There is not a switch-argument for this switch, but instead the user is prompted to enter one or more destination nodes/users. The second set of switches each performs the exact same task, and a switch-argument is required, which is a list of destination nodes/users. Some people think of these destination machines as *hosts*, so I added the **-h** and **-H** switches. Other people think of the destination machines as *nodes*, so I added the **-n** and **-N** switches. This way both sets of users can have it their way.

Using getopts to Parse the Command Line

Now we have a bunch of command-line switches, and some of these switches require a switch-argument. This is a job for **getopts**! As we have studied before, the **getopts** command is used in a **while** loop statement. Within the **while** loop there is a **case** statement that allows us to take some useful action when a command-line switch is encountered. Whenever a switch is encountered that requires a switch-argument, the argument that is found is assigned to the $OPTARG variable. This $OPTARG is a variable that is build into the **getopts** command. Let's look at the **getopts** command statement and the code segment with the enclosed **case** statement in Listing 25.2.

```
# Parse the command-line arguments for any switches. A command-
# line switch must begin with a hyphen (-).

# A colon (:) AFTER a variable (below) means that the switch
# must have a switch-argument on the command line

while getopts ":mMh:H:n:N:g:G:" ARGUMENT
   do
      case $ARGUMENT in

         m|M)   echo "\nEnter One or More Nodes to Send This Message:"
                echo "\nPress ENTER when finished \n\n"
                echo "Node List ==> \c"
                read  WINLIST
                ;;
         h|H|n|N)  WINLIST=$OPTARG
                ;;
         g|G)  GROUP=$OPTARG # $OPTARG is the value of the switch-argument!
```

Listing 25.2   Using getopts to parse the command-line switches.

```
                  # Make sure that the group has been defined

                  for G in $GROUP
                  do
                         echo "$GROUPLIST" | grep -q $G || group_error $G
                  done
                  # All of the groups are valid if you get here!
                  WINLIST=             # NULL out the WINLIST variable
                  # Loop through each group in the $GROUP
                  # and build a list of nodes to send the message to.

                  for GRP in $GROUP
                  do
                       # Use "eval" to show what a variable is pointing to!
                       # Make sure that each group has a non-empty list file

                       if [ -s $(eval echo \$"$GRP") ]
                       then
                           WINLIST="$WINLIST $(eval cat \$"$GRP" |grep -v ^# \
                                       | awk '{print $1}')"
                       else
                           group_file_error $(eval echo \$"$GRP")
                       fi
                  done
                  ;;
          \?)     echo "\nERROR: Invalid Augument(s)!"
                  usage
                  exit 1
                  ;;
      esac
done
```

Listing 25.2   Using getopts to parse the command-line switches. *(continued)*

Don't run away yet! The code segment in Listing 25.2 is not too hard to understand when it is explained. In the **getopts** statement, shown here, we define the valid switches and which switches require a switch-argument and which ones have a meaning without a switch-argument.

```
while getopts ":mMh:H:n:N:g:G:" ARGUMENT
```

In this **getopts** statement the switch definitions list, ":mMh:H:n:N:g:G:", begins with a colon (:). This first colon has a special meaning. If an undefined switch is encountered, which must begin with a hyphen (-), the undefined switch causes a question mark (?) to be assigned to the ARGUMENT variable (you can use any variable name here). This is the mechanism that finds the switch errors entered on the command line.

In the **getopts** statement the **-m** and **-M** switches do *not* have a switch argument and the **-h**, **-H**, **-n**, **-N**, **-g**, and **-G** switches *do* require a switch-argument. Whether or not a switch requires an argument is determined by the placement of colons in the definition statement. If a colon (:) appears *after* the switch in the definition, then that switch requires a switch-argument; if a switch does not have a colon after the switch definition, then the switch does not have a switch-argument. This is really all there is to using the **getopts** command.

Inside the **while** loop we have an embedded **case** statement. It is in the **case** statement that we do something useful with the command-line arguments that are switches. Just remember, **getopts** does not care *what* is on the command line unless it has a hyphen (–). This is why we need to test for valid arguments supplied on the command line.

In our **case** statement in Listing 25.2 we take action or make assignments when a valid switch is encountered. When a **-M**, or **-m**, switch is found we prompt the user for a list of one or more destination nodes to send the message. When a **-h**, **-H**, **-n**, or **-N** switch is found, we assign the $OPTARG variable to the WINLIST, which is a list of target users/nodes. When **getopts** finds **-g**, or **-G**, we assign the $OPTARG variable to the GROUP variable. When an undefined switch is found, a question mark (?) is assigned to the ARGUMENT variable. In this situation we give the user an ERROR message, show the usage function, and **exit** the shell script with a return code of 1, one.

Using the eval Function with Variables

Let's go back to the GROUP variable in Listing 25.2 for a minute. Remember that we can have group names assigned to the GROUPLIST variable. Each group assigned to the GROUPLIST variable must have a filename assigned to it that contains a list of destination machines. Now if you think about this you should notice that we have to work with a variable pointing to another variable, which points to a filename. The file contains the list of destination machines. Just how do we point *directly* to the filename? This is a job for the **eval** function. The **eval** function is a Korn shell built-in, and we use it to solve our little dilemma.

The **eval** function works like this in our code. We have the GROUP variable that is one or more groups that the user entered on the command line as a switch-argument to the **-G**, or **-g**, switch. Each group that is assigned to the GROUP variable is a pointer to a filename that holds a list of destination machines. To *directly* access the filename we have to use the **eval** function. Let's look at the code segment that uses the **eval** function in the **getopts** loop in Listing 25.3.

```
for GRP in $GROUP
do
    # Use "eval" to show the value of what a variable is pointing
    # to! Make sure that each group has a nonempty list file

    if [ -s $(eval echo \$"$GRP") ]
    then
        WINLIST="$WINLIST $(eval cat \$"$GRP" |grep -v ^# \
```

Listing 25.3   Using eval to evaluate double pointing variables.

```
                   | awk '{print $1}' | uniq)"
    else
        group_file_error $(eval echo \$"$GRP")
    fi
done
```

Listing 25.3   Using eval to evaluate double pointing variables. *(continued)*

We first start a **for** loop to process each group assigned to the GROUP variable, which is assigned to the GRP variable on each loop iteration. Inside the **for** loop we first test to see if the group has a group file assigned and if this file size is greater than zero. To do this we use the following command:

```
if [ -s $(eval echo \$"$GRP") ]
```

The command substitution, $(eval echo \$"$GRP"), points directly to the file name of the group. We could also use the command substitution, $(eval echo '$'$GRP), to directly access the filename. Both statements produce the same result. This **eval** statement is saying "tell me what this other variable is pointing to, in this statement."

Notice that we use **eval** two more times in Listing 25.3. We first use **eval** to assign the destination machine listed in the list file to the WINLIST variable in the command shown here.

```
WINLIST="$WINLIST $(eval cat \$"$GRP" | grep -v ^# \
                    | awk '{print $1}' | uniq)"
```

In this case we are listing the file with **cat** and then using **grep** and **awk** to filter the output, and **uniq** to remove any duplicate entries. The next instance of **eval** is in the error notification. The group_file_error function requires one argument, the group list filename. In this step we are building a list of destination machines if more than one group was given on the command line.

Testing User Input

For any shell script it is extremely important that the information provided by the user is valid. In the broadcast.ksh shell script we have the opportunity to check a lot of user input. Starting at BEGINNING OF MAIN several tests of data need to be made.

Testing and Prompting for WINLIST Data

The first test of user input is a test to ensure that the WINLIST variable is not empty, or NULL. To make this test we use an **until** loop to prompt the user for a list of destination nodes if the WINLIST is empty. I created a function called check_for_null_winlist that is used as the loop criteria for prompting the user for a node list input. This function is shown in Listing 25.4.

```
function check_for_null_winlist
{
if [[ -z "$WINLIST" && "$WINLIST" = "" ]]
then
     return 1
else
     return 0
fi
}
```

Listing 25.4   Function to check for a Null WINLIST variable.

The only thing that the check_for_null_winlist function in Listing 23.4 does is **return** a **1**, one, as a return code if the $WINLIST variable is empty, or NULL, and **return** a **0**, zero, if the $WINLIST has data assigned. Using this function as the loop criteria in an **until** loop is easy to do, as shown in the code segment in Listing 25.5.

```
# Ensure that at least one node is defined to send the message.
# If not stay in this loop until one or more nodes are entered
# on the command line

until check_for_null_winlist
do
     echo "\n\nEnter One or More Nodes to Send This Message:"
     echo "\n Press ENTER when finished \n\n"
     echo "Node List ==> \c"
     read  WINLIST
done
```

Listing 25.5   Using an until loop with check_for_null_winlist.

This **until** loop will continue to execute until the user either enters data or presses CTRL-C.

Testing and Prompting for Message Data

Like the WINLIST data, the MESSAGE variable must have at least one character to send as a message, or we need to prompt the user for the message to send. We use the same type of technique as we did for the WINLIST data. We created the check_for_null _message function to test the MESSAGE variable to ensure that it is not empty, or

NULL. This function returns a 1, one, if the MESSAGE variable is empty and returns a 0, zero, if the MESSAGE variable has data. Check out the function in Listing 25.6.

```
function check_for_null_message
{
if [[ -z "$MESSAGE" && "$MESSAGE" = "" ]]
then
     return 1
else
     return 0
fi
}
```

Listing 25.6   Function to check for a Null MESSAGE variable.

Using the check_for_null_message function in Listing 25.6 we can execute an **until** loop until the MESSAGE variable has at least one character. The loop exits when the function returns a 0, zero, for a return code. Look at the **until** loop in the code segment shown in Listing 25.7.

```
# Prompt the user for a message to send. Loop until the
# user has entered at least one character for the message
# to send.

until check_for_null_message
do
     echo "\nEnter the message to send:"
     echo "\nPress ENTER when finished\n\n"
     echo "Message ==> \c"
     read MESSAGE
done
```

Listing 25.7   Using an until loop with check_for_null_message.

If the MESSAGE variable already has data assigned, then the **until** loop will not prompt the user for any input. This is just a test to look for at least one character of data in the $MESSAGE variable.

Sending the Message

At this point we have validated that we have a list of one or more nodes/users to send the message and that the message is at least one character long. As stated before, the $MESSAGE will be truncated at 1600 characters (1600 bytes), which should not be an issue for a pop-up message. If the message is long, then an email is more appropriate.

We have already seen the basics of sending a message with the **smbclient** command, which is part of the Samba suite of programs. We are going to use the same technique here to send the message. Now we have the list of destination nodes assigned to the WINLIST variable. Let's look at the code segment to send the message in Listing 25.8.

```
echo "\nSending the Message...\n"

# Loop through each host in the $WINLIST and send the pop-up message

for NODE in $WINLIST
do
        echo "Sending to ==> $NODE"
        echo $MESSAGE | $SMBCLIENT -M $NODE # 1>/dev/null
        if (($? == 0))
        then
                echo "Sent OK    ==> $NODE"
        else
                echo "FAILED to  ==> $NODE Failed"
        fi
done

echo "\n"
```

Listing 25.8   Code segment to send a message to a list of nodes.

We added a few lines of code to the **for** loop in Listing 25.8. Notice on each loop iteration that the user is informed of the destination for the current loop iteration. When we send the message using the **smbclient** command we check the return code to see if the message was sent successfully. A 0, zero, return code does not guarantee that the target machine received the message. For example, if the target is a Windows 95 machine and **winpopup** is not running, then the message is lost and no error message is received back to let you know that the message was not displayed. You will receive a nonzero return code if the machine is not powered up or if the destination machine-name cannot be resolved.

Also notice the commented-out redirection to /dev/null, after the **smbclient** command statement. This output redirection to the bit bucket is commented out so that the user can see the result of sending each message. If there is a problem sending a message, then the **smbclient** event notifications provide better information than a return code for the **smbclient** command itself. If you want to hide this connection information, uncomment this redirection to the bit bucket.

Putting It All Together

Now that we have covered most of the individual pieces that make up the broadcast.ksh shell script, let's look at the whole shell script and see how the pieces fit together. The entire shell script is shown in Listing 25.9. Please pay particular attention to the boldface text.

```
#!/bin/ksh
#
# SCRIPT: broadcast.ksh
# AUTHOR: Randy Michael
#         Systems Administrator
# DATE: 1/12/2000
# REV: 1.2.P
# PLATFORM: Not platform dependent but requires Samba
#
# PURPOSE: This script is used to broadcast a pop-up message to
# Windows desktops. The Windows machines must be defined in
# the $WINNODEFILE file, which is where the master list of
# nodes is defined. The $WINNODELIST filename is defined in the
# variable definitions section of this shell script.
#
# You also have the ability of setting up individual GROUPS of
# users/nodes by defining the group name to the GROUPLIST variable.
# Then define the filename of the group. For example, to define a
# Unix and DBA group the following entries need to be made in this
# shell script:
#
#    GROUPLIST="UNIX DBA"
#    UNIX="/scripts/UNIXlist"
#    DBA="/scripts/DBAlist"
#
# Assuming that the filenames presented above are acceptable to you.
#
# There are four options for sending a message:
#
#    1) Execute this script without any argument prompts for the
#       message to send and then send the message to all nodes
#       defined in the $WINNODEFILE.
#    2) Specify the "-M" switch if you want to send a message to a
#       specific node or a list of nodes. The user is prompted for
#       the message to send.
#    3) Specify the -N or -H switches to specify the specific nodes
#       to receive the message. Add the node list after the -N or
#       -H switch.
#    4) Specify the -G switch, followed by the group name, that the
#       message is intended be sent.
#
#    EXAMPLES:
#          To send a message to all nodes defined in the $WINNODEFILE:
#
#          # broadcast.ksh
#
#          To send a message to only the "booboo" and "yogi" machines:
#
#          # broadcast.ksh -H "booboo yogi"
```

Listing 25.9   broadcast.ksh shell script listing. *(continues)*

```
#           OR
#           # broadcast.ksh -N "booboo yogi"
#
#           To send a message to specific machines without specifying
#           each one on the command line:
#
#           # broadcast.ksh -M
#
#           To send a message to all users in the Unix and DBA
#           groups only:
#
#           # broadcast.ksh -G "UNIX DBA"
#
#           Each switch is valid in uppercase or lowercase.
#
#   NOTE: This script uses SAMBA!!!  SAMBA must be installed
#         and configured on this system for this shell script
#         to function!
#
# EXIT CODES:   0 ==> Normal Execution
#               1 ==> Usage Error
#               2 ==> Missing Node List File
#               3 ==> The "smbclient" program is not in the $PATH
#               4 ==> The "smbclient" program is not executable
#
# REV LIST:
#
#
# set -x # Uncomment to debug this script
# set -n # Uncomment to check syntax without any execution
#
###############################################################
####### DEFINE BROADCAST GROUPS AND GROUP FILES HERE #######
###############################################################

# Define the file directory for this shell script.

GRP_DIR="/usr/local/bin"

# Define all valid groups to send messages

GROUPLIST="UNIX SAP ORACLE DBA APPA APPB"

# Define all of the Group files

UNIX="${GRP_DIR}/Unixlist"
SAP="${GRP_DIR}/SAPlist"
```

Listing 25.9 broadcast.ksh shell script listing.

```
ORACLE="${GRP_DIR}/ORACLElist"
DBA="${GRP_DIR}/DBAlist"
APPA="${GRP_DIR}/APPAlist"
APPB="${GRP_DIR}/APPBlist"

# File that contains the master list of nodes

WINNODEFILE="${GRP_DIR}/WINlist"


###########################################################
################ DEFINE FUNCTIONS HERE ####################
###########################################################

function display_listfile_error
{
# The function is used to inform the users that the
# $WINNODEFILE file does not exist. The $WINNODEFILE
# filename is defined in the main body of the shell script.

echo "\n\tERROR: ...MISSING NODE LIST FILE..."
echo "\nCannot find the $WINNODEFILE node list file!"
echo "\nThe $WINNODEFILE file is a file that contains a list of"
echo "nodes to broadcast a message. Create this file with"
echo "one node name per line and save the file.\n\n"

exit 2
}


###########################################################

function usage
{
echo "\nUSAGE: $THISSCRIPT [-M] [-H Host List] [-N Node List] \
[-G Group List]\n\n"
echo "EXAMPLES:"
echo "\nTo send a message to all nodes defined in the master list"
echo "$WINNODEFILE file enter the scriptname without any options:"
echo "\n$THISSCRIPT"
echo "\nTo send a message to one or more nodes only,"
echo "enter the following command:"
echo "\n$THISSCRIPT -M"
echo "\nTo specify the nodes to send the message to on"
echo "the command-line enter the following command:"
echo "\n$THISSCRIPT -H \"yogi booboo dino\" "
echo "\nTo send a message to one or more groups use the"
echo "following command syntax:"
echo "\n$THISSCRIPT -G \"UNIX DBA\" \n\n"
```

Listing 25.9   broadcast.ksh shell script listing. *(continues)*

```
}

################################################################

function check_for_null_message
{
if [[ -z "$MESSAGE" && "$MESSAGE" = "" ]]
then
     return 1
else
     return 0
fi
}

################################################################

function check_for_null_winlist
{
if [[ -z "$WINLIST" && "$WINLIST" = "" ]]
then
     return 1
else
     return 0
fi
}

################################################################

function group_error
{
(($# != 1)) && (echo "ERROR: function group_error expects \
an argument"; exit 1)
GRP=$1
echo "\nERROR: Undefined Group - $GRP"
usage
exit 1
}

################################################################

function group_file_error
{
(($# != 1)) && (echo "ERROR: function group_file_error expects \
an argument"; exit 1)

GPF=$1
echo "\nERROR: Missing group file - $GPF\n"
usage
```

Listing 25.9   broadcast.ksh shell script listing.

```
exit 1
}


#############################################################

function check_for_smbclient_command
{
# Check to ensure that the "smbclient" command is in the $PATH

SMBCLIENT=$(which smbclient)

# If the $SMBCLIENT variable begins with "which:" or "no" for
# Solaris and HP-UX then the command is not in the $PATH on
# this system. A correct result would be something like:
# "/usr/local/bin/smbclient" or "/usr/bin/smbclient".

if [[ $(echo $SMBCLIENT | awk '{print $1}') = 'which:' ]] || \
   [[ $(echo $SMBCLIENT | awk '{print $1}') = 'no' ]]
then
      echo "\n\nERROR: This script requires Samba to be installed
and configure. Specifically, this script requires that the
\"sbmclient\" program is in the \$PATH. Please correct this problem
and send your message again.\n"

      echo "\n\t...EXITING...\n"

      exit 3
elif [  ! -x $SMBCLIENT ]
then
      echo "\nERROR: $SMBCLIENT command is not executable\n"
      echo "Please correct this problem and try again\n"
      exit 4
fi
}


#############################################################
################ DEFINE VARIABLES HERE ####################
#############################################################

THISSCRIPT=$(basename $0) # The name of this shell script

MESSAGE=    # Initialize the MESSAGE variable to NULL

WINLIST=    # Initialize the list of node to NULL


#############################################################
############### TEST USER INPUT HERE ####################
#############################################################
```

Listing 25.9 broadcast.ksh shell script listing. *(continues)*

```
# Check for the "smbclient" command's existence

check_for_smbclient_command

# If no command-line arguments are present then test for
# the master $WINNODEFILE, which is defined at the top
# of this shell script.

if (($# == 0)) # No command-line arguments - Use the master list
then
     [ -s $WINNODEFILE ] || display_listfile_error

     # Load the file data into the WINLIST variable ignoring
     # any line in the file that begins with a # sign.

     WINLIST=$(cat $WINNODEFILE | grep -v ^# \
              | awk '{print $1}' | uniq)
else
   # Parse the command-line arguments for any switches. A command
   # line switch must begin with a hyphen (-).

   # A colon (:) AFTER a variable (below) means that the switch
   # must have a switch-argument on the command line

   while getopts ":mMh:H:n:N:g:G:" ARGUMENT
   do
     case $ARGUMENT in

        m|M)   echo "\nEnter One or More Nodes to Send This Message:"
               echo "\nPress ENTER when finished \n\n"
               echo "Node List ==> \c"
               read WINLIST
               ;;
        h|H|n|N)   WINLIST=$OPTARG
               ;;
        g|G)   GROUP=$OPTARG # $OPTARG is the value of
                             # the switch-argument!

               # Make sure that the group has been defined
               for G in $GROUP
               do
                   echo "$GROUPLIST" | grep -q $G || group_error $G
               done
               # All of the groups are valid if you get here!
               WINLIST=              # NULL out the WINLIST variable
               # Loop through each group in the $GROUP
```

Listing 25.9   broadcast.ksh shell script listing.

```
                    # and build a list of nodes to send the message to.

               for GRP in $GROUP
               do
                    # Use "eval" to show what a variable is pointing to!
                    # Make sure that each group has a non-empty list
                    # file

                    if [ -s $(eval echo \$"$GRP") ]
                    then
                         WINLIST="$WINLIST $(eval cat \$"$GRP" \
                                    | grep -v ^# | awk '{print $1}' \
                                    | uniq)"
                    else
                         group_file_error $(eval echo \$"$GRP")
                    fi
               done
               ;;
          \?)  echo "\nERROR: Invalid Argument(s)!"
               usage
               exit 1
               ;;
     esac
done


###############################################################
################## BEGINNING OF MAIN ########################
###############################################################

# Ensure that at least one node is defined to send the message.
# If not stay in this loop until one or more nodes are entered
# on the command line

until check_for_null_winlist
do
   echo "\n\nEnter One or More Nodes to Send This Message:"
   echo "\n Press ENTER when finished \n\n"
   echo "Node List ==> \c"
   read  WINLIST
done


#############################################################


fi  # End of "if (($# == 0))" test.

# Prompt the user for a message to send. Loop until the
```

Listing 25.9   broadcast.ksh shell script listing. *(continues)*

```
# user has entered at least one character for the message
# to send.

until check_for_null_message
do
    echo "\nEnter the message to send:"
    echo "\nPress ENTER when finished\n\n"
    echo "Message ==> \c"
    read MESSAGE
done

##############################################################

# Inform the user of the host list this message is sent to...

echo "\nSending message to the following hosts:\n"
echo "\nWIN_HOSTS:\n$WINLIST\n\n"

##############################################################

echo "\nSending the Message...\n"

# Loop through each host in the $WINLIST and send the pop-up message

for NODE in $WINLIST
do
    echo "Sending to ==> $NODE"
    echo $MESSAGE | $SMBCLIENT -M $NODE # 1>/dev/null
    if (($? == 0))
    then
        echo "Sent OK    ==> $NODE"
    else
        echo "FAILED to  ==> $NODE Failed"
    fi
done

echo "\n"

##############################################################
#
# This code segment is commented out by default
#
# Send the message to the Unix machines too using "wall"
# and "rwall" if you desire to do so. This code is commented
# out by default.
#
# echo "\nSending Message to the Unix machines...\n"
#
# echo $MESSAGE | rwall -h $UnixHOSTLIST
```

Listing 25.9   broadcast.ksh shell script listing.

```
# echo $MESSAGE | wall
# echo "\n\nMessage sent...\n\n"
#
##############################################################

# Remove the message file from the system

rm -f $MESSAGE
```

Listing 25.9   broadcast.ksh shell script listing. *(continued)*

As you study the script in Listing 25.9 I hope that you can see how the pieces are put together to produce a logical flow. You may have noticed that there is a larger **if** statement that skips all of the command-line parsing if there are no command-line arguments present. If we do not have anything to parse through, we just use the default master list of machine destinations.

I also want to point out a function that is called at the BEGINNING OF MAIN. The check_for_smbclient_command function looks for the **smbclient** command in the $PATH. Check out this function in Listing 25.10.

```
function check_for_smbclient_command
{
# Check to ensure that the "smbclient" command is in the $PATH

SMBCLIENT=$(which smbclient)

# If the $SMBCLIENT variable begins with "which:" or "no" for
# Solaris and HP-UX then the command is not in the $PATH on
# this system. A correct result would be something like:
# "/usr/local/bin/smbclient" or "/usr/bin/smbclient".

if [[ $(echo $SMBCLIENT | awk '{print $1}') = 'which:' ]] || \
   [[ $(echo $SMBCLIENT | awk '{print $1}') = 'no' ]]
then
     echo "\n\nERROR: This script requires Samba to be installed
and configured. Specifically, this script requires that the
\"sbmclient\" program is in the \$PATH. Please correct this problem
and send your message again.\n"

     echo "\n\t...EXITING...\n"

     exit 3
elif [  ! -x $SMBCLIENT ]
then
```

Listing 25.10   check_for_smbclient_command function listing. *(continues)*

```
        echo "\nERROR: $SMBCLIENT command is not executable\n"
        echo "Please correct this problem and try again\n"
        exit 4
fi
}
```

Listing 25.10 check_for_smbclient_command function listing. *(continued)*

Notice that we use the **which** command in Listing 25.10 to find the **smbclient** command in the $PATH. The **which** command will respond with either the full pathname of the **smbclient** command or an error message. The two messages look like the following:

```
# which smbclient
/usr/local/samba/bin/smbclient

OR

# which smbclient
which: 0652-141 There is no smbclient in /usr/bin /etc /usr/sbin
/usr/ucb /usr/bin/X11 /sbin /usr/local/bin /usr/local/samba/bin
/usr/local/bin /usr/dt/bin/ /usr/opt/ifor/ls/os/aix/bin .
```

If we receive the second message, then the **smbclient** command cannot be found. Note that this second response begins with which: just before the error code. This is true for AIX and Linux; however, on Solaris and HP-UX the result begins with no as opposed to which:. Using this response we give the user an error message that the **smbclient** command cannot be found.

Watching the broadcast.ksh Script in Action

You can see the broadcast.ksh shell script in action in Listing 25.11. In this listing we use the **-M** option to specify that we want to be prompted for both a list of destination machines and a message.

```
[root:yogi]@/scripts# ./broadcast.ksh -M

Enter One or More Nodes to Send This Message:

Press ENTER when finished

Node List ==> booboo

Enter the message to send:

Press ENTER when finished


Message ==> Please log out at lunch for a system reboot.

Sending message to the following hosts:


WIN_HOSTS:
booboo


Sending the Message...

Sending to ==> booboo
added interface ip=10.10.10.1 bcast=10.10.255.255 nmask=255.255.0.0
Connected. Type your message, ending it with a Control-D
sent 45 bytes
Sent OK    ==> booboo
```

Listing 25.11　broadcast.ksh shell script in action.

My **booboo** machine is an NT 4 box. The pop-up message that I received is shown in Figure 25.1.

The pop-up message in Figure 25.1 is typical for most machines except for Windows 95 and 98. For these two versions of Windows the **winpopup** program must be running. Most other machines have a similar pop-up message, as shown in Figure 25.1.

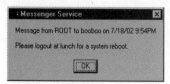

Figure 25.1   Pop_Up message sent to a Windows desktop.

Downloading and Installing Samba

You can download the latest version of Samba from the following URL: www
.samba.org/samba.

From the main page select a download site. Download sites from around the world
are available. This page has a link, `samba-latest.tar.gx`, to the latest version of
the source code. If you download the source code you need a C compiler to compile the
Samba release. The `./configure` file is looking for either **gcc** or **cc** when you begin
the compilation process. If a suitable C compiler is not found you cannot install the
Samba code. For our purposes we can download the available precompiled binary
versions of the code. Some of these are back releases, but the **smbclient** command
works just fine.

When you download the Samba *source* code follow these steps to compile the code
on your machine. Follow the link to the latest version of Samba. Download the code
into a directory on the Unix machine that has plenty of space, at least 500MB. Next,
uncompress the release. The code that I downloaded was a **tar** file that was compressed
with **gzip**, which has a **.gz** filename extension. Let's say that you downloaded the
Samba code into the `/usr/local` directory with the filename `samba.2.7.latest`
`.tar.gz`. You can name it anything you want when you download the file. The
following commands in Listing 25.12 are used to uncompress, untar, and install the
Samba code.

```
[root:yogi]@/usr/local > gunzip samba.2.7.latest.tar.gz

[root:yogi]@/usr/local > tar -xvf samba.2.7.latest.tar

[root:yogi]@/usr/local > cd samba.2.7

[root:yogi]@/usr/local/samba.2.7 > ./configure

[root:yogi]@/usr/local/samba.2.7 > make

[root:yogi]@/usr/local/samba.2.7 > make install
```

Listing 25.12   Samba source code installation.

Once the installation is complete you can remove the /usr/local/samba.2.7 directory to regain your disk space. Be aware that your file/directory names and release may differ from the commands shown in Listing 25.12. This source code installation does not create a smb.conf file. In the procedure that is presented in Listing 25.12, the smb.conf file is located in /usr/local/samba/lib/smb.conf. Please refer to the Samba documentation of the release you installed to know where to put this configuration file. For our purposes, and for security, make the file simple! The **smbclient** command works with a smb.conf file with only a single semicolon, (;). No other entry is required! The semicolon (;) and hash mark (#) are both comment specifications in this file. If you want to use any of the other functionality of Samba you are on your own, and the Samba documentation is your best resource for additional information.

Testing the smbclient Program the First Time

Before you start creating the master list file and a bunch of group list files, do a few tests to ensure that you have the correct format, the destination machines are reachable, and the name resolution is resolved for each node. Initially have a list of about five machines. The machines may be referenced in the NetBios world as a machine name or a username. This name resolution varies depending on the Windows network in your environment.

My home network does not have NetBios running, so I had to do a little research and I found that there is a file, which coexists with the smb.conf file, that works like a /etc/hosts file. This file is called lmhosts, and you make machine entries into this file just like a regular hosts file, except that the machine-names are entered in uppercase characters.

First try the following test. Let's suppose that I have five *users* named JohnB, CindySue, Bubba, JonnyLee, and BobbyJoe. For each user in the list we run the following commands.

```
echo "Hello World" | smbclient -M JohnB
echo "Hello World" | smbclient -M CindySue
echo "Hello World" | smbclient -M Bubba
echo "Hello World" | smbclient -M JonnyLee
echo "Hello World" | smbclient -M BobbyJoe
```

Ideally, the response should look something like the following output:

```
added interface ip=10.10.10.1 bcast=10.10.255.255 nmask=255.255.0.0
Connected. Type your message, ending it with a Control-D
sent 13 bytes
added interface ip=10.10.10.1 bcast=10.10.255.255 nmask=255.255.0.0
Connected. Type your message, ending it with a Control-D
sent 13 bytes
added interface ip=10.10.10.1 bcast=10.10.255.255 nmask=255.255.0.0
Connected. Type your message, ending it with a Control-D
sent 13 bytes
added interface ip=10.10.10.1 bcast=10.10.255.255 nmask=255.255.0.0
```

```
Connected. Type your message, ending it with a Control-D
sent 13 bytes
added interface ip=10.10.10.1 bcast=10.10.255.255 nmask=255.255.0.0
Connected. Type your message, ending it with a Control-D
sent 13 bytes
```

If you get responses like the ones shown here, then everything is as we want it to be. If you get output more like the next set of **smbclient** output, then we have a problem, Houston!

```
added interface ip=10.10.10.1 bcast=10.10.255.255 nmask=255.255.0.0
timeout connecting to 10.10.10.4:139
Error connecting to 10.10.10.4 (Operation already in progress)
Connection to JohnB failed
added interface ip=10.10.10.1 bcast=10.10.255.255 nmask=255.255.0.0
Connection to CindySue failed
added interface ip=10.10.10.1 bcast=10.10.255.255 nmask=255.255.0.0
Connection to Bubba failed
added interface ip=10.10.10.1 bcast=10.10.255.255 nmask=255.255.0.0
Connection to JonnyLee failed
added interface ip=10.10.10.1 bcast=10.10.255.255 nmask=255.255.0.0
Connection to BobbyJoe failed
```

Notice that the first attempt, to JohnB, timed out on connection. This is good! We know that there is name resolution to this machine but the machine is currently unreachable. I know it is unreachable because I turned the machine off. If a node is not powered up, this is the type of message that we receive.

On the other hand, the next four attempts to reach CindySue, Bubba, JonnyLee, and BobbyJoe failed. This is usually an indication that there is no name resolution to get to these machines. When you have this problem, first try to reach the machine by the node name instead of the user name. You can get the name of the machine by left-clicking on the **My Computer** icon on the Windows desktop. Then select **properties**. Try the same process of sending the message again, this time using node names. If you still have a problem, consult the Windows Systems Administrators to see if they can help.

The other solution is to maintain a lmhosts file, which is a pain to do. The lmhosts file is located in the same directory as the smb.conf file, which is in /usr/local/samba/lib if you downloaded and compiled the distribution from the Samba site. The lmhosts file does not exist by default, so you will have to create the file using the same format as the /etc/hosts file. This problem with this solution is that you have an extra step when you add a node to both the list files for the broadcast.ksh shell script and the lmhosts file.

Other Options to Consider

This is one of those shell scripts that you can do a lot of different things with. Here are a few things that I thought of. Use your imagination, and I'm sure that you can add to this list.

Producing Error Notifications

A very good use of this shell script is to set up as many groups as you need to do error notification to users responsible for maintaining particular machines, programs, databases, and applications. When an error is detected in one of the monitoring shell scripts, just send a pop-up message as an immediate notification; the email notification is just gravy on the potatoes. You can make this a powerful tool if you desire.

Add Logging of Unreachable Machines

If you redirect the output of the **smbclient** command in the shell script to a log file and parse the log file for connection and name resolution errors, you can find out who is not getting some messages, but not all. If a user's machine is turned off, the message is lost and there is no notification. Even if a message is refused by the host, the return code from the **smbclient** command is still 0, zero. Keeping a log of the activity and automatically parsing the log after each message is sent can help you find where the rejections occur. Just remember to keep it simple!

Create Two-Way Messaging

I wanted to figure out how to send the message from the Windows machines back to the Unix boxes, but I ran out of time to meet my due date. I am sure that this is not a hard task to solve. This is a good project for you to play around with; I am going to work on this one, too.

Summary

I sure hope that you enjoyed this chapter, and the whole book. The process of writing this book has been a thrill for me. Every time I started a new chapter I had a firm idea of what I wanted to accomplish, but usually along the way I got these little brain storms that help me build on the basic idea that I started with. Some five-page chapters turned into some of the longest chapters in the book. In every case, though, I always tried to hit the scripting techniques from a different angle. Sometimes this resulted in a long script or roundabout way of accomplishing the task. I really did do this on purpose. There is always more than one way to solve a challenge in Unix, and I always aimed to make each chapter different and interesting. I appreciate that you bought this book, and in return I hope I have given you valuable knowledge and insight into solving any problem that comes along. Now you can really say that the solution to any challenge is *intuitively obvious*! Thank you for reading, and best regards.

APPENDIX

A

What's on the Web Site

This Appendix shows a list of the shell scripts and functions that are include on the Web site. Each of the shell scripts and functions has a brief description of the purpose.

Shell Scripts

Chapter 2

```
12_ways_to_parse.ksh:
```

This script shows the different ways of reading a file line by line. Again there is not just one way to read a file line by line and some are faster than others and some are more intuitive than others.

```
mk_large_file.ksh:
```

This script is used to create a text file that is has a specified number of lines that is specified on the command line.

Chapter 3

No shell scripts to list in Chapter 3.

Chapter 4

`rotate.ksh:`

This shell script is used as a progress indicator with the appearance of a rotating line.

`countdown.ksh:`

This shell script is used as a progress indicator with a countdown to zero.

Chapter 5

`fs_mon_AIX.ksh:`

This shell script is used to monitor an AIX system for full filesystems using the percentage method.

`fs_mon_AIX_MBFREE.ksh:`

This shell script is used to monitor an AIX system for full filesystems using the MB free method.

`fs_mon_AIX_MBFREE_excep.ksh:`

This shell script is used to monitor an AIX system for full filesystems using the MB free method with exceptions capability.

`fs_mon_AIX_PC_MBFREE.ksh:`

This shell script is used to monitor an AIX system for full filesystems using the percentage method with exceptions capability.

`fs_mon_AIX_excep.ksh:`

Basic AIX filesystem monitoring using the percent method with exceptions capability.

`fs_mon_ALL_OS.ksh:`

This shell script auto detects the UNIX flavor and monitors the filesystems using both percent and MB free techniques with an auto detection to switch between methods.

`fs_mon_HPUX.ksh:`

This shell script is used to monitor a HP-UX system for full filesystems using the percentage method.

`fs_mon_HPUX_MBFREE.ksh:`

This shell script is used to monitor an HP-UX system for full filesystems using the MB free method.

`fs_mon_HPUX_MBFREE_excep.ksh:`

This shell script is used to monitor an HP-UX system for full filesystems using the percentage method with exceptions capability.

`fs_mon_HPUX_PC_MBFREE.ksh:`

This shell script is used to monitor an HP-UX system for full filesystems using the percentage method with exceptions capability.

`fs_mon_HPUX_excep.ksh:`

Basic HP-UX filesystem monitoring using the percent method with exceptions capability.

`fs_mon_LINUX.ksh:`

This shell script is used to monitor a Linux system for full filesystems using the percentage method.

`fs_mon_LINUX_MBFREE.ksh:`

This shell script is used to monitor a Linux system for full filesystems using the MB free method.

`fs_mon_LINUX_MBFREE_excep.ksh:`

This shell script is used to monitor a Linux system for full filesystems using the percentage method with exceptions capability.

`fs_mon_LINUX_PC_MBFREE.ksh:`

This shell script is used to monitor a Linux system for full filesystems using the percentage method with exceptions capability.

`fs_mon_LINUX_excep.ksh:`

Basic Linux filesystem monitoring using the percent method with exceptions capability.

`fs_mon_SUNOS.ksh:`

This shell script is used to monitor a SunOS system for full filesystems using the percentage method.

`fs_mon_SUNOS_MBFREE.ksh:`

This shell script is used to monitor a SunOS system for full filesystems using the MB free method.

`fs_mon_SUNOS_MBFREE_excep.ksh:`

This shell script is used to monitor a SunOS system for full filesystems using the percentage method with exceptions capability.

`fs_mon_SUNOS_PC_MBFREE.ksh:`

This shell script is used to monitor a SunOS system for full filesystems using the percentage method with exceptions capability.

`fs_mon_SUNOS_excep.ksh:`

Basic SunOS filesystem monitoring using the percent method with exceptions capability.

Chapter 6

`AIX_paging_mon.ksh:`

Shell script to monitor AIX paging space.

`HP-UX_swap_mon.ksh:`

Shell script to monitor HP-UX swap space.

`Linux_swap_mon.ksh`

Shell script to monitor Linux swap space.

`SUN_swap_mon.ksh:`

Shell script to monitor SunOS swap space.

`all-in-one_swapmon.ksh:`

Shell script to monitor AIX, HP-UX, Linux, and SunOS swap/paging space.

Chapter 7

`uptime_loadmon.ksh:`

System load monitor using the **uptime** command.

`uptime_fieldtest.ksh:`

Script to test the location of the latest uptime load information as it changes based on time.

`sar_loadmon.ksh:`

Load monitor using the **sar** command.

`iostat_loadmon.ksh:`

Load monitor using the **iostat** command.

`vmstat_loadmon.ksh:`

Load monitor using the **vmstat** command.

Chapter 8

`proc_mon.ksh:`

Process monitor that informs the user when the process ends.

`proc_wait.ksh:`

Process monitor that informs the user when the process starts.

`proc_watch.ksh:`

Process monitor that monitors a process as it starts and stops.

`proc_watch_timed.ksh:`

Process monitor that monitors a process for a user specified amount of time.

Chapter 9

There are no shell scripts to list in Chapter 9.

Chapter 10

`mk_passwd.ksh:`

This shell script is used to create pseudo-random passwords.

Chapter 11

`stale_LV_mon.ksh:`

This shell script is used to monitor AIX stale Logical Volumes.

`stale_PP_mon.ksh:`

This shell script is used to monitor AIX stale Physical Partitions.

`stale_VG_PV_LV_PP_mon.ksh:`

This shell script is used to monitor AIX stale partitions in Volume Groups, Physical Volumes, Logical Volumes, and Physical Partitions.

Chapter 12

`pingnodes.ksh:`

This shell script is used to **ping** nodes. The operating system can be AIX, HP-UX, Linux, or SunOS.

Chapter 13

`AIXsysconfig.ksh:`

This shell script is used to gather information about an AIX system's configuration.

Chapter 14

`chpwd_menu.ksh:`

This shell script uses **sudo** to allow support personnel to change passwords.

`sudo-1.6.3p7.tar.gz:`

This is a tar ball of the **sudo** source code.

Chapter 15

`hgrep.ksh:`

This shell script works similar to grep except that it shows the entire file with the pattern match highlighted in reverse video.

Chapter 16

enable_AIX_classic.ksh:

Enables all AIX "classic" print queues.

print_UP_AIX.ksh:

Enables all AIX System V printers and queues.

print_UP_HP-UX.ksh:

Enables all HP-UX System V printers and queues.

print_UP_Linux.ksh:

Enables all Linux System V printers and queues.

printing_only_UP_Linux.ksh:

Enables printing on Linux System V printers.

queuing_only_UP_Linux.ksh:

Enables queuing on Linux System V printers.

print_UP_SUN.ksh:

Enables all SunOS System V printers and queues.

PQ_all_in_one.ksh:

Enables all printing and queuing on AIX, HP-UX, Linux, and SunOS by auto detecting the UNIX flavor.

Chapter 17

tst_ftp.ksh:

Simple FTP automated file transfer test script.

get_remote_dir_listing.ksh:

Script to get a remote directory listing using FTP.

get_ftp_files.ksh:

Shell script to retrieve files from a remote machine using FTP.

`put_ftp_files.ksh:`

Shell script to upload files to a remote machine using FTP.

`get_remote_dir_listing_pw_var.ksh:`

Script to get a directory listing from a remote machine using FTP. The passwords are stored in an environment file somewhere on the system, defined in the script.

`get_ftp_files_pw_var.ksh:`

Script to retrieve files from a remote machine using FTP. This script gets its password from an environment file somewhere on the system, defined in the script.

`put_ftp_files_pw_var.ksh:`

Script to upload files to a remote machine using FTP. This script gets its password from an environment file somewhere on the system, defined in the script.

Chapter 18

`findlarge.ksh:`

This shell script is used to find "large" files. The file size limit is supplied on the command line and the search begins in the current directory.

Chapter 19

`broot:`

Shell script to capture keystrokes of anyone gaining root access.

`banybody:`

Shell script to capture keystrokes of any user defined in the shell script.

`log_keystrokes.ksh:`

Shell script to log a user's keystrokes as they type on the keyboard.

Chapter 20

`SSAidentify.ksh:`

Shell script to control SSA disk subsystem disk identification lights.

Chapter 21

`mk_unique_filename.ksh:`

This shell script creates unique filenames.

Chapter 22

`float_add.ksh:`

Adds a series of floating point numbers together using the **bc** utility.

`float_subtract.ksh:`

Subtracts floating point numbers using the **bc** utility.

`float_multiply.ksh:`

Multiplies a series of floating point numbers together using the **bc** utility.

`float_divide.ksh:`

Divides two floating point numbers using the **bc** utility.

`float_average.ksh:`

Averages a series of floating point numbers using the **bc** utility.

Chapter 23

`mk_swkey.ksh:`

Shell script to create a software license key using the hexadecimal representation of the IP address.

`equate_any_base.ksh:`

Converts numbers between any base.

`equate_base_2_to_16.ksh:`

Converts numbers from base 2 to base 16.

`equate_base_16_to_2.ksh:`

Converts numbers from base 16 to base 2.

```
equate_base_10_to_16.ksh:
```

Converts numbers from base 10 to base 16.

```
equate_base_16_to_10.ksh:
```

Concerts numbers from base 16 to base 2.

```
equate_base_10_to_2.ksh:
```

Converts numbers from base 10 to base 2.

```
equate_base_2_to_10.ksh:
```

Converts numbers from base 2 to base 10.

```
equate_base_10_to_8.ksh:
```

Converts numbers from base 10 to base 8.

```
equate_base_8_to_10.ksh:
```

Converts numbers from base 8 to base 10.

Chapter 24

```
operations_menu.ksh:
```

Shell script menu for an Operations staff.

Chaper 25

```
broadcast.ksh:
```

Shell script to send pop-up messages to Windows desktops. This shell script requires Samba to be installed on the UNIX machine.

Functions

Chapter 2

All of the following 12 functions are different methods to process a file line by line. The two fastest methods are tied for first place and are highlighted in boldface text.

```
while_read_LINE
while_read_LINE_bottom
cat_while_LINE_line
while_line_LINE
while_LINE_line_bottom
while_LINE_line_cmdsub2
while_LINE_line_bottom_cmdsub2
while_read_LINE_FD
while_LINE_line_FD
while_LINE_line_cmdsub2_FD
while_line_LINE_FD
```

Chapter 3

`send_notification:`

This function is used to send an email notification to a list of email addresses, specified by the `MAILLIST` variable defined in the main body of the shell script.

Chapter 4

`dots:`

This function is used as a progress indicator showing a series of dots every 10 seconds, or so.

`rotate:`

This function is used as a progress indicator showing the appearance of a rotating line.

Chapter 5

There are no functions to list in Chapter 5.

Chapter 6

`AIX_paging_mon:`

Function to monitor AIX paging space.

`HP_UX_swap_mon:`

Function to monitor HP-UX swap space.

```
Linux_swap_mon:
```

Function to monitor Linux swap space.

```
SUN_swap_mon:
```

Function to monitor SunOS swap space.

Chapter 7

There are no functions to list in Chapter 7.

Chapter 8

There are no functions to list in Chapter 8.

Chapter 9

```
check_HTTP_server:
```

This function is used to check an application Web server and application URL pages.

Chapter 10

```
in_range_random_number:
```

This function creates pseudo-random numbers within one and a "max value".

```
load_default_keyboard:
```

This function is used to load a USA 102-key board layout into a keyboard file.

```
check_for_and_create_keyboard_file:
```

If the $KEYBOARD_FILE does not exist then ask the user to load the "standard" keyboard layout, which is done with the `load_default_keyboard` function.

```
build_manager_password_report:
```

Build a file to print for the secure envelope.

Chapter 11

There are no functions to list in Chapter 11.

Chapter 12

```
ping_host:
```

This function executes the correct ping command based on UNIX, the UNIX flavor, AIX, HP-UX, Linux, or SunOS.

```
ping_nodes:
```

This function is used to ping a list of nodes stored in a file. This function requires the ping_host function.

Chapter 13

All of these functions are used in gathering system information from an AIX system. Refer to Chapter 13 for more details in the `AIXsysconfig.ksh` shell script.

```
get_host
get_OS
get_OS_level
get_ML_for_AIX
get_TZ
get_real_mem
get_arch
get_devices
get_long_devdir_listing
get_tape_drives
get_cdrom
get_adapters
get_routes
get_netstats
get_fs_stats
get_VGs
get_varied_on_VGs
get_LV_info
get_paging_space
get_disk_info
get_VG_disk_info
get_HACMP_info
get_printer_info
get_process_info
get_sna_info
get_udp_x25_procs
get_sys_cfg
get_long_sys_config
get_installed_filesets
check_for_broken_filesets
last_logins
```

Chapter 14

There are no functions to list in Chapter 14.

Chapter 15

There are no functions to list in Chapter 15.

Chapter 16

`AIX_classic_printing:`

Enables AIX print queues using the AIX "classic" printer subsystem.

`AIX_SYSV_printing:`

Enables AIX printers and queues using System V printing subsystem.

`HP_UX_printing:`

Enables HP-UX printers and print queues using System V printing.

`Linux_printing:`

Enables Linux printers and print queues using System V printing.

`Solaris_printing:`

Enables SunOS printers and print queues using System V printing.

Chapter 17

`pre_event:`

Function to allow for pre events before processing.

`post_event:`

Function to allow for post events after processing.

Chapter 18

There are no functions to list in Chapter 18.

Chapter 19

There are no functions to list in Chapter 19.

Chapter 20

`man_page:`

Function to create man page type information about the proper usage of the `SSAidentify.ksh` shell script.

`twirl:`

Progress indicator that looks like a "twirling", or rotating line.

`all_defined_pdisks:`

Function that lights all disk identification lights for all defined pdisks.

`all_varied_on_pdisks:`

Function that lights all disk identification lights that are in varied-on Volume Groups.

`list_of_disks:`

Function that acts on each pdisk by turning on/off the SSA disk identification lights.

Chapter 21

`get_random_number:`

This function produces a pseudo-random between 1 and 32,767.

`in_range_random_number:`

Create a pseudo-random number less than or equal to the `$UPPER_LIMIT` value, which is user defined.

Chapter 22

There are no functions to list in Chapter 22.

Chapter 23

There are no functions to list in Chapter 23.

Chapter 24

There are no functions to list in Chapter 24.

Chapter 25

```
check_for_null_message:
```

Checks to see if a variable is empty.

```
check_for_null_winlist:
```

Checks to see if a variable is empty.

```
check_for_smbclient_command:
```

Checks for the existence of the **smbclient** command and ensures the file is executable.

Index

SYMBOLS

* (asterisk), 28
\ (backslash), 2, 103, 265
` (back tic mark), 16
^ (caret), 105, 207, 622
$? (check return code), 25–26
: (colon)
  checking NFS for, 113–118
  getopts command and, 229, 562, 604
{} (curly braces), 104, 541
. (decimal point), 554
$ (dollar sign)
  numeric test comparison and, 120
  variable name and, 13, 151
&& (double ampersands), 407
$$ (double dollar signs), 524
== (double equal signs), 217
|| (double pipes), 407
" (double quotes)
  multiword string patterns and, 392
  uses of, 16
  variable and, 115
/ (forward slash), 471
' (forward tic mark), 2, 16
(hash mark), 5
- (hyphen), 562
- (minus) sign, 554
: (no-op), 58
% (percent) character, 103, 526

|& (pipe ampersand), 232
+ (plus) sign, 554
# (pound) operator, 527
? (question mark), 28, 562

A

accessing
  value of $# positional parameter, 45
  variable data, 13
adding list of numbers, 547–551, 555
AIX
  classic printer subsystem, 38, 404–408
  df -k command output, 130, 131
  iostat command output, 186
  Logical Volume Manager (LVM), 298
  lsps command, 146–147
  paging monitor, 149–155
  ping command syntax, 320
  pwdadm command, 385–389
  sar command output, 188–189
  system monitoring, 98–103
  system snapshot commands, 338–340
  system snapshot listing, 341–351
  system snapshot report output, 353–366
  System V output, 426
  System V printing, 408–414
  uptime command output, 180–181
  vmstat command output, 191
  See also stale disk partition, monitoring
    for

663

aliases for /etc/sudoers file, 384, 488
all_defined_pdisks function, 501–503
all_varied_on_pdisks function, 503–505
API (application program interface), 261
application monitoring
  APIs and SNMP traps, 261
  HTTP server, checking, 259–260
  local processes, 252–254
  Open Secure Shell and, 254–256
  Oracle databases, checking for, 256–259
  overview of, 251, 260
application program interface (API), 261
arguments, command switch and, 229.
    See also command-line arguments
arithmetic operators
  modulo, 267, 526
  overview of, 17
array
  creating, 418–419
  loading, 46–47, 264, 265–266, 280–281
  one-dimensional, 265
  uses of, 425
  working with, 419–420
array pointer, 264
ASCII text, 2
assigning variable, 13
asterisk (*), 28
at command, 28, 96
auditing root access, 476, 483–486
auto-detect techniques, 118
automated event notification
  basics of, 79–81
  file system monitoring and, 143–144
  techniques for, 79
automated FTP file transfer, 39
automated host pinging, 37
averaging series of numbers, 579–582
awk statement, 100, 307

B

background, co-process and, 245–246
backslash (\), 2, 103, 265
back tic mark (`), 16
basename command, 94–95
basename $0 command, 530
bc command and floating-point math,
    40–41, 545

bc utility
  float_add script, 546–552
  float_average script, 579–582
  float_divide script, 573–579
  float_multiply script, 565–570
  float_subtract script, 556–561
  functions, creating, 582–583
  here document, using, 555–556, 564–565
  Linux swap space monitor and, 160–161
  math statement, building, 554–555,
      563–564
  overview of, 545
  parsing command-line arguments with
      getopts, 561–563
  parsing command line for valid
      numbers, 570–572
  scale, removing from scripts, 582
  scale, setting, 161, 165, 556
  Solaris swap space monitor and, 165
  syntax, 545–546
  testing for integers and floating-point
      numbers, 552–554
bdf command, 132–133
bin directory, 103
blank line, removing from file, 44
boot logical volume, 300
bounce account, 480
break command, 9
broadcasting message
  to all users, 621–622
  error notifications, 645
  groups, adding, 623
  to individual destinations, 623–627
  log file and, 645
  overview of, 43, 619
  script for, 631–639
  sending message, 629–630
  testing user input, 627–629
build_manager_password_report function,
    271–274
built-in tests, 26

C

calling function, 2
capturing
  large list of files, 39
  user keystrokes, 40, 475–476, 480–483

caret (^), 105, 207, 622
case sensitivity, 1
case statement, 8, 437–438
catching delayed command output, 32–33
cat command, 57–58
cc, 371
CD-ROM
 files, script stub and, 5–6
 monitoring and, 98–99
check_exceptions function, 114
check_for_and_create_keyboard_file
  function, 270–271
check_for_null_message function, 629
check_for_null_winlist function, 628
check_for_smbclient_command function,
  639–640
check_HTTP_server function, 259–260
check return code ($?), 25–26
chmod command, 18–20
cleanup function, 500–501
colon (:)
 checking NFS for, 113–118
 getopts command and, 229, 562, 604
columns heading, removing in command
  output, 45–46
command-line arguments
 overview of, 13–14
 parsing with getopts, 29–30, 244–245,
   561–563, 602–604, 624–626
 special parameters and, 15–16
 testing and parsing, 275–279
commands
 at, 28, 96
 AIX classic print control, 404–408
 AIX System V print control, 408–414
 basename, 94–95
 basename $0, 530
 bc, 40–41, 545
 break, 9
 cat, 57–58
 catching delayed output, 32–33
 chmod, 18–20
 compress, 493
 configure, 371–375
 crontab, 27
 cut, 150
 date, 467, 472, 540
 df -k, 98, 130–132

disk subsystem, 298–299
echo, 35, 88, 89, 498–499, 524–525
echo $#, 275
enq -A, 404–405
env, 456
executing in sub-shell, 417
exit, 9, 483
find, 39, 465, 466–473
free (Linux), 148
ftp, 442, 443, 463
gunzip, 371
gzip, 493
hostname, 467, 478
HP-UX print control, 414–417
iostat, 179, 186–188, 203–208
kill, 500–501
last, 22–23
line, 54, 58–62
Linux print control, 417–422
list of, 10–12
lpc (AIX), 408–412
lpc (Linux), 417–418
lpc (Solaris), 425–429
lpstat (AIX), 412–414
lpstat (HP-UX), 414–417
lpstat (Solaris), 429–431
lsdev, 501–503
lslv, 299
lsps (AIX), 146–147
lspv, 299, 304, 504
lsvg, 298, 299, 308
lsvg -o, 504
mail notification, 34–35, 80–83
make, 371, 375–377
make install, 377
manual page, printing, 465
more, 392, 393, 399, 471
number base conversion, 41–42
pg or page, 392, 393, 399
ping, 37–38, 251, 319
printf, 41–42, 586–587
ps, 23
ps auxw, 179, 213–214
ps -ef, 216, 252, 257
pwd, 466, 467, 471
pwdadm, 385–389
read, 53–54, 60
real-time user communication, 24

commands *(continued)*
  remote, running, 255–256
  removing columns heading in output,
      45–46
  return, 9
  rsh, 20–21
  running on remote host, 20–21
  rwall, 24
  sar, 179, 188–191, 197–203, 214
  select, 42–43
  sendmail, 34–35, 83–84, 330
  set -A, 46–47, 265, 418
  shift, 14–15, 571, 607
  smbclient, 619–621, 630
  Solaris print control, 425–431
  sqlplus, 257–258
  ssaidentify, 496–497, 503
  ssaxlate, 315–316, 496, 504
  ssh, 254
  sudo program and, 369–370
  su (switch user), 478, 492
  swapinfo (HP-UX), 147–148
  swap (Solaris), 148–149
  symbol commands, 13
  system snapshot for AIX, 338–340
  tail, 45–46, 405
  talk, 24
  tee, 223
  tee -a, 352, 422
  time, 56, 67
  touch, 446
  tput, 38, 389, 400–401
  tput rmso, 392
  tput smso, 154, 392
  tr, 24–25
  tty, 223
  typeset, 24–25, 41, 529, 585–586
  uname, 128, 176
  uniq, 43–44, 622
  uptime, 179, 180–186, 194–197
  user information, 22–23
  vmstat, 179, 191–193, 208–212
  w, 22
  wall, 24
  which, 640
  who, 22
  write, 24
  See also getopts command; script
      command

command substitution
  back tics and, 16
  description of, 60
  experiment using, 393
  options for, 323
  timing methods of, 77–78
comments, 4–6
communicating with users, 23–24
compiling sudo, 371–372
compress command, 493
compressing file, 493
configure command, 371–375
configuring sudo, 378–384
continue, 9
control structures, 6–8
converting numbers between bases
  base 2 (binary) to base 16 (hexadecimal),
      587–590
  base 8 to base 16, 586
  base 10 (decimal) to base 16
      (hexadecimal), 590–593
  base 10 to base 16, 586
  base 10 to hexadecimal, 587
  base 10 to octal, 587
  beginning of main, 606–608
  overview of, 41–42, 585
  parsing command-line argument with
      getopts, 602–604
  sanity checks, 604–606
  software key, creating, 594–597, 608
  translation between any base, 597–608
  typeset command syntax, 585–586
co-process
  with background function, making,
      30–32
  process monitoring and, 245–246
  setting up, 230–231
countdown indicator, 91–96
COUNT variable, 570
CPU load monitoring. *See* system load
  monitoring
cron table
  automated hosts pinging and, 335
  file system monitoring and, 143–144
  overview of, 27–28
  pinging and, 321
  printing, queuing, and, 409, 418
  silent running and, 29
curly braces ({}), 104, 541

current directory, searching and, 472
cut command, 150

D

date command, 467, 472, 540
debug mode, automated FTP and, 463
decimal point (.), 554
declaring
  function, 3
  shell, 3–4
default shell, 3
defining
  function, 120, 340–341, 351
  trigger value, 118
/dev/random, 524
df -k command
  AIX output, 130, 131
  Linux output, 131
  overview of, 98
  SUN/Solaris output, 132
dial-out modem software, 84–85
directory, adding to path, 466
directory listing, saving remote, 444–446
dividing numbers, 573–579
dollar sign ($)
  numeric test comparison and, 120
  variable name and, 13, 151
dotting filename, 456–457
double ampersands (&&), 407
double bracket test for character data, 73
double dollar signs ($$), 524
double equal signs (==), 217
double parentheses mathematical test, 73,
  151
double pipes (| |), 407
double quotes (")
  multiword string patterns and, 392
  uses of, 16
  variable and, 115
downloading
  Samba, 642–643
  sudo program, 370–371

E

echo command
  cursor control commands for, 498–499
  RANDOM environment variable and,
    524–525
  series of dots and, 35, 88, 89

echo $# command, 275
egrep statement
  file system monitoring and, 144
  grep compared to, 99, 410
  -v argument, 99–100, 133–134
email as repository for log files, 479–480,
  486, 493
enclosures, 16
encryption key, 254
enq -A command, 404–405
enterprise management tool, 85, 86, 261
env command, 456
EOF character string, 555, 564
error log, 520
error notification, 645
escaping special character, 2, 265
/etc/motd file, 23
/etc/sudoers file
  samples, 378–384, 486–488
  troubleshooting, 494
eval function, 626–627
event notification
  basics of, 79–81
  file system monitoring and, 143
  monitoring for stale disk partition, 316
  swap space monitoring and, 177
  techniques for, 79
events, pre, startup, and/or post, running,
  228–229, 249
exceptions capability
  exceptions file, 103–110
  MB of free space with exceptions
    method, 113–118
  print queue and, 439
executing
  command in sub-shell, 417
  shell script recursively, 485–486
exit command, 9, 483
exit criteria, 616
exit signals, 21
exporting password variable, 456

F

file descriptors
  overview of, 54
  parsing file with, 63–66
  timing data and, 67, 73
filename
  creating unique, 535–543
  dotting, 456–457

filename *(continued)*
  log files, 478
  See also pseudo-random number, creating
files
  aliases for sendmail, 83
  capturing large list of, 39
  CD-ROM, 5–6
  compressing, 493
  .forward, 82–83, 480
  gzip, 371
  highlighting text in, 38
  large, finding, 465
  permissions and chmod command, 18–20
  processing line by line, 33
  .profile, ownership of, 477
  searching for newly created, 473
  See also filename; find command
file system monitoring
  automated execution, 143–144
  command syntax, 98–103
  egrep statement, modifying, 144
  event notification, 143
  exceptions capability, adding, 103–110
  full, defining, 100–101
  MB of free space method, 110–113
  MB of free space with exceptions
    method, 113–118
  percentage used-MB free combination,
    118–128
  techniques for, 97
  Unix flavors and, 128–130
  See also operating system (OS)
File Transfer Protocol. *See* FTP
find command
  large file script, creating, 466–472
  options for searching, 472–473
  overview of, 39, 465
  syntax, 466
flexibility in scripting, 249
floating-point math
  float_add script, 546–552
  float_average script, 579–582
  float_divide script, 573–579
  float_multiply script, 565–570
  float_subtract script, 556–561
  functions, creating, 582–583
  here document, using, 555–556, 564–565
  Linux swap space monitor and, 160–161
  math statement, building, 554–555,
    563–564

  overview of, 545
  parsing command-line arguments with
    getopts, 561–563
  parsing command line for valid
    numbers, 570–572
  scale, removing from scripts, 582
  scale, setting, 161, 165, 556
  Solaris swap space monitor and, 165
  syntax, 545–546
  testing for integers and floating-point
    numbers, 552–554
floating printer, 439
for ... in statement, 7
.forward file, 82–83, 480
forward slash (/), 471
forward tic mark ('), 2, 16
free command (Linux), 148
FTP (File Transfer Protocol)
  automation of, 39, 441, 444
  controlling execution with command-line
    switches, 463
  debug mode, adding, 463
  getting files from remote system, 446–450
  here document and, 442–443
  log file, adding, 463
  modifying script to use password
    variables, 456–463
  pre and post events, 449
  replacing hard-coded passwords with
    variables, 452–456
  saving remote directory listing, 444–446
  syntax for, 441–444
  typical file download, 442
  uploading files to remote system,
    450–452
ftp command, 442, 443, 463
full pathname, 471
functions
  all_defined_pdisks, 501–503
  all_varied_on_pdisks, 503–505
  build_manager_password_report,
    271–274
  calling, 119
  check_exceptions, 114
  check_for_and_create_keyboard_file,
    270–271
  check_for_null_message, 629
  check_for_null_winlist, 628
  check_for_smbclient_command, 639–640
  check_HTTP_server, 259–260

cleanup, 500–501
converting shell script into, 175–176
declaring, 3
defining, 120, 340–341, 351
eval, 626–627
form of, 3
get_max, 212–213
getopts, 278
get_random_number, 525
in_range_fixed_length_random_number,
    527–528
in_range_random_number, 267–268
as interpreted, 2
list_of_disks, 506–507
load_default_keyboard, 268–270
man_page, 499
mathematical, built-in, 18
overview of, 2–3
positional parameters and, 14
send_notification, 83–84
show_all_instances_status, 257
show_oratab_instances, 256
simple_SQL_query, 258
trap_exit, 275
twirl, 499–500
usage, 274–275, 497–498
on Web site for book, 656–662

G
gcc, 371
get_max function, 212–213
getopts command
  automating FTP and, 463
  limitations of, 246
  parsing command-line arguments with,
    29–30, 244–245, 278–279, 561–563,
    602–604, 624–626
  process monitoring and, 218, 228,
    229–230
getopts function, 212–213
get_random_number function, 525
global variable, 582
goal of script, 2
grep statement
  egrep compared to, 99
  exceptions capability and, 104–105
  process monitoring and, 214
  ps -ef command and, 216
  rows and, 307

uptime field test solution and, 184–186
  See also hgrep (highlighted grep)
group, broadcasting message to, 623
gunzip command, 371
gzip command, 493
gzip file, 371

H
hash mark (#), 5
hdisk#
  cross-referencing to pdisk#, 520
  overview of, 495
  translating to pdisk#, 496
here document
  bc utility and, 545–546, 555–556, 564–565
  FTP process and, 442–443
  swap space monitor and, 161, 165–166
  syntax for, 9–10
hgrep (highlighted grep)
  building shell script, 393–394
  listing, 394–399
  overview of, 391
  reverse video control, 392–393
highlighting text in file, 38
$HOME/.profile, 617
hostname command, 467, 478
HP-UX
  bdf command output, 132–133
  iostat command output, 186–187
  ping command syntax, 320
  print control commands, 414–417
  sar command output, 189
  swapinfo command, 147–148
  swap space monitor, 155–160
  uptime command output, 181–182
  vmstat command output, 191
HTTP server, checking, 259–260
hyphen (-), 562

I
identifying
  hardware components, Unix flavor and,
    495
  SSA disk, 496–497
if statement, tests used in, 330
if ... then ... elif ... (else) statement, 7
if ... then ... else statement, 6
if ... then ... fi statement, 417
if ... then statement, 6

input redirection, 58
in_range_fixed_length_random_number
function, 527–528
in_range_random_number function,
267–268
integer, testing for, 552–554
iostat command, 179, 186–188, 203–208
IP address, creating software key based
on, 594–597, 608

J
job control, 28–32
junk variable, 420

K
kill command, 500–501

L
large file, searching for, 466–473
last command, 22–23
$LENGTH, testing for integer value,
277–278
line, rotating, creating, 35–36, 89–91, 95–96,
499–500
line command, 54, 58–62
Linux
controlling queuing and printing
individually, 422–425
df -k command output, 131
free command, 148
iostat command output, 187
ping command syntax, 320
print control commands, 417–422
sar command output, 189
swap space monitor, 160–164
System V output, 409, 426
uptime command output, 182
vmstat command output, 192
linx command-line browser, 259–260
listings
AIX lsps -s data gathering, 150
AIX paging monitor, 151–153, 154
AIX system snapshot commands,
338–340
AIX System V printing, 411–412
all_defined_pdisks function, 503
all-in-one paging and swap space
monitor, 169–175

automated FTP, 444
averaging list of numbers, 581
base 2 (binary) to base 16 (hexadecimal)
conversion, 588–589
base 10 (decimal) to base 16
(hexadecimal) conversion, 590–592
broadcasting message, 621–622
build_manager_password_report
function, 272
case statement for iostat fields of data, 188
case statement for sar fields of data, 190
case statement for vmstat fields of data,
192–193
cat $FILENAME | while line LINE
method, 60
cat $FILENAME | while LINE=$(line)
method, 62
cat $FILENAME | while LINE=`line`
method, 59
cat $FILENAME | while read LINE
method, 57
check_exceptions function, 114
check_for_and_create_keyboard_file
function, 270–271
check_for_null_message function, 629
check_for_null_winlist function, 628
check_for_smbclient_command function,
639–640
check_HTTP_server function, 259–260
cleanup function, 501
configure command output, 371–375
controlling case statement to pick OS,
437–438
co-process, 231
countdown indicator, 92–94
cursor control using echo command, 499
dividend and divisor, extracting, 573–574
equate_any_base, 598–601
/etc/sudoers file samples, 378–381,
381–384, 486–488
exceptions file, 109
exceptions file that worked best with
testers, 127–128
filename, creating unique, 536–539,
541–543
file system monitoring for AIX, 101–102
file system monitoring for AIX with
exceptions capability, 106–109

finding large file, 467–470, 471–472

fixed-length random number output, 528

float_add script, 547–551, 555

float_average script in action, 581

float_divide script, 574–579

float_multiply script, 565–570, 572

float_subtract script, 556–561, 565

for loop enabling classic AIX print queues, 406–407

FTP file download, 442

full filesystem on yogi script, 110

full filesystem script, 103

getopts command line parsing, 279

getopts command usage, 229–230

getopts function, 278

get_random_number function, 525

get remote directory listing, 445

get remote directory listing, hard-coded passwords removed, 457–458

getting files from remote system, 446–448, 449–450

getting files from remote system, hard-coded passwords removed, 458–460

grep mistake, 104–105

here document for FTP, 442–443

hgrep, 394–399

HP-UX print control, 416

HP-UX swapinfo -tm command output, 155

HP-UX swap space monitor, 157–158

HP-UX swap space report, 159–160

in_range_fixed_length_random_number function, 527–528

in_range_random_number function, 268, 526

iostat load monitoring, 203–205, 207–208

$LENGTH, testing for integer value, 277–278

Linux, controlling printing individually, 422–423

Linux, controlling queuing individually, 424

Linux print control, 420–421

Linux swap space monitor, 162–163, 164

list_of_disks function, 506–507

load_default_keyboard function, 268–269

loading KEYS array, 280–281

logging keystrokes, 480–482

logging root access, 483–485

logic code for large and small filesystem freespace script, 119

looping in background, 88

loop list, building, 281–282

lpstat command output, 413, 429–430

lpstat command using -a and -p, 414, 430

lpstat or enq -A command output, 404

lpstat -W or enq -AW command output, 405

lsdev listing of pdisks, 502

lsvg -l appvg2 rootvg command output, 300

LV, loop to show number of stale PPs from each, 302

LV statistics, 301

mail code segment, 81

mail service, testing, 82

make command output, 375–377

make install command output, 377

MB of free space method, 111–113

MB of free space with exceptions method, 115–118

monitor all OS, 134–141

monitoring administration users, 489–492

monitoring application process, 253

my_sql_query.sql, 257

operating system test, 129

operations menu, 612–616

paging and swap space report, 146

parsing command line, 606–607

parsing command-line switches with getopts, 624–625

parsing numbers from command line, 572

password file with variable exported, 453–454

password file with variable not exported, 454

password report, 273–274

password report, printing, 283–284

password, testing visibility of, 455

percentage free-MB free combination, 121–127

pinging, automated hosts, with notification, 324–328, 331

pop-up messages, sending to Windows, 631–639, 641

listings *(continued)*
  printing and queuing all-in-one, 431–436
  process monitoring, 218–222, 223
  process monitoring and logging,
      224–227, 228
  process monitoring timed execution,
      232–244
  process monitoring timed execution in
      action, 248
  process startup loop, 216–217
  process wait, 218
  progress indicator background function,
      89
  pseudo-random number, creating,
      531–535
  pseudo-random password, 284–294
  pseudo-random password, building new,
      282
  PV statistics, 305
  reverse video menu options, 610–611
  reverse video message bar, 611
  rotate function, 90, 91
  running remote command, 255–256
  running total of numbers, 580–581
  Samba source code installation, 642
  sar load monitoring, 198–200, 202
  script for timing of line by line
      processing, 55–56
  script session, command-line, 476–477
  secure shell login, 254–255
  sending message to list of nodes, 630
  send_notification function, 83–84, 331
  shell script starter file, 5–6
  shift command, 14–15
  show_all_instances_status function, 257
  show_oratab_instances function, 256
  simple_SQL_query function, 258
  software key, creating, 594–595
  Solaris print commands, 427–428
  Solaris swap space monitor, 166–168, 169
  sorted timing data by method, 75–76
  SQL+ Oracle query, 258–259
  SSA identify, 507–519
  stale LV monitoring, 303–304
  stale PP monitoring, 305–306
  sudo, using first time, 385
  sudo, using in shell script, 386–388
  sudo log file, 389–390
  system snapshot for AIX, 341–351

  system snapshot for AIX report output,
      353–366
  testing command input, 72
  testing command-line arguments,
      276–277
  testing for integers and floating-point
      numbers, 552–553
  timing command substitution methods,
      77
  timing data for each method, 73–75
  timing script, 67–72
  twirl function, 500
  typeset command in random number
      function, 529
  typeset command to fix length of
      variable, 529
  uploading files to remote system,
      450–452
  uploading files to remote system, hard-
      coded passwords removed, 460–462
  uptime field test solution, 184–185
  uptime load monitoring, 194–196, 197
  usage function, 274, 497–498
  /usr/local/bin/exceptions file, 142
  verifying number base variables, 604–605
  VG, LV, and PV monitoring with resync,
      308–313
  vmstat load monitoring, 208–212
  while_line_LINE_Bottom method, 59, 76
  while LINE=`line` from Bottom, 61
  while LINE=$(line) from Bottom method,
      62
  while line LINE with file descriptors
      method, 66
  while LINE=$(line) with file descriptors
      method, 65
  while LINE='line' with file descriptors
      method, 64–65
  while read $FILENAME from Bottom, 58
  while read LINE method, 64
list_of_disks function, 506–507
load_default_keyboard function, 268–270
loading
  array, 46–47, 264, 265–266, 280–281
  default keyboard layout, 268
log file
  automated FTP and, 463
  automated hosts pinging, adding to,
      333–334

emailing, 479–480, 486, 493
filename, 478
monitoring for stale disk partition, 316
pop-up message and, 645
print queue and, 439
sudo program, 389–390
swap space monitoring and, 177
user activity and, 478–479
logging process starts and stops, 223–228
logical AND, 17, 407
logical OR, 17, 407
Logical Volume Manager (LVM, AIX), 298
loop counter, 410
looping techniques for parsing file line by
    line
  cat $FILENAME | while line LINE
     method, 60–61
  cat $FILENAME | while LINE=$(line)
     method, 61–62
  cat $FILENAME | while LINE=`line`
     method, 59–60
  cat $FILENAME | while read LINE
     method, 57–58, 77
  command syntax, 53–54
  file for testing timing of, 54–56
  techniques for, 33
  timing command substitution methods,
    77–78
  timing data for each method, 73–77
  timing methods, 66–67
  timing script, 67–72
  while_line_LINE_Bottom method, 58–59,
    76
  while LINE=`line` from Bottom, 61
  while LINE=$(line) from Bottom method,
    62
  while line LINE with file descriptors
    method, 66
  while LINE=$(line) with file descriptors
    method, 65–66
  while LINE='line' with file descriptors
    method, 64–65
  while read $FILENAME from Bottom
    method, 58
  while read LINE with file descriptors
    method, 63–64, 76–77
lpc command
  AIX, 408–412
  Linux, 417–418
  Solaris, 425–429

lpstat command
  AIX, 404–405, 412–414
  HP-UX, 414–417
  Solaris, 429–431
lsdev command, 501–503
lslv command, 299
lsps command (AIX), 146–147
lspv command, 299, 304, 504
lsvg command, 298, 299, 308
lsvg -o command, 504

M

mail command
  automated event notification with, 80–81
  syntax, 34
  -v switch, 82–83
mail notification techniques, 34–35
mailx command
  automated event notification with, 80
  syntax, 34
  -v switch, 82–83
maintenance window
  communicating with users and, 23
  printing and, 439
make command, 371, 375–377
Makefile, configuring, 371–375
make install command, 377
man_page function, 499
manual page, printing, 465
math
  bc command for floating-point, 40–41,
    545
  functions, built-in, 18
  modulo operator, 267, 526
  operators, 17
  See also bc utility
MB (megabytes), size of, 473
measurement type, 111
memory, paging and swap space and,
  145–146
memory leak, 153
menu, creating
  for Operations staff, 609–618
  select command and, 42–43
message, broadcasting. *See* pop-up
  messages, sending to Windows
message bar, creating, 611–612
mget subcommand, 449
MIB (Management Information Base), 86
Miller, Todd, 370, 378

minus (-) sign, 554
model dialing software, 84–85
modulo arithmetic operator, 267, 526
monitoring. *See* application monitoring;
　file system monitoring; process
　monitoring; script command; system
　load monitoring
more command, 392, 393, 399, 471
multiplying list of numbers, 565–570, 572

N
named pipe, creating, 493
nlist subcommand, 444–446
no-op (:), 58
notification of event. *See* event notification
null value check, 114
null variable, testing for, 44, 115
number. *See* bc utility; pseudo-random
　number, creating
number base conversion
　base 2 (binary) to base 16 (hexadecimal),
　　587–590
　base 8 to base 16, 586
　base 10 (decimal) to base 16
　　(hexadecimal), 590–593
　base 10 to base 16, 586
　base 10 to hexadecimal, 587
　base 10 to octal, 587
　beginning of main, 606–608
　overview of, 41–42, 585
　parsing command-line argument with
　　getopts, 602–604
　sanity checks, 604–606
　software key, creating, 594–597, 608
　translation between any base, 597–608
　typeset command syntax, 585–586
numeric test comparison, 120

O
Open Secure Shell (OpenSSH), 21, 254–256
operating system (OS)
　command syntax, output, and, 130–134
　controlling case statement to pick,
　　437–438
　exceptions file listing, 142
　file system monitoring and, 128–130
　/home filesystem, 142–143
　monitor all OS listing, 134–141
　See also specific operating systems

Operations staff, menu for
　overview of, 609
　reverse video syntax, 610–618
operators
　math, 17
　modulo arithmetic, 267, 526
　numeric, 120
　pound (#), 527
Oracle database, checking for, 256–259
OS. *See* operating system
outbound mail, problems with, 82–84
output control, 28–32

P
padding number with leading zeros,
　527–530
page command, 392, 393, 399
pager notification, 143
paging space. *See* swap space
parameters
　positional, 13–14, 45, 601–602
　special, 15–16
parsing
　command-line arguments, 29–30,
　　275–279
　command-line arguments with getopts,
　　244–245, 561–563, 602–604, 624–626
　command line for valid numbers,
　　570–572
　file with file descriptors, 63–66
　file with line command, 54, 58–62
　See also processing file line by line
passwords
　hard-coded, 446
　hard-coded, replacing, 452–456
　page of, printing, 264, 271–272, 283–284,
　　294
　password environment file, creating,
　　456–457
　pwdadm command, 385–389
　randomness and, 263
　root, auditing, 476, 483–486
　root, protecting, 369
　secure, 264, 273
　selecting, 295
　sudo program and, 369–370
　See also pseudo-random password
path, adding directory to, 466
pattern matching and set statement, 391

pdisk#
  all_defined_pdisks function, 501–503
  all_varied_on_pdisks function, 503–505
  cross-referencing to hdisk#, 520
  list_of_disks function, 506–507
  lsdev command and, 501–502
  overview of, 495
  translating hdisk# to, 496
percent (%) character, 103, 526
pg command, 392, 393, 399
PID (process ID), 263, 524
ping command, 37–38, 251, 319
pinging, automated hosts, with notification
  cron table entry and, 335
  /etc/hosts file compared to list file, 333
  functions, 329–331
  listing, 324–328
  logging capability, adding, 333–334
  options for convenience, 321
  overview of, 319
  pager notification, 334–335
  $PINGLIST variable length limit
      problem, 332–333
  script in action listing, 331
  syntax, 320
  trap, creating, 323
  "unknown host" and, 334
  variables, defining, 321–323
pipe ampersand (| &), 232
piping
  to background, 231, 232
  co-process to background, 31–32
  file output to while loop, 57–58
  to tee -a command, 352
plus (+) sign, 554
pop-up messages, sending to Windows
  to all users, 621–622
  error notifications, 645
  groups, adding, 623
  to individual destinations, 623–627
  log file and, 645
  overview of, 43, 619
  script for, 631–639
  sending message, 629–630
  testing user input, 627–629
positional parameters
  accessing value of $#, 45
  overview of, 13–14
  referring to, 601–602

pound (#) operator, 527
printers
  AIX classic print control commands,
      404–408
  AIX System V print control commands,
      408–414
  controlling case statement to pick OS,
      437–438
  exceptions capability and, 439
  HP-UX print control commands, 414–417
  keeping enabled, 38–39
  Linux, controlling queuing and printing
      individually, 422–425
  Linux print control commands, 417–422
  log file and, 439
  maintenance and, 439
  printing and queuing all-in-one listing,
      431–436
  scheduling, 439
  Solaris print control commands, 425–431
  status information, 413–414
  See also printing
printf command, 41–42, 586–587
printing
  manual page, 465
  page of passwords, 264, 271–272,
      283–284, 294
  See also printers; System V printing
process ID (PID), 263, 524
processing file line by line
  cat $FILENAME | while line LINE
      method, 60–61
  cat $FILENAME | while LINE=$(line)
      method, 61–62
  cat $FILENAME | while LINE=`line`
      method, 59–60
  cat $FILENAME | while read LINE
      method, 57–58, 77
  command syntax, 53–54
  file for testing timing of, 54–56
  techniques for, 33
  timing command substitution methods,
      77–78
  timing data for each method, 73–77
  timing methods, 66–67
  timing script, 67–72
  while_line_LINE_Bottom method, 58–59,
      76
  while LINE=`line` from Bottom, 61

processing file line by line *(continued)*
  while LINE=$(line) from Bottom method, 62
  while line LINE with file descriptors method, 66
  while LINE=$(line) with file descriptors method, 65–66
  while LINE='line' with file descriptors method, 64–65
  while read $FILENAME from Bottom method, 58
  while read LINE with file descriptors method, 63–64, 76–77
process monitoring
  common uses of scripts, 248
  end of process, 218–223
  logging starts and stops, 223–228
  modifications to scripts, 248–249
  overview of, 215–216
  startup loop, 216–218
  timed execution, 228–230
.profile file, ownership of, 477
progress indicator
  countdown indicator, 91–96
  creating, 35–36
  overview of, 87
  rotating line, 89–91
  series of dots, 87–89, 95
ps auxw command, 179, 213–214
ps command, 23
ps -ef command, 216, 252, 257
pseudo-random number, creating
  filename, creating unique, 535–543
  fixed-length numbers between 1 and user-defined maximum, 527–530
  numbers between 0 and 32,767, 525–526
  numbers between 1 and user-defined maximum, 526
  overview of, 36, 523, 524
  random number, description of, 523–524
  shell script listing, 531–535
  shell script overview, 530–531
  software key creation and, 608
  techniques for, 524
pseudo-random password
  array, loading, 280–281
  building new, 282–283
  creating, 264

functions, defining, 267–275
  keyboard file, checking for, 280
  listing, 284–294
  loop list, building, 281–282
  page of, printing, 264, 271–272, 283–284, 294
  syntax, 264–266
  testing and parsing command-line arguments, 275–279
  trap, setting, 280
  variables, defining, 266–267
pwdadm command, 385–389
pwd command, 466, 467, 471

Q
querying system for name of shell script, 530
question mark (?), 28, 562
queuing. *See* printers

R
random number, 523–524. *See also* pseudo-random number, creating
read command, 53–54, 60
rebooting system, 337
redirecting standard error to standard output, 366
relative pathname, 470–471
remote command, running, 255–256
remote host, running commands on, 20–21
removing
  blank lines in file, 44
  columns heading in command output, 45–46
  repeated lines in file, 43–44
repeated line, removing from file, 43–44
resyncing, 313
return code, checking, 25–26
return command, 9
reverse video
  control commands, 392–393
  highlighting text using, 391
  Operations menu, 610–618
  turning on and off, 154
root access, auditing, 476, 483–486
root access, restricted. *See* sudo (superuser do) program
rsh command, 20–21

running
  commands on remote host, 20–21
  pre, startup, and/or post events,
      228–229, 249
  printers, 38–39
  remote command, 255–256
  shell script, 3–4
  silent, 28–29, 63
run queue, 194
rwall command, 24

S

Samba
  downloading, 642–643
  overview of, 24, 619
  testing smbclient program, 643–644
  See also smbclient command
sanity check, 113–115
sar command, 179, 188–191, 197–203, 214
saving remote directory listing with FTP,
    444–446
scale
  description of, 545
  removing from scripts, 582
  setting, 161, 165, 556
scheduling
  monitoring, 177
  printers, 439
scope of variable, 14, 120
script command
  emailing audit logs, 493
  logging user activity, 40, 478–479, 480–483
  monitoring administration users, 489–492
  options, 493–494
  overview of, 475
  repository for log files, 479–480
  starting monitoring session, 479
  syntax, 476–477
  uses of, 477
searching for large file, 466–473
security
  monitoring user action, 475–476
  pseudo-random numbers and, 543
  See also passwords
sed statement
  character substitution and removal and,
      101, 102–103
  highlighting text in file and, 38

pattern matching and, 391
  removing blank lines from file and, 44
  reverse video control and, 392
seed, 267, 524
select command, 42–43
sending pop-up messages to Windows.
    See pop-up messages, sending to
    Windows
sendmail command, 34–35, 83–84, 330
Serial Storage Architecture (SSA)
  control functions, 501–507
  disk identification, 495
  error log, 520
  executing commands, 520–521
  identifying disks listing, 507–519
  identifying disks listing explanation,
      519–520
  syntax, 496–497
  usage and user feedback functions,
      497–501
set -A command, 46–47, 265, 418
set statement, 391
sgid, 18
shell, 2
shell script
  comments and style in, 4–6
  as interpreted, 2
  running, 3–4
shift command, 14–15, 571, 607
show_all_instances_status function, 257
show_oratab_instances function, 256
silent running, 28–29, 63
simple_SQL_query function, 258
smbclient command, 619–621, 630
snapshot information
  AIX commands listing, 338–340
  commands, selecting, 337–338
  determining statistics to include, 367
  functions, defining, 340–341, 352
  listing, 341–351
  listing explanation, 351–353
  report output, 353–366
  storing, 337
  variables, defining, 352
SNMP (Simple Network Management
    Protocol), 86
SNMP trap, 85–86, 261

software
  dial-out modem, 84–85
  license key, creating, 594–597, 608
  See also Samba; sudo (superuser do)
      program
Solaris
  df -k command output, 132
  iostat command output, 187
  ping command syntax, 320
  print control commands, 425–431
  sar command output, 190
  swap command, 148–149
  swap space monitor, 164–169
  System V output, 409, 426
  uptime command output, 183
  vmstat command output, 192
special characters, escaping, 2
special parameters, 15–16
SQL+ database query, 258–259
sqlplus command, 257–258
SSA. *See* Serial Storage Architecture
ssaidentify command, 496–497, 503
ssaxlate command, 315–316, 496, 504
ssh command, 254
stale disk partition, monitoring for
  automated execution, 316
  disk subsystem commands, 298–299
  event notification, 316–317
  Logical Volume Manager (LVM), 298
  LV level, stale PPs at, 299–304
  overview of, 37, 297
  PV level, stale PPs at, 304–307
  SSA disks, 315–316
  VG, LV, and PV monitoring with resync,
      308–315
starting and stopping all printing and
  queuing, 409
startup event, 228–229, 249
stderr file descriptor, 54, 63
stdin file descriptor, 54, 63
stdout file descriptor, 54, 63
sticky bit, setting, 18
storing log file, 479, 493
string, testing, 47–50
style, 4–6
sub-shell, executing command in, 417
subtracting list of numbers, 556–561, 565

sudo (superuser do) program
  compiling, 371–377
  configure command output, 371–375
  configuring, 378–384
  downloading, 370–371
  /etc/sudoers file samples, 378–381,
      381–384, 486–488
  installing, 377
  lecture message, 385
  log file, 389–390
  make command output, 375–377
  monitoring administration users and, 492
  need for, 369–370
  Operations menu and, 618
  overview of, 367, 369
  script command and, 475, 476
  using first time, 384–385
  using in shell script, 385–389
suid, 18
SUN/Solaris. *See* Solaris
su (switch user) command, 478, 492
swap command (Solaris), 148–149
swapinfo command (HP-UX), 147–148
swap space
  AIX paging monitor, 149–155
  all-in-one paging and swap space
      monitor, 169–176
  command syntax, 146–149
  HP-UX swap space monitor, 155–160
  Linux swap space monitor, 160–164
  memory and, 145
  options for, 176–177
  paging space compared to, 145–146
  Solaris swap space monitor, 164–169
symbol commands, 13
system information, gathering.
    See snapshot information
system load monitoring
  detecting problems, 213
  gathering data for plotting, 214
  get_max function, 212–213
  iostat command syntax, 186–188
  iostat solution, 203–208
  overview of, 179, 193–194
  sar command syntax, 188–191
  sar solution, 197–203
  showing top CPU hogs, 213–214

uptime command syntax, 180–186
uptime solution, 194–197
vmstat command syntax, 191–193
vmstat solution, 208–212
System V printing
  AIX and, 408–414
  commands for, 39
  Linux and, 417–422
  Solaris and, 429–431

T

tail command, 45–46, 405
talk command, 24
tar format, 371
tee -a command, 352, 422
tee command, 223
testing
  binary numbers, 589–590
  built-in tests, 26
  character strings, 245
  command input, 72–73
  command-line arguments, 275–279
  integers and floating-point numbers,
    552–554
  mail service, 82
  null variable, 44, 115
  numeric test comparison, 120
  password file with variable exported,
    455–456
  password file with variable not exported,
    456
  response to system snapshot, 366
  sanity check, 113–115
  smbclient program, 643–644
  string, 47–50
  text strings, 24–25
  timing of line by line processing, 54–56
  user input, 627–629
text
  ASCII, 2
  finding in large file, 391
  highlighting in file, 38
  uppercase or lowercase, 24–25
thrashing, 145–146
threshold variable, setting, 111
time-based script execution, 27–28
time command, 56, 67

timed execution for process monitoring
  co-process, 230–231, 245–246
  getopts command, 218, 228, 229–230,
    244–245, 246
  in action listing, 248
  listing, 232–244
  overview of, 228
timeout, shell, 476, 486
time stamping process, 227
timing, at command and, 96
TOKEN variable, 570
top level down, 120
touch command, 446
tput command, 38, 389, 400–401
tput rmso command, 392
tput smso command, 154, 392
trap
  setting, 21, 280
  SNMP, 85–86, 261
trap_exit function, 275
tr command, 24–25
trigger value, defining, 118
troubleshooting
  /etc/sudoers file, 494
  proactive approach to, 403
  See also snapshot information
tty command, 223
twirl function, 499–500
typeset command
  number base conversion and, 41
  overview of, 24–25
  syntax, 585–586
  variable length, setting, 529

U

uname command, 128, 176
uniq command, 43–44, 622
Unix flavors. *See* AIX; HP-UX; Linux;
    Solaris
until loop, catching delayed command
    output with, 32–33
until statement, 7–8
uptime command
  AIX system and, 180–181
  field test solution, 184–186
  HP-UX system and, 181–182
  Linux system and, 182

uptime command *(continued)*
  OS common denominator, 183–184
  overview of, 179, 180
  Solaris system and, 183
  system load, measuring, 194–197
usage function, 274–275, 497–498
user
  capturing keystrokes of, 40, 475–476,
    480–483
  giving feedback to, 313
  informing about monitoring, 493–494
  logging activity of, 478–479
  monitoring administration, 489–492
  monitoring session, starting, 479
  sending pop-up message to, 621–622
user information commands, 22–23
/usr/local/bin directory, 466

V
/var, 493
variable
  COUNT, 570
  double quotes (") and, 16, 115, 392
  global, 582
  junk, 420
  length, setting, 529
  name of, and $ (dollar sign), 13, 151
  null, testing for, 44, 115
  overview of, 13
  password, 456–463
  RANDOM, 524–525
  replacing hard-coded password with,
    452–456

scope of, 14, 120
threshold, setting, 111
TOKEN, 570
verbose mode, 218, 222
Veritas filesystem, 495
viewing data assigned to variable, 13
visudo program, 378, 488
vmstat command, 179, 191–193, 208–212
volume group, 495

W
wall command, 24
w command, 22
Web site for book
  functions on, 656–662
  shell scripts on, 24, 647–656
Web sites
  Open Secure Shell code, 21
  Samba, 642
  sudo program, 370
which command, 640
while loop
  parsing file in, 53–54
  progress indicator and, 88, 89
while statement, 7
who command, 22
wildcards, 28
Windows, sending pop-up messages to.
    See pop-up messages, sending to
    Windows
Winpopup protocol, 620
write command, 24